THE OXFORD HANDBOOK OF

PHILOSOPHICAL THEOLOGY

THE OXFORD HANDBOOK OF

PHILOSOPHICAL THEOLOGY

Edited by

THOMAS P. FLINT

and

MICHAEL C. REA

OXFORD

UNIVERSITY PRESS

OXFORD
UNIVERSITY PRESS

Great Clarendon Street, Oxford OX2 6DP
Oxford University Press is a department of the University of Oxford.
It furthers the University's objective of excellence in research, scholarship,
and education by publishing worldwide in

Oxford New York

Athens Auckland Bangkok Bogotá Buenos Aires Cape Town
Chennai Dar es Salaam Delhi Florence Hong Kong Istanbul Karachi
Kolkata Kuala Lumpur Madrid Melbourne Mexico City Mumbai Nairobi
Paris São Paulo Shanghai Singapore Taipei Tokyo Toronto Warsaw
with associated companies in Berlin Ibadan

Oxford is a registered trade mark of Oxford University Press
in the UK and in certain other countries

Published in the United States
by Oxford University Press Inc., New York

British Library Cataloguing in Publication Data
Data available

Library of Congress Cataloging in Publication Data
The Oxford handbook of philosophical theology / edited by Thomas P. Flint.
p.   cm. – (Oxford handbooks in religion and theology)
Includes index.
ISBN 978–0–19–928920–2 (alk. paper)
1. Philosophical theology.   I. Flint, Thomas P.
BT40.094   2008
210–dc22   2008036033

Typeset by SPI Publisher Services, Pondicherry, India
Printed in Great Britain
on acid-free paper by
CPI Antony Rowe

ISBN   978–0–19–928920–2

1 3 5 7 9 10 8 6 4 2

To Michael J. Loux

CONTENTS

PART III   GOD AND CREATION

PART IV   TOPICS IN CHRISTIAN
PHILOSOPHICAL THEOLOGY

PART V   NON-CHRISTIAN PHILOSOPHICAL THEOLOGY

LIST OF CONTRIBUTORS

Michael Bergmann is Professor of Philosophy at Purdue University.

John H. Berthrong is Associate Professor of Comparative Theology at the Boston University School of Theology.

Jeffrey E. Brower is Associate Professor of Philosophy at Purdue University.

Robin Collins is Professor of Philosophy at Messiah College.

William Lane Craig is Research Professor of Philosophy at Talbot School of Theology.

Oliver D. Crisp is Lecturer in Theology at Bristol University.

Richard Cross is Reverend John A. O'Brien Professor of Philosophy at the University of Notre Dame.

Stephen T. Davis is Russell K. Pitzer Professor of Philosophy at Claremont McKenna College.

Scott A. Davison is Professor of Philosophy at Morehead State University.

Paul Draper is Professor of Philosophy at Purdue University.

Thomas P. Flint is Professor of Philosophy at the University of Notre Dame.

Daniel H. Frank is Professor of Philosophy at Purdue University.

Laura Garcia is Adjunct Assistant Professor of Philosophy at Boston College.

Hud Hudson is Professor of Philosophy at Western Washington University.

Oliver Leaman is Professor of Philosophy and Zantker Professor of Judaic Studies at the University of Kentucky.

Brian Leftow is the Nolloth Professor of the Philosophy of the Christian Religion at Oxford University.

Trenton Merricks is Cavaliers' Distinguished Teaching Professor of Philosophy at the University of Virginia.

Mark C. Murphy is Fr. Joseph T. Durkin, S. J. Professor of Philosophy at Georgetown University.

Michael J. Murray is Arthur and Katherine Shadek Professor in the Humanities and Philosophy at Franklin and Marshall College.

Alexander R. Pruss is Associate Professor of Philosophy at Baylor University.

Michael C. Rea is Professor of Philosophy at the University of Notre Dame.

Del Ratzsch is Professor of Philosophy at Calvin College.

Richard Swinburne is the Emeritus Nolloth Professor of the Philosophy of the Christian Religion at Oxford University.

William J. Wainwright is Distinguished Professor Emeritus in the Philosophy Department at the University of Wisconsin, Milwaukee.

Jerry L. Walls is Professor of Philosophy of Religion at Asbury Theological Seminary.

Edward Wierenga is Professor of Religion and of Philosophy at the University of Rochester.

INTRODUCTION

THOMAS P. FLINT
MICHAEL C. REA

THE first half of the twentieth century was a dark time for philosophical theology. Sharp divisions were developing among philosophers over the proper aims and ambitions for philosophical theorizing and the proper methods for approaching philosophical problems. But many philosophers were united in thinking, for different reasons, that the methods of philosophy are incapable of putting us in touch with theoretically interesting truths about God. To be sure, doubts of this sort never gained a sure foothold in Catholic universities, which maintained the theological focus evident from their founding. But, for a variety of reasons, the scholasticism practiced in these institutions went on in virtual isolation from the philosophical trends dominant at the great secular universities of Europe and America. There, doubt reigned about the possibility of fruitful interaction between philosophy and religion. Since philosophical theology (as we understand it) is aimed primarily at theoretical understanding of the nature and attributes of God, and God's relationship to the world and things in the world, the prevailing skepticism about our ability to learn about God through philosophical reasoning left philosophical theology on the wane.

A bit of history is needed to understand the genesis of this skepticism. It is common now to see the field of academic philosophy as divided broadly into two camps—'analytic' and 'Continental'—and to locate the origins of the division somewhere in the first half of the twentieth century. The two camps elude precise definition and cannot plausibly be seen as encompassing all philosophical work. Furthermore, it is misleading at best to treat them either as wholly discrete from one another or as anything more than very loosely unified within themselves. Still, at the risk of dramatically oversimplifying, we offer the following characterizations. The analytic tradition has, by and large, treated philosophy as an explanatory enterprise aimed at analyzing fundamental concepts ('person', 'action', 'law', etc.), and at using this analytic method to clarify and extend the theoretical work being done in the natural sciences. The Continental tradition, on the other hand, has viewed philosophy as an autonomous discipline aimed, more or less, at exploring and promoting our understanding of the human condition in creative and decidedly non-scientific (and not even mostly explanatory-theoretical) ways.

As the division between the two camps was developing, the aboriginal figures of the analytic tradition leaned strongly in an empiricist direction. By and large, they thought, in the words of Wilfrid Sellars, that 'science is the measure of all things: of what is that it is, and of what is not that it is not.'[1] Indeed, the logical empiricists—figures such as Otto Neurath, Moritz Schlick, Rudolf Carnap, and, a bit later, A. J. Ayer—went so far as to say that statements that do not admit of empirical verification (i.e. statements where no observations would be sufficient to determine their truth or falsity) are entirely meaningless. Carnap likened metaphysicians to 'musicians without musical ability':[2] not only are the noises they produce utterly devoid of propositional content, but the noises don't even manage to *sound* beautiful. Thus, since philosophical theology is a mostly non-empirical enterprise, the heyday of logical empiricism found philosophical theologians beating a hasty retreat.[3] Moreover, even those in the analytic tradition who were unwilling to endorse anything resembling a verifiability criterion of meaning were nevertheless very suspicious of anything that looked like theory-building that wasn't somehow grounded in the natural sciences. In short, the analytic tradition generally proved to be an inhospitable climate for religious theorizing.[4]

Matters were not much better on the Continental side either. Among Continental philosophers, at least two strains of thought tended to choke out philosophical theology. Some were so gripped by the transcendence of God that they came to think that God was beyond all human categories, even Being itself. In the eyes of these thinkers, the project of trying to arrive at *theoretical* understanding of God is just hopeless. Indeed, more than hopeless—it might even be idolatrous, since what we would inevitably end up talking about in trying to discuss God in terms of human concepts would be a 'simulacrum' of human creation rather than God himself.[5] On a closely related note, some were gripped more by human limitations, and came to despair of the possibility of arriving via philosophical methods at general, universally valid theoretical understanding of anything at all. The idea, roughly, was that our belief systems are so inevitably tied to our own very limited perspectives—perspectives conditioned by our biological make-up, our sociopolitical circumstances, our own particular experiences in life, and the like—that it is ridiculous (at best) to think that we might ever attain to any kind of undistorted 'absolute' knowledge or understanding that would be valid for all rational creatures from all points of view for all of eternity.[6] Given the prevalence of both these strands of thought throughout the Continental tradition, it is no surprise that philosophical theology did not flourish there either.

In the latter half of the twentieth century, however, there was a great revival of interest in the philosophy of religion in general and, in its wake, in philosophical theology in particular. It is common to locate the origin of this revival in the publication of Alasdair MacIntyre and Anthony Flew's landmark anthology, *New Essays in Philosophical Theology*.[7] In that volume, the main issues on the table were concerns about the meaningfulness of religious discourse and questions about the rationality of religious belief. In other words, the volume was oriented mainly toward objections to religious belief and discourse arising primarily out of the analytic tradition. These topics constituted a large proportion of the agenda for subsequent work in philosophy of religion for the next two or three decades.

In a recent essay, Nicholas Wolterstorff has argued persuasively that the revival just described was made possible *within the analytic tradition* by three major developments.[8] First, there was the death of logical empiricism during the 1960s. Logical empiricism was responsible for much of the anti-metaphysical bias within the analytic tradition. Thus, with the death of logical empiricism came a revival of interest in metaphysics more generally, and a corresponding openness to the theoretical investigation of religious topics.[9]

Moreover, according to Wolterstorff, the demise of logical empiricism also brought about a loss of interest in general questions about the origins of our concepts and the limits of human thought and judgement. This was the second major development. Whereas the Continental tradition remained (like the modern period through Kant, and like the logical empiricists) rather preoccupied with the idea that human limitations might entirely close off certain avenues of inquiry or render impossible meaningful thought or discourse about certain kinds of topics, the analytic tradition seems to have left such concerns behind, thereby opening the door even wider to all sorts of metaphysical inquiry, theological and otherwise.

Finally, the third development was the flowering of meta-epistemology—explicit reflection on and evaluation of alternative theories of knowledge. One of the main developments within meta-epistemology was the rejection of classical foundationalism (the view, roughly, that a belief is justified only if it is indubitable, incorrigible, evident to the senses, or deducible from beliefs that are indubitable, incorrigible, or evident to the senses). Classical foundationalism was an epistemological theory that many modern philosophers implicitly took for granted; and it has been shown to lie at the heart of objections against the rationality of religious belief leveled by a variety of thinkers, including Hume, Freud, Marx, W. K. Clifford, and others. The collapse of classical foundationalism made room for the flourishing of alternative epistemological theories, including some that were much more friendly to the idea that religious belief might be perfectly rational.[10]

In sum, then, the analytic tradition seems to have moved beyond several important biases that placed obstacles in the way of the growth of philosophical theology. As Wolterstorff notes, however, the same sort of thing has *not* happened within the Continental tradition. Thus, though there has surely been some measure of philosophical theology done within that tradition, the field of philosophical theology has been dominated by figures writing within the analytic tradition. This fact goes a long way toward explaining why the present volume is oriented in that direction as well.

We said earlier that the agenda set for philosophers of religion for a couple of decades placed heavy emphasis on discussion of the epistemology of religious belief and the meaningfulness of religious discourse. There was also quite a bit of discussion of the divine attributes (omnipotence, omniscience, perfect goodness, and the like), of traditional arguments for the existence of God, and of the most widely discussed argument against the existence of God—namely, the problem of evil. Over the past twenty years, however, philosophers of religion have begun to focus more of their attention on theological doctrines apart from those concerning the nature, rationality, and meaningfulness of theistic belief. Thus, for example, a great deal of attention has been devoted recently to philosophical problems arising out of the Christian doctrines of the Trinity, the Incarnation, and the Atonement; there has been an explosion of work on questions about the nature of divine providence and its implications for human freedom; and a fair bit of recent work has also been done on questions about the metaphysical possibility of the resurrection of the dead. Other topics are still ripe for discussion. For example, there is a (relatively) very small literature on the topic of divine revelation and the inspiration of Scripture, only a handful of works on the topics of prayer, original sin, and the nature of heaven and hell, and virtually nothing on the Christian doctrine of the Eucharist.

In the present handbook we have tried to provide articles covering most of the above topics. However, we have tried to avoid covering topics that have already been discussed in the *Oxford Handbook of Philosophy of Religion*. The most notable exceptions are in Parts II and III where we include chapters on omniscience, omnipotence, moral perfection, and the problem of evil. We include these topics for two reasons. First, we believe that readers of a handbook in philosophical theology would quite naturally expect to see these sorts of issues covered. Second, and perhaps more importantly, we believe that each of these topics deserves more extended and detailed treatment than it could sensibly have received in a more general philosophy of religion handbook. To take just one example: there is a vast literature on the problem of evil; but the *Oxford Handbook of Philosophy of Religion* devotes (sensibly) only one chapter to that issue. For our more narrow purposes here, however, we have seen fit to include distinct chapters on (*a*) the different versions and instances of the problem of evil (e.g. the logical problem, the evidential problem, the problem of divine hiddenness, and perhaps others), (*b*) the so-called 'skeptical theist' strategy for responding to the problem of evil, and (*c*) questions about the prospects for 'theodicy' (i.e. a response to the problem of evil that offers a complete story about why God in fact permits evil). Similar reasoning explains our decisions to include the few other topics in this handbook that have already received coverage in the *Oxford Handbook of Philosophy of Religion*.

The chapters that follow are divided into five parts covering five general topics:

   I. Theological Prolegomena
   II. Divine Attributes
   III. God and Creation
   IV. Topics in Christian Philosophical Theology
   V. Non-Christian Philosophical Theology

The chapters in the first part treat questions about the authority of scripture, tradition, and the church; the nature and mechanisms of divine revelation; and the nature of theology. We also include a chapter on theology and mystery, a topic that we think has not yet received its due in the analytic tradition.

Chapters in the second part focus on philosophical problems connected with the central divine attributes: aseity, omnipotence, omniscience, and the like. These have traditionally been among the most widely discussed topics in philosophical theology.

In the third part, we take up questions about God's relationship to creation. The chapters in this part explore theories of divine action and divine providence; questions about the purpose and efficacy of petitionary prayer; problems about divine authority and God's relationship to morality and moral standards; and, finally, various formulations of and responses to the problem of evil.

In the fourth part, we turn to topics in specifically Christian philosophy. In recent years there has been a surge of interest in philosophical problems that arise in connection with the Christian doctrines of the Trinity, the Incarnation, the Atonement, original sin, and resurrection. Other topics, the doctrine of Christ's real presence in the Eucharist, or the nature of heaven, are ripe for exploration but have not, as yet, received their due. Part IV provides coverage of all these issues.

Finally, in the fifth part, we have included three chapters on non-Christian philosophical theology—Jewish, Islamic, and Confucian. The vast majority of philosophers (in the English-speaking world, anyway) devoting their attention to philosophical theology tend to focus either on distinctively Christian doctrines or on topics that are common to all the theistic traditions. Thus, relatively few pay much, if any, attention to topics in philosophical theology that fall squarely outside the Christian tradition. Since the target audience of our handbook comprises English-speaking philosophers of religion mostly in the analytic tradition, it is appropriate that our handbook emphasize, as it does, topics that have occupied and will probably continue to occupy center stage in the major journals in the philosophy of religion. But we believe that it is both important and valuable more widely to expose precisely that group of philosophers to the work that is being done in philosophical theology outside the Christian tradition. Providing such exposure is the goal of our fifth part.[11]

Notes

1. Wilfrid Sellars, 'Empiricism and the Philosophy of Mind', in his *Science, Perception, and Reality* (London: Routledge & Kegan Paul), 127–96, at 173.

2. From 'The Elimination of Metaphysics Through Logical Analysis of Language', English translation in S. Sarkar (ed.), *Logical Empiricism at its Peak: Schlick, Carnap, and Neurath* (London: Routledge, 1996), 30.

3. We say only 'mostly' for two reasons. First, not *everything* that would count as philosophical theology is non-empirical. G. K. Chesterton famously remarked that the doctrine of original sin is the one doctrine of Christianity that admits of direct empirical verification. Or, more seriously, consider e.g. Richard Swinburne's defense of belief in the resurrection of Jesus in *The Resurrection of God Incarnate* (Oxford: Oxford University Press, 2003). Second, because even outside the aforementioned Catholic institutions, a number of scholars kept alive (though more in the popular than in the academic realm) the great perennial questions in philosophical theology, C. S. Lewis being the most prominent example.

4. Fuller versions of the brief account we have given here of the relationship between philosophical theology and analytic philosophy in the mid-twentieth century and before can be found in Alvin Plantinga's 'Advice to Christian Philosophers', *Faith and Philosophy* 1 (1984): 253–71 and, more recently, Nicholas Wolterstorff's 'How Philosophical Theology became Possible within the Analytic Tradition of Philosophy', in Oliver D. Crisp and Michael Rea (eds.), *Analytic Theology: New Essays in the Philosophy of Theology* (Oxford: Oxford University Press, 2009).

5. Heidegger is one locus of such thinking; though here, we are effectively reading Heidegger through the eyes of such contemporary philosophers as Merold Westphal and Jean-Luc Marion. See e.g. Westphal's 'Appropriating Post-Modernism', *ARC, The Journal of the Faculty of Religious Studies, McGill University* 25 (1997): 73–84, and 'Overcoming Onto-theology', in J. D. Caputo and M. J. Scanlon (eds.), *God, The Gift, and Postmodernism* (Bloomington: Indiana University Press, 1999), 146–69, both reprinted in Westphal, *Overcoming Onto-Theology: Toward a Postmodern Christian Faith* (New York: Fordham University Press, 2001), and Marion's *God Without Being*, trans. Thomas A. Carlson (Chicago: University of Chicago Press, 1991); 'Metaphysics and Phenomenology: A Relief for Theology', trans. Thomas A. Carlson, *Critical Inquiry* 20 (1994): 572–59; and 'The Idea of God', in D. Garber and M. Ayers (eds.), *The Cambridge History of Seventeenth-Century Philosophy* (Cambridge: Cambridge University Press, 1998), i. 265–304. This strand of thinking has also influenced twentieth-century systematic theology (which, historically, has significantly overlapped what we are calling philosophical theology). See e.g. Paul Tillich, *Systematic Theology* (Chicago: University of Chicago Press, 1951), i., esp. 235 ff.

6. For fuller articulation and development of this line of thinking, see K. J. Vanhoozer (ed.), *The Cambridge Companion to Postmodern Theology* (Cambridge: Cambridge University Press, 2003), M. Westphal, 'Taking Plantinga Seriously: Advice to Christian Philosophers', *Faith and Philosophy* 16/2 (1999); 'Appropriating Postmodernism'; and 'Father Abraham and his Feuding Sons', in *Overcoming Onto-Theology: Toward a Postmodern Christian Faith* (New York: Fordham University Press, 2001). A very useful collection of relevant primary sources is L. E. Cahoone (ed.), *From Modernism to Postmodernism*, 2nd edn. (Oxford: Wiley-Blackwell, 2003).

7. London: SCM, 1955. Again, cf. Plantinga, 'Advice to Christian Philosophers'.
8. 'How Philosophical Theology Became Possible within the Analytic Tradition of Philosophy'.
9. For a discussion of *this* revival, see the Introduction to Michael J. Loux and Dean W. Zimmerman (eds.), *The Oxford Handbook of Metaphysics* (Oxford: Oxford University Press, 2001).
10. Notoriously, postmodern philosophers have drawn very different lessons from the collapse of classical foundationalism. On this, see e.g. Richard Rorty, *Philosophy and the Mirror of Nature* (Princeton: Princeton University Press 1979), or, more recently and with specifically theological applications, Vanhoozer (ed.), *Cambridge Companion to Postmodern Theology*, and Stanley Grenz and John Franke, *Beyond Foundationalism* (Louisville: Westminster/John Knox, 2001).
11. The editors would like to thank Claire Brown for her excellent work on the index to this volume. Her endeavours were supported by a grant from the Institute for Scholarship in the Liberal Arts, College of Arts and Letters, University of Notre Dame.

PART I

THEOLOGICAL PROLEGOMENA

CHAPTER 1

AUTHORITY OF SCRIPTURE, TRADITION, AND THE CHURCH

RICHARD SWINBURNE

CHRISTIANITY, Islam, and Judaism all claim that God has given humans a revelation. Divine revelation may be either of God, or by God of propositional truth. Traditionally Christianity has claimed that the Christian revelation has involved both of these. God revealed himself in his acts in history; for example in the miracles by which he preserved the people of ancient Israel, and above all by becoming incarnate (that is human) as Jesus Christ, who was crucified and rose from the dead. And God also revealed to us propositional truths by the teaching of Jesus and his church. Some modern theologians have denied that Christianity involves any propositional revelation, but there can be little doubt that from the second century (and in my view from the first century) until the eighteenth century, Christians and non-Christians were virtually unanimous in supposing that it claimed to have such a revelation, and so it is worthwhile investigating its traditional claim. It is in any case very hard to see how it would be of great use to us for God to reveal himself in history (e.g. in the Exodus, or in the life, death, and resurrection of Jesus) unless we could understand the cosmic significance of what happened—e.g. that Jesus was God incarnate and that his life and death constituted an atonement for our sins. And how are we to know that unless with the history God provides its interpretation?

My concern in this chapter is with the Christian claim to have a propositional revelation. In the first section I shall describe the process by which Christians of past centuries have come to believe that certain propositions have been revealed. (My account of this process is a summary of the far fuller account given in my book *Revelation*,[1] where it is backed up by far more historical references than there is space to provide here.) Then in the second part of the chapter I shall assess alternative philosophical accounts of what constitutes a belief that such-and-such propositions have been revealed, being a 'justified' belief (or a 'warranted' or 'rational' one).

I

Although almost all Christians (until the eighteenth century) agreed that God has revealed propositional truths to various individuals and groups at various times, they also agreed that there was a major public revelation through the teaching of Jesus and his apostles, which included his (qualified) authentication of a revelation by God to ancient Israel. From the earliest days of the Christian church, Christians recognized what we now call the Old Testament as revealed truth— despite one major denial of this (by Marcion—see later), and despite differences about exactly which books belonged to the Old Testament. By the middle of the second century AD most Christians also agreed that there were sacred books that contained the record of the new revelation given by Jesus and his apostles; and that these books included the four Gospels, the Acts of the Apostles, and most of the letters attributed to St Paul in today's Bibles. They disagreed, however, for some further centuries about which other books should be included in what we now call the New Testament. In his book *The Canon of the New Testament* Bruce Metzger[2] analyses the three criteria that led church bodies to recognize some book as New Testament Scripture—its conformity with basic Christian tradition, its apostolicity (being written by an apostle, or someone closely connected with an apostle), and its widespread acceptance by the church at large. So a prior understanding of the general nature of the Christian revelation (of central Christian doctrines), evidence of historical reliability, and church authority operated to determine which books constituted the Bible, Old and New Testaments together.

Christians have disagreed about whether there was more to the 'deposit of faith', the record of God's revelation, than the Bible. For Protestants the 'deposit of faith' just is the Bible, and many Catholics and Orthodox today also hold this view. But in the past, as also today, many Catholics and Orthodox hold that the deposit of faith also includes 'unwritten traditions', traditions of the apostolic church (that is the church in the years immediately after its foundation) which were not written down at that time in any book. These traditions have been thought to include not merely traditions as to how to worship (e.g. how to celebrate the Eucharist), but doctrinal truths some of which might be implicit in the rules for worship.[3]

Nevertheless, despite these differences about the extent of the deposit of faith, Christians agreed that taken together the biblical books constituted God's 'word'. While the New Testament seems to make a fairly modest claim for the authority of the Old Testament, that 'all scripture is inspired by God and profitable for teaching, for reproof, for correction and for training in righteousness' (2 Timothy 3: 16), much stronger claims soon came to be made for the authority of Scripture. Gregory the Great wrote that Holy Scripture is 'a letter of God Almighty to his creature'.[4] Theologians did not wish to deny that these books were written by different human authors at different times, as was evident by the fact that so often there are references to 'I' who did certain things, which can only be construed as a reference to such an author (e.g. St Paul), and by the discrepancies of style of the different books. But theologians claimed that these books were divinely inspired, and divinely authorized—that is, God was the ultimate author who authorized these books to be published as his revelation.

The main disagreements between Christians concern the criteria for determining the meaning of biblical passages and for deriving doctrines from them; and (partly in consequence of the former disagreement) about what various passages mean and which doctrines can be derived. The disagreements about the meaning of biblical passages often turn on which ones should be taken in their most natural literal sense, which should be taken in a possible literal sense although not the most natural one, and which should be understood metaphorically. It might seem that this is something to be sorted out by careful historico-literary investigation; and Protestant scholars of the last four centuries have had this ideal of discovering by normal methods of historical inquiry the 'original meaning' of the text, as first written down by a human author. Hermeneutics consisted in discovering this original meaning; the text with this meaning—although originally directed at ancient Israelites and early Christians—was also 'God's word' to all humans ever.

This project, however, soon shows that, so understood, the Bible contains many obvious inconsistencies, major and minor, between and within biblical books. The most obvious of these is the apparent inconsistency between Israelite leaders (apparently on God's behalf) commending the extermination of the Canaanites, men, women, and children, and burning their cities by fire, as described in the Book of Judges; and Jesus's (apparently on God's behalf) commending non-violence in the Gospels. There are also many biblical passages taken in the sense most probably intended by their human authors that are manifestly inconsistent with established conclusions of science and history. If we treat the book of Genesis and the subsequent 'historical' books with the dates and numbers of years recorded there as literally true history, we can deduce that the period between the creation of Adam and the birth of Jesus lasted something of the order of 4,000 years. So it seems to be claiming that the human race began to exist about 4,000 BC. Yet archaeology has shown us human civilizations much older than that. Genesis records a flood that covered the whole earth; but while geology certainly provides evidence of extensive floods, there is not the slightest record of a universal flood after the appearance of humans. And so on.

These evident facts led many liberal-minded theologians of the twentieth century to cease to talk of the Bible being 'true', but to speak rather of it being 'useful' or 'insightful' if read in accord with some rule or other of interpretation; and there have evolved as many ways of interpreting as there have been theologians to do the interpreting. And saying this sort of thing about the Bible hardly gives it a special status—the same could be said of any great work of literature. A general fog settled over 'hermeneutics'.[5]

The church of the early centuries was, however, well aware of these problems. It was well aware that if certain passages of the Old Testament were understood in the most natural way, they represented God as commending much immoral conduct, and contained many false assertions about matters of science and history. The biblical picture of a flat earth covered by a dome was inconsistent with the picture of the world provided by the contemporary Greek science of a spherical earth, centred in the middle of a hollow sphere that rotated daily around the earth. And many of the educated theologians (the 'Fathers') believed what the Greeks had to say about science. And while they didn't have any knowledge of archaeology and geology that would show the falsity of the historical claims in Genesis and other biblical books taken in their most natural senses, they still rejected some of them on the theological grounds that they depicted too anthropomorphic a God.

The Marcionite controversy made theologians more acutely aware of the need to develop a theory about how to interpret the Bible. In the late second century Marcion, a priest at Rome convinced of the immorality of much of the conduct apparently commended in the Old Testament, campaigned for a Bible that had no Old Testament, and a New Testament consisting merely of an expurgated version of Luke's Gospel and ten Letters of St Paul. The orthodox reassertion of the Old Testament was led by St Irenaeus, who claimed that much of the Old Testament had merely temporary and symbolic significance. It was, if read in its most natural sense, a record of the growth of understanding of God by the Israelites; and also God's revelation to Christians, if read metaphorically. At the beginning of the third century Origen claimed that some of the Bible (New Testament as well as Old) was not literally true, but all of it contained deep metaphorical truth. This view, developed in the next century by Gregory of Nyssa and accepted by Augustine, became a standard view. Augustine's basic rule was the same as that of Origen and Gregory: 'We must show the way to find out whether a phrase is literal or figurative.

And the way is certainly as follows: whatever there is in the word of God that cannot, when taken literally, be referred either to purity of life or soundness of doctrine, you may set down as metaphorical.'[6]

In other words, the way to find out what the Bible meant was not to use secular historical methods to discover the 'original meaning' of the text as written of its human author. Since God was the ultimate author of the Bible, it was what he meant the text to mean that was its meaning as a revealed text. The Fathers did normally suppose that the human author also understood this, but they allowed that he might be writing something that he did not understand. To understand what God meant by the written word, we need to take into account God's beliefs. We know, the Fathers claimed, two kinds of beliefs that God has—God believes central Christian doctrines, and God believes all truths about history and science. (Secular science and history, when very well established, provides us with strong evidence about God's beliefs about the latter.) So if anything in Scripture seems to contradict these beliefs, they argued, it must be understood in a metaphorical way. This result follows from normal rules for understanding a sentence of ordinary human discourse. If someone utters some sentence which, taken literally, they know to be false, and they know that (much of) their audience knows to be false, then they cannot mean it to be taken literally. If I say to others about our human friend Larry, 'Larry is an elephant', this must be understood metaphorically. And so if God is the ultimate author of Scripture and its intended audience is not merely its original hearers and readers, but the church of many future centuries, then it must be interpreted in the light not merely of Christian doctrine, but of future scientific knowledge. But the Fathers would have said, if such a possibility had occurred to them, that in the case of a conflict as to how to interpret a Scriptural passage between an interpretation guided by their prior understanding of central Christian doctrines and an interpretation guided by current established 'scientific knowledge', that the former took precedence. For God had revealed central Christian doctrines to his church before ever the New Testament was written; purported scientific knowledge was fallible. But how most scriptural passages should be interpreted was not regarded as fixed by already recognized central Christian doctrines.

One verse that all the Fathers refused to take literally on the ground of its incompatibility with Christian moral teaching was Psalm 137: 9 which says of the Babylon which held the Jews in captivity, 'Happy shall they be who take your little ones and dash them against the rock.' A verse from the Psalms which some of the Fathers refused to take literally on scientific grounds was Psalm 136: 6 which gives thanks to God 'who spread out the earth on the waters' on the grounds that science showed that earth did not float on water.[7] And in a wide sense of 'science' it was on scientific grounds that some of the Fathers rejected the literal understanding of the Genesis 1 claim that God made the world in six days. For there could not, they claimed, be days before the sun existed, and Genesis claimed that the sun was created on the fourth day. Augustine's basic rule deriving from Origen was applied throughout the

Middle Ages. Beryl Smalley has written that 'to write a history of Origenist influence on the West would be tantamount to writing a history of Western exegesis',[8] and she could have added Eastern exegesis as well.

When any sentence is to be interpreted metaphorically, the normal (secular) rules for interpreting it are: take the words of the passage (apart from words that link it to its context) in their literal senses. Consider the objects or properties normally designated by these words, and objects or properties commonly associated with them. Interpret the words as designating some of these latter objects or properties instead. Take as the true interpretation that which interprets the words as designating objects or properties closely rather than remotely connected with their normal designata, in so far as this can be done in a way which makes the sentence appropriate to the context. In so far as there is more than one equally plausible interpretation, the passage is to be read as having both (or all) of these interpretations. Origen recognized three different kinds of sense possessed by most passages of Scripture, and Augustine recognized four.[9] The Christian Fathers had available to them a whole set of objects or properties commonly associated with the people, places, and actions referred to in the Old Testament, which provided symbolic meanings for the words that normally designated the latter. 'Moses' can refer to Jesus, since Jesus was the new Moses who was leading his people out of slavery to sin, in the way that Moses led them out of slavery to the Egyptians. And 'Joshua' can also refer to Jesus, since Jesus was the New Joshua (the Hebrew word for 'Jesus') who was leading his people to his kingdom, as Joshua led them to the promised land. Jesus Christ is also the 'rock' to which we can cling successfully when storms attack us. And since the Jews became enslaved in Babylon, 'Babylon' comes to represent evil generally.

Hence the blessing confessed in Psalm 137: 9 on those who take the 'little ones' of Babylon and dash them against the rock was naturally interpreted as a blessing on those who take the offspring of evil (Babylon), which are our evil inclinations, and destroy them through the power of Christ ('the rock').[10] And the command to the Israelites invading Canaan to exterminate the Canaanites, and some details of the invasion, may be interpreted in the same spirit.[11]

When you begin to interpret passages metaphorically, conflicting interpretations multiply, some of which are more plausible than others. To my mind the metaphorical interpretation nearest to the literal under which Genesis 1's talk of 'days' comes out as plausibly true, and so the preferred metaphorical interpretation, is derived by treating 'days' as long periods of time and the exact order of creation as not relevant to the truth of the chapter. Then the passage tells us that gradually God brought about the various facets of creation over long periods of time, no doubt through 'secondary causes' (i.e. the normal operation of scientific laws that God sustains), as Genesis 2 suggests. Augustine also took the passage metaphorically, but his interpretation is by comparison a very far-fetched one. He claimed that all the things described in Genesis 1 as created by God were created simultaneously, and that talk about 'days' is to be interpreted as talk about stages in the knowledge of creation possessed by the angels.[12] But 'days' are more like billennia than they are like logical stages in the growth of knowledge. My metaphorical interpretation is, therefore, by normal criteria for metaphorical interpretation, better than his.

Augustine's *De Genesi ad Litteram* contains so many different interpretations of passages (most but not all of them literal interpretations, but not perhaps the most natural literal interpretations) that he faced the objection: what have you achieved except to show that we cannot know what these passages of Scripture mean? His answer was: I have shown that Genesis is compatible with whatever physical science might show.[13] But he would have found it natural to add: so long as what physical science shows is not incompatible with already recognized central Christian doctrines.

As I have just noted, a crucial constraint on the interpretation of Scripture was that it should be interpreted consistently with the church's teaching. All the Fathers were well aware that without this constraint, Scripture was capable of a thousand different (and often incompatible) interpretations. But 'every word' of Scripture 'shall seem consistent' to someone, wrote Irenaeus, 'if he for his part diligently read the Scriptures in company with those who are presbyters in the church, among whom is the apostolic doctrine'.[14] And Tertullian comments that disputes between orthodox and heretics could not be settled by appeal to Scripture, since the meaning of Scripture was uncertain; the teaching of the church must first be identified and that will determine how Scripture should be interpreted.[15] The Reformation claim that Scripture should be interpreted without any external constraint constituted an enormous innovation in Christian thought. Because of the innumerable different ways in which Scripture can be interpreted, the Westminster Confession's assertion that 'the infallible rule of interpretation of Scripture is the Scripture itself'[16] seems to me quite hopeless. The unavoidability for the above reason of a 'theological perspective' for the interpretation of biblical texts is developed at some length in Jorge Gracia's book *How Can We Know What God Means?*[17]

But all Christians shared another view, which seems opposed to what I have just described—that all doctrine must be derived from Scripture (perhaps with the addition of unwritten traditions). Some doctrines of the Creed (e.g. the doctrines that Jesus 'was crucified . . . buried . . . and rose up on the third day') simply repeat Scripture, which—it was agreed—must be understood literally unless there is reason to deny the literal sense. But the doctrines of the Trinity and the Incarnation as stated in the Creed and as defined by the Ecumenical Councils of the fourth and fifth centuries clearly do not repeat Scripture. Nor can they be deduced from Scripture without the aid of some definitions of the philosophical terms that occur in the Creed, such as οὐσία (substance), ὑπόστασις (individual), φύσις (nature), and so on. Even so, they can be rendered consistent with certain scriptural passages only if those passages are read in a none too natural way. And while everyone accepted that Scripture should be read in a way constrained by established doctrine, that was of no help when it was still disputed what the doctrine was. And that was the case in the Arian controversy. The Catholics said that Jesus Christ was ὁμοούσιος (of the same substance) as the Father, in other words fully divine; and the Arians said that Jesus Christ was ὁμοιούσιος (of similar substance) to the Father, in other words semi-divine. Both parties could quote biblical passages in their support. St John's Gospel, speaking of Jesus, claims that 'the word was God'.[18] But it also quotes Jesus as saying 'The Father is greater than I',[19] and how could any being be greater than God? And various other quotations could be assembled on each side.

What was at issue was surely which position fits best the overall pattern of the teaching of the New Testament, whose content was itself determined by a prior understanding of the nature of central Christian doctrines. And the inference from scriptural passages to a doctrinal definition that fits best their overall pattern is not a deductive inference. It is a probabilistic inference of a kind used by historians of thought in their systematizations of the work of some thinker which fit most of what he is alleged to have affirmed (taken in its most natural sense) better than any other simple account, but which may not fit all of what he is alleged to have affirmed. The historian then deals with any such recalcitrant sentences in one of three ways. First, he may claim that the thinker must have understood the recalcitrant sentences in a way other than a normal way. Secondly, he may claim that the thinker did not write these sentences—the record is inaccurate. Or thirdly, the historian may claim that his suggested principles fit almost everything the thinker wrote so well, that the thinker would have come to deny the statements expressed by the recalcitrant sentences if their incompatibility with his general viewpoint was pointed out to him. But when dealing with the Bible, believed by conflicting interpreters to be a true record of the teaching of God, only the first way is available. A sentence, such as the saying of Jesus 'the Father is greater than I', incompatible with one such system-atization if understood in the most natural way, was interpreted in a less natural way than the most natural way—for example as reporting Jesus saying that the Father was greater than Jesus in so far as Jesus was human (that is, in his human nature).

But of course it is often none too obvious which systematization of biblical passages fits the overall message of the text best. And so the church used a further criterion for judging between plausible competing interpretations: a proposed doc-trinal definition must be compatible with the church's own past decisions (even if the issue was still disputed). Newman characterized the derivation of a new doctrinal definition as involving the perception of its 'congruity' with Scripture and with the 'intuitive sense of the Church'.[20] There were competing theories about how the church could reach such a binding conclusion—by the decision of an Ecumenical Council (itself recognized as 'Ecumenical' by its subsequent widespread acceptance in the church), by the decision of a council ratified by the Pope, or even by the Pope acting on his own. But the suggestion that Christians could start again to discover the meaning of biblical passages without being constrained by the way those passages had been interpreted in the past is wildly out of line with the tradition of Christianity's first 1,400 years.

And how was the church that had this vital role in establishing true doctrine to be identified? While certainly the fact that some ecclesial body gave the most plausible overall interpretation of the 'deposit of faith' was used as a criterion for determining the identity of the church and so for which new doctrine should be adopted, the criterion of that ecclesial body's past approval of some plausibly derived doctrine could not be used as the sole test for the identity of the church without hopeless circularity. There was a further criterion recognized by all. An ecclesial body was the church in so far as it had continuity of organization with the apostolic church: that is, in so far as its church leaders were commissioned by other church leaders and so on back to the apostles. Again there were differences about the kind of commissioning required. (Did bishops need to be ordained by bishops? Was the recognition of a bishop's authority by the Pope required for that authority to be legitimate?) But all agreed that some body was only part of the church in so far as it had some continuity with the apostolic church.

So, to summarize this historical section, for Christianity's first 1,400 years Christians have recognized as revealed truths those properly derived from Scripture (and perhaps also unwritten tradition). Scripture consisted of books recognized as such by the church. The meaning of scriptural passages was determined in part by the church's prior teaching, and the proper derivation of doctrines from Scripture was also determined in part by the church's recognition of that derivation. Despite all the many differences of doctrine and organization between ecclesial bodies, it is a significant fact that for the thousand years between the ninth and nineteenth centuries virtually all ecclesial bodies (Catholic, Orthodox, Protestant, and Oriental Orthodox—that is monophysites and 'Nestorians') with any case for continuity of organization with the apostolic church were committed to the Nicene Creed as containing the central doctrines of Christianity. (By the ninth century Arian opposition to the Creed had virtually died out, while after the nineteenth century some ecclesial bodies began to adopt liberal interpretations of credal doctrines very different from earlier interpretations.) If the church is the source of our knowledge of a revelation from God through Jesus, at the very least the doctrines of the Nicene Creed must be true. And without the church's selection and interpretation of biblical texts we would have no knowledge of the content of that revelation.

II

Christian doctrines about what God is like and how he has acted have come to us through the church's tradition of interpreting Scripture, and without the historical process I have described in section I there would be no Christian doctrines to assess. But why should we believe these doctrines to be true? No doubt in the case of some of them there are considerations of pure reason that make it to some extent probable that the doctrines are true. For example we might expect a God who saw us suffering to become incarnate (become a human) in order to show solidarity with us by sharing our suffering. But such a priori reasoning seldom seems conclusive; and it will not in any case tell us where and when any divine actions were done, for example in which human God became incarnate. God needs to reveal these truths to us. So the question remains why, if at all, we are justified in believing that Scripture interpreted in a certain way is God's revelation. For anyone's belief in Christian doctrines depends in large measure on such a belief.

Modern philosophical theories of what makes a belief 'justified' (or 'rational' or 'warranted') divide into internalist and externalist theories. There is no space in this chapter to discuss adequately the merits of these two kinds of theory, or of all their consequences for the justification of Christian doctrines. But it will be appropriate to outline and comment on examples of recent attempts to apply theories of one or the other kind to assessing the justification for believing that God has revealed truths through Jesus Christ that are contained in Scripture, and for regarding some particular interpretation of Scripture as the correct one. The most common kind of internalist view holds that a belief is justified if (and only if) it is rendered probable by all a believer's basic beliefs taken together, basic beliefs being ones that seem obviously true to the believer but not for the reason that they are rendered probable by other beliefs. They include beliefs about what the believer seems to be perceiving, or clearly remembers, or what other people tell him that they have perceived, or that everyone knowledgeable agrees about. If you have a basic belief that you have observed so-and-so, but also a basic belief that renders the former belief improbable (for example that someone else claims that they were at the relevant place at the relevant time and observed that so-and-so did not happen, or that they saw you at a different place at the relevant time), then you must discover what is made most probable by the balance of all your basic beliefs taken together, each basic belief being weighted by the strength of your initial degree of conviction that it is true. Many of your basic beliefs will be ones shared by most other people, and so constitute public evidence. Virtually no basic belief can be regarded as infallible; but some few basic beliefs, for example beliefs about what you were doing two minutes ago, are so strong (that is, seem so obviously true), as to deserve to be believed despite almost any conceivable counter-evidence. My own view is an internalist view of this kind.

It follows from this internalist view that if you have had an overwhelming religious experience on reading Scripture that God is 'three persons of one substance' you are justified in believing it. So too if everyone tells you that everyone who knows anything about the subject agrees that everything written in Scripture is true and that Scripture says that God is three persons of one substance. Calvin wrote that 'Scripture exhibits fully as clear evidence of its own truth as white and black things do of their colour, or sweet and bitter things do of their taste,'[21] and many Protestant theologians and confessions have said much the same: that Scripture wears its truth on its face. And since Calvin also held that it was in general obvious (at any rate to those who were both educated and unprejudiced) what Scripture meant—we did not need church councils to tell us this—he held that the truths of Christian doctrine could be read from the pages of Scripture.

But in my view in the twenty-first century, while quite a number of people have religious experiences of the presence of God, relatively few people reading Scripture have experiences of the truth of Christian doctrines; and those that do often have different understandings of those doctrines. But it must very seldom be the case that any individual has had an experience of this kind so strong that it needs no further support from publicly available evidence. And in the twenty-first century there must be very few communities in which everyone assures you and no one denies that everything written in Scripture (understood in a certain way) is true. Among the basic beliefs of all of us will be basic beliefs that many people who read Scripture find it highly implausible, and that many of those who believe that it contains much truth interpret it in different ways from ourselves. So we need to assess what is shown by the balance of our basic beliefs, and—in order to get a belief as probably true as we can get—we need to seek more relevant basic beliefs; and that means primarily getting to know about the large amount of relevant public evidence. Even those who have had some relevant, though not overwhelmingly strong, religious experience need also some public evidence for the truth of Christian doctrines if their belief that those doctrines are true is to be justified in the internalist sense of 'justified'.

I have argued (e.g. in *The Existence of God*[22]) that there is substantial general public evidence (in the form of the existence of the universe, its conformity to simple general laws, these laws being such as together with the boundary conditions of the universe to give rise to human beings, these human beings being conscious, etc. etc.) which makes it probable that there is a God (omnipotent, omniscient, perfectly free, and perfectly good). I argued (e.g. in *Revelation*) that God had good reason to become incarnate in order to identify with our suffering, make atonement for our sins, and reveal important truths to us about what God is like and how we ought to live in order to enjoy life with God in Heaven forever. If he did this, he would have to lead a life of a certain kind (e.g. a perfect human life under difficult conditions in which he showed that he believed that he was divine and was making atonement for our sins, and founded a church which continued his work). He would also need to have his actions and teaching culminated by a great miracle, a setting aside of the laws of nature that God alone can do; this miracle would constitute God's signature of approval on those actions and that teaching. All this background evidence makes it quite probable that God would become incarnate in a prophet who would live a life of a certain kind, which would be culminated by a great miracle.

So we need only a modest amount of detailed historical evidence in the form of witness testimony that one prophet did lead the right kind of life that was culminated by a great miracle (together with evidence that this was true of no other prophet) in order to make it probable that that prophet was God incarnate. I argued further in *Revelation* that that evidence is available; there is only one prophet in human history about whom there is a modest amount of evidence of a kind to be expected if he lived the right kind of life, and also only one prophet about whom there is a modest amount of evidence that his actions and teaching were culminated by a great miracle. It is unlikely that there would be this combination of evidence unless it was produced by God, who is most unlikely to have produced it unless the prophet was indeed God incarnate. The unique prophet of whom both these things were true was Jesus (the miracle culminating his work about which there is evidence being his resurrection). He founded a church to continue his work; and if God revealed truths through Jesus, he must be providing that church with continuing divine guidance to ensure that it teaches what he taught and what is implicit in that. Otherwise God's revelation through Jesus would have been largely pointless, for except for a few immediate disciples, no one would know what Jesus had taught. Given that the teaching of Jesus and the resulting teaching of the Christian church is not too improbable on other grounds (e.g. it does not teach that there is nothing wrong with rape and pillage), then the total evidence (the general public evidence for the existence of God together with detailed historical evidence about Jesus) makes it probable that Jesus was God incarnate who rose from the dead, and so that God authenticated his teaching and the teaching that the church derived from his teaching. (In this process the historical evidence is confined to that obtained by treating the New Testament like any normal historical source.)

It follows from all this that the fact that a doctrine has been developed by the church through the process of derivation from Scripture described in section I, which the church recognized as the proper process for this, is substantial reason for supposing that that doctrine is true. So Scripture turns out to have an authority far greater than that of a normal historical source. (I believe that the apparatus of the calculus of probability can be used to elucidate the structure of the above historical argument, and gives us reason to suppose that that argument gives a high probability to the truth of Christian doctrines. In *Warranted Christian Belief*[23] Alvin Plantinga produced an argument from 'dwindling probabilities' purporting to show that a historical argument of the type I have produced will give only a fairly low probability to Christian doctrines. In an Appendix to the second edition of *Revelation*, I claim that Plantinga's argument based on his criticism of the first edition of that book misunderstands my argument, and is not cogent.)

An approach somewhat similar to mine, emphasizing the cumulative effect of different kinds of evidence in supporting what he calls 'canonical theism' (theism as developed in the Christian church) characterizes the work of William Abraham—see, most recently, his *Crossing the Threshold of Divine Revelation*.[24]

For an externalist, however, a belief is 'justified' (or whatever) if the belief is caused by a process of the right kind, whether or not the believer is aware of what that process is or that it is of the right kind. The simplest form of externalism is reliabilism: a belief is justified if (and only if) it is produced by a reliable process, a reliable process being one that produces mostly true beliefs. Thus it may be said: my belief that I am perceiving my desk is justified if it is produced by perception and perception is a generally reliable process. There is an enormous problem (the 'generality problem') about how the type of process to which the token process (the particular process that operated on a particular occasion) belongs is to be selected. For suppose that I am a retired professor who has recently taken the drug LSD. Then is what makes my belief that I am now perceiving a desk justified or unjustified, the fact that this token process belongs to the type of perception by anyone, or the type of perception by me, or the type of perception by a retired professor, or the type of perception by a retired professor who has recently taken LSD, or what? For the success rate of each of these types will vary. Maybe perception as such is 90 per cent reliable, whereas perception by retired professors who have recently taken LSD is only 30 per cent reliable. According to the type to which the token belief is referred, so different consequences follow for whether the belief is justified or not. I do not think that pure reliabilism has any principled solution to this problem.

But there are forms of externalism that incorporate a reliabilist element that do have such a solution. The best-known form of externalism that has been applied to assessing the 'justification' (or, as he calls it, the 'warrant') of central Christian doctrines (what he calls 'the great things of the Gospel') is Alvin Plantinga's theory of warrant. For Plantinga,[25] a belief has warrant (subject to defeaters) if and only if: (1) it is produced by cognitive faculties functioning properly, (2) in a cognitive environment sufficiently similar to that for which the faculties were designed, (3) according to a design plan aimed at the production of true beliefs, when (4) there is a high statistical probability of such beliefs being true (that is, the process of production is highly reliable). By someone's cognitive faculties 'functioning properly', Plantinga understands them functioning 'in the way their creator (whoever or whatever that was) meant them to function'. If God made us, our faculties function properly if they function in the way God designed them to function; whereas if Evolution (uncaused by God) made us (the main alternative that Plantinga considers), then our faculties function properly if they function in the way that Evolution (in some sense) designed them to function. Now if God, who is an intentional agent, created us, there will be clear content to all four criteria. God's intentional actions will have caused the operation of a particular type of process that caused the token belief that there is a God. If he designed it to operate in the environment in which it is currently operating so as to lead to true beliefs, and if the process is reliable (which it will be if God designed it for that purpose), the belief will be warranted. The type to which a token belief should be referred to assess its reliability is fixed by God's intention to produce true beliefs by a process of that type. The normal type of process that according to Plantinga God uses to bring about true beliefs in the 'great things of the Gospel' is the operation of the Holy Spirit on our hearts 'directly', that is, in response to hearing these 'great things' preached or reading them in Scripture. He does however allow that in some people the Holy Spirit might operate indirectly, making them recognize the cogency of some argument for the truth of these great things.

If, however, God (or any other intentional agent) did not create us (and Plantinga is seeking an account of warrant that does not presuppose that God created us), then there is a big problem about how (1) is to be understood. For Evolution (or any other inanimate cause) is not an agent who has intentions (despite the incautious talk by some biologists about our organs having 'design plans'). The only sense I can give to claims that Evolution 'meant' something to function in a certain way, or that it 'designed' it to function in a certain environment or to produce certain beliefs, is that it caused it to function in that way in that environment so as to produce those beliefs. So cognitive faculties function properly if they function in the way Evolution causes them to function; their design plan is 'aimed' at the production of true beliefs only in so far as it does produce true beliefs in that environment; and an environment is 'sufficiently similar' to that for which the faculties were 'designed' only in so far as they produce true beliefs equally well in that new environment. And so the whole edifice collapses on to (4): a belief is warranted if it is produced by cognitive faculties in an environment in which they produce true beliefs as frequently as in their original environment in which they produced mostly true beliefs. This is a form of simple reliabilism—and the normal form of reliabilism that is open to the generality problem, for there is no creator's 'intention' by which the type of 'cognitive faculty' and the 'environment' in which it was originally reliable can be selected from the whole range of other types of cognitive faculty and types of environment to which the token process and the token environment in which it originally operated belong. (Is the cognitive faculty 'perception' or 'vision'? Is the environment the earth, or merely a particular human community? And so on.)

Plantinga, however, thinks that there is a God, and thus that Christian beliefs are warranted if they are produced by a God-created process designed to produce true beliefs, and that will normally be the operation of the Holy Spirit on our hearts producing those beliefs, often in response to reading Scripture. Plantinga allows that there could in principle be 'defeaters' to show that, despite the initial warrant of the belief, it is not really warranted after all. Such defeaters to the warrant of belief in Christian doctrines might include the results of New Testament historical scholarship, or the conclusions of postmodernist philosophy; but Plantinga does not consider that any such defeaters are very strong.

William Alston has in the past also advocated a mainly externalist theory—in his case a straightforwardly reliabilist theory—of the justification of belief in general, and applied it to religious belief (to include belief in Christian doctrines), in particular where it is produced by religious experience resulting from what he calls 'Christian mystical practice'.[26] He claims that the process of believing beliefs produced in this way is a reliable process (that is, produces mostly true beliefs) and so makes us 'justified' in believing any belief so produced (e.g. about the authority or interpretation of Scripture). He allows that religious experience may need support (to make it overall probable) from arguments from public evidence (presumably also to be justified on a reliabilist account). Alston's theory is open to the generality problem common to all reliabilist theories. Stephen Evans applies an externalism derived from Plantinga and Alston to the justification of Christian doctrines in his *The Historical Christ and the Jesus of Faith*.[27] Evans emphasizes the point that Plantinga allows as an occasional possibility that the Holy Spirit may operate on humans to produce a justified belief that Christian doctrines are true not in a direct way or in showing us that they are well supported by public evidence. Both Evans and Alston allow the possibility of defeaters to belief in Christian doctrines that might need to be taken seriously. A more hardline externalism is put forward by John Lamont in his *Divine Faith*.[28] For Lamont, divine 'faith' is belief in the testimony of God spoken to us through the teaching of the church; response to that testimony is the only way to Christian faith. He holds that 'a belief that is based on the motives of credibility [that is, arguments from public evidence] is . . . not Christian faith'; and once you have that faith, 'it is irrational . . . to take objections to faith seriously'.[29]

So for all these writers what makes a belief in the authority of Scripture justified is that our belief in that authority and so in the doctrines that Scripture contains is produced by the right God-created process, and not (as such) by any argument from historical evidence or even from some overwhelming experience of the truth of that authority. (Such an argument or experience should be trusted on an externalist view only if it was produced by the right process.) These different writers have different views about which Christian doctrines are contained in Scripture, and they must maintain that the justification not merely of their belief in the authority of Scripture but of their belief in their particular interpretation of Scripture depends on how those beliefs were produced. For the internalist, however, a believer's interpretation is justified in so far as it is rendered probable by evidence supporting one interpretation against another, and that may include evidence of the extent to which different interpretations have been authenticated by the church.

Some of the writers whom I have been discussing use 'faith' interchangeably with 'belief'; for Lamont, for example, Christian faith is used to mean a belief that certain central Christian doctrines are true. For others, Christian faith is the belief that these doctrines are true accompanied by some affective component (such as a love of God or hatred of one's sins), so long as it is produced in the right way (e.g. by the operation of the Holy Spirit). But, as theses about the kind of faith that on traditional Christian views is necessary for salvation, these positions need argument of a kind not fully developed in the writings I discuss. For there is a different view that Christian faith is a matter of acting on the assumption that (or trusting that) Christian doctrines are true, and perhaps also believing that they are true or perhaps without that belief. In my view the Christian tradition has had no clear view of the nature of faith. This is partly because the same Greek word πίστις and the same Latin word *fides* can be translated either as 'belief' or as 'trust'. A distinction between 'belief' and 'trust' can only be brought out by different ways in which the corresponding verb is used: πιστεύω ὅτι (or *credo ut*) means 'I believe that, whereas πιστεύω εἰς (or *credo in*) or the verb followed by a dative noun means 'I trust in'. In this context[30] I am treating all theories merely as theories about what makes a belief that Christian doctrines are true 'justified' (or 'warranted').

So—to return to the main theme—we all want to have true beliefs and no false beliefs, on all matters and above all on religious matters. We can seldom be absolutely certain that our beliefs (especially in the twenty-first century our beliefs about religious matters) are true, but we can have beliefs that are probably true, and we can look for and assess further evidence in order to get beliefs that are more probably true than the ones we now have. What people who want beliefs which are 'warranted' or 'justified' are, I suggest, normally looking for is beliefs that are probably true—on the evidence. But we have access to no other evidence than our own (though we can add to that). So in seeking such beliefs we are seeking beliefs that are probably true on our evidence (that is, our own basic beliefs taken together). It is more sensible to be guided in our conduct by beliefs that are probably true than by ones that are not probably true, for the reason that if we rely on the former we are more likely to attain our goals (e.g. the forgiveness of our sins, and making ourselves and our fellow humans fitted for the worship of God in Heaven) than if we rely on the latter. And the more probably true our beliefs are, the more sensible it is to rely on them. So it is clearly a good thing to have beliefs about Christian doctrine that are justified in the sense of being rendered probable by our evidence, that is, 'justified' in an internalist sense.

It might also be a good thing to have beliefs about Christian doctrines that are 'warranted' in Plantinga's or some similar externalist sense. But it would be foolish to rely on such beliefs unless we have reason to suppose that they are true. Of course if they are warranted in a Plantinga-type sense, they will be true. But again before we rely on them for this reason, we need reason to suppose that they are appropriately warranted; and that means having a belief that they are probably (on our evidence) thus warranted. That is, before we rely on them for the stated reason, we need an internally justified belief that our Christian beliefs are caused in the way in which Plantinga claims that they are—that is, by the 'internal instigation of the Holy Spirit' leading to our having relevant true beliefs. That will involve, to begin with, an (internally) justified belief that there is a God who produces some of our beliefs. If there is a God, he is responsible in large measure (though humans can influence these processes) for the operation of all natural processes including those which produce beliefs in us, and so he has a considerable responsibility both for the operation of processes that produce in some of us beliefs that Christian doctrines are false and for the operation of processes that produce in others of us beliefs that Christian doctrines are true. So in order to have a probably true belief that our Christian beliefs have been produced by the right process, we must see what our evidence indicates about this. And the only evidence we can have that the beliefs have been produced by the right process will be any evidence we have that makes it probable that they are true. How else could one distinguish beliefs produced by the Holy Spirit according to the design plan aimed at producing true beliefs about the content of God's revelation, except as those beliefs in this area that are (on our evidence) probably true? That evidence may, I repeat, be for some of us merely the intuitive obviousness of such beliefs, or the unanimous testimony of those known to us that every knowledgeable person holds these beliefs. But surely for almost all of us today public evidence of the kind I summarized earlier must play a significant role. Without evidence that Christian doctrines are probably true, and so 'justified' in an internalist sense, we can have no reason to believe that they have warrant in a Plantinga-type sense. Similar criticisms apply to other externalist theories of the justification of religious belief. Plantinga, as also Lamont, identifies the process of the production of our Christian beliefs in such a way that, if they are indeed produced in that way, they are very probably true. If the Holy Spirit causes us to believe that Scripture is true, then very probably Scripture is true. So we need evidence that the beliefs are produced by the relevant process. Alston by contrast describes the process of production of Christian beliefs in a non-question-begging way; 'Christian mystical practice' can still produce beliefs even if there is no God. What he assumes is that this process is reliable; and what we need is evidence that the process is reliable. Only then will it be probably true (on our evidence) that a belief it yields is justified. Yet in either case if we have an internally justified belief (however produced) that Christian doctrines are true, there seems no obvious need for a further belief that they were caused in us by a special type of reliable process (unlike that by which any other true beliefs are caused). More generally, I suggest, an externalist warrant for Christian beliefs has no role to play in our religious lives; but we certainly need an internalist justification for them if it is to be sensible to use them to guide our lives.

Notes

1. Second edn. (Oxford: Clarendon, 2007). I am grateful to the Oxford University Press for permission to use material from this book in this chapter.
2. (Oxford: Clarendon, 1987).
3. Thus St Basil of Caesarea wrote that 'time would fail me if I attempt to recount the unwritten mysteries of the church' (*On the Holy Spirit* 27. 67). Although the sample list of mysteries that he does recount are all mysteries of liturgical practice (e.g. signing a catechumen with the sign of the Cross, and blessing the water of baptism and the oil of

chrismation before their use), he argues that doctrine can be derived from liturgical practice. He makes this assertion in the course of arguing that if the divinity of the Holy Spirit were not explicitly stated in Scripture, that would not suffice to dismiss it as not an essential part of the Christian faith. For the divinity of the Spirit, he argues, is clearly implicit in the words used by the church when catechumens are baptized. The second Council of Nicaea, the seventh Ecumenical Council (recognized by both Orthodox and Roman Catholics), anathematized anyone who 'rejects any written or unwritten tradition of the church'.

4. *Epistolae* 4. 31.

5. For descriptions of different modern ways of interpreting the Old Testament, see John Barton, *Reading the Old Testament*. Barton defends explicitly the thesis that there is no privileged method of interpretation.

6. *De doctrina Christiana* 3. 10. 14.

7. Thus Augustine (*De Genesi ad Litteram* 2. 1. 4, translated by J. H. Taylor (New York: Newman, 1982)): 'Let no one think that because the Psalmist says "He established the earth above the water", we must use this testimony of Holy Scripture against those people who engage in learned discussions about the weights of the elements. They are not bound by the authority of our Bible; and, ignorant of the sense of these words, they will more readily scorn our sacred books than disavow the knowledge they have acquired by unassailable arguments or proved by the evidence of experience. The statement of the Psalmist can with good reason be understood figuratively.'

8. Beryl Smalley, *The Study of the Bible in the Middle Ages* (Oxford: Basil Blackwell, 1952), 14.

9. See Origen, *De Principiis* 4. 2. 4; and Augustine, *De Utilitate Credendi* 5–8.

10. See e.g. Jerome's *Commentary on the Psalms* 137:9—'"Little ones" means thoughts...the Rock is Christ.'

11. Origen interpreted the story of Joshua's brutal execution of the five kings in Josh. 10: 15–27 allegorically. See the comparison of his treatment of this story with that of others in R. P. C. Hanson, *Allegory and Event* (London: SCM, 1959), ch. 5.

12. *De Genesi ad Litteram* 4. 22.

13. Ibid. 1. 21.

14. *Adversus Haereses* 4. 32. 1.

15. Tertullian, *De Praescriptione Haereticorum*, 19.

16. Article 1. 9 of the Westminster Confession.

17. (New York: Palgrave, 2001).

18. John 1: 1.

19. John 14: 28.

20. J. H. Newman, *The Idea of the Development of Christian Doctrine*; expounded in Owen Chadwick, *From Bossuet to Newman* (Cambridge: Cambridge University Press, 1957), ch. 7. See p. 157.

21. John Calvin, *Institutes of the Christian Religion*, trans. F. L. Battles (Philadephia: Westminster, 1960), 1. 7. 2.

22. Second edn. (Oxford: Clarendon, 2004).

23. (Oxford: Oxford University Press, 2000). See pp. 268–80.

24. (Grand Rapids: Eerdmans, 2006).

25. For his general theory of warrant, see Alvin Plantinga, *Warrant: The Current Debate* and *Warrrant and Proper Function* (Oxford: Oxford University Press, 1993). In the text

I summarize Plantinga's summary of his theory, ibid. 194. For Plantinga's application of his theory to Christian doctrines, see his *Warranted Christian Belief* (Oxford: Oxford University Press, 2000).

26. See his collection of essays, *Epistemic Justification* (Ithaca: Cornell University Press, 1989), and in it in particular 'An Internalist Externalism'. For the application to the results of 'Christian mystical practice' see his *Perceiving God* (Ithaca: Cornell University Press, 1991). (Note his remarks on pp. 75–6 of this work about its relation to the previous essay.) Alston has, however, now abandoned the view that there is a unique true account (externalist or other) of epistemic 'justification', and presents a pluralist account of the different epistemic desiderata (externalist and internalist) that can be possessed by a belief, in his *Beyond 'Justification'* (Ithaca: Cornell University Press, 2005).

27. (Oxford: Clarendon, 1996).

28. (Aldershot: Ashgate, 2004). My quotations are from pp. 196 and 215.

29. Ibid. 209.

30. I discuss the kind of 'faith' necessary for salvation, and how this differs from belief, in my *Faith and Reason*, 2nd edn. (Oxford: Clarendon, 2005).

CHAPTER 2

REVELATION AND INSPIRATION

STEPHEN T. DAVIS

I

IN this chapter, we will consider the concepts of revelation and inspiration.[1] The two notions are distinct but closely connected in Christian theology; they come together preeminently in discussions of the Bible. There are three assumptions that form the basis of this chapter but will not be argued for: (1) God exists; (2) there is divine revelation; and (3) the Bible plays a crucial role in revelation. Let us begin with revelation and then turn to inspiration.

One way to grasp the importance of revelation is to consider a God who does not reveal, namely, the God of Deism. Deism was a loosely defined philosophical and religious movement that thrived in Europe and America in the eighteenth century. The Deists affirmed the existence of God and held that God created the universe, with its immutable natural laws. They had confidence in the power of human reason to reach proper conclusions about religion, which for the Deists consisted of a few simple truths about God, creation, and morality.

The Deists importantly differed from traditional Christian thought in their rejection of all robust notions of divine revelation (except 'natural revelation', i.e. conclusions about God and religion reached by unaided human reason). Indeed, they rejected all claims of divine intervention in the world—not only special revelation but also miracles, epiphanies, and incarnations. God—so they implied—is like someone who winds a clock and then lets it run on its own without interference.

Oddly, Deism has made a recent comeback, although its contemporary defenders do not use that term. Despite differences, there are striking similarities between the original Deists and those recent and contemporary religious thinkers who affirm God but deny divine intervention in the world.[2] Some contemporary Deists affirm a notion of revelation, although the concept ends up being quite unlike traditional notions of God speaking or being supernaturally manifested in the world. Their operative notion of revelation seems to be more like: (1) insight into religious mysteries gained by those blessed with the relevant sort of spiritual wisdom; (2) enlightenment gained from a crucial event in personal or communal history; or (3) new truth arrived at via interpersonal or interreligious dialogue, truth that the participants would not have discovered independently. So the idea is that God is 'revealed' through ordinary historical, cultural, intellectual, or scientific processes.

In contrast, Christians believe in a God many of whose revelatory acts constitute interventions in the ordinary course of history. But it must be emphasized that human beings have no moral right to be recipients of divine revelation, no claim on God that God *must* reveal himself. So Christians should still—if they understand matters rightly—feel a sense of wonder when they grasp the fact that God has chosen to be revealed. There was no imperative or necessity that God do so. God could have remained silent.

What would have been the consequences if God had remained unrevealed? Suppose that the Deists were correct: suppose that God did not much care about the affairs of the world and that God never gave us a law or sent us prophets or a Son. What would follow? Certainly human beings would still be interested in religious questions. The Philippian jailer posed with elegant simplicity the most important of them: 'Sirs, what must I do to be saved?' (Acts 16: 30). The obvious conclusion is that if God were silent, we would be left to our own resources when we tried to answer questions like this.

What types of answers to such religious questions might we come up with? One possibility is some sort of *legalism*, i.e. a religious system containing little more than a set of rules that human beings must obey. This sort of religion would say: obey the laws and you'll be saved; disobey them and you'll be lost. A second possibility would be *ritualism*. This sort of religion would say: if you follow the prescribed ceremonials, the gods will be placated and you'll be saved; if you fail to follow them, you'll be lost. A third possibility, much in the spirit of our age, is *relativism*. This sort of religion would generously suggest that it doesn't really matter what you believe or how you behave; what matters is whether you are sincere and try hard to behave according to your best lights. A fourth possibility might be some version of *nihilism*: this sort of theory would deny that there are any answers; even if God exists, there is no way of knowing God or anything else for sure; there are no ultimate values; there is no justice; death ends everything. The most we can do is try as best we can to make life a bit more endurable.

In short, if God were silent, i.e. if there were no revelation of any sort, it is most probable that human beings would come up with false religious ideas. When revelation is lacking or not recognized, the world sets the intellectual and religious agenda. We see this today: in many circles, religion is held to be relativistic, private, syncretistic, deistic, or maybe all four. Such notions, in my view, are mistaken. And they illustrate the point that apart from revelation, there is no sure answer, based on human wisdom alone, to the question of the Philippian jailer. If God were silent there would be little hope of salvation; we would be like those who 'go down to the Pit' (Psalm 28: 1).

II

What is the purpose of divine revelation? It is to achieve God's aims in creation. Pre-eminently, God desires that human beings freely love, worship, and obey God, and (as the answer to Question 1 of the Westminster Shorter Catechism says), 'enjoy him forever'. Revelation, then, is not primarily for the purpose of imparting information, issuing commands, or initiating ceremonies, although it does all those things. Revelation exists for the essential purpose of establishing a personal and loving relationship between God and human beings.

To *reveal* is to unveil, show, or disclose something that was hidden or unknown. Divine revelation is God disclosing things that were hidden from human beings or unknown to them. Revelation is a way for God to leap across the gap, so to speak, that separates God from human beings. More precisely, there exist three gaps—an *ontological* gap, an *epistemological* gap, and a *moral* gap. The first is due to the difference between a necessary, eternal, all-powerful creator and a dependent, temporal, feeble creature. The second is due to the difference between an omniscient being and an ignorant being. The third is due to the difference between a holy and morally perfect being and a depraved and self-centered being.

Because of these gaps, human beings naturally know little of God and God's requirements, or at least not enough to accomplish God's redemptive purposes. And even things that they do know or can learn on their own (perhaps that God exists, that murder is morally wrong, etc.) can be denied, forgotten, or ignored. We are ignorant of much that we need to know in order to be saved, and we are unable to save ourselves. If we are to attain saving knowledge of God and God's purposes, that knowledge must come from God. It must be revealed.

Scripture teaches that human beings were created 'in God's image' (Genesis 1: 26), which suggests that God and human beings are in some ways significantly similar. Since 'being similar to' is a symmetrical relationship (if A is similar to B, then B is similar to A), then if we are (in some ways) similar to God, it follows that God is (in some ways) similar to us. That significant similarity—whatever exactly it is—is the ontological basis of revelation. Unless God and human beings were importantly related in some such way (e.g. by both being *persons*), revelation would be impossible. God has made us to be receivers of revelation.[3]

Again, what God preeminently wants is for humans to come to love, worship, and obey God. (For convenience we'll lump all three together and say that God wants us to 'glorify God'.) Let us also suppose that what God wants is for humans *freely* to opt to glorify God. And the central obstacle that God faces in achieving these desires is that human beings are both ignorant and sinful. They need to be both taught and redeemed.

There are many areas in which humans are ignorant. We who are asked to glorify God will need answers to at least the following questions:

- Does God exist?
- If God exists, what is God like?
- Exactly how do human beings 'glorify God', i.e. how do they go about loving, worshipping, and obeying God? What exactly are they required to do?
- What are the consequences of glorifying God, and what are the consequences of not doing so?

Thus there are many things that human beings do not naturally know or at least cannot easily come to know on their own and that they must know, if God's aims are to be realized (1 Cor. 15: 1–4; Heb. 11: 6; 1 John 1: 1–3). Accordingly, one of the things that God must do is find a way to answer these and other questions.

The term 'revelation', then, preeminently refers to God's actions to answer for our benefit these sorts of questions. The claim that God reveals himself is one of the most crucial claims of Christian faith—as an act of sovereign grace, God reveals God to us. Thus the prophet Amos says: 'For lo, the one who forms the mountains, creates the wind, *reveals his thoughts to mortals*, makes the morning darkness, and treads on the heights of the earth—The Lord, the God of hosts, is his name!' (Amos 4: 13; italics added). Moreover, in Christian theology, human ignorance and human sinfulness are connected. Sin has the effect of darkening our eyes to the truth, especially to uncomfortable truth. So revelation has a redemptive purpose. God does not just reveal interesting information to human beings; revelation is God's action aimed at creating a new relationship between God and human beings and among human beings.

Whatever revelatory methods God uses, the aim will surely be to answer human questions in ways that are clear, lasting, and convincing. A revelation is *clear* if it is unambiguous, if its meaning is not easily mistakable. Of course any communication from one person to another can be misinterpreted. Yet naturally God will want the divine acts of revelation to be clear. A revelation is *lasting* if its content is fairly easily passed on from one person to another and from one generation to another. Now any revelatory act can be forgotten or garbled through time, but God will clearly want the divine acts of revelation to be lasting. A revelation is *convincing* if it is powerful, illuminating, and tends to produce conviction. Of course any revelatory act, no matter how convincing, can be rejected, even if that rejection results from sheer stupidity or stubbornness. Nevertheless, God will clearly want the divine acts of revelation to be convincing.

III

There are many ways in which God might choose to reveal a given message (let's call it M) to some human being (let's say Jones). Here are a few: (1) God might create Jones in such a way as to be naturally disposed to believe M. (2) God might telepathically cause Jones to think or come to believe or at least cognitively entertain M. (3) God might appoint someone as a spokesperson and cause that person to say or write M to Jones. (4) God might cause Jones to dream M. (5) God might miraculously bring it about that Jones sees M written on a wall. (6) God might do some non-linguistic deed or action whose proper interpretation or deep meaning is M.

Of possible modes of revelation, some are linguistic (i.e. primarily involve words and sentences) and some are non-linguistic (i.e. primarily involve deeds or actions). God's revelatory action of rescuing Israel at the Red Sea was primarily non-linguistic; it was an action that spoke to Israel about the character of God. The Decalogue that God gave to Israel via Moses was primarily linguistic; it consists of words. This raises a theological question—much discussed in the previous century—whether divine revelation is by words or deeds.[4] Some theologians denied that God reveals propositions: such things—so they claimed—are timeless, static, impersonal, and cold. God's primary mode of revelation—so they insisted—was through dynamic personal encounters; God is revealed in deeds or persons or events rather than words.[5]

It does seem, a priori, that there are both values and problems in either approach. Actions are sometimes more impressive, powerful, gripping, and graphic than words. Just saying that you love your spouse or child is typically less convincing than showing it. Yet the problem with revelatory actions is that they seem more readily susceptible to being misinterpreted, changed in the retelling of them, and (unless they are written down) forgotten over time. Perhaps words are often less powerful than deeds; but revelatory words are valuable because they are not quite so easily misinterpreted, are easier to preserve and pass on, and once preserved are not quite so easily forgotten. These last two points are important given God's redemptive aims, i.e. given the assumption that God would intend at least some revelations to be for the benefit of other folk beside the original receivers or witnesses (see Psalm 22: 29–31).

It seems clear that God has used both modes of revelation. Moreover, God's great revelatory actions have typically been accompanied by authoritative verbal interpretations.[6] Indeed, it is not easy to see how a bare event, action, or encounter could be revelatory in any clear sense without interpretation or explanation. Events do not interpret themselves. And as soon as an interpretation is offered, then we are talking about words and sentences. A bare uninterpreted encounter with God (e.g. in the Exodus) will be far more easily recognized as such if it is explained or at least conceptualized as an encounter with God, as of course it is in Exodus 11–15. And if a claim is made that there is *truth* involved in a revelatory act or deed, it follows that the revelatory act be expressible in propositions.

Concerning the debates about propositional versus non-propositional revelation, it must be said that God is indeed revealed in deeds, persons, and human experiences (see 2 Cor. 12: 1–4). But it seems absurd to deny that God reveals words. To experience an encounter with God logically presupposes the possession of at least some knowledge about God. Thus Avery Dulles says: 'If we had no confidence in the propositional teaching of the Bible, we could hardly put our trust in the persons or events of biblical history, or even in the God to whom the Bible bears witness.'[7]

The enemies of 'propositional revelation' argued that Christian faith is trust in the person of God or Christ rather than in any proposition. As noted, their view was that propositions are too abstract, impersonal, and static to constitute the proper objects of religious faith; they elicit or call for no genuine response. This criticism contains a kernel of truth, but only that. It is true that Christian faith—or at least that crucial aspect of it that involves trust (*fiducia* or faith *in*)—is in God rather than any proposition. But surely the belief aspect of faith (*fides* or faith *that*) does essentially involve acceptance of certain propositions as true. Moreover, believing the truth of a proposition is inextricably tied to trusting a person in those cases where the person trusted takes responsibility for the proposition, e.g. by saying or writing it.[8] My trust in (*fiducia*) my mother, for example, makes no sense unless it involves willingness to believe (*fides*) what she says to me.

It is misleading, then, to argue that propositions are too static and invoke no genuine response. Christians would make no positive response to God at all unless they accepted as true such propositions as: *God loves us*; *Christ died for our sins*; and *we should thank and praise God*. Furthermore, the Bible itself claims that God reveals words. God is revealed in the words of the Decalogue, the oracles of the prophets, the parables and other teachings of Jesus, and the epistles of Paul. And many of those words were grammatically configured as propositions. They convey cognitive information; they contain truths. It seems to me that those theologians who denied that revelation was propositional believed (in fact, if not officially) in propositional revelation. They simply did not like the propositions that more conservative interpreters of the Bible claimed to find there, and so (in effect, if not by admission) they looked for and—not surprisingly—found others.

IV

We have noted some ways in which God might have chosen to be revealed to humans. But how did God actually choose to be revealed? A distinction is often made between general and special revelation. *General revelation* consists of those things about God, human beings, morality, and religion that human beings can learn on their own, i.e. without any supernatural ('special') assistance from God. The Bible teaches that some such things can be learned in this way (cf. Psalm 19: 1; Acts 17: 22–9; Romans 1: 18–23). Theologians have suggested that we can see evidence for them, for example, in considering the beauty and grandeur of creation, in reasoning cogently about God, or maybe even in examining our own consciences. But natural revelation, even at best, is incomplete, hazy, and easily confused. It is in need of supplementation.

Special revelation consists of those things about God, human beings, morality, and religion that are relevant to our salvation and that we can learn only as the result of, or are difficult to learn apart from, some supernatural or special act of assistance by God. Typically these would consist of things revealed by God to some person or group through dreams, visions, epiphanies, prophecies, miracles, or (supremely) through the life, death, and resurrection of Jesus Christ. The Scriptures hold that there are such acts (cf. Matthew 16: 17; Luke 4: 18–19; John 1: 14; Galatians 1: 11–12; Hebrews 1: 1–4). Christians believe that reading Scripture can also, through the illumination of the Spirit, constitute revelation.

Under the heading of special revelation, let me distinguish among three sorts of revelatory acts on the part of God. I will call them *original revelation, recorded revelation*, and *appropriated revelation*.

Original revelation consists of divine revelatory actions in history, some in the form of events and some in the form of words. This sort of revelation would preeminently include: the Exodus, the giving of the Decalogue, the oracles of the prophets, the teachings and miracles of Jesus, and the crucifixion and resurrection of Jesus. These are divinely ordained events or divine words that appear, by God's initiative, in the history of the people of God. Although God is still at work in history, Christian tradition holds that original revelation ceased with the death of the last apostle.[9] Christians celebrate the fact that God still speaks to people, moves them, guides them, and works in various other ways in their lives. But these divine actions do not count as original revelation and are not theologically normative for all Christians.[10]

But original revelation will most likely be fleeting and unstable unless it is recorded in some way, such as being written down. Oral traditions can certainly endure with amazing accuracy and for long periods of time, and did so in the ancient world. Moreover, written records can be corrupted or lost and forgotten. Still, if it is God's intention that as many human beings as possible know about God's acts of original revelation, then those acts must be recorded and interpreted in some sort of authoritative written document. And this is *recorded revelation*.

The text that Christians call the Bible is in part a record and interpretation of original revelation. By reading the Bible it is possible to learn some of what God has done in the past. Much of what the biblical writers recorded need not have been supernaturally revealed to them—doubtless they learned about some of the events and words that they recorded by quite ordinary means. The standard Christian claim is that recorded revelation, like original revelation, ceased long ago—when the last book of the Bible was completed. Since then presumably other Christian writings—sermons, hymns, liturgies, creeds, and perhaps even theological essays— were written under God's influence. Pronouncements of some of the early ecumen- ical councils have, in my view, a certain degree of normativity for Christians. But, as a Protestant, I do not hold that they are theologically authoritative for all Christians in the same sense that the Bible is.[11]

But the Bible is not *merely* (as is claimed in some circles[12]) a record of previous divine revelation. The Bible itself is revelatory. Christians hold that, through the illumination of the Holy Spirit, God speaks to us in the Bible. When it is correctly interpreted, the Bible in and of itself constitutes a unique and authoritative divine revelation. As Paul Helm points out, probably some things that were not necessarily revealed to the biblical writers, things they learned quite naturally, do constitute revelation to us as we read them in the Bible.[13] When God does speak to us in Scripture, e.g. when a biblical text, for example, inspires a reader to repent of a certain sin or assist a certain needy person, this is *appropriated revelation*. It is simply recorded revelation speaking to the reader, as we might say, in God's voice. Appropriated revelation adds nothing to original and recorded revelation, nor did it cease with the death of the apostles, nor are its deliverances theologic- ally authoritative for all Christians. Not all Christian denominations or traditions would accept this strong statement; still, my own view is that no post-apostolic vision, prophecy, dream, exegesis, creed, pronouncement, sense of discernment, decision, or conviction is normative for all Christians. It is authoritative only to the person by whom the revelation is appropriated, to whom the Holy Spirit is speaking. Appropriated revelation is an act of God; when I correctly sense that God is speaking to me in Scripture, that is a supernatural act of the Spirit of God.

Suppose God wanted to be revealed to as many people as possible and to as many sorts of people as possible—young and old, men and women, black and white, Eskimos and Hottentots, scholars and peasants. If so, it would seem appropriate for God to decide that at least part of divine revelation would consist of, or be crucially located in, a book. Presumably God's intention in doing so would be to make the content of revelation available to as wide a population as possible, and not just to those present at the appropriate time, to an elite class of scholars, or to those initiated into mysteries. This population would surely include people in generations and centuries after the revelation was given. A book seems particularly well suited to accomplish these ends.

It is inevitable that such a book would appear in a certain historical, national, cultural, and linguistic context, and that those who lived in that context would at least initially have the easiest access to the book. We cannot explain why God would choose one human group rather than another to be the original home of the book we are envisioning.[14] Still, if the revelatory book that first appeared in a given context were readily translatable into other contexts, God's aims could still be achieved.

If something like this picture were indeed God's revelatory choice, it would seem that God would then superintend the process of the writing of the various documents of which the book would ultimately consist, ensuring that they contained, at least in large part, what God wanted them to contain. That is, enough of their content would have to correspond to God's revelatory intentions so that people could read them and be reasonably sure of learning what God wanted them to learn. It would also seem plausible to suppose that God would ensure the church's recognition of the book as Scripture as well as superintend the process of copying, translating, reproducing, and preserving the book. All this would occur so that those who read the book could be reasonably sure that what they read corresponded reliably, even if not perfectly, to what was originally intended. There would also have to be ways for the errors of copyists, translators, and printers to be detected and corrected.[15]

According to Christians, this is precisely what did occur. God actually did choose to be crucially and normatively revealed in a book, and that book is the Bible. God did supervise the creation, production, transmission, and preservation of the book in roughly the indicated ways. The fact of God's providential guidance of the history of the Bible makes it unique among all the books that have ever been written in the world's history. It reveals God in a unique and normative way.

However, the Bible, by itself, was not sufficient to accomplish God's redemptive goals. A community was needed in order to provide authoritative texts, translations, and interpretations of the Bible. In this way, the original revelation could best be preserved and communicated.[16] The notion, sometimes heard in Protestant circles, that the 'Bible alone' is sufficient to accomplish God's revelatory and salvific aims is quite mistaken.

This is not to deny the traditional Protestant notion or the clarity or perspicuity of Scripture. The Bible's basic message can be understood by nearly anyone who is open and attentive to it, even children. But it is obvious that not everything in Scripture is plain and that a method and tradition of interpretation (e.g. what the church Fathers called 'the rule of faith') is needed.[17]

V

Is revelation 'progressive'? Are later divine revelations more accurate and sophisticated than earlier ones? The concept of progressive revelation has been used to solve problems caused by the fact that some earlier revelations seem crude and even immoral when compared with later ones. Some have felt, for example, that this notion might be a way to reconcile (1) the insistence of the books of Deuteronomy (see 2: 31–5; 3: 1–8; 7: 2) and Joshua (see 6: 15–21; 8: 25–6; 11: 12) that it was God's will that the Israelites kill every Canaanite man, woman, and child with (2) the law of love of the New Testament. The argument would go something like this: the earlier revelation was the best that God could do at the time, the most that God could reveal, given the level of theological and moral sophistication of the post-Exodus Israelites; they would have been unable to understand the more complete revelation of God as found in the New Testament. But by the time of the first century, people were ready to hear and receive that fuller revelation of the divine nature and so were able to receive the teachings of Jesus.

There is both something right and something mistaken here. All revelation, both earlier and later, involves accommodation or even condescension on the part of God. To borrow Calvin's metaphors, God must 'stoop' and even 'lisp' (i.e. engage in a sort of baby-talk) to speak to us.[18] All revelation must meet us where we are. The ontological, epistemological, and moral gaps between God and human beings ensure that we cannot comprehend the fullness of God's nature and will. So all revelation is partial. As Paul says, we now know 'in part', not 'face to face' (1 Corinthians 13: 12). What God has revealed is trustworthy; we do indeed have knowledge of God. But it is only provisional, incomplete, and inchoate. Even as revealed, much about God remains mysterious to us.

What is mistaken in the concept of progressive revelation? It is the suggestion that the ancient Israelites were so morally or intellectually primitive that God could not get them to grasp the fuller revelation that appears in the New Testament— a revelation that the much more enlightened folk of the first century (as well as, of course, those of us in the twenty-first) are clever and moral enough to grasp. That is not a particularly convincing claim. There is a sense in which revelation is progressive, but it has nothing to do with any inability on God's part to teach certain folk things that they were too dumb to understand.

Revelation is progressive in that: (1) as a sovereign choice, God decided to be revealed over time rather than all at once, and in earlier times did make concessions to then prevalent views, allowing such things as slavery, polygamy, and divorce (Matthew 19: 3–9); (2) as a sovereign choice, God decided to be revealed in such a way that earlier revelations are interpreted by, incorporated within, and sometimes superseded by, later ones (see Matthew 5: 21–48); and (3) as a sovereign choice, God decided that normative revelation occurs only for a time and then ceases. Thus the picture of God and of God's will that revelation paints for us is indeed more complete at the end than it is at the beginning. All three points are contingent, however; God could have chosen to do otherwise.

To accept a revelation from God is to be subject to something like a paradigm shift. Revelation typically calls for a response, a response of repentance, obedience, commitment, or trust. But it is perfectly possible to receive a revelation from God, or to have reliable evidence of one, and remain unmoved. Even the 'signs and wonders' that accompany some revelatory acts—e.g. the Exodus or the resurrection of Jesus—can be explained away by those who are hard-hearted or spiritually blind. God structures all God's revelatory acts—even the Christ event—in such a way as to ensure our cognitive and moral freedom to say no. God does not coerce the proper response.

Again, the purpose of revelation is to bring it about that humans come into a personal relationship with God, one that involves freely chosen love (which cannot be coerced) as well as worship and obedience. I argued above that God's aim would be to make all acts of divine revelation clear, lasting, and convincing. But they cannot be so overwhelmingly convincing as to coerce consent—as, say, the existence of my computer is to me now. The evidence for its presence in front of me is so overwhelming that no sensible person in my shoes could reject it. If God (as I believe) wants us to be free rationally to say yes or no to God, then God's revelatory acts cannot be so convincing that no sensible person could reject them.[19]

Still, if revelation is accepted by someone who did not previously know God, there must be change. A new notion of God is provided, as well as a new notion of what we owe God. Indeed, there is usually a radically new way of looking at all human experience and reality. When this occurs in someone's life, it is the work of the Holy Spirit. That work marks the difference between merely receiving a new bit of information, a new command, or a new ritual, on the one hand, and receiving a divine revelation, on the other.[20]

How then can our spiritual questions be answered? How can we learn how to glorify God and thus satisfy God's redemptive aims in creation? The answer is: preeminently by accepting and attending to the revelation of God in Scripture. All

Christians affirm that Jesus Christ is the supreme revelation of God. They should also affirm that the Bible is the primary appointed place where Christians encounter Jesus Christ and learn the divine will.

VI

Let us turn to inspiration. In 1 Corinthians 7, Paul addressed himself to questions such as marriage, divorce, celibacy, and sexual relations. In doing so, he carefully distinguished between his own teachings and those of Jesus. When Paul turned to the topic of the freedom of widows to remarry (vv. 39–40), he noted that what he said constituted his own teaching ('in my judgment'); but he then added, 'I think that I too have the Spirit of God.' Paul seems to have been claiming, then, that he was teaching the Corinthians what the Spirit of God would have him teach, that the Spirit stood behind or validated his own teachings.

The much wider claim that the writers of the texts that we call the Bible were so guided that what they wrote was what the Spirit of God would have them write is called *inspiration*. Traditionally, inspiration has to do with the influence of the Holy Spirit on the writers of the Bible so that what they wrote was, in some sense, the word of God. Several of the biblical writers were convinced that inspiration occurs. In 1 Corinthians 2: 9–15, Paul quoted an Old Testament text, and then said: 'These things God has revealed to us through the Spirit.' And 2 Peter 1: 20–1 speaks of scriptural prophecy in this way: 'No prophecy ever came by human will, but men and women moved by the Holy Spirit spoke from God.'

But serious difficulties face those who wish to write about this topic. Most of them fall under this heading: the notion of inspiration must fit the kind of document that the Bible actually is.[21] First, an acceptable notion of inspiration must fit the fact that while some biblical writers (e.g. Paul, the Old Testament prophets) were at times conscious of having a 'word' from God, others were not. Some biblical writers seem to have been conscious simply of having gathered information from various sources, and some of those sources were incomplete or defective.[22] Second, an acceptable notion of inspiration must fit the fact that in the Bible there are distinct traditions about the same events and discrepancies between them.[23] There are not just numerical and historical discrepancies, and not just apparently misidentified or misinterpreted quotations of the Old Testament in the New Testament. There are also theological discrepancies, or at least apparent ones. Third, an acceptable notion of inspiration must fit the fact that some biblical books had a long history of composition and that the very notion of '*the* author' is irrelevant.

Traditional theories of inspiration have focused on the human author or authors of the text and the text itself. They fit what is called the 'prophetic model' of inspiration, i.e. the model that envisions a biblical author writing an inspired book or text under the influence of the Spirit. The central idea of this model is that God inspired the writers of the Bible in a similar way as God inspired the Old Testament prophets and gave them a 'word' from God to the people. But under this model, there are several ways of formulating a doctrine of inspiration. Let me mention several possible theories, starting with the strongest and moving toward the less robust ones.

1. *Dictation.* The strongest and simplest of the theories, dictation holds that God alone is the author of Scripture; God dictated to the human authors the very words that they wrote down, so that in the (text-critically acceptable) words of Scripture we have the unambiguous words of God. Now almost nobody who talks about biblical inspiration admits to believing in dictation, although some views of robust biblical inerrancy are not easy to disentangle from dictation. The compelling reason that dictation is seldom defended is that the many differences in style, vocabulary, genre, and even substantive content that exist in the various books and passages of Scripture seem inconsistent with dictation. Unless God made sure to dictate the words of Galatians to Paul in Paul's own distinctive style, and the words of Ecclesiastes to Qoheleth in Qoheleth's own very different style, the theory collapses. That is, it collapses as a general theory covering the whole of Scripture. But dictation may well be the most helpful theory of biblical inspiration for some texts (assuming they capture accurately what was originally revealed), e.g. the Ten Commandments, the teachings of Jesus, and perhaps even some prophetic oracles.[24]

2. *Inspired ideas.* On this view, God inspired the biblical writers by giving them the correct ideas or images, which those writers then fleshed out or expressed by means of their own words. God left the choosing of the words pretty much up to them. The Bible's good points, so to speak, are a result of the divinely supplied ideas or images; its bad points are a result of poorly chosen human words. But this theory has received little support.[25] Perhaps it has some vague relevance to some parts of scripture, e.g. descriptions or explanations of visions in Ezekiel or Revelation. But the basic problem is the philosophical point that words are too closely connected to the ideas they express for such a distinction as to their origin to be consistently made.

3. *Middle knowledge inspiration.* William L. Craig has recently proposed a theory of biblical inspiration that is both new and serious.[26] It is based on the notion of 'middle knowledge', a complex and somewhat controversial notion that it is not possible to explain here in any detail. Invented by the Jesuit philosopher Luis de Molina (1535–1600), the idea is that at the moment of creation, God knew three sorts of things. The first is God's 'natural knowledge', which is knowledge of all necessities and possibilities, i.e. of what *could* be (e.g. 'Possibly the world will contain no

ten-foot tall human beings') or *must* be (e.g. 'No triangles are four-sided'). The second is God's 'free knowledge', which is knowledge of all propositions that are or will be contingently true of the actual world (e.g. 'George W. Bush will be President of the United States'). Located between these two—so Molina claimed—is God's middle knowledge (also called counterfactual knowledge); it is knowledge of what would be the case if certain non-actual circumstances obtained, e.g. 'If Stephen Davis is offered a peanut butter cookie to vote for a certain candidate, he will refuse.'[27]

Note that via his middle knowledge, God can providentially control people without taking away their (libertarian) freedom and thus can bring about the results that he desires. Craig then holds that divine middle knowledge allows us to affirm that scriptural inspiration was *plenary* (all of Scripture, not parts of it, were inspired), *verbal* (the very words of Scripture, not just the ideas, were inspired), and *confluent* (both God and the human authors are the authors of Scripture). As middle knowledge applies to the Bible, Craig affirms that 'God knew, for example, that were he to create the Apostle Paul in just the circumstances he was in around AD55 [given Paul's background, personality, environment, and promptings and gifts of the Holy Spirit], he would freely write to the Corinthian church, saying just what he did in fact say.'[28] So the letter of 1 Corinthians is truly the work of Paul (he freely wrote; the words are Paul's, etc.) and of God (since the letter says exactly what God wanted said).

4. *Degrees of inspiration.* The idea here would be that there were levels of inspiration of the writers of Scripture, i.e. some biblical texts or writers were more directly or thoroughly inspired by the Holy Spirit than were others. Thus James Orr said: 'There were lower grades of inspiration in the form of special *charismata* (wisdom, artistic skill, physical powers), shading off till it becomes difficult to distinguish them from heightened natural endowment.'[29] As Paul Achtemeier points out, such a theory fits well to the claim—frequently made in mainstream denominational and neo-Orthodox circles—that the Bible is not in and of itself divine revelation, but is rather a human and in places fallible *record* of past acts of divine revelation.[30]

5. *Social inspiration.* Perhaps God inspired not an individual writer but a group of people, specifically the community that was responsible for bringing the biblical text in question into existence. But while there is no good reason to deny that God ever did such a thing, the notion of social inspiration does not help us much in understanding inspiration. The question remains in what precise ways God inspired the community or the individuals who made up the community.

6. *Secular inspiration.* Although this theory does not fall under the prophetic model of inspiration, there is another possibility along the route that we have been roughly traveling from stronger to less robust theories. Possibly the Bible is an entirely human book and, so far as origin is concerned, there is no intrinsic difference between the Bible and any other book. To the extent that biblical inspiration

occurred at all (and some liberal Protestants reject the notion entirely), perhaps the writers of the Bible were 'inspired' in some sense not unlike the way the writers of great but entirely secular books were inspired. Perhaps God uses the book called the Bible for religious purposes more than God uses other books; perhaps the church accepts the Bible as more authoritative than other books; but there was no special divine influence on the writings of the Bible per se. The reasons usually given for abandoning robust notions of inspiration are (1) the discrepancies in the Bible, and (2) the fact that the Bible seems to speak approvingly of such practices as slavery, the oppression of women, mass murder, the torture of prisoners, and polygamy.[31]

There are obviously other possible theories, and no one theory has gained universal acceptance. Indeed, the problems of arriving at an adequate theory of inspiration that is author-oriented or text-oriented are so serious that some contemporary authors seek to locate inspiration elsewhere. That is, some choose to abandon the prophetic model. Not only do many biblical authors seem unaware of having received any inspired 'word' from God, but it is sometimes unclear precisely who would have been inspired. The point here is not the truism that there are biblical books and passages whose authors are unknown to us (e.g. Hebrews); the deeper point is that the complicated textual history of some books (e.g. Isaiah, John) makes the notion of one writer, blessed by God with the gift of inspiration, apparently inapplicable. When so many people were involved in creating the text, who was the inspired author?

VII

Accordingly, some recent and contemporary scholars attempt to locate biblical inspiration elsewhere than with the author or the text. Obviously, we cannot discuss all such attempts; we will consider two such theories, one by a theologian and the other by a philosopher.

In his book, *Evangelical Theories of Biblical Inspiration: A Review and Proposal*,[32] Kern Robert Trembath argues that what we call biblical inspiration is a fact not about the Bible, but about the reader of the Bible, whether that be the church or the individual Christian. He says: 'I shall propose that "the inspiration of the Bible" should be taken to refer not to empirical characteristics of the Bible itself but rather to the fact that the church confesses the Bible as God's primary means of inspiring salvation within itself' (p. 5).

The Bible is thus the means of biblical inspiration rather than its locus or terminus. Biblical inspiration depends on the faith perspective of the reader of the Bible; it is the way in which a believer or Christian community recognizes the indispensable role of the Bible in redemption. Trembath admits that inspiration is not totally independent of the words of the Bible, 'but neither is it a property which applies exhaustively to those words'. The phrase 'biblical inspiration', he says, is an abbreviated reference to 'the experience of salvation by God through Christ as mediated through the Bible' (p. 111; see also p. 62).

What about scriptural authority? Trembath denies that the authority of Scripture is located in its words, 'as though they could have an authoritative status apart from their reception and appropriation by the believers' (p. 52). Scriptural authority is conditional upon the appropriation of its central message by believers; it is the Bible's 'indispensability in witnessing to the relationship which God establishes through the church' (p. 53). The words of the Bible can be said to be inspired only when they are received as God's word by the believing community (p. 116).

Trembath recognizes that the traditional Reformed doctrine of the inward testimony of the Holy Spirit is, as he says, the functional equivalent of his theory of biblical inspiration. But the question is whether it constitutes an adequate theory of what it purports to be, namely, biblical inspiration.[33] If Trembath insists on using the term 'biblical inspiration' in his preferred way, one might ask what new term we are to use to describe God's guidance (if there was any such guidance) of the process of the production of the book that we call the Bible.

Few Christians will allow that there was no such process. For if not, the Bible will have no special status among the world's books apart from the functional point about its having shaped the Christian experience of salvation more than any other book. Yet even if we grant that the Bible has this unique functional status for the church, the question remains whether it has any special ontological status. Is it or is it not intrinsically different from other books? Is the Bible, in and of itself, unique? After all, some people have been powerfully moved by *The Iliad* or *The Apology* or *Anna Karenina*. And some people's experience of Christian salvation has been powerfully shaped by the *Summa Theologica* or *The Institutes of the Christian Religion* or *Mere Christianity*.

Book-oriented theories of biblical inspiration[34] usually involve *verbal* inspiration, and this theory often leads to the notion that the verbal claims made in the Bible are certainly true. Trembath criticizes this notion on the grounds that certainty is not a property of words (as the people who hold to the doctrine appear to hold), but of the mind. He says: 'Certainty is the conclusion of a judgment, and judgments are acts of human minds rather than properties of objects such as words' (p. 91). But this claim is a frail reed on which to hang a rejection of verbal inspiration. For some configurations of words—e.g. 'Two plus two equals four' and 'Abraham Lincoln was president of the United States'—have the property of being certainly true. And this is surely what the friends of verbal inspiration want to say about the words of the Bible. As regards the Bible, Trembath says that 'certainty results from the mental determination which chooses the biblical accounts of redemption and salvation as those which best summarize the actual experience of salvation undergone by Christian believers' (p. 91). Again, there is truth here, but the problem is that there is much in the Bible that seems certainly true to many believers and that has little or nothing to do with describing their 'actual experience of salvation'.

In the end it is puzzling that Trembath devotes his book to a sustained discussion of the special status of the Bible in the Christian experience of salvation—making points that could fall under the rubric of the inward testimony of the Holy Spirit—without raising the question of the special intrinsic character of the Bible. This is curious because Trembath insists both that knowledge of God can only come from God (pp. 5, 85, 90, 93) and that the Christian community's beliefs about God have been preeminently shaped by the Bible (p. 111). Does this not at least suggest that the Bible is 'from God' in some interesting way? If so, in what precise way is the Bible 'from God'? This is the question that book-oriented discussions of biblical inspiration were designed to answer. And the central moral that I draw from Trembath's work is that discussions of biblical inspiration ought to continue to address the question of the intrinsic character of the Bible.

VIII

In his ground-breaking book *Divine Discourse*,[35] Nicholas Wolterstorff makes a suggestion that might be usable as part of a non-book-oriented theory of biblical inspiration. But we must first note that Wolterstorff's book is not primarily about inspiration or even revelation, but about the concept of God speaking. Still, one of the important points that he makes in his book is relevant to our purposes.

Wolterstorff points out that it occasionally occurs that a piece of speech or writing is correctly attributed to a given person even though it was composed by somebody else. Maybe a secretary who knows the mind of the boss is asked by the boss to compose a letter; the boss approves of the letter, signs it, and it then becomes the boss's letter. Ambassadors are entitled to 'speak in the name' of the head of state whom they represent. Naturally, there can be different modes and degrees of superintendence over the words and different degrees in which the final words of the text are authorized and accepted as her own by the person who counts as the author.

So far as the Bible is concerned, we do find in it the phenomenon of prophets who are deputized or commissioned by God to speak a message in God's name. Wolterstorff calls this 'appropriated discourse'; he suggests that the Christian claim that the Bible is God's book can naturally be understood, at least for much of the Bible, as divinely appropriated human discourse (p. 53). So maybe the Bible as a whole is God's book in the sense that God appropriates it. Accordingly, in the Bible God now speaks to us via words that were composed by other people, namely the Bible's human authors. God is the ultimate author of Scripture (pp. 186, 283).

Wolterstorff recognizes that the notion of appropriated divine discourse must be supplemented by a doctrine of inspiration (p. 187); it can't be that God had nothing whatever to do with the composition of the books of the Bible, saw them (so to speak) lying about, and simply decided to adopt the words as his own. Still, he insists that the books of the Bible, human discourse as they are, mediate to us God's speaking. (Wolterstorff never spells out the notion of inspiration that he admits his theory needs as a supplement.)

Wolterstorff's notion of divine appropriated discourse seems acceptable as a way of understanding how God speaks to us in the Bible, at least in many of its books and texts. It is significant, however, that Wolterstorff sees clearly the need for this notion to be supplemented by a theory of inspiration. That admission tends strongly to confirm the suspicion that reader-oriented theories of biblical inspiration, while valuable as far as they go, are insufficient in themselves. They do not say enough about the intrinsic properties of the Bible itself; they do not capture what most Christians want to say about the Bible.

IX

Is it possible then to develop a defensible theory of inspiration that concentrates on intrinsic properties of the Bible itself? Before trying, let me mention three items that I reject. First, I do not hold that the ideas of Scripture are inspired but the words are not. Second, I do not hold that some parts of Scripture (e.g. the ethical or religious parts, or the parts that pertain to its central salvific purpose) are inspired and the others are not. Third, I do not hold that some parts of the Bible are *more* inspired than other parts (although certainly some parts are more theologically crucial, religiously useful, and hermeneutically central than other parts).

An acceptable theory of inspiration must recognize the fact that the Bible is in some sense both the words of God and the words of its human authors. There is both divine and human agency involved in the production of the Bible. Accordingly, theories of inspiration at both extremes are excluded: dictation because it denies human agency and secular inspiration because it denies divine agency. The Bible, then, is both the words of human beings and the word of God.

It is not hard to imagine scenarios in which God and human beings work together to produce some result. The humans involved may or may not be aware of God's agency or influence. Indeed, it seems a clear presumption of biblical religion that this sort of double agency occurs. Not only historical events (such as the crucifixion of Jesus—Acts 2: 23) but also literary products (according to 1 Peter 1: 20–1) can be the result of God and humans working together: 'No prophecy of scripture...ever came by human will, but men and women moved by the Holy Spirit spoke from God.' That is, Scripture is the result of human beings speaking and writing, but they spoke as moved by the Spirit.

What then is biblical inspiration? Let me define it as *that influence of the Holy Spirit on the writing of the Bible that ensures that the words of its various texts are appropriate both for the role that they play in Scripture and for the overall salvific purpose of Scripture itself.* In other words, working in conjunction with the human author, God ensures that the words written are revelatory and fit God's purposes. Because of inspiration, God speaks to us in the Bible. Scripture is not just a record of revelation; it in itself is revelatory.[36]

Paul in 2 Timothy 3: 15–17 speaks of 'the sacred writings that are able to instruct you for salvation through faith in Jesus Christ'. The sacred writings referred to here are surely the books of the Old Testament; it then says: 'All scripture is inspired by God and is useful for teaching, for reproof, for correction, and for training in righteousness.' This text is one reason for holding, as argued above, that the purpose of revelation is redemptive, i.e. its purpose is that human beings come freely to glorify God. The word translated 'inspired' in 2 Timothy 3: 16 (*theopneustos*) means 'breathed out by God'. Thus one venerable way of affirming that the Scriptures are inspired is to claim that they are 'breathed out by God' for the purpose of guiding people to life in Christ.

But it is also important to emphasize the point about God working with the human author or authors. This means that inspiration has nothing to do with authors being temporarily freed from their human characteristics or limitations. It means that despite those limitations, the words of Scripture fit God's purposes for them. Nor does inspiration necessarily imply that the inspired human authors experienced unusual psychological states such as trances, visions, dreams, or the hearing of paranormal voices. In some cases inspiration may have involved some such states, but in other cases an observer would doubtless have noticed nothing unusual about the behavior of the inspired author or authors.

I have argued against theories that locate biblical inspiration and authority entirely in the reader. These notions must have something to do with intrinsic properties of the Bible itself. Christians hold that the primary reason that the Bible, in and of itself, is unique among all the world's books and theologically normative is because its writers were inspired. That is why they hold that this book in some sense originates from God, why they hold that God speaks to them through this book.

Let us return to the point that the various books of the Bible seem to have reached their final form in different ways, and that several such books had no one human author. In such cases, if biblical inspiration is to make any sense, it must be that several people were inspired, i.e. the Holy Spirit influenced more than one person. Perhaps inspiration affected, say, the original prophetic speaker (ensuring that the prophet spoke the words God intended to reveal), the final editor (assuming that this is a different person) of the biblical book (ensuring that what it says is appropriate for God's purposes for it), and perhaps other people between them.

James Barr, a formidable critic of conservative views of biblical authority, makes the following point:

If there is inspiration at all, then it must extend over the entire process of production that has led to the final text. Inspiration therefore must attach not to a small number of exceptional persons like St. Matthew or St. Paul: it must extend over a large number of anonymous persons, so much so that it must be considered to belong more to the community as a whole than to a group of exceptional persons who through unique inspiration 'gave' the scriptures to the community.[37]

In general, Barr's point is well taken. We must insist that the process can still include exceptional inspired persons who shape their communities. But Barr is right that if inspiration is to make any sense, it must mean that God superintends the whole process that led to the existence of the book that we call the Bible.

Note the many ways in which God's redemptive purposes tied up in a book could be unfulfilled. The original revelatory event might be misinterpreted. Over time, oral traditions about it might be lost or distorted beyond recognition. The original piece of writing might be inaccurate or misleading. Poor editing might make a fine original document unintelligible, unhelpful, or otherwise salvifically useless. Writings not intended by God for inclusion in the book might be included, and writings intended by God for inclusion in the book might be excluded. The book could be copied or transmitted so poorly that over time it became impossible to hear God's voice in it. The book, or crucial parts of it, might be subject to so much systematic misinterpretation or mistranslation as to be useless in achieving God's purposes for it.

Small mistakes, perhaps at any point in the process, might be consistent with the book's achieving God's purposes for it, especially if they were either correctable or else so unimportant as to be negligible. Still, the point stands: God must providentially superintend the whole process of the production of the book that we call the Bible. If the Bible is indeed an inspired book, then God has done this very thing.

Surely no one theory of biblical inspiration will cover the whole of the Bible. Different theories seem relevant to different texts. As noted above, dictation seems to be relevant to some passages. Social inspiration, at least in some cases, must have occurred. Middle knowledge seems promising as a way of understanding inspiration, although the notion has yet to be thoroughly explored by scholars. And Wolterstorff's notion of divinely appropriated discourse is also helpful.

X

There is a logical connection between the inspiration of the Bible, as traditionally conceived, and the authority of the Bible. This connection seems sensible: if a book has been so guided throughout the history of its production that God speaks to us in it and it fulfills God's redemptive purposes for it, then that book will naturally have a great deal of authority.

Authority has both a subjective and an objective sense. A given civil law might have no authority over me in the sense of guiding my behavior if I do not know about the law or do not submit to it. The law, as we might say, has no subjective authority over me. Some recent and contemporary scholars want to think of biblical authority in this way: the Bible has authority over Christians because they have chosen to receive and appropriate it as normative. But some authority relationships (objective ones) exist whether submitted to or not. Whether I know about or submit to the law or not, it still has authority over me in the sense that my behavior *ought* to be guided by it.

Similarly, Scripture has subjective authority over a person's life only if that person submits to Scripture. Sadly, many people today fail to live their lives under Scripture's authority. But because of inspiration, Scripture is revelatory; God speaks to us in Scripture. Accordingly, Scripture has objective authority over a person's life whether or not it is ever read, recognized, or submitted to. If in the Bible God speaks to us, then we *ought* to submit to Scripture. Indeed, as Swinburne points out, the Bible would have no authority for Christians if the Christian community did not recognize its inspiration.[38] Of course all authority is from God, and belongs to Jesus Christ (Matthew 28: 18); accordingly, the Bible's authority over Christian faith and practice is derived rather than original or absolute. Nevertheless, the Bible is and ought to be the central way in which God exercises authority over the Christian community.

Notes

I would like to thank Professors Tom Flint, Susan Peppers-Bates, Michael Rea, and Richard Swinburne for their helpful comments on an earlier draft of this chapter.

1. Some of the material in the first half of this chapter is a slightly revised version of my *Christian Philosophical Theology* (Oxford: Oxford University Press, 2006), 44–57.

2. It is possible to posit a robust notion of miracles that do not amount to interventions. For example, God might foreordain that certain events occur at certain points in time that would not otherwise have occurred. But I will ignore that possibility here.

3. This point is rightly insisted on by Kern R. Trembath in his *Divine Revelation: Our Moral Relation With God* (New York: Oxford University Press, 1991), pp. 4, 114–15, 136, 168–9.

4. The distinction that I am making between revelation by words and revelation by deeds is close to the distinction that George Mavrodes makes between the communication model of revelation and the manifestation model of revelation. See his helpful book *Revelation in Religious Belief* (Philadelphia: Temple University Press, 1988), 35.

5. See e.g. John Baillie, *The Idea of Revelation in Recent Thought* (New York: Columbia University Press, 1956), 49: 'what is fundamentally revealed is God Himself, not propositions about God'.

6. This point was emphasized even in the neo-Orthodox period by James D. Smart. See his *The Interpretation of Scripture* (Philadelphia: Westminster, 1961), 172–3.

7. Avery Dulles, SJ, *Models of Revelation* (Garden City: Doubleday, 1983), 205. See also William Abraham, *Divine Revelation and the Limits of Historical Criticism* (New York: Oxford University Press, 1982), 21, and Ronald H. Nash, *The Word of God and the Word of Man* (Grand Rapids: Zondervan, 1982), 43–54.

8. See Paul Helm, *The Divine Revelation* (Westchester: Crossway Books, 1982), 26.

9. See the Westminster Confession, I. 1, in John H. Leith (ed.), *Creeds of the Churches* (Garden City: Doubleday, 1963), 193.

10. See Richard Swinburne, *Revelation: From Metaphor to Analogy* (Oxford: Oxford University Press, 1972), 102. I should note that much of what I say in this section of the chapter presupposes the work of Swinburne.

11. My own more complete views on Scripture and tradition can be found in my *Christian Philosophical Theology*, 265–82.

12. See Swinburne, *Revelation*, 103: 'Holy Scripture must be regarded by Protestants as it is by Catholics, as no more than a true record of a revelation which existed before it.'

13. Helm, *Divine Revelation*, 70.

14. Ancient Israel was similarly puzzled over its election as God's people. In Deuteronomy 7: 7–8a, the best explanation that they could find was a kind of tautology: God loved Israel because God loved Israel.

15. Many of these points are rightly emphasized by Swinburne. See *Revelation*, 75–84.

16. I entirely agree with the emphasis placed on this point by Swinburne (see ibid. 81–4, 113, 119, 178, 183–4.) But I believe that he is led to his emphasis on the church for the wrong reason. He concedes too much to historical-critical biblical scholarship, and concludes that on historical grounds alone (that is, apart from authoritative church teaching) there is little that we can know, for example, of the life of Jesus. Note this telling remark: 'The task of discovering some vague outlines of what Jesus said and did and what happened to him is not, I suggest, an impossible one' (p. 105). On the other hand, in the second edition of the book, Swinburne will take the slightly stronger stand that we have a reasonable amount of historical evidence for believing quite a lot of what is said by and about Jesus in the Gospels.

17. See James Callahan, *The Clarity of Scripture* (Downers Grove: InterVarsity Press, 2001).

18. See John Calvin, *Corpus Reformatorum* (Calvin's works, ed. W. Baum, E. Cunitz, and E. Reuss [Braunschweig, 1865]), xxvi. 35, 312, 387.

19. This point is well argued in W. S. Anglin, *Free Will and Christian Faith* (Oxford: Oxford University Press, 1990), 187–92.

20. See Mavrodes, *Revelation in Religious Belief*, 150.

21. See Raymond Brown, *The Critical Meaning of the Bible* (New York: Paulist Press, 1981), 7–14.

22. See James Orr, *Revelation and Inspiration* (Grand Rapids: Baker Book House, 1969; original edn. London: Duckworth & Co., 1910), 164–5, 179–81.

23. See Paul J. Achtemeier, *The Inspiration of Scripture* (Philadelphia: Westminster, 1980), 58–74.

24. A variation on this theory would be dictation at the stage of editing rather than the stage of composing the text. That is, perhaps the Bible's human authors supplied both the ideas and the words but God occasionally intervened to correct mistaken or misleading expressions.

25. For a discussion of it, see Robert Gnuse, *The Authority of the Bible* (New York: Paulist Press, 1985), 42–6.

26. Craig's Theory is found in his ' "Men Moved by the Holy Spirit Spoke from God" (2 Peter 1: 21): A Middle Knowledge Perspective on Biblical Inspiration', *Philosophia Christi*, ser. 2, 1/1(1999), 45–82.

27. Counterfactuals can be true or false. According to the standard Lewis/Stalnaker theory, we test a counterfactual such as, 'If Bryant had not been injured, the Lakers would have won the game' by asking whether the Lakers do win the game in the closest possible world to the actual world in which Bryant is not injured. This analysis is somewhat controversial among logicians, and things quickly get more complex than this, but the point is that there do exist procedures for verifying or falsifying counterfactual claims.

28. Craig, 'Men Moved by the Holy Spirit', 72.

29. Orr, *Revelation and Inspiration*, 177.

30. Achtemeier, *The Inspiration of Scripture*, 43.

31. Those who affirm robust inspiration deny that the Bible, properly interpreted, approves of such practices. But this hermeneutical issue is outside the scope of this chapter.

32. (New York: Oxford University Press, 1987). References to this book will be placed in parentheses in the text.

33. John Reid's comment of some half-century ago is appropriate: 'Now it turns out that the Bible is being recommended, not because it is an inspired book, but because it is an inspiring book...This may indeed be all that some people require of biblical inspiration; but it is an impoverished conception.' *The Authority of Scripture* (New York: Harper & Row, 1957), 168.

34. One of Trembath's criticisms of book-oriented biblical inspiration gets nowhere. He says the idea that inspiration is an intrinsic property of the Bible is wrongheaded because properties of things normally hold independently of anybody's beliefs about them, but only the Christian community believes in inspiration; ergo, inspiration is not an intrinsic property of the Bible (p. 116). But it surely cannot be true that a property can be a belief-independent property of some object only if everybody accepts it as a property of that object.

35. Nicholas Wolterstorff, *Divine Discourse: Philosophical Reflections on the Claim that God Speaks* (Cambridge: Cambridge University Press, 1995). References to this work will be placed in parentheses in the text.

36. It should be pointed out that the definition of biblical inspiration just suggested might fit with various theories of precisely *how* the Bible or the biblical writers were inspired. The fact that the definition does not entail a commitment to any such theory and is thus somewhat flexible is, I believe, an asset.

37. James Barr, *Holy Scripture: Canon, Authority, Criticism* (Philadelphia: Westminster, 1983), 27.

38. Swinburne, *Revelation*, 192–3.

CHAPTER 3

SCIENCE AND RELIGION

DEL RATZSCH

INTRODUCTION

THE natural sciences have profoundly shaped modern life and have notoriously generated challenges for religious belief—even being credited by some with having destroyed religion's rational defensibility. Most people, however, see both science and religion as having important truths to tell us, and try to fit both into a coherent world-view. Among that wider group, some see science and religion as occupying separate, isolated territories, with any alleged conflicts resulting from failure to respect proper boundaries, while others see varying relationships and legitimate (or illegitimate) interactions between the two. The competing views arise from a history, of course—a history widely misconstrued.

Brief History

There is a widespread perception that whatever their present relation (if any), historically science and religion have continually been at each other's throats. That picture is far from accurate—indeed it is widely acknowledged that Christian theology and practice played a substantial, positive role in the birth and rise of modern science.[1] The overwhelming majority of sixteenth- and seventeenth-century scientists were committed Christian believers who deliberately mined their theology for concepts, principles, boundary conditions, models, and rational justifications for their fledgling science.[2] But as a science initially unsure of its place and powers gained confidence and competence, a divide began to develop between science (increasingly seen as the autonomous, authoritative voice on nature) and religion/theology (increasingly seen as the intellectually disconnected, nature-irrelevant authority only on spiritual and moral matters—if that). That divide, beginning in the eighteenth century, became increasingly prominent, peaking in the Positivist movement of the early to mid-twentieth century.

Although the conceptions of reality, of science, of religion, of philosophy, and of humans undergirding Positivist claims were subsequently recognized as inadequate and impoverished, a broad science/religion disjunction still dominates most academic and much popular discussion. In recent decades, however, a renewed science/religion discussion has become lively, widespread, and substantive, with numerous standpoints vociferously advocated. Resolution is not in the offing, but visible progress—and the unmasking of various loud errors—is taking place.

The Relata

Assessing science/religion proposals requires understanding the relata. One would thus think that the initial step would be to define *science* and *religion*. Unfortunately, that's not going to happen, because there is no settled, consensus definition for either, and the standard candidates all have known problems. For present purposes I take *religion* to involve belief in a transcendent supernatural being(s), plus (typically) closely associated moral codes, ritual practices, personal/group commitments, convictions concerning meaning, purpose, value, and post-death conscious existence, all integrated into an encompassing world-view.[3]

Science I take to be a deeply empirical project aimed most fundamentally at understanding and explaining the natural realm, typically in natural terms. Conceptions of science have varied widely over the centuries, changing as shortcomings of earlier conceptions became progressively evident.[4] Incorporating lessons of some of those previous failures, contemporary pictures of science recognize that theories can be neither generated, rigorously proven, nor rigorously falsified by any quantity of empirical data. It is further recognized that science does not have a rigid logical structure and that theories are creatively constructed and not inferred. Philosophers now almost universally acknowledge that observation is not passive, and that data to some (often exaggerated) degree carry undertones of the theories involved in their generation. Quite a few contemporary philosophers of science have become convinced that echoes of human gender, political, class, psychological, and societal structures are sometimes imported into scientific concepts as well as into scientifically essential metaphors and theories. And few would now deny that theory evaluation and selection inescapably involve a wide range of scientifically essential extra-empirical conceptual resources—e.g. presuppositions (uniformity of nature, appropriateness of human cognitive resources, etc.), epistemic values (e.g. fruitfulness, consistency, explanatory power, empirical adequacy, wider fit, simplicity), concepts (e.g. law, explanation, confirmation, truth), and so forth. Over all, the trajectory of recent decades is the growing awareness of the centrality of humanness to science—with the consequence that the standard perceived dichotomy between science and religion is increasingly blurred.

Although disagreeing on specifics, most mainline commentators argue that, despite the complexities and despite the ineradicable dependence of science upon human-shaped resources beyond just empirical data and reason, scientific results can nonetheless often rightly claim powerful rational justification and epistemic legitimacy. Rigor, objectivity, and warrant may be less than absolute and less than often wished and claimed, and science may have human fingerprints and human DNA traces all over it, but science can still give us rational reason to accept various scientific theories as true or probably true. A tempered or 'critical' realism (the position that science attempts and sometimes succeeds in uncovering genuine theoretical truth, and that *critically vetted* scientific results are rationally warranted) is still defensible.

PROVISIONAL TYPOLOGIES

Science and religion each have complex hierarchical internal structures involving multiple, multilevel components, with complex and varied internal connections between them. Indeed, science and religion each exhibit so many variations and such complex and dynamic internal structures that prospects of there being any simple, unitary account of the relationship(s) between science and religion seem dim.

Still, it seems worthwhile to try to identify *some* sort of gross order. There have been and continue to be numerous proposals concerning if and how science and religion relate to each other.[5] Most fall somewhere into one of three very broad categories:

A. *Independence* (or *separation*): Science and religion are both legitimate, justifiable, valuable human pursuits. Each has its own proper authority and domain (e.g., issues, methods, results), but the respective domains have no substantive overlap, connections or interactions. A person can be a competent practitioner of both with integrity.

B. *Conflict* (or *warfare*): Science and religion operate in the same (or overlapping) domains, make conflicting claims and/or demands. At most one of the two is rationally legitimate, their basic conflicts being ultimately irreconcilable. A person cannot, with competence and integrity, be a practitioner of both.

C. *Dialogue* (or *interaction, integration*): Science and religion are both legitimate, justifiable, valuable human pursuits, and while each has its own (possibly even over-lapping) authority and domain, science and religion each can and do substantively interact with, contribute to, and even properly self-correct in the light of the other, especially in such areas as foundations and interpretative stances, with apparent conflicts ultimately reconcilable.

As indicated, terminology is not uniform among science/religion scholars, and a number of influential proposals constitute subtypes of one (sometimes more) of the above. Brief discussion of major views follows.

Independence (Separation)

The popular cultural perception is that religion has not fared well in its contacts with science, and it is commonly suspected that religion's problem has resulted from attempts to speak in areas where it has no rightful authority or competence. But (on Independence views) were science and religion to stay in their appropriate domains, there would be no problem. The only issue would involve locating the relevant boundaries and identifying what lay within each.

There are indeed religious issues that appear to have no overlap with any scien-tific issues and vice versa. But Independence does not seem adequate as a general position. For one thing, as indicated earlier, not only were science and religion *not* independent historically, but had they been, the early history of science might have been quite different—and not in a positive way. For another, no one knows how to delineate hard boundaries to science (or religion)—demarcation issues being as intractable as ever.

Furthermore, the history of science contains numerous cases of fruitful cross-fertilization. Newton, for instance, was emboldened by the doctrine of divine omnipresence to countenance something very like the otherwise (at that point) proscribed concept of action at a distance—in his case, gravitational. And in his *Mysterium Cosmographicum*, Kepler said:

[T]here were three things above all for which I sought the cause as to why it was this way and not another—the number, the dimensions, and the motions of the orbs. I have dared to carry out this search because of the beautiful correspondence of the immobile Sun, the fixed stars, and the intermediate space with God the Father, the Son, and the Holy Spirit.[6]

On a more general level, science de facto takes the cosmos to be in relevant respects *like* a creation—uniform, orderly, intelligible, predictable, and even beau-tiful. And science de facto takes scientists to be in relevant respects *like* creatures made in God's image—rational, creative, knowing, capable of understanding.

And intriguingly, there is growing neurophysiological evidence that human cognition is not neatly compartmentalized—and that things typically taken as definitive of science (reason, perception, and so forth) and things popularly taken as definitive of religion (emotion, faith, and so forth) are inseparable cognitive functions. (More later.) That is at least *suggestive*, along the same lines as Einstein's remark that 'The compartments into which human thought is divided are not so watertight that fundamental progress in one is a matter of indifference to the rest.'[7]

Given these sorts of cross-talk, attempts sharply to separate science and religion almost inevitably do violence to one or the other—e.g. reducing religion to subjective value and morality, or reducing science close to a sterile positivism.

Methodological Naturalism

The currently most influential supporting thesis for Independence is *methodological naturalism*. According to this doctrine, science takes no position on *philosophical naturalism*,[8] but by its very nature (or alleged definition) restricts its methods, presuppositions, conceptual resources, and results wholly to the realm of nature and must proceed *as if* philosophical naturalism were true. As a strategic recommendation, this type of de facto prohibition might well be a harmless and indeed practically useful restriction. But that benignity fades when advocates forget that it is a stipulated prohibition and take the pronouncements of a science operating under that human prohibition as the unvarnished truth about nature. There is no *rational* reason why the supernatural might not exist and have a hand in the structure and running of nature at some points. *Were* that the case, any science confined to and driven to purely 'naturalistic' theories would go irretrievably wrong on such points. Thus, to merely *assume* that a methodological naturalistically restricted science generates truth would derail science at exactly all the places that a mistaken assumption of philosophical naturalism would. The following:

(C_1) T is the best theory consistent with philosophical naturalism

and

(C_2) T is the best theory

are not interchangeable and require different justifications—*unless*, for example, we take philosophical naturalism as defining the relevant (or normative) context for science. To *forget* the qualification thus smuggles a substantive and far from innocent philosophical doctrine into science. And that restriction is not scientifically essential. For example, science can be done—and historically sometimes was done—employing a non-naturalistic conception of law as regularities in God's immediate governance of the cosmos. Such views may even offer the only viable explanation of the unique logical characteristics of natural laws—i.e. their being located between material generalizations and necessities, their support of counterfactuals, etc.[9]

With all Independence views there could still be fights over exactly whose turf specific matters fell within—even *if* each side scrupulously avoided meddling in what it saw as the sovereign territory of the other. And exactly who is going to adjudicate *those* disputes and on what basis?

Complementarity

Complementarity—a subtype of Independence—is the most popular of the usual science/religion positions. In confining science and religion each to its own realm, Complementarity dictates that scientists and theologians tend their own level and not meddle in others, thereby precluding nasty science/religion turf wars. Complementarity also insists on the coordinateness of the truths arising from both pursuits, seeking a more cohering, unified picture of reality. Advocates also typically accept a *completeness* principle for both science and religion agreeing with van Huyssteen that

> [A]t its own level science is capable of providing adequate and complete explanations.[10]

and that

> [A]ll it [the universe] contains is explicable by the natural sciences.[11]

Large stretches of science and religion do seem orthogonal and autonomous. But how—or if—the claims work generally is problematic.

Boundaries

First, there would have to be a clear demarcation between the explanatory/causal economies of the two realms in question, as well as a *matching* disjunction between the results (and perhaps the methods, etc.) of the corresponding disciplines. I know of no non-question-begging case for either. Second, some complementarists hold that a theistic world-view provides the undergirding conceptual matrix required by science but that science and religion diverge past that point. That presents technical difficulties maintaining the required separations, and has consequences for the possibility of miracles, providence, and other things important to some religions.

Connections vs. Completeness

Given the precision, order, complexity, and generally staggering beauty of the cosmos, it seems wildly implausible that the sole purpose of the cosmos is to generate (as it inarguably does) charred Camel cigarette butts. The different levels of reality thus clearly have *some* inter-relevance—or *consonance*—bearing upon science and religion. Complementarists thus routinely claim that religion must 'take science seriously'.[12] But if religion is complete in the appropriate sense it can presumably in principle arrive at a complete *religious* picture purely on its own. Thus, if religion *should* pay attention to science, it is evidently for practical reasons—although if the realms are disjoint and complete, that practicality is puzzling.

But the typical requirement for science/religion consonance seems right, although involving different levels (as it must) it constitutes an awkwardness for completeness claims. If consonance really is a substantive requirement, then there could very well be specific religious claims that were not in the requisite way consonant with specific (purported) characteristics of the physical realm. Thus those specific religious claims could not be held without violating the consonance requirement. But given the stipulated *completeness*, religion is supposed to be complete and autonomous in its own realm and should thus have the right to make exactly the 'non-consonant' claim in question. There would thus be conflict, contrary to Complementarity. But if there can properly be no such conflict, consonance is a singularly tenuous demand.

Advocates frequently see such tenuous connections as 'science pointing beyond itself'—i.e. raising questions it cannot answer. (For instance, science can neither explain the ultimate origin of the natural laws or lawlike structures that it both investigates and uses in its investigations, nor explain the ultimate boundary conditions of the cosmos, nor explain the ultimate source of nature's intelligibility.) But if there are questions *in its own domain* that science cannot answer, then it is not *complete*. Thus those questions must fall *outside* the domain of science. But if science generates questions in other domains, then it must have *some* grip on resources and issues of relevance to that other domain, violating *separation*.

Complementarists want separation as a remedy for meddling hostilities, want completeness within each realm, and also want both consonance and science's pointing beyond itself so that science and religion can be laced into a whole picture whose components constitute a harmonious unity—not a compacted conceptual conglomerate or the fragmented compartmentalization of simple separation. It is not obvious that those are mutually realizable desiderata. Genuine unification will require smudging the boundary lines and softening the claims of completeness and autonomy. That, however, would involve moving into the area of various alternative modes of contact. To those we now turn.

Conflict (Warfare)

Once the barriers are lowered and science and religion are construed as potential competitors in the same (explanatory) tasks in the same arena, interaction and conflict become very real—some would say inevitable—possibilities. There is naturally disagreement over who gets eviscerated in such conflict, but some cautions are in order. First, conflict of content requires realist conceptions of both science and religion. (*Realist* views in this context are, roughly, those according to which truths and entities of the relevant sorts do exist, that discovering truths involving such entities constitutes an important aim, and that such truths or something near to them are sometimes actually secured.) Thus, neither *non*-realist views of science nor *non*-realist views of religion will serve the conflict thesis.[13] Second, neither outdated history and philosophy of science nor uninformed views of religion will do. Much of the perception of historical conflict is sheer invention. The *loci classici* for that perception (for instance Draper's and White's books[14]) are polemics with 'history' manipulated or manufactured to match preconceptions. And some purveyors of more recent popular screeds on science and religion have exhibited equal 'respect' for historical fact when it stands in the way of preconception.[15] Of course, the mere fact of science/religion conflict would not reveal which side was mistaken. Sorting *that* out would take further work.

Creationist/ID 'Conflict' Views

Creationists, Intelligent Design (ID) advocates, the church of Galileo's day, etc., are habitually (and polemically) cited as holding a Conflict thesis, but that is largely misrepresentation. On many views (e.g. Dialogue) there can be prima facie science/religion disputes—indeed, even legitimate interaction of nearly any sort creates the possibility of disagreement. The key difference is that on other views such disputes are ultimately legitimately resolvable whereas Conflict says that they are not—that conflicts partially *define* the relationship.

But creationists (and many ID advocates) insistently and flatly *deny* that *legitimate* science and *legitimate* religion are in any ultimate opposition whatever. In contrast to most others, some creationists do hold that religious/theological matters can not only play legitimate roles in science but take *precedence* in resolving apparent science/religion conflicts. But that is a very different issue from endorsing Conflict. Creationists and ID advocates typically claim that the only real conflict is between religion and an agenda-twisted, polemical, atheism-fueled faux 'science'—not *real* science.

Unfortunately, some, especially among popular creationists, have endorsed Baconian inductivism, according to which science involves only strict inductive inferences from pure observational data, have taken that as the criterion of scientific legitimacy, and have argued (correctly) that most contemporary theoretical science fails to meet Baconian conditions. But given the well-known and insurmountable difficulties with Baconian and allied conceptions of science, even if parts of contemporary science fail Baconian standards, nothing much follows.

Naturalist/Atheist Conflict Views

Contentions in this category come in several types, brief discussion of the more prominent of which follows.[16]

Foundations

Various commentators claim that science rests upon a presupposition of *philosophical* naturalism, note that that contradicts the belief of most religions in supernaturalism, and conclude that the very project of science is 'diametrically opposed' to any religious belief worth its salt.[17]

But that allegation is suspect.[18] For one thing, if science operates in a cosmos structured *like* a creation, if the historical roots of science lie in theology, and if the historical justification for essential scientific presuppositions or stances was theological, then contradiction between the *foundations* of science and religion seems implausible. Nor is it plausible that Newton, Boyle, Faraday and other major historical figures weren't quite perceptive enough to notice their own incoherence (unless, of course, in their religious 'commitments' they were just liars, cowards and/or hypocrites—also wildly implausible).

Deconstructing Religious Rationality

One common 'conflict' line attempts to defeat (specifically: undercut) the rational propriety of religious belief rather than directly attacking its truth. This challenge involves:

   a. citing purported causes/sources of religious belief;
   b. claiming that those causes/sources are aimed at something *other* than capturing truth;

then

   c. arguing that such causes/sources, so aimed, cannot provide rational justification for the beliefs generated.

As an historical example, Freud argued that religious belief represented wish fulfillment aimed at comfort and reassurance in a world where life was threatening and death terrifying. As the product of processes not reliably aimed at truth (wish fulfillment), religious beliefs would have no rational warrant.

But making a *case* here requires *showing* that the alleged source is the actual source, is not aimed at truth, is thus unreliable, etc. None is trivial, and Freud failed miserably on the first at least. More recently, there have been a number of attempts to defeat the rational legitimacy of religious belief by citing evolutionary theory as fully explaining the emergence, and/or the preservation, of religious beliefs. Explanatory proposals vary. For instance, some argue that religious belief is/was just an evolutionary spandrel,[19] with no special evolutionary upside.[20] Others, e.g. David Sloan Wilson, argue that religion was preserved for its group-selective advantages,[21] while Daniel Dennett argues that religion in the form of early animism arose out of a Hyperactive Agent Detection Device (HADD), and served fitness by making the welter of experiences of nature not only cognitively more manageable but even predictable.[22]

It is worth noting that all the evolutionary scenarios about religious belief currently on offer are highly speculative 'imaginative illustrations' (to borrow a term from Darwin). But suppose that one of them *was* prehistorically absolutely right. Exactly how is that supposed to undermine either the truth or the rational legitimacy of religious belief? That a propensity toward religious beliefs (and practices) should have arisen by evolutionary means (whether having direct fitness value or not) does not in the slightest imply that basic religious beliefs are *false* or *irrational*, any more than the fact that a propensity to believe our senses arose by evolutionary means implies that we should be deeply suspicious of that propensity.

One can perfectly sensibly, and consistently with everything science knows, maintain that evolution is the means by which humans were equipped to achieve recognition of some crucial religious realities. And if evolution has *preserved* those propensities, that strongly suggests that they have some (at least evolutionary) *value*. Given evolution, that religious propensities were both selected for *and* preserved as near-universals is nicely consistent with what one might expect were some basic religious outlook true. And the implied value is flatly contrary to what most foes of religion have stridently proclaimed for, literally, centuries.

Furthermore, if Darwin is right, then natural selection produced the faculties and mental structures with which we form *all* other beliefs, and by which we even pursue science. The governing aim of natural selection is reproductive success (*not* theoretical truth) as contemporary Darwinians acknowledge.[23] But if a belief-production mechanism having some governing aim and purpose *other than truth* means that the resultant beliefs are not rational legitimate, then *exactly* the same principle poses problems for scientific beliefs *and for anti-religious arguments* produced, as they must be if Darwin is correct, by the cognitive faculties developed *via* Darwinian processes ultimately pointed toward enhancing reproductive fitness—not truth. In fact, Darwin *himself* worried about his theory undercutting the mind's reliability.[24] Creation-based religion—with humans, however produced, reflecting God's image—may be in less trouble here than the 'blind, pitiless indifference' of Dawkins-style naturalism.[25]

Erosion of Religion—Closing Gaps

One challenge cites gradual historical erosion rather than specific decisive episodes. Religion, the story goes, supplied (perhaps then-reasonable) pre-scientific explanations, but science has progressively conquered those areas, evicting religion in the process. Thus, Alfred North Whitehead:

[F]or over two centuries religion has been on the defensive...The period has been one of unprecedented intellectual progress....Each such [advance] has found the religious thinkers unprepared. Something which has been proclaimed to be [theologically] vital, has finally, after struggle, distress, and anathema, been modified and otherwise interpreted....The...continuous repetition of this undignified retreat, during many generations, has at last almost entirely destroyed the intellectual authority of religious thinkers.[26]

On this view, the bits and pieces that have crumbled away from the religious conceptual scheme might not individually have been essential to religious belief, but over the longer haul they constitute a dismal track record of serial failure.

The most common way of packaging this challenge involves the 'God-of-the-gaps' picture. According to this picture, since religion arose as and remains nothing beyond a primitive attempt at explaining natural phenomena, believers inevitably attribute any phenomenon not understood at a given moment to divine activity, then interpret that phenomenon as empirical evidence for theism. In short, believers bridge any gaps in our understanding of nature—or any actual causal gaps in nature—by reference to divine activity. But, it is claimed, there is a recurring historical pattern of science hitting upon natural explanations of the relevant phenomena, and as religious 'explanations' are sequentially displaced by science, the available fields for religious explanations (gaps) continually shrink. Religion is thus reduced to fighting for its life in rearguard actions from within whatever gaps happen to be (as yet) unclosed. But even those temporary hideouts are well within the gunsights of scientific inevitability, spelling the inevitable doom of rational religious belief as its major substantive field of operation—explanation of natural phenomena—is wholly taken over by science.

A variant version is that while science has perhaps not rendered religious belief completely irrational, it has made explanatory appeal to any supernatural agency unnecessary—even pointless.[27] God is superfluous because his primary function is explanatory, and anything one might claim to explain theistically will ultimately be covered by alternative scientific explanations. Perhaps one *can* still accept religion if one wants, but religious belief does not provide resources for any essential explanatory work not equally (indeed, better) doable by science.

Many religious believers also reject God-of-the-gaps views, but for different reasons. They reject the whole underlying picture of religion as an explanatory scheme for natural phenomena. They accept the historical perception that religion has been serially displaced from earlier gaps, then argue (*a*) that when science *does* produce a natural explanation and religion is forced to retreat, religion is made to look foolish; (*b*) that the religious faith of anyone who rested their belief upon that now-discredited 'evidence' is thus weakened; and (*c*) that such gap theories involve a derogatory picture of God not getting things right initially and resorting to emergency tinkerings to keep things on track. Religion is thus indeed harmed and it would be vastly better for religion to avoid such vulnerability altogether by not being construed as in the business of providing competing explanations to begin with. It should rather be construed as having a wholly different, exclusively religious and moral content, structure, and purpose.

Despite their constituting (largely unargued) ritual incantations, all those objections strike me as seriously weak. First, it should be recognized that the *logic* of gap views is impeccable—*if* there is no other viable explanation, then divine activity must be the answer. Furthermore, science has a long track record of overturning *its own* positions, but that doesn't make those who held the earlier, overturned scientific views look foolish, lose their trust of science, or anything of the sort. Thus, the mere fact of exhibiting a history of having views overturned by science is not alone necessarily problematic for some doxastic region—religion as well as science. And perhaps God *likes* running the cosmos, and deliberately left dials he gets to turn from time to time. I know of no reason—aside from speculative supernatural psychology—for thinking that if only he *could* have, God *would* have produced a cosmos that precluded his special activity in running it.

The 'history' isn't exactly bulletproof either. Religion hasn't always been driven into gaps, and has in fact sometimes made substantive contributions. As mentioned earlier, Newton embraced a theory of gravitation involving the then-proscribed idea of action at a distance (short-range repulsion in this case) on the basis of his belief in God's omnipresence. Impetus theory, a crucial forerunner to inertial theories, was defended by Francis of Marchea on the basis of doctrines connected with the sacraments. Faraday's field theory was connected to his theology of God as creator and sustainer. Maxwell's field equations modeled his views concerning relationships within the Trinity. Further, religion-friendly aspects of contemporary cosmic fine-tuning cases cannot be dismissed as easily as some would like.

More generally, there still are gaps in our scientific pictures, and it takes a-historical hubris (or massively undersupported philosophically flavored induction) to claim that science has, does, can, or ever will explain *everything* having to do with the cosmos. Recurrent claims that we finally have in hand all necessary materials for completing the scientific picture have just as recurrently failed. Moreover, Kuhn argued that revolutionary advances sometimes *reopen* scientific issues previously thought to be settled. Closed gaps may thus be an unstable launching platform for critiques.

And in any case, an essential presupposition underlying the first two cases—that religion is merely explanatory—is *seriously* historically and theologically speculative, and controversial to boot.

Comparative track records—rampant success of science vs. visible stagnation of theology—also require caution. Most scientists take methodological naturalism as a norm for the acceptability of scientific theories. Thus any inadequate theory will by methodological policy be replaced by some alternative theory that also meets methodological naturalistic conditions—non-naturalistic theories being ruled out by fiat. Thus, *only naturalistic* theories can even be *candidates* for 'success'. The claim, then, that naturalism has a monopoly on scientific success bears some logical resemblance to that of the ruling party in a one-party country citing its history of electoral success—where only party members can run—as evidence of the voters' high regard.

Specific Scientific Results

The simplest challenge science could pose would be inarguable *results* of science contradicting fundamental religious beliefs. But while accepted scientific results may contradict specific doctrines of specific groups (e.g. young earth views), one cannot seriously hold that plate tectonics, biological or stellar evolution, relativity, or quantum mechanics entail the non-existence of God. Obviously, one could coherently claim that God *used* evolution, or that the world is quantum mechanical because that is the way God wanted it. Since those are *coherent* claims, then those theories do not contradict the existence of God.

a. *Inconsistency.* Mere inconsistency does not show *religion* mistaken unless science is given precedence in such conflicts. *Showing* that precedence is not trivial. And inconsistency is not automatically fatal even within science itself. It has been known for decades that general relativity and quantum mechanics are in tension with each other, but—rightly—no one seriously proposes abandoning either. Furthermore, the clash of ideas is often how truth emerges.

b. *Randomness.* It has also been claimed that the key role played by randomness in such central theories as evolution and quantum mechanics undermines the religiously central doctrine that the cosmos, life, and humans are products of deliberate *purpose.* That claim does not stand up to scrutiny,[28] and in fact (as will emerge later) the very randomness alleged to be religiously problematic can serve some theologically important functions.

Styles of Rationality

Many challenges to the rationality of religious belief assume that rational justification must conform to a 'scientific' model. Though that assumption is far from evident, some believe that religious belief does (or can) meet that standard.[29] Others have argued that there is no single canon of rationality—that different domains have their own characteristic rationality. If either contention is right, these objections fail, as they would were the proposed 'scientific' model mistaken.

Very recently, some scholars have argued that virtually none of our fundamental, common sense, life-governing beliefs are generated by argumentation, nor are they mere provisional explanatory hypotheses. A belief that one's spouse loves one is neither a hypothesis to explain puzzling behaviors, an induction, something to be empirically tested, a candidate for stringent falsification efforts, nor an empty irrelevancy. We simply do not acquire or justify beliefs that those around us have minds or that there has been a past via testing, confirmation, and argumentation. Nor could we—as the long history of failed philosophical attempts attests.

Yet such beliefs are surely sensible if any of our non-trivial beliefs are, and non-accidentally track the truth if any do. Rational justification here must have some different, deeper character, and artificially limiting acceptable sources to explanatory hypotheses, scientific argumentation, and the like, does serious violence to human rationality. Some have suggested analogously that artificially limiting rational justification for core religious beliefs to procedures (e.g. foundationalist procedures) that are demonstrably inadequate even for ordinary experience is equally misguided.[30]

Independence and Conflict can each point to historical and current episodes that illustrate their respective patterns. But despite these apparent successes, each is inadequate as a *general* approach, and formally inadequate for broader conceptual reasons. We must, then, look further.

Dialogue (Interaction, Integration)

Various Dialogue advocates argue that science and religion share normative patterns of inference, theory evaluation, evidence assessment, explanatory styles, and the like. On some views, those patterns are specialized, on others simply honed instances of ordinary, everyday patterns. Nancey Murphy argues that 'philosophy of science...provides the definitive account of the canons of probabilistic reasoning' but that '(potentially at least) theology is methodologically indistinguishable from the sciences'.[31] Others (e.g. Mikael Stenmark) argue that scientific rationality is parasitic on deeper structures of rationality. Thus science does not *define* canons of reason.[32]

Many Dialogue advocates argue that religion *supports* science by providing conceptual, presuppositional, meaning-assigning, and practical milieus within which science thrives and fits better than in any non-theistic foundation. Some see science reciprocating, offering discoveries (e.g. fine tuning) best explained by theism and thus providing indirect evidence for theism.

Some argue that science provides *models* for various religious matters. For instance, Peacocke and Clayton argue that while science's picture of nature as a 'seamless web' has undercut theology's traditional interventionist (or 'interfering') view of God's activity in the world, science's picture of dynamic emergence within nature (e.g. consciousness emerging from neural complexity) offers a new model of God's immanent activity[33]—a model with less need for a separate supernatural realm (and hence for an 'outside interventionist' model of God's action in the world) and which in turn fits best with panentheistic theology.[34] (This view involves an interesting partial reprise of some earlier views in that it sees 'even inner-worldly causality as (in at least some sense) a manifestation of divine agency...there [being] no *qualitative* or ontological difference between the regularity of natural law and the intentionality of special divine actions'.[35]) Similarly, evolutionary theory provided a primary model (and perhaps much of the impetus) for process theology. Some (e.g. Stump and Kretzmann) have argued that relativistic conceptions of simultaneity provide a model for what God's being outside time would look like.[36] And yet others (e.g. Torrance, Pannenberg) have tried to connect relativity and field theories to the specifically Christian doctrine of the Incarnation.

Although most Dialogue advocates decry scientism, the de facto position of most is that science can have decisive consequences for theological positions but that attempts to draw from religion or theology similar consequences for properly constituted scientific positions are 'interfering' with science.[37] Despite the science-heavy tilt of most advocates, the rejection of scientism is genuine—science (as noted earlier) being seen as incomplete in inevitably raising questions which it cannot answer, and which only religion has the resources to address.[38]

There are important exceptions to that tilt tendency. Murphy argues that there is 'no reason in principle why theories originating in theology cannot be included as auxiliary hypotheses in scientific research programs and vice versa'.[39] More significantly, she argues that 'We sometimes have to correct our theology as science advances.... But sometimes theology must correct science as well.'[40] On a parallel tack, Wolfhart Pannenberg believes that theology establishes that 'If God...is the creator of the universe, then it is not possible to understand fully...the process of nature without reference to God.'[41] Of course, science is now attempting that 'impossibility' and thus for its own sake needs redirection.

Dialogue views see science and religion as each maintaining its own recognizable identity, but with a permeable (or semi-permeable) interface or shared stratum on some level(s) rather than a sealed boundary between them. Such views, it seems to me, point in the right direction, but there are deeper interfusions between science and religion, which Dialogue proposals do not adequately acknowledge. (More shortly.)

One other Dialogue view tries to trace connections to a finer-grained level than most others. On this view, the fundamental indeterminacy of quantum mechanics means that the future is genuinely open, with multiple divergent, live, unknown futures. But God deliberately created the world that way. Thus, just as the clockwork Newtonian universe was taken as indicating a creator favoring mathematical precision, sharp distinctions, overriding micro-order, autonomous and static identities, and infinite predictability, some Dialogue advocates argue that the quantum world suggests a creator favoring openness, freedom, fuzzy edges, dynamic fluidity, interconnectedness, novelty, innovation, emergence, surprises. This openness, it is argued, allows for free will and also suggests new ways of conceptualizing God's immanentness.[42]

A number of authors (e.g. Polkinghorne, Murphy) have sought to locate some divine activity within the open causal interstices of quantum phenomena—seeing God as influencing otherwise indeterminate quantum events in directions leading toward desired ends.[43] While this idea would allow direct, special divine action in the world, such action need not *violate* probabilistic natural law and need not even be *scientifically* determinable. These are seen as virtues, because they avoid the objectionable (to many) idea of God 'interfering' in nature (a dislike often related to God-of-the-gaps worries noted earlier). And even many who don't object to intervention as such, nonetheless dislike the idea of God's action in nature being so 'heavy-handed' that even something so lacking in religious sensitivities as science can detect it.[44]

Those objections do not seem particularly fatal, meaning that the 'interstitial' view of this sort of divine action remains a live possibility.

Deeper Integration

Some commentators have argued that the connections between science and religion run even more profoundly deep—arguing that the two constitute an *indissoluble, intermingled unity*. Such philosophical or religious positions as coherentism, pantheism, process theology, and panentheism could quite organically accommodate such a view, but prominent advocates of those positions generally adopt a less extreme version of the Dialogue view. (Note that panentheists Clayton and Peacocke figured into the previous section.)

Some Candidates

Among the scholars who suggest this deeper Integration picture are theologian Thomas Torrance and philosopher Roy Clouser. I shall briefly describe Clouser's view in order to provide a glimpse of what such a theory might look like.

According to Clouser, any belief in something as *divine* is a religious belief, and to believe that something is divine just is to hold that thing to have unconditional, non-dependent existence. But all theories, according to Clouser, substantively embody presuppositions about the nature of reality (e.g. what kinds of things are real and upon which explanations *must* be grounded) and thus can't avoid presupposing something or other to have that unconditional, non-dependent status.

That means, says Clouser, that every theory (scientific, mathematical, or otherwise) carries the freight of some religious belief concerning a divinity. Further, every theory is regulated by some presupposition concerning what is divine, and every scientific theory and concept has its content bounded and colored by such divinity presuppositions. Those presuppositions play a 'pivotal' role in the construction, assessment, acceptance, or rejection of theories. The effects are pervasive, having implications for positions concerning 'human nature, destiny, values, happiness and so on'.[45] This does not necessarily make scientific theories themselves components of religion proper, but it means that every scientific explanatory theory is unavoidably and substantively affected by some religious (divinity) belief.[46]

Clouser further contends that attributing unconditional non-dependent existence to anything other than God leads inevitably to 'reductionistic' theories (in this case, theories restricted to conceptual resources too impoverished to encompass the relevant truths even in principle), and that any such will be partially (often subtly) false, since *its* internal religious shape will embody something other than the *non*-reductionistic truth that God alone is divine. Thus, the science of anyone not committed to God's being the only unconditional, non-dependent existent will be, strictly speaking, false. In fact, Clouser argues that similar conclusions hold for all truth, knowledge, and even concepts.[47] Thus religious believers and non-believers cannot share even *quite* the same scientific concepts.

Although we must recognize that intuitive conceptual boundaries are permeable, things get pushed a bit far here. I am suspicious of definitions that entail that belief that numbers and propositions exist necessarily is a *religious* belief. Nor does it seem to me that materialists do not *truly and fully* understand that the earth orbits the sun because their concept of the earth has a deeply buried, underlying intuition that the earth is composed of material substance which does not ultimately depend on God for its existence.[48]

Further Dialogue/Integration Exploration

Most philosophers of science believe that science cannot function without some underlying de facto metaphysical principles that are not consequences of science itself. Given science's contingency, there are a variety of broader matrices into which a science can be embedded. But no complete metaphysical system is neutral with respect to philosophical naturalism and theism, and it is not clear how that non-neutrality is to be prevented from seeping into science. The metaphysical foundations contribute *something* to science—otherwise they would not be essential—and that contribution is not merely in providing a generic, content-irrelevant platform for science to sit on. The consequences of science's fundamental presuppositions (or predispositions) for boundaries and initial conditions could provide a significant connection between the content of religious belief and the content of science. And theological developments that affected that content could in principle generate ripples into science.

Moreover, aspects of deeper levels can seep into other levels of the scientific hierarchy, and just as observational data are (widely taken to be) theory-laden, theories in this circumstance may be metaphysics- or even theology-laden.[49] And, as noted, science can function only in a world *like* a creation—coherent, uniform, intelligible, and so on. If, as is sometimes argued, structure is in subtle part content, then a science that requires a creation-like structure may have subtle creation-like content.

There are other possible factors as well. Human natural science is confined ultimately to humanly-accessible concepts and procedures. In creating and constructing theories, the concepts employed are nearly always imported or assembled from descriptive and theoretical contexts from other areas of cognition and experience. Typically, such imports drag more with them than the phenomenon specifically warrants. And where our human concepts don't quite map exactly onto reality (think quantum phenomena), we must do the best we can with the concepts we can manage, applied partially metaphorically.[50] In fact, Mary Hesse has argued (correctly, I think) that theoretical explanations just *are* 'metaphoric redescriptions' of relevant phenomena.[51]

Historically, theology has provided some of those concepts employed metaphorically. It has been argued more recently that conceptual imports into science include gender, political, class, psychological, and societal structures. If importation and employment of metaphoric content are cognitive and practical necessities, then scientific theories and concepts will inevitably be infused with humanness, and the standard prohibitions—meant originally to sieve out religion—aren't going to work.

There are additional facets of science that soften its (earlier-perceived) contours, making it less inconceivable that religion plays some role in science proper. Perception, recall, is an active process, and there are no obvious boundaries concerning what sorts of factors can affect (however subtly) the shape of perceptual content. Values and value judgments play an ineliminable role in the sciences. Science pursues intelligibility and explanation, but our recognition of both is in part via a cognitive phenomenology, as a particular *feel*, a particular *seeming*. Even our most rigorous reason—mathematics, logic—rests ultimately upon our human *intuitions* concerning deductiveness and entailment, on involuntarily embraced axioms, etc.

More surprisingly, the neurophysiological underpinnings of our cognition simply do not respect the dichotomies we try to impose. Recent research indicates that some of the very cognitive processes by which we judge *beauty* are also among those by which we judge *truth*.[52] And on a number of levels, reason and emotion function as a unit. As one example, various structures in the brain (e.g. tonically active neuron sites in the caudate) directly integrate reason inputs (from the prefrontal cortex) with emotion inputs (from the amygdala).[53] In some of those structures, integration occurs prior to our conscious access to the process. One upshot of all this is that certain sorts of rationality are compromised in the absence of emotion.

Antonio Damasio and others suspect that that pattern applies to scientific reasoning and mathematics.[54] Paul Thagard has argued that one important factor in scientific theory justification is whether acceptance of the theory maximizes coherence—including *emotional* coherence.[55] And Christopher Hookway has argued that felt emotional responses are one way that unarticulated *epistemic* evaluative criteria present themselves to us cognitively, and that 'effective *epistemic* evaluation could turn out to be impossible without . . . appropriate emotional responses' (my emphasis).[56]

Thus, some things often seen as closely linked to religion operate deep within—indeed, constitute operative components of—cognitive processes often seen as closely tied to science. Still deeper, our very selfhood may be involved. Physicist Sir Denys Haig Wilkinson asks, 'How do we then choose between alternative scientific hypotheses when we have used up all our scientific criteria? We are, of course, left face to face with ourselves. The only remaining criterion is what seems right to us . . . in the deepest seat of human feeling . . .'[57]

So values, intuitions, seemings, a sense of beauty, emotions, the deepest seat of human feeling—all are built into science. And into reason itself. Again none of them—much less Einstein's 'rapturous amazement at the harmony of the laws of nature'—are strangers to the religious domain of the cognitive landscape. And if the reality science studies is an *integrated creation*, the infusion nestled within any wholly successful science may well be theistic.

WIDER PICTURES

Each proposal above typically works in some cases but contorts other cases when pushed as universal. *Conflict* views are often agenda-driven and fail historical and philosophical scrutiny. *Independence* views often deny the real connectedness at various points, miss some basic human epistemic facts, and often involve impoverished views of religion and/or outdated conceptions of science. The *Complementarity* subtype represents an improvement, but does not give adequate weight to the depth of some connections, and often involves untenable pictures of both science and religion as having independent, substantive, and complete takes on everything in the natural realm. *Dialogue* gets a lot right, but often tilts toward science, limits the scope and level of interpenetration, overestimates science's scope and autonomy, and (like Complementarity) is often accompanied by nearly pathological fear of God-of-the-gaps. The *Deep Integration* subtype of *Dialogue* alone recognizes the depth of some crucial connections, but often overshoots the mark, and sometimes ignores the fact that religion really is irrelevant to some scientific contents and vice versa.

What procedures, principles, and criteria can we trust in trying to put science and religion together? We need a perspective broader than any of the usual candidates and ultimately broader than just science/religion interactions. Most humans ultimately seek a world-view that is *whole, unified,* and *satisfying*—one that includes science, religion, and an organic relationship between them. We look for inclusive unity because few could take rejection of science seriously, yet most believe that science alone cannot provide wholeness and satisfyingness—either intellectual or deeper.[58] And human judgments of *satisfactoriness* are bedrock even for science, mathematics, and reason itself. There being no escaping that, we had best learn to appropriate and employ it epistemically properly.[59]

With scientific theory, satisfactoriness has to do ultimately with certain sorts of theory-generated, science-relevant *successes*—making intelligible, unifying, explaining, predicting, and so on, relevant judgments and the standards themselves being embedded within a human-tinged conceptual, philosophical, and praxical matrix. A theory might be propped up artificially in the short term, but any theory or discipline that fails such success tests is not stable in the long term. With religion, the same thing holds. Any religion that fails to afford religiously-relevant success—making intelligible, unifying, explaining, generating social coherence, meaning, inner peace, hope, charity, love, gratitude, awe, and human flourishing—may be propped up artificially in the short term, but is not viable in the long term.

Viable world-views must achieve world-view-relevant successes. What those are is not wholly clear, but they must *include* something at least *like* the science-relevant and religion-relevant successes noted above. And any world-view that claims that its science-relevant successes demonstrate the impossibility of realizing important religion-relevant aims has failed. Any world-view that claims that its religion-relevant successes demonstrate the impossibility or impropriety of realizing important science-relevant aims has likewise failed. And any world-view that insists that the two are disconnected or irreconcilable has failed, having turned its back on some of the deeper drives of *both* science and religion—coherence, unification, system, wholeness.[60] Peacocke's remark that in our search for intelligibility and meaning science and religion are now 'inextricably interlocked...in the common human enterprise of seeking *both*'[61] is spot on.

The relevant successes are not just propositional. Satisfyingness is not merely, for instance, an axiomatic structure, even with respect to standard evaluative criteria for science—e.g. explanatory power. And some contemporary thinkers cite even broader than usual non-epistemic criteria for evaluating theory legitimacy—considerations having to do with human wellbeing, global human solidarity, democracy, social justice, equality, ecological concerns, and other 'progressive interests'. Marxists, many postmodernists, some feminists, and even some Darwinians fall into this category.

Although some of that involves (to use Darwin's wonderful phrase) 'mental rioting', broad, not very well-behaved criteria beyond propositionally linked considerations play substantive and legitimate roles in both religion and science. Criteria for science/religion interaction models and criteria will likely be at least as broad as that. And still other, farther-flung constraints involving an array of facets of human life will likely sift down from any world-view matrix in which that relationship is embedded.

CONCLUSION

All this inter-infusion conjoined with the lack of absolute boundaries between science and non-science means that science/religion issues will not be the clean, simple, no-strings-dangling phenomenon many would like them to be. There is unlikely to be any single elegant, all-encompassing solution—at least any available to us humans. Just as there may be aspects of nature forever beyond our cognitive capacities, just as there may be religious facts forever beyond our understanding, some facets of the actual relationship between science and religion may be forever beyond us as well. There may always be tensions and loose ends. But that is true in nearly every human endeavor—whether involving science, religion, theology, philosophy, or world-views. Indeed, given human history, propensities, and finitude, the slick tidiness of any proposed science/religion resolution (or dissolution) is very probably legitimate cause for epistemological alarm.

NOTES

I thank colleagues in the Calvin College Philosophy Department, and David van Baak of the Calvin Physics Department, as well as Michael Rea and Thomas Flint for their often disquieting and annoyingly correct criticisms.

1. A wide variety of prominent historians—R. Hooykaas, Eugene Klaarrens, and John Hedley Brooke—have developed this theme, which goes back at least to Collingwood.

2. The literature is huge, involving Newton, Kepler, Boyle, Descartes, Maxwell, Faraday, Mersenne, Von Helmont, and others.

3. That is, naturally, controversial. Some (e.g. the Wittgensteinian D. Z. Phillips) have challenged the essentiality of *belief* to religious faith, advancing a type of anti-realism according to which religious 'belief' involves minimal or no (theistic) metaphysical commitments or claims, but is rather a 'form of life'. Others argue that e.g. Buddhism is a religion although some forms of it involve no belief in the *supernatural*. While acknowledging such positions, I am restricting the present discussion to theistic religions.

4. Nearly any good introduction to philosophy of science will contain discussions of various past failures.

5. Many are descendants of Ian Barbour's typology developed in e.g. *Religion in an Age of Science* (San Francisco: HarperSanFrancisco, 1990).

6. For further historical discussion see e.g. John Hedley Brooke, *Science and Religion: Some Historical Perspectives* (New York: Cambridge University Press, 1991).

7. Max Jammer, *Einstein and Religion* (Princeton: Princeton University Press, 1999), 156.

8. *Philosophical naturalism* is the view that the natural realm is all that exists—that there is no supernatural realm.

9. See my 'Nomo(theo)logical Necessity', *Faith and Philosophy* 4 (1987), 383–402. Reprinted in Michael Beaty (ed.), *Christian Theism and the Problems of Philosophy* (Notre Dame: University of Notre Dame Press, 1990), 184–207.

10. J. Wentzel van Huyssteen employs this phrase more than once in *Duet or Duel: Theology and Science in a Postmodern World* (Harrisburg: Trinity), e.g. 56, 77. Many others, e.g. Alan G. Padgett, *Science and the Study of God* (Grand Rapids: Eerdmans, 2003), 81, concur.

11. Ibid. e.g. 55, 75.

12. e.g. van Huyssteen, *Duet or Duel*, 57, 78.

13. e.g. instrumentalist and some social constructivist views.

14. J. W. Draper, *History of the Conflict Between Religion and Science* (1875), and A. D. White, *History of the Warfare of Science with Theology in Christendom* (1896).

15. The Galileo, Scopes, Bruno, and other frequently cited cases contain in their currently popular versions vast quantities of invention.

16. Much of this section derives from my 'Demise of Religion: Greatly Exaggerated Reports from the Science/Religion "Wars"', in Michael Peterson and Raymond Van Arragon (eds.), *Contemporary Debates in the Philosophy of Religion* (Oxford: Blackwell, 2004), 72–87.

17. Norman F. and Lucia K. B. Hall, 'Is the War between Science and Religion Over?', *The Humanist* (May/June 1986), 26–8.

18. Although I will not pursue the issue here, some argue that there are—or can be—non-supernaturalistic religions. Buddhism is sometimes cited as an example, and some philosophers argue for the possibility of an 'anthropic theism' involving a 'deity' who while powerful, knowing, etc., is wholly natural (see e.g. Peter Forrest, *God without the Supernatural: A Defense of Scientific Theism* (Ithaca, NY: Cornell, 1996). However, I am restricting discussion to supernaturalistic systems.

19. In the evolutionary context, a spandrel is a mere by-product of the evolutionary production of some characteristic actually selected for (which may itself later be co-opted for some significant biological function).

20. Scott Atran, *In Gods We Trust* (New York: Oxford University Press, 2002), is often read this way.

21. *Darwin's Cathedral* (Chicago: University of Chicago Press, 2002).

22. *Breaking the Spell* (New York: Viking, 2006), 117.

23. Patricia Churchland, 'Epistemology in the Age of Neuroscience', *Journal of Philosophy* 84 (1987), 544–53 at 548–9.

24. See his 3 July 1881 letter to William Graham, in *The Life and Letters of Charles Darwin*, ed. Francis Darwin (New York: n.p., 1889).

25. Alvin Plantinga has precipitated quite a debate on this issue. See James Beilby (ed.), *Naturalism Defeated?* (Ithaca: Cornell University Press, 2002).

26. 'Religion and Science', in *Science and the Modern World* (Cambridge: Cambridge University Press, 1925).

27. Steven Weinberg, 'A Designer Universe?', *New York Review of Books* (21 October 1999), 48.

28. See my 'Design, Chance, and Theistic Evolution', in W. Dembski (ed.), *Mere Creation* (Downers Grove: InterVarsity Press, 1998), 289–312, and my 'Saturation, World Ensembles and Design', *Faith and Philosophy* 22 (2005), Special Issue; 'Proceedings of the Russian-Anglo-American Conference on Cosmology and Theology, Notre Dame', 667–86.

29. See e.g. Nancey Murphy, *Theology in the Age of Scientific Reasoning* (Ithaca: Cornell University Press, 1990), and Michael Banner, *The Justification of Science and the Rationality of Religious Belief* (Oxford: Clarendon, 1990).

30. Among these are a number of 'Reformed Epistemologists', including Alvin Plantinga, Nicholas Wolterstorff, and Kelly Clark, among others.

31. Murphy, *Theology*, 99, 198. Many others argue for a commonality of inference types, canons of reasonableness, etc.

32. See e.g. Mikael Stenmark *How to Relate Science and Religion* (Grand Rapids: Eerdmans, 2004), ch. 5.

33. See Philip Clayton and Arthur Peacocke (eds.), *In Whom We Live and Move and Have Our Being* (Grand Rapids: Eerdmans, 2004), e.g. pp. xix–xx (Peacocke) and 87 (Clayton).

34. Panentheists disagree about what the view is. The basic description is: 'the world is in God, but does not exhaust God'. But the 'in' is metaphorical, with no agreement on what the metaphor means. In discussing God's relation to and action in the world, panentheists often use the analogy of the world being 'God's body'—God's action in the world being analogous to the human mind's relation to the human body.

35. P. Clayton, 'The Case for Christian Panentheism', *Dialog* 37 (Summer 1998), 201–8 at 206.

36. See e.g. Eleonore Stump and Norman Kretzmann, 'Eternity', *Journal of Philosophy*, 78 (1991), 429–58.

37. John Haught, *Science and Religion*, e.g. 4, 18. Others, including e.g. Clayton, Polking-horne, van Huyssteen, and Peacocke, often sound like this.

38. Nancey Murphy, *Reconciling Theology and Science* (Kitchener: Pandora, 1997), e.g. ch. 1 pp. 46, 67, 79, *et passim*. Many others (e.g. Peacocke, 21; J. Polkinghorne, *Reason and Reality* (Philadelphia: Trinity, 1991), 75; *Serious Talk* (Philadelphia: Trinity, 1996), 7, T. F. Torrance, *The Christian Frame of Mind* (Edinburgh: Handsel, 1985), 77–8, van Huyssteen, *Duet or Duel*, 77) make similar claims.

39. See Murphy, *Reconciling Theology and Science*.

40. Ibid. 4.

41. See e.g. W. Pannenberg, *Toward a Theology of Nature*: *Essays on Science and Faith* (Philadelphia: Westminster/Knox, 1999), 17 ff., 30–1, *et passim*.

42. There are obvious connections to 'open theism'. Kelly James Clark describes open theism thus: According to open theists, God changes, cannot do certain things, is dependent on creatures for emotional states and will, and genuinely suffers along with his creation. More particularly, God does not know future contingents (especially those involving libertarian free will). All of this is taken to mean that the future is open both to God and to human beings, who work in partnership to carve out an unforeseen but hoped for future.

43. e.g. *Serious Talk*, 53–4; id., *Quarks, Chaos, and Christianity* (New York: Crossroads, 1994), 71. Polkinghorne in some places seems a bit ambivalent about this view.

44. Christian critics of ID routinely assert that nature is in fact designed, but that its designedness is not a scientifically determinable matter.

45. *Knowing With the Heart* (Downers Grove: InterVarsity, 1999), 41.

46. See e.g. ibid. 29.

47. R. Clouser, 'Prospects for Theistic Science', in *Perspectives on Science and Christian Faith* 58 (2006), 2–15 at 15 n. 25.

48. Note that on e.g. coherentist views, Independence advocates are mistaken in thinking that there is no conflict if both sides respect proper boundaries. Given the infusion of religious (or anti-religious) foundations into *everything*, conflict between believing and non- (or un-)believing conceptual systems would be global and pervasive.

49. Integration via the same foundational metaphysics influencing both science and religion is the basic idea underpinning Padgett's *mutuality model* (*Science and the Study of God*).

50. Mary Midgley has done particularly interesting work in this area. See e.g. her *Science as Salvation* (New York: Routledge, 1994).

51. See her *Revolutions and Reconstructions in the Philosophy of Science* (Bloomington: Indiana University Press, 1980).

52. Norbert Schwarz, 'On Judgments of Truth and Beauty', *Daedalus* 135 (2006), 136.

53. See e.g. J. M. Schwartz and S. Begley, *The Mind and the Brain* (New York: Regan, 2002), 67 ff., and Pinker, 371 ff., for discussion.

54. Damasio has written a number of interesting books dealing with this and related topics.

55. See e.g. his 'The Passionate Scientist: Emotion in Scientific Cognition', in Peter Carruthers, Stephen Stich, and Michael Siegal (eds.), *The Cognitive Basis of Science* (Cambridge: Cambridge University Press, 2002), 235–50. See also Gerald Clore and

Karen Gasper, 'Feeling is Believing: Some Affective Influences on Belief', in Nico Frijda, Antony S. R. Manstead, and Sacha Bem, *Emotions and Belief: How Feeling Influences Thought* (Cambridge: Cambridge, 2000), esp. 10–44, 24 ff., and Eddie Herman-Jones, 'A Cognitive Dissonance Theory Perspective on the Role of Emotion in the Maintenance and Change of Belief and Attitude', in Frijda, Manstead and Bem, ibid., 185–211.

56. 'Emotions and Epistemic Evaluations', in Carruthers, Stich, and Siegal (eds.), *Cognitive Basis*, 251–62 at 257. A related position is taken in Clore and Gasper, 'Feeling is Believing'.

57. Sir Denys Haig Wilkinson, 'The Quarks and Captain Ahab', Schiff Memorial Lecture, Stanford, 1977.

58. There are exceptions on both ends. For the former see e.g. Andrew Pickering, in *Constructing Quarks* (Chicago: University of Chicago Press, 1984), and for the latter see e.g. Richard Dawkins, Peter Atkins, et al.

59. That requires presumptive acceptance that our cognitive faculties are basically reliable, but *any* epistemological hope requires that, and the only workable way of securing that may be a doctrine of creation. Stenmark's theory of *presumptionism* is useful here (see Stenmark, *How to Relate Science and Religion*, p. 90 et passim), as are Alvin Plantinga's works on Reformed Epistemology.

60. Imre Lakatos, Larry Laudan, et al. have led important parts of the charge here.

61. *Theology for a Scientific Age*, 5

CHAPTER 4

THEOLOGY AND MYSTERY

WILLIAM J. WAINWRIGHT

CHRISTIANITY's critics have often accused it of mystery mongering. Hume, for example, says that

all popular theology, especially the scholastic, has a kind of appetite for absurdity and contradiction. If that theology went not beyond reason and common sense, her doctrines would
appear too easy and familiar. Amazement must of necessity be raised: Mystery affected:
Darkness and obscurity sought after: And a foundation of merit afforded to the devout
votaries, who desire an opportunity of subduing their rebellious reason, by the belief of the
most unintelligible sophisms.[1]

And John Toland asserts that Christian theologians and priests have gone even
further than the hierophants of the ancient mystery cults. The latter swore their initiates to secrecy but their mysteries were intelligible in themselves. Only Christians
dared maintain that their doctrines were mysterious in a more radical sense, 'that
is, inconceivable in themselves, however clearly revealed'.[2]

Hume's and Toland's explanations of this phenomenon differ.[3] Whatever one
thinks of their explanations, however, there is little doubt that the appeal to,
and adoration of, mystery is a characteristic feature of much Christian thought
and practice. The Pseudo-Dionysius, for example, begins his *Mystical Theology*
by asking the Trinity to guide him to the 'most exalted' and hidden secrets of
Scripture 'which exceedeth light and more than exceedeth knowledge, where...the
mysteries of heavenly truth lie hidden in the dazzling obscurity of the secret silence,
outshining all brilliance with the intensity of their darkness'.[4]

Nor are themes like these peculiar to Christian mystics and mystical theologians. They are commonplace in the Church Fathers and in a number of later Christian theologians. Two examples will suffice.

Consider first John Chrysostom. St Paul said,

'The Lord ... dwells in unapproachable light.' And pay heed to the accuracy with which Paul speaks ... He does not say: 'Who dwells in incomprehensible light,' but: 'in unapproachable light,' and this is much stronger than 'incomprehensible.' A thing is said to be 'incomprehensible' when those who seek after it fail to comprehend it, even after they have searched and sought to understand it. But it does not elude all inquiry and questioning. A thing is unapproachable which, from the start, cannot be investigated nor can anyone come near to it.[5]

Yet,

suppose ... we forget Paul and the prophets for the moment, [and] mount up to the heavens ... Do you think that the angels in heaven talk over and ask each other questions about the divine essence? By no means! What are the angels doing? They give glory to God, they adore him, they chant without ceasing their triumphal and mystical hymns with a deep feeling of religious awe. Some sing: 'Glory to God in the highest;' the seraphim chant: 'Holy, holy, holy,' and they turn away their eyes because they cannot endure God's presence as he comes down to adapt himself to them in condescension.   (Chrysostom 65–6)

My second example is from Jonathan Edwards, who concludes a philosophically sophisticated explication of the Trinity by saying: 'I don't pretend fully to explain how these things are, and I am sensible a hundred other objections may be made, and puzzling doubts and questions raised, that I can't solve. I am far from pretending to explain the Trinity so as to render it no longer a mystery,' or 'asserting that [my account of the Trinity is] any explication of this mystery that unfolds and removes the mysteriousness and incomprehensibleness of it: for I am sensible that however, by what has been said, some difficulties are lessened, others that are new appear; and the number of those things that appear mysterious, wonderful, and incomprehensible are increased by it'.[6]

As these examples illustrate, both Christians themselves and their critics have historically thought that the concept of mystery is central to Christian reflection and Christian worship. It is initially surprising, then, to find that the indices of four important recent reference works contain few if any references to mystery. None are found in the index to Philip Quinn and Charles Taliaferro's *A Companion to the Philosophy of Religion*, for example, and the indices to my *The Oxford Handbook of Philosophy of Religion* and to William Mann's *The Blackwell Guide to the Philosophy of Religion* contain only one each. What is perhaps most surprising is that the only reference to mystery in Peter Byrne and Leslie Houlden's massive *Companion Encyclopedia of Theology* is to a discussion of Rudolf Otto's numinous experience in my article on 'Religious Experience and Language' in that volume. What explains this?

Partly, I think, a not unreasonable fear of obfuscation—a suspicion that appeals to mystery can be an excuse for avoiding hard thought and a justification for obscurantism and superstition.

Part of the explanation may also be a suspicion that the apophatic tradition that fuels much classical discussion of mystery isn't really Christian or is not Christian enough.[7] But this, I believe, is a mistake. Even 'Dionysius is not without a sense of personal devotion to the God-man, as when he prays that his discourse may be guided "by Christ, by my Christ," at the beginning of [the] *Celestial Hierarchy*.'[8] Christ also plays an important role in Dionysius's mystical vision. For God reveals and communicates himself through the celestial and ecclesiastical hierarchies, and Christ is the head and inner power of both. And the centrality of Christ is even clearer in Dionysius's first major western disciple. For John the Scot, the end of creation as a whole is the Word of God. 'The beginning and the end of the world are in the Word of God, indeed, to speak more plainly, they are the Word itself, for It is manifold end without end and beginning without beginning...save for the Father.'[9] Moreover, only the Word *made flesh* makes the return of all things to God possible. 'God's Word cried out in the most remote solitude of divine Goodness...He cried out invisibly before the world came to be in order to have it come to be; he cried out visibly when he came into the world in order to save it.'[10] Or consider Pierre de Berulle, who 'never stopped drinking at the well of Dionysius',[11] yet more or less seamlessly wedded his mystical apophatism to a very rich Christ mysticism.

The most important reason for the neglect of mystery, however, may be this. William Alston begins his recent 'Two Cheers for Mystery' by observing that 'contemporary Anglo-American analytic philosophy of religion' exhibits 'a considerable degree of confidence in' its ability 'to determine what God is like; how to construe his basic attributes; and what his purposes, plans, standards, values and so on are'. No one 'thinks we can attain a *comprehensive* knowledge of God's nature and doings. But on many crucial points, there seems to be a widespread confidence in our ability to determine exactly how things are with God.'[12] And, of course, the more confident one is, the less one will see any need for according the concept of mystery a central place in one's reflections on God. But what if failing to do so distorts these reflections? The burden of this chapter is that it does.

I

Philosophical and theological discussions of the Christian mysteries are frequently confused by a failure to carefully distinguish distinct[13] religiously relevant uses of the term. Four seem to me particularly important.

First, a sense of mystery can refer to wonder, surprise, or astonishment at something the human mind did not expect, and could not have anticipated. For example, 'things beyond our seeing, things beyond our hearing, things beyond our imagining, prepared by God for those who love him' (1 Corinthians 9). Mysteries in this sense, however, need not (though they may) be things we can't know or understand once they have occurred or been revealed to us (the Resurrection, for example, or the new life in Christ).

Second, 'mysteries' may refer to doctrines that are either incongruent or formally inconsistent with 'common notions'. Jonathan Edwards uses 'mystery' in this sense when he says that we should expect a revelation of 'spiritual' or 'invisible' things to be attended with much mystery and difficulty since they are remote from 'the nature of things that language is chiefly formed to express—viz. things pertaining to the common affairs and vulgar business of life, things obvious to sense and men's direct view...and of an exceeding different nature from the things of this world...and not agreeable to such notions, imaginations, and ways of thinking that grow up with us and are connatural to us'.[14] Thus Edwards argues that without a love of holiness and its consequent horror of sin, the doctrine of hell will seem absurd (unfair, unjust, and, in that sense, irrational) since one fails to appreciate what makes infinite punishment appropriate.

Again, a common pagan reaction to the 'scandal' of the cross was that it was not 'God-befitting'. It is often assumed that what troubled reflective or philosophically minded pagans was the doctrine of a crucified God's seeming inconsistency with God's impassibility. Paul Gavrilyuk has convincingly shown, however, that, for the most part, pagan theologians did *not* think that the divine's impassibility precluded emotions (love or benevolence, for example), or an involvement in human affairs. What troubled them, rather, was the attribution of *suffering* to God, and the *kind* of involvement implied by the doctrine of the crucifixion. 'A slave's death on the cross was unanimously regarded as shameful and degrading.' Docetic forms of Christian Gnosticism were at least partly motivated by a desire to defuse this scandal. Thus, 'a Basilidean account of the crucifixion...puts the following confession into the mouth of Christ..."I did not die in reality but in appearance, lest I be put to *shame* by them..."' Similarly, 'in the docetic segment of the apocryphal *Acts of John*', Christ reveals himself to John on the Mount of Olives at the very moment at which the crucifixion is taking place at Golgotha as the cosmic being he really is, but says that others (namely orthodox Christians) ' "will call me something else, which is vile and not worthy of me." '[15]

Third, a doctrine or truth may seem absurd, unbelievable, or, at the very least, mysterious because we are deprived of relevant information. Suppose, for example, that it is true that God exists and that every evil is necessary for a greater good, and consider Rowe's example of a fawn who dies slowly and painfully in a raging forest fire. Even if we believe that because God exists, the fawn's death is necessary for a good that outweighs it, *how* it does so may well seem mysterious. But, the *reason* it seems mysterious is, arguably, that we are ignorant of certain relevant facts. Finite intellects or, in any case, finite intellects *in via*, cannot grasp all the relevant logical connections between goods and evils, and are unavoidably ignorant of some of the relevant goods and evils (either because they don't know what these goods and evils are or, if they do, fail to fully appreciate their goodness or badness). The truths in question are not *intrinsically* mysterious, however, since the mystery would be dispelled if we were to come into possession of the relevant information—through a special revelation, perhaps, or at the eschaton or divinely ordained denouement of the world's history. Thus, Edwards thinks that some central doctrines are 'very mysterious', and 'have difficulties in them, inexplicable by us'. The doctrine of predestination, for example, is 'very difficult to reconcile with the justice of God'. Nevertheless, 'the time is coming when these mysteries will all be unfolded, and the perplexing difficulties that have attended them will all be perfectly vanished away, as the shades of night before the sun in a serene hemisphere'.[16]

In other cases, however, the mystery may be uneliminable by any addition of information or strengthening of our intellectual powers. In cases of this sort the mystery is irreducible because its object is intrinsically mysterious. These are mysteries in Gabriel Marcel's sense. Marcel distinguishes 'problems' from 'mysteries'. Problems[17]—a chess problem or mathematical problem, for instance, or the puzzles brought to Sherlock Holmes—have solutions, although these solutions may never be discovered. If and when the solutions are discovered, however, the problems disappear. A mystery, on the other hand, *has* no solution. No matter how much we may come to learn about it, it remains as mysterious as it was before.[18] A mystery in Marcel's sense is more or less the same as what Rudolf Otto called the '*mysterium* . . . that which is "mysterious" ', 'in the religious sense', is 'the "wholly other," . . . that which is quite beyond the sphere of the usual, the intelligible, and the familiar, which therefore falls quite outside the limits of the "canny" [of what is 'within our ken'], and is contrasted with it, filling the mind with blank wonder and astonishment'.[19] The concept of mystery, like the concept of transcendence, is formally negative. 'On the side of the feeling-content', however, 'it is otherwise; that *is* in very truth positive in the highest degree, though . . . it cannot be rendered explicit in conceptual terms.'[20]

Mysteries in this fourth sense are, arguably, the subject of the passages from the Pseudo-Dionysius, John Chrysostom, and Jonathan Edwards that I quoted at the beginning of this chapter. They are also my primary concern in what follows.

II

Alston offers four reasons for what he calls the 'Divine Mystery Thesis', namely, that 'God is inevitably so *mysterious* to us, to our rational capacities . . . that nothing we can think, believe, or say about him is *strictly* true of God as he is in himself.' These reasons include the experiences of the great Christian mystics and the doctrine of simplicity to which I shall turn in a moment. The others are, first, 'the puzzles, paradoxes, and insoluble problems which theological thought [about the Trinity, for example] seems so frequently to lead'; and, second, our limited capacities: 'If we think about the relation of human cognitive powers to the absolutely infinite source of all that is other than itself, it seems reasonable to suppose that the former would not be in a position to get an account of the latter that is exactly correct, even in certain abstract respects'[21] (Alston 100–1). Or as Edwards argues: 'A very great superiority, even in beings of the same nature as ourselves', makes many of their actions, intentions, and assertions 'incomprehensible and attended with inexplicable intricacies'. Witness the relation that 'little children' bear to 'adult persons', for example, or the 'vulgar' to 'learned men, [or] great philosophers and mathematicians'. God 'is *infinitely* diverse from and above all in his nature', however. So if God vouchsafes a revelation of himself (of his triune nature, say) 'which is entirely diverse [not only] from anything we do now experience in our present state, but from anything that we can be conscious or immediately sensible of in any state whatsoever that our nature can be in, then especially may mysteries be expected in such a revelation'.[22]

Or consider Aquinas. In Part 4 of the *Summa Contra Gentiles*, Aquinas argues that because 'the human intellect' must 'derive its knowledge from sensible things, [it] is not able through itself to reach the vision of the divine substance in itself, which is above all sensible things and, indeed, improportionately above *all* other things'. Yet 'man's perfect good is that he somehow know God'. Therefore, because 'it was [but] a feeble knowledge of God that man could reach' by unassisted reason, 'God revealed certain things about himself that transcend the human intellect...These things [the doctrine of the Trinity, for example] are revealed to man as...not to be understood but only to be believed as heard, for the human intellect in this state...is connected with things sensible [and] cannot be elevated entirely to gaze upon things which exceed every proportion of sense', although 'when it shall have been freed from the connection with sensibles, then it will be elevated to gaze upon the things which are revealed'.[23] The arguments I have discussed so far focus on the relation between our necessarily limited intellects, on the one hand, and the divine, on the other. Other arguments focus more directly on God's own being.

According to John the Scot, for example, God *knows* himself but does not know *what* he is. John's reasons for this are essentially these: to know what God is, one would have to grasp God's essence; God 'is not essence', though, 'but More than Essence and the infinite Cause of all essences, and not only infinite but the Infinity of all infinite essence, and More than infinity'. God is beyond essence because essences are the sorts of thing that can be captured or expressed in definitions, and definitions proceed by marking out a thing's boundaries. God has no boundaries, however, since he is infinite or limitless. Not even God, then, can know what God is. But this does not imply that God is ignorant (because 'He does not understand of

Himself what He is') nor does it imply that God is impotent (because 'He is unable to define His Substance'). For God *has* no what.[24] Nor does it imply that 'God does not know himself', or know himself *as* infinite, and as indeed 'above every finite thing and every infinite thing and beyond finitude and infinity'.[25] (John the Scot, Bk. 2. 585A–590D).

John's case for the claim that God has no essence or 'what' depends on the following subargument. If a definition is to succeed in distinguishing its definiendum from other things, it must *exclude* the item being defined *from* other things. An 'absolutely infinite' God would exclude *nothing*, however, since if it did exclude something, it would have limits and thus not be '*absolutely*' infinite (or limitless).

This subargument has a certain (specious) plausibility if 'absolutely infinite' is construed in arithmetical or geometrical terms. The series of natural numbers excludes no natural numbers, for example, and an infinite line excludes none of its segments. Yet why should we construe 'absolutely infinite' in this fashion? Why not, instead, construe it as 'absolutely perfect'? If we were to do so, however, the subargument wouldn't go through because absolute perfection *does* exclude things, for it excludes *im*perfections such as ignorance and injustice and *mixed* perfections[26] such as repentance.[27] Let us turn, then, to another attempt to show that God's nature is such that he transcends what can be thought of him.

In *Proslogion* 15, Anselm exclaims: 'Lord, not only are you that than which a greater cannot be thought, but you are also something greater than can be thought. For since it is possible to think that there is such a one, if you were not this same being something greater than you could be thought—which cannot be.'[28]

Commenting on this passage, M. J. Charlesworth observes that Anselm is reminding us that 'even if we understand God to be "that than which nothing greater can be thought," we do not thereby have a *positive* or *determinate* knowledge of God';[29] and refers us to the reply to Gaunilo where Anselm says that just as one can think or understand 'the ineffable' though one can't 'specify [or describe] what is said to be ineffable; and just as one can think of [or understand] the inconceivable— although one cannot think of what "inconceivable" applies to—so also "that than which a greater cannot be thought" ... can be thought of and understood even if the thing itself cannot be thought and understood.'[30] But granting this, one may still wonder why Anselm thinks that a being *greater* than can be thought is greater or more perfect than one lacking this property.

Being such that one cannot think it is not *itself* a perfection if for no other reason than because our inability to think something (adequately capture it in concepts) may be a function of its *im*perfection. Plato's Receptacle, or Aristotle's or Plotinus's *hyle*, are examples.[31] Again, a thing might be too complicated or too hidden for our intellects to comprehend it. The true nature of the physical universe might be an example. It doesn't follow that its impenetrability to finite intellects is a good-making feature of it.

Being too *perfect* for us to conceive, on the other hand, might be a *second-order* perfection, that is, a perfection parasitic on a thing's other perfections. And perhaps God has this second-order property. Yet why think he does?

Well, perhaps because while we know that God's joy, for instance, or his knowledge, are perfect we don't have a good conceptual grasp of either of them. In the case of a degreed property that lacks an upper limit, such as joy, this might be because the bliss that God enjoys is incommensurable with any finite analogue of it.[32] Or in the case of a degreed property such as knowledge which *has* an intrinsic maximum (namely, maximal knowledge or omniscience), finite intellects may know *that* God knows all truths, and yet not know *how* he knows them, or just what his knowledge of them is like. Moreover, if God is simple, as much of the tradition maintains, then *no* positive characterization of God is strictly true of him since 'all our propositional thought and speech is necessarily carried on by making distinctions' (Alston 101). Or perhaps Karl Rahner is right, and mystery in Marcel's or Otto's sense is an intrinsic positive feature of the Godhead. (More on this later.)

But suppose we agree that being greater than can be thought is a consequence of (some of?) God's first-order perfections, or of the relation between them (that is, of his simplicity),[33] or of the fact that mystery is an intrinsic feature of the divine essence.[34] Does it straightforwardly follow that being greater than can be thought is not only a divine property but also a *divine perfection*? Only if we assume that any property entailed by a perfection is itself a perfection. And this assumption is false. Repentance entails a prior sin, and while the former is a perfection or good-making property, the latter is not. Again, intelligence trivially entails two plus two equaling four but two and two summing to four is not a perfection. Even so, since being greater than can be thought is arguably entailed by God's first-order perfections, if God were not greater than can be thought, he would necessarily lack one or more of those perfections and so would not be God, a being greater than which none can be thought.

There is reason to think, then, that God necessarily transcends what can be said and thought of him. Just *how* mysterious is he, though? We will turn to this question in the next section.

III

At one extreme are the views of deists such as Charles Blount who assert that 'that rule which is necessary for our future happiness ought to be generally made known to all men...Therefore, no revealed religion', with its attendant mysteries, 'is necessary for human happiness.'[35] John Toland and other deists think that, because God's perfection entails his 'justice and reasonableness', 'nothing in true Christianity... is either contrary to or above reason.... Nothing in true Christianity', therefore, 'can be a mystery—a proposition or notion impenetrable to ordinary, human intellectual capacities.'[36]

At the other extreme lies Pierre Bayle who professes faith in the Christian mysteries but insists on their contra-rationality. The doctrine of the Trinity, for example, contradicts the self-evident principle that if $x = y$ and $y = z$ then $x = y = z$, for any x, y, and z. And more generally, 'there is a clear incompatibility between accepting the Cartesian standard of clarity and distinctness', which Bayle believes to be appropriate in philosophy, 'and accepting the Christian doctrine[s] ... Mysteries... are necessarily non-evident'.[37] Hence, while faith 'produces a perfect certitude ... its object will never be evident. Knowledge, on the other hand, produces together both complete evidence of the object and full certitude of conviction.' So 'if a Christian ... undertakes to maintain the mystery of the Trinity', for instance, 'against a philosopher, he would oppose a non-evident object to evident objections'.[38]

Bayle claims that skeptical arguments drive us to faith. 'It is through a lively awareness' of 'the difficulties that surround the doctrines of the Christian religion...that one learns of the excellence of faith and the blessing of heaven. In the same way, one also learns of the necessity of mistrusting reason and having recourse to grace.' 'It has pleased the Father, and the Son, and the Holy Ghost, Christians ought to say, to lead us by the path of faith, and not by the path of knowledge and disputation ... We cannot lose our way with such guides. And *reason itself commands us to prefer them to its direction*' (Bayle 435, 423, my emphasis).

Yet can one 'assert doctrines while simultaneously holding that they contradict self-evident principles'?[39] Bayle thinks that one can. For in doing so, one is not inconsistently 'believing and not believing the same [proposition] at the same time'. Rather, one consistently believes that '(1) The light of reason teaches me that [the doctrine] is false; [yet] (2) I believe it nonetheless because I am convinced that this light is not infallible and because I prefer to submit...to the Word of God, than to a metaphysical demonstration' (Bayle 298). Is this coherent? Penelhum thinks that it isn't. For in spite of Bayle's explicit disclaimer, he *does* believe two inconsistent things. Through faith Bayle believes the doctrine of the Trinity, for example, and yet at the same time believes that the doctrine's falsity is entailed by self-evident principles. But because one can't believe that a proposition, p, is entailed by self-evident principles without believing p, Bayle must also believe that the doctrine of the Trinity is false.[40]

I do not find this objection compelling. Granted, one can't both *find* a set of principles self-evident and *find* that they self-evidently entail p, and not believe p. To rest on this, though, seems to miss Bayle's point, namely, that his radical skepticism has led him to *doubt* so-called self-evident principles. Since he no longer finds them self-evident, he no longer finds the propositions they entail evident either, and so does *not* inconsistently believe the doctrine of the Trinity, for instance, while simultaneously believing its denial.

Whether Bayle can escape *all* charges of incoherence is more doubtful. For if *all* principles of reason are called into question, it is difficult to see how Bayle can be justified in asserting that reason itself directs us to set reason aside.[41] As far as I can tell, Bayle has only two recourses. The first is to restrict his skepticism to only *some* of reason's self-evident principles. This seems to me a non-starter, however, for if his doubt extends to self-evident logical and mathematical principles, as his animadversions on the doctrine of the Trinity imply, it is difficult to see how he could retain his confidence in *any* principle of reason. The second is less obviously incoherent, and this is to regard the apparent bankruptcy of reason as a *cause of,* rather than a *reason for,* the flight to faith. Bayle's procedure would then bear some resemblance to that of the Buddhist Madhyamikas who employ reason to show the incoherency of reason, thereby, in their view, clearing a space for the occurrence of the non-dual, non-conceptual intuition of the Suchness of things.

There may also be another problem. John Toland characterizes views such as Bayle's thus: while doctrines such as the Trinity 'cannot in themselves be con-tradictory to the principles' of reason yet, because 'of our corrupt and limited understandings', they may *seem* to us to contradict them. On 'the authority of divine revelation', however, 'we are bound to believe…in them', and '*to adore what we cannot comprehend*' (Toland 24).

Toland has two responses to this position, the second of which is more telling,[42] namely, that we cannot understand what is or seems to be contradictory,[43] and can-not believe what we don't understand, although 'a man may give his *verbal* assent to he knows not what, out of fear, superstition…interest, and the like…motives'. 'For what I don't conceive, can no more give me right notions of God, or influence my actions, than a prayer delivered in an unknown tongue can excite my devotion' (Toland 35, 28, my emphasis). Of course, strictly speaking, Toland is mistaken be-cause we can and do understand contradictions. Indeed, it is just *because* we under-stand them, that we know they are necessarily false. In a larger sense, though, Toland is right. Because contradictions imply everything, in believing a contradiction I am implicitly committed to believing that God both is and is not evil, that we both should and shouldn't worship him, and the like, and it is difficult to see how a belief of this sort could give me right notions of God or guide my behavior. Moreover, this is true even if the doctrines proposed for our belief, while not contradictory, are wholly impenetrable by our understandings. The divine mysteries, then, cannot be contradictions and they cannot be totally opaque to finite intellects. So precisely what about them can't we understand?

Leibniz understands Bayle to say that while *God* can comprehend the mysteries of his own being (and so see that they involve no inconsistencies), they are contrary to human and, indeed, *any* finite understanding. He finds this incoherent, however. For, in his view, human reason is *part* of divine reason, and what is contrary to part of reason must be contrary to the whole of reason since the latter includes the former.[44] Why does Leibniz think this?

Some of the divine mysteries, at least, are necessary truths. The doctrine of the Trinity is an example.[45] Now Leibniz believes that a comprehension of necessary truths depends upon a proof or analysis that demonstrates or explicates their necessity. In the case of the divine mysteries, however, the required analysis or proof involves an infinite number of steps, and so God alone can perform it. Hence, while *God* can comprehend the mysteries of his own being, we cannot. We can, nonetheless, meaningfully and justifiably believe and assert them, and this for three reasons. First, we possess or have been given 'analogies'. The soul's union with its body, for instance, is an analog of the Word's union with a human nature. Second, even though we can't *prove* a mystery and, in that sense, comprehend it, we can refute objections to it. A 'defense of the mysteries' is similar in this respect 'to a defense of the consistency and completeness of arithmetic'. Kurt Gödel (1906–78) has shown that arithmetic's consistency and completeness can't be proved 'but this does not prevent one from [successfully] defending it against specific accusations of inconsistency'.[46] Finally, one has the standard 'motives of credibility' for believing the mysteries (miracles, fulfilled prophecy, and so on). Leibniz has thus explained, to his own satisfaction, how divine mysteries can be both incomprehensible to finite intellects and justifiably believed and asserted by them.

Leibniz's refutation of Bayle depends on his claim that human reason is not a mere analog of God's reason but literally a part of it. Why does he say this? 'When functioning properly, humankind's reasoning is simply "the linking together of truths and objections in due form" ... [and] as such cannot be mistaken'. Divine reason does not differ from human reason in kind but only in degree. Although the demonstration or analysis of the divine mysteries 'require[s] infinite cognitive power',[47] the *kind* of demonstration or analysis required is essentially the same. But this strikes me as doubtful at best and, in any case, not what the tradition as a whole has had in mind: the difference between God's nature and capacities and ours is not merely quantitative but qualitative, a difference of kind and not just of degree. Let us therefore try again.

Thomas Aquinas claims that some truths about God exceed 'the power of human reason'. In a paper published in 1988, George Mavrodes suggested that we gloss 'exceeds the power of human reason' thus: 'A truth exceeds the ability of all human reason if and only if it is not possible to prove that truth demonstratively.' Why think that, in this sense, the doctrine of the Trinity, say, exceeds the power of human reason? Perhaps because, as Aquinas suggests, there are only two ways of demonstrating a truth about something—by deducing it from our 'understanding of the substance [or essence] of the thing which is the subject of that knowledge' or from the thing's causal effects.[48] Truths about such things as the Trinity can't be demonstrated in this way, however. For we can't (prior to the beatific vision at least) grasp God's essence. And Aquinas assumes that 'the creative power of God is *common* to the whole Trinity, and hence ... belongs to the *unity* of the essence, and *not* to the distinction of the persons'. So while 'by natural reason we can know what belongs to the *unity of the essence*' from God's casual effects, we *cannot* know 'what belongs to the distinction of the persons' from them.[49]

Mavrodes' principal objection to this line of thought is that there are other no less reasonable interpretations of 'demonstration'. For example, following Plantinga and others, we might identify a demonstration with a sound, non-circular deductive or inductive argument from universally (or nearly universally) accepted premises. Or, following Mavrodes and Penelhum, we might identify a demonstration with a sound, non-circular argument from premises that its proponent or recipient knows to be true or has strong reasons to believe are true. Although it is unlikely that one can provide demonstrations in the first sense of the doctrine of the Trinity (or of any other interesting philosophical or theological truth for that matter), the prospects of doing so in the second may be brighter. And, in fact, Richard of St Victor, Jonathan Edwards, and Richard Swinburne claim to have provided demonstrations of the doctrine of the Trinity in the sense in question.[50]

The tradition does more or less unanimously attest that God's essence is unknown or unknowable by finite creatures.[51] The fact that a thing's substance or essence is unknown or unknowable does not entail that we can't rationally establish many truths about it, however. Locke thought that the substances or essences of physical objects were currently unknown but did not think that there were no well-grounded truths about them. Again, many truths about water were known before it was discovered that water is H_2O. Nor would matters obviously have been different if we had not discovered that water is H_2O or even if, for some reason, humans never *could* have discovered this.

Yet if God's essence or inner being is unknown or unknowable, what *can* we know about God? One of the most common answers hinges on a distinction between knowing *that* a proposition is true and knowing or understanding *how* it can be true. As Edwards observes in 'The Mind', 71, 'it is not impossible to believe or know the truth of mysteries, or propositions that we cannot comprehend, or see the manner how the several ideas that belong to the proposition are united ... we may perceive *that* they are united and know *that* they belong one to another, though we do not know the manner *how* they are tied together'.[52] In view of remarks Edwards makes elsewhere, it is clear that he is referring not only to propositions that we know to be true because their truth is attested by reliable authority but also to propositions that we can prove or demonstrate without fully comprehending them. In a late entry, for example, Edwards asserts that ' 'Tis not necessary that persons should have clear ideas of things that are the subject of a proposition, in order to being rationally convinced of the truth of the proposition,' and cites 'many truths of which mathematicians are convinced by strict demonstration ... concerning which they have no clear ideas', such as propositions about 'surd quantities and fluxions'.[53] It is in this sense, presumably, that after having given his rational account of just why

God must be triune, Edwards exclaimed 'I don't pretend fully to explain how these things are ... I am far from pretending to explaining the Trinity so as to render it no longer a mystery.'[54]

In what sense, though, can propositions which we know to be true elude our comprehension? Well, in some cases we may observe, and hence know, that an event has occurred without understanding how it *could* have occurred, or be cognizant of a phenomenon such as lightning or combustion yet be utterly baffled by it. In cases like these, what is lacking is a grasp of the occurrence's causes or of the mechanisms or internal structures underlying the phenomenon that puzzles us. Something like this may be involved in our understanding of God's providence, for example. As James Kellenberger observes in discussing Job's faith, one can believe or even know *that* God exists, is good and merciful, and the like without understanding *how* God is good and merciful, since 'his *ways* of goodness, mercy', and so on, 'are beyond our conceiving ... This source of mystery—the inconceivability of God's ways—would remain just as it is if it were *known that* there is a God, *that* he is good and *that* he is merciful.'[55] What Job lacks, in short, is an understanding of the *mechanisms* of divine providence. The extent to which divine providence is a mystery in this sense is a matter of debate, of course. Job confesses that he has 'obscured [God's] designs with [his] empty-headed words ... holding forth on matters [he] cannot understand, on marvels beyond [him] and [his] knowledge' (Job 42: 3). Edwards, on the other hand, thought that he *did* have a grasp of the mechanisms of providence, devoting an entire sermon series to an explication of the wondrous 'machine', composed of wheels within wheels, that underlies and constitutes the history of redemption.

Edwards's *Discourse on the Trinity* suggests a somewhat different sense of 'incomprehensibility'. He compares the Christian enquirer to a student of nature. When the latter 'looks on a plant', or an animal, 'or any other works of nature, at a great distance, [he] may see something in it wonderful and beyond his comprehension', and so desire to view it more closely. And if he does, he 'indeed understands more about them ... and yet the number of things that are wonderful and mysterious in them that appear to him are much more than before. And if he views them with a microscope, the number of the wonders that he sees will be much increased still. But yet the microscope gives him more of a true knowledge concerning them.'[56] What this comparison suggests is that while Christian divines' investigations of the Christian mysteries are progressive in the sense that more and more facets of these mysteries are revealed, more questions answered, and more puzzles removed, the knowledge that is gained only leads to new questions and new puzzles: 'However ... some difficulties are lessened, others that are new appear; and the number of those things that appear mysterious, wonderful and incomprehensible are increased by it.'[57] Edwards's point in this passage, I think, is not that some questions about the Trinity, for instance, are unanswerable (although they may be) but, rather, that any answers we may discover simply lead to more questions. The problem the passage isolates is thus quantitative rather than qualitative. But unlike some of the more optimistic estimates of the possibility of progress in science, Edwards seems to think that our mounting success in answering questions about the Christian mysteries takes us no closer to the goal of answering all questions about them.

Yet another sense of 'incomprehensibility' is suggested by 'Miscellany 839': divine mysteries 'are not only so above human comprehension that men can't easily apprehend all that is to be understood concerning them, but [they] are difficult to the understanding in that sense, that they are difficult to be received by the judgement or belief'.[58] Why is this the case? At least partly because the Christian mysteries are attended with 'paradoxes' and 'seeming contradictions'. Difficulties of this sort are not peculiar to divinity. 'The reasonings and conclusions of the best metaphysicians and mathematicians concerning infinities', for instance, are also 'attended with paradoxes and seeming inconsistencies'.[59] (Hilbert's hotel is an example.[60])[61] The problem is partly due to the limitations of language. As Edwards observes in 'Miscellany 83', 'The things of Christianity are so spiritual, so refined, so high and abstracted, and so much above the things we ordinarily converse with and our common affairs, to which we adapt our words,' that 'we are forced to use words...analogically...and therefore [does] religion [abound] with so many paradoxes and seeming contradictions.'[62] If I understand Edwards, however, the problem is not just with our language but with our imagination or sense of grasp.[63] Our analogies and metaphors are ultimately inadequate. We lack an adequate model or, perhaps more accurately, an adequate *unified* model of the deep things of God. Edwards sometimes employs an Augustinian psychological model of the Trinity, for example, while at other times employing patristic social models. He makes no attempt to unify them, however—presumably because he sees no way of doing so.[64]

IV

But suppose that we grant that the veil between God and ourselves cannot be removed in this life. Will we, indeed, can we, behold God unveiled in the next? Some texts suggest that we will. Paul, for example, asserts that while 'we now see only puzzling reflections in a mirror, we shall then see face to face'. Our 'knowledge now is partial' but 'then it will be whole, like God's knowledge of me' (1 Corinthians 13: 12). Does the beatific vision, then, include an unclouded vision of God's essence? Some Christian theologians, at least, have thought not.[65]

Thus, Aquinas says that 'since our mind is not proportionate to the divine substance, that which is the substance of God remains beyond our intellect and so is unknown to us. Hence the supreme knowledge which man has of God is to know that he does not know God, in so far as he knows that what God is surpasses all that we can understand of him.'[66] Rahner seems to me to be correct in arguing that, because 'the reason for saying' that knowing God involves knowing that one does not know God[67] 'holds good for the beatific vision' as well as for the veiled glimpses of God we have in this mortal life, 'there is no reason for not applying [it] to the knowledge of God in the beatific vision'[68] (Rahner 59).

Some of the things Edwards says have similar implications. Edwards believes that while many of the difficulties and perplexities surrounding Christian doctrines will be cleared up in the 'future appointed time of joy and glory to the church [on earth]...the perfect and full explication of these mysteries is part of the last and eternal state of the church [in heaven], to heighten the joy and praises of the wedding day of Christ and his church'.[69] It doesn't follow that *all* mystery will be dispelled, however, and at least some things Edwards says suggest that it won't. Thus, as we have seen, in 'Miscellany 1340' Edwards asserts that because God 'is infinitely diverse from and above all others in his nature', any revelation he chooses to vouchsafe of his intrinsic nature (of his triunity, say) will be so 'entirely diverse [not only] from anything that we do now experience in our present state, but from anything that we can be conscious or immediately sensible of *in any state whatsoever that our nature can be in*', that many 'mysteries may be expected in such a revelation'.[70] The clear implication is that even the light of heaven won't, and indeed cannot, dispel all mystery.

One of the most powerful statements of this view is given by John Chrysostom, who exclaims: 'let us call upon him, then, as the ineffable God who is beyond our intelligence, invisible, incomprehensible...Let us call on him as the God who is inscrutable to the angels, unseen by the Seraphim, inconceivable to the Cherubim, invisible to the principalities, to the powers, and to the virtues, in fact to *all* creatures without qualification, because he is known *only* by the Son and the Spirit' (Chrysostom 97, my emphases). Why do the Seraphim 'stretch forth their wings and cover their faces? For what other reason than that they cannot endure the sparkling flashes nor the lightning which shines from the throne. Yet they did not see the pure light itself nor the pure essence itself. What they saw was a condescension accommodated to their nature'[71] (Chrysostom 101). So unless the beatified see God more clearly than the angels do, they do not grasp God's essence. The mystery of God is thus ineluctable.

And, indeed, it is possible that it is ineluctable in an even stronger sense. For there may be a sense in which God's own knowledge of himself does not dispel the mystery. Karl Rahner points out that in post-medieval scholastic theology (and, I would add, in much if not most contemporary analytic philosophy of religion), mystery is a property statements have when they exceed our reason or cannot be fully understood. This conception of mystery has three noteworthy features. First, while it is admitted that the mystery of doctrinal statements is rooted in features of their object, the *focus* of scholastic theology's discussion of mystery is on the statements, rather than on what those statements are about. Second, mystery is regarded as a function of the relation of the propositions in question to human reason. Third, reason is construed in its modern sense as ratiocination or 'calculation', and thus sharply distinguished from the will and affections. Rahner thinks that each of these features reflects a mistake. In the first place, mystery is primarily a characteristic of the deep things of God—not of the doctrinal statements that express them. In the second, mystery is not (in the first instance at least) a function of the relation between certain propositions about God and finite intellects but, instead, an intrinsic property of God himself. Finally, we can cognize mystery by faith alone, and faith is an expression of our will and affections as well as our intellect. To recognize mystery is not just to acknowledge that certain propositions exceed our grasp; it is to prostrate ourselves in loving wonder before something which can't be comprehended by any sort of propositional cognition.

In short, as Rahner says, if God's incomprehensibility 'is the very substance of our vision and the very object of our blissful love', then 'vision must mean grasping and being grasped by the mystery, and the supreme act of knowledge is not the abolition or diminution of the mystery, but its final assertion' (Rahner 41). The beatific 'vision of God face to face' does remove many mysteries, 'but this only means that *what* [the mysteries] express is manifested in its own being and substance, is experienced therefore in itself and must no longer rely for its manifestation on the [authoritative] word that does duty for it[72] ... Nonetheless, these mysteries [that is, what one now directly beholds] remain mysterious and incomprehensible' (Rahner 56). The Greek Fathers are thus right when they speak of 'the highest stage of life and knowledge' as entering 'into the darkness in which God is' (Pseudo-Dionysius), or a not-knowing which is 'the supra-rational knowledge' (Maximus the Confessor), or tell us that 'to enter the holy of holies is to be encompassed by the divine darkness' (Gregory of Nyssa) (Rahner 58).

But all this, if correct, has a potentially startling consequence. For if mystery is not, in the first instance, a function of the relation between God and finite intellects but, rather, an intrinsic property of God's own nature, then God's complete and perfect knowledge of himself must include a recognition of it. 'The absolutely clear self-awareness of' God may thus include 'something positive which does not appertain to the [propositional] intellect[73] but to the mystery in contradistinction from such an intellect.' If this is so, then mystery 'appertains to God's knowledge [of himself], essentially, in a preeminent and analogous sense' (Rahner 48–9). There may thus be a sense in which God himself can't comprehend his own essence[74] but must enter into the 'divine darkness', knowing himself, or aspects of himself, through a 'not-knowing' that is at one and the same time a supreme 'supra-rational knowledge' of the deep things of his own being.

To see why this suggestion isn't outrageous, we need to say more about the *kind* of knowledge involved in apprehending a mystery in Marcel's or Rahner's sense.

An awareness of mystery in the sense in question is perhaps best construed as a species of appreciation or knowledge by acquaintance.[75] Other examples of this sort of knowledge are my knowledge of what strawberries taste like or silk feels like, my awareness of a thunderstorm's sublimity or the beauty of a Bach fugue, or my knowing what it is like to suffer or to love. Notice that these forms of knowledge by acquaintance are related analogically, and vary with their objects. Our appreciation of beauty, for instance, is importantly different from our acquaintance with sense modalities such as the taste of strawberries or the feel of silk, and both differ significantly from a first-hand knowledge of the horror of war or what Kierkegaard calls 'first love'.

Instances of knowledge by acquaintance aren't just differentiated by their objects, however. Consider the wonder over her own beauty that Semele expresses in an aria in Handel's opera of the same name, or the Greeks' wonder at the world (the fact of its being),[76] or the Christian's or Muslim's or Sri Vaisnava's wonder at the glory of God. These instances of wonder differ not only in object but in phenomenological quality or feel. Semele's wonder, for example, is qualitatively different from the Greeks' wonder at the world, and both differ qualitatively from the theists' wonder at the glory of God.[77]

The object of a sense of mystery in Marcel's or Rahner's sense is God's own being or nature, and the best description of its phenomenological character is probably Otto's—'blank wonder, an astonishment that strikes us dumb, amazement absolute', occasioned by coming 'upon something inherently "wholly other," whose kind and character are incommensurable with our own, and before which we therefore recoil in a wonder that strikes us chill and numb', but whose 'feeling-content' is 'positive in the highest degree'.[78]

Does a sense of mystery in this sense entail lack of understanding or grasp? The answer is 'Yes' *if* understanding or grasp is defined in terms of *conceptual* grasp or *propositional* knowledge (knowledge that). The answer is 'No' if an affirmative answer is understood to imply the existence of a gap in understanding that could in principle be filled in, or that the sort of knowledge involved in this and other instances of knowledge by acquaintance isn't adequate to its object.

Are there two quite different senses of mystery,[79] then, which we might call epistemological mysteries and ontological mysteries, respectively? (Epistemological because the mysteries in question are a function of the relation between God's nature or being, on the one hand, and the limitations of created intellects, on the other. Ontological because the mystery this expression gestures at is an intrinsic aspect of God's own being rather than a feature of human or divine knowledge of it.) These senses of mystery *are* at home in very different places. Discussions of epistemological mysteries are at home in philosophical theology, for example, and are the principal subject of this chapter's first three sections. The ontological sense of mystery, on the other hand, is perhaps most at home in liturgical worship and the prayer of adoration.[80] But the two senses of 'mystery' are not entirely equivocal. For both senses are partly defined by a lack of conceptual mastery. Epistemological mysteries and ontological mysteries elude conceptualization in very different ways, however, and for very different reasons. Epistemological mysteries elude it because while adequate concepts are in principle available (if only to God), they are *not* available *to us*. Ontological mysteries elude conceptualization because *no* concepts can fully express them. They are best (albeit imperfectly) expressed by symbols, images, songs, poetry, and, perhaps ultimately, by the silence of mystical prayer.

The question raised by Rahner's claim that 'mystery appertains to God's knowledge' of himself is thus roughly equivalent to this. Can God adopt the attitudes described by Otto toward himself? On the whole,[81] I don't see why not. Even if we understood everything about ourselves that can be conceptually grasped we might still wonder at, or be amazed or astonished by, our own being. ('We are fearfully and wonderfully made' (Psalm 139: 14)) Why, then, can't God wonder at, or be amazed by, *his* being? Moreover, that God can adopt these attitudes toward himself seems even clearer in a Trinitarian context. A standard eucharistic prayer concludes, 'All this we ask through your Son Jesus Christ. *By him, and with him, and in him*, in the unity of the Holy Spirit, all honor and glory are yours, Almighty Father, now and forever' (my emphasis). Just as we adore or glorify God, so the Father and Son and Holy Spirit adore and glorify each other. Nor do I see why the Father's and the Son's and the Holy Spirit's mutual adoration can't be tinged with awe, wonder, and (even) astonishment.

So in precisely what sense does mystery 'appertain to God's knowledge' of himself? God, I suggest, knows everything that can be propositionally known about himself[82] through an analog of propositional cognition. But other aspects of God's being (those which are mysteries in Marcel's or Rahner's sense) can't be grasped in this way even in principle, and God knows these by an analog of appreciation or knowledge by acquaintance. Nothing about God is thus unknown to God. He is neither 'baffled' nor 'puzzled' nor 'mystified' by his own being.[83] Nevertheless, God's nature is for him an object of an amazement, wonder, and awe, which are the felt aspects, as it were, of a perfect experiential acquaintance with depths of his own being that necessarily elude even his own complete conceptual comprehension.[84]

Notes

1. David Hume, *The Natural History of Religion* (London: Adam & Charles Black, 1956), 54 (henceforth Hume).
2. John Toland, *Christianity Not Mysterious* (London, 1696; repr. New York: Garland, 1978), 73 (henceforth Toland). I have modernized Toland's spelling and capitalization.

3. Toland ultimately explains it by the activity of 'cunning priests' who exploited people's gullibility for 'their own advantage' (Toland 70). Hume traces its origin to people's fear of God and of his ill favor; and who, 'supposing him to be pleased, like themselves with praise and flattery', spare 'no eulogy or exaggeration...in their addresses to him...Thus they proceed; till at last they arrive at infinity itself...And it is well, if, in striving to get farther...they run not into inexplicable mystery, and destroy the intelligent nature of their deity, on which alone any rational worship or adoration can be founded' (Hume 43).

4. *Dionysius the Areopagite on The Divine Names and The Mystical Theology*, trans. with introduction by C. E. Rolt (London: Macmillan, 1957), 191 (henceforth Dionysius).

5. John Chrysostom, *On the Incomprehensible Nature of God*, trans. Paul W. Harkins, Fathers of the Church (Washington: The Catholic University of America Press, 1984), 100 (henceforth Chrysostom).

6. Jonathan Edwards, *Discourse on the Trinity*, in *The Works of Jonathan Edwards* (New Haven: Yale University Press, 1957–), xxi. 134, 139.

7. The apophatic tradition (or tradition of negative theology) insists that God is most accurately described by saying what God is not.

8. Bernard McGinn, *The Foundations of Mysticism: Origins to the Fifth Century* (New York: Crossroad, 2003), 180.

9. Johannes Scotus Erigena, *Periphyseon: The Division of Nature*, trans. I. P. Sheldon-Williams, rev. John J. O'Meara (Montreal: Bellarmin, 1987), Book 5. 893A (henceforth John the Scot).

10. John the Scot, *Commentary on John*. Quoted in Bernard McGinn, *The Growth of Mysticism: Gregory the Great through the 12th Century* (New York: Crossroad, 2004), 108.

11. William L. Thompson (ed.), *Berulle and the French School: Selected Writings*, intro. (New York: Paulist Press, 1989), 14.

12. William P. Alston, 'Two Cheers for Mystery', in Andrew Dole and Andrew Chignell (eds.), *God and the Ethics of Belief: New Essays in Philosophy of Religion* (New York: Cambridge University Press), 99 (henceforth Alston).

13. Distinct, though not necessarily mutually exclusive.

14. Jonathan Edwards, 'Miscellany 1340', in *Works*, xxiii. 368.

15. Paul Govrilyuk, *The Suffering of the Impassible God* (Oxford: Oxford University Press, 2004), 81–2. 'Many apologists considered an open attack upon the prevailing [sentiments and] social conventions to be the most successful defense strategy.' They admitted 'that the divine birth, suffering, and crucifixion were unseemly, scandalous, and offensive in the eyes of the world', but insisted that what the world deemed shameful and offensive is in fact a most God-befitting way of securing the redemption of a ruined creation since only by assuming flesh and suffering and death could God redeem them (ibid. 87). I would only add that scandals in this sense don't entirely disappear upon conversion. For old sentiments and habits of evaluation linger on even though they no longer dominate one's life and outlook. In so far as they do, the sense of offense and scandal isn't entirely eradicated.

16. Jonathan Edwards, 'Miscellany 654', *Works*, xviii. 195–6.

17. At least when well formed.

18. A mystery, in this sense, should be distinguished from the 'unknowable', for the latter is a purely negative notion. 'The recognition of mystery', on the other hand, 'is an essentially positive act of the mind' (Gabriel Marcel, *Being and Having* (New York: Harper & Row, 1965), 118).

19. Rudolf Otto, *The Idea of the Holy*, trans. John W. Harvey (New York: Oxford University Press, 1958), 26.

20. Ibid. 30. Although it *can* be expressed in images and symbols. Otto is explicitly speaking in this passage of the concepts of transcendence and the supernatural. The context makes it clear, however, that what Otto says of the concepts of transcendence and the supernatural also applies to the concept of mystery.

21. Alston asks us to consider, in this connection, how difficult it is to even craft 'a picture of the physical world ... the complete correctness of which we can be assured' (Alston 100).

22. Jonathan Edwards, 'Miscellany 1340', *Works*, xviii. 370–1, my emphasis.

23. Thomas Aquinas, *On the Truth of the Catholic Faith, Book Four: Salvation*, trans. Charles J. O'Neil (Garden City: Doubleday, 1957), 35–7, my emphasis. While the general thrust of this passage is clear enough, it does raise an important question to which we will return later. For if God 'improportionately' transcends *all* finite things, as Aquinas says, why think that freedom from connection with sensibles will be sufficient to remove the mystery or darkness that surrounds God's nature?

24. So there is nothing God has that God doesn't know, and no task that someone could perform (such as defining God's essence) that God cannot do.

25. The idea here is presumably this. Finitude and infinity contrast with, and hence circumscribe, each other. An infinite line or quantity isn't a finite line or quantity, and vice versa, and is, in that sense, limited. Infinite lines or quantities are thus only limitless in certain respects. God, by contrast, is limitless in *all* respects.

26. Mixed perfections are good-making properties that entail an imperfection.

27. John's claim that God has no essence also rests upon the traditional notion that a good definition states a thing's genus and differentia and/or proceeds by locating the definiendum within the Aristotelian categories. If God is simple and/or transcends the Aristotelian categories, then neither of these requirements can be met. What is unclear, however, is just why definitions must meet either of these requirements. Does 'God = df. a being greater than which none can be thought' do so, for example? I doubt that it does, but a traditionalist could reply that it doesn't capture God's essence either and, for that reason, isn't a so-called 'real definition'.

28. Anselm, *St. Anselm's Proslogion, with a Reply on Behalf of the Fool by Gaunilo and the Author's Reply to Gaunilo*, trans. M. J. Charlesworth (Oxford: Clarendon, 1965), 137.

29. Ibid. 81, my emphases.

30. Ibid. 189.

31. Matter for Plotinus, for example, is 'not an independently existing principle, but the point at which the outflow of reality from the One fades away into utter darkness'; or, alternatively, the point at which the process of fragmentation reaches its logical limit, a plurality without any unity at all—and hence not even a real plurality, since a real plurality is 'always a plurality of [determinate] things, each of which is one'. Matter is thus sheer formless indeterminacy. Matter is below being (although not non-existent) just as the One is above it. Since only what has being and form can be conceptualized,

both matter and the One elude our intellect (R. T. Wallis, *Neoplatonism* (New York: Charles Scribner's Sons, 1972), 48–50).

32. Not only is God's joy or happiness greater than any finite joy or happiness, no finite joy or happiness is half as great, or two-thirds as great, or almost as great as God's.

33. If simplicity *supervenes* on the relations between God's first-order properties, being greater than can be thought would be a third-order divine property: being greater than can be thought supervenes on God's simplicity, which supervenes in turn on the relations between his first-order properties. If, however, God's simplicity is simply *identical* with the relations between his first-order properties, then being greater than can be thought would presumably be a second-order divine property.

34. Strictly speaking, the latter two cases are also cases in which being greater than can be thought is a consequence of God's first-order properties. For (as we saw in n. 33), since God's simplicity depends on his first-order properties, so too does the property of being greater than can be thought which is a consequence of it; and mystery, in Rahner's view, is presumably a first-order property of the divine essence (?).

35. Charles Blount, *Oracles of Reason*, 198–9. Quoted in Peter Byrne, *Natural Religion and the History of Religion: The Legacy of Deism* (London: Routledge, 1989), 53–4.

36. Byrne, ibid. 54, 71. Toland allowed that revelation might be a 'source' of true propositions but insisted that 'once such truths come to my notice by revelation', they must pass the bar of human reason, i.e. I must be able to make out their truth for myself on the basis of publicly available evidence. More radical questioners of revealed religion refused to grant 'even this limited role to' tradition since doing so would preclude some people from salvation (those who lived before the decisive moment or *kairos*, for example) (ibid. 72–4).

   But even if God's justice and reasonableness were to preclude his making human salvation *depend* on assent to mystery, why should it preclude either the possibility that certain truths about him are irreducibly mysterious or his communicating those truths to us? Perhaps it wouldn't. But the deists' confidence in the transparency of a just and reasonable religion doesn't comport well with either the existence or communication of irreducibly mysterious truths. In any case, if knowledge of them isn't necessary for salvation, then (from the deists' point of view) their communication is superfluous at best and, at worst, a distraction from what is truly important.

37. Terence Penelhum, *God and Skepticism* (Dordrecht: D. Reidel, 1983), 27.

38. Pierre Bayle, *Historical and Critical Dictionary: Selections*, trans. Richard H. Popkin (Indianapolis: Bobbs-Merrill, 1965), 414 (henceforth Bayle).

39. Penelhum, *God and Skepticism*, 28.

40. Ibid. 56–9.

41. For a related objection see Toland: 'The very supposition, that reason might authorize one thing, and the Spirit of God [Scripture] another, throws us into inevitable skepticism.' For if contradictions can be true, the authority of reason is called into question. And if the authority of reason is called into question, then so too is the authority of Scripture since the latter rests on the former. 'We believe the Scripture to be divine, not upon its own bare assertion [or upon an inner impulse or intuition, or the so-called testimony of the Holy Spirit], but from a real testimony consisting in the evidence of the thing contained therein; from undoubted effects, and not from words and letters' (Toland 30, 32). We believe Scripture, in other words, because what it tells us—that God exists, that we are immortal, that the best offering we can give God

is a moral life—is intrinsically evident to reason. However inadequate this account of the authority of Scripture may be, Toland has put his thumb on a real problem. For calling reason's authority into question undercuts any attempt to offer rational arguments for relying on Scripture, including not only standard appeals to miracles, fulfilled prophecy, and so on, but also existential or pragmatic arguments such as Bayle's.

42. Toland's first response is this: to the claim that while doctrines such as the Trinity are indeed 'not contrary to sound reason...*no man's reason is sound*', Toland objects that even though the reason of most people is indeed unsound, the de facto defects of human reason can be remedied without divine assistance. For we can learn to 'compare ideas, distinguish clear from obscure conceptions, suspend our judgments about uncertainties, and yield only to evidence' (Toland 57, 60). One may reasonably doubt whether these measures are sufficient to restore an impaired or fallen intellect, however. They clearly are not if, as I have argued elsewhere, a rightly disposed heart is needed to reason rightly about religion and other value-laden matters. See my *Reason and the Heart: A Prolegomena to a Critique of Passional Reason* (Ithaca, NY: Cornell University Press, 1995).

43. And 'a seeming contradiction is *to us* as good as a real one' (Toland 34, my emphasis).

44. Leibniz's idea, I think, is that the set of propositions certified by human reason (that is, that seem clearly true to a properly functioning human reason) is a proper subset of the set of propositions that are certified by reason as such. The set of propositions that are certified by reason as such, however, is identical with the set of propositions that are certified by *divine* reason. If so, then if it were to seem clearly true to a properly functioning human reason that (e.g.) God can't be one and three, then 'God can't be one and three' would be a member of the set of propositions that are certified by divine reason. Since, by hypothesis, the divine reason *also* certifies 'God *is* three and one,' the set of propositions certified by divine reason would be inconsistent.

45. This is not absurd since presumably, if God is triune, he is necessarily triune. It is more difficult to see how the doctrine of the Incarnation is a necessary truth, however, except on the peculiarly Leibnizian view that *all* truths are analytic.

46. Adrian Bardon, 'Leibniz on the Epistemic Status of the Mysteries', *Philosophy and Theology* 13 (2001), 153.

47. Ibid. The internal quote is from Leibniz's *Theodicy*, trans. E. M. Huggard (La Salle: Open Court, 1985), 108.

48. George Mavrodes, ' "It is Beyond the Power of Human Reason" ', *Philosophical Topics* 16 (1988), 77.

49. Thomas Aquinas, *Summa Theologica* I q. 32 a. 1, trans. the Fathers of the English Dominican Province (New York: Benziger Brothers, 1947), i (my emphases).

50. Indeed, if we follow Locke, Swinburne, and others who believe that a rationally compelling case can be made for the authority of the Christian revelation, and that that revelation includes the doctrine of the Trinity, and if we broaden the concept of proof or demonstration to include proofs from testimony, then reason *can* prove or demonstrate that God is triune. As Jonathan Edwards says, 'divine testimony' cannot be opposed to reason, evidence, and argument because it is a *rule* of reason, a *kind* of evidence, and a *type* of argument like the 'human testimony of credible eye-witnesses', 'credible history', 'memory', 'present experience', or 'arithmetical calculation' (Jonathan Edwards, 'Miscellaneous Observations', *The Works of President*

Edwards (New York: B. Franklin, 1968); repr. of the Leeds edn. reissued with a 2-vol. supplement in Edinburgh (1847), 228. While Edwards doesn't clearly distinguish between evidence, argument, and rule of reason, the distinction is presumably this: apparent memories, for example, are a type of evidence, justifying claims by appeal to memory is a type of argument, and the appropriate rule is 'one's memories are normally reliable'. Similarly, the contents of Scripture are a type of evidence, justifying claims by appealing to Scripture is a type of argument, and the appropriate rule is 'Scripture is trustworthy.') 'Scripture is reliable' resembles such rules as 'The testimony of our senses may be depended on,' 'The agreed testimony of all we see and converse with continually is to be credited,' and the like (Edwards, 'Miscellany 1340', *Works*, xviii. 361). Principles such as these can be established, or at least certified, by reason and then used to establish other truths that cannot be established without their help. However, that reason can appropriately be used to establish the credentials of a rule of reason, and that that rule can in turn be used to establish other truths that can't be demonstrated without it, does *not* imply that opinions formed by a reason that does not employ the rule can be used to determine the truth or falsity of opinions established only *by* its means. The naked eye, for example, 'determines the goodness and sufficiency' of the optic glass, yet it would be absurd for someone to 'credit no representation made by the glass, wherein the glass differs from his eye', and to refuse to believe 'that the blood consists partly of red particles and partly of limpid liquor because it all appears red to the naked eye' ('Miscellaneous Observations', *Works of President Edwards*, 227). Similarly, the fact (if it is a fact) that the credibility of Scripture can be established by a sound non-circular deductive or inductive argument does not show that every truth the Scripture contains can be demonstrated in the same fashion.

51. As we shall see, e.g. John Chrysostom clearly thinks that God's essence can't be known by even the most exalted of creatures. The cherubim and seraphim themselves know God only by 'figures'.

52. Jonathan Edwards, 'The Mind', *Works*, vi. 385.

53. Jonathan Edwards, 'Miscellany 1100', *Works*, xx. 485. Propositions about infinities and, perhaps, quantum mechanics provide other examples.

54. Jonathan Edwards, *Discourse on the Trinity*, *Works*, xxi. 134.

55. James Kellenberger, 'God and Mystery', *American Philosophical Quarterly* 11 (1974), 99.

56. Jonathan Edwards, *Discourse*, *Works*, xxi. 140.

57. Jonathan Edwards, ibid 139.

58. Jonathan Edwards, 'Miscellany 839', *Works*, xx. 54–5.

59. Jonathan Edwards, 'Miscellany 1340', ibid. xviii. 371.

60. David Hilbert described a hotel with an infinite number of rooms, each of which is occupied. Yet even though the hotel is full, its proprietor can accommodate an infinite number of new guests. If Jones requests a room, for example, the proprietor can simply move the guest in room number 1 to room number 2, the guest in room number 2 to room number 3, the guest in room number 3 to room number 4, etc., and assign Jones room number 1. And the process can be repeated for each new arrival.

61. Or again, in discussing some of the implications of idealism (which he thinks is not only coherent but true), Edwards asserts, 'But we have got so far beyond those things for which language was chiefly contrived, that unless we use extreme caution, we

cannot speak, except we speak exceedingly unintelligibly, without literally contradict-ing ourselves', and adds the following corollary: 'No wonder, therefore, that the high and abstract mysteries of the Deity, the prime and most abstract of all beings, imply so many seeming contradictions' ('The Mind', sect. 35, *Works*, vi. 355).

62. Jonathan Edwards, 'Miscellany 83', ibid. xiii. 249.

63. The two are not unrelated of course.

64. See e.g. William J. Danaher, Jr., *The Trinitarian Ethics of Jonathan Edwards* (Louisville: Westminster John Knox, 2004). Cf. Amy Plantinga Pauw, *The Supreme Harmony of All: The Trinitarian Theology of Jonathan Edwards* (Grand Rapids: William B. Eerdmans, 2002).

65. Or, more cautiously, have said things that imply that it doesn't.

66. Thomas Aquinas, *de Potentia*, q. 7 a. 5. Quoted in Karl Rahner, 'The Concept of Mystery in Catholic Theology', *Theological Investigations* (New York: Seabury, 1974), iv. 58–9 (henceforth Rahner).

67. Namely, that our minds are 'not proportionate to the divine substance'.

68. Aquinas, of course, thinks that the redeemed in heaven have a direct vision of God's essence. Yet how is this possible if 'no proportion exists between the created intellect and God' because of the 'infinite distance between them'? His answer is that while there is no *quantitative* proportion between God and created intellects (God isn't twice as great, or four times as great, or a thousand times as great, or…as created intellects), '*every* relation of one thing to another is called proportion', and created intellects are related to God as effects to their cause (*Summa Theologica*, I q. 12, a. 1, my emphasis). Whether this response is adequate seems to me doubtful. It may be sufficient to show that created intellects are capable of knowing *that* there is a first cause and that that cause must have those properties entailed by its being first cause. It isn't clearly sufficient to show that created intellects are capable of directly beholding God's *essence*. But even if they are, Aquinas is clear that the lack of 'quantitative' proportion between created intellects and God implies that God's essence can't be known by created intellects *as God himself knows it*, namely, 'in an infinite degree'. The beatified see God 'wholly', and there is nothing 'of him [which] is not seen'. But he is not seen 'perfectly'. Aquinas illustrates the distinction between knowing a whole in its entirety yet not knowing it perfectly by contrasting two ways of knowing that a triangle's angles are equal to two right angles, the first resting on a 'probable reason' and the second on a 'scientific demonstration'. A person possessing the latter '*comprehends*' the truth while someone who only possesses the former does not. Yet it 'does not follow that any part of [the truth] is unknown [to the former], either the subject, or the predicate, or the composition; but [only] that it is not as perfectly known as it is capable of being known' (ibid. I q. 12 a. 7) Aquinas's point, I think, is not that certain truths about God's essence necessarily elude the saints in heaven but, rather, that their apprehension of them is unavoidably imperfect or obscure to one degree or another. The *object* of the saints' vision (the divine essence) is apprehended directly (without a medium) and in its entirety, but the *manner* in which they behold it is necessarily imperfect. None of this, as far as I can see, is inconsistent with the thesis of this section, namely, that there are aspects of God that can't be fully captured by the propositional or conceptual intellect.

69. Jonathan Edwards, 'Miscellany 654', *Works*, xviii. 196.

70. Jonathan Edwards, 'Miscellany 1340', *Works*, xxiii. 370–1, my emphasis.

71. 'God condescends whenever he is not seen as he is, but in the way one incapable of beholding him is able to look upon him,' that is, by images, visions (including, presumably, so-called intellectual visions), and the like (Chrysostom 101).
72. Namely, the Bible, creeds, and the like.
73. That is, to concepts or their divine analogs.
74. That is, doesn't know himself by any analog of propositional knowledge.
75. I owe this suggestion to Alvin Plantinga.
76. See e.g. Michael B. Foster, *Mystery and Philosophy* (London: SCM, 1957), ch. 2.
77. Note that appreciation should not be construed as a purely subjective reaction to something that can, in principle, be fully captured in concepts. The taste of strawberries, for example, or the nature of first love elude adequate conceptualization although both *can* be expressed in poetry or song.
78. Otto, *Idea of the Holy*, 26, 28, and 30.
79. As Plantinga also suggested to me.
80. See e.g. the eucharistic hymn adapted from the *Liturgy of St James* that begins 'Let all mortal flesh keep silence and with fear and trembling stand.'
81. On the whole, because God presumably isn't 'numbed' or 'chilled' by the sight of his own being.
82. That he is omnipotent, say, or good.
83. Reactions, which notice, are only appropriate to puzzles in Marcel's sense, i.e. to problems that would be resolved by the acquisition of the right propositional knowledge.
84. Thus, to put the point in terms of the distinction introduced earlier, God is not an epistemological mystery to himself but does regard his own being as an ontological mystery.

PART II

DIVINE ATTRIBUTES

CHAPTER 5

....

SIMPLICITY
AND ASEITY

....

JEFFREY E. BROWER

THERE is a traditional theistic doctrine, known as the doctrine of divine simplicity, according to which God is an absolutely simple being, completely devoid of any metaphysical complexity. On the standard understanding of this doctrine—as epitomized in the work of philosophers such as Augustine, Anselm, and Aquinas—there are no distinctions to be drawn between God and his nature, goodness, power, or wisdom. On the contrary, God is identical with each of these things, along with anything else that can be predicated of him intrinsically.[1]

Although divine simplicity was once regarded as an essential part of philosophical theology, having been upheld for over a millennium by a veritable army of philosophical theologians—not only Christian, but also Jewish and Islamic—the doctrine has, in more recent history, fallen on hard times. Philosophers and theologians now seldom speak of divine simplicity, and when they do, their remarks are almost always critical. Indeed, contemporary analytic theists often take themselves to have conclusive reasons for rejecting it. 'The trouble with the idea', C. B. Martin once remarked, 'is just that it is hogwash.'[2] Many others would agree, perhaps even be willing to go so far as to claim, with Quentin Smith, that divine simplicity is not only 'plainly self-contradictory' but actually 'testifies to the predominance of faith over intellectual coherence'.[3]

In this chapter, I take the first steps necessary for restoring the doctrine of divine simplicity to its former glory, arguing that its widespread rejection in contemporary philosophy and theology is certainly premature, perhaps ultimately unwarranted. There can be no question that this doctrine comes with substantial and controversial commitments in metaphysics. But in each case, I shall argue, these commitments are perfectly respectable, having been ably defended and taken very seriously on independent grounds in the contemporary literature. If my argument is successful, it will be clear that this doctrine—together with the conception of divine aseity that traditionally motivates it—deserves more attention than it has yet received at the hands of contemporary philosophers and theologians.

My discussion is divided into three main parts. In sect. 1, I provide a brief introduction to divine simplicity, describing its chief motivation historically and explaining why, on the standard contemporary interpretation, the doctrine looks incoherent. In sect. 2, I articulate and defend an alternative interpretation of divine simplicity, one calculated to avoid the problems plaguing the standard interpretation and to establish the doctrine's coherence. In sect. 3, I show how my preferred interpretation can be extended to deal with what is perhaps the chief objection to simplicity from within traditional theism itself—namely, that it appears to exclude the possibility of contingent divine volition and knowledge.

1. THE DOCTRINE OF DIVINE SIMPLICITY

The doctrine of divine simplicity arises from philosophical reflection on a traditional conception of God—one that is common both to philosophers of antiquity and to adherents of the world's three great monotheistic religions: Judaism, Christianity, and Islam. In order to clarify this doctrine, as well as to prepare for a discussion of the main objections to it, it will be useful to approach simplicity via the traditional theistic conception from which it arises.

1.1. Personhood, Aseity, and Simplicity

Traditional theism has many ingredients, including among others that God is an omnipotent, omniscient, perfectly good (or loving), eternal, necessarily existing, divine being. Obviously, this list is not exhaustive. But it is sufficient to highlight one of the most important assumptions of traditional theism—namely, that God is a *person*, at least in the broad sense of an entity possessing the sorts of mental states generally regarded as constitutive of personhood.[4] For as the foregoing list makes clear, the God of traditional theism possesses intellectual states such as knowledge (in virtue of which he is omniscient), and appetitive states such as desires or volitions (in virtue of which he is perfectly good or loving).

Traditional theists disagree among themselves about how exactly to think of divine personhood. Some ancient Greeks, for example, claim that God possesses each of his mental states essentially, so that he could not have known or willed anything other than he actually knows or wills. By contrast, other traditional theists, including most orthodox Jews, Christians, and Muslims, insist that God possesses at least some of his mental states contingently, so that he could, for example, have chosen to create a universe different from the actual one—or none at all. Even so, these differences occur within the traditional conception of God as a person in the broad sense sketched above.

There is another ingredient of traditional theism that is especially important for our discussion in what follows. In addition to thinking of God in broadly personal terms, traditional theists also habitually think of him as an absolutely independent being—that is, as a being who is *first* or *primary* in the sense that he does not depend on anything distinct from himself. Such a being, it is often said, exists entirely from himself (*a se*). Hence, traditional theists often characterize God's absolute independence in terms of his *aseity*.

Here again, there are disagreements to be noted among traditional theists. Some, influenced by the philosophical theology of Aristotle, regard divine aseity as among the most basic or fundamental features of our conception of God. Aquinas's famous 'five ways', for example, are specifically designed to establish the existence of a being who is primary in just the sense described above—a being which, he says, 'everyone calls God'.[5] Others, influenced more by Neoplatonic considerations, take divine goodness or perfection to be God's most basic feature, arguing that divine aseity follows directly from it. Thus, both Augustine and Anselm defend divine aseity on the grounds that *dependency on another* is always an imperfection, and hence must be excluded from our conception of God. But here again the differences among traditional theists arise from a common commitment—in this case, to the view that divine aseity is somehow essential to God.

The reason that divine aseity is especially important for our purposes here is that it provides divine simplicity's chief motivation historically. As Aquinas points out, in the section of his *Summa Theologiae* immediately following the 'five ways', it is a very short step from aseity to simplicity: 'Every composite thing is posterior to its components and dependent on them. But, as was shown above, God is the first being [and hence not dependent on anything]' (*Summa Theologiae* 1. 3. 7). The basic pattern of reasoning that Aquinas invokes here helps to explain why, on the traditional doctrine of divine simplicity, God must lack not only proper parts or constituents, but even distinct properties or attributes. If God exists entirely *a se*, he cannot depend on anything in any way at all, not even in the way that a subject depends on its properties (in order to exemplify them). As Aquinas says in his other *Summa*: 'In every simple thing, its being and *that which it is* are the same. For if the one were not the other, simplicity would be removed. As we have shown, however, God is absolutely simple. Hence, in God, being good is not anything distinct from him; he *is* his goodness' (*Summa Contra Gentiles* 1. 38).

This same basic pattern of reasoning pervades traditional philosophical theology, and lies behind not only Aquinas's Aristotelian-based formulation of divine simplicity, but also standard Neoplatonic formulations of the doctrine. Thus,

Augustine, inspired by the very same considerations, says in a passage much quoted in the contemporary literature:

> We speak of God in many ways—as great, good, wise, blessed, true, and whatever else does not seem unworthily said of him. Nonetheless, God is identical with his greatness, which is his wisdom (since he is not great by virtue of quantity, but by virtue of power); and he is identical with his goodness, which is his wisdom and his greatness; and he is identical with his truth, which is all of these things. For in him it is not one thing to be blessed and another to be great, or wise, or true, or to be good, or to be altogether himself.   (*De Trinitate* 6. 7. 8)

Following Augustine in this regard, Anselm says in a well-known passage of his *Proslogion*: 'Life, wisdom, and all the rest are not parts of you, but all are one, and each of them is the whole of what you are and the whole of what the others are' (*Proslogion* 18). And similar such remarks can be found in the works of other traditional theists, not only in the Latin-speaking Christian west, but also in the Arabic-speaking Jewish and Islamic east. In short, it can be found wherever there is support for the traditional understanding of divine aseity.[6]

1.2. Simplicity and Its Interpretation

On the standard contemporary interpretation, the doctrine of divine simplicity requires that God is identical with each of his intrinsic properties. Nor is it hard to see why. What else could it mean to say that God is identical with his nature, goodness, power, and so on? The problem with this standard interpretation, however, is that it appears to lead directly to incoherence. If God is identical with each of his properties, then God must himself be a property. But *that* seems absurd. As we have seen, one of the most obvious things about God, on traditional theism, is that he is a person. But no person can be a property. For properties are, by their very nature, *exemplifiable*—that is, things that can be possessed, instantiated, or had. But no person could be a thing of that sort. Indeed, insofar as divine simplicity requires God to be a property, it appears to be not merely absurd, but guilty of a category mistake—that of placing a non-exemplifiable thing (namely, God) into the category of exemplifiables (namely, properties).[7]

If we take a closer look at traditional formulations of divine simplicity, however, we can see that there is nothing in them that requires the identification of God with a *property*. On the contrary, all they require is that if a predication such as 'God is good' is true, then there exists an entity, *God's goodness*, that is identical with God; likewise, if 'God is powerful' is true, then *God's power* exists and is identical with God; and so on for all other such divine predications. More precisely, what traditional formulations of the doctrine require is the following:

(DS) If an intrinsic predication of the form 'God is *F*' is true, then *God's F-ness* exists and is identical with God.

So understood, the doctrine of divine simplicity takes no stand whatsoever on the precise nature of the entities with which it identifies God. It does assume that there are (or at least could be) entities corresponding to expressions such as 'God's goodness', 'God's power', and 'God's wisdom'.[8] Nonetheless, it says nothing about the specific ontological category to which they belong. But this just goes to show that the claim that God is identical with a property results not from the doctrine of divine simplicity itself, but rather from its conjunction with something like the following 'property account' of predication and abstract reference:

(PA) If an intrinsic predication of the form '*a* is *F*' is true, then *a*'s *F-ness* exists, where this entity is to be understood as a property.[9]

Although contemporary defenders of divine simplicity often recognize that something like PA is at the root of contemporary difficulties with the doctrine, they are extremely reluctant to abandon it. Indeed, they prefer (almost to a person) to defend the coherence of the standard interpretation (i.e. the conjunction of DS and PA) rather than develop an account of predication and abstract reference in terms of something other than properties.[10] This seems to me to be a mistake—indeed, one that explains the general failure of contemporary defenses of divine simplicity. Even so, there are at least two things that explain the contemporary resistance to abandoning PA.

First, this account strikes many as extremely intuitive. We habitually speak *as if* for any true (atomic) predication, there is a subject of predication (e.g. Socrates), there is property (e.g. Socrates's wisdom or wisdom in general), and the subject exemplifies the property (e.g. Socrates *is* wise). In fact, this account is so intuitive that many find it difficult to imagine how expressions of the form '*a*'s *F-ness*' could refer to anything but properties.[11]

Second, many traditional proponents of divine simplicity say things that appear to commit them to PA. To take just one example, consider the following passage from Anselm's *Monologion*, which involves a comparison of divine and human justice:

A human being cannot *be* his justice, though he can *have* his justice. For the same reason, a just human being is not understood as *being* his justice (*existens iustitia*), but as *having* his justice. By contrast, it is not properly said that the supreme nature *has* its justice, but *is* its justice. Hence when the supreme nature is called just, it is properly understood as *being* its justice, rather than as *having* its justice.[12]   (*Monologion* 16)

Here Anselm suggests that, if we want to explain the justice of a human being, we must appeal to a property exemplified by that human being. Thus, if Socrates is just, this is because he has his justice. Like other traditional proponents of simplicity, therefore, Anselm seems to take for granted that at least some creaturely predications of the form '*a* is *F*' entail the existence of properties, which can in turn be referred to by expressions of the form '*a*'s *F-ness*'. But if expressions of the form '*a*'s *F-ness*' refer to properties in the case of creatures, we might expect them to behave similarly in the case of God. To the extent that traditional proponents of divine simplicity suppose that at least some creaturely predications imply the existence of properties, therefore, it is natural to suppose they do so because they accept the property account at PA.

There are, then, some considerations that make it tempting to accept the standard interpretation of divine simplicity in terms of PA. Even so, I maintain, we must not give in to this temptation. For the claim that God is identical with a property really is absurd, and hence any interpretation of simplicity that requires its truth must be rejected as incoherent. I realize, of course, that there are some who want to resist this conclusion.[13] But since I have defended it at length elsewhere, I will not repeat my arguments for it here.[14] Instead, I will simply present my own preferred alternative to the standard interpretation, and then argue that it not only renders the doctrine of divine simplicity perfectly coherent, but also fits well with the view that there is contingent divine volition and knowledge.

2. SIMPLICITY AND COHERENCE

The standard interpretation of divine simplicity assumes that expressions such as 'God's nature', 'God's goodness', and 'God's power' refer to properties. If we are to reject the standard interpretation, then we must find an alternative interpretation according to which these expressions refer to entities of some other type. But what other type of entities can they plausibly be taken to refer to? The answer, I suggest, is to entities of a broadly functional type—namely, *truthmakers*.[15]

2.1. Truthmakers, Predication, and Ontological Neutrality

'Truthmaker' is something of a term of art in contemporary philosophy, but the idea behind it is perfectly intuitive. Many of the predications we make about the world are true. That much seems obvious. But many of us also think it is obvious that when such predications are true, their truth must be a function of the way the world is. That is to say, when a predication of the form '*a* is *F*' is true, there must be something that *makes* it true—or better, some thing (or plurality of things) which *explains* its truth or *in virtue of* which it is true. As these qualifications indicate, the notion of 'making' at work here is not causal, but explanatory.[16]

How exactly are we to understand the notion of explanation involved in truth-making? Most contemporary philosophers take it to be a form of broadly logical necessitation or entailment, so that if an entity E is a truthmaker for a predication P, then E necessitates that P.[17] Although truthmaking and entailment are closely allied notions, we must be careful not to identify them, since that would lead to obvious absurdities, including the claim that truths expressed by necessary predications—such as '2 is an even number'—have anything whatsoever for their truthmaker. But, then, if truthmaking is not to be identified with entailment, how exactly are we to understand it? This is a notoriously difficult question to answer. My own view is that the truthmaking is a primitive or *sui generis* form of necessitation, one that does not admit of (non-circular) analysis or definition.[18] But other answers to the question have been given in the literature.[19] Fortunately, we needn't insist on the correctness of any of the answers here. For our purposes, it will suffice to note that truthmaking must involve *some form* of broadly logical necessitation, so that even if E's necessitating that P does not, by itself, *guarantee* that E is P's truthmaker, it does make E a candidate—perhaps even a prima facie good candidate—for playing this role.

Whatever else we say about the notion of a truthmaker, it should be clear that it is intended to be an ontologically neutral notion. To characterize an entity as a truthmaker, as we've just seen, is to characterize it in terms of a certain metaphysical function or role it plays—that of necessitating (in a certain way) the truth of the predications it makes true. But such a 'functional' characterization places no restriction on the specific nature or ontological category to which a truthmaker can belong. Indeed, it leaves open the possibility that truthmakers can belong to ontological categories of very different kinds, including both *concrete individuals* (such as persons) and *properties*.

Consider, for example, an essential predication such as 'Socrates is human.' In this particular case, it is possible to identify its truthmaker with the subject of the predication itself. For the existence of the concrete individual, Socrates, is by itself sufficient for the truth of 'Socrates is human,' and hence a candidate for its truthmaker. Generalizing on this sort of case, some philosophers have been led to think that concrete individuals are the truthmakers for all of their true essential predications—that is, for each predication whose truth they entail.[20] But that seems too strong. Entailment, as we've seen, is necessary but not sufficient for truthmaking. Even so, it does seem plausible to think that a concrete individual can be the truthmaker for a proper subset of its true essential predications—namely, each of its true *intrinsic* essential predications. Thus, Socrates himself, just in virtue of being the concrete individual he is, can be regarded as the truthmaker for 'Socrates is human,' 'Socrates is an animal,' 'Socrates is a material object,' 'Socrates exists,' 'Socrates is identical with himself,' and so on.

What if we turn now to contingent predications, such as 'Socrates is wise' or 'Socrates is just'? Here things get more complicated. The mere existence of Socrates, it would seem, is not sufficient for the truth of these predications; hence he cannot himself be their truthmaker. But then what are we to say about their truthmakers? There is more than one way to answer this question, but the two most common ways of answering it both appeal to properties. First of all, we can say, as David

Armstrong does, that the truthmakers for contingent predications are facts (or concrete states of affairs) that include properties as constituents.[21] In that case, the truthmaker for 'Socrates is just' will be the *fact that Socrates is just*, which includes the property *justice* as a constituent. Alternatively, we can say, as C. B. Martin does, that the truthmakers for contingent predications are non-transferable tropes (or concrete individual properties essentially dependent on the subjects of which they are the properties).[22] In that case, the truthmaker for 'Socrates is just' will not be the *fact that Socrates is just*, but *Socrates's justice*—an entity such that, in all possible worlds in which it exists, Socrates exists and is just.

2.2. Truthmakers and Divine Simplicity

The relevance of all this for divine simplicity is perhaps already obvious. As we have seen, this doctrine requires us to identify God with each of the things that can be intrinsically predicated of him:

> (DS) If an intrinsic predication of the form 'God is *F*' is true, then *God's F-ness* exists and is identical with God.

As we have also seen, however, the doctrine takes no stand on the precise nature of the entities with which it identifies God. Thus, if we are to understand what the doctrine amounts to, we must adopt an interpretation that takes such a stand (but does so without also rendering the doctrine incoherent). Suppose, therefore, we adopt the following 'truthmaker account' of predication, modeled after the property account given earlier:

> (TA) If an intrinsic predication of the form '*a* is *F*' is true, then *a's F-ness* exists, where this entity is to be understood as the truthmaker for '*a* is *F*'.

Interpreted in light of TA, the doctrine of divine simplicity entails that God is identical with the truthmaker of each of the true intrinsic predications that can be made about him. Thus, if God is divine, he is identical with that which makes him divine; if he is good, he is identical with that which makes him good; and so on in every other such case. On this interpretation, therefore, divine simplicity just amounts to the claim that God is the truthmaker for each of his true intrinsic predications.[23]

It should be clear already that the truthmaker interpretation goes a considerable distance toward rendering the doctrine of divine simplicity coherent. On this interpretation, for example, the doctrine does not require that God is identical with each of his properties, and hence is himself a property. In fact, it does not even require that God has any properties at all (in the ontologically loaded sense of exemplifiables). On the contrary, all the doctrine requires is that, for every true intrinsic divine predication, there is a truthmaker and God is identical with that truthmaker. But there is nothing obviously absurd about that. Indeed, on the assumption that each of God's intrinsic predications is also essential, this interpretation renders the doctrine quite plausible in certain respects (more on this below).

Finally, we should note that the truthmaker interpretation allows us to make sense of the claim, endorsed by traditional proponents of simplicity, that abstract expressions such as 'a's justice' can refer both to concrete individual persons (in the case of God) and to properties or exemplifiables (in the case of creatures). For according to TA, expressions of this form will refer to whatever it is that makes predications such as 'a is just' true. But in the case of creatures, unlike that of God, such predications will often be plausibly regarded as contingent. In order to supply a truthmaker for it, therefore, we must appeal to something like particular properties (or non-transferable tropes). And this, I think, is exactly what traditional proponents of simplicity such as Augustine, Anselm, and Aquinas do.[24]

For all these reasons, it should be clear that the truthmaker interpretation provides us with an account of divine simplicity that is at least prima facie coherent. Of course, even if this interpretation avoids the standard difficulty with the doctrine, there might still be concerns about its own coherence or plausibility. In order to complete my defense, therefore, I need to respond to the objections most likely to threaten TA itself. In decreasing order of strength, these would seem to be the following: (1) truths do not have truthmakers; (2) truthmakers can't serve as referents for expressions of the form 'a's F-ness'; (3) a single thing cannot be the truthmaker for many distinct truths; and (4) a simple God cannot be the truthmaker for all his true intrinsic predications.[25]

Objection 1: In the course of developing my preferred interpretation of divine simplicity, I have appealed to the thesis that truths have truthmakers—that is, to the claim that when a given predication is true, there is some entity (or plurality of entities) in the world that explains its truth. Although initially intuitive, this appeal might seem problematic, since it runs into difficulty when applied to predications such as 'Homer is blind' and 'Unicorns are not real,' whose logical structure seems to be of the form 'a is not F' and 'there are no Fs'. Indeed, predications of this sort are often thought to be the undoing of truthmaker theory, since the only candidate truthmakers for them appear to be negative facts such as *a's not being F* and *there not being any Fs*, and yet negative facts strike many as extremely implausible. As David Lewis says: 'It seems, offhand, that [such predications] are true not because things of some kind *do* exist, but rather because counterexamples *don't* exist' (Lewis 1999: 204).

It is important to emphasize, however, that my interpretation of simplicity does not require the general thesis that *all truths have truthmakers*. On the contrary, it requires only a restricted version of it—namely, the thesis that *all positive (atomic) predications of the form 'a is F' have truthmakers* (cf. TA above). This more restricted thesis, however, is extremely plausible. It appears, for example, to be what motivates the traditional problem of universals, which is plausibly regarded as that of specifying the truthmakers for positive atomic predications of the form 'a is F'.[26] Indeed, this understanding of the problem of universals appears to be the one driving the 'property account' of predication (at PA above), in terms of which divine simplicity is standardly interpreted. The property account takes for granted that whenever a predication of the form 'a is F' is true, there is a subject, there is a property, and the subject exemplifies the property. But this just appears to be a specification of the restricted truthmaker thesis, a way of saying that the truthmakers for positive (atomic) predications share a common structure or ontology.

But perhaps it will be worried that once we abandon the general truthmaker thesis, we lose all motivation for holding the restricted version of it. 'If any truths can lack truthmakers,' it might be said, 'then surely some positive atomic truths can, however initially plausible it seemed to deny this.' But if that's right, then my interpretation will be committed to the general truthmaker thesis after all.

It is not clear to me how serious this worry is. A number of philosophers have argued that a principled account can be given of why certain truths (including negative existentials) lack truthmakers, even though all positive atomic truths require them.[27] But even if their argument fails, and no such principled account can be given, it isn't obvious what follows for my interpretation. For other philosophers have argued equally strenuously for the general truthmaker thesis, insisting in particular that we are perfectly within our rights to allow truthmakers even for negative existentials.[28]

Obviously, these issues are too large to be resolved here. Let us simply grant, therefore, that it's a cost of my interpretation that it requires the success of truthmaker theory *in some form or other*. In the present context, this seems to me a perfectly acceptable cost. In fact, I would regard it as a major advance for the doctrine of divine simplicity if contemporary philosophers came to regard its plausibility as on a par with truthmaker theory.

Objection 2: Although truthmaker theory has received considerable attention from contemporary philosophers, it is not typically developed in connection with any particular view of abstract reference in mind. On my interpretation, however, truthmakers are required not only to explain the truth of true predications of the form 'a is F', but also to serve as the referents for their abstract counterparts— that is, expressions of the form 'a's F-ness'. This might seem problematic. For it is natural to assume that such abstract expressions can only refer to properties.[29] Indeed, I suspect it's the naturalness of this assumption that has always made the property interpretation so tempting.

As far as I can tell, however, there is nothing to prevent us from rejecting this assumption, despite its naturalness, and simply stipulating, as my interpretation does, that expressions of the form 'a's F-ness' are technical terms whose referents are the truthmakers for the corresponding predications (in this case, 'a is F'). Of course, it might be objected that this stipulation is arbitrary. But such an objection would seem to have little force. A truthmaker theorist will, presumably, need some way of referring to truthmakers for particular predications and TA gives us just what is needed. To refer to the truthmaker for '*a* is *F*', qua truthmaker, it tells us, simply construct the corresponding sentential nominalization, '*a*'s *F*-ness'.

Again, it might be objected that in adopting such a stipulation we are departing from common sense, or at least the common practice of a large number of philosophers. As we've seen, many traditional philosophers have reserved expressions of the form '*a*'s *F*-ness' for properties, and hence for things that can be exemplified. And the same could be said of many contemporary philosophers. But even granting this, it's not clear that the objection has much force. As we have seen, the stipulation in question allows—indeed, is designed to allow—that expressions of the form '*a*'s *F*-ness' still refer to properties in many cases (e.g. *Socrates's justice*). Indeed, insofar as philosophers have traditionally taken these sorts of cases as paradigmatic, it should come as no surprise that they would think all such expressions refer to properties. In any case, we shouldn't balk at some regimentation of ordinary (philosophical) language, especially in the service of a large-scale metaphysical view such as truthmaker theory.[30]

Objection 3: But even if we allow that all predications of the form '*a* is *F*' have truthmakers, and that such truthmakers can be referred to by expressions of the form '*a*'s *F*-ness', there might still appear to be something problematic about my interpretation of simplicity. For if this interpretation is true, then God himself turns out to be the truthmaker for a large number of conceptually distinct predications—including 'God is divine,' 'God is good,' 'God is powerful,' and 'God is wise.' But can a single thing really be the truthmaker for many conceptually distinct truths?

This objection would have some force if truthmakers were intended to provide the conceptual content or meaning of predications. But they are not. Indeed, it is part-and-parcel of contemporary truthmaker theory to deny that truthmakers stand in a one-to-one correspondence with the predications they make true. And such a denial is plausible in particular cases. Consider, for example, the following predications:

(S1) Socrates is human.
(S2) Socrates is an animal.
(S3) Socrates is a material object.
(S4) Socrates exists.
(S5) Socrates is identical with himself.

As noted earlier, it seems perfectly plausible to suppose that Socrates himself is the truthmaker for each of these, despite the fact that they differ in meaning and logical form. But if that is right, then there can be no objection in principle to saying that God is the truthmaker for many distinct predications.

Objection 4: But even if a single thing can, in principle, be the truthmaker for many distinct predications, it might be said that my interpretation stretches credulity insofar as it requires not only this, but also that an *absolutely simple thing* can make true *the specific variety* of predications that are supposed to be true of

God on traditional theism. Let us consider what can be said in response to this objection.

To begin, let us note that there doesn't appear to be anything particularly objectionable about saying that even a simple thing can be the truthmaker for a number of distinct predications. Suppose there exists a particular property or trope of Socrates—say, Socrates's whiteness. Now consider the following set of predications that can be made about it, modeled on those stated above (at S1–S5):

(T1) Socrates's whiteness is a whiteness trope.
(T2) Socrates's whiteness is a color trope.
(T3) Socrates's whiteness is a trope.
(T4) Socrates's whiteness exists.
(T5) Socrates's whiteness is identical with itself.

Here, as above, it seems plausible to say that a single thing—namely, Socrates's whiteness—is the truthmaker for all these predications, despite the fact that Socrates's whiteness is a trope and tropes are standardly regarded to be simple beings. If there is something objectionable about the truthmaker interpretation, therefore, it must have something to do with the specific variety of predications it requires a simple being to make true.

Initially, there does appear to be something worrisome about the specific variety of predications for which the God of traditional theism is supposed to be the truthmaker. In order to see why, compare the two sets of predications we've considered so far (at S1–S5 and T1–T5). In each case, we have three predications that subsume their subject under increasingly general sortals (namely, 'human', 'animal', and 'material object' in S1–S3, and 'whiteness trope', 'color trope', and 'trope' in T1–T3), and two predications whose truth appears to follow from purely formal features of reality (namely, S4–S5 and T4–T5, since everything is such that it both exists and is identical with itself). Given the relationship between the members of these two sets, it seems plausible to say that anything that makes true the first member (S1 or T1) will thereby make true the others (S2–S5 or T2–T5).

Now contrast these two sets of predication, where it is plausible to suppose we have a single truthmaker, with the following sorts of predication, which are supposed to be true of God on traditional theism:

(G1) God is divine.
(G2) God is good.
(G3) God is powerful.
(G4) God is wise.
(G5) God is just.

Unlike the members of the other two sets of predications we've considered, G1–G5 do not appear to involve sortals related as general to specific; nor do any of them appear to be true solely in virtue of purely formal features of reality. We could, of course, always *add* further predications to this effect, but that wouldn't help with an explanation of how God can be the truthmaker for each of the predications already listed.

A little reflection, however, reveals that G1–G5 are more closely connected than they might initially seem. Traditional theists standardly derive the intrinsic divine attributes (or better, the truth of predications involving them) from their under- standing of the divine nature. That is to say, they take God to be not only good, powerful, wise, and just, but to be all these things *in virtue of* being divine.[31]

Of course, there is a real question whether the list of divine attributes we arrive at following either of these two procedures will include all the things traditional theists have wanted to say about God. For our purposes, however, that is neither here nor there. Provided we insist—as traditional theists have, and as certainly seems *coherent* to do—that all God's (non-formal) intrinsic attributes derive from the divine nature, then it will follow that predications such as those at G1–G5 are related in roughly the way that predications subsuming their subject under increasingly general sortals are related. That is to say, they will be related in such a way that anything making the first predication true will also make the others true.

In the end, therefore, there would appear to be nothing absurd or incoherent about asserting any of the following claims: (1) the truths expressed by positive atomic predications have truthmakers; (2) that such truthmakers can be referred to by the corresponding abstract terms; (3) that a single thing is the truthmaker for many distinct truths; and (4) a simple God is the truthmaker for all his true intrinsic predications, provided that the truth of these predications either follows from purely formal features of reality (as in the case of 'God exists' or 'God is identical with himself') or can be explained in terms of the truthmaker of the predication 'God is divine.' And since the coherence of these claims is all that's required to secure the coherence of the truthmaker interpretation of divine simplicity, I conclude that this interpretation provides us with all we need to resolve the chief contemporary difficulty with the doctrine.

3. SIMPLICITY AND CONTINGENCY

Apart from questions about its coherence, the main contemporary objection to divine simplicity has focused on its apparent exclusion of contingent divine voli- tion and knowledge.[32] As indicated earlier, most traditional Jews, Christians, and Muslims believe that God possesses certain of his mental states contingently— more specifically, that he could have chosen to create a universe different from the actual one (or none at all), and hence could have known different things than he actually knows. But this seems incompatible with divine simplicity. For in order to will or know something different, it would seem that God himself would have to be different. But divine simplicity requires that he be the same across all possible worlds.

It is important to see that this problem is not one that the truthmaker interpretation can, by itself, resolve. If God possesses certain acts of will or knowledge contingently, then it would seem to follow that there are true divine predications that are both intrinsic and contingent:

(G6) God freely chooses to create the universe.
(G7) God knows that p, where p is a contingent truth.

Insofar as these predications are intrinsic, my interpretation requires God himself to be their truthmaker. But insofar as these same predications are contingent, it would also seem that God cannot be their truthmaker. For as already indicated, truthmaking is a form of broadly logical necessitation. Hence, if an entity E is a truthmaker for a predication P, then E must necessitate that P.

Let us call this 'the problem of contingency'. In this section, I respond to the problem by denying that predications such as G6 and G7 must be regarded as genuinely intrinsic. As will become clear, once this has been denied the truthmaker interpretation fits well with the assumption that God is capable of contingent volition and knowledge.

3.1. Contingent Divine Volition

To begin, let us focus on predications such as G6, which involve the ascription of contingent divine volitions. It is natural to think of such volitions as intrinsic features of God, especially if we are thinking of them on the model of contingent human volitions. But this is not the only way to think of them. In order to see why, let us approach the matter somewhat indirectly—via a comparison of two different accounts of human volition.

Suppose some agent A freely chooses on some occasion to perform a specific action, even though A could just as easily have chosen to do something else. We might describe this situation by saying that, in the actual world, w_1, A has volition V_1, even though in another possible world, w_2, A has volition V_2—where V_1 and V_2, let us grant, are distinct intrinsic states of A. Now, if we think about such volitions on a libertarian—or more specifically, an agent-causal—model according to which volitions are the irreducible products of free agents, it will turn out that w_1 and w_2 share the same causal history and laws of nature, and yet differ because in $w_1 A$ directly causes V_1, whereas in $w_2 A$ directly causes V_2 (see Fig. 5.1). No doubt this understanding of the difference between w_1 and w_2, like the agent-causal model of volition it presupposes, is controversial. But we can, I think, safely presuppose

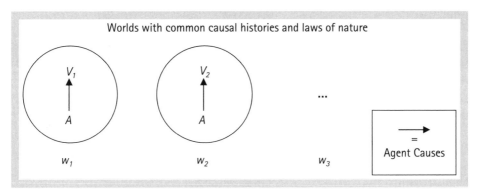

Figure 5.1. Agent-causal model of volition

its coherence here. For once again, it would be a major advance for the doctrine if critics were forced to admit that its plausibility is on a par with that of agent causation.

How is all this relevant to the contingency problem? Note first of all that on the agent-causal model, there are no intrinsic differences in virtue of which A causes its volitions. That is to say, if we want to distinguish worlds w_1 and w_2, we have no choice but to appeal to the immediate effects of A's agent-causal activity in these worlds—namely, volitions V_1 and V_2. Now up to this point I've been assuming that V_1 and V_2 are intrinsic features of A—that is, properties or states possessed by but distinct from A. Given this, the model is obviously inapplicable to a *simple* God. Nonetheless, it is easy enough to modify the model so as to make it applicable: simply 'kick away' the distinct volitions and think of our agents as directly causing the effects themselves.[33] Initially, such a kicking away might seem implausible. Since our volitions are not ordinarily sufficient to produce their immediate effects, we have no choice but to distinguish the direct objects of our agent-causal activity (the volitions) from the effects that indirectly (and perhaps only partially) come about via them. But let us suppose—as seems plausible at least in the case of certain agents, such as God—that the connection between the objects of our agent-causal activity and their effects is non-contingent. In that case, it will be possible to kick away the volitions and thus to revise our original account of the difference between worlds w_1 and w_2 as follows: in w_1 A directly causes E_1, whereas in w_2 A directly causes E_2, where E_1 and E_2 are what we might earlier have described as the immediate effects of V_1 and V_2 (see Fig. 5.2).

On this revised agent-causal model, there are no distinct volitions (or for that matter, any distinct intrinsic features whatsoever) in virtue of which A causes its effects. Even so, it would be a mistake to deny that A freely brings about its effects on this model—especially if we add, as often seems plausible, that A has some reasons that partly explain (in the only way that reasons can explain actions on an

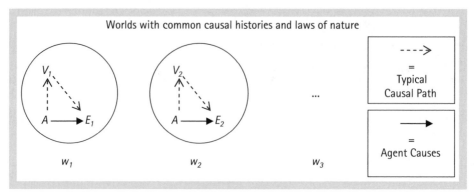

Figure 5.2. Revised agent–causal model of volition

agent-causal theory) the specific effects it brings about.[34] Rather than deny that *A* has any volitions or choices on this model, therefore, we can instead simply identify *A*'s volitions or choices with *A*'s direct acts of agent causing.[35]

By now it should be clear that the revised agent-causal model provides a straightforward way of handling contingent divine volition, one that violates nei-ther the spirit nor the letter of divine simplicity as I've interpreted it. Consider again our representative example of a predication involving contingent divine volition:

(G6) God freely chooses to create the universe.

On the revised agent-causal model, this predication turns out to be straightfor-wardly extrinsic. To say that God freely chooses to create the universe is just to say that he stands in a certain relation to something wholly distinct from himself—namely, the relation of *agent causation*. But as we have seen, this is a relation in which an agent can stand to different things in different worlds, despite any lack of intrinsic differences across those worlds.[36] In any case, once G6 is taken to be extrinsic, there is no pressure to interpret God alone as its truthmaker. Indeed, as far as my interpretation of simplicity is concerned, there is no pressure to say it has any truthmaker at all (since my interpretation requires truthmakers only for positive atomic predications of the form '*a* is *F*'). Even so, there is a truthmaker ready to hand, if one is wanted—namely, God, the universe, and the relation of agent causation. Nor is there any danger of this truthmaker's violating divine aseity, since both the universe and God's relation to it contingently depend for their existence (or obtaining) on God rather than the other way around. Assuming, therefore, as seems plausible, that other predications involving contingent divine volition can be handled similarly to G6, we appear to have a perfectly general solution to the problem of contingency for divine volitions.

3.2. Contingent Divine Knowledge

But we are not quite out of the woods yet. For as we have seen, the problem of contingency arises for ascriptions of contingent divine knowledge as well as volition. Initially, the problem here might seem no more worrisome than in the case of divine volition. Just as we can treat predications involving contingent divine volition as extrinsic, so too it might seem that we can do the same in the case of contingent divine knowledge. Consider a specific instance of the type mentioned at G7 above:

(G7a) God knows that *human beings exist.*

The truth of a predication like G7a would seem to require only two things: (1) that God stand in a certain cognitive relation to the contingent truth that human beings exist; and (2) that human beings do in fact exist. But if that's right, then predications such as G7a will be extrinsic after all. And assuming our treatment of this sort of predication generalizes, we would appear to have a general solution to the problem of contingency for divine knowledge as well as for divine volition.[37]

But note that there is a question that arises here that does not arise for our treatment of divine volition—one that has to do with the consistency of this account with divine aseity. For whether or not predications such as G7a are extrinsic, they appear to make God dependent on something distinct from himself—namely, the objects of his contingent knowledge. After all, if God knows that human beings exist, he seems to know this *because* they exist.

Now, in the case of certain predications, including G7a itself, the appearance of dependency can perhaps be avoided by noting that the objects of God's contingent knowledge depend for their existence on God himself. For example, since human beings exist (at least in the first place) only because God has freely chosen to create a universe containing them, we can perhaps say that, strictly speaking, what God depends on for his knowledge that human beings exist is not anything distinct from himself (namely, human beings themselves), but only his own free acts of will or choice.

This strategy will not obviously work, however, for all predications involving contingent divine knowledge. Suppose that instead of G7a, we consider the following predication:

(G7b) God knows that *Smith is freely choosing to mow his lawn.*

It is considerably more difficult to treat this predication in the way we treated G7a above. For unlike the existence of human beings in general, it's hard to see how Smith's free choice to mow his lawn could depend solely on the divine will—unless, of course, we are prepared to accept some form of compatibilism about human freedom. If we are, then we can treat G7b in the same way we treated G7a. For in that case, we can adopt a compatibilist model of human volition—that is, one according to which free choices are not the irreducible products of agents, but the causal consequences of deterministic processes. Then we can say that Smith's free choice to mow his lawn depends on God in roughly the same way that the existence of human beings in general does—namely, by depending on God's choice to create a certain kind of universe (in this case, one having a certain causal history and laws of nature). And likewise for all the free choices of all human agents. Of course, it might seem odd to adopt a compatibilist account of human volition, but not of divine volition. But perhaps not (or perhaps the compatibilist will want to extend the account to divine volitions as well). In any case, once we adopt a compatibilist account of human volition, the problem vanishes.

But what if we are not prepared to accept any form of compatibilism? In that case, it is hard to avoid the conclusion that the truth of G7b violates divine aseity. For in that case, we certainly won't be able to say that Smith's choice depends entirely on God's will—since it is a contradiction to say that God causes an agent to freely choose (in the incompatibilist or libertarian sense) to perform some action. But what else, besides Smith's free choice itself, could God's knowledge in G7b be said to depend on? The only obvious suggestion here is that made by the so-called Molinists (i.e. the followers of the sixteenth-century Spanish Jesuit, Luis de Molina): God's knowledge here depends not only on his will (or more specifically, on his choice to create a universe with Smith in his current circumstances), but also on his knowledge of what Smith would freely do in any circumstances in which he is created and left free. Rather than solve our problem with G7b, however, it merely pushes it back a step. For now we have a new predication involving contingent divine knowledge that needs explaining:

(G7c) God knows that *Smith would freely choose to mow his lawn, if created and placed in his current circumstances.*

And here we seem to run up against a predication whose truth really does violate divine aseity. For what Smith would freely do, if created and placed in various circumstances, is generally taken by Molinists to be a brute contingent truth about Smith (or better, about Smith's individual essence, which is an abstract object existing independently of God). Evidently, therefore, the truth of G7c, and hence the truth of G7b, ultimately requires God to be dependent on something distinct from himself.[38]

What all of this shows is that a full solution to the problem of contingency— that is, one that not only takes care of worries about contingent divine volition and knowledge, but also is fully consistent with the chief motivation for divine simplicity historically—carries a significant cost. It requires the truth of compatibilism (about human, though not divine freedom). Is this cost prohibitive? No doubt, many will think it is, seeing in it sufficient grounds if not for rejecting divine simplicity wholesale, then at least for detaching it from its traditional moorings in divine aseity. But we mustn't be too hasty here. Such an attitude would be justified if compatibilism were obviously incoherent, absurd, or false. But it isn't. Compatibilism has a rich history of supporters, both within and outside traditional philosophical theology. Indeed, the former often see compatibilism as a natural consequence of theological doctrines just as well established as that of creation (most notably, providence, foreknowledge, predestination, and election). If we are going to evaluate divine simplicity, therefore, especially in the context of its original motivation, then we must engage in the kind of complicated cost–benefit analysis that we have come to expect for the evaluation of any large-scale metaphysical theory. In such an analysis, compatibilism will certainly be one, but it will not be— or at least, shouldn't be—the only deciding factor.

4. Conclusion

My aim in this chapter has been to show that the doctrine of divine simplicity deserves further consideration than it has yet received from contemporary philosophers and theologians. If I have achieved my aim, it will be clear that the standard objections to this doctrine can all be answered: the doctrine is neither incoherent nor incompatible with contingent divine volition and knowledge. Of course, this by itself does not give us reason to accept the doctrine as true. But it does, I hope, go considerable distance toward showing its acceptability. Moreover, insofar as negative attitudes toward simplicity have contributed to the neglect of the considerations motivating it historically, I hope that my defense will also encourage their reevaluation. Contemporary philosophers and theologians often reject traditional views about divine aseity precisely because they lead to the doctrine of divine simplicity. But this is a mistake. Indeed, quite apart from simplicity, such views deserve our attention insofar as they lie at the very heart of the traditional theism, which is still widely taken for granted, both by those who follow Anselm in thinking of God as 'that than which nothing greater can be conceived' and by those who follow Aquinas in thinking of him as 'that which explains all motion, change, and contingency'.

Notes

A portion of this chapter was presented at a meeting of the International Society of Thomas Aquinas in Prague 2006. I am grateful to the audience on that occasion for stimulating comments and discussion. I am also grateful to Michael Bergmann, Susan Brower-Toland, Thomas Flint, Wesley Morriston, Daniel Novotny, Alexander Pruss, and Michael Rea for helpful comments and criticism on earlier drafts. Finally, I owe a special debt of gratitude to Wesley Morriston for extended correspondence that resulted in substantial clarification of the views developed and defended here.

1. Let us say that an *intrinsic* predication characterizes things 'in virtue of the way they themselves are', whereas an *extrinsic* predication characterizes them 'in virtue of their relations or lack of relations to other things' (cf. Lewis 1986: 61). This distinction, though pervasive in philosophy, is notoriously resistant to analysis. In what follows, therefore, I shall have to rely on the intuitive understanding of it. I would only add that it must be kept separate from two other familiar distinctions—namely, (*a*) that between essential and contingent predication, and (*b*) that between non-relational and relational predication. Intrinsic predications can be either essential (e.g. 'God is wise') or contingent (e.g. 'Socrates is wise'). And, even if most intrinsic predications are non-relational, there are some intrinsic *relational* predications (e.g. 'God is identical with himself', 'Socrates chooses to go to the marketplace', 'Socrates has parts').

2. Martin 1976: 40.

3. Q. Smith 1988: 524 n. 3. The *locus classicus* for contemporary difficulties with simplicity is Plantinga 1980. There are, however, a number of works that have contributed in important ways to the contemporary understanding of these difficulties, including the following: Mann 1982, 1983; Morris 1985; and Stump and Kretzmann 1985.

4. In certain contexts, it might be better to speak of the God of traditional theism as an entity possessing the sorts of mental state generally regarded as constitutive of a *personal being* rather than a *person*, so as to leave open the possibility, insisted on by traditional Christian theists, that there is more than one person in God. I shall ignore this complication here, since it is not relevant for my purposes, but cf. Michael Rea's contribution to this volume, Ch. 18.

5. *Summa Theologiae* 1. 2. 3.

6. Cf. Jordan 1983 for further discussion and references, especially to Plotinus, who is an important source for thinkers in the east and west.

7. Again, cf. Plantinga 1980 for the *locus classicus* for this sort of objection.

8. Thus, traditional formulations of the doctrine are inconsistent with certain forms of nominalism—namely, all those that deny that expressions of the form '*a*'s F-ness' can function as genuinely referring devices.

9. Since proponents of divine simplicity typically speak of God being identical with *his* goodness, *his* power, and *his* wisdom (rather than with goodness, power, wisdom *tout court*), I have stated the property account in such a way that it introduces properties using expressions of the form '*a*'s F-ness' (rather than of the form 'F-ness'). Those philosophers who think of properties as particular (i.e. the so-called trope theorists) will, of course, have no difficulty with this, but those who think of properties as universals may find it puzzling. It should be noted, however, that strictly speaking PA is neutral as regards the specific nature of the properties. If Socrates and Plato are both human, then according to PA they must each have a property of humanity. Even so, PA takes no stand on the question of whether Socrates's humanity is identical with Plato's (and hence whether properties are particular or universal).

10. Cf. e.g. Leftow 1999; Mann 1982, 1983; Rogers 1996; Stump and Kretzmann 1985; Vallicella 1992.

11. It is sometimes suggested that these expressions could refer to states of affairs—that is, to the exemplification of the properties by their subjects (cf. Plantinga 1980). But this suggestion is of little use, from the point of view of divine simplicity, since identifying

God with a state of affairs seems just as absurd as identifying him with a property. For further discussion, cf. Brower 2008.

12. The possessive pronouns do not explicitly occur in the Latin, but I think they are best understood as implicit here (as they often are in Latin)—especially in light of Anselm's insistence that God's goodness, power, wisdom, and so on must be conceived of as distinct from our own. For discussion of Anselm's theory of properties, in the case of both God and human beings, see Brower 2004.

13. Cf. again the references cited in n. 10.

14. Cf. Brower 2008.

15. This answer is apparently one whose time has come. Cf. e.g. Bergmann and Brower 2006; Pruss forthcoming; and Oppy 2003. For a defense of the claim that truthmakers are not only sufficient, but also necessary for making sense of divine simplicity, cf. Brower 2008.

16. It would, perhaps, be better to speak of *truth-explainers* rather than *truthmakers*, but the terminology of truthmaking has become so well entrenched that to do so would require a departure from standard usage.

17. Assuming, of course, that *P* exists. For simplicity's sake, I shall hereafter ignore this complication and speak of truthmakers as entities that *actually* make predications true rather than as entities that *would* make such predications true, if they existed. In doing so, I don't mean to beg any questions about the ultimate nature of truth-bearers or to assume that truthmakers require the existence of corresponding truths.

18. Here I follow Rodriguez-Pereyra 2002: 34, who argues that the best we can do is to say that an entity *E* is a truthmaker for a predication *P* if and only if *E* is an entity *in virtue of which P* is true, and then illustrate what we mean by 'being true in virtue of' with examples.

19. E.g. Restall 1996 suggests that we can define truthmaking in terms of the notion of non-classical or 'relevant' entailment, and B. Smith 1999 and 2002 claim that we can define it in terms of *representation* or *projection*, which is the dual of necessitation.

20. E.g. Bigelow 1988: 128.

21. Cf. Armstrong 1997, 1989.

22. Cf. Armstrong 1989, esp. 116–19. For a more complete development and defense of this view, cf. Mulligan, Simons, and Smith 1984.

23. Following Pruss forthcoming, we can put this point more precisely by saying that, on the truthmaker interpretation, God is the *minimal* truthmaker for each of his true intrinsic predications—where an entity *E* is a minimal truthmaker for a predication *P* just in case *E* is such that no proper part of it also makes *P* true. As Pruss points out, this qualification is needed since on some theories of truthmaking, if *E* is a truthmaker for *P*, then so is anything of which *E* is a part. Once the qualification is added, however, the absolute simplicity of God follows immediately. For if God had any proper parts, there would be true intrinsic divine predications (namely, about these parts) whose minimal truthmakers would not be God (but the parts).

24. Cf. Fox 1987 for defense of the claim that medieval philosophers operate within some form of truthmaker account of predication. Cf. Klima 2004 for a defense of the claim that they also typically adopt some form of trope theory of properties.

25. For discussion of some of the other objections facing TA, including worries about the relationship between divine and human 'attributes' on TA, cf. Brower 2008.

26. Cf. Rodriguez-Pereyra 2000 and 2002, ch. 1.

27. Cf. e.g. Bigelow 1988: 128–34 and Lewis 2001 for an account in terms of the super-venience of truth on being.

28. Cf. e.g. Armstrong 1997 and Rodriguez-Pereyra 2005.

29. Again, once we've ruled out the possibility of their referring to states of affairs. Cf. n. 11 above.

30. It may be wondered how, on the truthmaker interpretation, such expressions as '*a*'s *F*-ness' are related to more general expressions of the form '*F*-ness', which are also typically taken to refer to properties (or better, universals). The most natural answer, it seems to me, is to say that whereas such expressions as '*a*'s *F*-ness' refer to truthmakers for specific predications—namely, predications of the form '*a* is *F*'—expressions such as '*F*-ness' refer to truthmakers for some predication or other of the form '*x* is *F*'. In that case, the truthmaker interpretation will allow us to say not only that God is identical with *his* goodness (i.e. the truthmaker for 'God is good'), but also that he is identical with goodness—or better, *a* goodness (i.e. a truthmaker for some statement of the form '*x* is good').

31. As I mentioned earlier, traditional theists differ among themselves about how exactly the divine nature is to be conceived. Some, such as Anselm, conceive of the divine nature in terms of absolute perfection, as that than which nothing greater can be conceived. For such theists, the predication at G1 will be shorthand for the claim that God is an absolutely perfect being, and the predications at G2–G5, as well as any other intrinsic divine predications, will involve specification of particular perfections. Others, such as Aquinas, conceive of the divine nature in terms of aseity. For theists of this sort, the predication at G1 will be shorthand for something like the claim that God is an absolutely independent being, and the derivation of particular divine attributes will be more indirect (e.g. Aquinas himself derives complete actuality from independence, and derives the other attributes from this, arguing that a being who is completely actual will have all perfections, without limit, and hence be all good, powerful, wise, and just).

32. Cf. e.g. Craig 2001; O'Connor 1999; Pruss forthcoming; Stump and Kretzmann 1985; and Stump 2003. This objection is also taken seriously by traditional proponents of simplicity. Cf. e.g. Aquinas's discussion in *Summa Theologiae* 1. 19. 3.

33. According to McCann 2005 (esp. 144–5), something like this model is required to make sense of God's creating anything at all.

34. I'm assuming that in God's case his reasons for creating remain the same across all possible worlds, and hence that the only thing that varies is the particular set of reasons he acts on.

35. For a theory of reasons explanation that fits with agent-causation in general, cf. O'Connor 1995; and for an attempt to modify this theory to fit with something like the revised agent-causal model, cf. O'Connor 1999 and also Pruss forthcoming.

36. This is perhaps the idea behind the traditional description of the difference between worlds in which God creates different creatures (or none at all) as a difference in the effect.

37. Indeed, assuming (as I shall throughout) that divine beliefs can be explained along the same lines as divine knowledge, we would appear to have a solution to the problem of contingency for them (and perhaps all contingent divine mental states) as well. For a different account of divine beliefs, one which treats them differently from divine

knowledge and requires a fairly radical form of externalism about content, cf. Pruss forthcoming.

38. One could try to avoid this problem by adopting a form of what is known as 'theistic activism'—that is, the view that all abstracta (including individual essences) are mental states of God. In that case, what Smith would freely do, if created and placed in various circumstances, would be a brute contingent truth about God (or God's mental states). Although this might seem to help from the point of view of divine aseity (though cf. Bergmann and Brower 2006 for reservations even about this), it would be of no use for preserving divine simplicity. For such brute truths would appear to involve true predications of God (or God's ideas) that are not only contingent but also intrinsic. As we have seen, however, these are precisely the sorts of predications about God that divine simplicity excludes.

REFERENCES

ARMSTRONG, DAVID (1989). *Universals: An Opinionated Introduction.* Boulder: Westview
—— (1997). *A World of States of Affairs.* Cambridge: Cambridge University Press.
BERGMANN, MICHAEL, and BROWER, JEFFREY E. (2006). 'A Theistic Argument against Platonism (and in Support of Truthmakers and Divine Simplicity)', *Oxford Studies in Metaphysics* 2: 357–86.
BIGELOW, JOHN (1988). *The Reality of Numbers: A Physicalist's Philosophy of Mathematics.* Oxford: Clarendon.
BROWER, JEFFREY E. (2004). 'Anselm's Ethics', in Brian Davies and Brian Leftow (eds.), *The Cambridge Companion to Anselm.* Cambridge: Cambridge University Press, 222–56.
—— (2008). 'Making Sense of Divine Simplicity', *Faith and Philosophy* 25: 3–30.
CRAIG, WILLIAM L. (2001). *God, Time, and Eternity.* Dordrecht: Kluwer Academic.
FOX, JOHN (1987). 'Truthmaker', *Australasian Journal of Philosophy* 65: 188–207.
JORDAN, MARK D. (1983). 'The Names of God and the Being of Names', in Alfred J. Freddoso (ed.), *The Existence and Nature of God.* Notre Dame: University of Notre Dame Press, 161–90.
KLIMA, GYULA (2004). 'The Medieval Problem of Universals', in Edward N. Zalta (ed.), *The Stanford Encyclopedia of Philosophy (Winter 2004 Edition)*, <http://plato.stanford.edu/archives/win2004/entries/universals-medieval/>, accessed 13 May 2008.
LEFTOW, BRIAN (1999). 'Is God an Abstract Object', *Noûs* 24: 581–98.
LEWIS, DAVID (1986). *On the Plurality of Worlds.* Oxford: Blackwell.
—— (2001). 'Truthmaking and Difference-Making', *Noûs* 35: 602–15.
MCCANN, HUGH J. (2005). 'The Author of Sin?', *Faith and Philosophy* 22: 144–59.
MANN, WILLIAM (1982). 'Divine Simplicity', *Religious Studies* 18: 451–71.
—— (1983). 'Simplicity and Immutability in God', *International Philosophical Quarterly* 23: 267–76.
MARTIN, C. B. (1976). 'God, the Null Set and Divine Simplicity', in John King-Farlow (ed.), *The Challenge of Religion Today.* New York: Science History Publications, 138–43.

MORRIS, THOMAS V. (1985). 'On God and Mann: A View of Divine Simplicity', *Religious Studies* 21: 299–318.

MULLIGAN, KEVIN, SIMONS, PETER, and SMITH, BARRY (1984). 'Truthmakers', *Philosophy and Phenomenological Research* 44: 287–321.

O'CONNOR, TIMOTHY (1995). 'Agent Causation', in Timothy O'Connor (ed.), *Agents, Causes, and Events: Essays on Indeterminism and Free Will*. New York: Oxford University Press.

——(1999). 'Simplicity and Creation', *Faith and Philosophy* 16: 405–12.

OPPY, GRAHAM (2003). 'The Devilish Complexities of Divine Simplicity', *Philo* 6: 10–22.

PLANTINGA, ALVIN (1980). *Does God Have a Nature?* Milwaukee: Marquette University Press.

PRUSS, ALEXANDER R. (forthcoming). 'On Two Problems of Divine Simplicity', in Jonathan Kvanvig (ed.), *Oxford Studies in Philosophy of Religion*, i.

RESTALL, GREG (1996). 'Truthmakers, Entailment and Necessity', *Australasian Journal of Philosophy* 74: 331–40.

RODRIGUEZ-PEREYRA, GONZALO (2000). 'What is the Problem of Universals?' *Mind* 109: 255–73.

——(2002). *Resemblance Nominalism: A Solution to the Problem of Universals*. Oxford: Oxford University Press.

——(2005). 'Why Truthmakers?' in Helen Beebee and Juliane Dodd (eds.), *Truthmakers: The Contemporary Debate*. Oxford: Clarendon.

ROGERS, KATHERIN (1996). 'The Traditional Doctrine of Divine Simplicity', *Religious Studies* 32: 165–86.

SMITH, BARRY (1999). 'Truthmaker Realism', *Australasian Journal of Philosophy* 77: 274–91.

—— (2002). 'Truthmaker Realism: Response to Gregory', *Australasian Journal of Philosophy* 80: 231–4.

SMITH, QUENTIN (1988). 'An Analysis of Holiness', *Religious Studies* 24: 511–27.

STUMP, ELEONORE (2003). *Aquinas*. London: Routledge.

—— and KRETZMANN, NORMAN (1985). 'Absolute Simplicity', *Faith and Philosophy* 2: 353–82.

VALLICELLA, WILLIAM (1992). 'Divine Simplicity: A New Defense', *Faith and Philosophy* 9: 508–25.

CHAPTER 6

OMNISCIENCE

EDWARD WIERENGA

OMNISCIENCE is the divine attribute of possessing complete or unlimited knowledge. In this chapter we will examine motivations for taking such a property to be a divine attribute, attempts to define or analyze omniscience, possible limitations on the extent of divine knowledge, and, finally, objections either to the coherence of the concept or to its compatibility with other divine attributes or with widely accepted claims.

SOURCES OF THE IDEA THAT GOD IS OMNISCIENT

Among the principal sources of the idea that God is omniscient are the numerous biblical passages that attribute vast knowledge to God. Thomas Aquinas, in his discussion of the knowledge of God (1945 *Summa Theologiae* (*ST*) I q. 14), cites such texts as Rom. 11: 33 ('O the depths of the riches and wisdom and knowledge of God!'), Job 12: 13 ('With God are wisdom and strength; he has counsel and understanding.'), and Heb. 4: 13 ('And before him no creature is hidden, but all are naked and laid bare to [his] eyes...').

Another source of the attribution of omniscience to God derives from 'perfect being theology', usually attributed to St Anselm. Anselm's ontological argument attempts to prove the existence of a being than which no greater can be thought.

Reflection on the concept of a greatest conceivable or a greatest possible being yields the conclusion that such a being possesses all perfections. In Anselm's formulation, 'God is whatever it is better to be than not' (1998*b*: 5), and although the intellectual attribute Anselm derived from this formula is that God is *wise* (1998*a*: 15), later philosophers included complete knowledge among the perfections.

The requirements of one or another theological doctrine provide a third source of the idea that God is omniscient. Prominent among these is the doctrine of divine providence. This doctrine holds that God has a plan for the world according to which all things are in his care and work out according to his good will. In Thomas Flint's formulation, 'to see God as provident is to see him as knowingly and lovingly directing each and every event involving each and every creature toward the ends he has ordained for them' (1998: 12). It is hard to see how God could order things according to such a detailed plan without having vast, if not unlimited, knowledge.

Defining Omniscience

Standard accounts of omniscience take it to be knowledge of all truths. That lends itself to the following straightforward definition:

(D1)   S is *omniscient* $=_{df}$ for every proposition p, if p is true, then S knows p.

Several philosophers have proposed variants of this definition. For example, Alvin Plantinga (1974: 68) and Stephen Davis (1983: 26) implicitly or explicitly accept

(D2)   S is *omniscient* $=_{df}$ for every proposition p, if p is true then S knows p, and if p is false then S does not believe p.

Unless it is possible to know all truths and yet believe some falsehood, (D2) is equivalent to (D1). But it seems highly implausible that someone could have knowledge of all truths and nevertheless believe the denial of one of the propositions he or she knows to be true. Believing the denial of a proposition would seem to undermine knowledge of it, and in any event, it seems implausible to think that someone could know some proposition p, know that he or she knows, and, hence, believes p, and also know that he or she believes *not-p*. But this would have to be possible in order for someone to know all truths and yet believe a falsehood.

Another variant is stated by Linda Zagzebski (2007: 262):

(D3)   S is *omniscient* $=_{df}$ for every proposition p, either S knows that p is true or S knows that p is false.

(D3) is also equivalent to (D1), because if S knows all true propositions, then for any false proposition, p, S knows *that p is false*; in other words, if S knows all true propositions and p is false, then S knows *not-p* and so knows that p is false.

ADDITIONAL PROPERTIES OF
GOD'S KNOWLEDGE

Another recent proposed definition of omniscience turns out not to be equivalent to the ones we have been considering, but it is useful for what it suggests about another feature of God's knowledge. Peter van Inwagen (2006: 26) suggests

> (D4) S is *omniscient* $=_{df}$ for every proposition p, S either believes p or the denial of p and it is metaphysically impossible that there is a proposition q such that S believes q and q is false.

(Van Inwagen actually endorses a restricted version of (D4).) The condition that it be impossible for an omniscient being to believe mistakenly adds a modal element; a being who believed all and only truths but who in some non-actual situation believed a falsehood would not satisfy this condition. Believing, or better, knowing, all and only truths would seem to constitute complete knowledge, so the modal clause seems not to be required for omniscience. This sort of immunity from error, *infallibility*, does seem to be an epistemic perfection, however. So a complete account of perfect knowledge would attribute not only omniscience but infallibility as well.

There is a related attribute that also seems to be part of perfect knowledge, namely, *essential omniscience*. Someone who is essentially omniscient is not merely omniscient but in addition could not possibly exist without being omniscient. Infallibility does not entail essential omniscience, because, at least in theory, someone could be infallible while failing to believe *all* truths. But essential omniscience does entail infallibility; someone who is essentially omniscient could not possibly have a false belief.

Another question that arises about God's knowledge is whether it is all *occurrent* knowledge or whether some of his knowledge is *dispositional*. Knowledge of a proposition is occurrent just in case the knower has that proposition in mind or is currently aware of it. Knowledge of a proposition is dispositional, very roughly, if the subject knows the proposition but is not currently thinking of it or aware of it. Dispositional knowledge is thus a sort of standing knowledge of which the subject need not be aware. Aquinas recognized two kinds of *discursion* in knowledge, the first of which is related to dispositional knowledge. One kind of discursion, then, is 'according to succession only, as when we have actually understood anything, we turn ourselves to understand something else' (1945 *ST* I q. 14 a. 7). But he denies that God's knowledge is like this, because 'God sees all things together and not successively' (ibid.). So Aquinas denies that God's knowledge is ever merely dispositional, and that seems to have been the view of most philosophers who have considered the matter. Recently, however, David Hunt (1995) has argued that taking God's knowledge of the future to be dispositional can help with the problem of reconciling divine foreknowledge and human free action (see below). But it is difficult to see how God could fail to be aware of what he knows and it is not clear why the standard arguments for the incompatibility of foreknowledge and free action cannot be adapted to the case of dispositional knowledge.

Aquinas identified a second way in which knowledge can be dispositional, namely, 'according to causality, as when through principles we arrive at the knowledge of conclusions'. Aquinas held that from the fact that God's knowledge is not discursive in the first sense, of first attending to one proposition and then to another, it follows that God's knowledge is not discursive in the second, either. Two qualifications are in order. First, if God knows propositions, they certainly stand in logical relations to one another, and that includes standing in the relation of premises to conclusion. Aquinas's claim is that God does not *arrive* at a conclusion by deriving it from premises. Second, Aquinas allows that God can know effects by knowing a cause, but this is not so much deriving the effect from the cause as having such complete knowledge of a cause that it can be 'resolved' into its effects. More puzzling, however, is Aquinas's further claim that God can know everything there is to know through knowledge of his own essence. On this view there is a certain unity to God's knowledge—it is not fragmented into different pieces—and he does not obtain his knowledge by being the passive recipient of causal factors in the world. But it is difficult to see how his essence, which presumably is the same in every possible world, could nevertheless reflect or reveal different contingent facts in different possible worlds.

Is God's Knowledge Justified True Belief?

The traditional accounts of omniscience treat it as a special case of knowledge, although perhaps a very special sort of knowledge, including infallibility, being essential, and being global or unified in a way no human knowledge is. Despite this focus on knowledge, however, very little philosophical attention has been devoted to exploring the application of traditional accounts of knowledge to the divine case. For example, knowledge is traditionally thought to involve justified true belief, plus a 'fourth condition' to avoid counterexamples. (See, for example, Chisholm 1977.) More recent accounts of justification or of warrant (justification plus something else) have emphasized reliably produced beliefs or the proper functioning of one's epistemic faculties in conditions for which they were designed. (See Alston 1989*b* and Plantinga 1993, respectively.) But, with only a few exceptions, philosophers have not inquired into the status of God's beliefs or the nature of his justification.

One exception is William Alston (1989*a*), who defends the view that God does not have beliefs, that beliefs are not 'constituents of divine knowledge'. Alston considers two ways of developing this claim. According to the first, God 'is in no state that embodies the complexity of [a] proposition', so God does not believe any propositions. But on this account, God does not *know* any propositions, either. So, unless belief but not knowledge is essentially propositional, Alston's first suggestion seems less a departure from the traditional account of knowledge than an implicit departure from the traditional account of omniscience. Alston's second proposal holds that 'knowledge is a different psychological state from belief (judgment); it is not a belief that meets certain further conditions' (ibid. 188). Knowledge, on this view, is 'intuitive'. It is 'immediate awareness' of a fact. This sort of knowledge does apparently yield propositional knowledge, since Alston writes that 'God's immediate awareness that *p* is itself His knowledge that *p*.' Alston thinks that such knowledge need not involve belief, that it need not be of the '*true belief* + variety.' It could just as easily be the case, however, that the psychological state of having this direct awareness *is* a state of belief. What makes it special is that the other conditions for knowledge—truth, justification, etc.—are automatically satisfied in the case of this kind of belief. In any event, most philosophers have not followed Alston in this regard and have continued to conceive of God's knowledge as including belief.

A second, less explicit, respect in which philosophers have treated God's knowledge as satisfying the traditional account is by asking how God arrives at his knowledge. This may be understood as a way of asking what justifies God in his beliefs. Alfred Freddoso inquires with respect to future contingents (propositions about the future that are contingently true), 'what is the source of and explanation for the fact that God knows future contingents . . . ?' (1988: 1). Freddoso's constraint on an answer to this question, stated in his development of the views of Aquinas, Molina, and Bañez, but presumably one he accepts, is that 'an adequate answer to the source-question must essentially appeal to God's active causal role in the created world and must eschew even the faintest suggestion that God's knowledge of effects produced in the created world is causally dependent on the activity of His creatures'. So what justifies God in his beliefs, on this view, is quite different from what justifies us in many of our beliefs. God is not causally impinged upon and thus is not justified in his beliefs by being affected by anything other than himself.

THE EXTENT OF OMNISCIENCE AND PHILOSOPHICAL OBJECTIONS

Questions may be asked about the extent of God's omniscience, about exactly what is included in knowledge of all truths, whether this knowledge leaves anything out, and whether it is compatible with other attributes of God or with other claims we take to be true.

Knowledge *de re*

Knowledge (and belief) can be knowledge with respect to a thing that it has a certain property. Someone can have this *de re* knowledge without having the corresponding propositional or *de dicto* knowledge. For example, not recognizing the Provost in a dark alley, Ralph may know of the Provost that he appears suspicious without believing, and hence not knowing, that the Provost appears suspicious. In his discussion of omniscience, Arthur Prior (1962) called attention to the phenomenon of *de re* knowledge and gave several examples 'which a believer in God's omniscience would wish to maintain'. If omniscience should thus extend to knowledge *de re*, the question arises as to whether our definition (D1), which only requires knowledge of true propositions, captures such knowledge.

Philosophers have disagreed as to what exactly is required to acquire *de re* belief with respect to an object, but typically they assume that it is by bearing a relation of acquaintance with the object, to be epistemically *en rapport* with it, and then to have some *de dicto* belief attributing a property to the object in a way appropriately connected to that relation. Proposals for bearing the right relation of acquaintance range from having an appropriate concept of the object to being in the right causal relation to the object. (See Chisholm 1976; Lewis 1979; Kaplan 1968.) On all these accounts, knowledge *de re* is a species of knowledge *de dicto* together with a relation of acquaintance. It might be tempting to think that whatever that relation of acquaintance should turn out to be, God bears it to every thing and, thus, has complete *de re* knowledge. But that would not be right, in view of the claim in the last section, if the relevant relation requires being causally impinged upon by the object. Nevertheless, a related claim seems plausible: for any object x, whatever relation is such that standing in it to x is sufficient (together with the appropriate *de dicto* belief) for having a *de re* belief about x, God bears a relation to x that is at least as intimate, one that is at least as good for supporting a *de re* belief. God's creating, sustaining, and direct awareness of contingent things put him epistemically *en rapport* with them. So if *de re* knowledge is reducible to *de dicto* knowledge, then God's satisfying (D1) gives him complete *de re* knowledge.

Of course, if it turns out that *de re* knowledge is not thus reducible to *de dicto* knowledge, it would be a simple matter to revise (D1) so as explicitly to extend omniscience to knowledge *de re*, namely, by adding the following second clause to (D1), 'and for any x and property P, if x has P, then S knows of x that x has P'.

Indexicals, Temporal Knowledge, and First-Person Knowledge

What we know changes as time goes by. And what we know when we use present-tense sentences, or sentences with such temporal indexicals as 'now' or 'today', often seems particularly fleeting or ephemeral. We can use a sentence such as

(1) It is sunny today

to express a truth one day, and a falsehood the next. Moreover, what we express with (1) on a given occasion of use seems not to be equivalent to anything we could express with the corresponding sentence with the time-indication made explicit, for example, with

(2) It is sunny on 16 June 2008.

If omniscience requires knowledge of all truths, then God must know whatever proposition we express with a given use of (1), as well as that expressed by (2), if those propositions are true. So, our first question is whether omniscience extends to knowledge *de praesenti*, the kind of knowledge we have when we use (1) to express a truth.

In addition, many philosophers have claimed that the phenomenon of temporal knowledge can be used to show that if God is omniscient then he lacks one of the divine attributes traditionally ascribed to him. For example, Norman Kretzmann (1966) argued that omniscience is incompatible with immutability, Nicholas Wolterstorff (1975) claimed that omniscience is incompatible with divine eternity, and Stephen Davis (1983) held that omniscience is incompatible with divine timelessness. Other philosophers who urge a version of this claim include Arthur Prior (1962), Anthony Kenny (1979), and Patrick Grim (1985).

It is instructive that a parallel issue arises for first-person knowledge or knowledge of propositions expressed by sentences containing such first-person indexicals as 'I' or 'me'. To cite an example given by Kretzmann (1966), there is a difference between the proposition Jones expresses by the sentence

(3) 'I am in hospital'

and the proposition

(4) Jones is in hospital.

If Jones is hospitalized for amnesia, he might well believe the proposition expressed by his use of (3) without believing (4). And, similarly amnesiac but ignorant of his location, Jones can believe (4) without believing the proposition he would express by (3), if he reads a newspaper account of his hospitalization. So propositions we express by sentences using the first-person personal pronoun ('first-person propositions') do not seem to be equivalent to the corresponding propositions we express without using a first-person indexical.

Kretzmann took the first-person proposition Jones knows when he knows the proposition his use of (3) expresses to be one that no one other than Jones could know. This leads to the objection that if omniscience requires knowledge of all true propositions, then the existence of an omniscient God is incompatible with the existence of any other person with self-knowledge or knowledge *de se*. Alternatively, in a formulation closer to that given by Patrick Grim (1985), given that we do have knowledge *de se*, there is no God who knows all true propositions.

As in the case of knowledge *de praesenti*, we face the question of whether omniscience extends to knowledge *de se*, in particular to such first-person knowledge of others. And there is the further question of whether facts about knowledge *de se* lead to good objections to there being an omniscient God.

The structural similarity between the two types of knowledge, as well as the sorts of problems they are supposed to create for omniscience, suggests that they might be given similar rejoinders, and indeed they have. From the fact that the propositions we know change over time, it does not follow that the propositions we know when we know what day it is are not eternally true or that they cannot be known at other times. Similarly, from the fact that we know certain propositions about ourselves *as ourselves*, it does not follow that the propositions in question could not be known by someone else. In each case, what is missing in the objection is an account of exactly what the objects of knowledge and belief are, an account according to which there are special propositions believable only at certain times or by certain individuals.

Jonathan Kvanvig (1986) has given an account of the objects of knowledge according to which what is unique about knowledge *de praesenti* and knowledge *de se* is not a special proposition graspable only at certain times or by certain individuals but rather a special kind of access to or grasping of ordinary propositions. According to Kvanvig, what is involved in knowledge of the present or of oneself is a 'direct grasp' of a proposition—which leaves it open that God could believe the same propositions without ending up with knowledge *de praesenti* or knowledge *de se* of someone other than himself.

Edward Wierenga (1989) has made a slightly different proposal according to which sentences containing the first-person personal pronoun typically express a proposition involving the *haecceity* or individual essence of the person using the sentence. Believing a proposition involving one's own haecceity gives one belief *de se*. Although, as a matter of fact, we never grasp the propositions involving the haecceities of others, nothing prevents God from grasping or believing them. He would end up with a belief *de se* in the process only if the haecceity in question were his own. Similarly, if somewhat less plausibly, sentences with present-time indexicals express, at a given time of use, propositions involving the haecceity or individual essence of that time. Believing such a proposition at its time gives one a belief *de praesenti*. Although we never grasp such propositions at any other time, nothing prevents God from grasping or believing them. He would acquire a *de praesenti* belief only if he were present at the time in question. On this proposal, whether God is in time or timeless, or whether he is immutable, is not settled by whether he is omniscient but instead by whether he has his beliefs in time.

Another account of the objects of knowledge and belief is available, one that does not appeal to a special kind of grasping or an exotic type of proposition. It is the claim that many propositions are perspectival. A proposition can be true at one time and false at another. More generally, a proposition can be true at one *index*, consisting of a person and a time (and perhaps a place and a world), and false at another. Consider

(5) I am in hospital.

On the present proposal, (5) might be true at the index <Jones, 4.30 p.m. on 16 June 1967>, when amnesiac Jones is in hospital, but false at the index <Jones, 10.30 a.m. on 14 October 2007> by which time Jones has been cured and discharged. (See Sosa 1983 and Kaplan 1989.)

If propositions are perspectival in this way, there is a distinction between *believing that a proposition is true at an index* and *believing at an index that a proposition is true*. An example of the former is believing

(6) *I am in hospital* is true at <Jones, 4.30 p.m. on 16 June 1967>.

An example of the latter is believing (5) *at the index* <Jones, 4.30 p.m. on 16 June 1967>. Anyone can have the former belief; only someone at the index in question can have the latter. In particular, only Jones can have beliefs at that index, and even that he can only do at the time of the index. In our story, Jones did believe (5) at <Jones, 4.30 p.m. on 16 June 1967>, but he did not believe (6) then, for at that time he did not know that he was Jones. Belief *de praesenti* is thus belief in any proposition at an index, and belief *de se* is belief in a first-person proposition at an index; both are instances of believing a perspectival proposition at an index.

Wierenga (2002) has shown how this account may be applied to omniscience. God should not be expected to have beliefs impossible for him to have. Thus, he should not be expected, even though omniscient, to believe (5) at <Jones, 4.30 p.m. on 16 June 1967>, because that is possible only for Jones. Omniscience would require him to know only those perspectival propositions true at whatever indices he is at. Thus, we could revise (D1) as

(D4) *S* is omniscient $=_{df}$ for any proposition p and perspective $<x, t>$, (i) if p is true at $<x, t>$ then *S* knows that p is true at $<x, t>$, and (ii) if *S* is at $<x, t>$ and p is true at $<x, t>$, then at $<x, t>$ *S* knows that p.

According to (D4), God can be omniscient without having the *de se* beliefs of others, and it would follow from his omniscience that he is in time only on the additional assumption that he has his beliefs at temporal indices. But of course if it could be shown that God has beliefs at temporal indices, it would follow straightaway that he is in time, and arguing for that conclusion by way of appeal to omniscience is simply otiose.

Foreknowledge and Free Action

If omniscience requires knowledge of all truths and there are truths about the future, then omniscience includes foreknowledge. The simplest argument for this conclusion, considered by both Augustine and Boethius, can be stated as:

(7) If God knows in advance that a person will perform a certain action, then that person must perform it.

(8) If a person must perform an action, then the person does not do so freely.

(9) If God knows in advance that a person will perform a certain action, then the person does not do so freely.

Although this argument enjoys occasional support, its flaw had been identified by Aquinas (1945: i. 14, 13, *ad* 3). The first premise is ambiguous. It may be taken as

(7′) Necessarily, if God knows that a person will perform a certain action, then the person will do so,

which is true, but so taken the conclusion does not follow. The conclusion does follow if the premise is

(7″) If God knows that a person will perform a certain action, then the proposition that the person will perform that action is necessarily true,

but this premise is false. So neither interpretation yields an argument that is both logically valid and has true premises.

A considerably more difficult argument for the incompatibility of divine foreknowledge and free human action appeals to the apparent fixity or necessity of the past, what William of Ockham called the *accidental necessity of the past*. This argument requires three principles about accidental necessity:

(10) True contingent propositions reporting God's past beliefs are forever after accidentally necessary.

(11) A contingent proposition entailed by an accidentally necessary proposition is itself accidentally necessary.

(12) If a proposition is accidentally necessary at a time, then no one is able at any later time to make it false.

Suppose, to take an example introduced into the literature by Nelson Pike (1965), that eighty years ago God believed that Jones will mow his lawn tomorrow. Since this is a contingently true proposition reporting a past belief of God's, by (10), it is accidentally necessary, that is,

(13) It is accidentally necessary that eighty years ago God believed that Jones will mow his lawn tomorrow.

At this point the argument needs a slightly stronger assumption than that God is omniscient. It requires the assumption either that God is essentially omniscient or that he is infallible (see sect. 3 above). Inasmuch as perfect knowledge includes essential omniscience, let us make this assumption. Then the proposition that eighty years ago God believed that Jones will mow his lawn tomorrow entails that Jones will mow his lawn tomorrow. So by (11), the principle that accidental necessity is closed under (contingent) entailment, it follows that

(14) It is accidentally necessary that Jones will mow his lawn tomorrow.

But from (14) and (12) it follows that there is nothing anyone can do to make (14) false. In particular, there is nothing Jones himself can do to make (14) false. Mowing his lawn tomorrow is a chore he is unable to shirk. So Jones is not free with respect to mowing his lawn tomorrow. This argument may, of course, be generalized to cover any human action that God has foreknown.

The philosophical literature on this topic is voluminous. Many important papers are collected in Fischer (1989); see also Hasker (1989), Zagzebski (1991), and Wierenga (1989) for engagement with and further references to that literature. Responses fall into several different categories. One response is to accept the conclusion that divine foreknowledge is incompatible with human free action but to attempt to mitigate it by claiming that God's omniscience does not include foreknowledge. This was the response of Boethius (1999), who held that God's mode of existence was that of eternity, 'the complete possession all at once of illimitable life' (see Stump and Kretzmann, 1981). Thus, although God knows everything that ever happens, it is not *foreknowledge* from his eternal perspective. Aquinas, too, seemed to have thought that the correct response to the problem was to appeal to divine eternity. More recently, Stump and Kretzmann (1991) speak of 'the eternity solution'. But, as several philosophers have argued (Plantinga 1986; Zagzebski 1991; Wierenga 1989), whatever the merits of the doctrine of divine eternity, it does not by itself solve the problem raised by this argument. The reason is that an exactly analogous argument can be constructed in terms of the past truth of God's eternal knowledge of propositions about our future. The defender of divine eternity would need to say something about *that* argument, so we should find out what that is so that we can see whether it applies to the present argument.

Another response also accepts the conclusion of the argument but denies both that God has foreknowledge and that he has any other way of knowing the future free actions of creatures. This view has become increasingly popular in recent years. A limited version of it was defended by Peter Geach (1977), who held that God lacks foreknowledge of future free actions of creatures unless those actions result from 'present trends and tendencies'. Swinburne (1993) agrees, at least on the assumption that God is contingent, that he does not have knowledge of future free actions. Hoffman and Rosenkrantz (2002) develop a detailed analysis of omniscience, intentionally limiting God's knowledge of the contingent future to those truths that are 'causally inevitable'. Finally, William Hasker (1989) and others associated with the 'Open Theism' movement (see Pinnock et al. (1994)) are insistent that God leaves the future open so as to leave room for human freedom. Nevertheless, denying that God has foreknowledge (without substituting eternal knowledge or some other kind of cognition for it) seems a retreat from the traditional conception of the God of the philosophers, and it certainly seems difficult to see how a significant doctrine of providence could be developed without including knowledge of the future in omniscience.

Appealing to divine eternity and abandoning foreknowledge of future free actions are two options open to philosophers who accept the argument above. Philosophers who do not want to accept the conclusion of that argument will have to deny one or more of its assumptions (10), (11), and (12). Ockhamism denies that propositions reporting God's past beliefs about the future need be accidentally necessary. Ockhamists notably include, in addition to William of Ockham (1969) himself, Alvin Plantinga (1986). They hold that propositions reporting God's past beliefs may be partly about the future, just as

(15) Twenty years ago Ralph correctly believed that the sun will rise on 1 January 2010

is not wholly about the past. It has turned out to be remarkably difficult to give a satisfactory account of the key concepts of accidental necessity or of being wholly about the past. Nevertheless, if God's past beliefs about the past are not now accidentally necessary, the Ockhamist has found a premise of the argument to deny with some plausibility.

Molinists deny (11), the claim that accidental necessity is closed under entailment of contingent propositions. Molinism, to be discussed in the next section, defends the claim that God has 'middle knowledge', and it provides a plausible explanation of how God could know the future free actions of human beings without causing those actions or otherwise destroying their freedom. This central feature of Molinism seems independent of any of the premises of the argument under review, so it is not clear why Molinism picks (11) to deny. Nevertheless, Freddoso (1988: 58), himself a convert to Molinism, has found a passage in Molina that pretty clearly seems to deny (11). There seems to be a good reason to accept (11), however. If accidental necessity is indeed a well-behaved modality it must obey two principles. The first is that

(16) Any proposition that is logically equivalent to an accidentally necessary proposition is itself accidentally necessary.

If a proposition p is fixed and unalterable in virtue of what has happened, if there is nothing anyone can do that would render p false, then it is hard to conceive how a proposition q that is logically equivalent to p is not similarly fixed and beyond anyone's ability to render false. The second principle is that

(17) Any conjunction that has as a conjunct a contingent proposition that is not accidentally necessary is itself not accidentally necessary.

Suppose there is something you could do that would make p false. If you were to do it, then for any proposition q, the conjunction $p \& q$ would be false, too; so the truth of the conjunction is not fixed or unalterable. If accidental necessity satisfies these two modest and intuitive principles, then it is closed under (contingent) entailment. To see this, suppose that p is accidentally necessary and that it entails a proposition q (where q is possibly false). Since p entails q, p is logically equivalent to the conjunction of $p \& q$. By (16), then, this conjunction is accidentally necessary. But if this conjunction is accidentally necessary, then by (17) it does not have any contingent conjuncts that are not accidentally necessary. By assumption, q is a contingent conjunct of the conjunction $p \& q$. So q is accidentally necessary. Hence, if p is accidentally necessary and entails a contingent proposition q, then q is accidentally necessary. So accidental necessity is closed under (contingent) entailment.

The final option is to deny (12), the claim that no one can make an accidentally necessary proposition false. More carefully, it is open to hold that from the fact that there is nothing Jones can do to make

(14) It is accidentally necessary that Jones will mow his lawn tomorrow

false, it does not follow that he is not free with respect to mowing his lawn tomorrow. This response will be congenial to compatibilists—those who hold that free action is compatible with causal determinism. But it will be much less palatable to those who think that free will is libertarian.

Middle Knowledge

A final question about the extent of God's knowledge is whether it extends to include middle knowledge. This is a question that requires some explanation. Luis de Molina (Freddoso 1988) and other late-medieval philosophers divided God's knowledge into several categories. Part of what God knows is *natural* knowledge, that is, knowledge of necessary truths, of possibilities, and of the natures of things. Two features of natural knowledge are that it is of propositions that are both necessarily true and independent of God's will or decision to create. Another category is *free* knowledge, knowledge of propositions true because God decides to have them be true. So this category includes propositions that are both contingent and dependent upon God's will. An especially interesting category of propositions are those that describe what free agents would freely do in a variety of situations ('counterfactuals of freedom'). Molina's insight was to categorize these propositions as intermediate between the other two categories, in two dimensions: they are contingently true but independent of God's will. Hence, knowledge of propositions such as these is naturally thought of as *middle* knowledge, in the middle of natural and free knowledge.

Thomas Flint (1998) has described how on Molinism God's knowledge 'grows' through four 'logical moments'. First, God has 'natural knowledge', that is, knowledge of necessary truths. Second, he has middle knowledge, knowledge, that is, of contingent truths beyond his control, preeminently, counterfactuals of creaturely freedom. Third, God decides upon a particular divine creative act of will, and thus knows what his direct contribution to the world is. Finally, by using his knowledge of his own creative action as well as his knowledge of what would happen if he were to do that action, God arrives at knowledge of all remaining contingent truths. This final category includes propositions describing what free agents will do in the future. But it is clear from the way God arrives at this knowledge that his knowledge exerts no causal or determining influence on the actions of free agents.

Attributing middle knowledge to God has been employed in ways that have been enormously fruitful in recent philosophy of religion, ranging from a response to the problem of evil (see Ch. 15), to an account of God's knowledge of future contingents, to a developed account of divine providence (see Ch. 12). But the claim that omniscience includes middle knowledge has been controversial. Molina's sixteenth-century opponents denied that counterfactuals of freedom really were independent of God's will. Contemporary opponents deny that they are true, or that they are true soon enough to be of use to God in deciding what to create (Adams 1977; Hasker 1986; Kenny 1979). Philosophers who hold that the counterfactuals of freedom needed to guide God's creation decision are not true typically claim that they are not 'grounded', that prior to creation there is nothing that would make them true (Adams 1977). Proponents often deny that all contingent propositions need a ground of truth. But consideration of this dispute is beyond the scope of this chapter.

Conclusion

Omniscience may be understood as perfect knowledge and, thus, as knowledge of all truths. Perfect knowledge would also have additional features, such as, infallibility, being essential, and being whole or non-discursive. It is a matter of controversy as to whether omniscience extends to such particular cases as knowledge *de praesenti*, knowledge *de se*, knowledge of the future, including future free actions, and middle knowledge, especially knowledge of what free creatures would do in alternative circumstances. On these topics, philosophers have taken opposing sides and debate continues.

References

ADAMS, R. M. (1977). 'Middle Knowledge and the Problem of Evil', *American Philosophical Quarterly* 14: 109–17.

ALSTON, W. P. (1989a). 'Does God Have Beliefs?', in id., *Divine Nature and Human Language*. Ithaca: Cornell University Press.

—— (1989b). *Epistemic Justification: Essays in the Theory of Knowledge*. Ithaca: Cornell University Press.

ANSELM (1998a). *Monologion*, in B. Davies and G. R. Evans (eds.), *Anselm of Canterbury: The Major Works*. Oxford: Oxford University Press.

—— (1998b). *Proslogion*, in B. Davies and G. R. Evans (eds.), *Anselm of Canterbury: The Major Works*. Oxford: Oxford University Press.

AQUINAS, THOMAS (1945). *The Basic Writings of Thomas Aquinas*, ed. A. C. Pegis, 2 vols. New York: Random House.

BOETHIUS (1999). *The Consolation of Philosophy*, trans. P. G. Walsh. Oxford: Oxford University Press.

CHISHOLM, R. (1976), 'Knowledge and Belief: "De Dicto" and "De Se"', *Philosophical Studies* 29: 1–20.

—— (1977). *Theory of Knowledge*, 2nd edn. Englewood Cliffs: Prentice-Hall.

DAVIS, S. (1983). *Logic and the Nature of God*. Grand Rapids: Wm. B. Eerdmans.

FISCHER, J. M. (1989). *God, Foreknowledge, and Freedom*. Stanford: Stanford University Press.

FLINT, T. (1998). *Divine Providence: The Molinist Account*. Ithaca: Cornell University Press.

FREDDOSO, A. (1988). 'Introduction' to Luis Molina, *On Divine Foreknowledge: Part IV of the Concordia*. Ithaca: Cornell University Press.

GEACH, P. (1977). *Providence and Evil*. Cambridge: Cambridge University Press.

GRIM, P. (1985). 'Against Omniscience: The Case from Essential Indexicals', *Noûs* 19: 151–80.

HASKER, W. (1986). 'A Refutation of Middle Knowledge', *Noûs* 20: 545–57.

—— (1989). *God, Time, and Knowledge*. Ithaca: Cornell University Press.

HOFFMAN, J., and ROSENKRANTZ, G. (2002). *The Divine Attributes*. Oxford: Blackwell, ch. 6.

HUNT, D. (1995). 'Dispositional Omniscience', *Philosophical Studies* 80: 243–78.

KAPLAN, D. (1968). 'Quantifying In', *Synthese* 29: 178–214.

—— (1989). 'Demonstratives' (with 'Afterthoughts'), in J. Almog, J. Perry, and H. Wettstein (eds.), *Themes from Kaplan*. New York: Oxford University Press.

KENNY, A. (1979). *The God of the Philosophers*. Oxford: Clarendon.

KRETZMANN, N. (1966). 'Omniscience and Immutability', *Journal of Philosophy* 63: 409–21.

KVANVIG, J. (1986). *The Possibility of an All-Knowing God*. New York: St Martin's.

LEWIS, D. (1979). 'Attitudes *De Dicto* and *De Se*', *Philosophical Review* 88: 513–43.

PIKE, N. (1965). 'Divine Omniscience and Voluntary Action', *Philosophical Review* 74: 27–46.

PINNOCK, C., et al. (1994). *The Openness of God*. Downers Grove: InterVarsity Press.

PLANTINGA, A. (1974). *God, Freedom, and Evil*. rpt. Grand Rapids: Wm. B. Eerdmans, 1977.

—— (1986). 'On Ockham's Way Out', *Faith and Philosophy* 3: 235–69.

—— (1993). *Warrant and Proper Function*. New York: Oxford University Press.

PRIOR, A. N. (1962). 'Formalities of Omniscience', in id., *Papers on Time and Tense*. Oxford: Oxford University Press.

Sosa, E. (1983). 'Consciousness of the Self and of the Present', in J. Tomberlin (ed.), *Agent, Language, and the Structure of the World*. Indianapolis: Hackett.

Stump, E., and Kretzmann, N. (1981). 'Eternity', *The Journal of Philosophy* 78: 429–58.

——(1991). 'Prophecy, Past Truth, and Eternity', in J. Tomberlin (ed.), *Philosophical Perspectives* 5: 395–424.

Swinburne, R. (1993). *The Coherence of Theism*. rev. edn. Oxford: Clarendon, ch. 10.

van Inwagen, P. (2006). *The Problem of Evil: The Gifford Lectures Delivered in the University of St Andrews in 2003*. Oxford: Clarendon.

Wierenga, E. (1989). *The Nature of God*. Ithaca: Cornell University Press.

——(2002). 'Timelessness out of Mind', in G. Ganssle and D. Woodruff (eds.), *God and Time: Essays on the Divine Nature*. New York: Oxford University Press.

William of Ockham (1969). *Predestination, God's Foreknowledge, and Future Contingents*, trans. M. M. Adams and N. Kretzmann. New York: Appleton-Century-Crofts.

Wolterstorff, N. (1975). 'God Everlasting', in C. Orlebeke and L. Smedes (eds.), *God and the Good: Essays in Honor of Henry Stob*. Grand Rapids: Wm. Eerdmans.

Zagzebski, L. (1991). *The Dilemma of Freedom and Foreknowledge*. New York: Oxford University Press.

——(2007). 'Omniscience', in C. Meister and P. Copan (eds.), *The Routledge Companion to Philosophy of Religion*. London: Routledge, 261–9.

CHAPTER 7

DIVINE ETERNITY

WILLIAM LANE CRAIG

'God', declares the prophet Isaiah, 'is the high and lofty One who inhabits eternity' (Isa. 57: 15). But being a prophet and not a philosophical theologian, Isaiah did not pause to reflect upon the *nature* of divine eternity. Minimally, to be eternal means to exist without beginning and end. To say that God is eternal means minimally that he never came into being and will never go out of being. To exist eternally is to exist permanently.[1]

There are, however, at least two ways in which something could exist eternally. One way would be to exist omnitemporally throughout infinite time. In this case God would have an immemorial and everlasting temporal duration. The other way in which a being could exist eternally would be by existing timelessly. In this case God would completely transcend time, having neither temporal location nor temporal extension. He would simply exist in an undifferentiated, timeless state.

If we take Scripture as our guide in matters of theology, the initial question we must ask is: does biblical teaching on divine eternity favor either one of these views? The question turns out to be surprisingly difficult to answer. On the one hand, it is indisputable that the biblical writers typically portray God as engaged in temporal activities, including foreknowing the future and remembering the past, and when they speak directly of God's eternal existence they do so in terms of beginningless and endless temporal duration. The data are not wholly one-sided, however. There is some evidence, at least, that when God is considered in relation to creation he must be thought of as the transcendent creator of time and the ages and therefore as existing beyond time (Gen. 1: 1; Prov. 8: 22–3; 1 Cor. 2: 7; 2 Tim. 1: 9; Titus 1: 2–3; Jude 25). So the biblical data are underdeterminative, and one seems forced to conclude with James Barr that 'if such a thing as a Christian doctrine of time has to be developed, the work of discussing it and developing it must belong not to biblical but to philosophical theology'.[2]

At issue here is God's relationship to time: Does God exist temporally or atemporally? God exists temporally if and only if he exists in time, that is to say, if and only if his duration has phases that are related to each other as earlier and later. In that case, God, as a personal being, has experientially a past, a present, and a future. No matter what moment in time we pick, given God's permanence, the assertion, 'God exists now', were we to make it, would be literally true.

By contrast, God exists atemporally if and only if he is not temporal. This definition makes it evident that temporality and timelessness are contradictories: an entity must exist one way or the other and cannot exist both ways at once. If, then, God exists atemporally, he has no past, present, and future. At any moment in time it would be true to assert, 'God exists', in the tenseless sense of 'exists', as when one says, 'The natural numbers exist', but not true to assert, 'God exists now'.

Philosophical theologians have been sharply divided with respect to God's relationship to time. What are the principal arguments they have offered for divine timelessness and temporality?

ARGUMENTS FOR DIVINE TIMELESSNESS

Argument from Simplicity or Immutability

Consider first the view that God exists timelessly. Traditionally Christian theologians such as Thomas Aquinas argued for God's timelessness on the basis of his absolute simplicity and immutability (*Summa theologiae* (*ST*) Ia q. 10 a. 3). The argument can be simply formulated. As a first premise, we assume either

(1) God is simple

or

(1') God is immutable.

Then we add

(2) If God is simple or immutable, then he is not temporal,

from which it follows that

(3) Therefore, God is not temporal.

Since temporality and timelessness are contradictories, it follows that

(4) Therefore, God is timeless.

Is this a cogent argument? Consider (2). The doctrine of divine simplicity implies not merely that God does not have parts, but that he does not possess even distinct attributes. In some mysterious way his omnipotence is his goodness, for example. He stands in no relations whatsoever. His nature or essence is not even distinct from his existence. He is, Aquinas tells us, the pure act of existing (ST Ia q. 3 a. 4). Now if God is simple in the way described, it obviously follows that he cannot be temporal. For a temporal being is related to the various times at which it exists: it exists at t_1 and at t_2, for example. But a simple being stands in no real relations. Moreover, a temporal being has phases of its life that are not identical but rather are related to one another as earlier and later. But an absolutely simple being could not stand in such relations and so must have its life, as Boethius put it, 'all at once' (totum simul) (Philosophiae consolationis 5 pr. 6. 9–11).

Similarly, if God is immutable, then even if he is not simple, he cannot be temporal. Like simplicity, the immutability affirmed by the medieval theologians is a radical concept: God cannot change in *any* respect. God not only cannot undergo intrinsic change, but he also cannot change extrinsically by being related to changing things.[3] But obviously a temporal being undergoes at least extrinsic change in that it exists at different moments of time and, given the reality of the temporal world, coexists with different temporal beings as they undergo intrinsic change. Even if we relax the definition of 'immutable' to mean 'incapable of intrinsic change' or the even weaker concept 'intrinsically changeless', an immutable God cannot be temporal. For if God is temporal, God will be constantly changing in his knowledge, knowing first that 'It is now t_1' and later that 'It is now t_2.' God's foreknowledge and memory must also be steadily changing, as anticipated events transpire and become past. God will constantly be performing new actions, at t_1 causing events at t_1 and at t_2 causing events at t_2. Thus, a temporal God cannot be changeless. It follows, then, that if God is immutable, he is timeless.

Thus, God's timelessness can be deduced from either his simplicity or immutability. Is this a good reason for thinking that God is timeless? That depends on whether we have any good reason to affirm (1) or (1'). Here we run into severe difficulties. For doctrines of divine simplicity and immutability that are sufficiently strong to support divine timelessness are even more controverted than the doctrine of divine timelessness itself. These strong doctrines find no explicit support in Scripture, which at most speaks of God's immutability in terms of his faithfulness and unchanging character (Mal. 3: 6; Jas. 1: 17), and philosophically there seem to be no good reasons to embrace these doctrines but weighty objections against them.[4] These cannot be discussed here; the point is that (1) and (1') are even more difficult to prove than (4), so that they do not constitute good grounds for believing (4). Thus, while we may freely admit that a simple or immutable God must be timeless, we have even less reason to think God simple or immutable than to think him timeless and so can hardly hold that he is timeless on the basis of those doctrines.

Argument from Divine Knowledge of Future Contingents

In contrast to divine simplicity and immutability, divine omniscience is clearly a great-making property and enjoys considerable Scriptural warrant. An argument for divine timelessness predicated upon God's omniscience would therefore have a more secure theological foundation. Many thinkers have argued that God's knowledge of future contingent events, for example, future human free actions, implies divine timelessness. The reasoning seems to go as follows:

(5) A temporal being cannot know future contingent events.
(6) God knows future contingent events.
(7) Therefore, God is not a temporal being.

Again, if God is not a temporal being, then (4) follows as before.

Despite the denial of (6) on the part of a wide range of contemporary thinkers from process theologians to 'open' theists, a biblical doctrine of divine omniscience makes (6) incumbent upon an orthodox theologian.[5] The argument hinges, therefore, on the truth of (5). On behalf of (5) it is usually claimed that contingent events, not being deducible from present causes, can be known only insofar as they are real or existent. Given (6), it follows that future contingent events are real or existent for God. Defenders of divine timelessness such as Boethius, Anselm, and Aquinas thus typically maintained that all events in time are real to God and therefore can be known by him via his *scientia visionis* (knowledge of vision).

How can we make sense of this claim? The most plausible move for the defender of divine timelessness to make will be to hold that the four-dimensional spacetime manifold exists tenselessly and that God transcends that manifold. A good many physicists and philosophers of time and space embrace such a tenseless view of time (spacetime realism). Such a view makes sense of the traditional claim that all events in time are present to God and therefore known to him via his *scientia visionis*.

The drawback is that there is a high price to be paid philosophically and theologically for such a tenseless theory of time.[6] Therefore, the claim that contingent events can be known only insofar as they are real or existent comes at a considerable cost for the biblical theist. One is therefore inclined to be sceptical of the argument on behalf of (5).

Moreover, (5) can be directly challenged as well. In assessing the question of how God knows truths about temporal events, we may distinguish two models of divine cognition: the *perceptualist* model and the *conceptualist* model. The perceptualist model construes divine knowledge on the analogy of sense perception: God looks and sees what is there. Such a model patently underlies the classic doctrine of *scientia visionis* and is implicitly assumed when people speak of God's 'foreseeing' the future. The perceptualist model of divine cognition does encounter difficulty concerning God's knowledge of future contingents, for, if future events do not exist, there is nothing there to perceive.[7]

By contrast, on a conceptualist model of divine knowledge, God does not acquire his knowledge of the world by anything like perception. His knowledge of the future is not based on his 'looking' ahead and 'seeing' what lies in the future (a terribly anthropomorphic notion in any case). Rather God's knowledge is more like a mind's knowledge of innate ideas. It is therefore inappropriate to speak of God's *acquiring* knowledge at all. Rather as an omniscient being, God has essentially the property of knowing all truths; there are truths about future events; *ergo*, God knows all truths concerning future events. So long as we are not seduced into thinking of divine foreknowledge on the model of perception, it is no longer evident why knowledge of future contingents should be impossible.

We can go further, however. For the doctrine of middle knowledge (*scientia media*) is a version of the conceptualist model that allows us to say considerably more about the basis of God's foreknowledge of future contingents. Divine fore-knowledge is based on (1) God's middle knowledge of what every creature would freely do under any circumstances and (2) his knowledge of the divine decree to create certain sets of circumstances and to place certain creatures in them. Given middle knowledge and the divine decree, foreknowledge follows automatically as a result without any perception of the created world. This complex and interesting doctrine must be pursued in an independent discussion (see Ch. 12, Divine Provi-dence).

In sum, while the argument from God's knowledge of future contingents has some force in motivating a doctrine of divine timelessness, that force is mitigated by the availability of viable alternatives and the high price exacted by a tenseless theory of time.

Argument from Special Relativity

A third argument for divine timelessness arises from the concept of time in Ein-stein's Special Theory of Relativity (STR). According to this theory there is no unique, universal time and so no unique, worldwide 'now'. Each inertial frame has its own time and its own present moment, and there is no overarching, absolute time in which all these diverse times are integrated into one. So if God is in time, then the obvious question raised by STR is: *Whose time is he in?*

The defender of divine timelessness maintains that there is no acceptable answer to this question. We cannot plausibly pick out some inertial frame and identify its time as God's time because God is not a physical object in uniform motion, and so the choice of any such frame would be wholly arbitrary. Moreover, it is difficult to see how God, confined to the time of one inertial frame, could be causally sustaining events that are real relative to other inertial frames but are future or past relative to God's frame. Similarly, God's knowledge of what is happening now would be restricted to the temporal perspective of his frame, leaving him ignorant of what is actually going on in other frames. In any case, if God were to be associated with a particular inertial frame, then surely, as God's time, the time of that frame would be privileged. It would be the equivalent of the privileged frame of the aether in classical physics. So long as we maintain, with Einstein, that no frame is privileged, then we cannot identify the time of any inertial frame as God's time.

Neither can we say that God exists in the 'now' associated with the time of every inertial frame, for this would obliterate the unity of God's consciousness. In order to preserve God's personal consciousness, it must not be fragmented and scattered among the inertial frames in the universe. But if God's time cannot be identified with the time of a single frame or of a plurality of frames, then God must not be in time at all; that is to say, he exists timelessly.

We can summarize this reasoning as follows:

(8) STR is correct in its description of time.

(9) If STR is correct in its description of time, then if God is temporal, he exists in either the time associated with a single inertial frame or the times associated with a plurality of inertial frames.

(10) Therefore, if God is temporal, he exists in either the time associated with a single inertial frame or the times associated with a plurality of inertial frames.

(11) God does not exist in either the time associated with a single inertial frame or the times associated with a plurality of inertial frames.

(12) Therefore, God is not temporal.

What can be said in response to this argument? Although it may come as something of a shock to many, the most dubious premise of the argument is (8). For STR's concept of time rests upon decrepit epistemological foundations. Einstein's redefinition of simultaneity in terms of clock synchronization by light signals simply assumes that the time light takes to travel between two relatively stationary observers A and B is the same from A to B as from B to A in a round-trip journey. That assumption presupposes that A and B, while at relative rest, are not both in absolute motion, or in other words that neither absolute space nor a privileged inertial frame exists. What justification did Einstein have for so radical a presupposition? The answer, in a word, is verificationism. It is empirically impossible to distinguish uniform motion from rest relative to such a frame, and Einstein believed that if absolute space and absolute motion or rest are undetectable empirically, they therefore do not exist (and may even be said to be meaningless). Historians of science have shown that at the philosophical roots of Einstein's theory lies a verificationist epistemology, mediated to the young physicist chiefly through the influence of Ernst Mach, which comes to expression in Einstein's analysis of the concepts of time and space.[8]

The untenability of verificationism is so universally acknowledged that it will not be necessary to rehearse the objections against it here.[9] Verificationism provides no justification for thinking that Newton erred, for example, in holding that absolute time, grounded in God's sempiternal duration, exists independently of our physical measures of it and may or may not be accurately registered by them. With the demise of verificationism, the philosophical underpinnings of STR have collapsed. In short, there is no reason to think that (8) is true.

But what about (9)? The difficulty with this premise is that it fails to take into account the fact that STR is a *restricted* theory of relativity and therefore is correct only within prescribed limits. It is a theory that deals with uniform motion only. The analysis of non-uniform motion, such as acceleration and rotation, is provided by the General Theory of Relativity (GTR). STR cannot therefore be expected to give us the final word about the nature of time and space; indeed, within the context of GTR a new and important conception of time emerges.

GTR serves to introduce into Relativity Theory a cosmic perspective, enabling us to draft cosmological models of the universe governed by the gravitational field equations of GTR. Within the context of such cosmological models, the issue of time resurfaces dramatically. All contemporary cosmological models derive from Russian physicist Alexander Friedman's 1922 model of an expanding, material universe characterized by ideal homogeneity and isotropy. Although GTR does not itself mandate any formula for how to slice up spacetime into a temporally ordered foliation, nevertheless certain models of spacetime, such as the Friedman model, have a dynamical, evolving spatial geometry whose natural symmetries guide the construction of a cosmic time; in order to ensure a smooth development of this geometry, it will be necessary to construct a time parameter based on a preferred slicing of spacetime. Now as a parameter independent of spatial coordinates, cosmic time measures the duration of the universe as a whole in an observer-independent way; that is to say, the lapse of cosmic time is the same for all observers.

Based on a cosmological, rather than a local, perspective, cosmic time serves to restore the classical notions of universal time and absolute simultaneity that STR denied. The defender of divine temporality may accordingly hold that God exists in cosmic time.[10] Hence, contrary to (9), it does not follow from the correctness of STR that if God is in time, then he is in the time of one or more inertial frames. Because space itself is expanding, there is no universal inertial frame with which God can be associated, even though there does exist a preferred foliation of spacetime and so a cosmic time in which God can be conceived to exist.[11]

Argument from the Incompleteness of Temporal Life

An important argument in favor of divine timelessness is based on the incompleteness of temporal life. Brian Leftow, as well as Eleonore Stump and Norman Kretzmann, argues that the fleeting nature of temporal life is incompatible with the life of a most perfect being such as God. A temporal being is unable to enjoy what is past or future for it, possessing only the fleeting present. The passage of time thus renders it impossible for any temporal being, even God, to possess all its life at once. By contrast a timeless God lives all his life at once because he literally has no past or future and so suffers no loss. Therefore, since God is the most perfect being, he is timeless.

We can formulate this argument as follows:

(13) God is the most perfect being.
(14) The most perfect being has the most perfect mode of existence.
(15) Therefore, God has the most perfect mode of existence.
(16) Temporal existence is a less perfect mode of existence than timeless existence.
(17) Therefore, God has a timeless mode of existence.

The key premise here is (16), which rests on very powerful intuitions about the irretrievable loss that arises through the experience of temporal passage, a loss that intuitively should not characterize the experience of a most perfect being. Some philosophers of time might try to avert the force of this consideration by adopting a tenseless view of time according to which things and events do not in fact come to be or pass away. The difference between past, present, and future is a subjective illusion of consciousness. On this view of time, no temporal being ever really loses its past or has not yet acquired its future; it (or its temporal parts) just exists tenselessly at its various temporal locations. A temporal God would exist at all temporal locations without beginning or end and so would not lose or acquire portions of his life.

The problem with this escape route is that it fails to appreciate that the argument is based on the *experience* of temporal passage, rather than on the objective reality of temporal passage itself. Even if the future never becomes and the past is never really lost, the fact remains that for a temporal person the past is lost *to him* and the future is not accessible *to him*. For this reason, it would be futile to attempt to elude the force of this argument by postulating a temporal deity in a tenseless time.

Perhaps, however, the realization that the argument is essentially experiential in character opens the door for a temporalist alternative. When we recall that God is perfectly omniscient and so forgets nothing of the past and knows everything about the future, then time's passage is not so tragic for him. His past experiences do not fade as ours do, and he has perfect prescience of what the future holds. So it is far from obvious that the experience of temporal passage is so melancholy an affair for an omniscient God as it is for us. Moreover, the life of a perfect person may have to be characterized by the incompleteness that would in other contexts be considered an imperfection. There is some evidence that consciousness of time's flow can actually be an enriching experience, as in music appreciation.[12] Timelessness may not be the most perfect mode of existence of a perfect person. All this goes to call into question (16). Still, this last argument, like the argument from divine foreknowledge, does have some force and so needs to be weighed against whatever arguments can be offered on behalf of divine temporality.

ARGUMENTS FOR DIVINE TEMPORALITY

Argument from the Impossibility of Atemporal Personhood

What arguments, then, might be offered for divine temporality? One argument frequently raised in the literature is that timelessness and personhood are incompatible. Some philosophers have denied that a timeless God can be a self-conscious, rational being because he could not exhibit certain forms of consciousness that we normally associate with personal beings (namely, ourselves). For example, Robert Coburn has written,

Surely it is a necessary condition of anything's being a person that it should be capable (logically) of, among other things, doing at least some of the following: remembering, anticipating, reflecting, deliberating, deciding, intending, and acting intentionally. To see that this is so one need but ask oneself whether anything which necessarily lacked all of the capacities noted would, under any conceivable circumstances, count as a person. But now an eternal being would necessarily lack all of these capacities in as much as their exercise by a being clearly requires that the being exist in time. ... Hence, no eternal being, it would seem, could be a person.[13]

Since God is essentially personal, he therefore cannot be timeless.

We can formulate this argument as follows (using x, y, z to represent certain properties allegedly essential to personhood):

(18) Necessarily, if God is timeless, he does not have the properties x, y, z.
(19) Necessarily, if God does not have the properties x, y, z, then God is not personal.
(20) Necessarily, God is personal.
(21) Therefore, necessarily, God is not timeless.

The defender of divine timelessness may attempt to turn back this argument either by challenging the claim that the properties in question are necessary conditions of personhood or by showing that a timeless God could possess the relevant properties after all. With respect to the second strategy, even if Coburn were correct that a personal being must be capable of exhibiting the forms of consciousness he lists, it does not follow that a timeless God cannot be personal. For God could be *capable* of exhibiting such forms of consciousness but be timeless just in case he does not *in fact* exhibit any of them. In other words, the hidden assumption behind Coburn's reasoning is that God's being timeless or temporal is an essential property of God. But that assumption seems dubious. Suppose, for the sake of argument, that God is in fact temporal. Is it logically impossible that God could have been timeless instead? Since God's decision to create is free, we can conceive of a possible world in which God alone exists. If he is unchanging in such a world, then on any relational view of time God would be timeless. In such an atemporal world God would lack certain properties which we have supposed him to have in the actual world—for example, the property of *knowing what time it is* or the property of *coexisting with temporal creatures*—and he would have other properties that he lacks in the actual world—for example, the property of *being alone* or of *knowing that he is alone*—but none of these differences seems significant enough to deny that God could be timeless yet still be the same being. But then it seems that there are possible worlds in which God exists temporally and possible worlds in which he exists timelessly. God's temporal status is thus plausibly a contingent rather than essential property. So (apart from highly controversial claims on behalf of divine simplicity or immutability) there seems to be no reason to think that God is either *essentially* temporal or *essentially* timeless.

So if timelessness is a merely contingent property of God, he could be entirely capable of remembering, anticipating, reflecting, and so on; only were he to do so, then he would not be timeless. So long as he freely refrains from such activities he is timeless, even though he has the *capacity* to engage in those activities. Thus, by Coburn's own lights God must be regarded as personal.

At a more fundamental level, it is in any case pretty widely recognized that most of the forms of consciousness mentioned by Coburn are not essential to personhood—indeed, not even the capacity for them is essential to personhood. Take remembering, for example. Any temporal individual who lacked memory would be mentally ill or less than human. But if an individual exists timelessly, then he has no past to remember. Similarly with regard to anticipation: since a timeless individual has no future, there just is nothing to anticipate. Nevertheless, given his omniscience, God would still know what takes place (tenselessly) at every time.

As for reflecting and deliberating, these are ruled out not so much by God's time-lessness as by his omniscience. An omniscient being cannot reflect and deliberate because he already knows the conclusions to be derived. Even if God is temporal, he does not engage in reflection and deliberation. But he is surely not impersonal as a result.

What about deciding, intending, and acting intentionally? All these forms of consciousness are exhibited by a timeless God. With respect to deciding, again omniscience alone precludes God's deciding in the sense of making up his mind after a period of indecision. Even a temporal God does not decide in that sense. But God does decide in the sense that his will inclines toward one alternative rather than another and does so freely. It is up to God what he does; he could have willed otherwise. This is the strongest sense of libertarian freedom of the will. In God's case, because he is omniscient, his free decisions are either sempiternal or timeless rather than preceded by a period of ignorance and indecision.

As for intending or acting intentionally, there is no reason to think that intentions are necessarily future-directed. One can direct one's intentions at one's present state. God, as the Good, can timelessly desire and will his own infinite goodness.

Such a changeless intention can be as timeless as God's knowing his own essence. Moreover, in the empty world we have envisioned, God may timelessly will and intend to refrain from creating a universe. God's willing to refrain from creation should not be confused with the mere absence of the intention to create. A stone is characterized by the absence of any intention to create but cannot be said to will to refrain from creating. In a world in which God freely refrains from creation, his abstaining from creating is a result of a free act of the will on his part. Hence, it seems that God can timelessly intend, will, and choose what he does.

In short, the argument for divine temporality based on God's personhood cannot be deemed a success. On the contrary, a timeless God can be plausibly said to be a self-conscious, rational individual endowed with freedom of the will and therefore a person.

Argument from Divine Action in the World

In our thought experiment above, we abstracted from the actual existence of the temporal world and considered God existing alone without creation and asked whether he could exist timelessly. But, of course, the temporal world does exist. The question therefore arises whether God can stand in relation to a temporal world and yet remain timeless. It is very difficult to see how he can. Imagine once more God existing changelessly alone without creation, but with a changeless determination of his will to create a temporal world with a beginning. Since God is omnipotent, his will is done, and a temporal world comes into existence. Can God remain untouched by the world's temporality? It seems not. For at the first moment of time, God stands in a new relation, one in which he did not stand before (indeed, there was no 'before'). Even if in creating the world God undergoes no *intrinsic* change, he at least undergoes an *extrinsic* change. For at the moment of creation, God comes into the relation of *sustaining* the universe or, at the very least, of *coexisting with* the universe, relations in which he did not stand before. Since he is free to refrain from creation, God could have never stood in those relations, had he so willed. But in virtue of his creating a temporal world, God comes into a relation with that world the moment it springs into being. Thus, even if it is not the case that God is temporal prior to his creation of the world, he nonetheless undergoes an extrinsic change at the moment of creation that draws him into time in virtue of his real relation to the world. So even if God is timeless without creation, his free decision to create a temporal world also constitutes a free decision on his part to exist temporally.

The argument can be summarized as follows:

(22) God is creatively active in the temporal world.
(23) If God is creatively active in the temporal world, God is really related to the temporal world.

(24) If God is really related to the temporal world, God is temporal.

(25) Therefore, God is temporal.

This argument, if successful, does not prove that God is essentially temporal, but that if he is a creator of a temporal world—as he in fact is—then he is temporal.

One way to escape this argument is to deny (23). This might not appear to be a very promising strategy, since it seems obvious that God is related to his creatures insofar as he sustains them, knows them, and loves them. Remarkably, however, it was precisely this premise that medieval theologians such as Aquinas denied. Thomas agrees with (24). On his view, relational properties involving God and creatures, like God's *being Lord*, first begin to exist at the moment at which the creatures come into being (*ST* Ia q. 13 a. 7). Hence, if God stands in real relations to his creatures, he acquires those relational properties *de novo* at the moment of creation and thus undergoes change. And anything that changes, even extrinsically, must be in time. Thomas escapes the conclusion that God is therefore temporal by denying that God stands in any real relation to the world. Since God is absolutely simple, he stands in no relations to anything, for relations would introduce complexity into God's being. Aquinas holds, paradoxically, that while creatures are really related to God, God is not really related to creatures. The relation of God to creatures exists only in our minds, not in reality. On Aquinas's view, then, God undergoes no extrinsic change in creating the world. He just exists, and creation is creatures' coming into existence with a real relation to God of being caused by God.

This is certainly an extraordinary doctrine. Wholly apart from its reliance on divine simplicity, the doctrine of no real relations is very problematic. God's sustaining the world is a causal relation rooted in the active power and intrinsic properties of God as First Cause. Thus, to say the world is really related to God by the relation *is sustained by*, but that God is not really related to the world by the relation *is sustaining*, seems unintelligible. It is to say that one can have real effects without a real cause—which seems self-contradictory or incomprehensible.

Moreover, God is surely really related to his creatures in the following sense: in different possible worlds, God's will, knowledge, and love are different than they actually are. For example, if God had not chosen to create a universe at all, he would surely have a different will than that which he has (for he would not will to create the universe); he would know different truths than the ones he knows (for example, he would not know *The universe exists*); he would not love the same creatures he actually loves (since no creatures would exist). It is the implication of Aquinas's view, however, that God is perfectly similar in every possible world: he never wills differently, he never acts differently, he never knows differently, he never loves differently. Whether the world is empty or chock-full of creatures of every sort, there is no difference in God. But then it becomes unintelligible why this universe or any universe exists rather than just nothing. The reason cannot lie in God, for he is perfectly similar in all possible worlds. Nor can the reason lie in creatures, for we are asking for some explanation of their existence. Thus, on Aquinas's view there just is no reason for why this universe or any universe at all exists. Therefore, Aquinas's attempt to evade the present argument by denying (23) is implausible.

Recent defenders of timeless eternity have turned their guns on (24) instead. They have tried to craft theories of divine eternity that would permit God to be really related to the temporal world and yet to exist timelessly.

For example, Eleonore Stump and the late Norman Kretzmann attempted to craft a new simultaneity relation, which they believed would allow a timeless God to relate to his creation.[14] They propose to treat modes of existence as analogous to reference frames in STR and to construct a definition of ET-simultaneity in terms of two reference frames (timelessness and temporality) and two observers (one in eternity and one in time). Their basic idea is: take some eternal being x and some temporal being y. These two are ET-simultaneous just in case relative to some hypothetical observer in the eternal reference frame x is eternally present and y is observed as temporally present, and relative to some hypothetical observer in any temporal reference frame y is temporally present and x is observed as eternally present.[15]

On the basis of their definition of ET-simultaneity, Stump and Kretzmann believe themselves to have solved the problem of how a timeless being can be really related to a temporal world. For relative to the eternal reference frame, any temporal entity that exists at any time is observed to be present, and relative to any moment of time God is observed to be present. The metaphysical relativity postulated by ET-simultaneity implies that all events are present to God in eternity and therefore open to his timeless causal influence. Every action of God is ET-simultaneous with its temporal effect.

Unfortunately, as many critics have pointed out, the language of observation employed in the definition is wholly obscure.[16] In STR very specific physical content is given to the notion of observation through Einstein's operational definitions of distant simultaneity. But in the definition of ET-simultaneity, no hint is given as to what is meant, for example, by x's being observed as eternally present relative to some moment of time. In the absence of any procedure for determining ET-simultaneity, the definition reduces to the assertion that relative to the reference frame of eternity x is eternally present and y is temporally present and that relative to some temporal reference frame y is temporally present and x is eternally present—which is only a restatement of the problem! Worse, if y is temporally present to God, then God and y are not ET-simultaneous at all, but temporally simultaneous. Thus, God would be temporally simultaneous with every temporal event, which is to sacrifice divine timelessness.

To their credit, Stump and Kretzmann later revised their definition of ET-simultaneity so as to free it from observation language.[17] Basically, their new account tries to define ET-simultaneity in terms of causal relations. On the new definition, x and y are ET-simultaneous just in case relative to an observer in the eternal reference frame, x is eternally present and y is temporally present, and the observer can enter into direct causal relations with both x and y; and relative to an observer in any temporal reference frame, x is eternally present and y is at the same time as the observer, and the observer can enter into direct causal relations with both x and y.

The fundamental problem with this new account of ET-simultaneity is that it is viciously circular. For ET-simultaneity was originally invoked to explain how a timeless God could be causally active in time; but now ET-simultaneity is defined in terms of a timeless being's ability to be causally active in time. Our original problem was to explain how God could be both timeless and yet creatively active in the world. That is hardly explained by saying that a timeless God is ET-simultaneous with his effects in time and then defining ET-simultaneity in terms of the ability of a timeless being to be causally related to temporal effects. This amounts to saying that God can be causally active in time because he can be causally active in time. Since their first definition was explanatorily vacuous and their second definition viciously circular, Stump and Kretzmann must be judged to have failed in their attempt to undercut (24).

Leftow has offered a different account of divine eternity in order to refute (24).[18] On the Stump–Kretzmann model, there is no common reference frame or mode of existence shared by timeless and temporal beings. As a result, Stump and Kretzmann were unable to explain how such beings could be causally related. The essence of Leftow's proposal is to remedy this defect by maintaining that temporal beings do exist in eternity; they share God's mode of existence and so can be causally related to God. But, he insists, this does not imply that time or temporal existence is illusory, for temporal beings also have a temporal mode of existence.

How can it be shown that temporal beings exist in timeless eternity? Leftow's argument is based on three theses:

(I)   The distance between God and everything in space is zero.
(II) Spatial things do not change in any way unless there is a change of place (a motion involving a material thing).
(III) If something is in time, it is also in space.

On the basis of these theses Leftow argues as follows: there can be no change of place relative to God because the distance between God and everything in space is zero. But if there is no change of place relative to God, there can be no change of any sort on the part of spatial things relative to God. Moreover, since anything that is temporal is also spatial, it follows that there are no temporal, non-spatial beings. The only temporal beings there are exist in space, and none of these changes relative to God. Assuming, then, some relational view of time, it follows that all temporal beings exist timelessly relative to God. Thus, relative to God all things are timelessly present and so can be causally related to God.

The problem with this reasoning is that all three of its foundational theses seem false, some obviously so. (I), for example, rests pretty obviously on a category mistake. When we say that there is no distance between God and creatures, we do not mean that there is a distance and its measure is zero. Rather we mean that the category of distance does not even apply to the relations between a non-spatial being such as God and things in space. What about (II)? This thesis is false if time is 'tensed'. For then spatial things can change even if there is no spatial motion by changing in their temporal properties. For example, some spatial object can change by being one year old and then becoming two years old, even if no change of place has occurred. Even most relationalists are today willing to admit that time can go on during periods of spatial changelessness. So even if the entire universe were frozen into immobility, there would still be change relative to God, namely, change of temporal properties. Thus, if time is tensed—and Leftow allows that may be—then his theory is nullified. Finally, consider (III). Leftow needs this thesis, lest someone say that there are non-spatial, temporal beings such as angels that are changing relative to God. Such beings would (on Leftow's analysis) have a zero distance from God and yet not be changeless relative to God. Thus, they would not exist in eternity. So in order to sustain his claim that temporal beings exist in eternity, Leftow has to get rid of such beings. But we have every reason to reject this radical thesis. Even in the absence of a physical universe, God could choose to entertain a succession of thoughts or to create an angelic being that experiences a stream of consciousness, and such a series of mental events alone is sufficient for such entities' being in time. Thus, all Leftow's key theses are at least dubious, if not clearly false. We have little choice but to conclude that he has given no good grounds for thinking that temporal beings exist in timeless eternity.

In summary, it seems that we have here a powerful argument for divine temporality. Classical attempts such as Aquinas's to deny that God is really related to the world and contemporary attempts such as those of Stump, Kretzmann, and Leftow to deny that God's real relation to the world involves him in time all appear in the end to be less plausible than the premises of the argument itself.

Argument from Divine Knowledge of Tensed Facts

We have seen that God's action in the temporal world gives us good grounds for concluding God to be temporal in view of the extrinsic change he undergoes through his changing relations with the world. But the existence of a temporal world also seems to entail intrinsic change in God in view of his knowledge of what is happening in the temporal world. For since what is happening in the world is in constant flux, so also must God's knowledge be in constant flux. Defenders of divine temporality have argued that a timeless God cannot know certain tensed facts about the world—for example, what is happening now—and therefore, since God is omniscient, he must be temporal.

We can formulate the argument as follows:

(26) A temporal world exists.

(27) God is omniscient.

(28) If a temporal world exists, then if God is omniscient, God knows tensed facts.

(29) If God is timeless, he does not know tensed facts.

(30) Therefore, God is not timeless.

Again, this argument does not prove that God is essentially temporal, but, if successful, it does show that if a temporal world exists, then God is temporal.

Defenders of divine timelessness have attempted to refute this argument either by arguing that a timeless God can know tensed facts or by arguing that God may still qualify as omniscient even if he is ignorant of tensed facts.

Let us look first at the plausibility of denying (29). Can a timeless God know tensed facts? Although Jonathan Kvanvig, Edward Wierenga, and Leftow have all argued that God can know the facts expressed by tensed sentences, an analysis of their respective positions reveals that in the end they all embrace the view that the factual content expressed by tensed sentences is tenseless.[19] Despite first appearances to the contrary, they all accept the truth of (29). Kvanvig, Wierenga, and Leftow's accounts are the most sophisticated attempts to explain how a timeless God can know the facts expressed by tensed sentences, yet they all finally deny that God knows tensed facts. Thus, (29) seems secure.

Defenders of divine timelessness have no recourse, then, but to deny (28). They must deny that omniscience entails a knowledge of tensed facts. They can do this either by revising the traditional definition of omniscience or else by maintaining that tense, while an objective feature of time, does not strictly belong to the factual content expressed by tensed sentences. Let us examine each strategy in turn.

The general problem with the strategy of revising the traditional definition of omniscience is that any adequate definition of a concept must be in line with our intuitive understanding of that concept. We are not free simply to 'cook' the definition just to solve some problem under discussion. According to the traditional definition, a person S is omniscient if and only if, for every fact, S knows that fact and does not believe its contradictory. On such a definition, if there are tensed facts, an omniscient person must know them. What plausible alternative definition of omniscience might the defender of divine timelessness offer?

Wierenga offers a revised account of omniscience that would not require an omniscient person to know tensed facts. Some facts, he says, are facts only from a particular perspective. They must be known to an omniscient being only if he shares that particular perspective. Thus, a person is omniscient if and only if, for every fact and every perspective, if something is a fact from a certain perspective, then that person must know that it is a fact from that perspective, and if he shares that perspective, then he must know the fact in question. Wierenga treats moments of time as perspectives relative to which tensed facts exist. So while a temporal person existing on 8 December 1941 must (if he is omniscient) know the fact *Yesterday the Japanese attacked Pearl Harbor,* a timeless person must know only that from the perspective of 8 December 1941, it is a fact that *Yesterday the Japanese attacked Pearl Harbor.* On this definition God's being omniscient does not require that he know the tensed fact, but only the tenseless fact that from a certain perspective a certain tensed fact exists.

Wierenga's revised definition of omniscience seems to be unacceptably cooked. Wierenga is not denying that there are tensed facts. Rather he wants to allow that there really are tensed facts but to maintain that an omniscient being need not know them. This claim seems quite implausible. On Wierenga's view temporal persons know an incalculable multitude of facts about the world of which a supposedly omniscient being is ignorant. Temporal persons know that the Japanese attack on Pearl Harbor is over; God has no idea whether it has occurred or not. Since he does not know what time it actually is, he does not know any tensed facts. This is an unacceptably limited field of knowledge to qualify as omniscience.

Leftow also entertains the idea of revising the definition of omniscience in such a way that omniscience does not entail knowledge of all truths. He argues, in effect, that there are many sorts of truths that God cannot know, so there is no harm in admitting one more class of truths (namely, tensed truths) of which God is ignorant. But, again, such a consideration should not affect the definition of 'omniscience' as such. Besides, should it turn out that there are truths God cannot know, that is no reason for further eroding the extent of his knowledge by denying him knowledge of tensed truths. In any case, does Leftow succeed in showing that there are truths which God cannot know? It seems not. His examples of things God cannot know include how it feels to be oneself a failure or a sinner. But Leftow has confused *knowing how* with *knowing that. Knowing how* does not take truths as its object. God can know such truths as *Being a failure feels lousy, Sinners feel guilty and hopeless,* and so on. God's not knowing how it feels to be himself a failure or a sinner is not an example of truths he fails to know and so does not constitute a restriction on his omniscience. Leftow furnishes no example of any truth which might be conjoined with 'knows that' such that we cannot say, 'God knows that—,' where the blank is filled by the truth in question. Therefore, he has not adequately motivated denying that knowledge of tensed truths properly belongs to omniscience.

It seems, therefore, that no adequate grounds have been given for thinking that someone could be omniscient and yet not know tensed truths. The traditional definition of omniscience requires it, and we have no grounds that do not involve special pleading for revising the usual definition.

So what about the second strategy for denying (28), namely, maintaining that tense does not, strictly speaking, belong to the factual content expressed by tensed sentences, even though tense is an objective feature of the world? Tense might be analyzed as a feature of the mode in which the factual content is presented to someone expressing it, or of the way in which a person grasps the factual content, or of the context of someone's believing the factual content. Alternatively, tense could be understood in terms of a person's ascribing to himself in a present-tense way the property of being such as the factual content expressed by the sentence specifies. On such analyses, an omniscient being could be timeless because omniscience is traditionally defined in terms of factual knowledge and tense is not part of the factual content of tensed sentences. Tense is an objective feature of the world, but since it does not belong to the factual content of a sentence, a being which knew only tenseless facts could on the traditional definition count as omniscient.

Even though such analyses are plausible and attractive, they do not ultimately save the day for the defender of divine timelessness. For as the greatest conceivable being, God is not merely factually omniscient, but also maximally excellent cognitively. On the theories under discussion a merely factually omniscient God would know such things as *God is omnipotent, God loves his creatures, God created the universe*, and so on. But he would not have to possess any first-person indexical beliefs such as 'I am omnipotent', 'I love my creatures', 'I created the universe', and so forth. A machine could count as omniscient under such analyses. But such a God or machine would clearly not have maximum cognitive excellence. In order to qualify as maximally excellent cognitively, God would have to entertain all and only the appropriate, true first-person beliefs about himself. This would furnish him with knowledge *de se* (first-person self-knowledge) in addition to mere knowledge *de re* (knowledge of a thing from a third-person perspective). In order to be maximally excellent cognitively, God would not have to possess all knowledge *de se* in the world, but only such knowledge *de se* as is appropriate to himself. It would be a cognitive defect, not a perfection, for God to have the belief 'I am Napoleon', though for Napoleon such a belief would be a perfection. The point is that omniscience (on these theories) is not enough for perfect-being theology; God must be maximally excellent cognitively.

Now in the same way, it is a cognitive perfection to know what time it is, what is actually happening in the universe. A being whose knowledge is composed exclusively of tenseless facts is less excellent cognitively than a being who also knows what has occurred, what is occurring, and what will occur in the world. This latter person knows infinitely more than the former and is involved in no cognitive defect in so knowing. On the analogy of knowledge *de se*, we can refer to such knowledge as knowledge *de praesenti* (knowledge of the present). A being that lacks such knowledge is more ignorant and less excellent cognitively than a being that possesses it. Therefore, if we adopt views according to which tense is extraneous to the factual content expressed by a tensed sentence, we should simply revise premise (28) to read

(28′) If a temporal world exists, then if God is maximally excellent cognitively, then God has knowledge *de praesenti*

and, with appropriate revisions, the argument goes through as before.

The attempt to deny (28) thus seems to fare no better than the effort to refute (29). If God is omniscient, then given the existence of a temporal world, he cannot be ignorant of tensed facts. It follows that God is not timeless, which is to say, he is temporal. So in addition to the argument from divine action in the world, we now have a second powerful argument based on God's changing knowledge of tensed facts for thinking that God is in time.

ETERNITY AND THE NATURE OF TIME

On the basis of our foregoing discussion, we have seen comparatively weak grounds for affirming divine timelessness but two powerful arguments in favor of divine temporality. It would seem, then, that we should conclude that God is temporal. But such a conclusion would be premature. For there does remain one way of escape still open for defenders of divine timelessness. The argument based on God's action in the world assumed the objective reality of temporal becoming, and the argument based on God's knowledge of the temporal world assumed the objective reality of tensed facts. If one denies the objective reality of temporal becoming and tensed facts, then the arguments are undercut. For in that case, nothing to which God is related ever comes into or passes out of being, and all facts exist tenselessly, so that God undergoes neither extrinsic nor intrinsic change. He can be the immutable, omniscient Sustainer and Knower of all things and, hence, exist timelessly.

In short, the defender of divine timelessness can escape the arguments for divine temporality by embracing the tenseless theory of time. It is noteworthy, however, that almost no defender of divine timelessness has taken this route. Virtually the only proponent of timeless eternity to embrace consciously the tenseless theory of time in defending God's timelessness is Paul Helm.[20]

It seems, then, that in order to adjudicate the question of the nature of divine eternity and God's relationship to time, philosophical theologians have no choice but to grapple with a further question, one of the most profound and controverted issues of metaphysics: is time tensed or tenseless? This is difficult and mysterious territory. But we have no choice: if we are to understand eternity, we must first understand time.

Notes

1. For an analysis of what it means to be permanent, see Brian Leftow, *Time and Eternity*, Cornell Studies in the Philosophy of Religion (Ithaca: Cornell University Press, 1991), 133; cf. Quentin Smith, 'A New Typology of Temporal and Atemporal Permanence', *Noûs* 23 (1989), 307–30. According to Leftow an entity is permanent if and only if it exists and has no first or last finite period of existence, and there are no moments before or after it exists.

2. James Barr, *Biblical Words for Time* (London: SCM, 1962), 149.

3. An intrinsic change is a non-relational change, involving only the subject. For example, an apple changes from green to red. An extrinsic change is a relational change, involving something else in relation to which the subject changes. For example, a man becomes shorter than his son, not by undergoing an intrinsic change in his own height, but by being related to his son as his son undergoes intrinsic change in his height.

4. See discussion in Thomas V. Morris, *Anselmian Explorations* (Notre Dame: University of Notre Dame Press, 1987), 98–123; Christopher Hughes, *On a Complex Theory of a Simple God*, Cornell Studies in Philosophy of Religion (Ithaca: Cornell University Press, 1989).

5. I take for granted that there are contingent events such as human free acts; see Ch. 12 in this volume on divine providence. See also my *The Only Wise God: The Compatibility of Divine Foreknowledge and Human Freedom* (Grand Rapids: Baker Bookhouse, 1987).

6. See my *The Tenseless Theory of Time: A Critical Examination*, Synthese Library 294 (Dordrecht: Kluwer Academic, 2000).

7. Notice, however, that if we think of statements or facts as within God's perceptual purview, then even on a perceptualist model, God must know the future, so long as the Principle of Bivalence holds for future-tense statements. For he perceives which future-tense statements presently have the property of truth inhering in them or which future-tense facts presently exist. Thus, by means of his perception of presently existing realities he knows the truth about the future.

8. See especially Gerald J. Holton, 'Mach, Einstein and the Search for Reality', in *Ernst Mach: Physicist and Philosopher*, Boston Studies in the Philosophy of Science 6 (Dordrecht: D. Reidel, 1970), 165–99; id., 'Where Is Reality? The Answers of Einstein', in *Science and Synthesis,* ed. UNESCO (Berlin: Springer-Verlag, 1971), 45–69; and the essays collected together in id., *Thematic Origins of Scientific Thought* (Cambridge: Harvard University Press). See also Lawrence Sklar, 'Time, Reality, and Relativity', in Richard Healey (ed.), *Reduction, Time and Reality* (Cambridge: Cambridge University Press, 1981), 141.

9. Verificationism proposed a criterion of meaning that was so restrictive that it would consign vast tracts of apparently perfectly intelligible discourse to the trash heap of

nonsense; moreover, the criterion seemed to be self-refuting. See the excellent discussion in Frederick Suppe, 'The Search for Philosophical Understanding of Scientific Theories', in id. (ed.), *The Structure of Scientific Theories*, 2nd edn. (Urbana: University of Illinois Press, 1977), 3–118.

10. Unless there exists a multiverse in which our observable universe is but one domain, in which case God exists in the global time of the multiverse.

11. Cosmic time is related to the local times of a special group of observers called 'fundamental observers'. These are hypothetical observers, associated with the galaxies, who are at rest with respect to the expansion of space itself. As the expansion of space proceeds, each fundamental observer remains in the same place, though his spatial separation from fellow fundamental observers increases. Cosmic time relates to these observers in that their local times all coincide with cosmic time in their vicinity. Because of their mutual recession, the class of fundamental observers does not serve to define a global inertial frame, technically speaking, even though all of them are at rest. But since each fundamental observer is at rest with respect to space, the events he calculates to be simultaneous will coincide locally with the events that are simultaneous in cosmic time. One could say that God exists in the time of the inertial frame of every fundamental observer; but then there is no problem, since all their local times fuse into one cosmic time.

12. See the very interesting piece by R. W. Hepburn, 'Time-Transcendence and Some Related Phenomena in the Arts', in H. D. Lewis (ed.), *Contemporary British Philosophy*, 4th series, Muirhead Library of Philosophy (London: George Allen & Unwin, 1976), 152–73.

13. Robert C. Coburn, 'Professor Malcolm on God', *Australasian Journal of Philosophy* 41 (1963), 155.

14. Eleonore Stump and Norman Kretzmann, 'Eternity', *Journal of Philosophy* 78 (1981), 429–58.

15. A word of clarification: by 'eternal' Stump and Kretzmann mean 'timeless', and by 'temporal reference frame' they mean 'moment of time'. It is also worth noting that this definition is not really analogous to simultaneity in STR at all. A better analogy would be to say that x and y are ET-simultaneous just in case they both exist at the same eternal present relative to the eternal reference frame and both exist at the same moment of time relative to the temporal reference frame. But then God would be temporal relative to our mode of existence, which Stump and Kretzmann do not want to say.

16. Stephen T. Davis, *Logic and the Nature of God* (Grand Rapids: Wm. B. Eerdmans, 1983), 20; Delmas Lewis, 'Eternity Again: A Reply to Stump and Kretzmann', *International Journal for Philosophy of Religion* 15 (1984), 74–6; Paul Helm, *Eternal God* (Oxford: Clarendon, 1988), 32–3; William Hasker, *God, Time, and Knowledge* (Ithaca: Cornell University Press, 1989), 164–6; John C. Yates, *The Timelessness of God* (Lanham: University Press of America, 1990), 128–30; Brian Leftow, *Time and Eternity*, Cornell Studies in Philosophy of Religion (Ithaca: Cornell University Press, 1991), 170–2; Garrett J. DeWeese, *God and the Nature of Time*, Ashgate Philosophy of Religion Series (Aldershot: Ashgate, 2004), 164.

17. Eleonore Stump and Norman Kretzmann, 'Eternity, Awareness, and Action', *Faith and Philosophy* 9 (1992), 477–8.

18. Brian Leftow, 'Eternity and Simultaneity', *Faith and Philosophy* 8 (1991), 148–79; cf. id., *Time and Eternity*, ch. 10.

19. Jonathan L. Kvanvig, *The Possibility of an All-Knowing God* (New York: St Martin's, 1986), 150–65; Edward R. Wierenga, *The Nature of God: An Inquiry into Divine Attributes*, Cornell Studies in Philosophy of Religion (Ithaca: Cornell University Press, 1989), 179–85; Leftow, *Time and Eternity*, 312–37. See also Jonathan L. Kvanvig, 'Omniscience and Eternity: A Reply to Craig', *Faith and Philosophy* 18 (2003), 369–76; Edward R. Wierenga, 'Omniscience and Time, One More Time: A Reply to Craig', *Faith and Philosophy* 21 (2004), 90–7.

20. Paul Helm, 'Eternal Creation: The Doctrine of the Two Standpoints', in Colin Gunton (ed.), *The Doctrine of Creation* (Edinburgh: T. & T. Clark, 1997), 42–3; Helm, *Eternal God*, 25–7, 44, 47, 52, 79.

CHAPTER 8

....

OMNIPOTENCE

....

BRIAN LEFTOW

THE doctrine that God is omnipotent takes its rise from Scriptural texts:

Lord . . . nothing is too hard for you.   (Jer. 32: 17)

Our God is in heaven; He does whatever pleases Him.   (Ps. 115: 3, 135: 6)

the Lord . . . can do all things.   (Job 42: 2)

nothing is impossible with God.   (Luke 1: 37)

with God all things are possible.   (Matt. 19: 26).

These texts concern two linked topics. One is how much power God has to put behind actions: enough that nothing is too hard, enough to do whatever he pleases. Let's call this 'how strong God is'.[1] The other is how much God can do: 'all things'. The link is obvious: we measure strength by what tasks it is adequate to perform, and God is so strong he can do all things. There are two distinct topics here because strength does not consist in or entail abilities to accomplish tasks. I might be physically and mentally strong enough to win a chess match, but be unable to do so because I do not know the rules or have not practiced. I might be strong enough to lift a skunk, but unable because an allergic reaction causes me to pass out when I get within range. Again, two people might be able to accomplish the same tasks; if one does them easily and the other strains to equal the first, there is a difference between them, which intuitively does not consist in the range of tasks they are able to perform.[2]

The Christian philosophical theologian who seeks to explicate omnipotence seeks a convincing account of the reality beneath the 'phenomena' of Scripture. I now look briefly at some historic accounts of omnipotence. It emerges that the early history of the concept emphasized strength more than range of action, with range coming to prominence in Aquinas's day. I next consider three recent attempts to define omnipotence. I find them all wanting, but draw morals that help me hazard my own definition. Treatments of omnipotence typically test such definitions against putative problem cases, but space restrictions force me to forgo this for the present.

OMNIPOTENCE: EARLY ACCOUNTS

Some Patristic writers treat omnipotence simply as power over all things. So Cyril of Jerusalem (c.315–86): 'he is almighty who rules all things, who has power over all things.'[3] Origen (185–254) went so far as to argue that 'God cannot be...omnipotent unless there exist those over whom He may exercise His power; and therefore, that God may be...almighty, it is necessary that all things should exist.'[4] The eternity of some world or other, then, followed from the claim that God is eternally omnipotent. One could avoid this by treating omnipotence as the disposition to have power over whatever else exists. Surprisingly, Origen saw it as conceivable or even possible for there to be too many things for God to have power over: God 'made creatures according to some definite number...creatures have...a limit, because where there is no limit there can be neither any comprehension nor any limitation. Now if this were the case...created things could neither be restrained nor administered by God.'[5] To be omnipotent, then, is to have enough power (strength) to control all other things. Augustine (354–430) wrote that God 'does whatever He wills: that is omnipotence.'[6] Swinburne recently echoed this: 'God is omnipotent in that whatever he chooses to do, he succeeds in doing.'[7] There are problems here. On this account, even a rather weak being could come out omnipotent by carefully choosing to do only things at which it was guaranteed to succeed. Perhaps what's intended is that an omnipotent being is incapable of choosing to bring something about and failing to do so, but then a being able to choose to bring about only one thing, but guaranteed to bring it about if it does, would come out omnipotent. Again, nothing would seem to stop an ill-informed omnipotent being from choosing to do something it is metaphysically impossible to do.

Augustine often discusses the paradox that a God who 'can do all things' can't do some things we can do. He writes that God

is omnipotent to make all things He may have willed to make. [But] He cannot die [or] sin [or] deceive [or] be deceived...were He able to do these, He would not be omnipotent.[8]

Neither is His power diminished when we say that He cannot die or [err]—for this is in such a way impossible to Him, that if it were possible for Him, He would be of less power.

But…He is rightly called omnipotent though He can neither die nor [err]. For He is called omnipotent on account of His doing what He wills, not on account of His suffering what He wills not; for if that should befall Him, He would by no means be omnipotent. Wherefore He cannot do something for the very reason that He is omnipotent.[9]

The inabilities come from Scripture, which tells us that God is immortal (1 Tim. 6: 16), omniscient about what we do and think (Ps. 139), and cannot be so much as tempted to do evil (Jas. 1: 13). Augustine tries to rationalize these. I suggest that he is working with a strength account in these passages. He probably has such thoughts as these in the background: *ceteris paribus*, no one wants to err. No one perfectly rational and informed whose existence would on balance be worth continuing would want to die. No one all-good would want to sin or deceive. The only question for someone with God's other attributes, then, is whether he has strength enough to have what he wants and not get what he does not want. Given God's other traits, only a lack of power could explain his sinning, erring, etc., and so these are 'in such a way impossible to Him, that if (they) were possible for Him, he would be of less power'. So God is of maximal strength, Augustine may think, only if he is so far from having these befall him that they literally cannot happen to him. The tie to strength became clearer when Anselm (1033–1109) reworked Augustine in *Proslogion* 7:

He who can do these things [be corrupted, lie, etc.] can do what is not good for himself and what he ought not to do. And the more he can do these things…the less power he has against…adversity and perversity. He, therefore, who can do such things, can do them not by power but by impotence.[10]

With the strength-notion (and other texts of Augustine) in mind, Peter Lombard (1095/1100–1160) made it a 'sign' of omnipotence that God can suffer nothing and cannot be impeded when he acts.[11] In his *Sentences*, which became the standard theological textbook till the 1300s, Lombard wrote that God is omnipotent because he 'can do all things being able to do which belongs to power',[12] having previously suggested along Augustine's line that lying, sinning, dying, failing, being defeated, and being miserable are things 'ability' to do which is really a matter of impotence, not power. William of Auxerre (1140–1231)—a household name then as now—wrote that 'God is omnipotent because He can do from Himself and through Himself whatever He wills to do. By "whatever" is understood a fullness which is not determined to some particular effect…"from Himself and through Himself" removes need of extrinsic helps, and compulsion, and extrinsic impediment.'[13] 'Whatever He wills to do' harks back to Augustine. Here the note of strength predominates, though the account of 'whatever' tries to suggest at least that God can do other than he in fact does.[14] The denial of extrinsic impediment, present also in Lombard, becomes important below.

The *Summa Theologiae* of Thomas Aquinas (1224–74) took over from the *Sentences* as standard textbook. There we find an influential range-centered account. Philosophers tend to misread it, likely by focusing only on the paragraph in which

Thomas states it and ignoring his explications, arguments, and qualifications else-where. With these taken into account, his definition turns out to be that

God is omnipotent at t = df. God can bring about all states of affairs that can be produced at t,[15]

where something can be produced at t only if its being produced is compatible with there having been the past there actually has been.[16] Thomas provides a reasonable gloss on the scriptural texts. It's not true that 'all things are possible' with God—God can't make round squares. Rather, Aquinas suggests, all products that *are* producible as of t are 'possible with God'—God has power enough to actualize the whole range of the producible, whatever that is. Aquinas pushes the strength-notion to explain certain apparent lacks of ability, writing that God can't be moved because this would imply lack of power, and so can't walk: thus suggesting that God can't walk because he is omnipotent.[17] This might suggest that one walks because one lacks the power to stay still. But Aquinas's thought may instead be that being omnipresent, God has no place to go—he already is everywhere. Thomas cashes out the claim that God is everywhere *inter alia* in terms of his having complete power over all places and their contents.[18] If this is correct, God could move—be first only in some places and then only in others—only due to a lack of power. Walking is an issue because God is omnipotent (and so, we'd think, can walk) but lacks a body (and so can't). Yet walking is actually an easy case to handle. Either it is or it is not absolutely possible that God take on a body. If it is, he has the power to walk, even if he currently lacks a body. One has the power to walk if (so to speak) one can just will it and be walking—if walking is just a volition away.[19] For God, this is so—but the volition would be to make a walking body and be incarnate in it mid-stride. If it is not absolutely possible that God take on a body, being unable to walk doesn't count against his omnipotence, as omnipotence doesn't require being able to bring about the impossible.[20]

Duns Scotus took Aquinas's definition to give a necessary but not sufficient condition of omnipotence: he added that something is omnipotent only if it can produce all that it can produce immediately rather than through some helping cause.[21] This built into the definition a claim from William of Ockham that Aquinas in fact held.[22] Ockham gives Aquinas's account in a *Quodlibet*,[23] and commits himself to Scotus's *addendum* in another.[24] Aquinas's definition as modified by Scotus and Ockham became the consensus medieval account of omnipotence, and has remained influential. Almost all recent attempts at definition continue its stress on range to the exclusion of strength, and most seek to hew closely to it.[25] To see what the consensus medieval account comes to, and whether it is viable, I now turn to two recent attempts to define omnipotence which try merely to update it.

WIERENGA

Edward Wierenga's definition is that

> A being x is omnipotent in a world W at a time $t =_{df}$. (i) it is true in W that possibly x strongly actualizes some state of affairs at t, and (ii) it is true in W that for every state of affairs A, if it is possible that both there has been the initial segment of W up to t and x strongly actualizes A at t, then at t x can strongly actualize A.[26]

Wierenga does not define 'strongly actualizes', telling us only that if one causes a state of affairs to obtain, one strongly actualizes it.[27] Nor does he define 'initial segment', saying only that an initial segment of W up to t consists of all states of affairs in W that occur before t save those that depend in the wrong way on events after t (e.g. God's foreknowing them at t).[28] (i) seeks to keep things that cannot strongly actualize anything from trivially satisfying the definition. As Wierenga does not specify that one strongly actualizes A only if one directly, immediately causes A to obtain, this is Aquinas's account with one key difference: Aquinas's version of (ii) would have 'up to t and that there exist some y that strongly actualizes A at t ...' Aquinas does not say *by whom* A is to be strongly actualized.

In (ii), a quantifier within the scope of 'it is true in W' governs a free-variabled sentence, (it is possible that both there has been the initial segment of W up to t and x strongly actualizes A at t) $\supset$ (at t x can strongly actualize A).[29] As it occurs within the scope of 'it is true in W', this open sentence really amounts to

(1) (it is possible in W that both there has been the initial segment of W up to t and x strongly actualizes A at t) $\supset$ (at t in W x can strongly actualize A).

(1)'s antecedent asserts that in W there is a possible world in which there has been the initial segment of W up to t and x strongly actualizes A at t. We might read (1)'s consequent in three ways:

(a) as that at t in W there is a possible world with W's initial segment up to t in which x strongly actualizes A. So read, (1)'s consequent is identical with (1)'s antecedent, save for asserting that this world is possible in W at one particular time. Most would see this difference as vacuous, as most would think that what is metaphysically possible in a world does not vary over the course of its history. So on this reading, (ii) is vacuous.

(b) as that at t in W there is a possible world in which x strongly actualizes A. But this would be true if there were a world with an initial segment other than W's in which x does A at t. This wouldn't entail that x was able to do A in a world with W's initial segment—e.g. W itself. It would entail that at t in W, x could have strongly actualized A, not that x can. If there is a state of affairs S x could have strongly actualized but cannot, x is less powerful than x might be, unless gaining the power to actualize S would have cost x an at least equivalent amount of power. But there is no reason to expect this to be true in general, and if there is one state of affairs x could have actualized for which it is not true, x has less power than x might. Nothing with less than its greatest possible power is omnipotent. So on this reading, (ii) is arguably not sufficient for omnipotence at t in W.

(c) as involving a thicker notion than the modal '◇', a primitive power-locution, entailing not that in some possible world x does, but that in the world under discussion x has the power to bring about. On this reading (i) doesn't after all keep things that can't strongly actualize anything from satisfying the definition: for then it could be true both that possibly x strongly actualizes some state of affairs at t and that x can't—i.e. lacks the power to—actualize anything at t in W.[30]

Wierenga's clause (ii) also faces McEar problems.[31] McEar is essentially able only to scratch his left ear. As McEar has this ability essentially, if McEar exists at t in W, he satisfies (i). As this is McEar's only possible action, if he can do it at t in W, he also satisfies (ii). But if McEar has this ability essentially, he can scratch his ear at t in W. So on Wierenga's account, McEar is omnipotent. Wierenga sees the difficulty, and replies that if someone can scratch his ear, then he can also do indefinitely many other things—move his arm, move his hand, scratch his ear at t, from t to t*, etc.—and so McEar isn't a possible being.[32] But to make it clear that McEar is possible, we need only adjust his description: he's essentially unable to accomplish anything save as part of or as a logical consequence of scratching his ear.[33] Wierenga adds a general doubt about essential limitations: surely, he suggests, for any agent who lacks certain abilities, it is possible that God give it those abilities.[34] But the general doubt can be resisted. If some agents have non-trivial essential properties (that is, essential properties other than those like being self-identical or a being that are shared with all possible things), and even one of these essential properties entails the lack of some power, there *are* essentially limited agents. I shortly suggest it to be plausible that both premises are true, but first I must note that for Christians, at least, problems crop up here from an unexpected direction.

Christians believe that one human, Jesus, was also divine. The orthodox Chalcedonian view has been that this entails that one human was omnipotent; those with this sort of Christology, then, can't claim that being human is incompatible with being omnipotent, and so, one might think, can't say that being human entails the lack of any power whatsoever. Further, the same will hold for any nature God the Son might have taken on. However, even if being human is compatible with being omnipotent, it does not follow that just any human could have been omnipotent. In fact, no human not actually assumed by a divine Person could have been. For God is no body-snatcher. But had God the Son taken over the body and soul that would otherwise have been mine to make himself human, he would in effect have stolen my natural endowment. Further, actual humans are actually substances. Jesus' body and soul do not on their own constitute a substance. They are not independent existents; they exist only as adjuncts supported in being by the substance who is God the Son. It is implausible that being a substance is a contingent property—that something that is a substance could have failed to be one. If this is correct, one can't use the Incarnation to argue against there actually being essentially limited agents: no actual human could have been omnipotent in virtue of having been the vehicle of a divine incarnation. One can see this more simply still: had my body and soul been used for the Incarnation, *I* would not have existed. The person in my body would have been not me, but God the Son. So God's becoming incarnate in my body and soul would not entail that *I* was omnipotent.

Again, one strand of Christianity might see the claim that some agents are essentially limited as controversial. Picking up on a few New Testament texts, Eastern Orthodoxy believes that salvation involves eventual 'deification'. Richard Swinburne approvingly interprets Maximus the Confessor's version of this as implying that the blessed in heaven become omniscient, omnipotent, and perfectly good.[35] But if God can make us so, the question arises of whether there are any sorts of agent he can't do this for: perhaps he could deify rabbits, frogs.... Be this as it may, much turns on how the idea of being made omnipotent is parsed out. A perfectly good God would not grant omnipotence without also granting sufficient knowledge and goodness to use it properly or else hemming in its use by a use of his own power: an omnipotent but evil, partly corrupt, or partly ignorant being left free to act as it pleased would be an evil too great to reconcile with God's existence. On a weak reading, becoming omnipotent could mean simply that God so reforms the blessed's characters and informs their knowledge that they no longer make prayers whose granting would in the long run go counter to the best good God has in mind, and God accordingly grants all their prayers: anything they choose to bring about in this way, they succeed in bringing about. *This* sort of 'becoming omnipotent' would be limited to things possibly with sufficient cognitive complexity to pray, and would leave any essential intrinsic limitations an agent had in place, since the agent's intrinsic powers would not be heightened one whit. And it is not in my view genuine omnipotence at all: the agents in question remain intrinsically of a sort to be frustrated by external limitations, and can succeed in what they do only by external help. True omnipotence, I suggest below, is not compatible with these things.

On a strong reading, being made omnipotent would mean being granted a new intrinsic property in virtue of which one henceforth has that much power.[36] Duns Scotus and others would argue that this is impossible—that there cannot be two such omnipotent beings—but I cannot delve into this here. Still, what could this intrinsic property be? Being omnipotent is a matter of having powers. One has powers in virtue of having an underlying categorical attribute which supports or subvenes them.[37] In God's case, the underlying categorical is deity. It is not clear or at all intuitive that any other underlying nature could support omnipotence. But to bestow a case of deity on a creature would be to make a created thing a God. It is plausibly part of the divine nature to be uncreated. I therefore suggest that God just cannot make another being intrinsically omnipotent. It follows that every non-divine nature essentially involves some limitation of power: even if there is no particular power such that the nature guarantees that the being bearing it lacks that one, the nature guarantees that there are some powers the being does not have. It follows further that for every non-divine being, there can be powers such that God cannot give that being those powers: if I were improved up to (so to speak) one power short of omnipotence, God couldn't give me that last power. Further, if I'm right in this last, every created being has at least the non-trivial essential property of being non-divine, and this suffices, as I've said, to involve essential limitation. But of course it's plausible that we have other, positive non-trivial essential properties. I am human. So while any chicken embryo has the ability to grow by natural processes into a chicken, I do not; while any cat has the ability to clean its own cat-fur, I do not. Plausibly I am essentially human; if I am, God can't give either ability to me. We can also generate essential limitations without substantive essentialism about non-world-indexed properties. I have not just abilities, but world-indexed abilities: if in W I can run, I also can-run-in-W. All world-indexed attributes are essential. Thus any world-indexed ability I lack, even God can't give me. Finally, Wierenga's claim, again, is that for any agent who lacks certain abilities, it is possible that God give it those abilities. But God, as we've seen, lacks abilities to die and err. If he is essentially eternal and omniscient, he cannot give himself these. Thus Wierenga's response fails, and on his definition, McEar is omnipotent.

Flint/Freddoso

Like Wierenga, Flint and Freddoso seek to explicate the consensus medieval account. They suggest that

(FF) S is omnipotent at t in W if and only if for any state of affairs p and world-type-for-S Ls such that p is not a member of Ls, if there is a world W^* such that

I Ls is true in both W and W^*, and

II W^* shares the same history with W at t, and

III at t in W^* someone actualizes p,

then S has the power at t in W to actualize p.[38]

A world-type is a set of subjunctive conditionals about how agents would freely act in various circumstances—'counterfactuals of freedom' (CFs) about those agents—such that for every CF P, either P or $\neg P$ is a member of the set.[39] A true world-type is one all of whose members are true. A world-type-for-S is a subset of a true world-type, containing only CFs about agents other than S.[40] Roughly, W and W^* share the same history at t just if they share all non-future-dependent states of affairs at t: that is, just if all that is and was the case at t in W which is not a consequence of what will be the case after t also is and was the case at t in W^*. So if world-types are non-future-dependent, as in standard Molinism, (I) is redundant. *Modulo* the introduction of world-types, this is Aquinas's account, with 'that can be produced' specified (in (III)) to 'that someone can produce'. I read 'someone' as 'at least one agent', on the assumption that it is the ordinary-language version of an existential quantifier.

Hoffman and Rosenkrantz offer the following counter-example to (FF). Consider possible worlds W and W^*, sharing the same history up to t, such that in W a contingently omnipotent being is omnipotent for the first time at t. In W^*, no omnipotent agent ever exists. So, they suggest, someone in W^* can bring it about at t that a ball rolls and no omnipotent being ever exists. But the omnipotent being in W can't bring this about at t. So (they conclude) there is an omnipotent being in W, and it can be the case that at t in W^* someone actualizes p, but it is false that the omnipotent being has at t in W the power to actualize p. Now they infer that someone in W^* brings it about that a ball rolls and no omnipotent being ever exists *via* the claim that

(HR)   if S brings about p, q obtains, and $\neg q$ is not in the power of anyone other than S, S brings it about that $(p \cdot q)$.[41]

But this principle is dubious. Booth brought it about that Lincoln no longer exists. One hundred years later, let's say, it came about uncaused that q, where $\neg q$ is necessarily uncaused. Is it plausible that 100 years after his own death, Booth brought it about that Lincoln no longer exists and q? If q was uncaused, it seems more plausible that this conjunction has no full cause: that nothing brought it about, though Booth brought about one conjunct. According to Duns Scotus, God brought it about that $2 + 2 = 4$, but bringing about the opposite was and is in no one's power. Suppose for the nonce that Scotus was right. On (HR), it would then follow that Booth brought it about that Lincoln no longer exists and $2 + 2 = 4$. But this would be false were Scotus correct: the cause of a conjunctive state of affairs both of whose conjuncts are caused is the composite consisting of their causes. Again, suppose we live in a physically deterministic universe. Then it obtains (say) that I will eat eggs for breakfast tomorrow, and the opposite is in no one's power, even God's. (Were God able to bring about the opposite, it would not be the case that given the past (which includes the physical laws' obtaining) there is just one physically possible future, and so the universe would not be physically deterministic.) Then on (HR), Booth brought it about that Lincoln no longer exists and I will eat eggs. But Booth would have had no effect on my breakfast at all, at any time; again, the cause of this conjunctive state of affairs is the composite of the conjuncts' causes. So I take it that (HR) is false, and the example fails.

Oppy offers the following counterexamples to (FF):

> Consider the conjunctive state of affairs *the cat comes in and if Jones were in C at t, he would freely decide at t to let out the dog*...suppose now that S is omnipotent. Since [this] state of affairs...does not belong to Ls, it follows from (FF) that an omnipotent being can bring (it) about...though it cannot bring about one of the conjuncts...consider...the disjunctive state of affairs *if Jones were in C at t, he would freely decide at t to let out the dog or if Jones were in C at t, he would freely decide at t to go to the bathroom*...(this) does not belong to Ls, and so it follows from (FF) that an omnipotent being can bring [it] about...even though (it) can bring about neither of the disjuncts. Not good.[42]

The first is a problem given the falsity of (HR), for this suggests that something can bring about a conjunctive state of affairs only by bringing about both conjuncts or something relevantly like bringing about both conjuncts.[43] One can address both by asking how CFs get included in a true world-type. In standard counterfactual logics, if $p \cdot q$, then $p > q$. So it seems that by making $p \cdot q$ true, one makes it true that $p > q$. Flint and Freddoso allow this in the case of CFs at one point:

> Any free being will have some say in determining which world-type is true...since Jones is free to decide whether...to write...to his wife, it is up to him whether the true world-type includes (that) if Jones were in C at t, he would freely decide at t to (write) to his wife...However, the vast majority of the counterfactuals which go to make up a world-type relate to beings other than Jones, and Jones...is powerless to make such counterfactuals true or false.[44]

Flint and Freddoso deny that anyone other than Jones can affect the truth-value of a CF about Jones.[45] But they also allow that 'a person's power is...in large measure...his ability to influence the free actions of others...e.g. by restricting their options...or by persuading or dissuading them'.[46] If so, then if there *are* CFs about Jones, someone not Jones can bring it about that a CF about Jones is true. Let's distinguish complete from incomplete circumstances of a free choice. A complete circumstance of a free choice K is the entire history (in Flint and Freddoso's sense) of the world prior to t, plus those states of affairs obtaining at t whose obtaining in no way depends on what is freely chosen in K. If complete circumstances are sets of states of affairs, an incomplete circumstance for K is any non-empty subset of its complete circumstance. There are CFs for both complete and incomplete circumstances. Someone not Jones can bring it about that a CF for an incomplete circumstance is true. Let the incompleteness in the circumstance for K be that it excludes everything I do so to persuade Jones, not in C, that

(2) were Jones in C, he would freely do A.

Suppose I give Jones good reasons R to do A if in C. It is possible that he accept them voluntarily and freely. Perhaps, for instance, part of his reason to accept them is that he trusts me on certain matters, he would not accept them if he did not trust me, and his experience of me is such as to leave this trust an attitude he freely adopts. Again, if I give him evidence in favor of doing A in C, the strength of the evidence may not be such as to coerce (as it were) belief: he may be left with a decision about whether the reasons are good enough. Again, even if Jones is caused to form the belief that R are good reasons to do A, Jones is able not to adopt R and make them *his own* reasons to do A. He must consent at least implicitly to their influencing his action, rather than (say) stubbornly giving greater weight to reasons he had had against doing A, and this consent can only be voluntary. Suppose, then, that Jones freely accepts the reasons, nothing other than my giving them being relevant to his doing so, I do not cause him to do so, but given that he has accepted them, he now is such that (2) is true. Then the following seems a legitimate chain of full explanations: (2) is true because Jones freely accepted R, Jones freely accepted R because R seemed good to him, and R seemed good to him because I presented them persuasively. It seems to follow that (2) is true because I presented R persuasively: which is to say that in some appropriate sense of the term, I brought it about that (2) is true. This is not a case of strongly or weakly actualizing the truth of (2), as Flint and Freddoso define these terms, but their definitions do not exhaust all ways of bringing something about. Perhaps no one can bring it about that a CF for a complete circumstance is true—at any rate that's a further issue. But where C does not include the persuading, a persuader can affect what Jones would do in C. [47] Omnipotent beings can doubtless be very persuasive. So it is not the case, I submit, that an omnipotent being is unable to bring about the problem conjuncts and disjuncts.

Oppy raises a question for (III):

Suppose that S is omnipotent at t in W (and) leaving S aside...no agent in W...acting alone, can bring it about that p in any world W* that shares its history with W, but...a group of agents in W...acting together, can bring it about that p in...W*...Suppose (e.g.) that no human acting alone can bring...it about...that a particular car is raised one metre above the ground using nothing but human muscle power...but that there are groups of four people who (can). As things stand, (FF) would allow that S is omnipotent even if it cannot bring it about that this particular car is raised one metre above the ground using nothing but human muscle power. And this seems wrong. [48]

The thought is that (III) only requires someone omnipotent to be able to do what any one other agent can, not what groups of agents can. I'm not sure this reads (III) correctly. Many, I think, would render 'someone' in (III) as $(\exists x)(x$ actualizes ... $)$, which would in turn translate as 'at least one agent...' Further, something Flint and Freddoso say about strong actualization could help here. They first say that one who strongly actualizes it that P causally determines it that P, then add 'i.e. does something which in conjunction with other operative causal factors constitutes a sufficient causal condition for p's obtaining'. [49] The second permits that one who strongly actualizes it that P be only one causally contributing part of the sufficient causal condition, rather than on its own causally determining it that P. On this account, any one of the four humans can strongly actualize the car's rising etc., the other humans counting as 'other operative causal factors'. So a being able to do what any one other agent can do will be able to strongly actualize this too—even absent any other causal factors. And there are no states of affairs essentially able to be strongly actualized only by many agents: whatever one agent can actualize in conjunction with other agents, the one agent can in (FF)'s sense strongly actualize. Oppy has noted in correspondence that this creates a problem: we wind up saying that it is in an agent's power to strongly actualize it that P even if the agent requires significant help to do so—say, the help of 20 million other voters in electing a government—and this is a bit unintuitive. But only a bit: 'strongly actualizes' is an artificial, technical term, without an established sense to violate, and without this, it's not clear what intuitions we really have on the subject.

Still, there are more-than-exegetical points to make here. The humans don't move the car solely by muscle-power. Their moving the car also depends on non-muscular events such as the synaptic firings involved in executively intending to lift the car. If that's compatible with its being the case that human muscles supply the only lifting power involved, it's not clear why an omnipotent being's volition that four humans move the car by muscle-power alone could not play a parallel role. In this scenario, the causal chain resulting in the car's rising would have a further link, a divine volition that sets off the executive intending, or perhaps overdetermines its first effect. Or perhaps the divine volition could just usurp the brain's place and stimulate the muscles directly. We might also suppose that God induces in himself a liability to be affected by the four's volitions, so that when they will to lift the car, he so wills as partly to usurp the brain's place in the causal chain, providing some link between their intentions and the motion of their muscles. It would need some doing to show that such a causal chain (particularly if lawlike) is incompatible with the lifting's being an action. The lifting that results would not be free in the first case, but might be so in the second—Frankfurt questions arise here. But free or not, in the first, second, and fourth cases the lifting would be an action ascribable to the four, and in the third and fourth, the omnipotent being would lift the car using only human muscles. In none of these scenarios does an omnipotent being's willing add any lifting power other than human muscle. But then why couldn't an omnipotent being have four humans lift the car by muscle-power alone?

One might reply that this is irrelevant, because what Oppy has in mind is not whose the lifting power is, but rather the bringing-about of the state of affairs *four humans lift the car by their muscle power and nothing, including an omnipotent being, helps them*. But if an omnipotent being is part of W's history, as Oppy assumes, in no possible world sharing W's history at t do four humans bring this about by themselves. Humans cannot block the influence of someone omnipotent: if S chose to help them, they could do nothing about it. Thus four humans raise the car by their own muscle-power only if S cooperates by leaving them alone—only if S's refraining from action is part of the causal history of their joint action. With S lurking in the background, humans cannot effect the second conjunct—and if p obtains and one brings about q, that is not sufficient to entail that one brings it about that $p \cdot q$. So this is not a state of affairs they can bring about by human muscle-power alone. If S cannot do so either, then, this counts nothing against S's omnipotence on (FF), for this state of affairs fails (III). Oppy replies:

> When I am at the gym, I lift a weight unaided provided that no one helps me ... I can lift the weight using my muscle power *alone* even though ... my trainer could prevent me from lifting the weight ... it doesn't seem right to me to say that since his consent is required—he has to refrain from intervening to prevent me from lifting the weight—I can't lift the weight using my muscle power alone.[50]

But the question here is not whether only my muscles provide lifting power but whether I can bring it about that only my muscles do so, i.e. whether I can prevent my being helped. I can, at the gym: if need be I can shoot the trainer. His consent is not required.

Again, Gellman asks us to consider S's doing A while no one other than S actualizes it that S does A. This, he claims, is something S can actualize but an omnipotent being other than S cannot.[51] But this is a conjunctive state of affairs, and the claim that S can actualize it requires either something like (HR) or that S itself be able to bring it about that no one other than S actualizes that S does A. If an omnipotent being coexists with S, S cannot on S's own bring it about that this being does not actualize S's doing A. This is true even if our basic actions consist in what we agent-cause and nothing can cause an agent cause to cause whatever it causes. For in this case it is the nature of agent causation and human agency that accounts for the fact that the omnipotent being can't bring it about that S does A. And S cannot bring it about that this is the true story about human agency. But if this story about agent causation is not the reason S can't bring it about that the omnipotent being does not actualize S's doing A, the omnipotent being must cooperate, and so S can at most causally contribute to this.

Thus (FF) survives some arguments in the literature. But it still has problems. Flint and Freddoso let part of an omnipotent being's power consist in power to weakly actualize states of affairs, where S weakly actualizes it that P just if S strongly actualizes it that some S^* is in a circumstance C such that $(S^*$ is in $C) > (S^*$ freely strongly actualizes it that $P)$: again, 'a person's power is ... in large measure ... his ability to influence the free actions of others'.[52] But suppose Whitehead's metaphysics were true. Then everything, even quarks, would be conscious in some way, and open to divine persuasion. On Whitehead's account, God can strongly actualize only what is necessary to persuade and to some extent limit options: he can directly cause other things to apprehend possibilities, and make some possibilities seem more attractive or relevant than others, and this is all he can directly do. God must bring about everything else he brings about through others' help. Whitehead does not appear to believe in CFs. But even if there were such CFs as let God get his way in the end—that is, even if he offers reasons R to Jones in C knowing that were Jones in C and presented with R, Jones would do A—would such a God be omnipotent? Surely it's reasonable to require an omnipotent being to be able to strongly actualize more than this. For Whitehead's God, in effect, can't do anything directly or on his own but talk to others. Yet (FF) does not require this: 'actualize' is in both occurrences the disjunctive 'strongly or weakly actualize'.[53] Thus if Whitehead had the necessary metaphysical truth about the nature of things, his deity could well come out omnipotent on (FF).[54]

Scotus's addendum to Aquinas assures that omnipotence entails the greatest possible range of power strongly to actualize at t. An omnipotent being must have this. Suppose that God and Schmod are both omnipotent per (FF), but God can strongly actualize more than Schmod can, because God can bring about on his own some things Schmod can bring about only by persuading free agents to do them or perhaps manipulating them into doing them by the use of CFs. If this is so and God and Schmod are otherwise equal, God seems more powerful than Schmod. But nothing can be more powerful than an omnipotent being. Thus only a being of maximal strong-actualization range can be omnipotent, and (FF) fails for allowing that something can be more powerful than someone omnipotent. I've suggested that an omnipotent being can influence the content of its world-type. As this is so, but (FF) is entirely in terms of ability to actualize states of affairs not included in world-types, (FF) lets one omnipotent being be more powerful than another in a second way: there could be two beings satisfying (FF), only one of which was able to persuade Jones, and so one of which had the ability to render true a CF the other could not.[55] But again, nothing can be more powerful than an omnipotent being.

Omnipotence, then, must entail maximal power to strongly actualize. I now argue that such power exhausts it: that powers to persuade or weakly actualize are not of the right sort to help constitute a being as omnipotent. First, power to per- suade: if this is power over others' libertarian-free actions, it seems the wrong sort to figure in a definition of omnipotence.[56] 'Persuade' is a success term: I persuade you only if I succeed in my attempt to do so. How much persuading I can do depends on how hard the hearts are around me. So power to persuade is not intrinsic: having it depends on what is the case outside the agent. This is necessarily the case; it is a matter of what it is to persuade. But omnipotence is an intrinsic attribute. William of Auxerre held that an omnipotent agent needs no help to do what its omnipotence gives it power to do. This became part of the consensus medieval account, and is plausible. But if a being can achieve an effect only by exercising a power whose possession must be partly determined extrinsically, it necessarily needs the help of those extrinsic circumstances that help give it the power to achieve that effect. This is true even if the circumstances obtain necessarily. If they obtain contingently, there is another problem. Plausibly only the limits of logic, other metaphysical necessities (e.g. that there be no ideas that sleep furiously), the content of possibility (if this is not itself metaphysically necessary), and perhaps its own decrees or the will of another omnipotent being can impede the will of an omnipotent being. But if a being can achieve an effect only by exercising a power whose possession must be partly determined extrinsically, and the relevant circumstances can fail to obtain, lack of those circumstances is another impeding factor to which it is subject.[57] It could seem to follow that no one can be omnipotent, since any reasonable candidate for omnipotence would be able to persuade. But another moral is that any being is omnipotent only if powers of this sort are irrelevant to whether one is omnipotent—and they are so only if their presence would not help constitute one as omnipotent. An omnipotent being needs no help to do what powers constituting it as omnipotent empower it to do. Persuaders need help. So the power to persuade is not one of those powers.

Again, power to persuade is not guaranteed to produce the desired effect. If those I'm trying to persuade have libertarian freedom, it is beyond my control whether I succeed, though it is in my control (of course) greatly to raise the odds that I do. Suppose that Zod and God offer the same blandishments to Smith in the same way on two occasions, Smith being in the same relevant internal state in both. Displaying the notorious persnicketyness of free agents, Smith accedes to Zod but not God. It is unintuitive that this shows Zod to have more power of any relevant sort, for Zod has done only what God has. I'm not claiming that an omnipotent being would not as such have the powers to speak, to offer reasons, and so on. These are the purely intrinsic powers that are exercised in cases of persuasion. But power to persuade is not intrinsic, not independent of circumstances. If God is omnipotent, he doesn't depend for his omnipotence on the lucky break of having easily persuadable people around him, or more generally on circumstances being propitious. So I suggest that while it is part of what makes God omnipotent to be able to do all those things which are his contribution to a case of persuasion, it is not part of what makes him omnipotent to be able to persuade. If omnipotence is intrinsic, it is not even partly constituted by non-intrinsic powers.

But then what of power weakly to actualize? Flint and Freddoso see persuasion as one instance of this, and so it is, if the relevant CFs are true. Suppose that Zod offers Smith the same blandishments in two possible worlds featuring different true CFs, and due to the differences, Smith does as Zod asks in just one world. Again, it is unintuitive that this shows Zod to have more power of any relevant sort in that world. Our intuitions about persuasion shouldn't change if we learn that it sometimes takes advantage (as it were) of CFs. Power to weakly actualize is power to accomplish certain things only by means of extrinsic helps (the contingent presence of propitious CFs). So it can't help constitute an intrinsic attribute. Omnipotence, then, is power simply to strongly actualize, or cause to be the case.

(FF) avoids Wierenga's McEar problem by speaking in (III) of someone's actual-izing *p* rather than the omnipotent being's actualizing *p*. But (FF) has difficulty with Lonely McEar. LM can only scratch his left ear, but exists only in worlds in which he is the only agent. In one such world, LM scratches his ear. So LM comes out omnipotent on (FF).[58] Further, LM suggests a series of omnipotent beings one more powerful than the other: for there are Lonely McEars. McEar-Nose-and-Throat, etc.[59] Now there is a dialectical problem here, in that LM and kin are possible just if God is not a necessary being, and theists tend to believe the latter. But God can exist only if someone can be omnipotent, and we're considering whether there *is* an adequate account of omnipotence, a claim relevant to whether there is a property of omnipotence to be had. So it's not clearly legitimate to invoke the necessary existence of God to block appeal to LM. Further, even if we do, we can treat the Lonely McEar argument as trading on significant counterpossible conditionals—something common in philosophy.

We can now draw a more general moral. The high-medieval consensus view defined omnipotence in terms of states of affairs strongly actualizable at *t*. This nat-urally raises the question 'by what or whom?' Wierenga's answer 'by the omnipotent being' and (FF)'s answer 'by something'—which is to say by anything, or on a reasonable interpretation even any group—face McEar problems. The only other reasonable answer would be 'by something(s) other than the omnipotent being'. But this would fail for reasons Aquinas saw: if nothing else at *t* in any possible world sharing *W*'s history can do a miracle out of its own natural powers, it would follow that one could be omnipotent without being able to do miracles out of one's own natural powers.[60] We thus have yet to find a parsing of the high-medieval consensus view that can handle McEar.

A way out is not hard to spot. We must answer the question 'by what or whom?' as (FF) does. But we must also jettison Wierenga and (FF)'s claim that to assess omnipotence in *W* at *t*, only worlds which share *W*'s history at *t* matter. This is what makes Lonely McEar difficult. The thought behind the claim is that it is now impossible to bring about anything incompatible with the past's having been as it was: if it was the case that *P*, now or in the future nothing can occur that entails that it was the case that ¬*P*, nor can the contents of the past be shifted. As this is so, Wierenga and (FF) think, it does not count against someone's claim to omnipotence that he/she is unable to do so.[61] They infer that the only power that matters for being omnipotent at *t* in *W* is power having which is compatible with *t*'s past in *W*. But there are other ways to deal with the fixity of the past. One is simply to note that power to bring about (say) that the Germans lost World War II (or anything entailing this) is not intrinsic: to have this power, one must be sited either before World War II or outside time, and so whether one has it depends on one's circumstances. As we've seen, intrinsic power alone counts for omnipotence; extrinsic powers, or their lack, are irrelevant. This being so, there is no need to jigger one's definition of omnipotence to allow for the past's fixity. What matters is simply that the omnipotent being have all such intrinsic powers as would allow it to bring about a German loss were it appropriately sited. To parse the consensus view, then, let us simply speak of states of affairs with the modal property of being strongly actualized in some possible world. If the states of affairs relevant for counting as omnipotent are those actualized in some possible world, not in some possible world sharing history with *W*, this keeps McEar at bay.

STRENGTH VS. RANGE

Still, the consensus view on its own won't do, however parsed. The most basic problem with (FF) is one it shares with almost all definitions of omnipotence since Aquinas: it speaks only of the omnipotent being's range of action, not its strength or power. We can agree in advance of any detailed account of omnipotence that an omnipotent being is as powerful as it is possible to be: no one could be more powerful than someone omnipotent. But now consider two deities, Schmod and God. Schmod 'can do all things', but finds some of them hard (though not 'too hard'). God can do all Schmod can, but finds none of it hard. One legitimate explanation of this is that God is stronger. If someone is stronger than Schmod, Schmod is not omnipotent, even if Schmod 'can do all things'. If this is a coherent example, a definition of omnipotence needs to assure maximal strength; talk of range alone is inadequate.

Two things in this argument need explicating: what 'strength' or power can mean in talk of God, and what it consists in for Schmod to find something hard. Neither is a physical notion in this case, but not all power is on its surface physical, and not everything we find hard seems hard to us due to what seems to us a physical lack. Some people are smarter than others. Perhaps this has a purely brain-based explanation, but we don't need to know this to make sense of talk of the smarter having more powerful minds. As long as we have a *concept* of power that does not *conceptually* involve a physical basis, we can ascribe power (as vs. powers) to someone we consider non-physical. Again, if Jones finds doing calculus hard, this may be because Jones's brain does not make certain electrical connections easily, but making sense of 'this is hard for Jones and easier for others' doesn't depend on such notions.

Many powers can act with varying intensity: a light can shine more brightly, a trumpet sound more loudly, a muscle contract or a mind concentrate harder. These all vary the *power* of the powers involved. How much strength/power is associated with a power is a matter of how intensely one can exercise it, how long one can sustain that intensity and how easily one can summon it. The last involve *inter alia* whatever feelings of pain or effort may accompany the effort and psychologically or physically discourage eliciting or continuing that intensity. This capsule account of strength suggests what hardness might be for Schmod. Perhaps Schmod simply has to concentrate harder to make a decision, or exercise any of his powers. Perhaps, unless he concentrates very hard, he occasionally wills slightly the wrong thing, or his power does not accomplish quite what he wants it to. Perhaps when Schmod wills to do certain things, he feels just what we feel phenomenologically when we exert effort and accomplish something with difficulty. Perhaps Schmod tires: gradually, as he wills first one and then another effect, it takes more effort to concentrate, painful fatigue sensations increase, his attempts become gradually more inaccurate, etc. We can understand this in many ways we would with ourselves that do not *a priori* imply the presence of a physical substrate for the mental activity or effort. But perhaps too Schmod has a body, and can do certain things only by exerting its muscles,[62] these muscles tire unless he consciously wills to keep them fresh, and he does not always remember to do this. I suggest, then, that there is no insuperable objection to talk of strength as well as range here.

A defender of a pure range account might reply that Schmod counts as nonomnipotent on a pure range basis, and so we needn't invoke a separate strength consideration to explain this. Consider a state of affairs S God can bring about without effort, which Schmod finds hard. There is in addition to S the possible state of affairs *S's being brought about easily*. God can actualize this. Schmod can't—unless by easily persuading God to bring about S.[63] But then there is still a related state of affairs only God can manage, *S's being brought about easily without persuading someone else to bring about S*. So Schmod is not omnipotent, it would seem, having a less than maximal range of action. (If only range counts for omnipotence, and it is not possible to be more powerful than someone omnipotent, being omnipotent entails having the maximal range.) But this sort of counter creates problems for God too. There is also the possible state of affairs *S's being brought about with difficulty*. Schmod can strongly actualize this. God can do so only if he can make this difficult for himself or else cause someone else to bring S about with difficulty. The claim that an omnipotent being can make something difficult for himself courts paradox: can God make a stone so heavy that he can lift it only with difficulty? If he can't, the paradox would say, he is not omnipotent, unless the reason for this lies in some limitation it is acceptable for an omnipotent being to face (e.g. that this would entail a contradiction). But if he can, he can have difficulty lifting something, and that (so the paradox would say) doesn't befit omnipotence either. Be that as it may, first making something difficult and then having difficulty dealing with it is not the same thing as just having difficulty *ab initio*, and so there still seems to be a possible state of affairs Schmod can and God can't actualize, *S's being brought about with non-self-imposed difficulty*. God could get this one done by causing or persuading Schmod to bring about S, as Schmod could co-opt God above. But then as above there would be another problem state of affairs, *S's being brought about with non-self-imposed difficulty and without persuading or causing someone else to bring S about.* So if the objection we're considering is good reason to consider Schmod non-omnipotent, it might also be good reason to consider God so. On the other hand, if Schmod and God thus tie, we might just as easily say they are both omnipotent, as both (we may suppose) have the maximal possible range of action. For neither can bring about all possible states of affairs, and for each one Schmod can't manage because it is too hard, there is one God can't, of some such form as we've seen, and every other possible being (we can suppose) has a lesser range of action. Either way, we lose the contrast between Schmod and God we wanted to preserve and explain—that just one is omnipotent. If their ranges of action are equal, talk of range of action doesn't capture their difference in strength or power. So states of affairs like *S's being brought about easily* do not rescue range accounts.

WIELENBERG

If the note of strength is needed, it is natural to wonder whether talk of an omnipotent being's strength suffices on its own for a definition. Erik Wielenberg suggests that 'x is omnipotent if and only if it is not the case that there is some state of affairs...x is unable to bring about...at least partially because of a lack of power...'[64] This is a pure strength definition; range isn't mentioned. A range of action is not even implicit, because Wielenberg allows that many sorts of things might prevent x's *using* this power in various ways. Wielenberg has it expressly in view that a metaphysical impossibility of using one's strength in a particular way does not preclude being omnipotent, as long as the metaphysical impossibility in no way involves a lack of power.[65] Even if it is metaphysically impossible that Hercules lift a particular stone, Wielenberg insists, it makes perfectly good sense to say that he is strong enough to do so. (Hercules would then lack the ability for some non-power reason.) McEar is thus a problem for Wielenberg: we can imagine that McEar satisfies Wielenberg's definition but is metaphysically incapable of using his great power to do anything but scratch his ear.[66] However strong McEar is, we jib at calling him omnipotent. This suggests that strength alone is insufficient for omnipotence. An adequate definition must contain both a strength- and a range-clause. Below, I take Wielenberg's *definiens* as one conjunct in my final account. This entails that whatever an omnipotent being does, is done easily. It is not implausible that the 'ability' to find things hard is a mark not of power but of weakness, and that an omnipotent being needn't have it.

If there is a *prima facie* case for both sorts of clause in an adequate definition of omnipotence, a natural question is whether one is basic, the other derived, and whether one can therefore reduce in the end to the other. It's plausible that if God can do all things, this is at least partly because he is so strong. One might suggest to the contrary that God's strength consists in his ability to do all things. But that God can do all things is a fact about how God can *use* his strength rather than something which constitutes his having it. Ability to do a thing arises from at least three things more basic, having power enough, having knowledge enough, and possibly having the desire to do it.[67] Further, since it takes more than power to generate an ability, and so to include various states of affairs in one's range of action, facts about range don't in the end reduce to facts about strength. This is why a good definition of omnipotence must mention both.

RANGE

As a first pass at what a maximal range of action is, we might suggest

> At t, S's range of action is maximal $=_{df.}$ at t, $(P)(\Diamond(\text{something(s) cause(s) it to}$ be the case that $P) \supset (\text{S is all-things-considered able to bring it about that } P))$.

This ascribes to S not ability to bring about whatever is metaphysically possible at t, but ability to bring about whatever it is metaphysically possible to bring about at t. It leaves space for the possibility that some states of affairs cannot be brought about at t. If they cannot, of course, this doesn't entail that S has a less than maximal range of action. If a state of affairs can't be brought about, it is not in any possible range of action. Nor does it follow that S lacks some ability: there is no such thing as ability to do what metaphysically cannot be done (though there may be such a thing as being strong enough—God cannot sin but is strong enough to do so). Nor does it entail that S is less than maximally strong—nothing about one's strength follows from one's being all-things-considered unable to bring about what cannot be brought about. However, a problem with this account is that it requires being all-things-considered able. This is a sort of ability that includes having the opportunity to act. At times later than t, no one later than t is all-things-considered able to bring about states of affairs at t, unless backward causation is possible. So all-things-considered ability varies over time, and is extrinsic. Thus it is the wrong sort of thing to figure in an account of omnipotence. As a second pass, one might suggest

> At t, S's range of action is maximal $=_{df.}$ at t, $(P)(\Diamond(\text{something(s) at some time(s)}$ or timelessly cause(s) it to be the case that $P) \supset (\text{S is intrinsically such as to bring}$ it about that $P))$.

Omnipotence is a matter of S's intrinsic power. If S has intrinsically a large enough range of action to count as omnipotent, then if at some time S cannot bring about some state of affairs that at other times someone could bring about, this is due to a lack of opportunity which does not entail a lack of (intrinsic) power.

The second-pass condition won't do either. It is at least possible that some agents are incompatibilistically free. Someone can bring it about that someone other than an omnipotent being does an incompatibilistically free action—that free agent brings it about. But an omnipotent being can't bring this about. No one else can causally determine me to do an act I do with incompatibilist freedom. This would amount to bringing it about that someone is causally determined to do an act he is not causally determined to do. If it would imply a contradiction to causally determine me to do an act with incompatibilist freedom, an omnipotent being can't do this—but it is an acceptable limitation on an omnipotent being's power not to be able to do it (if the principle of non-contradiction itself is an acceptable limit). My second-pass range condition is in terms of states of affairs someone can bring about. So I introduce a qualification for this in my final account of omnipotence.

We are not yet finished, though. Even a range clause and a strength clause, I now suggest, do not suffice for a full account of omnipotence.

MODALITY AND GOD'S POWER

Intuitively, if God is omnipotent, his power is unlimited. Philosophers add at once, though, that God can do only the absolutely possible, i.e. bring about or help establish only absolutely possible facts.[68] This is well motivated. Were God able to bring about the impossible, it would not *be* impossible. It would be something God possibly brings about. Yet when philosophers introduce such claims to (say) first-year university students, the frosh tend to reply, 'doesn't that "only" limit God's power? If God is omnipotent, how can there be things he can't do?'

Some try to meet the students' concern by arguing that there are no 'things God can't do', because if a state of affairs is absolutely impossible, there is no act or task of bringing it about. Actions or tasks (they say) are by definition things someone *can* do. If a state of affairs is absolutely impossible, nobody can bring it about. So there is no act or task of doing this[69]—and so, the argument concludes, no act or task God cannot do. But students tend not to feel comfortable with this. And perhaps there is something to their feeling. For one thing, it's now more usual to define omnipotence in terms of the range of states of affairs God can bring about.[70] Discomfort with acts or tasks God can't do may well transmit itself to talk of states of affairs he can't bring about, and there is no way to deal with this analogous to the act/task move. Moreover, perhaps the modal part of our description of an act or task ('*can* do') smuggles something in illicitly. We have the sentence

(RS) It is not the case that something is both round and square.

(RS) says something true. The contradictory of a truth is not nonsense but a falsehood. So (RS)'s contradictory,

(¬RS) something is both round and square,

says something false—and so it says something. It is not nonsense. We understand what it says, though not in the fullest possible way. (We can't picture what would make it true.) If we do, there is something it says—a proposition it expresses, whatever our theory of propositions be. (¬RS) expresses a proposition. If (¬RS) expresses a proposition, so does

(¬RS*) something is round and square and made by someone.

For we understand this in whatever way we understand (¬RS). (¬RS*) describes the result of performing a task. In whatever sense we can conceive of this, we can conceive of the task being performed. So *prima facie*,

(SM) someone makes it the case that (¬RS)

expresses a proposition, one closely related to (¬RS*). If (SM) expresses a proposition, it describes the doing of an act or task, if not one whose results we can picture, or one someone possibly does. So to the extent that we understand (SM), we may be conceiving (in some sense) an act or task God cannot do. To allow for this, we could just say that an act (task) is something an act- (task-)description would describe, and an act- (task-)description is a sentence-frame whose main verb is a verb of agency, which yields a comprehensible sentence if one fills its gap with a term for an agent (e.g. '—is feeding a bird'). 'Would describe' brings merely possible actions under this rubric, and the notion of an action can be understood without a modal element: an act is something of a sort to be done, or such as to be done, and so agency-verbs express things of a sort for someone to do, etc.[71] If we say only this, the bare form of an act- (task-)description does not rule out impossible actions (tasks). '—is making a round square' yields comprehensible sentences given the right terms in its gap, though not possibly true sentences, or sentences whose truth we can picture, or sentences we can understand in the *fullest* way. So it's not as if there is no alternative to saying that an act (task) is a thing someone can do. As there is an alternative, one can't just suppose without further ado that the notion of an action (task) must have a modal element. And so it is worth asking why the notion of an action (task) must have a modal element. Might there be something question-begging in that?

More basically, though, the idea of acts an omnipotent being can't do may not be what disturbs the frosh; many are after all content to say both that God is omnipotent and that God cannot do evil. The act/task move supposes that some states of affairs *are* metaphysically impossible even if an omnipotent being exists.

This may well be precisely what bothers the students. They may wonder how anything can truly *be* impossible if an omnipotent being exists. If we are charitable, we will not take them to be supposing that nothing really is impossible, or that no omnipotent being can exist if anything is impossible: rather, they wonder how the two fit together, how an unlimited power can face limits set by the bounds of metaphysical possibility.

One source of the feeling that it limits God's power if he can do only what is absolutely possible, I think, may be that talk of absolute possibility has no obvious connection with God. The limits of the possible seem wholly independent of God. So if they are the boundaries of his power, these boundaries seem imposed on him from without. So it seems that what God can and cannot do is determined from without—and this, I submit, may be the real root of the frosh unease.[72] For what determines this from without places an extrinsic limit on God's power: it is something outside him to which even an omnipotent power must bow. This does not seem to comport with omnipotence. The Frosh Intuition, then, is that

(FI) (x)(if x is omnipotent, nothing independent of x determines what x can do).

The limits of absolute possibility are in a sense the weakest constraint an omnipotent being could operate under: anything else (having to respect natural law, say) would seem even less appropriate. So (FI) denies not just this sort of constraint but any other. Again, it would not be appropriate to omnipotence if something independent of an omnipotent being, while not determining what it could do, made some of its alternatives a good deal harder than others. For an omnipotent being, nothing should be at all hard. If this is intuitive, then intuitively

(FI*) (x)(if x is omnipotent, nothing independent of x to any degree constrains x's actions).

One way to respect (FI) is to adopt the claim that

(G) (x)(if x is omnipotent, every possible state of affairs is possible and every impossible state of affairs is impossible due to x, x's being in some intrinsic state or items x brings to be).

On (G), what states of affairs are possible is not independent of an omnipotent God. Instead, God as it were stretches out the realm of possibility, and its having a certain extent is just his stretching it so far and no further. The extent of the possible just expresses God's own nature, power, or activity. So if God can bring about only the absolutely possible, this does not fence God in from without. Given (G), God can do only what is possible because God can do just what he makes it possible that he do. It is not the possible that places limits on God, but God who delimits the possible.

(G) gives us (I claim) the best account of the relation between God's omnipotence and absolute possibility. We have two intuitions, (FI) and that God can do only what is absolutely possible. These seem to clash. (G) lets them coexist harmoniously. For God's nature, power, and action are not matters independent of God. If only these bound God's power, God meets (FI)'s condition on omnipotence. Thus we can preserve both intuitions if we adopt (G). The harder it is to find other ways to do so, the more of these two intuitions' force (G) inherits.[73]

Now some could object that far from helping an account of omnipotence, (G) trivializes omnipotence or could expel it from God's nature altogether. Suppose that God is omnipotent. Suppose (G) too, and that it is in God to have the entire range of the possible consist of (say) his existing, being as he is, setting his power, and there being one apple. Then God would count as omnipotent even if all he could do is set the range of his power and make an apple. But this trivializes omnipotence: an omnipotent being must be able to do more. Suppose on the other hand that omnipotence precludes a range of power this limited, but on (G) it is in God to have the range of the possible come out this small. Then (G) entails that it is in God to bring it about that he is not omnipotent. If so, being omnipotent is not part of his nature. Further, it's in him to bring it about either that omnipotence is not part of deity or that he is not divine. As it's not clear that properties can have inessential parts—that deity could contain omnipotence in some possible worlds but not all—it seems to follow that it is in him not to be divine.

The shortest answer here is that (G) says nothing at all about whether it is in God to have the range of the possible other than it actually is. So (G) carries none of the suggested consequences. Further, if (G) is true *and* it is in God to make the range of the possible other than it actually is, it does not follow that it is in God to make the range of the possible so small as to threaten his omnipotence.[74] Even if it is in God to have the range of the possible be other than it is, his nature could constrain the way he could vary its range. Further, if there is a problem here, it arises as we consider restricted ranges for the possible, whether or not God is the reason for them. If the real problem is making God's power hostage to the range of the possible, one could be pardoned for seeing (G) precisely as an antidote to this. Thus I take (G) as one conjunct in my final account of omnipotence.

An Account of Omnipotence

At this point I am ready to hazard an account. I propose

x is omnipotent at t if and only if (i) it is not the case at t that there is some state of affairs x is unable to bring about at least partially due to lack of power, (ii) all truthmakers of modal truths are either x, x's being in some intrinsic state or items x brings to be,[75] (iii) at t, $(P)(\Diamond(\text{something}(s)$ at some time(s) or timelessly cause(s) it to be the case that P and P is not the doing of an action with incompatibilist freedom by someone distinct from x) $\supset$ (x is intrinsically such as to strongly actualize it that P)).

All three clauses are necessary. As I've argued, definitions purely in terms of strength or range are inadequate just because they are such, and (ii) is needed for the best account of an omnipotent being's relation to modal truth. This definition can't be called too weak to capture an 'intuitive' sense of omnipotence (supposing for the nonce that we have one). (i) guarantees that an omnipotent being has all power—that its strength is without defect. If (i) is true, there is no state of affairs, even an impossible one, such that x cannot bring it about even partly because x is not strong enough. This implies that an omnipotent being has enough raw power to do even what is in fact absolutely impossible. If states of affairs are impossible, it does not wind up possibly bringing them about—but *per* (ii), the reason for this will be some constraint either entirely internal to itself, rooted in its nature, or rooted in its action. A greater degree of power over the states of affairs there are is inconceivable.[76] (ii) secures the definition against the most general external constraint problem. (iii) is the late-medieval consensus account, with a needed qualification. The qualification is consistent with (i): it is not due to lack of power in anyone that nothing but its agent can cause an incompatibilistically free action.

NOTES

1. Hill often links power and strength, as at 2005: 149, but he's not consistent: ibid. 134.
2. Later we see that things are not quite this straightforward.
3. Cyril (1994: 48), *Catechetical Lecture* 8. 3.
4. Origen (1994: 289), *De Principiis* 2. 9. 1. I owe the reference to Mark Edwards.
5. Ibid. 249–50, *De Princ.* 1. 2. 10. I owe the reference to Mark Edwards.
6. *De Symbolo* 2, my translation.
7. Swinburne (1994: 129). This account intends to allow there to be multiple omnipotent beings, with restricted ranges of choice.
8. Augustine, *Sermon* 213, PL 38, 1061. My translation.
9. Augustine (1950: 156–7) 5. 10.
10. And Pike's (1969: 210) suggestion that Anselm is speaking of mere 'moral weakness' is (I submit) just off the mark.
11. *I Sent.* d. 42 c. 3.
12. Ibid. d. 42 c. 3, my translation.
13. William of Auxerre (1986), 4. 215.
14. William likely has Abelard's denial of this primarily in view.
15. *ST* Ia q. 25 a. 3; *SCG* lib. 2d. 25. For full discussion see my 'Aquinas on Omnipotence', in Stump and Davies (eds.) (forthcoming).
16. e.g. *ST* Ia q. 25 a. 4.

17. *QD de Potentia* 1. 6.
18. So e.g. Aquinas, *ST* Ia q. 8.
19. More precisely, this is sufficient for having the all-things-considered power, power in the fullest sense. There are lesser degrees or sorts of power. A baby has the power to walk before it has learned, since it can learn, but this is not all-things-considered power.
20. I owe the 'can't' part of this disjunctive approach to Davis 1983: 81. Note incidentally that taking on a body isn't something we can do—since it would require that we first exist bodiless, and we do not. Nor is it even something that can happen to us: we are not first spirits who then fall into bodies despite ourselves; if we and our bodies come to be at once, we do not take on bodies, but rather simply come to be in them; if first our bodies exist and then we do, we do not take our bodies on, but rather they acquire us.
21. See Duns Scotus 1950– , xvii. 524–5, *Lectura* I d. 42 q. 1 n. 11; ibid. ii. 343–4, *Ordinatio*, d. 42 q. 1 n. 9.
22. See e.g. *ST* Ia q. 105.
23. no. 6 q. 1. See also *Ordinatio* I d. 20 q. 1, in *Opera Theologiae*, iv. 36.
24. no. 4 q. 22, *Opera Theologiae*, ix. 404.
25. Thus when Patrick Grim writes that the 'genuinely traditional and unlimited notion of omnipotence' is that of being able to perform any task specifiable without contradiction and that 'the task of defending' this 'seems to have been abandoned' (2007: 204, 200, 201), he makes at least two mistakes. If anything qualifies as a traditional concept of omnipotence, it is not what Grim says. I'm tempted to say that Grim's concept does not go back further than twentieth-century misreadings of Aquinas. And the task of defending the genuine traditional account, or an only slightly cleaned-up version of it, is still ongoing.
26. Wierenga (1989: 25). I've rearranged this a bit.
27. Ibid. 19–21, 27.
28. Discussions of freedom and foreknowledge frequently try to make out a distinction between 'hard' and 'soft' facts. (See e.g. many pieces collected in Fischer 1989.) Wierenga might mean that initial segments up to *t* consist of all 'hard facts' up to *t*—but he doesn't say so.
29. Wierenga (1989: 25). I've rearranged this a bit.
30. Tom Flint pointed out the third reading, and the problem that ensues on it.
31. Mackie (in Urban and Walton 1978: 77–8) raised the issue McEar raises without making up an example involving a particular individual. Plantinga (1967: 170) introduced McEar without naming him. LaCroix (1977: 187) added the name. Mavrodes (1977: 280) pointed out the importance of McEar's having his limits essentially. Flint and Freddoso (1983: 110 n. 4) discovered McEar's medieval ancestry.
32. Wierenga 1989: 29.
33. For the 'part of' part of this see also Hill (2005: 136 n. 19).
34. Wierenga (1989: 29).
35. Swinburne (1998: 251 n. 17).
36. On the definition I offer below, if there are things other than oneself, it would not be possible to be made omnipotent unless one had already been the creator of everything other than oneself: no being who had not been creator could satisfy (ii). But those failing this condition would not for any such reason be disqualified from

satisfying (i) and (iii), and this would be enough to count as omnipotent in many eyes.

37. Or else the power and its base are really just two aspects of a single attribute. As this qualification does not affect the rest of my argument, I henceforth ignore it.

38. Flint and Freddoso (1983: 99).

39. Ibid. 96.

40. Ibid. 97.

41. Hoffman and Rosenkrantz (1988: 297 ff).

42. Oppy (2005: 72–3).

43. If S brings it about that p, and it is the case that $p \cdot q$, but S did not bring it about that q, q has no cause, a full cause other than S, a partial cause not including S, or a partial cause including S. If no cause, one can infer that S brings it about that $p \cdot q$ only *via* something relevantly like (HR). If q has a full cause other than S, then as we've seen, it is not the case that S brought it about that $p \cdot q$. If q has only a partial cause not including S, what to say will be a function of what we say in cases where there is no cause and cases in which there is a full cause other than S, and so whether S brought it about that $p \cdot q$ again will hinge partly on the fate of (HR) and relevantly similar principles: if (HR) is false, and relevantly similar principles are false, then S did not bring it about that $p \cdot q$, given that where there is a full cause other than S, S did not bring it about that $p \cdot q$. If q has only a partial cause including S, the possibilities multiply dizzyingly:

(I) q has no components and has only a partial cause as a whole.

(II) q has components and has only a partial cause because of the causal stories behind those components' obtaining.

(II-a) the causal story is that some bits of q have full causes and other bits have only partial causes or no cause.

(II-b) the causal story is that all bits have only partial causes or no cause.

For simplicity's sake, let's discuss a case where $q = (r \cdot t)$.

(II-a1) r has a full cause, which is S.

(II-a2) r has a full cause, which is a composite $(S + u)$. This alternative yields an infinity of others, since every u may itself be a composite, and composites may be involved because r may be conjunctive. The way to deal with further iterations should be clear from what I say about simpler cases.

(II-a3) r has a full cause which does not include S.

(II-a1a1) t's partial cause is S.

(II-a1a2) t's partial cause is a composite, $(S + v)$.

(II-a1a3) t's partial cause does not include S.

(II-a1a4) t has no cause.

(II-a2a1) t's partial cause is S.

(II-a2a2) t's partial cause is a composite, $(S + v)$.

(II-a2a3) t's partial cause does not include S.

(II-a2a4) t has no cause.

(II-a3a1) t's partial cause is S.

(II-a3a2) t's partial cause is a composite, $(S + v)$.

(II-a3a3) t's partial cause does not include S.

(II-a3a4) t has no cause.

Obviously alternatives multiply similarly under the assumptions that r has no cause or only a partial cause which does or doesn't include S, but the ways to deal with these will be displayed in discussing the other alternatives, and so there will be no need (thankfully) to take them up.

As to (I), if q has no components and only a partial cause, S, then the overall scenario is that S fully causes p, S partially causes q and nothing else contributes causally to $(p \cdot q)$. My intuition here is that S counts as bringing about $(p \cdot q)$, on analogy to the case where S fully causes it that p and fully causes it that q. Under (II), there are these terminal possibilities to consider:

(II-a1a1) S fully causes p, $q = (r \cdot t)$. S fully causes r and partially causes t; nothing else causally contributes to t. Here it seems clear that S brings it about that $(p \cdot q)$, on analogy to the case where S fully causes it that p and fully causes it that q.

(II-a1a2) S fully causes p, $q = (r \cdot t)$. S fully causes r. t's partial cause is a composite, S $+ u$. There is not just one sort of case here, because partial causes can divide up causal responsibility in many ways. If S is mostly (i.e. way more than half) responsible for t, the case is enough like one in which S fully causes both conjuncts to warrant the claim that S brings it about that $(p \cdot q)$. If most responsibility lies with u, one would need something like (HR), and so can't conclude that S brings it about that $(p \cdot q)$. And there will be a gray zone in which intuition just is not clear. In the gray zone, though, it will at least not *clearly* be warranted to say that S brings it about that $(p \cdot q)$.

(II-a1a3) S fully causes p, $q = (r \cdot t)$. S fully causes r. t has a partial cause which does not include S. This seems to parallel the case in which S causes p and something else causes q. So my intuition is that in this case S does not bring it about that $(p \cdot q)$.

(II-a1a4) S fully causes p, $q = (r \cdot t)$. S fully causes r, t has no cause. One could have it that S brings it about that $(p \cdot q)$ in this case only *via* something like (HR).

(II-a2a1) S fully causes p, $q = (r \cdot t)$. r has a full cause, $(s + u)$. t has a partial cause, s. Here again all will depend on the degree of S's causal responsibility for r and t.

(II-a2a2) S fully causes p. $q = (r \cdot t)$, r has a full cause, $(S + u)$. t has a partial cause, $S + v$.

Again we face partial-cause unclarity.

(II-a2a3) S fully causes p, $q = (r \cdot t)$. r has a full cause, $(S + u)$. t has a partial cause which does not include S. One could have it that S brings it about that $(p \cdot q)$ in this case only *via* something like (HR).

(II-a3a1) S fully causes p, $q = (r \cdot t)$. r has a full cause which does not include S. S partially causes t; nothing else causally contributes to t. Here and in a3a2–4 it seems plain that S does not bring it about that $(p \cdot q)$.

44. Flint and Freddoso (1983: 97, 94). Note 22 could be read as expressing an intention to be neutral on this issue, but the text does not seem neutral. If the text does let us make some CFs true, Flint's later writing on Molinism retracts this.

45. Ibid. 95.

46. Ibid. 86.

47. This also vitiates one of Oppy's examples. Accepting the Flint–Freddoso claim that only Jones can affect (2)'s truth-value, Oppy suggests that the state of affairs (everyone in the room is free with respect to giving to Oxfam at t) > (everyone in the room freely chooses to give to Oxfam at t) can only be brought about jointly by everyone in the room. But one sufficiently persuasive person can bring it about. The persuader need merely cause the emotional dispositions of those in the room so to change that were they asked, they would give—or else give reasons they all freely adopt.

48. Oppy 2005: 74.

49. Flint and Freddoso (1983: 85).

50. Personal correspondence.

51. Gellman (1989: 333).

52. Flint and Freddoso (1983: 86).

53. Oppy (2005: 75–6) makes a closely related point, independently.

54. If there were some non-Whiteheadian possible worlds, they too would count for (FF)'s purposes, and the result might well be that Whitehead's God was not omnipotent. But Whiteheadianism is hardly the sort of thing to come out contingently true, so assuming even one Whitehead-world is tantamount to assuming for illustration's sake that all worlds are Whiteheadian. If we assume this, it is *not* germane to point out that Whitehead's God would have the maximal Whiteheadian power in any possible world. My point is rather that we, from our non-Whiteheadian vantage, see this as not power enough.

55. One might ask here why just one has this ability if both satisfy (FF). One answer might be that Jones strongly likes one of them and strongly dislikes another. Of course both, being omnipotent, might easily efface Jones's likes and dislikes, but this would be relevantly like brainwashing and so would defeat the claims that Jones freely accepts reasons given and that the case is purely one of persuasion.

56. This does not disqualify the persuading-Jones example just given against (FF), because Flint and Freddoso accept weak actualization as partly constitutive of omnipotence and see persuasion as a sort of weak actualization.

57. If there are true CFs, and an omnipotent being does not wholly control their truth-value, these are contingent and can impede its will too. I suggest that the right conclusion here is that a Molinist God cannot be omnipotent.

58. This is essentially what Oppy (2005: 76) calls a 'tempting objection' to (FF), framed so as to get around his problem with it, but I hit on it independently.

59. I owe the thought of a series of godlets to Wielenberg (2000: 36–7).

60. *ST* Ia q. 25 a. 3.

61. Flint and Freddoso (1983: 87–9); Wierenga (1989: 16–17, 25–6).

62. I owe this suggestion to an audience-member at the British Society for Philosophy of Religion.

63. Here I'm indebted to a related suggestion by Tom Flint, in correspondence.

64. Wielenberg (2000: 42).

65. Ibid. 37–8, 39–40, 43–4.

66. There is also thus a puzzle in Wielenberg's use of his 'series of deities' objection against Wierenga and Flint–Freddoso. The objection turns on the intuition that if a deity is less powerful than something else, it is not omnipotent (surely correct), but takes it as sufficient for being less powerful that the deity have a more restricted range of

action than the other thing (ibid. 30, 36–7). On Wielenberg's own showing, this is not sufficient.

67. There seems intuitively to be a difference between the modal status of the three. Is Hugo able to lift 300lbs? Intuition replies: not if he is not strong enough. Perhaps he is able to be able, since he can develop the strength over time, but he is not able *now*: able to be able doesn't entail able. Again, not if he does not know how to lift. If he is able to learn to lift, he is still no more than able to be able to lift. But if he has strength and knowledge enough to lift it, we do not require in addition that he should actually want to lift 300lbs. It seems enough that he might want to—that he can 'trigger' the action simply by having a desire. If Hugo literally cannot be made to desire to lift 300lbs., though, is he able to lift it? If he cannot, in no possible world does he lift 300lbs., even involuntarily. (Perhaps his body does, acting under someone else's control.) In no possible world is an act of lifting ascribable to him: one requisite for a desire-belief action-explanation is not there, and so we can't treat his body-movements as an action. So it seems to me that if Hugo can't want to lift 300lbs., he can't lift it, though perhaps his body can.

68. 'Help' allows for facts God cannot establish on his own: for it to be a fact that I feed some fish, I must do the feeding.

69. So Swinburne (1993: 153).

70. So e.g. Hoffman and Rosenkrantz (1988); Flint and Freddoso (1983); Wierenga (1989).

71. Some might say they can't understand this save by tacitly introducing the modal 'can do' again. If this is your plight, we might approach this in terms of conditional modalities. All possible tasks are tasks someone could do just if (RS) were true. Impossible tasks are those someone could do just if (RS) were false.

72. At any rate, it's the most cogent root I can ascribe to it. Worries based on biblical texts such as 'with God all things are possible' (Matt. 19: 26) seem to me misplaced. For nothing in such texts suggests a particular reading of 'all things'.

73. (FI) is not the only intuition we have in this vicinity. We might also think that

(O) if God is omnipotent, his power is unlimited, and
(U) if God's power is unlimited, he does not limit it himself.

(O), (U), and (G) are co-tenable, for it is co-tenable with (G) that it not be up to God what states of affairs there are and that God have placed every state of affairs in his power's range. Had he done so, he would have set no limits to his power, and everything would be possible. Conflict emerges if we conjoin (O), (U), (G), and the claim that some states of affairs are impossible. But in this conflict, if there are any impossibilities, (O) or (U) should lose. If we reject (G), God's power is limited from without by facts of impossibility—and intuitively limits imposed from without, over which one has no control, are worse than self-imposed limits whose extent one in some way controls. One might object that there being a stock of states of affairs whose content is not up to God is itself a non-self-imposed limit. But if this is right, then equally any stock whose content God set would constitute a self-imposed limit on his power. As one or another must be the case, it would seem to follow that any extent of divine power involves some limitation—in which case either (O) is false or omnipotence is impossible. I incline either to reject (O) or to question the objection.

74. If it were necessary (due to God's nature and that of omnipotence, say) that the possible have a range of a certain size, it would not follow that any particular state

of affairs had to be included in this. It could still be the case that any candidate state of affairs (perhaps any candidate meeting some conditions, e.g. not being an explicit contradiction) could wind up possible.

75. My talk of truthmakers is meant in a very weak sense. There are truthmakers of *some* sort on any non-deflationary theory of truth—be they corresponding facts, cohering bodies of propositions, convention-setting decisions, or what have you. Equally, there are truthmaking relations on each such theory—correspondence, coherence, etc. What I mean by saying that truths have truthmakers is that for each truth, there is at least one truthmaking relation which links it to the sort of truthmaker allotted it in some non-deflationary theory of truth. In effect, then, my talk of truthmakers commits me to no more than some disjunction of non-deflationary theories of truth being true. My truthmaking relations are those specified in theories of truth, rather than being any sort of entailment. This matters. Any fact entails that $2 + 2 = 4$. But not every fact is linked to this truth by all truthmaking relations. So I am not committed to the claim that every fact (etc.) whatever truthmakes every necessary truth.

76. One could hold that a greater degree of power still would consist in being able to add to the stock of states of affairs available to bear modal status. I would happily redo the definition so as to include this note.

REFERENCES

AQUINAS, THOMAS, *QD de Potentia*.
—— *Summa Theologiae*.
—— *Summa Contra Gentiles*.
AUGUSTINE, *De Symbolo*.
—— (1950). *The City of God*, trans. Marcus Dods. New York: Random House.
—— *Sermon* 213, PL 38.
CYRIL OF JERUSALEM (1994). *Catechetical Lecture* 8, trans. E. Gifford, in P. Schaff and H. Wace (eds.), *Nicene and Ante-Nicene Fathers*, 2nd ser. Peabody: Hendrickson, v. 7.
DAVIS, STEPHEN (1983). *Logic and the Nature of God*. Grand Rapids: Eerdmans.
DUNS SCOTUS, JOHN (1950–). *Lectura*, in *Opera Omnia*, ed. C. Balic et al. Vatican City: Typis Polyglottis Vaticana, xvii.
—— (1950–). *Ordinatio*, in *Opera Omnia*, ed. C. Balic et al. Vatican City: Typis Polyglottis Vaticana, ii.
FISCHER, JOHN M. (ed.) (1989). *God, Foreknowledge and Freedom*. Stanford: Stanford University Press.
FLINT, THOMAS, and FREDDOSO, ALFRED (1983). 'Maximal Power', in Alfred Freddoso (ed.), *The Existence and Nature of God*. Notre Dame: University of Notre Dame Press, 81–113.
GELLMAN, JEROME (1989).'The Limits of Maximal Power', *Philosophical Studies* 55: 329–36.
GRIM, PATRICK (2007). 'Impossibility Arguments', in Michael Martin (ed.), *The Cambridge Companion to Atheism*. Cambridge: Cambridge University Press, 199–214.
HILL, DANIEL (2005). *Divinity and Maximal Greatness*. London: Routledge.

Hoffman, Joshua, and Rosenkrantz, Gary (1988). 'Omnipotence Redux', *Philosophy and Phenomenological Research* 49: 283–301.

LaCroix, Richard (1977). 'The Impossibility of Defining "Omnipotence"', *Philosophical Studies* 32: 181–90.

Mavrodes, George (1977). 'Defining Omnipotence', *Philosophical Studies* 32: 191–202.

Oppy, Graham (2005). 'Omnipotence', *Philosophy and Phenomenological Research* 71: 58–84.

Origen (1994). *De Principiis*, trans. F. Crombie, in P. Schaff and H. Wace (eds.), *Nicene and Ante-Nicene Fathers*, 2nd series. Peabody: Hendrickson, v. 7.

Pike, Nelson (1969). 'Omnipotence and God's Ability to Sin', *American Philosophical Quarterly* 6: 208–16.

Plantinga, Alvin (1967). *God and Other Minds*. Ithaca: Cornell University Press.

Stump, E., and Davies, B. (eds.) (forthcoming). *The Oxford Handbook of Aquinas*. Oxford: Oxford University Press.

Swinburne, Richard (1994). *The Christian God*. Oxford: Oxford University Press.

—— (1993). *The Coherence of Theism*, rev. edn. Oxford: Oxford University Press.

—— (1968). *Space and Time*. London: Macmillan and Co., Ltd.

—— (1998). *Providence and the Problem of Evil*. Oxford: Oxford University Press.

Urban, Linwood, and Walton, Douglas (eds.) (1978). *The Power of God*. Oxford: Oxford University Press.

Wielenberg, Erik J. (2000). 'Omnipotence Again', *Faith and Philosophy* 17: 26–47.

Wierenga, Edward (1989). *The Nature of God*. Ithaca: Cornell University Press.

William of Auxerre (1986). *Summa Aurea*, ed. J. Ribailler. Paris: CNRS.

William of Ockham, *Ordinatio*, *Opera Theologiae* v. IV.

—— *Quodlibeta*, *Opera Theologiae* v. IX.

CHAPTER 9

OMNIPRESENCE

HUD HUDSON

Do not I fill heaven and earth? saith the Lord.

Jeremiah 23: 24.[1]

I. PRELIMINARIES

ACCORDING to the tradition of western theism, God is said to enjoy the attribute of being everywhere present. But what is it, exactly, for God to manifest ubiquitous presence? Well, presumably, it is for God to bear a certain relation—the 'being present at' relation—to every place.

Quarreling about the alleged relata of this preliminary response can generate a pair of dismissive answers to a rather natural follow-up question—'And in just what manner does this "being present at" relation relate God to places?'

'In no way at all,' says the atheist, 'for no divine being exists.' 'In no way at all,' says the relationalist, 'for regions do not exist.'[2] Let us put on hold these dismissive answers in the ensuing discussion and openly acknowledge a working assumption of theism and substantivalism for the remainder of the chapter. Thus, for present purposes, we shall count ourselves among the realists about God and regions.[3]

Most of us who subscribe to some kind of region realism do so because we countenance a substantivalist spacetime. Historically, however, it is more accurate to construe omnipresence as a relation between God and space, rather than as a relation between God and spacetime. Similarly (and for obvious reasons) eternality has been historically conceived as a relation between God and time, rather than as a relation between God and spacetime. In the discussion to follow I will attempt to respect this historical antecedent where I can, asking after a variety of relations that might be thought to bind God to spaces (on the supposition that there are such things).

In this chapter, then, I intend primarily to focus my discussion on the 'being present at' relation that figures so prominently in the divine attribute of omnipresence, on both fundamental and derivative readings of that relation, and on a host of philosophical problems that arise for each reading. The chapter will be divided between a discussion of the historical positions of Anselm and Aquinas, a note on the controversy stirred up by the modern contributions of Hartshorne, Swinburne, Taliaferro, and Wierenga, a brief glance at two curious and underexplored approaches, an investigation of the promising prospects for further inquiry afforded by recent work on the metaphysics of location, and some concluding comments on special problems of occupation for the Christian theist.

II. Two Historical Views and a Recent Controversy

One would think the 'being present at' relation is a thoroughly straightforward one, in current idiom—a perfectly natural and fundamental, external relation of *occupation* between objects and regions. At each moment they are present, for example, this die occupies a roughly cubical region, that tower a roughly cylindrical region, and the Earth a roughly spherical region. Such a simple occupation reading of omnipresence, however, has often been avoided for fear that it would conflict with other divine attributes.

In his *Monologium* and in his *Proslogium*, St Anselm explores some of these conflicts.[4] Anselm begins in ch. 20 of the *Monologium*—'[God] exists in every place at every time'—by recognizing a need to assert some kind of presence relation or other on the grounds that nothing can be good or even exist (not even the regions themselves) where God is not. Thus, he endorses the claim that God exists everywhere. But in ch. 21—'[God] exists in no place or time'—he also recognizes a need to deny the most familiar kind of presence relation on the grounds that it either violates the doctrine of divine simplicity with God's being partly here partly there or else leads to the impossibility of God's being wholly present at two different places, a trick that might be pulled off by a universal but not by a non-repeatable substance. Thus, he endorses the claim that God exists nowhere. Reconciliation in ch. 22—'How [God] exists in every place and time, and in none'—is achieved by noting two different senses of 'being present at a place'. The first sense, enjoyed by the die, tower, and planet in the example above, is just the fundamental and familiar occupation relation. Anselm dismisses this reading of God's omnipresence, adding to the difficulties of simplicity and impossibility just mentioned a third problem of unacceptably confining the divine being by the constraints that seem wedded to being literally located, restrictions that are appropriate for creaturely items but not for their creator. (An association of certain kinds of predication with unacceptable confinement was once more common than perhaps it is today and was responsible for much medieval mischief in motivating attempts to show that God is extra-categorial.) The second sense, the acceptable and derivative one, is then endorsed but largely left in mystery.

Edward Wierenga has cast some light on this mystery.[5] Taking as clues certain passages in the *Proslogium*, Wierenga finds in Anselm the double view that souls, like God, exhibit the acceptable form of being wholly present in more places than one and that this kind of multi-presence is wedded to sensations that are themselves related to different places. Wierenga then floats the promising hypothesis that Anselm's positive and preferred account of God's being at every place and time amounts to God's sensing or perceiving at each place and time. To avoid the issue of embodiment, a precondition of certain kinds of perception, Wierenga redescribes the relation as a kind of inner sense or immediate knowledge of the goings-on at the relevant location. Omnipresence for Anselm, then, is ultimately reducible to a kind of knowledge, immediate and localized for every region.

In addition to proposing an analysis of omnipresence in terms of knowledge, Anselm has identified three puzzles for anyone who wishes to champion the alternative, literal occupation account: *The problem of simplicity*—how can something that is not mereologically composite occupy more than one region? *The problem of multilocation*—how can something occupy (in the 'wholly present' sense) two numerically distinct regions? *The problem of containment*—if to occupy a region is to be contained by it, how can something that is essentially free of the constraints that bind all creaturely things occupy a region?

In his *Summa contra Gentiles*, St Thomas Aquinas offers an interpretation of omnipresence that analyzes divine presence by appeal to power rather than knowledge.[6] Like Anselm's, this account should be distinguished from the fundamental occupation relation, and unless it is so distinguished it may well give rise to a nest of further problems clashing with the Thomistic reading of eternity as atemporality.[7] Echoing Anselm, Aquinas argues first, that God must be present in all things insofar as he must sustain them in existence (which in a sparsely populated world falls short of omnipresence, unless the regions themselves are similarly sustained), and second, that insofar as the presence of an incorporeal being is a function of its power, God's infinite power ensures that he is everywhere.[8] Aquinas both clarifies and supplements this emphasis on power in the later *Summa Theologiae*.[9] Not just one kind of power, but two are at issue: the preserving or sustaining of a creaturely thing and an absolute and immediate control over all such things. Thus God is in all things, 'giving them being, power, and operation', which for Aquinas necessitates a relation of direct contact. Again, though, the kind of presence afforded through the contact of power is different from that of the contact of 'dimensive quantity' or simple location for corporeal things, for unless power can take the place of a fundamental occupation relation, Aquinas seems to concede that God's incorporeality and the ban on the literal co-location of bodies would both be in jeopardy. So long as God is present by contact of power and not by contact of dimensive quantity, a necessary condition of God's causality is insured while the genuine problems of co-location are kept at bay. Moreover, in addition to these two sorts of power, a kind of accessibility makes the list which Aquinas glosses with the scriptural metaphor, 'all things are bare and open to His eyes' (Hebrews 4: 13), suggesting an incorporation of the unmediated knowledge that characterized the Anselmian proposal. It is unclear whether the vision metaphor introduces a part of the analysis of omnipresence or merely observes a consequence of it with respect to knowledge, and since the primary emphasis is clearly on power, it seems best to regard Aquinas as putting a new interpretation on the table; whereas for Anselm omnipresence is primarily a kind of knowledge, for Aquinas it is primarily a kind of power.

Reflecting on this brief rehearsal of the Thomistic position can help us add three more entries on our list of puzzles to be addressed by anyone who wishes to champion the alternative, literal occupation account: *The problem of timelessness*—how can something occupy a region and be atemporal? *The problem of incorporeality*—how can something occupy a region and fail to have a body? *The problem of co-location*—how can two numerically distinct things each occupy the same region?

As Wierenga has noted, both Anselm and Aquinas develop accounts of omnipresence and its characteristic 'being present at' relation that are parasitic on our understanding of the straightforward, non-mysterious occupation relation with which we are all familiar. In other words, the special way in which God is credited with being everywhere is tantamount to God's having knowledge or control over and sustaining in existence those items that stand in fundamental occupation relations to places. Owing to their derivative nature, I will henceforth refer to these historical conceptions as 'non-occupation accounts' of omnipresence.[10]

The non-occupation accounts of omnipresence have been influential, and new variants have been formulated, expanded, and advocated by recent writers in the philosophy of religion. Four prominent contributors on this theme over the last century include Charles Hartshorne, Richard Swinburne, Charles Taliaferro, and Edward Wierenga.[11] Despite the advantages of the historical and derivative conceptions of presence, a version of the problem of incorporeality resurfaces to divide these authors. Swinburne, for example, joined the debate as a non-occupation theorist of a Thomistic stripe who wished to illuminate the consequences of acknowledging the sort of universal power that makes for divine omnipresence. Following (to a degree) the lead of Hartshorne, this investigation led him to the question of God's embodiment. Hartshorne had earlier endorsed the rather surprising thesis that the immediacy that characterized God's knowledge of and power over everything found in the world doubled as a guarantee that the world thus conceived is God's body.[12] Accordingly, to the extent that omnipresence is read as knowledge and power, God's omnipresence determines God's embodiment. Hartshorne's conclusion rests on the dubitable foundation that a mind has as its own whichever body it both knows and controls in a non-mediated way, a premise that seems at once too weak and too strong: too weak for it fails to secure my exclusive relation to my body (since both God and I presumably meet the relevant criteria) and too strong for, plausibly, there exist parts of my body that I have no non-mediated power over and no knowledge of at all—mediated or otherwise. Swinburne's discussion is more modest and more nuanced than Hartshorne's, but nevertheless accords to God a restricted form of embodiment, allegedly compatible with 'the traditional theistic view that God has no body'.[13] On Swinburne's view, restricted embodiment means both that God is able to move directly any object (capable of motion) without the benefit of causal intermediaries and that he knows directly (again without causal intermediaries) the qualities exemplified in any region at any time. Thus, restricted embodiment is a consequence of a combination of Anselmian and Thomistic themes. According to Swinburne, the embodiment is limited insofar as God has no particular orientation or restricted point of view on the world (as we do) and since God is not pained by disturbances in material bodies nor affected in thought by the states of those objects (as we are).

But for some, limited embodiment is problem enough. Taliaferro, for instance, vigorously resists the suggestion to see the world as God's body, citing the sort of immediacy essential to the non-occupancy accounts of omnipresence as altogether different in kind from the relations that we bear to our own bodies.[14] Wierenga has also taken to task the embodiment theses found in Hartshorne and Swinburne on the grounds that whereas Aquinas stressed God's presence as a presence in things that stand in fundamental occupation relations to regions, these later theorists extend the relevant doctrines of knowledge and power to the regions themselves, whether occupied or not. But, complains Wierenga, it would be unmotivated to take God's knowledge and power of and over a region that happens to be occupied by some material object as a reason to count that object among the parts of God's body, when the knowledge and power in question are indifferent to whether the region is occupied at all. The object isn't doing any work, so to speak, in providing access to the region, and thus fails to have even a diminished claim on being an instrument or body through which God knows or can manifest power.[15]

On the strength of this four-way discussion between Hartshorne, Swinburne, Taliaferro, and Wierenga, it is rather interesting to note that one of the most compelling motivations backing non-occupation accounts of omnipresence—namely, that they permit an adherence to the incorporeality of God untroubled by qualifications and partial concessions—is much less secure than it is often taken to be.

III. A Brief Glance at Two
Under-Explored Non-Occupation
Relations

Before renewing an investigation into the prospects of reviving an account of omnipresence featuring a fundamental (rather than derived) occupation relation, perhaps it would be worthwhile to note two other rather underexplored non-occupation relations that (unlike the accounts emphasizing knowledge and power) do not as easily raise the question of regarding the world as God's body. Curiously, each proposal has some genuine purchase on the notion of being everywhere present. Both suggestions are admittedly bizarre, but the detour through them won't take much time and they are fun and interesting to entertain.

The first takes the relation between God and region to be mereological. Not, as some pantheism might have it, with God claiming the regions (as well as everything else) as proper parts, but the other way around. That is to say, each region (as well as everything else) would have God as a proper part. By occupying the unique position of being a locus of universal overlap all the while remaining a mereological simple, God would thus turn out to manifest exactly the right qualifications to function as the null individual—that elusive counterpart to the null set in set theory whose most salient characteristic is being a proper part of anything distinct from it. Omnipresence would thus amount to being a proper part of each region.[16]

The second takes the relation between God and spacetime to be that of numerical identity. Locations have locations, even if they cannot be properly said to occupy or fill those locations; spacetime itself, then, has an arguable claim on omnipresence. On this view, our substantivalist spacetime would (despite current opinion) be without beginning or end and a necessarily existing entity, as well as being the subject of omnipotence, omniscience, perfect goodness, and the lot. Spinoza's monism (under at least one plausible reading) presents itself as a historical candidate for such an interpretation, and perhaps there is also something of a stoic precedent in all of this, as well. Compare the many-sided imagery of Acts 17: 27–8: 'God is not far from each one of us. For in him we live and move and have our being.' Moreover, it is worth noting that there is somewhat less pressure to deny divine attributes of the receptacle than to deny them of the fusion of its material contents (as is more common in the literature on embodiment and the corporeality of God). Finally, such an identification would ground one straightforward interpretation of the immanence of God and would effectively sidestep the increasingly common complaint of the incoherence of taking God to be outside spacetime (but at a considerable price!). Omnipresence would thus amount to being everywhere not in the sense of occupying a region but in the sense of being identical to the most inclusive region.[17]

IV. An Old-Time Revival

What of reviving the literal occupation account of omnipresence? Again, insofar as the derivative readings proffered by Anselm and Aquinas are parasitic on this fundamental relation, it is not as if a proponent of one of those historical camps or of their descendants lacks the conceptual resources to entertain the view. Moreover, many of the advantages of the historical views need not be lost, and they may be improved upon. Not only may omnipresence be significantly related to omnipotence and omniscience, literal occupation of every place may go some considerable distance toward resolving some of those perplexing 'how-is-that-possible' questions that threaten such incredible claims of direct and unmediated knowledge and power. To put it another way: rather than having knowledge and power as components of its analysis, omnipresence may receive an explanation quite independent of omniscience and omnipotence, but then be available as a tool to explore the possibility (and mechanics) of these other divine attributes.

Still, we must not forget our list of puzzles, which have certainly discouraged any appeal to the perfectly natural and fundamental, external relation of occupation as the key to omnipresence. A reminder:

The problem of simplicity—how can something that is not mereologically composite occupy more than one region?

The problem of multilocation—how can something occupy (in the 'wholly present' sense) two numerically distinct regions?

The problem of containment—if to occupy a region is to be contained by it, how can something that is essentially free of the constraints that bind all creaturely things occupy a region?

The problem of timelessness—how can something occupy a region and be atemporal?

The problem of incorporeality—how can something occupy a region and fail to have a body?

The problem of co-location—how can two numerically distinct things each occupy the same region?

Fortunately, recent work in contemporary analytic metaphysics offers some hope of intelligibly addressing these worries and of reestablishing the fundamental occupation relation as one of the candidates for providing the proper analysis of omnipresence.[18]

V. Occupation Relations

Ordinary objects stand in a variety of location relations. In this section, I propose to explore different candidate-descriptions of these kinds of occupation that have emerged in the recent literature, descriptions that presuppose a primitive and fundamental occupation relation. Although occasioned more or less exclusively by work on the metaphysics of material objects, the attention that has recently been devoted to the metaphysics of location relations may provide some genuinely valuable insights into the nature of omnipresence.[19]

There are many ways into our topic. Let us begin by posing a pair of questions about locations:

(Q1) When an object, x, is located at a non-point-sized region, r, is x thereby located at each of the subregions of r, as well?

(Q2) When an object, x, is located at each of two regions, r and r^*, is x thereby located at the fusion of r and r^*, as well?

Affirmative answers to (Q1) can be rooted in very different kinds of theory. To get a sense of the debate in question it will help to have some machinery before us. What follows is certainly not exhaustive but is nevertheless representative of some of the ways relations between objects and regions have been recently conceived. Consider the following five definitions deriving from work by Josh Parsons.[20]

'x is entirely located at r' $=_{df}$ x is located at r and there is no region of spacetime disjoint from r at which x is located.

'x is wholly located at r' $=_{df}$ x is located at r and there is no proper part of x not located at r.

'x is partly located at r' $=_{df}$ x has a proper part entirely located at r.

'x pertends' $=_{df}$ x is an object that is entirely located at a non-point-sized region, r, and for each proper subregion of r, r^*, x has a proper part entirely located at r^*.[21]

'x entends' $=_{df}$ x is an object that is wholly and entirely located at a non-point-sized region, r, and for each proper subregion of r, r^*, x is wholly located at r^*.[22]

Take someone who thinks that all non-point-sized objects are composite and pertend. Given the definitions of 'partly located' and 'pertending' this theorist holds that strictly speaking the answer to (Q1) is negative; an object always has exactly one location. But he can explain why we might tend to regard it as affirmative, since when an object, x, is located at a non-point-sized region, r, x is partly located at each of the subregions of r as well (even if x is neither wholly nor entirely located at those regions). The pertension theorist, however, should be careful to add that 'being partly located at region r' does not entail 'being located at region r'—for despite what is suggested by its name, being partly located is not a species of location.

A theorist who would unqualifiedly answer (Q1) in the affirmative is one who thinks that some non-point-sized objects are composite and pertend while others are simple and entend. What one may have thought was exclusively an a priori battlefield has recently been an arena in which a posteriori arguments from contemporary physics have provided unexpected support favoring recognition of some entending objects.[23] One thing that emerges, then, is that these two theorists disagree about whether an object's occupying a non-point-sized region guarantees that it sports proper parts, with our entension theorist leaving open the exotic possibility of extended simples.

On the other hand, a kind of theorist who would answer (Q1) clearly in the negative is one who thinks that some non-point-sized objects are spanners.

'x spans' $=_{df}$ x is an object that is wholly and entirely located at exactly one non-point-sized region, r, and there is no proper subregion of r, r^*, such that any part of x is located at r^*.[24]

Although the proponents of spanning objects accept (as do the friends of entension) the possibility of non-point-sized mereological simples, they deny (against both the pertension and entension theorists) that an object's occupying a non-point-sized region guarantees that it either occupies or partly occupies each of that region's proper subregions. Spanners do not enjoy any variety of multiple location.

Recall our second question:

(Q2) When an object, x, is located at each of two regions, r and r^*, is x thereby located at the fusion of r and r^*, as well?

Affirmative answers to (Q2) might initially seem automatic and inescapable. One who thinks that all objects pertend is likely to imagine cases in which (Q2)'s corresponding conditional is vacuously satisfied on the grounds that pertending objects are never located at more than one region (at best being partly located at more than one region). One who thinks that some objects entend may consider cases in which the non-point-sized simple itself makes both the antecedent and consequent of (Q2)'s corresponding conditional true. Finally, one who thinks that some objects span will not thereby see any threat to an affirmative answer, for a spanner also satisfies (Q2)'s corresponding conditional vacuously.

Nevertheless, I think that the same sorts of consideration that lead some to take entension seriously may also lead to uncovering a neglected notion of occupation and to a negative answer to (Q2). If we begin thinking of 'being located at' as a one–one relation, we are left with a choice between pertension and spanning for non-point-sized objects (and with some minor explaining to do involving partial-occupying, if we opt for pertension). Indeed, thinking that location is one–one and accepting the possibility of non-point-sized simples would be one straightforward motivation for accepting the possibility of spanners. But 'being located at' is a perfectly natural external relation, and without some argument to the contrary, perhaps one should take as a default position that a single object can bear this relation to more than one region. Accordingly, the possibility of entension appears to gain some plausibility.[25] But once one is willing to grant that 'being located at' can hold in a one–many pattern, one should not restrict that pattern without good reason, and entension embodies a restriction.

According to our account of entension above, when an object entends it is wholly located at each of the regions where it is located at all. But if we are willing to claim that occupation is a one–many relation, we might briefly consider a maximally liberal proposal according to which any set of regions is such that there could be a single object that occupies all and only the members of that set. Consider, for example, an object that bears this perfectly natural external relation of occupation to a cubical region, S, and also to another cubical region, S* (where S and S* do not overlap), and to no other regions. Moreover, let us add that our object is a simple and thus fails to be partly located at any region. By hypothesis, this object is neither located nor partly located at proper subregions of S and S* and it also fails to be located at the fusion of S and S*. Such an object would ensure a negative answer to (Q2).

Objects of this kind would nevertheless enjoy multiple location. The simples of this species would in one respect be like entending objects (since they would be wholly located at more than one region) but could in another respect be like spanners (for they could in fact be located at a non-point-sized region without also having themselves or their parts located at any of its proper subregions). The composites of this species would in one respect be like entending objects (since they would be located at more than one region) but could in another respect be like pertending objects (since they could be partly located in some regions). Let us then add one final definition.

'x multiply locates' =$_{df}$ (i) x is an object that is located at more than one region, and (ii) x is not located at the fusion of the regions at which x is located.

Entending, spanning, and multiply located objects would be (or in the case of multiple locaters would occasionally be) non-point-sized or even extended mereo-logical simples. There are some long-standing friends of the possibility (and per-haps of the actuality) of extended simples, and the number of their supporters is ever increasing. Philosophers who endorse the possibility of extended simples (on non-theistic grounds) include John Bigelow, Ned Markosian, Fraser MacBride,

Kris McDaniel, Josh Parsons, Ted Sider, and Peter Simons.[26] On the working assumption, then, that we have a number of conceptual possibilities alive in the
contemporary literature now clearly displayed, how can we make use of any of this
machinery to revive a literal occupation account of omnipresence?

VI. Occupation Accounts of
Omnipresence and Our Six Puzzles

Pertension, entension, spanning, and multiple location provide us with four clearly
different ways to conceive of God's relation to regions.

Recall our first puzzle: *the problem of simplicity*—how can something that is not
mereologically composite occupy more than one region? Assuming divine simplicity, this is exactly the sort of question that historically has proved worrisome for
a literal occupation account of omnipresence, for pertension is the natural default
understanding of literal occupation. So reasoned Anselm, for example, as he took
the occupation of an extended region to require proper parts. Let us soften Anselm's
rejection, though, to disqualify pertension only and leave untouched the other three
conceptions that accommodate simplicity.

Spanning, like pertension, is a one–one relation, and although it does not require
proper parts, this conception would require a unique region at which God would
be located, all others (whether sub-or-super-regions of the privileged region) being
thereby rendered ineligible to host the divine presence. On the grounds that this
conception is too restrictive, let us also disqualify a spanning conception of omnipresence.

Multiple location appears rather better off in this regard, at least at first blush.
As it says right on the label, multiple location is not one–one, and a single object
enjoying this feature can be found at several regions. But not at all of them. A
definitional constraint on multiple location as it appears above ensures that such an
object is not located at the fusion of the regions at which it is located. Consequently,
whereas this conception would be infinitely more liberal than spanning, it would
ban the most inclusive region from being among those that can host God. On the
grounds that this conception is likewise too restrictive, let us disqualify a multiple
location conception of omnipresence.

Accordingly, let us understand our literal occupation account of omnipresence
as ubiquitous entension. Once again, to entend is to be wholly and entirely located
at some non-point-sized region (in the case of omnipresence, at the maximally
inclusive region) and to be wholly located at each of that region's proper subregions
(in the case of omnipresence, at every other region there is).[27] Whereas our earlier
definition of being 'entirely located' would then require that there be no region

disjoint from the maximally inclusive region at which God is also located, it should be obvious that this condition is automatically satisfied. Moreover, our earlier definition of being 'wholly located' would then require that for every region there is, God does not have any part that fails to be at that region, but again assuming the mereological simplicity of God it should be obvious that this condition is automatically satisfied as well. Recall, then, our second puzzle: *the problem of multilocation—* how can something occupy (in the 'wholly present' sense) two numerically distinct regions? In exactly the same way God can occupy more than one region without forfeiting mereological simplicity—by entending.

Two of Anselm's three worries thus receive answers, but what of the third puzzle we extracted from our discussion of Anselm: *the problem of containment—*if to occupy a region is to be contained by it, how can something that is essentially free of the constraints that bind all creaturely things occupy a region? I think the best the entension theorist of omnipresence can hope for here is to insist that freedom from the constraint of location consists in God's bearing occupation relations accidentally rather than essentially. That is to say, whereas God is wholly present at every region there is—a type of presence that embeds the perfectly natural and fundamental location relation—God would have existed even if there had been no regions at all. In this respect, God enjoys a freedom from occupation that many of God's creatures do not; for creatures, but not their creator, occupation proves to be an ontological condition.

A similar sort of concession seems equally appropriate in response to our fourth difficulty: *the problem of timelessness—*how can something occupy a region and be atemporal? Despite the inventive and ingenious literature on atemporality, perhaps nothing can.[28] It would seem that occupying a region of spacetime is sufficient for having some temporal location or other and to that extent also ensures some literal temporal predication, but once again, this may well be among God's accidental rather than his essential features. Had there been no spacetime, God would still have existed. Mystery that it is, this verdict is no worse than the declaration that God is atemporal to begin with—it only serves to show that those who do not care for an essential tie between God and time do not have to accept one on the entension reading of omnipresence. And if an accidental tie is deemed unacceptable on the grounds that God would thereby once again forfeit simplicity, we may simply note that this complaint is better directed at the temporal-parts commitments of pertension, not the mereologically neutral stance of entension.

Our fifth problem strikes me as considerably more difficult: *the problem of incorporeality—*how can something occupy a region and fail to have a body? My own view of the matter is that anything that occupies a region is a material object, and that the occupier inherits the shape, size, dimensionality, topology, and boundaries of the region in which it is entirely located.[29] Anyone similarly attracted to the simple occupancy analysis of 'material object' and these related theses has a bullet to bite if he wants to endorse an entension-based reading of omnipresence, for God will then exemplify the shape, size, dimensionality, topology, and boundaries of whatever is the most inclusive region. We can again tender our previous reassurance and declare that these are merely accidental and extrinsic characteristics of God, but undoubtedly the concession will be declined by many who think that these properties cannot be accommodated in any form. It would seem that some kind of embodiment will turn out to be an unavoidable cost of the present hypothesis, but as we observed in the debate between Hartshorne, Swinburne, Taliaferro, and Wierenga (explored in sect. II above), it may be a cost borne by adherents of traditional non-occupancy accounts as well. To be fair, however, the simple occupancy analysis of 'material object' is certainly controversial (and negotiable for the traditional theist). Moreover, it would be a reasonable rejoinder that these are simply not the same kind of 'body problem' in any event and that there is precious little support to be garnered on this matter from Hartshorne and Swinburne's earlier and hedged embodiment theses.

Finally, recall our sixth puzzle: *the problem of co-location*—how can two numerically distinct things each occupy the same region? A common answer is that they can do so provided that they are of fundamentally different kinds. The 'fundamentally' seems required, for 'being a co-located thing' is a kind, and unsurprisingly all coincident entities (if there are any) are at least of that sort. What, though, are the fundamental kinds? Do objects divide at the most basic level into the concrete and the abstract? Or perhaps into substances, properties/relations, and facts? Or maybe into the material and the immaterial? Or into objects, stuff, and spacetime? Or into the divine and the non-divine? Of course, one could dodge the heavy burden of giving a full-blown answer to the question at hand and maintain that whatever the correct response turns out to be—God is of a fundamental kind all his own. Accordingly, whereas God's omnipresence would ensure God's being co-located with every other thing, such coincidence would always be of the harmless and acceptable variety. It is worth noting, though, that even with such widespread space-sharing, appeals to location might still be able to serve their historical individuating function. Since the entension theorist recognizes occupation as a one–many relation, it should come as no surprise to learn that she may be attracted to an individuation principle for located objects that says—necessarily, for any located objects, x and y, x is located at all and only the same regions as y iff $x = y$.[30]

VII. Some Concluding Remarks on Omnipresence and Christianity

What additional puzzles might confront the Christian theorist tempted by entension and its apparently satisfying reading of omnipresence? It depends.

Recall the final suggestion of the preceding section: namely, that the entension theorist may be attracted to an individuation principle for located objects that says—necessarily, for any located objects, x and y, x is located at all and only the same regions as y iff $x = y$. If our Christian theist is a Trinitarian recognizing three numerically distinct persons each of whom is omnipresent, perhaps she will hesitate over that individuation principle. Or what if our Christian theorist accepts the Incarnation and holds that there is a special sense in which the Son but not the Father was hanging on the cross, despite the fact that both were and are omnipresent? Or what if our Christian theorist maintains that the Son is literally present in the consecrated bread and wine, while the similarly omnipresent Father and the Holy Spirit are not?

These are excellent and difficult questions, and I have neither the space nor expertise to enter here the controversies with which they are associated. I will remark in closing, however, that once again the relation of entension may serve as a promising source of resolution for some of those debates. Even if one took the Anselmian/Thomistic accounts to suffice for omnipresence, entension remains available to provide partial readings of additional special claims of location such as Christ's presence in the Eucharist or the specific comings and goings of the Holy Spirit. Accordingly, if the 'located at' in the principle noted above ranges over these very different types of occupation, even the Trinitarian may embrace the individuation principle without apology.

At the outset of this chapter, I noted that according to the tradition of western theism God is said to enjoy the attribute of being everywhere present, and I asked—'what is it, exactly, for God to manifest ubiquitous presence?' As we have seen, for Anselm it is a kind of knowledge, for Aquinas a kind of power, and for many of their intellectual descendants a kind of mixture of knowledge and power. On the strength of recent work in the metaphysics of location relations, however, some western theists (and especially some Christian theists) may wish to entertain with full seriousness that God's omnipresence involves a non-derivative and literal location relation—the relation of entension.

Notes

For comments and criticism on earlier versions of this paper I thank Michael Rea, Thomas Flint, Andrew Arlig, Joseph Jedwab, Robert Pasnau, Jonathan Schaffer, Edward Wierenga, Dean Zimmerman, the participants at the 2006 Mereology, Topology, and Location conference at Rutgers University and the philosophy departments at the University of Colorado at Boulder, Baylor University, and West Virginia University.

1. Compare Psalm 139: 7–8: 'Whither shall I go from thy spirit? Or whither shall I flee from thy presence? If I ascend up into heaven, thou art there: if I make my bed in hell, behold, thou art there.'

2. Theorists other than relationalists can give the second dismissive answer, too, so long as they do not include regions in their ontology (i.e. so long as like the relationalists they do not take spacetime to be an independent *thing* partially filled or occupied by other entities).

3. With the hope of remaining as neutral as possible on the debate about the nature of the divine being as conceived in western theism, I will say very little on the term 'God'; nevertheless, in the subsequent discussion I will have occasion to comment on the relation between omnipresence and other commonly ascribed divine attributes such as simplicity, eternality, incorporeality, omnipotence, and omniscience. On relationalism and substantivalism see Earman 1989 and Nerlich 1994. Of course I'm not suggesting that the relationalist need turn atheist, but I will not be investigating relationalist reconstruals of occupation relations in what follows.

4. Especially, *Monologium* chs. 20–2 and *Proslogium* ch. 13, in Anselm 1948.

5. Wierenga 1988. I owe much of my understanding of Anselm and Aquinas on omnipresence to Wierenga from the days when I was among his students. I am delighted to acknowledge that here.

6. *Summa contra Gentiles*, lib. 3 d. 68 in Aquinas 1975.

7. For a discussion of the tension between Aquinas's doctrines of omnipresence and eternity see La Croix 1982.

8. Perhaps there is a questionable move in sliding from 'infinite' to 'all' (e.g. one can think about infinitely many natural numbers without thinking about them all and presumably, one could bear infinitely many such presence-as-power relations without bearing them to all of the regions). But let that go.

9. *Summa Theologiae* I. q. 8 in Aquinas 1975.

10. Wierenga 2006 and 1997. For the record, scholars are divided on whether Anselm and Aquinas really advocate the non-occupation accounts as a substitution for (as opposed to an addition to) a literal reading of omnipresence, and Robert Pasnau (in private communication) has made an interesting case for the combined view.

11. Hartshorne 1941; Swinburne 1977; Taliaferro 1994 and 1997; and Wierenga 1988, 1997, and 2006.

12. Hartshorne 1941.

13. Swinburne 1977: 102–4.

14. Taliaferro 1994 and 1997.

15. Wierenga 1988, 1997, and 2006.

16. For a more comprehensive discussion of the null individual, its friends and foes, its philosophical profile, and the prospects of and obstacles to identifying it with God, see Hudson (forthcoming *a*).

17. Note, however, that mereological simplicity seems irredeemably forfeit on this proposal, and unless divine simplicity is reinterpreted as something like there being no difference between subject and attribute or between essence and existence in God, that undesirable consequence may be enough to do it in.

18. The material in the next section 'Occupation Relations', which introduces and discusses a number of alleged kinds of literal occupation, is drawn largely from ch. 4 of my 2006. In that work, I focus on material objects, but the present section differs from its predecessor by omitting the adjective 'material'.

19. For accessible and interesting examples of this literature see Casati and Varzi 1999; Gilmore 2003 and forthcoming; McDaniel 2003; and Parsons forthcoming.

20. Parsons (unpublished). The first two definitions (i.e. of 'entirely located' and 'wholly located') and the fourth and fifth definitions (i.e. of 'pertending' and 'entending'), while inspired by Parsons, use a different primitive and have different content than the definitions given to those phrases by him. Note that the definition of 'entirely located' involves a claim about the non-existence of a certain kind of region, while that of 'wholly located' involves a claim about the non-existence of a certain kind of object. Parsons is to be commended for noting and correctly emphasizing the importance of this crucial distinction.

21. In this and the definitions to follow, I use 'non-point-sized' rather than 'extended' in order to be neutral (i.e. in order to leave open the possibility of a receptacle that is the fusion of at-least-two-yet-no-more-than-countably-many point-sized regions—a region which would then be both non-point-sized and non-extended).

22. Why the fanciness? Why not just say 'x entends' means 'x is located at a non-point-sized region and is a mereological simple'? This won't do, for the proposed definiens would then apply to three of the four different ways an object may be thought to be related to regions (to be discussed below), and one of the main aims of this section is to clearly distinguish those different ways.

23. See the discussion of non-locality and quantum mechanics in Parsons (unpublished). See also the support for entension contributed by the null individual in Hudson (forthcoming a).

24. See McDaniel (forthcoming a) from which I borrow the term 'spanners'. My characterization, however, differs from his in using 'entirely located at exactly one' and in replacing 'continuous region' with 'non-point-sized region' so as not to prejudge the possibility of spatially or temporally disconnected simples.

25. See Sider (forthcoming) who argues in this fashion not only for the possibility of a single object occupying more than one region but also for the possibility of a single region hosting more than one object. Again, though, perhaps this establishes at best a presumption in favor of the relevant thesis which may be trumped by good arguments against multiple occupancy or co-location.

26. Bigelow 1995; Markosian 1998; MacBride 1998; McDaniel (forthcoming b); Parsons 2004 and (unpublished); Sider (forthcoming); Simons 2004.

27. One qualification: should it turn out that there is no maximally inclusive region (i.e. if every space is a proper subregion of a larger space), then entension is disqualified owing to its definitional link to being entirely located somewhere or other, and omnipresence would simply amount to being wholly present at each of the infinitely many contained regions.

28. An exception to this rule: Perhaps something can occupy a region without being temporal if the world at which the region is to be found is a space-only world. For a brief discussion of this issue see Hudson (forthcoming b).

29. See the Introduction to Hudson 2006 and Markosian 2000. Note that I did not say 'of *the* region in which it is wholly located', for the entension theorist doesn't think there is any such unique region. For a discussion of what to say about shape properties for the pertension, entension, spanning, and multiple location theorists, see 'the problem of shapes' in ch. 4 of my 2006.

30. Of course, the pertension theorist attracted to location-as-individuation principles could say this too, and ignore what from his point of view is idle complexity in talk of regions in the plural. For more on location and individuation principles, see 'the problem of diachoric identity' in ch. 4 of my 2006.

References

ANSELM (1948). *St. Anselm: Proslogium; Monologium*, trans. Sidney Norton Deane. La Salle: Open Court.

AQUINAS, ST THOMAS (1945). *Summa Theologiae*, in *Basic Writings of Saint Thomas Aquinas*, ed. Anton Pegis, 2 vols. New York: Random House.

——(1975). *Summa contra Gentiles*, trans. James F. Anderson. Notre Dame: University of Notre Dame Press.

BIGELOW, JOHN (1995). *The Reality of Numbers*. Oxford: Oxford University Press.

CASATI, ROBERTO, and VARZI, ACHILLE (1999). *Parts and Places: The Structures of Spatial Representation*. Cambridge, Mass.: Bradford Books.

EARMAN, JOHN (1989). *World Enough and Space-time: Absolute Versus Relational Theories of Space and Time*. Cambridge: MIT.

GILMORE, CODY (2003). 'In Defense of Spatially Related Universals', *Australasian Journal of Philosophy* 81: 420–8.

——(forthcoming). 'Time Travel, Coinciding Objects, and Persistence', in Dean Zimmermen (ed.), *Oxford Studies in Metaphysics*. Oxford: Oxford University Press.

HARTSHORNE, CHARLES (1941). *Man's Vision of God and the Logic of Theism*. Chicago: Willett, Clark.

HUDSON, HUD (forthcoming *a*). 'Confining Composition', *The Journal of Philosophy*.

——(forthcoming *b*). 'Lesser Kinds Quartet', *The Monist*.

——(2006). *The Metaphysics of Hyperspace*. Oxford: Oxford University Press.

LA CROIX, RICHARD R. (1982). 'Aquinas on God's Omnipresence and Timelessness', *Philosophy and Phenomenological Research* 42: 391–9.

MACBRIDE, FRASER (1998). 'Where are Particulars and Universals?', *Dialectica* 52: 203–27.

MCDANIEL, KRIS (2003). 'No Paradox of Multi-Location', *Analysis* 63: 309–11.

——(forthcoming *a*). 'Brutal Simples', in Zimmerman (ed.), *Oxford Studies in Metaphysics*.

——(forthcoming *b*). 'Extended Simples', *Philosophical Studies*.

MARKOSIAN, NED (1998). 'Simples', *Australasian Journal of Philosophy* 76: 213–26.

——(2000). 'What Are Physical Objects?' *Philosophy and Phenomenological Research* 61: 375–95.

NERLICH, GRAHAM (1994). *What Spacetime Explains*. Cambridge: Cambridge University Press.

PARSONS, JOSH (2004). 'Distributional Properties', in Frank Jackson and Graham Priest (eds.). *Lewisian Themes*. Oxford: Oxford University Press, 173–80.

——'Entension', Unpublished manuscript.

——(forthcoming). 'Theories of Location', in Zimmerman (ed.), *Oxford Studies in Metaphysics*.

SIDER, THEODORE (forthcoming). 'Parthood', *Philosophical Review*.

SIMONS, PETER (2004). 'Extended Simples: A Third Way Between Atoms and Gunk', *The Monist* 87: 371–84.

SWINBURNE, RICHARD (1977). *The Coherence of Theism*. Oxford: Oxford University Press.

TALIAFERRO, CHARLES (1994). *Consciousness and the Mind of God*. Cambridge: Cambridge University Press.

—— (1997). 'Incorporeality', in Philip L. Quinn and Charles Taliaferro (eds.), *A Companion to the Philosophy of Religion*. Oxford: Blackwell, 271–8.

WIERENGA, EDWARD (1988). 'Anselm on Omnipresence', *New Scholasticism* 52: 30–41.

—— (1997). 'Omnipresence', in Quinn and Taliaferro (eds.), *A Companion to the Philosophy of Religion*.

—— (2006). 'Omnipresence', Edward N. Zalta (ed.), *The Stanford Encyclopedia of Philosophy (Spring ed.)*. <http://plato.stanford.edu/archives/spr2006/entries/omnipresence/>, accessed 16 May 2008.

CHAPTER 10

....

MORAL
PERFECTION

....

LAURA GARCIA

PERFECT goodness is one of those attributes included in the conception of God as
the greatest conceivable being. Some refer to this as the Anselmian concept of God,
in honor of the eleventh-century monk St Anselm who claimed to have discovered
a proof for God's existence based simply on the definition of God as a being
than which none greater can be conceived. Anselm's definition can be rephrased
in modal terms, as the claim that God is the greatest possible being. The version
of theism that operates from this definition of God we might call 'perfect-being
theology'. Traditional proofs for the existence of God seek to provide strong rational
support to the claim that there is such a perfect being, and familiar objections to
God's existence (e.g. the problem of evil) aim to demonstrate that no such being
exists.

In the 1970s Alvin Plantinga made use of the Anselmian concept of God to
develop a modal version of Anselm's ontological argument for God's existence. His
definition describes the God of perfect-being theology as one that exists necessarily
and is essentially omnipotent, omniscient, and morally perfect, and this definition
has become standard in discussions about the nature and existence of the God of
western theism. Hence these discussions operate with a relatively thin conception
of God, since many of the key terms in the definition, including essential moral
perfection, remain undefined. Philosophers find this attractive in some ways, since
it permits (even invites) an a priori approach to explicating the divine perfections.
In fact, proposed definitions or analyses of each divine attribute abound in the
philosophical literature. Striving for compossibility among the perfections steers

these discussions toward ever leaner definitions that will present fewer potential conflicts with the definitions of other attributes.

One drawback for the minimalist approach, however, is that it can impede the effort to connect philosophical theology with religious faith. In his treatise on the Anselmian concept of God, philosopher Thomas Morris defends his claim that the God of the philosophers (the God of perfect-being theology) is the God of Scripture: 'If the object of worship in the western tradition of theology is intended to be the ultimate reality, and if the Anselmian conception of God is coherent, if maximal perfection is possibly exemplified, then the God of religious devotion is the God of the philosophers.'[1] The number of conditions here is daunting to say the least. But many philosophers believe that there is enough shared content in the western (or at least in the Judaeo-Christian) concept of God to provide at least a starting point for philosophical analysis of that concept. In what follows, we will discuss three major ways of modeling divine moral perfection and consider some of the major objections to the claim that God is necessarily morally perfect.

THE POSSIBILITY OF MORAL PERFECTION

For most theists, moral perfection is the attribute most essential to a divine being. If it turns out that moral perfection is incompatible with omnipotence or omniscience, theists are more likely to surrender the latter than to question divine goodness. One reason is that only a perfectly good being is worthy of worship, while a being who (for some plausible reason) has limited power or knowledge might still be worthy of worship, as long as that being has as much power or knowledge as it is possible for a being to have. Peter Geach defends a non-Anselmian conception of God owing to his belief that future contingent propositions about what humans will freely choose are (at present) neither true nor false, and so cannot be known (now) with certainty even by an omniscient being.[2] It also follows from Geach's view that there are some things God cannot prevent (free choices), though he can of course prevent the typical effects of those choices from occurring. Geach contends that since God has perfect goodness and can carry out his plan for the world no matter which choices free creatures make, he remains worthy of worship. Eschewing the traditional doctrine of omnipotence, Geach proposes that God is *almighty*, having as much power as a being can possibly have in a world containing other genuinely free creatures.

Perfect-being advocates criticize Geach's proposal as inadequate to the traditional theistic understanding of God, though objections focus primarily on Geach's view about future contingent propositions. That view requires that some propositions are neither true nor false, which violates a basic assumption of logic, the law of bivalence, which states that every genuine proposition has a truth-value. While many theists agree that propositions about future free choices are genuinely contingent and that finite creatures cannot know their truth-value with certainty, they insist nonetheless that God knows with certainty for each such proposition whether it is true or false. If Geach is correct in asserting that knowledge of future contingent propositions is logically impossible, this will require revisions in definitions of divine omniscience and omnipotence. Divine moral perfection remains untouched, however, since presumably a morally perfect being will always choose the good, whatever the extent of his knowledge and power.

But the moral attributes of God have come under attack as well. William Rowe argues that perfect being theology is logically incompatible with divine freedom.[3] His case for this claim requires the following two principles:

    (a) Where possible world x is better than possible world y, God's act of creating x will be better than his act of creating y.

    (b) If one action is better than another, then God cannot choose the less perfect action over the more perfect action.[4]

Principle (a) assumes that there is some way of assessing the overall value or desirability of possible worlds. Rowe admits that it may be logically impossible for there to be a best of all possible worlds, but he concludes from this that, given principles (a) and (b), God is not free to create a world at all. In such a situation, God cannot choose something less than the best, yet necessarily any world he creates will be less good than some other one he could create. If it turns out that, contrary to what we've assumed so far, there is a best possible world, then God is morally required to create that world. He will not be free to refrain from creating, nor will he be free to choose among a variety of logically possible alternative worlds.

Rowe anticipates the objection that if God is a necessary being, every possible world includes God, so it is never the case that one possible world is better than another in terms of overall value—every one already has infinite value. In reply, Rowe makes a distinction between quantitative value and qualitative value, claiming that even if every possible world contains the same amount of quantitative value (an infinite amount), worlds with creatures or with a variety of creatures are qualitatively more valuable than a world with only God. That is, such worlds contain more kinds of value. Against this it might be said that a world's quality can be assessed in more than one way. Some philosophers, in the tradition of the Greek philosopher Parmenides, considered a world with only one perfect being to be the summit of perfection and saw the existence of lesser beings as undermining the overall quality of a world. But Rowe could grant the Parmenidean conception of quality without surrendering his argument for divine necessitation, since by (a) and (b) a Parmenidean God would be morally obliged to refrain from creating.

Most of Rowe's theistic interlocutors grant principles (a) and (b) and so find themselves hard pressed to maintain both God's moral perfection and his perfect freedom. It may be useful to consider a parallel dilemma that arises within perfect being theology. Paul Helm and some others in the Reformed theological tradition propose that among the criteria for rationality is the following principle: a rational agent must always have a reason for acting, a reason that justifies choosing this specific action over every alternative action.[5] Given this principle and the assumptions that God is perfectly rational and that he created the actual world, God must have a reason to create rather than not create and a reason to prefer creating the actual world to creating any alternative possible world. It follows in turn that the actual world is the only possible world (understanding possibility here as metaphysical possibility rather than as mere logical possibility or as conceivability). Since creating the actual world was the best action God could perform, he is not free to choose any alternative course of action. While such a view is logically coherent, it is disturbingly counterintuitive. In my opinion, this is a reason to reject the rationality requirements proposed above and to allow that a rational agent may choose any satisfactory means to accomplish his or her ends. If several satisfactory means are available, a rational agent needs no additional reason for choosing one of them *rather than* the others. If this leaves some free choices partially unexplained (other than by saying they were chosen for the desired end), then so be it.

For similar reasons, theists may wish to reject Rowe's principle (a), at least as he understands it. Theists in the Thomistic tradition conceive of God as containing all the perfections found in creatures (but in a much higher way). This means that a world with God in it is already maximally excellent, not just quantitatively but qualitatively as well. Creatures reflect the perfections of God and participate in them to a greater or lesser degree, but the addition of creatures neither increases nor decreases the qualitative goodness of the world in Thomas's perspective. Whatever God's reasons for creating, this theological tradition emphatically denies that they include making the world a better place in some way.

Theists in the Anselmian tradition should be equally suspicious about the claim that a moral agent has a duty to perform the best action he can, as Rowe's principle (b) requires. One troubling aspect of this claim is that the 'best action' is understood in the context of principle (a) as the action that achieves the best outcome. This simply assumes that the moral evaluation of actions is based primarily on their results, an assumption that is highly questionable and that many theists reject. Without (a) and (b), the claim that divine moral perfection is logically incompatible with divine freedom does not succeed. Further, as we shall see below, the virtue theory of morality provides a different model for understanding God's motives in creating a world, a model that preserves a place for divine freedom.

MODELS OF MORAL PERFECTION

Conceptions of divine goodness are generally modeled on conceptions of human goodness. Different moral theories, then, give rise to different analyses of moral perfection for humans and so, by extension, for God. Historically speaking, the Big Three moral theories are the virtue theory, developed by Aristotle and St Thomas Aquinas, the duty theory, with Immanuel Kant as its main champion, and the utility theory, advocated by Jeremy Bentham and John Stuart Mill, and sometimes defended these days under the more inclusive banner of consequentialism. Recent discussions of divine goodness rely almost exclusively on the latter two theories, defining moral perfection either as doing the best thing one can do (either all told or for each person affected) or fulfilling all one's duties. As we shall see, neither of these theories works well as an account of divine goodness. Virtue-based theories show more promise, depending on what role is assigned to the virtues in assessing the moral quality of actions and persons.

Maximizing the Good

Utilitarian and consequentialist moral theories treat certain desirable states of affairs as the primary locus of value. Generally the valuable states of affairs involve persons having positive experiences of some kind, such as feeling pleasure or getting things they want. Actions are good if they produce more value or less disvalue than any alternative action available to the agent. In order to avoid egoism, most consequentialist theories require that a good action produce more total value for everyone affected, not just for the agent. (How this value should be distributed among persons affected by the act is a matter of dispute among consequentialists.) Given the difficulties involved in calculating the probable effects of each action, some consequentialists modify the theory to allow that an action is good if it is *of a type* generally known to produce the most value in situations similar to the present one. For the most part, morally good persons will be those who consistently choose morally good actions. Virtues may be treated as morally relevant as well, but only if (and because) they increase an agent's tendency to produce good actions.

Consequentialism is open to many lines of criticism. First, there is something odd about treating moral value as simply a function of non-moral value (the value of various states of affairs). While that move has the advantage of providing an objective and quasi-empirical basis for moral judgments, it overlooks the importance we ascribe to motivations in assessing moral agents and their actions. Second, it is difficult if not impossible for a human agent to calculate the total effects of her actions even in the short term, much less over the course of her lifetime and beyond. Third, this theory conflicts with one of our firmly rooted moral intuitions, that in our actions we should be motivated by concern for others and their true welfare rather than by an attempt to calculate the optimific action (the one that optimizes the proportion of value over disvalue). In fact, we want others to care about us and our welfare even if they can do nothing to help us or are relatively inept in their efforts to help.

Some of these criticisms lose their relevance when we turn to consider divine moral perfection. Presumably an omniscient moral agent can anticipate all of the effects of each of his actions[6] and an omnipotent agent can see to it that his actions have only the effects he wants them to have. Taking valuable states of affairs as primary then, a divine agent should be able both to maximize value in the universe and to maximize value for each created human being. Unfortunately, the task of maximizing non-moral value is not logically possible and so is not one that even God can perform. For any amount of such value, i.e. for any number of creatures and their pleasures or satisfactions, there could always be more—more creatures, more pleasures, or more varieties of pleasure. Similar problems have plagued the project of defining the best of all possible worlds. For any world God creates, surely there could be a world with one more creature in it, one extra day, and so on.[7] If we omit the requirement that God maximize value overall, perhaps we could retain the lesser requirement that God must maximize value for each of his creatures (or each of his rational creatures). But the same paradox of maximization applies in the individual case as well, since there could always be more and different positive experiences.

One way to get around the difficulties involved in maximizing benefits to individuals would be to understand benefits primarily in terms of moral value. Perhaps the focus of a morally perfect being should be on maximizing the amount of moral good in the universe, where moral good is a result of the morally right actions of free agents. On this view, the truly valuable states of affairs (creatures' morally good actions) necessarily incorporate states of affairs (free choices) that are not up to God. God cannot directly cause creatures to choose what is morally right without removing their freedom.[8] In his free will defense against the problem of evil, Alvin Plantinga makes use of this conception of moral good as consisting in the number of morally good choices made by creatures. He contends that it is logically possible that God cannot create a world with as much moral good as that found in the actual world without permitting an amount of moral evil at least as great as what is present in the actual world.[9] If Plantinga is correct, then God's moral perfection is not compromised by the existence of moral evil in the amount we find in our world. But we are still left with a maximization problem, since it seems possible for God to have created additional moral good in the world simply by creating more creatures with moral freedom, even if this also means permitting additional moral evil. Beyond this, some will contend that a perfectly good being should maximize both moral and non-moral good for his creatures, which will again raise the paradoxes of maximization that William Rowe has pointed out.

Plantinga may well be onto something in focusing on moral good, however. It does seem to most theists that maximizing the non-moral value in a person's life is not necessarily the best thing to do for him. As John Henry Newman explains:

The Church...regards this world, and all that is in it, as a mere shadow, as dust and ashes, compared with the value of one single soul. She holds that, unless she can, in her own way, do good to souls, it is no use her doing anything; she holds that it were better for sun and moon to drop from heaven, for the earth to fail, and for all the many millions who are upon it to die of starvation in extremest agony, so far as temporal affliction goes, than that one soul, I will not say, should be lost, but should commit one single venial sin, should tell one willful untruth, though it harmed no one, or steal one poor farthing without excuse. She considers the action of this world and the action of the soul simply incommensurate, viewed in their respective spheres.[10]

This passage suggests that the most important goods for human persons are ones that cannot be achieved without their free participation. St Augustine claims that 'God, who created you without you, will not save you without you.'[11] On this view, maximizing the good for a given person requires that person's free cooperation and continues to depend upon it throughout his or her earthly life. Further, one person's hardships may be an occasion for another person's moral growth or conversion, so that a divine being must choose among many different kinds of goods—maximizing some may be incompatible with maximizing others, and there is no guarantee that different kinds of goods will be commensurable with one another. Given these difficulties within the consequentialist model, then, there is reason to search for a more satisfactory explication of divine moral perfection.

Doing One's Duty

Duty-based theories of morality treat actions as the primary locus of moral value, evaluating actions as good or bad, right or wrong, depending on whether they accord with what the moral law prescribes. Duties themselves are variously grounded. Immanuel Kant claims that the fundamental moral law, the Categorical Imperative, draws its authority from reason. Acting against this law leads a person into contradictions and incoherence. Other duty theorists claim that some basic moral laws expressing absolute moral duties are known immediately through intuition. Among intuition theorists, some hold that intuition yields particular judgments about which actions are right or wrong, while others claim it only tells us which *kinds* of action are right or wrong. A third group claims that we intuit only which things are intrinsically good, so that principles of right and wrong action must be derived subsequently.[12]

Divine command theories of morality hold that the moral law rests on God's commands, so that following God's will (generally as revealed in Scripture) is what duty requires. Similarly, for God to do his duty is for him to act according to his will. The result, of course, is that since God always and necessarily acts according to his own will, he is necessarily morally perfect. On the other hand, since there is no independent source to give content to the concept of moral goodness, this theory cannot rule out the possibility of divine actions that we would consider cruel or malevolent. Indeed, on this theory such actions would actually be morally good. This outcome has led many philosophers to reject the divine command theory of morality, though some continue to support versions of it that purport to escape the unpleasant implications just noted.[13] In what follows, we will assume that there is some objective basis for ascertaining one's moral duties independently of God's commands, and that humans do in fact know what duty demands of them in most situations. The Ten Commandments might serve as a brief summary of these duties.

Duty theories of morality do not require the maximizing calculations involved in the various versions of consequentialism. As long as one can apply a universal moral norm to a specific instance, one will know whether a given action is right or wrong. Lying is wrong; to omit this income from my tax return would be lying; hence, it is wrong for me to omit it. But the duty theory faces difficulties of its own. One of these stems from cases of conflicting duties, where it seems one has a strong duty to do two (or more) actions that are incompatible with each other. Perhaps Smith is kayaking with her daughter and the daughter's friend when the girls' kayak overturns; she is obliged to try to rescue both, but an approaching waterfall makes it possible to rescue only one person, and the daughter's friend is the one nearest to her. Some duty theories provide rules for resolving conflicts between duties, though these can be controversial and difficult to defend, and they introduce complications into the theory. Kant famously denied any moral importance to so-called 'special relations', which seems to imply that in the case of the kayak incident, Smith should try to save the friend rather than her daughter. If one disagrees with Kant and allows some relevance to special relations, this complicates the moral theory and makes it more difficult to apply.

A separate criticism of duty theories is that they place insufficient emphasis on the agent's motives and intentions in acting. Kant offered a negative criterion here, arguing that an action is morally good only if the agent acts out of respect for the moral law alone, but this requirement seems both impossible and misguided. Presumably Smith's daughter would not be consoled to find that her mother had saved her life purely out of respect for the moral law, because it was her duty to do so. She would rightly feel that love should also have played a role, and not just a supporting one. Finally, our moral intuitions suggest that fulfilling one's duties is a kind of minimum in the moral life, and that a truly good person would go far beyond what duty requires in her dealings with other people. She would often do things that were beyond the call of duty, that were 'supererogatory'. But since every good deed that exceeds what duty requires falls into this category, it is hard to say just how much extra good one must do in order to qualify as a really good person, much less a perfectly good person.

Applying the duty model to divine goodness results in something like the following definition: God's moral perfection consists in his perfectly fulfilling all his moral duties. Thomas Morris treats this as capturing at least part of the concept of divine goodness. However, he anticipates a major obstacle to applying the duty theory to God, since that model assumes that an agent has a duty to act in a certain way only if he or she is free to do otherwise. According to perfect-being theology, God *necessarily* acts in accordance with moral principles. While humans can fail in their duties, it is logically impossible for God to lie, to break his promises, and the like. Morris's solution is to claim that the duty model of moral goodness applies to God only analogically. God always acts in the way that a being with moral duties *would act* in his situation, even though strictly speaking he has no moral duties.

Morris is reluctant to call this a definition of divine moral perfection however, since he endorses the standard duty theory as the correct analysis of our concept of moral goodness, and he also believes that Scripture ascribes duties to God in a fairly straightforward way. 'In the biblical tradition, God has been experienced as one who makes and keeps promises, who enters into covenant relations, and who does not lie.'[14] (Of course, the biblical tradition also presents God as a being who *cannot* lie and *cannot* do evil, so it is not clear that the biblical tradition helps resolve the philosophical question of whether God has duties.) Morris concludes that while God's fulfillment of his duties is not *morally* good, it is nonetheless good in a way that is not reducible to metaphysical (i.e. non-moral) goodness. He introduces the term 'volitional goodness', which is 'goodness residing in or arising out of a being's will or character when that will or character is not itself causally determined in that respect by anything independent of that being'.[15] Volitional goodness covers both actions that fulfill duties God would have were he subject to duties and supererogatory acts for which other courses of action were metaphysically possible for God. This preserves the duty model as the primary analysis of moral goodness without surrendering the claim that God is perfectly good, since volitional goodness includes both moral goodness and acts of supererogation, and God has more volitional goodness than any other being.

While this represents a valiant attempt to reconcile divine goodness with the standard duty model of morality, it is not a complete success. For on this view God's acting in accordance with duty is not *morally good*. It may be good in some metaphysical way—what Morris calls 'axiological goodness'—but it is not indicative of God's *moral* perfection.[16] On Morris's duty model, an act can be morally good only if it derives from the kind of *free choice among alternatives* that a perfect being lacks when that being is subject to moral requirements. Volitionally good acts are not freely chosen, but are necessitated by the divine nature. Even though divine acts of supererogation do count as morally good (because freely chosen), they are not morally good according to the standard duty-based concept of moral goodness.

Morris attempts to bypass this problem by suggesting that 'when religious people claim that God is morally good, meaning that he acts in accord with moral principles, they are merely using that axiological conception with which they are most familiar, moral goodness, to describe or model an aspect of divinity functionally isomorphic with, though ontologically different from, human goodness'.[17] Religious people might well respond that they thought they were using the ordinary (human) concept of moral goodness in claiming that God is perfectly good. But it is possible to preserve the standard (ordinary) duty model of moral goodness for God only if one surrenders the claim that having moral duties requires being able to act against them, and Morris believes that claim is essential to the duty model.

Even if Morris's modified duty model (the volitional interpretation of divine goodness) succeeds, it generates a problem of its own. Including acts of supererogation within moral perfection introduces the maximizing principle once again; if some number of gracious, supererogatory deeds is good, wouldn't more of them be even better? This point is pressed at some length by Earl Conee, who claims that supererogatory acts are in fact essential to the concept of moral perfection: 'Nothing less than the best is perfect. The agent of a morally imperfect act is not a morally perfect agent. An act is morally imperfect if its agent thereby neglects one that is morally better. And supererogatory acts are precisely those which are morally better than others that are right'.[18] Conee anticipates the objection that supererogatory acts are not morally required and so do not belong to the concept of *moral* perfection as such. Colin McGinn, for example, contends that 'surely if an agent always conforms his actions to the moral norms that apply to him, there can be no room left for moral imperfection to creep in'.[19] Conee replies that the *anticipated consequences* of one's actions clearly contribute in some way to the moral value of those actions, and that the value of these consequences has no intrinsic maximum. If the duty theorist accepts the moral relevance of an action's accurately foreseen effects, then I believe Conee's argument succeeds. He concludes (along with Rowe) that it is impossible for any being to exhibit moral perfection, since for any given value of an action's foreseen consequences, there could in principle be an action that yields a higher value. Hence the duty-plus-supererogation model of divine moral perfection succumbs to the same maximization problems that beset the consequentialist model.

If the duty theorist retreats from the difficulties raised by supererogatory acts back into the duty model *simpliciter*, still further obstacles lie in the path of explicating divine goodness by way of the duty model. First among these is Conee's contention that a perfectly good being would not be content simply to fulfill his duties, since even human moral goodness often goes beyond this to include acts of heroic generosity and selflessness. Further, some believers deny that God has any duties at all, since he is the sovereign lord of the universe and every creature owes its existence and all of its powers to him. While there is much that creatures owe to God, what could the sovereign creator owe to creatures? Part of the strangeness in the idea that God has duties stems from this vast asymmetry in the relationship between God and humans, and part of it is due to the felt absurdity of saying that there are things God *should* do, as though there were a chance that he might not do them. These considerations make it difficult (though perhaps not impossible) to formulate an adequate definition of divine moral perfection within the confines of the standard duty model.

A Combination Theory

Some philosophers, aware of the difficulties in both the duty and the consequential-ist models, attempt to combine the two in the hope of counteracting the weaknesses of each with the strengths of the other. One such attempt is sketched in some detail by T. J. Mawson: 'God's perfect goodness then is his perfectly fulfilling his duties toward his creatures and, furthermore, whenever there is a logically possible best thing for him to do for them, his doing that too, his perfectly loving them.'[20] Mawson takes it for granted that God fulfills all his duties, and that he fulfills them necessarily, so he disagrees with Morris's claim that having duties requires that one is free to act against them. Both Morris and Mawson note that an omnipotent and omniscient being necessarily fulfills his duties, then, but Mawson claims this is not because God lacks an important kind of freedom but because he has perfect freedom. 'These properties [omnipotence and omniscience] entail that there is nothing that constrains God's actions (no external power that can trump his will and no ignorance that can misdirect it).'[21] Hence a perfectly free being necessarily fulfills all his duties. The effectiveness of this solution depends on whether one finds it essential to the concept of a morally good action that the agent be free to fail to perform it, since on Mawson's view God acts dutifully as an automatic and logically necessary effect of his recognizing the right action to perform and having the power to perform it.

One difficulty for Mawson's 'best-action' model of divine goodness is that it requires God to choose whatever is best for each creature. For now we may set aside the problems that beset maximizing requirements in general, since Mawson requires that God act for the best vis-à-vis each person only when a best action is logically possible. Still, God's plans for the universe or for the human race might be such that the best action in a given situation has little to do with benefits to this specific individual (except insofar as having a part in an excellent overall plan counts as a benefit). Must God benefit a particular person at the expense of other important values, including benefits for other persons? Further, the best-action model requires that it is possible to assign a relative value to benefits and harms in order to determine, say, whether a benefit that lasts for all eternity outweighs a temporal harm. If benefits of very diverse kinds *are* commensurable in this way, no doubt an omniscient being can make the calculations, perhaps even minimizing the harm-to-help ratio for each creature. Nonetheless, Mawson's theory confronts three further obstacles: maximizing benefits for one person may not be compatible with maximizing benefits for others; many important personal benefits cannot be effected by God's actions alone (moral growth, friendship, etc.); and God on this theory would be acting immorally in preferring some other valuable state of affairs to maximizing benefits for each human being.

Finally, both duty models and consequentialist models of morality focus on right actions to the neglect of other important features of moral agents such as their attitudes and intentions. On both theories, reason determines what is the right action in a given situation either by anticipating the outcome of the action or by assessing its conformity with the moral law (or some combination of both). The role of the will is simply to choose the action that reason commends. On consequence-based theories, the assumption is often that there is one best action, thus limiting God's options to a single alternative. Duty theories allow God a wider range of choices, as long as none of his actions violate any duties. But if God has a duty to do the best he can (as Conee suggests), then in the divine case the duty model collapses into the consequentialist model. That is, if God must choose the overall best action (the action producing the best consequences), assuming that such an action (in God's case) will never be one that violates a duty, the duty criterion can simply be omitted.[22]

One advantage to an intellect-centered approach to moral evaluation is that it simplifies the argument for divine moral perfection. As Richard Swinburne points out, since an omniscient being necessarily knows what is the right thing to do and an omnipotent being necessarily has the power to do what is right, God's moral perfection is entailed by his omniscience and omnipotence.[23] The disadvantage of this intellect-based approach is that it seems to make moral motivation entirely a matter of rationality. Indeed, Immanuel Kant claimed that reason *should* be the only motive for right action, as other motives can conflict with the directives of reason. But it seems that the human will is naturally drawn toward the good (that is, by non-moral values such as existence, beauty, pleasure, fulfillment, and knowledge) and that we make choices for the sake of such good ends. So perhaps moral excellence consists at least partly in what kinds of goods a person wills (or seeks) and whether he or she values them appropriately. Such considerations lead in the direction of virtue theories of ethics as potential models for conceiving of divine moral perfection.

Acting Virtuously

Virtue theories treat various internal features of moral agents as the locus of moral value, especially traits of character, intentions, motives, and the like. Morally good traits are those that dispose a person to choose and act well. Acting well is generally defined in terms of seeking what furthers the genuine good of persons, either that of the agent herself or, when others are the objects of an action, their genuine good.

Some read Aristotle's ethical theory as a virtue-based theory that attempts to show that seeking one's own genuine good (or flourishing) requires that one also seek the genuine good of others for their own sake. Whether or not that claim is true, we will take it for granted in this discussion that to act virtuously is to act solely from virtuous intentions, desiring, favoring, and hoping to attain what is truly good for the person (or persons) who is the object of one's actions. A virtuous person also takes into account the effect of her act on any persons she foresees will be affected by it, aware unintended but foreseen harm to others may render an otherwise virtuous action vicious in a particular instance. This is the subject of the much-maligned and widely misunderstood doctrine of *double effect*.

Well-being or flourishing is of course a type of non-moral good, but it is not the locus of moral value for virtue theories. It can be given content by reflecting on what Aristotle called the final cause of a thing—its goal or full development, flourishing, wellness, etc. Aristotle defines the virtues as settled dispositions or states of character that incline a person to feel, respond, and act in ways that serve the flourishing of persons. More recently, Jorge Garcia proposed a different way to give content to the goal of virtuous actions, defining the virtues in connection with the roles we fill in the lives of persons (ourselves and others). On Garcia's view, virtues are the states of character (dispositions to feel, respond, intend, act, etc.) that make us good in our morally significant roles, as parent, friend, colleague, and so on. In order to know what traits make an agent good in a role, we can reflect on what we (humans) naturally expect from those who fill that role in our lives. Garcia argues that what we most want and expect from other persons is that they be motivated by goodwill toward us, that they be concerned for our genuine well-being for its own sake. When we assess their character and their actions from a moral point of view, their motives and intentions are the key to our assessments. Persons of good will may fail to actually benefit us, owing to ignorance, ineptitude, lack of opportunity, or other factors outside their control, but we do not condemn them morally for this kind of failure.[24]

Lists of moral virtues (and corresponding vices) go back at least as far as Socrates, and there is a surprising amount of agreement among them. Such personal virtues as temperance and courage (or fortitude) typically appear along with interpersonal virtues such as fairness, generosity, and friendliness. The influence of Christianity on western thought has added such qualities as compassion and humility to the list. While this presents a rather daunting moral program, Garcia's virtue theory claims that the whole set can be reduced to one overarching virtue—genuine concern for the well-being or good of persons, especially of all the persons affected by or in the scope of one's actions. An action performed from this intention (and from no harmful or neglectful intentions) is a morally good act regardless of whether it is successful (that is, whether it actually benefits the person or persons involved). On this view, love of persons is both the root and key component in all the virtues.

One common criticism of virtue theories is that they cannot accommodate the kind of moral absolutes that one finds within duty theories of morality, and especially within the moral teaching of the major theistic religions. Striving to acquire the virtues is a gradual process, one that evokes the image of a sliding scale rather than of a line that cannot be crossed. Garcia replies that virtue theories do support moral absolutes, since some actions are such that it is always wrong to intend them—taking an innocent human life, treating a person with ridicule or contempt, and so on. Deliberately acting in this way is acting from a motive directly opposed to the virtue of love or goodwill, and such actions are always wrong. The extent to which one's motives depart from care and goodwill determines the degree of their viciousness and so the degree to which they are morally blameworthy. While it is wrong to remain indifferent to another's suffering, it is worse to purposely inflict suffering on an innocent person. To inflict suffering on one's own child is more blameworthy still, given the greater love and care that is properly owed to a son or daughter.

A virtue theory along these lines can be extended to provide a conception of divine moral goodness, though the transition is not exactly seamless. Perhaps the most obvious definition of divine moral perfection in terms of the virtues is to say that a morally perfect being perfectly exemplifies all the (standard) moral virtues. But this will not do. Some human virtues, such as temperance or courage, have no obvious divine equivalent,[25] and others, such as humility, seem inappropriate for God. Further, unlike human agents, a divine agent cannot fail to act from virtuous motives or intentions. This last point raises Morris's worry about whether a trait exemplified necessarily by an agent can be properly included in an account of that agent's *moral* perfection. Human virtues must be acquired gradually by acting well in various situations and thereby developing the right habits. Nothing like this process could characterize divine virtues.

On the positive side, virtue theories locate moral perfection in the will rather than in the intellect, treating right actions as those that are properly motivated and directed toward the right ends. This model allows room for freedom to operate even for a perfectly good being, since there are many different ends that can be chosen for the right reasons. Without the maximizing requirement of consequentialist theories or the rationality requirement of duty theories, God is left free to create or not to create, and to create any number of worlds that reflect his glory out of his gracious generosity. This in turn suggests a more promising definition of divine moral perfection, understood not in terms of perfectly exemplifying the whole list of virtues but as exemplifying perfect love. If love is at the root of the human virtues, this definition has the further advantage of providing a clear analogy between human and divine moral goodness.

St Augustine and St Thomas Aquinas both endorse a concept of moral perfection along these lines. Thomas argues that God wills the existence of creatures out of his goodness, but that he does not create out of necessity:

Accordingly as to things willed by God, we must observe that He wills something of absolute necessity: but this is not true of all that He wills. For the divine will has a necessary relation to the divine goodness, since that is its proper object. Hence God wills His own goodness necessarily, even as we will our own happiness necessarily.... [But] since the goodness of God is perfect, and can exist without other things inasmuch as no perfection can accrue to Him from them, it follows that His willing things apart from Himself is not absolutely necessary.[26]

While God has no need to create, Thomas does say that, having created human beings, God necessarily wills their good. He cannot hate anything that he has made.[27] Since God is the highest good, the greatest good for human persons is to know and love God and to live in his presence forever. Hence, this is the destiny that God wills for each person.

We saw earlier that the duty model of divine goodness hit a snag over the question of whether a perfect being could be free to act *against* a requirement of duty. Perfect-being theologians are inclined to answer this question in the negative, though this puts a strain on the idea that God has duties in the ordinary sense. There are at least four possible solutions to that problem. First, retain the standard duty model and surrender perfect-being theology, so that it is possible for God to act against a moral duty (adding perhaps that he never actually does so). While some theistic philosophers might find this acceptable, those committed to perfect-being theology would vigorously oppose it. Second, retain the essential moral perfection of God and surrender the freedom requirement of the duty model, so that even a being who necessarily fulfills his duties qualifies as morally perfect. While this move is attractive in some ways, it sits uneasily with important components of the duty model, e.g., that fulfilling one's duties is worthy of moral praise, or that duties are inherently prescriptive (since for a perfect being they will simply be descriptive). A third solution, that of Thomas Morris, retains both perfect-being theology and the freedom requirement of the duty model but argues that a being who necessarily acts according to duty can still be called perfectly good by extension, as long as his actions are not coerced by anything outside his nature. This solution has promise, but it runs counter to the spirit of the duty model. Any necessitation of one's actions, whether from without or within, undermines the prescriptive element essential to the duty model.

Fourth, one could retain perfect-being theology and jettison the duty model of moral perfection. Morris objects to this move in part on the grounds that the Bible describes God as having duties that he can be counted on to fulfill. But virtue-based moral theories can also accept the language of moral duties, defining these in terms of the virtues. For instance, if all one's actions should be motivated by genuine concern for the good of others, then one has a duty not to intend harm to them. Admittedly, there is a difficulty in ascribing duties to God in this way. Does God have a duty not to harm the persons that he has created? Putting the question like this, I believe, shows both what is right and what is wrong about the duty model of divine goodness. On the one hand, traditional theists want to say that God must not harm his creatures, and on the other hand they want to say that of course God could never do such a thing anyway. Why? I believe the answer is not that God is necessarily dutiful but that he is necessarily virtuous, necessarily loving. Indeed, love is one of the names of God. Creatures are not virtuous by nature and can be tempted toward vicious actions of one kind or another, so the language of duties (especially as prohibiting certain kinds of actions) is appropriate for them. But God as perfectly virtuous cannot act viciously, so to say that he has a duty not to act badly makes little sense.

As we saw earlier, Morris acknowledges that there is a clear tension between divine perfection and the language of duties, and he sides with perfect-being theology in claiming that moral goodness is essential to God. Putting these two together, Morris arrives at a picture of a God who first *knows* what his duties are vis-à-vis other beings in the universe and then necessarily *wills* in accordance with that knowledge. Of course this vastly underdetermines an agent's choices even for finite agents. It tells us not to do anything wrong, but little about the good that we should do. As such, it hardly seems a recipe for exemplary moral achievement. 'Doing one's duty' can even carry negative connotations, since conforming one's actions to a rule may be done for a wide variety of motives. This is one reason for supplementing the duty model, giving moral extra credit for supererogatory actions that go beyond the call of duty. But if supererogatory actions are the real key to moral excellence, it appears that duty is not the most fundamental moral concept after all. A virtue theory, on the other hand, can explain what is good about supererogatory acts, since they go beyond the demands of justice to include heroic and self-sacrificing actions motivated by love and compassion.

EVALUATING MORAL AGENTS

Consequence-based and duty theories of morality share a common limitation in focusing on actions rather than on agents. While actions are more accessible for moral evaluation, they present only part of the picture. In evaluating the moral caliber of a person, emphasis falls on his or her character—desires, concerns, affections, intentions, humility, perseverance, and the like. Part of the work of reason in the moral life is to determine what is the right action in a specific situation. Aristotle calls this the work of practical reason, applying general principles to the particular circumstances one confronts. Among the influences on practical reason are a person's formed attitudes, habitual responses, and guiding concerns, and these are the province of the virtues. Hence, even if the benefits model or the duty model of morality can provide an acceptable theory of right action, both would fall short of providing a full moral assessment of the agent. But when we are attempting to explicate divine moral perfection, this is precisely the kind of assessment that is needed.

Focusing on the intentions of moral agents rather than on their actions also makes it possible to define God's moral perfection without compromising his freedom. While God necessarily wills his own being and goodness, he already possesses these, so nothing compels him to create. Also, since any universe would be created out of love, there are few limits on which worlds God can create. There may be limitations beyond simple logical ones, perhaps moral or aesthetic considerations, but infinitely many worlds will be compatible with these requirements. With respect to individual creatures, Thomas says that non-rational creatures exist for the sake of the perfect ordering of the universe as a whole, and also for the sake of human beings who are entrusted with the care, cultivation, and proper use of the natural world. Humans, on the other hand, are willed for their own sake; that is, they are not a proper object of use by anyone (including God), since they are intrinsically good and not merely instrumentally good. God desires the true good of persons, which is that they should live forever in communion with him and with one another, free from pain and sorrow and death.

It may seem that there are easy counterexamples to this last claim, since human beings are not free from pain and sorrow in this life and may (because of age or some other impediment) fail to seek communion with God. The reply to this objection is complex. First, recall that the good for persons is one that cannot be realized apart from their free cooperation, since there is no genuine love or communion that is coerced. Second, while God does not will evil to any person, he may allow pain and suffering that result from humans' misuse of freedom, from disturbances in the natural order (perhaps as an effect of original sin), from the ordinary operation of physical laws, and so on. The compatibility of these forms of pain and suffering with God's perfect goodness is defended in theistic responses to the problem of evil. Third, as William Alston has argued persuasively, it is difficult for finite minds to assess all the kinds of positive goods or values there are (especially if some take place in the next life) or to understand the many connections there may be between the pains of this life and highly significant goods, known and unknown.[28] The Christian Scriptures claim that God can make every situation in a person's life conducive to this end, though perhaps not without that person's free cooperation (or at least consent).[29]

The virtue theory of divine moral perfection entails that God's love for each person is unconditional and unimpeded by incompatible motives. But what is it that love requires with respect to each person? Presumably, God desires that each one should come to enjoy communion with God and with other persons. Can this end be reached by a person who has not freely chosen it? If the answer is yes, then God is not required to provide for each person an opportunity to make such a choice. If the answer is no, then presumably God does provide such an opportunity for each person, either before or after death.

On this point, Thomas Flint raises the following objection: 'Once God creates [a person], can he have perfect concern for [her] if he chooses to put [her] in situations less conducive to [her] happiness than he might have? Maximizing concerns may be less here than they are for the consequentialist, but it's not obvious that they have totally evaporated.'[30] A virtue theorist might reply that what is morally significant is that God wills the true good of each person and that he uses every available means toward that end. But it is also important to note that the end in view is not exactly the same for each person. Each soul is unique, and each is given gifts and graces, challenges and trials, that are known to that person and to God alone. Perhaps persons in heaven are not experiencing some kind of generic human bliss, but are aware of God's beauty, truth, joy, and mercy as it is reflected in (the whole of) her life and in other unique ways in the lives of countless others. At least it seems safe to assume that what might be called God's courtship of each person involves a complex and delicate interplay among things in that person's life that are chosen and things that are not. But it is not obvious that there is one situation or set of situations that would be *maximally* conducive to bringing a given person into loving union with God. A scenario truly maximally conducive toward this end would be one that removes the person's freedom to resist, but then the goal of genuine loving communion is lost. Surely a person who is the recipient of infinite and unconditional love should be more free, not less so. If God aims to win a person's heart and will, his consent to what God wills, perhaps any situation that is an occasion for this consent will serve as well as any other. One of the strengths of Aristotle's virtue theory of morality is that it allows for many ways of living a virtuous life, and I believe it is one of the strengths of the virtue analysis of moral perfection that it allows for many ways of arriving at eternal happiness.

CONCLUSION

Treating God's goodness as a feature primarily of his will, as virtue theories suggest, rather than as a feature primarily of his intellect, sustains a more positive understanding of divine freedom. Richard Swinburne and others define perfect freedom negatively, as freedom *from* external coercion and *from* forces that could interfere with or prevent what one wills. This is surely an important aspect of freedom, but it neglects the Thomistic insight that the will is appetitive, that is oriented toward the good. In perfect freedom, then, the will seeks the highest good and perfectly possesses what it wills.[31] While Thomas does not use this language, it is surely consistent with his view to say that the first principle of morality is the law of love. God loves his own being and goodness, and wills everything else 'for the sake of his goodness' as Thomas puts it. But finite persons (angels and humans) are created as ends in themselves (as intrinsically good), not as a *means* to divine goodness, since God already possesses that end (his own goodness) and cannot possess it any more perfectly. Rather, creation is ordered to God's goodness in the sense that it reflects and reveals his goodness, beauty, and wisdom, and has its end in God.

What the apostle Paul says to the early Christians is also the purpose of all created things, that they 'exist for the praise of his glory'.[32] St Thomas adds that human persons arrive at this end only by imitating the moral perfection of God, loving him above all, loving ourselves as we ought, and loving others as God does, for their own sake. Wishing others well, in this perspective, means especially wanting them to obtain the highest of all goods, friendship with God. Some criticize Christians for a perceived lack of attention to the material and economic needs of those around them, and certainly these are essential to a person's welfare. But one cannot blame Christians for working even harder to bring others closer to God, to a good that is unsurpassable, imperishable, and can never be taken away. Using St Paul's language, C. S. Lewis spoke eloquently about the 'weight of glory', the infinite value and eternal destiny of each human being that requires us to treat others with respect, and even with a form of reverence.[33] Since divine goodness is, among other things, a model for human goodness, our attitudes toward others should be more like those of God, ready to offer mercy and forgiveness, to share the burdens and sorrows of those around us, to reach out to those in need, and to defend the weak and despised. While our efforts may not always succeed, believers hope in a God who uses all their efforts to accomplish his will and whose love for each human being is beyond our imagining.

Notes

I am grateful to Jorge Garcia and to the editors of this volume, Michael Rea and Thomas Flint, for their many valuable comments and suggestions on earlier versions of this chapter. Eileen Sweeney and Oliva Blanchette provided helpful discussions of the Thomistic understanding of creation. Any flaws or shortcomings are, of course, my own responsibility.

1. Thomas V. Morris, *Anselmian Explorations: Essays in Philosophical Theology* (Notre Dame: University of Notre Dame Press, 1987), 20.
2. See Peter Geach, *Providence and Evil: The Stanton Lectures 1971–2* (London: Cambridge University Press, 1977), 58. 'God, like some grand master of chess, can carry out his plan even if he has announced it beforehand. . . . No line of play that finite players may think of can force God to improvise: his knowledge of the game already embraces all the possible variant lines of play, theirs does not.' Geach also points

out that God can have strongly justified beliefs about future contingents because he knows each person's character thoroughly and knows the way things are presently tending.

3. See William Rowe, *Can God Be Free?* (Oxford: Clarendon, 2004) and his critique of the standard theistic replies in his article 'Freedom, Divine' in E. Craig (ed.), *Routledge Encyclopedia of Philosophy* (London: Routledge, 1998); <http://www.rep.routledge.com/article/K025SECT3>, accessed 15 January 2008.

4. Rowe, *Can God Be Free?*, 128.

5. This rationality requirement is more complicated in the case of finite persons, since presumably the alternatives must be ones that the agent knows about (or perhaps should know about) and that he or she has considered (or should have considered). For God, the requirement can be stated more simply.

6. Thomas Flint points out that this is true only if God knows the truth-values of counterfactuals of freedom, i.e. propositions of the form: *In circumstances C, agent S freely chooses action A.* As we have seen, Peter Geach (and some others) denies that God can know with certainty the truth-values of such propositions.

7. For an introduction to this issue see Robert M. Adams, 'Must God Create the Best?', *Philosophical Review* 81 (1972), 317–32, and Alvin Plantinga, *God, Freedom and Evil* (New York: Harper & Row, 1974), 89–91. In considering Gaunilo's objection to Anselm's ontological argument for God, Plantinga notes that some descriptions of the form 'the greatest X' are logically incoherent, as when X denotes a being with properties that have no intrinsic maximum. His examples are 'the greatest number' and 'the greatest island'. The phrase 'the greatest being' escapes this problem, since the qualities such a being would have—knowledge, power, and goodness—do have intrinsic maxima; e.g. to know (immediately and infallibly) the truth-value of every proposition is to have maximal knowledge, and to be able to bring about any logically possible state of affairs (or something along these lines) is to have maximal power.

8. Here I assume that compatibilism is false. Compatibilists claim that a person can be morally responsible for one of her actions even if that action is causally necessitated by a chain of prior events that originates outside her.

9. Plantinga, *God Freedom and Evil*, 7–57. The key claim is on p. 56: 'It's possible that every world containing as much moral good as the actual world, but less moral evil, [is such that] God could not have created it.'

10. John Henry Cardinal Newman, Lecture 8, in *Certain Difficulties Felt by Anglicans in Catholic Teaching*, i. 239–40; <www.newmanreader.org/works/anglicans/volume1/lecture8.html>, accessed 9 October 2007.

11. St Augustine, Sermon 169, 13 (PL 38. 923).

12. A clear and succinct summary of these varieties of moral intuitionism can be found in Robert L. Frazier, 'Intuitionism in Ethics', in E. Craig (ed.), *Routledge Encyclopedia of Philosophy* (London: Routledge, 1998); <http://www.rep.routledge.com/article/L041>, accessed 14 January 2008. According to Frazier, H. A. Prichard, Joseph Butler, and W. D. Ross are intuitionists of the first sort, Richard Price, Thomas Reid, and Henry Sidgwick examples of the second type of intuitionist, and G. E. Moore a representative of the third. Further, while Price and Moore think of intuition as an intellectual capacity, Prichard and Thomas Reid describe it as closer to a type of perception.

13. See Janine Idziak (ed.), *Divine Command Morality: Historical and Contemporary Readings* (New York: Edwin Mellen, 1979), especially the essay by Philip Quinn. Also see Robert M. Adams, 'Divine Command Metaethics Modified Again', *Journal of Religious Ethics* 7 (1979), 71–9, and William P. Alston, 'What Euthyphro Should Have Said', in William Craig (ed.), *Philosophy of Religion: A Reader and Guide* (New Brunswick: Rutgers University Press, 2002), 283–98.

14. Thomas V. Morris, 'Duty and Divine Goodness', *American Philosophical Quarterly* 21 (1984), 264.

15. Thomas V. Morris, *Our Idea of God: An Introduction to Philosophical Theology* (Notre Dame: University of Notre Dame Press, 1991), 62.

16. Axiology is the branch of philosophy that deals with questions about value, and includes ethics (the good for persons), politics (the good for communities or nations), and aesthetics (the nature of beauty). Morris uses the term here to indicate a kind of goodness of being that is more than just moral goodness and (it seems) more than just duty-fulfillment.

17. Ibid. 62–3.

18. Earl Conee, 'The Nature and Impossibility of Moral Perfection', *Philosophy and Phenomenological Research* 54 (1994), 815–25.

19. Colin McGinn, 'Must I Be Morally Perfect?', *Analysis* 52 (1992), 32–4. McGinn's answer is 'yes' since he interprets moral perfection as a matter of having no moral defects (never violating one's moral duties), which is a goal that is possible to achieve (at least in principle).

20. T. M. Mawson, *Belief in God: An Introduction to Philosophy of Religion* (Oxford: Clarendon, 2005), 59.

21. Ibid. 67.

22. On the other hand, if God's duties to each individual might prevent him from maximizing overall value (or from achieving the relevant consequentialist objective), the duty model could result in a different outcome than the consequentialist model.

23. Richard Swinburne, *The Coherence of Theism* (Oxford: Clarendon, 1977), 202.

24. For a fuller explication and defense of this virtue theory see J. L. A. Garcia, 'Interpersonal Virtues: Whose Interest Do They Serve?', *American Catholic Philosophical Quarterly* 71 (1997), 31–60.

25. Christian theologians may of course appeal to the doctrine of the Incarnation as a counterexample to this claim. But presumably even though Jesus *as man* experienced emotions and desires and so could exemplify the virtues of courage and temperance, it would be odd to say that he exemplified these virtues *as God*. There is an extended sense of the term in which one might describe God as exhibiting humility in deigning to come among us as a man (in the Incarnation), but this strikes me as an analogical use of the term.

26. St Thomas Aquinas, *Summa Theologiae* I q. 19 a. 3.

27. Unless having duties is compatible with necessarily fulfilling them, God does not have a duty to will the good of each person. On Thomas's view, God's perfect goodness entails that it is logically impossible for him to create a person without willing that person's good.

28. William P. Alston, 'Some Temporarily Final Thoughts on Evidential Arguments From Evil', in Daniel Howard-Snyder (ed.), *The Evidential Argument from Evil* (Bloomington: Indiana University Press, 1996), 311–32.

29. 'We know that all things work together for those who love God, who are called according to his purpose.' Romans 8: 28.

30. Thomas Flint, in editorial comments on an earlier version of this chapter, February 2008.

31. Such freedom wills the highest good (namely, God) and necessarily possesses this good, as being one and the same with it.

32. Ephesians 1: 12.

33. C. S. Lewis, 'The Weight of Glory', in *The Weight of Glory and Other Essays* (New York: HarperCollins, 1949, 1976, 1980), 25–46.

PART III

GOD AND CREATION

CHAPTER 11

DIVINE ACTION AND EVOLUTION

ROBIN COLLINS

I. INTRODUCTION

ALTHOUGH many issues relate to divine action—such as the doctrine of creation, God's relation to human beings, God's relation to time, the intrinsic nature of God, and the like—the issue of divine action as it specifically relates to evolution can be divided into two major issues: (1) that of understanding the ways in which God might have influenced the evolutionary process, if at all, and (2) that of attempting to gain insight into God's ultimate purposes in creating the universe and life by means of an evolutionary process. This chapter will primarily focus on (2), an issue that has largely been neglected by philosophers writing on divine action. This issue is particularly important given that the broadly evolutionary picture—namely that the universe, life, and human culture have gone through a long developmental process—is now beyond reasonable doubt and yet at the same time constitutes a drastic shift in our understanding of the universe.

The literature on issue (1) has largely focused on whether it is possible to provide a satisfactory 'non-interventionist' account of God's interaction with the world.[1] The typical requirement for a non-interventionist account is that God's interaction should not 'break' the laws of nature, though what exactly this means is typically not spelled out. One widely discussed proposal along these lines is that God influences the course of the world by determining the outcome of some, if not all, quantum events. Purportedly, this does not break the laws of nature since the laws of physics do not determine which quantum events will occur.

One major problem with the literature is the lack of well-developed, convincing arguments for rejecting an 'interventionist' account of the laws of nature. Robert Russell (2006: 584), for instance, claims that a major problem with interventionism is that 'it suggests that God is normally absent from the web of natural processes, acting only in the gaps that God causes'. The force of this objection is highly questionable, however, since it is unclear why God could not act *both* through natural processes and by means of occasional divine interventions, something Christians have traditionally held. Typically, little further argument is offered in support of this, and related, objections to interventionism. In any case, philosopher William Alston (1994) has carefully examined the major objections commonly offered to interventionism and concludes that he can find no reasons to reject this view. At least for those who hold a traditional view of God in which God has the ability to intervene, I agree with Alston that the reasons typically offered against interventionism are unconvincing, unless one already makes highly controversial assumptions about God's purposes in creation.

What often fails to be explicitly recognized is that whether we should seek for non-interventionist accounts of divine action, and what constraints we should put on such accounts, largely depend on the view we have of God's purposes in creation. If, for example, one of God's primary purposes was to display his power over nature, then a natural way for God to do this would be for God to suspend the normal operation of nature. An advocate of such a view, therefore, would likely have no problem with the claim that God has intervened in cosmic history on a regular basis. On the other hand, if one of God's primary purposes in creating the world was to allow creation to 'make itself', a position taken by most of the current major writers on divine action and evolution (see below, sect. II), then one would at most allow very limited divine intervention. Or, if one thinks that God creates the world by an evolutionary process to secure an epistemic distance between God and humans, as some have proposed (see below, sect. II), then one might be happy with divine intervention, as long as it could not be detected. Accordingly, once we have some understanding of what God's purposes for creation might be, then we can ask whether a particular mode of divine action will help fulfill that purpose or not; without such an understanding, the only constraints for Christians seem to be Scripture, Church tradition, and logical coherence, constraints the traditional interventionist accounts seem to meet. As Keith Ward (1990: 269) notes, God's ultimate purpose for creation 'provides the rationale for all particular Divine actions which continually shape and direct the temporal process of the universe'. Thus, this chapter will be devoted to addressing this prior and key question of what God's ultimate purposes might be for creating the world, particularly focusing on what

God's purpose might have been in creating the world via a seemingly partly chance-driven evolutionary process.

Throughout this chapter, I take it as a well-established theory that life on earth arose through the process of biological evolution, by which I mean the process of descent with modification from the first cell. I will leave open, however, the question of whether this process was guided by God.

The Issue

To many, evolution provides evidence against the existence of God, and for others, at least a theological perplexity. As theologian John Haught (2006: 702–3) has eloquently summarized the problem:

It is the absence of purposive design and the presence of accident that seem to rule out the existence of God.... Evolution requires enough time for a sufficiently large number of minute random variations to supply the mindless process of natural selection with adaptable outcomes. The fact that so much time is required for this unwieldy epic to transpire, and so much death occurs along the way, and so many mistakes and monstrosities appear, only to be discarded renders evolution all the more devoid of purpose apparently. Any creator who would 'fool around' so inefficiently for billions of years in order to produce living and thinking beings seems much less competent than the most mediocre human engineers.

This perplexity can be broken down into two questions: (1) Why did God create a world that had to undergo a very long developmental process to give rise to life, and then conscious, moral agents, instead of creating a world that was fully formed from the beginning? And (2) Why did this developmental process, whether or not it was guided by God, involve so many apparent accidents and chance events, which has led to so much suffering and death over millions of years? Doesn't this seem contrary to the character of an all good, all loving God who has a providential purpose for creation?

Although one could respond to these questions by leaving it a 'mystery' as to why God created the universe in this way (similar to the strategy of what is often labeled a 'defense' in the case of the evidential problem of evil), if overused such a strategy undermines the claim that the theistic hypothesis provides a fruitful basis for understanding the existence and nature of the universe and human experience. In any case, I will pursue another strategy in this chapter, that of attempting to offer a plausible speculation as to why God might have created the world through an evolutionary process. Apart from apologetic purposes, engaging in such speculation, I believe, is important in its own right for gaining a clearer theological and philosophical understanding of what God's purposes might be for the universe and ourselves.

II. Major Current Accounts
of God's Purposes

The Autonomy of Creation Explanation

In the last twenty years, the most common answer given by those writing in the area of science and religion as to why God used a partly chance-driven evolutionary process to create the world is that such a process is required for creation to be truly independent of God. Scientist-theologian John Polkinghorne, for example, says that he believes the only possible solution to the wastefulness of evolution and other sorts of natural evil 'lies in a variation of the free-will defence, applied to the whole created order. In his great act of creation I believe that God allows the physical world to be itself, not in Manichaean opposition to him, but in that independence which is Love's gift of freedom to the one beloved. . . . The cosmos is given the opportunity to be itself (1989: 67). On the next page, Polkinghorne goes on to state that 'God accords to the processes of the world the same respect he accords to the actions of humanity' (ibid. 68). Elsewhere Polkinghorne (1998: 14) summarizes his free process defence as the claim that 'a world allowed to make itself is better than the puppet theatre of a Cosmic Tyrant'. Polkinghorne's free-process defence, therefore, is an attempt to extend the free will theodicy—the idea that God has given his creatures free will and thus must allow them to do evil—to creation as a whole.[2]

John Haught, currently the leading theologian writing on evolution and Christian theology, presents a similar explanation. According to Haught (2003: 168),

an instantaneously finished universe, one from which our present condition of historical becoming and existential ambiguity could be envisaged as a subsequent estrangement, would in principle have been only an emanation or appendage of deity and not something truly other than God. A world that is not clearly distinct from God could not be the recipient of divine love. And an instantaneously completed world could never have established an independent existence vis-à-vis its creator.

Michael Murray criticizes Haught's claim that the universe could not be truly independent of God if God created it in an instant. As Murray (forthcoming, ch. 6) rightly points out, if an artist creates a fully-formed painting, the painting is still a truly distinct entity from the artist. Although Haught is not explicit about what exactly he means by autonomy, perhaps a more charitable interpretation of Haught's idea of independence is that the universe be allowed to 'make itself'. As Haught (2000: 41) says elsewhere, 'A world given a lease to become more and more autonomous, even to help create itself and eventually attain the status of human consciousness, has much more integrity and value than any conceivable world determined in every respect by a "divine designer".' Under this interpretation, Haught could be seen as extending both the free will theodicy and the soul-making theodicy to the universe itself (as Polkinghorne also seems to do). In the soul-making theodicy, God creates a universe in which natural and moral evil can occur so that human beings can develop a freely formed virtuous character by acting virtuously in response to evil. If God simply created our characters fully formed, then we would not have been allowed to 'make ourselves'. Indeed, the soul-making theodicy can be seen as an extension of the free will theodicy: it could be argued that one major reason that free will is valuable is that it gives us the opportunity partly to choose our own character.

One outstanding problem with Polkinghorne's and Haught's explanation is that of understanding what is meant by creation 'making itself' or being 'autonomous'. The whole appeal of this idea, it seems, arises because the metaphors of 'making itself' and 'autonomy' tempt us to endow nature with the sort of will and choice we find in ourselves. Assuming that non-human creation does not have a will to decide its own destiny, it is hard to see what these concepts could mean when applied to the non-human world, other than that creation simply unfolds in accordance with the deterministic and statistical laws with which God endowed it. Clearly, merely to follow a statistical law is not the same as free choice: presumably, a radioactive atom that decays does not 'decide' to decay but merely follows the statistical rules of quantum mechanics.

The worry here is that both Polkinghorne and Haught are overly anthropomorphizing nature: eliminate the semi-anthropomorphic metaphors, and the idea of creation 'making itself' seems to lose much, if not all, of its appeal. The reason is that it is unclear what is supposed to be good about creation making itself, once we de-anthropomorphize nature. In the case of human freedom, we have a strong intuition that moral responsibility requires free will and that moral agency is a great good in and of itself. Further, arguably, beings without free will could not authentically love God (or even one another) if God determined all their choices. Presumably, however, non-human creation neither has moral agency nor does it love God (except, perhaps, some higher non-human animals), or at least not unless one adopts a radically different view of nature than delivered by modern science: namely, a view in which non-human, non-higher-animal creation does have a will and can make choices. Neither Haught nor Polkinghorne, however, advocates such a view.[3]

One response to the above criticisms is to argue that God's creating the universe and life through an evolutionary process is more consistent with the kenotic, self-emptying, non-compelling character of God's love as revealed in Jesus, even if it is not required by it. As Lutheran theologian George Murphy (2003: 372) states, 'if the character of the true God is shown to us in the saving work of the cross, then we may expect that all of the divine activity will be consistent with this character. We should not be surprised if this God in his creative and providential work "makes himself nothing" ... and "humbles himself" rather than overwhelm the world with arbitrarily exercised power.' The problem with this response is that it is once again difficult to see how, without a highly anthropomorphic view of nature, it would be in any way inconsistent with God's character as revealed in Jesus to create the universe in an instant with its future development determined by natural law. For instance, it is not in any way inconsistent for one to treat other human beings in a loving way that respects their autonomy, while being a 'tyrant' with one's car or computer. At best, this 'kenosis' response seems to provide only a weak reason for God's creating by means of an evolutionary process—namely, that everything else being equal, we would expect creation to reflect the creator's character, much as we might expect an artwork to reflect the character of the artist.

Divine Hiddenness as an Explanation

Another explanation for God's using an evolutionary process is that this is necessary to keep God's existence from being too evident. If God's existence were obvious, that would take away from human free choice, much as seeing a police officer in the rear-view mirror takes away—or at least severely reduces—the choice of obeying the speed limit for its own sake. As Murray points out, one major problem with this view is that until the last two centuries, the theory of evolution did not exist, and people saw what they considered powerful evidence of design all around them. Yet, presumably they had the freedom to believe or disbelieve in God. Further, Christians should at least be cautious concerning this argument since it seems to be in tension, if not conflict, with various statements in the New Testament. For example, the Apostle Paul states that God's existence is evident from the things that are made (Romans 1: 20) and the book of James says that 'even the demons believe—and shudder' (2: 19, NRSV). Thus, even if one is convinced that God exists, much room still seems to be left open with regard to believing in God, in the sense of trusting, relying on, and committing oneself to God.

The Chaos to Order Proposal

After reviewing and rejecting as seriously flawed several other proposals for why God created a universe via an evolutionary process that results in so much animal suffering, Michael Murray (forthcoming, chs. 5 and 6) proposes as a viable possibility the idea that bringing about a universe from a state of chaos to order via lawlike means is intrinsically valuable (ibid. ch. 6). One problem with this idea is technical: from the perspective of the second law of thermodynamics, the early universe was in a very low entropy state and hence actually highly ordered, at least by the technical definition of order given by statistical mechanics. (Statistical mechanics provides the standard physicist's understanding of the laws of thermodynamics.) One could circumvent this problem, however, simply by claiming that what is intrinsically valuable is for God to bring about a universe by a developmental process that partly involves seemingly chance occurrences. The other problem is justifying such a claim. Murray supports this claim by noting that there is a significant thread of past Christian thinkers (such as St Augustine) who claimed that it would be grander for God to create the world in a developmental way instead of fully formed. This claim seems correct as far as it goes: it does seem to be a greater accomplishment to create a universe that 'forms itself' into stars and galaxies from an initial fireball than to create a fully formed universe. Arguably, a universe that forms itself also would be aesthetically richer since it would not only contain a greater variety of states, but these states would coherently build on each other.

Although a combination of the value of expressing God's grandeur and aesthetic values could plausibly be thought to be sufficient reason for God to create a universe that required billions of years to develop, one might doubt (1) whether it could adequately explain why seemingly chance processes have played such a major role in the universe's evolution and (2) whether it is sufficient to offset the seeming dis-value of the suffering of non-human sentient life during the evolutionary process. These doubts, I believe, should be sufficient to motivate us to search for additional reasons, whether or not such reasons ultimately can be found.

III. My Own Proposal

My own highly speculative proposal begins with the claim that the evolutionary process allows for certain types of interconnection between humans and non-human creation that are potentially of significant value. I do not claim that these interconnections provide the sole reason for God's creating by means of a seemingly chance-driven evolutionary process, only that they provide one reason. We will first explicate what these interconnections are, and then present some reasons for thinking that they are of value. The three types of interconnections that we will consider are what I will call *emergent*, *ancestral*, and *redemptive* interconnections.

Before proceeding, however, a brief explanation should be given about what is meant by 'interconnection'. To begin, an interconnection is a special sort of relation between persons or between persons and non-personal aspects of creation. Why hypothesize the existence of such a special relationship? The basis for this hypothesis is that people commonly claim to feel deeply connected to other human beings, such as their parents, their spouses, or someone who has greatly helped them in times of suffering and hardship. Further, many people, particularly people in indigenous societies, claim to feel a profound connection to the surrounding earth and animals. This common human experience is the basis for claiming that there is this sort of special and significant relationship which in common discourse is often called a 'connection'.

People commonly experience the persons/entities that they are connected to, and the connections themselves, as being 'part' of their selves. Thus, it could plausibly be argued that this idea of interconnection presupposes that the self is partly constituted by its relations to other entities. Since one can be more or less connected with another person or entity, this in turn presupposes that the self does not have definite boundaries: some relations can be a deeper part of the self than others. Why make this presupposition? Once again we can appeal to experience. People commonly experience their relations with other persons, or even parts of non-human creation, as both profoundly important and as being in some way deeply significant to what they are as human beings. Further, the loss of one of these relations is often experienced as a loss of an aspect of one's self. For example, the loss of a loved one—particularly a spouse—is often experienced as a loss of some part of one's own self. Once again, indigenous peoples often claim this sort of thing about the land. Even if this talk of another entity or our relation to it as being part of one's very selfhood is only metaphorical, the metaphor is still picking out some special relation that people find of great significance, which is all that we require for the argument in this chapter.

Emergent Interconnection

An emergent interconnection refers to a sort of interconnection that occurs under the hypothesis that, at least in part, the human body and soul emerge out of the basic materials of the universe. I define a *weak emergent connection* as an emergent connection that occurs if the human body is the result of an evolutionary process, but the human soul is directly created by God. On the other hand, I define a *strong emergent connection* as an emergent connection that occurs if the human soul itself—including its libertarian agency—is formed in some way out of what is already present, in nascent form, in the universe itself. If this latter a view of the human person is correct, then our consciousness and libertarian agency would be more deeply interconnected with the universe than under a traditional substance dualist account of the soul. Further, if libertarian agency emerges out of the matter in some way, then it seems that indeterminism would have to be built into the very fabric of the cosmos. Given that a strong emergent connection results in greater value than a weak emergent connection, this would provide one reason for why God created the universe by means of an *indeterministic* evolutionary process instead of a deterministic evolutionary process. We will explore the value of emergent connections more below.

Although I believe emergent interconnections are important, I do not want to promote a physicalist view of the mind, since I believe that there are powerful arguments for some form of dualism in which the self is partly a separate entity from the brain, whether that be a classical form of substance dualism, an emergentist form in which the partially independent soul is generated from the brain, or some sort of Thomistic view.[4] Exactly how one should view the relationship between the mind and the brain is a very deep issue that we cannot explore here. Instead, I simply note that the existence of even a strong sort of emergent connection seems compatible with some forms of dualism in which the human person is partly separable from the body.

Ancestral Interconnections

Emergent interconnections could be realized by God creating a world with fully formed animal and plant life with human and animal souls somehow arising out of matter. In such a world, however, a certain sort of connection would be missing, what I will call an *ancestral* connection. An ancestral connection occurs when one being shares a common ancestor with another—e.g. according to the theory of evolution, human and apes both arose by common descent from the primate group called prosimians. Many thinkers writing in the areas of evolutionary theory and ecology intuit a special value in the fact that we are ancestrally connected with other living organisms. For example, Stanford University evolutionary biologist Joan Roughgarden (2006: 18) writes: 'Our material continuity with the rest of living creation is not a threat to Christian beliefs. Just the opposite... Evolution's discovery of a single tree of life extends a Christian view of the body and family beyond humans out to all of living creation.'

Redemptive Interconnections

By 'redemptive interconnection' I mean the sort of interconnection that would occur between humans and creation if, through God's grace, human beings help 'redeem' the world by helping make God present in creation in such a way that creation more fully participates in the life of God.[5] To explain this more, we will first need to sketch a Christian eschatology that I believe is suggested by the New Testament.

Many New Testament scriptures speak of the ultimate fulfillment or redemption of creation. Romans 8: 21, for example, tells us that 'creation itself will be set free from its bondage to decay and will obtain the freedom of the glory of the children of God' (NRSV). Similarly, other scriptures speak of God's ultimate purpose being directed toward the redemption of all creation. In Ephesians 1: 10, this ultimate purpose is to 'gather all things in him [Christ], both in heaven and earth'; in

Ephesians 4: 10 it is for Christ to 'fill all things'; in Colossians 1: 20 it is to 'reconcile to himself all things, whether on earth or in heaven'; and finally, in 1 Corinthians 15: 28 it is for God to be 'all in all'. These scriptures suggest, if not imply, that God's ultimate purpose for the material cosmos is that it become a full participant in the divine life.

This idea of the entire created order ultimately participating in the life of God is particularly emphasized in Eastern Orthodox. According to standard Eastern Orthodox theology, this complete participation of humans and creation in the divine life is understood as participation in what the Orthodox call the 'energies' of God in contrast to the essence of God (Lossky 1976: 74–5, 97–101, 133–4). For the Orthodox, the energies of God refer to the life of God—that is, 'God in his activity and self-manifestation' (Ware 1976: 22)—whereas the essence of God refers to God's innermost self, which is forever inaccessible to us. Using this distinction, Orthodox theologians claim to be able to affirm the eventual complete participation of re-deemed humanity *and* creation in the divine life while at the same time excluding 'any pantheistic identification between God and creation' (ibid. 23).[6]

Within the context of the New Testament, the passages cited above suggest that this redemption will take place through the actions of human beings. In the New Testament, Christians are referred to as the 'body of Christ', which suggests that one primary way in which Christ acts in the world is through human beings, just as we act through our bodies. Hence if God's purposes are to redeem all creation—as is clear, I believe, from the scriptures cited above—it makes sense that it will be at least in part through his 'body', which consists of human beings. Our redemption comes to us first, and then spreads out to all creation through us.[7] In any case, I agree with philosopher and theologian Keith Ward (2001: 165) when he states that 'I can think of nothing more important for the Christian faith in our day than to recover the truly cosmic sense of redemption that was characteristic both of the biblical writings and of the Church Fathers. Redemption will not be seen as a saving of a few human beings from destruction of one small planet. It will be seen as a reconstituting of the whole cosmos in the presence of God, in a more glorious form.'

How will this redemption work? One can only speculate. I speculate that it will be through both the action of God through human beings and the activation of subtle orders in nature of which we are presently unaware, though this particular speculation is not essential to my overall proposal in this chapter. Two analogies might make this more plausible. First, consider the case of metamorphosis, in which one organism undergoes a radical transformation in its morphology, such as a tadpole becoming a frog or a caterpillar becoming a butterfly. If we had not seen this happen, we would have never predicted it; clearly it involves subtle processes that we do not understand very well yet. Whether metamorphosis can be understood by current chemistry or requires some new sort of science—such as the non-local 'morphic fields' suggested by biologist Rupert Sheldrake (1988)—is unclear. The suggestion is that in analogy to cases of metamorphosis, the universe itself will undergo a radical, currently unimaginable transformation and yet still be the same universe, just as a caterpillar could be thought to remain the same entity through its radical transformation to a butterfly; the caterpillar does not die and is then replaced by a butterfly, but instead transforms into a butterfly, implying a retention of its identity.

The second analogy is the development of life and finally conscious beings. If we imagine ourselves as disembodied physicists existing in the first minute of the big bang, we probably never would have predicted the eventual emergence of life and consciousness using only our current knowledge of physics. We probably would have thought the idea was absurd. Finally, the revolutions of quantum theory and general relativity have taught us that nature is full of surprises and matter is much more mysterious than we thought; consequently, one must be extremely careful when extrapolating the future of the universe based on our current understanding of physics.

Although not essential to my argument concerning redemptive interconnections, I further speculate that the universe's being 'subject to decay' is the result of the universe's operation being governed mostly by law, instead of God's being more fully involved in its operation beyond sustaining its laws. To elaborate on this idea, consider the second law of thermodynamics. The second law states that within a closed system, the entropy of a system always increases. Within statistical mechanics, this notion of entropy is given a precise definition in terms of probabilities over what physicists call 'phase space'. In the standard explanation of the second law, the claim that the entropy of a closed system must always increase is reduced to the claim that the system proceeds from a less probable macroscopic state to a more probable macroscopic state. The example of perfume in a bottle nicely illustrates this idea. If one opens a bottle of perfume, the molecules eventually will evaporate and become distributed throughout the room. In order for this to happen, no special initial distribution of the positions and velocities of the molecules in the bottle is required; virtually all initial distributions would yield the same result. In contrast, unless the perfume molecules had just the right enormously improbable configuration of positions and velocities in the room, the perfume has a virtually zero chance of returning to the bottle (within any reasonable period of time) apart from some intervention such as the room being cooled causing the perfume to condense. This leads to the following suggestion: without some sort of external intervention or exactly the right initial conditions, the laws of probability dictate that any sufficiently complex closed system that both obeys laws similar to those in our universe and contains systems of enormous complexity, will tend, however slowly, to move from order to disorder; or at least this occurrence is highly probable. Of course, it might be possible for God to circumvent this movement from order to disorder by creating a universe with radically different laws or initial conditions, but we cannot say what other goods might be lacking in such a universe.

Under this idea, therefore, the fact that the universe is 'subject to decay'—and hence suffering and death occur in it—is because it is governed by a set of laws, whether those laws are deterministic or indeterministic. Only if God becomes directly and constantly involved with the universe (beyond simply sustaining it) could this process of decay be stopped; even by God's carefully choosing the universe's laws and initial conditions, avoiding some sort of imperfection might be impossible.[8] My suggestion, therefore, is that God has left it up to human beings to help bring about this further divine involvement with the universe that is necessary for it not to be subject to decay.

My proposal is that by our first sharing in the divine life through Christ, this life is able to spread throughout all creation and hence reverse the decay. This proposal fits well with Romans 8: 20–1, since this passage suggests that God created nature to be 'subject to frustration' so that it would participate in the new life of redeemed humanity. According to the NRSV version of this passage (which does not relevantly vary among translations), 'the creation was subjected to futility, not of its own will but by the will of the one who subjected it, *in hope that* creation itself will be set free from its bondage to decay and will obtain the freedom of the glory of the children of God'. Notice that the passage suggests that God subjected it to futility ('by the will of the one who subjected it') for the purpose that it be set free, as indicated by the phrase 'in hope that'.

What will this sharing in the divine life be like? Beyond the claim that the universe would no longer be subject to decay, one can only speculate. Perhaps the fabric of the universe would be in perfect harmony with the wills and thoughts of resurrected human beings. Further, perhaps all sufficiently sentient animals will become fully conscious in some way, taking on new forms that are in continuity with their current bodies, but which are also radically different, with current forms of metamorphosis being only a foretaste. It might even be the case that the universe itself gains a 'soul' of some sort, with which human beings could be in communion.[9]

Why think this scenario is at all plausible? First, such a scenario is suggested by the Apostle Paul's statement that creation itself will share 'in the glorious liberty of the children of God'. More importantly, however, given that this sort of scenario would result in a richer and more valuable universe, then theists would have good reason to believe that this is God's ultimate destiny for the universe, unless we had some reason to believe it was either contrary to some well-established knowledge about the nature of the universe or in some way impossible for God to bring about, neither of which we have good reason to believe. In any case, it seems plausible to suppose that in such a transformed creation, there would be a deep intercommunion between non-human creation and human beings. Further, the interconnections hypothesized above would become particularly valuable, as now they would involve interconnections between conscious beings. For example, these redeemed non-human creatures would have a connection of appreciation for being redeemed from decay. (See more below for the value of this sort of interconnection.) Finally, such a scenario would provide additional resources for understanding why an all good, loving God would create a world that would involve so much animal suffering and pain. This issue becomes particularly pressing with regard to the redemptive status of highly evolved non-human hominids such as Neanderthals and *homo erectus*. The existence of such beings—which have a form of sentience between currently existing non-human primates and humans—really presses the case, I believe, for including all God's creation in God's redemptive plan.

At this point, one might ask: couldn't we still play a major role in creation's ultimate fulfillment even if God created it in a perfect state? For example, through watering and tending an oak tree from its being a seedling to a fully mature tree, one can contribute to its final perfection as a fully grown oak, even though at every stage of the oak's development it could be said to be perfect for that stage of development. By analogy, then, it seems that God could have created the universe in an immature, yet perfect state, and then have given human beings the opportunity to become co-creators with God to bring it to fulfillment.

One response to this objection is that the depth of redemptive interconnection would not be as great. It seems to involve a deeper interconnection actually to be the instrument by which the divine life becomes fully present in creation, which involves a much more radical transformation. Bringing creation from a state of 'bondage to corruption' to sharing fully in the divine life would involve contributing to the fulfillment of creation in a greater way than simply helping it come to maturity from one state of perfection to another. To help see this, imagine that creation (or perhaps just the higher animals) became self-conscious: creation would appreciate our work of bringing it to fulfillment more if we brought it from a state of bondage to decay to sharing in the divine life than if we simply helped it come to maturity, since the former involves a much greater transition.

Summary

It should be clear from the foregoing that a world created to evolve and eventually produce human beings in a partially chance-driven way allows for the realization of emergent, ancestral, and redemptive interconnections. Further, it is at least difficult to conceive of how God could have created the world by some alternative means and at the same time for these interconnections to be realized to as great an extent. Thus, given that these interconnections are of significant value, they provide a reason for an all good God to have created the world in this way.

IV. The Value of Interconnections

Why think these connections are valuable? To answer this question, we will begin by considering the value of interconnections between persons. First, an essential part of love seems to be interconnection, at least insofar as it goes beyond mere benevolence: the lover desires to be deeply connected with the beloved, to participate in the life of the beloved in some way. Without this interconnection, love is in some important sense incomplete. Second, we all value interconnection. Few of us would think that a life lived alone, without significant and deep interconnections with others, would be ideal; rather, we would think it was missing something of great value. Third, part of traditional theism, especially Christian theism, is the idea of the great value of communion with God and with others in the body of Christ. This is taken as one of the major reasons that God created other beings with free will. Finally, further hints regarding the significance we attach to certain sorts of connections abound, from adopted children looking for their biological parents and people expending great effort to determine their family tree, to claims of the importance of apostolic succession, which involves a purported mystical connection in the body of Christ.

Our next question is: why think that the three types of interconnections with creation elaborated above would be of value? One answer is that such interconnections pave the way for a deeper intercommunion with creation, an intercommunion in which creation in some sense becomes part of what we are, and ultimately through us is taken into the divine life. To see how this might take place, we will begin by looking at four analogies.

The first analogy is that of the purported value of soul-making, as one would find in the soul-making theodicy. This analogy will particularly illustrate the value of redemptive interconnections. Unlike some appeals to the universe 'making itself', our use of the soul-making theodicy will not involve any anthropomorphism of nature, at least not of the current pre-redeemed nature. As mentioned above, the idea behind the soul-making theodicy is that there is some great good in human beings having a major part in determining their future character, instead of God simply endowing them with a perfect character from the beginning. This goes beyond the mere value of free will, since God could have created us with a perfect character and then simply given us the choice of good over evil, something many think was the case with angelic beings.

I suggest that the core value in being partly responsible for our own souls is that our character becomes more fully our own in a way that would otherwise not be possible. The reason, I suggest, is that our 'deepest choosing self'—that is, our self considered as the underlying agent that makes choices—gets interwoven and connected with those aspects of our character that we help develop through our actions.[10] Finally, by co-creating our character with God's grace in Christ, there is an interweaving between Christ, our agency, and our character, so that not only does our character become deeply our own, but in some sense through Christ God's character and life also become deeply our own.

Applied to creation, our choosing to co-create the world with God from a state of 'frustration' to one of 'liberty' means that we become interwoven and inter-connected with creation, and it becomes a joint work both of God and of us. In analogy to our character traits becoming our own, this interconnection helps creation become part of who we are, and so leads to an expansion of our selves. The claims here parallel part of Karl Marx's insights concerning the alienation of labor: through the efforts and toil we put into the products of our labor, they become an extension (objectification) of ourselves, and further by others enjoying the fruits of our labors, a means of sharing ourselves with others. This important connection between our self and our labor is something Marx saw the capitalist system as undercutting, hence resulting in the 'alienation' of labor.

A second analogy for seeing how the interconnections discussed above form the basis for a particularly deep communion between humans and creation is that of being deeply involved in the lives of other persons. When we are deeply involved in the lives of others in a truly loving way, their joys become our joys, and their sorrows become our sorrows. Likewise, it is plausible to think that our deep involvement with creation—especially our redemptive involvement—paves the way for its joys, pains, and sufferings to become, in some significant sense, our joys, pains, and sufferings, and thus through us to be taken up into the very life of Christ.

A third analogy is that of the relation we have with our own body. Traditional Christian theology holds that even though the soul survives bodily death, the soul is incomplete, if not radically incomplete, without the body. Why is this? One plausible reason seems to be that the body is 'part' of what we are, at least in some significant metaphorical sense. A further question is: what makes the body part of what we are? One answer is that we are deeply interconnected in this life with our bodies: it is through our bodies that we become conscious and interact in the world. Indeed, the interconnections with our bodies seem to be analogous or parallel to the emergent and redemptive interconnections described above: our self is at least in part formed from our bodies and we in turn shape and transform the nature of our own bodies. In analogy to how these interconnections with our body make it part of our very self, I propose that the emergent, ancestral, and redemptive interconnections hypothesized above could plausibly be thought to pave the way for the non-human creation becoming 'part' of what we are. If this is correct, then it is at least plausible to hold that the full redemption of humans will require the full redemption of the creation itself. This gains plausibility when we consider that our bodies are intertwined with the rest of creation, and thus it makes sense that the full redemption of our bodies in the resurrection will involve—and hence be simultaneous with—the redemption of the cosmos (e.g. see Romans 8: 23). As John Haught (2003: 155) has stated, 'as long as the universe is unfinished, so also is each one of us. Because of the intricate way each organism is tied into the cosmic story...no living being can attain a satisfying fulfillment independently of the cosmos. Our personal redemption awaits the salvation of the whole.'

The last analogy is that of the connection we have to our parents, and to our relatives. People commonly perceive that familial connections are deeply important to their own identity. One reason might be that these connections make those related in this way part of what we are as persons. So, perhaps the emergent and ancestral connections with the rest of creation, particularly the higher-level animals, help make them in some significant way part of what we are; we are in some sense one family with creation. This in turn helps pave the way for an even deeper intercommunion that results from establishing redemptive interconnections with creation.

Finally, I propose that these interconnections gain their full value by being taken up into conscious experience, specifically our conscious experience, God's conscious experience, and if non-human creation becomes conscious, its conscious experience. For example, the internal interconnections and interweavings that are a result of the universe's long evolutionary history would move from being an externally realized aesthetic value to an internally, consciously realized beauty and richness. Thus, the richer the universe is—both synchronically and diachronically—the richer we will be. If, moreover, the higher animals, or even possibly the creation itself, become conscious, they will also share in this richness, and moreover, there will be a bond of appreciation for being redeemed, something I assume is of intrinsic value. (I discuss the intrinsic value of this sort of bond more below when I briefly outline my 'connection-building theodicy'.) Finally, I propose, this will in turn enrich God. As Keith Ward (2001: 158–9) notes, through creation 'God realizes, makes actual, aspects of the divine being that otherwise would have remained potential. Entering into relationship and communion, and cooperating in realizing new forms of finite value, are realizations of great values in and for the divine nature itself.' Similarly, George Murphy (2003, p. 385) surmises that 'by assuming our common humanity in the incarnation, God took on these evolutionary relationships [that we have with the animals] and became a participant in this history [of life on earth]'.

At this point, one might ask: couldn't the creation be part of who we are even if God made it instantaneously and fully formed? Yes, to a certain extent, since it would be connected to us: our bodily existence would be dependent on the material processes around us, and in turn we would affect the universe. It is plausible to suppose, however, that in this circumstance its connection with us would not be nearly as deep: it would lack the ancestral and redemptive interconnection discussed above. This would, I suggest, take away from the depth of intercommunion with creation and the depth to which it would become part of our own selves, at least given the assumption that intercommunion is built off the right sort of previously established interconnections. Of course, as mentioned previously, an incomplete but non-evolutionary world could still have similar redemptive interconnections, but it would still lack the ancestral interconnections discussed above.

Interconnection, Original Sin, and Theodicy

Not only can one make the sort of case in the last section for interconnections being important, but this idea of certain kinds of interconnection being intrinsically valuable is also a highly fruitful one in other areas. As our first example, the importance of interconnections makes sense of why God created human beings to go through a developmental process, and why humans in general are deeply interconnected and interdependent on each other, especially through time. Not only are we each dependent on our parents (or some equivalent group of human beings) for our existence, and our development into adulthood, but our entire present human culture is dependent on the choices made by previous generations.

Further, this idea can help make sense of why God allows evil and the doctrine of original sin. Elsewhere, I have constructed both a theodicy and an account of original sin based on this idea, both of which I will briefly summarize here.[11] I call my theodicy the *connection-building theodicy* (CBT) and claim that it offers at least a partial explanation for God's allowing evil. This theodicy begins with the assumption that positive connections between individuals, such as connections of appreciation for being helped in times of suffering, of being forgiven of sin, of being helped out of spiritual and moral darkness, and the like, are of intrinsic value, a value in which all the parties involved in the connection share. Further, it hypothesizes that these connections of appreciation and intimacy have the potential of being an ongoing part of one's life for all eternity. For example, when all things are brought to light, we will have an ongoing appreciation for those who self-sacrificially helped us in times of suffering, since we will always remember what they did. Accordingly, I claim, the goodness of this connection keeps growing, becoming of very large, if not of infinite, value, thus outweighing the finite evils that God must allow in order for the types of connections in question to exist.

One way of understanding this theodicy is to see it as greatly adding to the virtuous-response theodicy, in which evil allows for certain sorts of virtuous responses such as self-sacrificial love. One problem with this theodicy is that the hypothesized greater goods are the virtuous responses themselves, which are of finite temporal duration and thus arguably not of great enough value to compensate for the evils in the world. In contrast, the CBT postulates that these virtuous responses give rise to further positive special relations between two persons that become part of each person's ongoing selfhood. Because of this, the value of these connections is not restricted to the time at which they were formed, but can keep growing. The CBT, therefore, can be seen as postulating something of potentially great extrinsic value resulting from many of our virtuous responses, thereby significantly strengthening the virtuous-response theodicy and similar theodicies, such as that advocated by Richard Swinburne (2004: ch. 11).

Finally, the above explanation for why God used an evolutionary process can be seen as an extension of this theodicy to the natural world, even though the purpose of this chapter is not to address the problem of evil per se. As an extension of this theodicy, it can be seen to provide at least one reason for thinking that the value of the connections that evolution makes possible outweighs the suffering that occurs in the process: since the connections are eternal, their value could be thought to be very large or infinite, thus outweighing the finite suffering that necessarily result from the evolutionary process.

This idea of the importance of interconnections also helps makes sense of the idea of original sin in an evolutionary context, as I argue in more detail elsewhere (Collins 2003). If we think of original sin as a sort of negative spiritual inheritance resulting from previous sinful acts of human beings—such as the sort of spiritual darkness that the Apostle Paul claims has fallen on the human race because of human evil (see Romans 1: 18–21)—then the idea of original sin makes good sense even in the context of evolutionary theory; the existence of original sin can be seen as a logical consequence of the spiritual interconnection of all human beings and of their having morally significant libertarian free will.

V. Conclusion

I have argued that God's creating human beings and other living organisms through an evolutionary process allows for richer and deeper sorts of interconnections between humans and non-human creation than would otherwise be possible. I have presented reasons for thinking that these interconnections are of significant value, the main reason being that they allow for creation to become more deeply united with ourselves, in fact so united that there exists a deep communion between us and the rest of creation. This communion is not only an intrinsic good, but it enriches us, since part of this communion is creation becoming part of our very self, and thus we consciously share in the richness of creation. As a final comment, it is important to note that this idea that communion with nature is a great good and an ideal to be sought after has made intuitive sense to many people in the past and across cultures, although of course they did not view it from within an evolutionary framework. For instance, consider the *Western Inscription*. Written by Chang Tsai (1020–79), this was one of the most influential writings in China, especially for the Neo-Confucian philosophy that dominated Chinese thought from around AD 1000 until the early twentieth century. This text proclaims that 'Heaven is my father and Earth is my mother, and even such a small creature as I finds an intimate place in their midst. Therefore that which fills the universe I regard as my body and that which directs the universe I consider as my nature. All people are my brothers and sisters, and all things are my companions.' (Quoted in Chan 1963: 497.) The modern academic West has largely lost touch with this intuition since being in the grip of an overly mechanical, reductive view of nature, a view that I argue elsewhere is severely called into question by quantum mechanics and general relativity (Collins 2006).[12]

NOTES

I would like to thank Thomas Flint, Michael Rea, Keith Ward, David Schenk, John Polkinghorne, and John Haught for comments on an earlier draft of this chapter.

1. For a good overview of this literature on divine action as it relates to issue (1), see Tracy 2006.
2. Polkinghorne has retained this explanation in later writings. See e.g. his 2001: 94–6.
3. In his book *Faith of a Physicist*, Polkinghorne (1994: 85) briefly addresses this criticism. His reply is to suggest another reason why God might have created a world by means of an evolutionary process, namely that 'only a world endowed with its own spontaneity and its own reliability could have given rise to beings able to exercise choice'. As he notes, this idea bears a 'cousinly relation' to the idea of emergent interconnection that I develop below (private communication). An outstanding issue is why such an 'emergent interconnection' would be of value, something I address below.

    Finally, to be fair to Haught, he does offer other reasons, such as aesthetic reasons, for why God created a world that develops by an evolutionary process. Nonetheless, a core reason running throughout his writings is that a loving God would allow the universe to make itself. As Haught 2000: 137 says, 'The notion of God as defenseless and vulnerable love provides...an *ultimate* explanation of nature's evolutionary character.' Although I think that this aspect of both Polkinghorne's and Haught's explanations are subject to the above criticisms, I think their books are valuable contributions and well worth reading.
4. For a defense of dualism, see Plantinga 2006.
5. If extraterrestrial embodied moral agents exist in our universe, they might also contribute to its redemption, in which case the human contribution might be restricted to some localized region. We will not discuss this issue here, however.
6. See David Bradshaw 2004 for lengthy philosophical and historical discussion of how this participation is supposed to occur.
7. Further evidence that the redemption of creation comes through humans is given by two of the scriptures cited above: Romans 8: 21, which says that creation shares in *our* redemption, not something separate, and Colossians 1: 20, which appears to imply

that creation's redemption is 'through the blood of the Cross', which presumably only had a direct redemptive effect on humans.

8. To see this, suppose that one has a set of deterministic laws L and at some time t^*, a state $S(t^*)$ would be the perfect state. Running the laws backward, one would obtain an initial state $S(t_0)$ which, when the laws are played forward, would yield $S(t^*)$. Thus, God could guarantee $S(t^*)$ by creating the universe in an initial state $S(t_0)$. Furthermore, for any arbitrarily chosen time t', the initial state $S(t_0)$ will result in a state $S(t')$ at time t'. There is no reason, however, to think that in general the state $S(t')$ will be a perfect state. Of course, God will have much flexibility: God can create different laws L, and there will typically be more than one perfect state at any given time. Even with this flexibility, however, it is unclear whether God could bring it about that at every time t a perfect state is realized merely by creating the right initial state. It is especially unclear if the laws of nature must meet certain other criteria, such as having enough regularity for them to support free action by human beings and having enough simplicity and other features for us to discover them and hence develop technology. The closest we come in our universe to a preprogrammed development of a complex system is that of living organisms, such as a tree; such development, however, is never perfect, and always requires a compensating increase in entropy in the surrounding environment. Thus, it at least seems plausible to suppose that not even God could create a perfect world whose behavior was solely determined by the previous states of the world and the laws of nature.

9. For a somewhat different proposal concerning the redemption of all creation, see Polkinghorne 2003: ch 10.

10. Further, I suggest, this interweaving is deeper if the formation of the character occurs over many choices, instead of in a few choices, although this is not essential to my argument.

11. The theodicy is explicated in a yet to be published manuscript. For the account of original sin, see Collins 2003.

12. Lest I be misunderstood, I do not claim that quantum mechanics or general relativity show that this more organic view of nature is correct, only that they undercut the reductive, mechanical view of nature and indicate that at some level nature is deeply interconnected; this at least opens the door for taking a more 'organic view' of nature as a viable possibility. (For those who read this critique in Collins 2006, it should be noted that the explication of David Bohm's interpretation of quantum mechanics fails to mention the 'classical potential', thus resulting in a significant error in one of the critiques of Bohm. This error, however, does not affect the argumentation in the rest of the chapter.)

References

ALSTON, WILLIAM (1994). 'Divine Action: Shadow or Substance?', in Thomas Tracy (ed.), *The God Who Acts: Philosophical and Theological Explorations.* University Park, Pa.: Pennsylvania State University Press.

BRADSHAW, DAVID (2004). *Aristotle East and West: Metaphysics and the Division of Christendom*. Cambridge: Cambridge University Press.

CHAN, WING-TSIT (1963). *A Source Book in Chinese Philosophy*. Princeton: Princeton University Press.

COLLINS, ROBIN (2003). 'Evolution and Original Sin', in Keith Miller (ed.), *Perspectives on an Evolving Creation*. Grand Rapids: Eerdmans, 496–501.

—— (2006). 'Philosophy of Science and Religion', in Philip Clayton and Zachary Simpson (eds.), *The Oxford Handbook of Religion and Science*. Oxford: Oxford University Press, ch. 20, 328–44.

HAUGHT, JOHN (2000). *God After Darwin: A Theology of Evolution*. Boulder: Westview.

—— (2003). *Deeper than Darwin*. Boulder: Westview.

—— (2006). 'God and Evolution', in Philip Clayton and Zachary Simpson (eds.), *The Oxford Handbook of Religion and Science*. Oxford: Oxford University Press, ch. 41, 697–712.

LOSSKY, VLADIMIR (1976). *The Mystical Theology of the Eastern Church*. Crestwood: St Vladimir's Seminary Press.

MURPHY, GEORGE (2003) 'Christology, Evolution, and the Cross', in Keith Miller (ed.), *Perspectives on an Evolving Creation*. Grand Rapids: Eerdmans, 370–89.

MURRAY, MICHAEL (forthcoming). *Creation, Providence, and the Problem of Animal Suffering*. Oxford: Oxford University Press.

PLANTINGA, ALVIN (2006). 'Against Materialism', in *Faith and Philosophy* 23/1: 3–32.

POLKINGHORNE, JOHN (1989). *Science and Providence: God's Interaction with the World*. Boston: Shambhala Publications [New Science Library].

—— (1994). The *Faith of a Physicist: Reflections of a Bottom-Up Thinker*. Minneapolis: Fortress.

—— (1998). *Belief in God in an Age of Science*. New Haven: Yale University Press.

—— (2001). 'Kenotic Creation and Divine Action', in id. (ed.), *The Work of Love: Creation as Kenosis*. Grand Rapids: Eerdmans, 90–106.

—— (2002). *The God of Hope and the End of the World*. New Haven: Yale University Press.

ROUGHGARDEN, JOAN (2006). *Evolution and the Christian Faith: Reflections of an Evolutionary Biologist*. Washington: Island.

RUSSELL, ROBERT (2006). 'Quantum Physics and Divine Action', in Philip Clayton and Zachary Simpson (eds.), *The Oxford Handbook of Religion and Science*. Oxford: Oxford University Press, ch. 34, 579–95.

SHELDRAKE, RUPERT (1988). *The Presence of the Past: Morphic Resonance and the Habits of Nature*. New York: Vintage Books.

SWINBURNE, RICHARD (2004). *The Existence of God*, 2nd edn. Oxford: Oxford University Press.

TRACY, THOMAS (2006). 'Theologies of Divine Action', in Philip Clayton and Zachary Simpson (eds.), *The Oxford Handbook of Science and Religion*. Oxford: Oxford University Press, ch 35, 596–611.

WARD, KEITH. *Divine Action*. London: Collins.

—— (2001). 'Cosmos and Kenosis', in John Polkinghorne (ed.), *The Work of Love: Creation as Kenosis*. Grand Rapids: Eerdmans, 152–66.

WARE, KALLISTOS (1976). *The Orthodox Way*, rev. edn. Crestwood: St Vladimir's Seminary Press.

CHAPTER 12

·····

DIVINE
PROVIDENCE

·····

THOMAS P. FLINT

INTRODUCTION

·····

THROUGHOUT history, most Christians, like most Jews and Muslims, have consistently professed their belief in divine providence.[1] Our creator is not a distant demiurge who fashioned us without caring how we turn out or who left us to fend for ourselves. On the contrary, God is a creator whose omniscience, omnipotence, and perfect love are manifested in the care he shows for his creatures, a care exhibited in his plan to bring his beloved children to a good end.

Traditionally, two elements of this notion of providence have been highlighted. First, God is in *control* of his universe. Everything that occurs is either intended or at least permitted by him; nothing takes place that is beyond his power to prevent. Hence, the world, with all its inhabitants and all their doings, is radically dependent upon God. Second, God *knows* all there is to know about his universe. Nothing in the past is noetically lost to him; nothing in the future is beyond his cognitive reach.

Theories of providence arise because the two elements just noted appear to lead to problems, especially problems concerning the freedom of God's creatures. Take first the notion of God's sovereignty. If we are genuinely free, how can God be genuinely in control? Doesn't our freedom set limits to his sovereignty? Isn't the world dependent on us, not just on God, for its features and its history? Mustn't God's plan be constantly revised in response to our actions?

The questions that freedom poses for divine control are thus varied and serious. No less serious are those that freedom raises for God's knowledge. If we're free, don't we have to set definite limits to God's knowledge, especially to his foreknowledge? How could he know what a free being is going to do before that free being decides to do it? If God already knows, infallibly and unchangeably, what I'm going to do long before I do it—even long before I'm born—how could I possibly do otherwise? Mustn't we, then, concede that a God who leaves some of his creatures free surrenders not only the control, but also the knowledge that the traditional picture of providence affords him?

Christian advocates of providence have not been blind to such questions, and through the years have offered a number of different responses. Though categorizing responses is always a dangerous (and potentially quite misleading) business, I don't think it would be overly simplistic to see the attempts to deal with these questions as falling into three broad categories.

First, some Christians have suggested that the problems arise from our assuming a misguided picture of freedom—that which is often called *libertarianism*. Abandon this picture—acknowledge that it is both philosophically bankrupt and theologically untenable—and our problems dissolve; human freedom, *properly understood*, is fully compatible with God's complete control and universal foreknowledge.[2] Though a number of names have been ascribed to this school of thought (including the *Augustinian* view, the *Banezian*, the *Calvinist*, and others), I will (with some trepidation) follow the tradition among many Catholic thinkers in referring to this as the *Thomist* solution.

Second, other Christians, insisting that the libertarian picture of freedom ought not be surrendered, have claimed that our notion of providence needs to be modified in order to meet the objections. If we acknowledge that God's control over his world is more limited than past enthusiasts have affirmed, and if we recognize that *perfect* knowledge does not entail *fore*knowledge, we see that true-blue human freedom is not endangered. In recent years, the most ardent advocates of this approach have called themselves *Open Theists*, the name I also will use in this chapter (along with the shorter *Openists*).[3]

Finally, a third group of Christian theorists holds that *neither* the strong, traditional picture of providence *nor* the libertarian notion of freedom is negotiable; each is manifestly supported by reason and/or by revelation. But, these Christians say, the appearance of conflict between providence and freedom is *merely* an appearance. Once we see that God's sovereign control would operate *through* his creatures' free decisions, and (more specifically) through his knowledge of what those decisions would be, we see that none of the radical moves advocated by the two camps described above needs to be made. This attempt to reconcile freedom and providence is usually called *Molinism*.[4]

In this chapter, I will attempt to spell out more clearly the Thomist, the Openist, and (especially) the Molinist approaches to divine providence, and to indicate as objectively as I can the strengths and weaknesses of these three positions.[5] Before doing so, however, let me say just a bit more about both the traditional notion of divine providence and the libertarian picture of freedom.

TRADITIONAL PROVIDENCE AND LIBERTARIAN FREEDOM

The heart of the traditional Christian notion of providence is nicely stated at the start of ch. 5 of the Westminster Confession:

God, the great Creator of all things, doth uphold, direct, dispose, and govern all creatures, actions, and things, from the greatest even to the least, by his most wise and holy providence, according to his infallible foreknowledge, and the free and immutable counsel of his own will, to the praise of the glory of his wisdom, power, justice, goodness, and mercy.

According to this tradition, God is not merely the one who brought all things into being. All aspects of his creation depend upon his sustaining presence, and all (great and small) are subject to his control. As the last line of the passage makes clear, God's plan for the world is not merely all-encompassing, but fully in accord with the divine perfections of justice, goodness, and mercy. And that plan, the quotation clearly implies, is not one that God makes up as he goes along. Rather, he foreknows all that will occur, and thus (one would assume) is neither surprised by what happens nor forced to alter his intentions as events move in directions unanticipated by him.

This picture of providence has been dominant throughout the history of Christianity, though (as we shall see) it has been called into question in recent years by the rise of Open Theism. On reflection, it's not difficult to see why such a picture (which has its roots both in biblical and in classical Greek sources) should seem at least prima facie attractive to thoughtful Christians. After all, the heart of Western monotheism is a conviction that God is the all-knowing, all-powerful, all-good creator of all that is. How, one might wonder, *could* such a deity who chooses to create not know precisely what he's doing and what he could have done? How could he have created a world that wasn't crafted to mirror his infinite power, wisdom, and love? Mustn't we assume that, in Cardinal Newman's memorable phrase, 'He knows what He is about',[6] and can't we rest confident both in his overall plan and in our place therein?

As we have seen, part of this picture is that God governs all in accord with 'the free and immutable counsel of his will'. This, of course, assumes that God *has* free will. And this assumption naturally leads those of a philosophical bent to reflect upon just what freedom might amount to, in God's case or in ours. As noted above, many (though hardly all) Christians throughout history have insisted that the notion of freedom now commonly referred to as libertarianism is the one that is most consonant with a Christian outlook. Let's now consider, just a bit more carefully, the characteristic features of libertarian freedom.

Though a complete and precise characterization of libertarianism is notoriously difficult to provide, the basic idea is that external determination of a person's action (especially causal determination by some factor not subject to the person's causal control) is incompatible with that action's being free. Libertarians insist that some of our actions are free; hence, they deny that those actions are determined, mediately or immediately, by events not under our causal control. And what goes for us goes for God as well; his freedom too must be understood in this libertarian way.

The central idea here seems to be that *my* actions (or at least my *free* actions) are the ones that I initiate and control. And equally central, at least for most libertarians, is the connection between freedom so understood and moral responsibility. Actions caused by something or someone external to me simply couldn't be actions for which I am responsible—for which I could properly be praised or blamed. If I program an automaton to kill an innocent person, I, not the automaton, am guilty of murder—assuming, of course, that I'm not an automaton myself!

Again, what we've offered here is a fairly coarse-grained depiction of the libertarian picture. Libertarians disagree about many things: the precise nature and degree of causal relations present within a free act; the precise connection between the beliefs and desires we have and the actions we perform; the frequency (or infrequency) of free acts; whether some genuine actions are unfree; and so on. But enough, I hope, has been said for readers to grasp the type of position on freedom that libertarians champion.

I hope as well that enough has been said to see why there at least appears to be a tension between providence (understood in the strong traditional manner delineated above) and freedom (interpreted in a libertarian manner). On the one hand, providence postulates complete divine foreknowledge of and control over all that occurs, including human actions. Libertarianism, on the other hand, insists that external determination of an action is incompatible with that action's being free. To endorse providence, then, it seems we need to deny that there are any free actions, at least as understood by libertarians; to endorse libertarian freedom, it seems we must deny (or at least limit) God's providence. Given this apparent tension, it is not surprising that Christians have attempted to rectify matters by surrendering (or at least significantly modifying) one or the other of the two positions that seem to lead to our quandary. Let us now turn to the two directions in which these attempts might be taken.

ABANDONING LIBERTARIANISM: THE
THOMIST ALTERNATIVE

As with the other pictures of providence we will examine, speaking of *the* Thomist alternative is a bit misleading, since it implies a degree of uniformity that simply does not exist. Still, what I am calling the Thomist position, though a *big* tent covering a wide variety of positions, is still *a* tent, one that shelters those who respond to our quandary by saying that it is the libertarian account of freedom, or at least the standard version of that account,[7] that is causing our problems. Liberate ourselves from libertarianism, they say, and the problem of freedom and providence dissolves.

Libertarianism causes problems, the Thomists say, because it conflicts with one of the most central and indispensable principles of traditional Christian belief: that God is genuinely in control of everything that goes on in his universe. Libertarianism suggests that we free creatures and God are competitors in a zero-sum game of actualizing the world.[8] God performs certain free actions, and there's nothing we can do about them. We perform other free actions, and there's nothing he can do about them (short, of course, of simply putting us out of the free-action-performing business entirely). Increase divine free activity and the sphere for free human activity shrinks; magnify human freedom, and divine sovereignty and control wanes. No true Christian, the Thomist says, can comfortably accept so radical a diminishment of the creator. Hugh McCann, one of the foremost contemporary advocates of the Thomist view, nicely summarizes and expands upon this point:

to the extent God does not exert active control over my decisions, whether through other events or direct involvement, He does not control them at all. He can therefore achieve His ends only by reacting to what I do, and to that extent His plans are subordinated to mine. In addition to weakening His sovereignty, this situation also threatens God's omniscience. It suggests He can know how I will act in the circumstances in which I am placed only by observing my actions. As creator, He is in the dark. He can know what the possibilities are, but if my freedom makes for more than one, then even His knowledge of the world He is creating appears to depend on my action—an unsatisfactory situation to say the least. These problems can be avoided if God is able to exercise creative control in my actual choice.[9]

For the Thomist, then, God's sovereignty requires that God have control over our actions greater than libertarians have typically allowed. Some Thomists suggest that God's arranging of natural causes that determine our actions is fully in accord with their freedom. But this, to my understanding, has never been more than a minority view among Thomists. Libertarians are right, they say, in resisting the common contemporary compatibilist view of freedom—the view that actions that are functions of the laws of nature and prior states of the natural world can still be free provided that the crucial determining events are of the right sort (such as the agent's own, fully embraced beliefs and desires) and bring about the action in the normal way.[10] What libertarians have failed fully to appreciate, though, is that God is not just another natural cause. God's relation to his universe is utterly unique, and his determining of his creatures' actions no more robs them of their freedom than does (say) Euripides' authorial determination of Medea's actions mean that she lacks freedom within the world of the play. As Aquinas famously put it:

it does not of necessity belong to liberty that what is free should be the first cause of itself, as neither for one thing to be cause of another need it be the first cause. God, therefore, is the first cause, Who moves causes both natural and voluntary. And just as by moving natural causes He does not prevent their actions from being natural, so by moving voluntary causes He does not deprive their actions of being voluntary; but rather is He the cause of this very thing in them, for He operates in each thing according to its own nature.[11]

Many Thomists feel comfortable (as Aquinas seems to here) speaking of God as the source of the very being both of ourselves and of our actions, and hence as the one whose will supernaturally *causes* the free actions we perform. Others feel that such language is at best misleading; God determines our decisions, they believe, without there being any causal connection between his act of will and our decisions. But whatever the precise explanation embraced here (and I don't mean to imply that the choice of explanation is insignificant), Thomists concur in maintaining that the type of 'absolute metaphysical freedom' endorsed by most libertarians, a view that insists that I, not God, am the 'final ontological arbiter' of my actions, cannot be sustained by the circumspect Christian.[12]

Two other elements of the Thomist position, both at least suggested by the McCann quotation above, are worthy of mention. First, Thomists insist that a God who truly enacts a plan for his world does not need to look at that world to see how things are going in it. If the creator is truly in charge, then the fact that something (call it X) is incorporated into his plan just entails that X occurs, and occurs when and as God wills. (And, of course, for the typical Thomist, no event is *not* part of his overall plan.) Once God determines his own will—once he decides upon a providential plan for creation—he has no need to observe the world to see what occurs. To the extent that libertarians imply that God's knowledge is dependent upon such observation, their picture of freedom diminishes the nature and the quality of that knowledge.

The second element is closely related to the first. In making his providential plans for the world, God's will determines how it is that his free creatures will in fact use their freedom. But there's no reason to think that God's knowledge of creaturely freedom is exhausted by his recognition of how creatures will actually perform. He knows not only what they *will* do, but also what they *could* have done. And most Thomists will take this a step further. God knows not only what they *could* have done, but also what they *would* have done had he placed them in other situations. Take a certain free creature named Framboise who visits an ice cream shop tomorrow, and assume that she'll freely order a raspberry sundae. She does so, says the Thomist, because of God's will that she order the sundae. Consequent to forming his plan, God knows, of course, that Framboise *will* order the raspberry sundae. But he also knows that she *could* have ordered a strawberry sundae instead. And perhaps he also knows that, if the ice cream shop hadn't offered raspberry sundaes, Framboise would freely have ordered a hot fudge sundae instead. He might well know such a *counterfactual of creaturely freedom*, but if he does know it, he knows it only because its truth was also determined by his all-sovereign will; i.e. part of that all-encompassing act of will was that Framboise would have freely ordered the hot fudge sundae were raspberry unavailable. Again, none of this knowledge depends upon his observing what goes on in the world.

Critics of the Thomist view raise both metaphysical and moral objections to its picture of God and his relation to creation. The picture of freedom that it offers, they suggest, is hopelessly flawed. As noted above, Thomists offer a variety of explanations of the relation of God's will to our actions. Some say that the former initiates a causal chain that ends with the latter; others suggest that a unique type of supernatural causal connection immediately relates the two; still others maintain that our very actions are the content of God's act of will, and thus not strictly speaking causally connected to it. Most libertarians respond by saying that the differences here, though of arcane metaphysical interest, are uniformly unhelpful in safeguarding human freedom. Whichever of the various Thomist schemes we adopt, doesn't it remain the case that, with regard to human actions, it's *God and God alone* who's really calling the shots here, not us? Even if there's no external *event* that's causing me to act as I do, isn't the existence of an external *agent* whose will fully and inevitably determines my action sufficient to rob that event of freedom?

The moral objections have seemed, to most critics of the Thomist position, even more severe than the metaphysical ones. For what the Thomist position implies is that there were no non-logical limitations upon God's creative activity. Assuming (as Thomists do) that God is necessarily sovereign, it follows that any world that is so much as possible is a world God could have created, since all contingent events are determined by his will.[13] But if this is so, how can we possibly account for the presence, the amount, and the horrendous nature of the evil in our world? If God is as unfettered as the Thomists say, if he could have created any possible world whatsoever, then it seems he had available to him worlds much better than the one in which we live. Adam freely ate the apple, and the result was unlimited suffering for himself and for his descendants. But why did he make that free choice? According to the Thomist, the ultimate explanation lies in God's will. But then, why did God will as he did? Why didn't he will that Adam resist temptation, and maintain the sinless status of the Garden with which he was entrusted? Don't the Thomists, in seeking to magnify the power and sovereign control of the deity, make him alone ultimately responsible for the evil that his creatures do, thereby belittling his moral grandeur? Indeed, by suggesting (as most Thomists, being traditional

Christians, do) that God would punish for eternity those whom *he* has determined will never repent for the sins he has *also* determined that they commit, haven't Thomists depicted a God whose actions display not the loving-kindness of the God of the Bible, but rather (as Molina puts it) 'cruelty and wickedness'?[14]

Thomists are not without responses here. Perplexity with regard to the motivations behind God's permission of evil or uncertainty concerning the correct analysis of freedom, some suggest, shouldn't lead us to soften our conviction that God is truly in charge of all that occurs.[15] As the so-called skeptical theists of today remind us (see ch. 17 on 'Skeptical Theism' in this volume), we should hardly expect to understand why God acts as he does; hence, our inability to answer the questions posed above gives us no reason to think there aren't sufficient responses that simply lie beyond our ability to grasp. Others have suggested that perhaps we *can* understand why God wills evil: to create a world in which both his mercy (in saving sinners) and his retributive justice (in punishing unrepentant evildoers) are graphically apparent.[16] And others have reminded us that the efficacy of God's will is perfectly consistent with the existence of genuine created causes. Suppose that Pamplemousse, a young French statesman eager to follow in the ways of his mentors, cheats on his wife. God's willing that Pamplemousse be unfaithful determines the cheating; still, it's Pamplemousse, not God, who's doing the cheating, and it's Pamplemousse, not God, who's morally accountable for that sinful act.[17]

There are, then, many directions in which the Thomist might go, and the arguments quickly and predictably become quite complex.[18] Still, many (probably most) Christians find this approach unsatisfactory. For them, surrendering a libertarian picture of freedom is too high a price to pay to resolve the tension between freedom and providence. If one still feels that the apparent incompatibility between the two is genuine, the only remaining route of escape is to amend the strong, traditional notion of providence that we earlier described. And this route takes us to Open Theism.

AMENDING PROVIDENCE: THE OPEN THEIST ALTERNATIVE

Open Theism, as an explicit alternative to the Thomist and Molinist accounts of providence, is a fairly new position. Because the strong, traditional notion of providence seemed so central a part of orthodox Christian belief, defending Christianity by altering our picture of providence struck many as a pointless endeavor, or at least would so have struck them had they even considered it, which few did. But within the last few decades, many philosophers and theologians have argued that it is only by revising our idea of how God interacts with his creatures that we can offer a coherent account of providence while avoiding the metaphysical and moral perplexities that both Thomists and Molinists face.

As Openists see it, affirming divine sovereignty in so strong a fashion as Thomists (or, as we'll see, Molinists) do is simply incompatible with our freedom, which can plausibly be understood only along libertarian lines. Divine foreknowledge of and control over our free actions both need to be understood in a modified way if our status as free agents is to be safeguarded. But these modifications, they insist, should not be seen as denying God's status as the all-knowing, provident lord of the universe. On the contrary, they allow us to fashion a picture of a perfect creator that is both more solidly based in Scripture and more resilient in the face of philosophical objections.

Let's first consider the limitations on God's knowledge that Open Theists embrace. Unlike most Thomists and many Molinists, Openists typically see God as a temporal being; the idea of an eternal God who has no relation to the temporal realm is, they argue, unbiblical or philosophically untenable or both. But if God is in time, can he foreknow what we will freely do? Openists argue that he cannot. Though developed arguments for this conclusion generally get rather complex,[19] the basic idea is easy enough to understand. Open Theists agree with the traditional ascription of perfection to God, including doxastic perfection: there's no way God can believe a proposition which isn't true. So suppose God had always known, and hence always believed, that Framboise would order that raspberry sundae tomorrow. Since his belief is infallible, there's no way he could have this belief and Framboise *not* order the sundae. So, when Framboise enters the ice cream shop, there's a fact about the past (regarding God's prior belief) that entails her action. How, then, could she be free? If she could change what it was that God believed in the past, perhaps we could make sense of her having real alternatives. But how could she do something tomorrow to change what it was God believed thousands of years ago? What God believed back then is a settled fact about the past; hence, it's incoherent to think that there's something she can do about it tomorrow. So God's believing in advance that a free action will be performed entails that the action in question isn't free after all. And from this it follows that such belief isn't possible at all.[20]

So divine foreknowledge has to be denied to make room for human freedom. But it's not only knowledge of what *will* happen that needs to go. Remember those conditional propositions that, as we saw, Thomists typically see God as determining— propositions (counterfactuals of creaturely freedom, as we called them) not about what *will* happen, but about what *would* happen under various hypotheses. Such conditionals can be seen as answers to questions about potential creaturely actions. If Framboise were to go to the ice cream shop, what would she freely order? If Framboise were to find the ice cream shop had no raspberry sundaes, what would she freely order instead? Thomists generally want to insist that there are definite answers to such questions, answers dependent upon God's will. But Open Theists reject the claim that there are true counterfactuals of this type. For suppose there were such truths, and suppose that God, being omniscient, knew them—all of them. This means that God would know what any free being would do in any situation in which it might be placed. But if God knew a counterfactual such as *If Adam were to be placed in the Garden, he would eat the apple*, and then were to decide to place Adam in the Garden, he would know that Adam will eat the apple. In other words, divine foreknowledge seems undeniable once we grant there are true counterfactuals of creaturely freedom known by God. And since we've already seen (according to Open Theists) that foreknowledge is incompatible with our freedom, we need to reject counterfactuals of creaturely freedom as well.[21]

Now, it might seem that the Openists' God, knowing neither what *will* happen nor what *would* happen (under various hypotheses), would have scant providential control over his world. But Open Theists suggest that God, though not the all-controlling deity of the Thomists, would still have enough to go on. For even if God doesn't know what Adam *would* do if placed in the Garden, he might well know what Adam would *probably* do. And knowledge of such 'would-probably' conditionals, say Openists, gives God enough information to operate providentially. Take Framboise once again. Perhaps God believes that Framboise (and others) would benefit greatly were she to meet a marriageable young gent. And maybe he sees that there's a situation he can put her in such that, if in that situation, she'd *probably* freely decide to go to the ice cream shop. Once there, she'd *probably* freely decide to order a raspberry sundae. And, upon ordering it, she'd *probably* strike up a conversation with that nice young sundae-maker (and raspberry afficionado) Maraschino, who'd *probably* ask her out on a date, which (since God sees that the two are in fact a perfect match) she'd *probably* accept, and so on. The point is that knowledge of probabilities is enough for God to act knowingly to achieve his good ends.

Note, though, that there are no guarantees in this picture of providence. God can't (as the Thomists' God can) simply decide how Framboise will freely react in these various situations. And, since improbable things do happen, there's a genuine possibility that Framboise will act so as to frustrate God's good plan for her. So the God of Open Theism is a genuine risk-taker. He aims for the best, but with the full knowledge that his free creatures may disappoint him, and block his endeavors to lead us toward what is best for ourselves and for his world. The moral evil that occurs in the world is to be explained not via the contortions needed to justify the all-determining God of the Thomists, but as the all-but-inevitable result of God's gracious creation of beings whose free actions he can neither foresee nor control.

Openists can develop this picture of a risk-taking God in a number of different directions. Some embrace it rather reluctantly and try to minimize the degree of risk God faces, by curtailing the quantity of significant free actions or by maximizing the probabilities God knows. (If God knows that there's a .999999998 probability of Framboise's ordering a raspberry sundae, he knows there's not *much* of a chance that she'll escape Maraschino's attention.) Others openly prefer the picture of a God who values our freedom so much that he's willing to share with his free creatures a very large degree of the responsibility for fashioning our world. Openists also differ on how exactly God would utilize his knowledge of would-probably conditionals. Some think that God would from the start develop an unlimited number of contingency plans ready to be enacted should things take an unexpected turn. ('OK, I'm going to get Framboise into that ice cream shop tomorrow. She'll *probably* order a raspberry sundae, getting Maraschino's attention. But if she *doesn't*, I'll arrange for her to spill her water glass. That will *probably* get Maraschino to come over and try to make a joke of it, thereby getting them to talk. But if he *doesn't* come over, then I'll. . . .')[22] Many Open Theists, though, seem to feel that such extensive pre-planning would be neither necessary nor fitting for God. On their view, God has ample resources, given his knowledge of would-probably conditionals, to respond to any surprising development if and when it occurs. Rather than meticulously pre-programming his reactions, he responds to his creatures in real time, using all the knowledge he has to nudge humankind toward the good no matter how they might behave.[23]

So Open Theism can be developed in a number of different directions; as with Thomism and (as we'll see) Molinism, a multitude of distinct positions are available. Still, the heart of the Openist view is clear enough: with respect to free creaturely actions, God has in advance only would-probably knowledge, and thus must take risks in his providential interactions with the free beings he creates.

The development of Open Theism over the past two or three decades has led to stormy debates, especially within certain evangelical organizations and colleges. The debates have often enough turned to practical as well as theoretical issues: membership for Open Theists within Christian academic societies has been called into question, and teaching jobs have been lost. Though unseemly, these conflicts are in a sense unsurprising. For Open Theism constitutes a radical break with the picture of providence that has been dominant within Christianity throughout its history. And defenders of that dominant picture have not been reticent in pointing to what they see as the religious and philosophical deficiencies of the Openist alternative.

Many critics of Open Theism charge that the view, though allegedly developed in part to offer a more biblically accurate picture of God's relationship to his people, in fact does the opposite. The strong, traditional picture of providence, these critics insist, is actually demanded by the Bible; the hesitant, odds-playing God of the Openists, they say, can hardly be reconciled with the meticulous providence so evident in Scripture, and so repeatedly endorsed by councils and catechisms throughout the history of the church. Part, though not all, of this criticism centers on the question of prophecy. If God doesn't *know* what someone will freely do, how can he *reveal* what he will do? If no one can know how Peter will freely react to Christ's arrest, how can Jesus so confidently predict Peter's denials? Open Theists have offered several responses to this criticism. Some predictions may be of actions that are not in fact free. Some may be implicitly conditional; e.g. what Jesus was really telling Peter was that *if* the apostle acted in accord with the character he'd formed up to that point, he'd deny Jesus. And some prophecies may be revealing what God intends to do regardless of how his creatures act. Not surprisingly, critics of Open Theism have not been persuaded by such responses.[24]

Equally questionable, from the traditionalists' perspective, is the role God's knowledge of probabilities plays in the Openists' account of providence. Some critics have called into question whether an Openist can consistently affirm that God knows even would-probably conditionals.[25] Even if such objections can be parried, though, serious questions arise when we consider the level of the probabilities of which God is supposedly aware. For God to be a genuine risk-taker of the sort so many Openists celebrate, the probabilities God knows cannot uniformly be extremely high. Again, if the probability of Framboise's ordering a raspberry sundae if she goes to the ice cream shop is .999999998, God (assuming he wants her to order the sundae) isn't taking much of a risk if he gets her to go. If all the probabilities God knew were of this type, he would be *nearly* as manipulative and controlling as is (according to Openists) the God of the Thomists—and evil would remain *nearly* as big a problem. On the other hand, if the probabilities God knows are more varied, it's hard to see how God could have anything more than a very short-range plan for his world, and thus anything more than an extremely emaciated type of providential control.[26]

As one might expect, the Open Theists' embrace of a risk-taking deity has also proved controversial. While we may admire humans who are willing to take risks to benefit others, few of us (the critics say) see risk-taking as inherently valuable, especially with respect to matters of life and death. The heart surgeon who employs a risky new procedure when a (comparatively) risk-free one is available would be viewed not as courageous or daring, but as foolish and perhaps even malevolent. A God who (*pace* Einstein) does play dice with the universe, at least with free macro-objects if not with undetermined micro-ones, is more to be pitied than acclaimed. Indeed, far from lessening the problem of evil, the Openist stance actually intensifies it. For God could surely make a wonderful world without including free creatures in it. If the cost of creaturely freedom is the genuine possibility that some, or most, or all of his creatures will use their freedom to make things worse and worse for themselves and for their fellows, a truly loving God would deem such a cost too high.[27]

Open Theists have, of course, responded to these and other criticisms of their position.[28] While their spirited defense of this view has led to many converts, many (probably most) Christians who have considered the issues retain grave doubts about the adequacy of the Openist alternative. For those who harbor such doubts but who also cannot bring themselves to accept the Thomist position, the only remaining live candidate for their consideration is Molinism.

LIBERTARIANISM *AND* TRADITIONAL PROVIDENCE: THE MOLINIST ALTERNATIVE

As our discussion has already indicated, Molinism is the position of those who decline to surrender either the libertarian notion of freedom or the traditional picture of providence—and who insist that the two can be combined without contradiction. Let me briefly describe the Molinist view and then indicate how, according to Molinists, it dissolves the alleged tension between freedom and divine sovereignty.[29]

Like their Thomist brethren, Molinists believe that the alterations to the notion of providence advocated by Open Theists are unacceptable. Divine control over all that occurs, along with both foreknowledge and knowledge of counterfactuals of creaturely freedom, are non-negotiable elements of a sound doctrine of providence. But, as libertarians, Molinists side with their Openist brethren in condemning the Thomist embrace of an all-determining divine will. What we need to see, say Molinists, is that God's knowledge and control operate through creatures who enjoy full libertarian freedom.

Consider, Molinists say, God's knowledge of his world. Some of the truths God knows—e.g. mathematical truths such as *two plus three equals five*—are necessary truths, ones that could not have been other than they are and that are in no sense the result of any free decision on God's part. Knowing such truths can be seen as part of God's very nature; hence, Molina labeled this God's *natural knowledge*. On the other hand, many truths of which God is aware—e.g. *Framboise will freely order a raspberry sundae tomorrow*—are neither necessary nor beyond God's power to control. There are many possible worlds in which Framboise never has a sundae tomorrow, and there are many ways in which God could have prevented her having one (most radically, by deciding never to create Framboise at all). Contingent truths of this sort, then, are true only because God freely allowed them to be true. Such propositions, said Molina, are elements of God's *free knowledge*. And this, obviously, is where foreknowledge of what will occur in the world belongs.

But where do the counterfactuals of creaturely freedom fit in? Recall that, on the Thomist picture, God knows what any free creature would do in any situation in which it might be placed. If Framboise were to go to the ice cream shop tomorrow and find that raspberry sundaes were unavailable, there's a fact of the matter as to what she would freely do (e.g. order a hot fudge sundae), and God, being omniscient, knows that fact. Molinists agree, but (unlike Thomists) believe that the existence of such truths force us to posit a third category of divine knowledge. For these conditionals, like elements of free knowledge, are contingent truths; but, like elements of natural knowledge, they're not in any way under God's control, given the fact that the creatures they are about have libertarian freedom. (As Molinists are wont to say, such truths are *prevolitional*, meaning simply that they're true independent of any exercise of God's free will.) So the contingent but prevolitional truths really belong in a middle category between the necessary, prevolitional truths that make up natural knowledge and the contingent, postvolitional (i.e. those that *are* subject to God's will) truths that constitute free knowledge. Not surprisingly, Molina gave the name *middle knowledge* to this third category.

The notion of middle knowledge is the cornerstone of the Molinist position. For it allows us to see how God can both foreknow and exercise control over all that occurs. Since both natural knowledge and free knowledge are prevolitional, they can be thought of as present to God when he's deciding what creative act to perform.[30] Given his middle knowledge, God knows exactly how his free creatures would react in any situation in which he might place them. He knows, for example, that if he were to create Framboise and she were to visit the ice cream shop, she'd freely order a raspberry sundae; he knows that if raspberry were unavailable, she'd opt for hot fudge instead; and so on. God knows such truths about every possible creature and every situation in which she might be placed.[31] So, once he decides which creatures to create and which situations to place them in, he foreknows exactly what that creature will do. For example, by middle knowledge, he knows what Framboise *would* do if she were in the ice cream shop; once God decides to put her in the ice cream shop, it follows that he knows what she *will* do. So middle knowledge, when combined with God's full creative decision (concerning which beings to create in which circumstances), simply *entails* foreknowledge. Given middle knowledge, then, foreknowledge no longer appears to be a mystery.

Nor does it seem to be a threat to our freedom. For foreknowledge is not (as with the Thomists) simply a function of God's free choice; rather, it's a function of his choice concerning what to create (over which he *does* have control) and truths about what we would freely do (truths over which he has *no* control whatsoever). If one thought of the counterfactuals about Framboise as utterly beyond *her* control, one might have doubts about whether or not middle knowledge safeguards her freedom. But no Molinist worth his or her salt thinks of the counterfactuals that refer to a creature as manacles she is powerless to escape. For such conditionals say only what the creature *would in fact* freely do, not what she would *have to* freely do. It may be true that Framboise would freely order a raspberry sundae, but it's also true that, when in the ice cream shop, she has full libertarian freedom to (say) order a vanilla milkshake instead, and were she to do so, the counterfactual that is in fact true about her would never have been true. In other words, God is powerless regarding which counterfactuals of creaturely freedom are true, but we aren't.[32] Hence, middle knowledge is fully consistent with our freedom.

Furthermore, say Molinists, it's also consistent with a strong notion of divine providential control. True, given the reality of libertarian freedom, God can't exercise the type of unilateral control promoted by the Thomists. Even so, say Molinists, middle knowledge affords God a much stronger type of control than the emaciated Openist version. For the Molinist God, thanks to middle knowledge, *isn't* a risk-taker. He never has to deal with acting in situations where he knows only what *probably* will result from his actions. Rather, he knows *precisely* how his free creatures would react to any action on his part. If he were to put Framboise in situation A, she'd freely do X; if he were to put her in situation B, she'd do Y; and so on. God can then decide which situation to put her in (say, A or B) depending upon which result (X or Y) can more readily be woven into a world that satisfies his creative intentions. God needn't worry about things heading off in an unintended direction—about his being surprised by unexpected actions on the part of his creatures. With middle knowledge, he truly does know what he is about; by exercising his providential control through the free actions of his creatures, he (and we) are assured that the world that results will fully manifest his wisdom and love.

The advantages of the Molinist view (in saving both the libertarian notion of freedom and the classical picture of providence) are evident, and attempts to apply it to a number of specific Christian beliefs—the problem of evil, prophecy, petitionary prayer, biblical inspiration, original sin, and the salvation of the unevangelized, among others—have been offered by a number of Molinists.[33] Potentially the most fruitful such application may prove to be a Molinist Christology, which alone seems to offer the prospect of providing us a coherent picture of the incarnate Son that ensures both his genuine libertarian freedom and his true impeccability.[34] Further reflection on the implications of this Christology (which is controversial even among Molinists) can be expected in the coming years. Much light might be thrown on the ultimate destiny of those who make up the Body of Christ.

Molinism has always been an extremely controversial position, and disagreements concerning the coherence and the plausibility of the view continue. Before turning to the major objection that has been raised, let me first note two less-discussed but significant questions concerning this theory of providence.

First, what exactly is to be included in the antecedent of a counterfactual of creaturely freedom? Molinists have typically argued that the basic elements of middle knowledge should be conditionals with *complete* antecedents. To see what they mean by this, note that most everyday counterfactuals are radically *incomplete* with respect to their antecedents, though the context usually makes the direction in which completion would be made relatively easy to see, even if impossible for us fully to state. For example, with conditionals such as

If I'd asked you at noon yesterday to join me for lunch, you'd have agreed

we naturally assume that the idea is that, had the world gone as it in fact did up until noon yesterday, and had I then asked you to join me, you'd have agreed. We're not, for example, asking how you would have reacted had I asked you to lunch at noon after performing some action (say, insulting you vilely at 11:45) that, as a matter of fact, I didn't perform. With some counterfactuals, of course, the consequent is stated in a manner no more precise than the antecedent. Take, for example, the memorable words sung by Tevye in *Fiddler on the Roof*:

> If I were a rich man,
> Ya ha deedle deedle, bubba bubba deedle deedle dum.
> All day long I'd biddy biddy bum.
> If I were a wealthy man.[35]

The general thrust of Tevye's counterfactual may be clear enough to us, but its precise meaning is tough to discern.

None of these interpretative problems, it seems clear, could plague the counterfactuals God knows via his middle knowledge. The counterfactuals would need to have complete antecedents, in part because, at the logical moment when such conditionals are of use to God, there *is* no fact of the matter as to how the world has gone up to the relevant point in time, and thus no way for the context to allow completion of the antecedent. Besides, one would think that God's creative decisions would best be guided by (and could adequately be guided *only* by) conditionals with the widest antecedents and the most exact consequents—'If I were to create a world in which things had gone *precisely* this way up to time t, and Tevye were free at t, he'd freely do *exactly* X.'

Nevertheless, determining what that 'precisely' amounts to—i.e. specifying exactly what goes into the antecedent C of a counterfactual of creaturely freedom (which we might represent as $C \rightarrow A$)—is no mean feat, one to which Molinists have heretofore perhaps devoted less time than the task deserves, and one on which there is no reason to think all Molinists will agree. It makes sense to think that God's foreknowledge of the relevant action would not be included in the antecedent of such conditionals. If C includes 'God foreknows that A', then $(C \rightarrow A)$ will be necessarily true; if it includes 'God foreknows that $\sim$A', then it will be necessarily false. In neither case will it be the type of contingent, prevolitional conditional that would seem to be of much action-guiding use for God. Furthermore, for the Molinist, foreknowledge is simply an effect of God's middle knowledge and creative action, not part of the situation in which the action is performed, and thus seems peculiar to include in the antecedent. So leaving foreknowledge out of C makes sense. But what, for example, of cases of prophecy? Here one could see Molinists torn in both directions. On the one hand, a prophet's publicly declaring 'You will do A' seems an obvious actual-world exercise of causal power on his or her part, and thus an exceedingly odd factor to exclude from C. On the other hand, a genuinely prophetic utterance, if included in C, would give us an antecedent that entails the consequent as surely as would including divine foreknowledge, and thus would render the conditional necessarily true, and so no part of middle knowledge.

More careful and detailed consideration of this issue by Molinists seems to be called for.[36]

Another issue Molinists might well need to face more directly is a challenge suggesting that they have given insufficient reason to reject the Thomist view that sees God as the cause of the truth of contingent counterfactuals of creaturely freedom.[37] As noted above, Molinists typically say that God knows which such counterfactuals are true, but that their truth in no sense constrains the relevant agents, since they retain (Molinists say) counterfactual power over their truth. Even if $(C \rightarrow A)$ is true, the agent in question, if placed in C, retains the power to do something (i.e. bring it about that $\sim A$) such that the counterfactual would have been false. But then, the challenge goes, why not just say that God flat-out *causes* certain counterfactuals to be true, but that his causing in no way constrains the relevant agents, since they retain counterfactual power over their truth? For example, God, prior to creation, causes $(C \rightarrow A)$ to be true, but the agent in question, if placed in C, retains the power to do something (bring it about that $\sim A$) such that the counterfactual would have been false. Of course, the counterfactual's being false would entail that God never caused it to be true, and so having counterfactual power over *its* truth would entail having counterfactual power over *God's* prior causal activity. But many Molinists have been willing to countenance such power in other instances—take, for example, Plantinga's celebrated example of Jones's having the power to act in such a way that God would have done something he in fact didn't do, namely, prevent some ants from moving into Jones's yard yesterday.[38] Molinists, it would seem, can parry this Thomist thrust only if they can offer strong reasons to think that we couldn't have counterfactual power over God's causation of counterfactuals. Though I suspect that such reasons can be offered, it is admittedly a task that no Molinist has yet fully undertaken.

Rather than focus on such questions, though, opponents of Molinism have over the last thirty years devoted most of their attention to the 'grounding' problem. Counterfactuals of creaturely freedom are supposed to be true prior to the actions (or even the existing) of the agents in question. How, the skeptics ask, could such conditionals be true at all? What would *cause*, or *bring about*, or *ground* their truth? God, traditional Molinists have insisted, can't make the conditionals that are true to be true; he knows but doesn't control their truth. But no one and nothing else exists at the logical moment (prior to creation) when God knows and uses these truths in his creative deliberations. But then, how could anyone or anything make these propositions to be true? And if there is no ground, no truthmaker, no cause of truth that we can identify, how can we possibly allow that there are any such truths?

Now, speaking of *the* grounding objection, as some critics of Molinism tend to do, is obviously misleading, since such terms as *ground, bring about, cause, make true,* and so on are not clearly synonymous, and since each individually can be interpreted in a number of different ways. Trying to spell out all the available variations on the basic form of the grounding objection by considering all such interpretations would in all likelihood be a tiresome venture—and, I suspect, one that's not worth the effort. After all, hardly anyone claims that his or her grounding argument constitutes a refutation of middle knowledge, and even the most ardent proponents of the grounding objection acknowledge that there are responses available to render Molinism coherent.[39] Still, looking at one recent version of the argument may be helpful insofar as it offers a decent idea of the types of move each side makes in this sometimes tedious debate.

William Hasker has suggested that the key intuition of the grounding objector might be captured via the following principle:

> (GP) Any true contingent proposition is true in virtue of the existence or non-existence of some concrete state of affairs.[40]

Hasker explains that by a *concrete* state of affairs he means 'the exemplification of an occurrent property by a substance at a time, or of an occurrent relation by two or more substances at a time'. The notion of existence in (GP), Hasker says, is to be taken 'trans-temporally': 'a thing "exists" if it exists *now*, or *has* existed, or *will* exist'. The 'in virtue of' relation is left unexplicated.[41]

Given (GP), Hasker argues, it follows that there can be no true counterfactuals of creaturely freedom. For such conditionals (if true at all) would have to be contingent truths, yet there are no concrete states of affairs in virtue of which they are true. This is, perhaps, most glaringly true (he suggests) for counterfactuals with antecedents that turn out to be false. If, for example, Framboise *isn't* in the situation of being told that raspberry sundaes are unavailable, then there simply isn't anything that she (or anyone else) does that could be seen as grounding any counterfactual of freedom about what she would do. So all such conditionals, Hasker concludes, are necessarily false.

In response to any grounding objection, there are two directions in which a Molinist might be inclined to go. Grounding objections are akin to shouts, directed at the Molinist, of 'Your Conditionals Aren't Grounded!' where some specific grounding principle such as (GP) is assumed.[42] Responses are then apt to be akin to counter-shouts either of 'Are So!' or of 'So What?' Sometimes, in fact, Molinists might be inclined to offer *both* ripostes, indicating that one is appropriate if the argument is taken one plausible way, the other if the argument is understood in a different plausible way. Let's see which (if either) of these two replies the Molinist might reasonably use against Hasker.

Could an 'Are So!' response be offered? That is, could a Molinist plausibly claim that (GP) is true, but that counterfactuals of creaturely freedom pass the (GP) test for grounding? That depends in part upon how that unanalyzed relation 'in virtue of' is understood. Alas, constraints of space preclude a full discussion of this matter. My own guess, though, is that, with regard to *this* version of the grounding objection, 'Are So!' replies probably would ring hollow.

Would 'So What?' counter-shouts be more viable? That is, is it plausible to claim that counterfactuals of creaturely freedom are ruled out by (GP), but that this doesn't matter, since (GP) is false? There is much that might be said here about whether, say, 'would-probably' conditionals or laws of nature do in fact (as Hasker asserts) pass muster under (GP). Should they fail to do so, the plausibility of (GP) would obviously be reduced. Discussion of these issues, though, would take us too far afield. Let us instead focus on a different approach a Molinist might take to call (GP) into question.

Recall that Hasker relies upon a 'trans-temporal' reading of the notion of existence in (GP); the concrete state or event in virtue of which a proposition is true 'exists *now*, or *has* existed, or *will* exist'. For clarity's sake, let's rephrase (GP), with the transtemporality of 'existence' made explicit, thus:

(GP) Any true contingent proposition is true in virtue of some concrete state of affairs that does exist, or has existed, or will exist.

Now, pretend that you (*un*like Hasker) are a skeptic concerning *non*-conditional future contingent propositions (such as *Framboise will freely order a raspberry sundae tomorrow*). You're perfectly willing to agree that things *were* and *are* a certain way, but not willing (because of human freedom and/or God's freedom and/or quantum indeterminacy and/or whatever) to grant that things *will be* a certain way. If so, you'd be apt to think that (GP) is unduly complicated, for there *are* no concrete states of affairs that *will* exist. (There are lots that *might* exist, but none that definitely *will*.) So you decide to help Hasker out. Instead of saying that a thing 'exists' just in case it 'exists *now*, or *has* existed, or *will* exist', you suggest, we should really say that something 'exists' if and only if it exists *now* or *has* existed—period. Instead of the painfully swollen (GP), you say, all we need is a thinner, more modest principle:

(GP−) Any true contingent proposition is true in virtue of some concrete state of affairs that does exist or has existed.

(GP−), you note, seems to work just as well against the Molinist as the original (GP) did. So Hasker, you conclude, should look upon the move to (GP−) as but a friendly amendment strengthening his argument.

It's fairly obvious, though, that Hasker would view this alteration as anything but friendly. *Excluding* counterfactuals of creaturely freedom from the realm of the contingently true is not enough to make a grounding principle plausible for Hasker; it also needs to *include* all those contingent propositions that *should* rank as grounded. Since (GP−) *wouldn't* allow us to say that *Framboise will freely order a raspberry sundae tomorrow* is true, and since we need a grounding principle that *does* allow such truths, we need the beefier (GP), not the comparatively emaciated (GP−).

Now, I would have no complaints about Hasker's responding in such a manner. But note what it suggests about grounding principles. Starting with the assumption that contingent truths need grounding, we further assume that we know at least some of the more important *classes* of such truths. We know, for example, that there are non-conditional contingent truths about the past and about the present; we know (Hasker assumes) that there are laws of nature and 'would-probably' conditionals; *and we know that there are non-conditional contingent truths about the future*. We don't *start* with a grounding principle and use *it* to decide whether or not the members of one of these classes of propositions are in fact contingent truths. Things work the other way around. We *start* with the classes of propositions we feel confident about and fashion a grounding principle that will (at a minimum) not rule out any of them. Contingent truths about the future *would be* ungrounded if (GP−) were an adequate account of grounding, but so what? *Because* it doesn't let them in, it follows that it's *not* adequate.

But, of course, what's good for the Openist goose is good for the Molinist gander. Suppose the Molinist assumes that contingent truths need grounding. He, like Hasker, will assume as well that he knows some of the major classes of such truths. He knows that there are non-conditional contingent truths about the past and about the present; he knows (let's assume) that there are laws of nature and 'would-probably' conditionals; he knows that there are non-conditional contingent truths about the future; *and he knows that there are true counterfactuals of creaturely freedom*. Like Hasker, then, he won't *start* with a grounding principle and use *it* to decide whether or not the members of one of these classes of propositions are in fact contingent truths. Things work the other way around. He'll *start* with the classes of propositions he feels confident about and fashion a grounding principle that will (at a minimum) not rule any of them out. Counterfactuals of creaturely freedom *would be* ungrounded if (GP) were an adequate account of grounding, but so what? Since it doesn't let them in, it just follows that it's *not* adequate. What we need is a beefier principle, one that acknowledges that grounding states or events include not only ones that do, did, or will exist, but ones that *would* exist (under specified conditions). What we need, in other words, is something more on the order of

(GP+) Any true contingent proposition is true in virtue of some concrete state of affairs that does exist, or has existed, or will exist, or would exist (under specified conditions).

And with (GP+), of course, we have a principle that the Molinist can endorse without hesitation.

Not every version of the grounding objection, again, can be met by the Molinist with the same response. A Molinist needs to look very carefully at the details of a specific grounding objection before determining what response is appropriate. Still, for every version of the grounding objection of which I am aware, some elaboration of the 'Are So!' or of the 'So What?' response can be made by the Molinist. Hence, though one can safely predict that variations on the grounding objection will continue to appear, and that a significant number of philosophers will find one or another of them convincing, the Molinists' track record in coming up with responses suggests that variations on prior responses will likely be available.

CONCLUSION

I have argued that theories of divine providence are of three basic types. Each such type has its advantages and its disadvantages. Each has had numerous able and creative defenders. As with most philosophical disputes, one can hardly expect this debate to come to an end. I suspect that the field of battle may shift more clearly in the coming years to considerations of which view, when applied to specific doctrines (such as the Incarnation), offers us the most satisfying overall position. Still, it seems quite likely that all three positions will continue to be defended (and attacked) for the foreseeable future.

NOTES

I am grateful to Mike Rea for comments on an earlier draft of this chapter.

1. For the rest of this chapter, I will speak of the Christian notion of providence. In general (though with some obvious exceptions), what I say would apply equally well within the Jewish or Muslim traditions.
2. By foreknowledge I mean knowledge of what lies in our future. Whether God is best to be thought of as existing in time is a much disputed question, one that I think can be largely ignored for our discussion.
3. Process theists, who differ from Open Theists in a number of respects, would also fit into this general category. My discussion, though, will ignore process theism, largely because (as I see it) Open Theism offers the more promising (and, in recent years, surely the more discussed) version of this general approach to providence. It's also, perhaps, worth noting that a number of features characteristic of (even if not essential to) Open Theism—e.g. the general rejection among Open Theists of such traditional divine attributes as eternity and simplicity—will be largely ignored in our discussion.
4. The name comes from Luis de Molina, the sixteenth-century Jesuit theologian who first explicitly proposed this solution.
5. Readers should be forewarned that perfect objectivity may be too much to expect from the author of a book called *Divine Providence: The Molinist Account* (Ithaca: Cornell University Press, 1998). Though I am unabashedly an advocate of the Molinist position, and though I shall devote more space to discussing that position than to the two alternatives, I shall not endeavor to underestimate the real challenges that Molinism continues to face, nor to ignore the genuinely alluring elements offered by its rivals.

6. John Henry Newman, *Prayers, Verses and Meditations* (Ft. Collins: Ignatius Press, 2002), 339.

7. I will, by and large, henceforth dispense with this qualifier, but the reader should understand it to be tacitly present in most of the following discussion.

8. The language here is borrowed from my colleague David Burrell. See e.g. his *Freedom and Creation in Three Traditions* (Notre Dame: University of Notre Dame Press, 1993), 112.

9. Hugh McCann, 'Divine Sovereignty and the Freedom of the Will', *Faith and Philosophy* 12 (1995), 586.

10. For a clear expression of the Thomist rejection of contemporary compatibilism, see e.g. Theodore J. Kondoleon, 'The Free Will Defense: New and Old', *The Thomist* 46 (1983), 19.

11. Thomas Aquinas, *Summa Theologica*, I q. 83 a. 1 ad 3. Translation by the Fathers of the English Dominican Province.

12. The words quoted are from McCann, 'Divine Sovereignty', 593.

13. I assume, here and throughout this discussion, the standard contemporary notion of a possible world. For a magisterial explication of possible worlds, see Alvin Plantinga, *The Nature of Necessity* (Oxford: Clarendon, 1974), esp. ch. 4.

14. Luis de Molina, *On Divine Foreknowledge: Part IV of the Concordia*, trans. Alfred J. Freddoso (Ithaca: Cornell University Press, 1988), disp. 50 sect. 14 (p. 139).

15. See e.g. the classic discussion in Reginald Garrigou-Lagrange, *The One God*, trans. Dom. Bede Rose (St Louis: B. Herder, 1944), 469–71.

16. For further discussion and references, see my 'Two Accounts of Providence', in Thomas V. Morris (ed.), *Divine and Human Action: Essays in the Metaphysics of Theism* (Ithaca: Cornell University Press, 1988), 168–70.

17. For an interesting recent exchange on this point, see Hugh McCann, 'The Author of Sin?', *Faith and Philosophy* 22 (2005), 144–59, and Katherin Rogers, 'God is Not the Author of Sin: An Anselmian Response to McCann', *Faith and Philosophy* 24 (2007), 300–10.

18. For a fuller discussion, see my *Divine Providence*, 84–94.

19. See e.g. William Hasker, 'Foreknowledge and Necessity', *Faith and Philosophy* 2 (1985), 121–57. For one response, see my 'In Defense of Theological Compatibilism', *Faith and Philosophy* 8 (1991), 237–43.

20. Though Openists agree that God cannot know (or even believe) propositions about what free creatures will freely do, they differ as to whether or not there are any such propositions that are in fact true. For an interesting discussion of the alternatives, see Dale Tuggy, 'Three Roads to Open Theism', *Faith and Philosophy* 24 (2007), 28–51.

21. Note that the picture isn't of a God who is ignorant of something that could be known. Openists are united on this point: there simply isn't anything that could be known here. Could an Openist believe that there *are* true counterfactuals of creaturely freedom, but that they're one and all necessarily unknowable, even by God? Technically, yes. But this is not a popular Openist stance.

22. Such an approach is at least suggested in Gregory Boyd, *God of the Possible* (Grand Rapids: Baker Books, 2001), 61, 127. See also Thomas Oden, *The Living God: Systematic Theology, Volume One* (San Francisco: Harper, 1987), 306. For a discussion of the advantages and disadvantages of such an approach, see my review of William Hasker's *Providence, Evil and the Openness of God*, in *Philosophia Christi* 8 (2006), 493–6.

23. It's also worth noting that an Open Theist could view a God who constantly uses his knowledge of would-probably conditionals to interfere with human events as a tad too manipulative. For an interesting presentation of such a view, see James Rissler, 'Open Theism: Does God Risk or Hope?', *Religious Studies* 42 (2006), 63–74.

24. For a fuller discussion of this issue, see William Hasker, *God, Time, and Knowledge* (Ithaca: Cornell University Press, 1988), 194–6, and my *Divine Providence*, 100–2.

25. See Michael Robinson, 'Why Divine Foreknowledge?', *Religious Studies* 36 (2000), 251–75, and Jennifer Jensen, 'The Grounding Objection to Molinism' (Doctoral dissertation, University of Notre Dame, 2008), ch. 5. Hasker has responded to Robinson in *Providence, Evil and the Openness of God* (London: Routledge, 2004), 206–11.

26. For more on this topic, see my *Divine Providence*, 102–5.

27. For a fuller discussion of these issues, see ibid. 105–7.

28. See especially Hasker, *Providence, Evil and the Openness of God*, 'Appendix: Replies to My Critics'.

29. For a much more extensive and detailed presentation of the Molinist position, see my *Divine Providence*, especially ch. 2.

30. The language here suggests that God is in time—that there's a time when he's deciding what to do, and a later time at which he does it. Many Molinists, though, think of God as atemporal, and view the use of temporal metaphors (based, obviously, on the fact that our decision-making is typically a temporally extended process) as a useful but potentially misleading way of describing what is essentially a dependence relation, not essentially a temporal one. For more on this point, see ibid. 37, 174–6.

31. I'm speaking a bit loosely here in referring to *possible creatures*. Molinists are not committed to the odd claim that, in addition to all the *actual* creatures in existence, there are also a horde of *merely possible* creatures hanging around! For a stricter statement of the Molinist view, see ibid. 46–7.

32. At least, we aren't powerless with respect to counterfactuals with true antecedents. Molinists needn't think that Framboise can do something about counterfactuals where the antecedent describes a situation she's in fact never in. All they need insist is that, if she were in such a situation, she would have power over both the counterfactual and her own action.

33. In addition to chs. 8–11 of *Divine Providence*, see esp. William Lane Craig, ' "No Other Name": A Middle Knowledge Perspective on the Exclusivity of Salvation Through Christ', *Faith and Philosophy* 6 (1989), 172–88, as well as his ' "Men Moved by The Holy Spirit Spoke from God" (2 Peter 1: 21): A Middle Knowledge Perspective on Biblical Inspiration', *Philosophia Christi* 1 (1999), 45–82. Regarding original sin, see Michael C. Rea, 'The Metaphysics of Original Sin', in Peter van Inwagen and Dean Zimmerman (eds.), *Persons: Human and Divine* (Oxford: Clarendon, 2007), 319–56. For the classic presentation of a 'free will defense' in response to the argument from evil, see Plantinga's *The Nature of Necessity*, ch. 9.

34. See e.g. my ' "A Death He Freely Accepted": Molinist Reflections on the Incarnation', *Faith and Philosophy* 18 (2001), 3–20, as well as my 'The Possibilities of Incarnation: Some Radical Molinist Suggestions', *Religious Studies* 37 (2001), 125–39. For a very different Molinist view, see William Lane Craig, 'Flint's Radical Molinist Christology Not Radical Enough', *Faith and Philosophy* 23 (2006), 55–64.

35. The lyrics are by Sheldon Harnick.

36. My preference is to include instances of prophecy in the antecedents. Space constraints, though, preclude a fuller discussion of this issue.

37. My thinking on this subject has been prompted by remarks by Brian Leftow and Robin Collins.

38. See Alvin Plantinga, 'On Ockham's Way Out', *Faith and Philosophy* 3 (1986), 235–69.

39. See e.g. Robert Adams's remark in n. 22 of the version of 'Middle Knowledge and the Problem of Evil' printed in his *The Virtue of Faith and Other Essays in Philosophical Theology* (New York: Oxford University Press, 1987), 77–93. See also Hasker's *Providence, Evil and the Openness of God*, 197.

40. Hasker, *Providence, Evil and the Openness of God*, 195.

41. Ibid. 195.

42. For a sustained argument to this effect, see Jensen, *The Grounding Objection to Molinism*.

CHAPTER 13

....

PETITIONARY
PRAYER

....

SCOTT A. DAVISON

TRADITIONAL theists believe that there exists an all-knowing, all-powerful, perfectly loving, and perfectly good God. They also believe that God created the world, sustains it in being from moment to moment, and providentially guides all events, in accordance with a plan, toward a good ending. Historically, most traditional theists have believed that God sometimes answers prayers for particular things. In keeping with the literature on this subject, I shall call such prayers 'petitionary prayers'.

In this chapter, I discuss several problems related to the concept of the traditional theistic God's answering petitionary prayers. To simplify matters, and for the sake of convenience, I shall speak as if traditional theism were true, but I should not be understood to be arguing or claiming this is so.[1] Also, I shall not discuss here any specific teachings about petitionary prayer derived from any particular theistic religious traditions.[2] Finally, wherever possible, I shall avoid specific assumptions about what traditional theists should say about the nature and extent of divine power, knowledge, and goodness, although at certain junctures in the argument it may be impossible to avoid some commitments in these areas.

1. SOME FLAWED ACCOUNTS OF ANSWERED PRAYER

In what circumstances might it be true to say that God has answered a prayer? Discussions of the difficulties surrounding petitionary prayer in the literature typically ignore the complexities involved in providing an adequate answer to this most basic question. I shall begin with a simple example.

Suppose that a particular person prays that a certain event happen, and that the event in question actually happens. Should we say, in this kind of case, that God has answered the prayer? Not necessarily. For example, suppose that you and I are competing in a science contest, and I pray that you will be struck by lightning and incapacitated so that I can win the contest. Imagine now that you are struck by lightning and incapacitated, exactly as I imagined you might be when I prayed about it. Does this mean that God answered my prayer?

No. It is an important restriction on answered prayers that they concern only good things. This restriction follows from the nature of God's moral perfection. God would not cooperate in the production of evil for its own sake, or for bad reasons. In terms of the example just described, it would be wrong for God to strike you with lightning and incapacitate you just so that I could win the science contest, unless something else were at stake in this situation. So if people pray for bad things to happen, and they actually do happen, then we should not conclude that the prayers in question were answered. In other words, what we might call a 'pure correlation' account of answered prayer is mistaken. God answers only good prayers, we might say, or at least prayers for things that are not bad. (Someone might suppose that there are neutral things, things that are neither good nor bad; I shall ignore this point in what follows, because nothing of substance turns on it.) It is just a coincidence that bad things sometimes happen after people have prayed for them to happen.

Consider instead the following suggestion about when it is true to say that God answers a prayer: whenever a person prays for something good to happen, and it happens, then God has answered a prayer. We could call this a 'modified correlation' account of answered prayer. Is this suggestion satisfactory? Not really. After all, in the same way that there can be coincidences involving prayers for bad things, there can be coincidences involving prayers for good things, too. It could happen, for example, that the event in question was a very important part of God's plan for the world, in such a way that God's bringing it about was not related at all to anyone's prayers.

So just because a person prays for something good and it happens, this by itself is not sufficient for saying that the person's prayer was answered. What else is necessary? Taking a cue from the cases of coincidence mentioned above, perhaps what is needed is some condition such as this: in order for God to answer a prayer, it must be the case that if the person had not prayed for the event in question, then it would not have occurred. Let us call this a 'counterfactual dependence' account of answered prayer. Almost every treatment of the topic of petitionary prayer in the literature endorses (or assumes) something like the counterfactual dependence account.[3] Is this approach satisfactory?

No. On the one hand, this account demands too much. Imagine—just for the sake of the argument; I shall argue below that this scenario is problematic—that I pray for a certain person to recover from a serious illness, and that God answers my prayer by healing this person. But suppose that as it happens, if I had not prayed for this, then you would have prayed for it instead, and God would have answered your prayer by healing this person in exactly the same way. Do we really want to say that my prayer was not answered in the actual sequence of things, just because the recovery in question would have happened even if I had not prayed for it? Clearly not. So in order for a prayer to be answered, it is not necessary that if the person had not prayed for the event in question, then it would not have occurred.[4]

On the other hand, the suggested account is also too weak. Suppose that I pray for something to happen, and it does, and it would not have happened if I had not prayed for it to happen. This is not sufficient for saying that my prayer was answered, because there are many ways in which it might be true that the event in question would not have happened if I had not prayed for it to happen. For example, it might be the case that the event in question was somehow caused by my very act of praying. Lawrence Masek (2000: 279) provides an example of this (unintentionally, I believe) in the following passage, which is about helping distant victims of a hurricane:

Perhaps my prayer for the hurricane victims makes me more aware of their suffering, which leads me to donate money to help them. My friend might see this action and donate money, and his friend might see his action and do likewise. Hence, my prayer can lead to comfort for the hurricane victims that would not have occurred without my prayer.

If something like this were to happen, then it would be true that the event in question would not have happened if I had not prayed for it. But in this kind of case, we need not say that my prayer was *answered by God*, since the very act of praying for the victims could lead to comfort for the hurricane victims all by itself, even if God did not exist.[5] So in order for a prayer to be answered, it is not sufficient that if the person had not prayed for the event in question, then it would not have occurred.

What we should say here, I think, is something like the following: A person's prayer for something is answered by God if and only if (1) the person prays for the thing in question, (2) the thing in question is good,[6] (3) God brings about the thing in question, and (4) God brings about the thing in question at least in part because the person prays for it.[7] In order to make sense of condition (4), we will need to appeal to something like God's reasons for doing things.[8] I shall call this type of account a 'reasons account' of answered prayer.

2. A Reasons Account

A reasons account of answered prayer is clearly superior to a pure correlation account, a modified correlation account, and a counterfactual dependence account. But it isn't completely clear as it stands. The most pressing problem involves trying to make sense of condition (4): what does the word 'because' mean here? One of the difficulties we face stems from the fact that creatures have no direct causal impact upon God, at least as traditionally conceived. Another, more pressing difficulty stems from the fact that since God is good, God already has a reason to bring about all good events, whether or not anyone ever prays for them to occur. So condition (2), which requires that answered prayers concern only good events, actually makes it harder to understand the word 'because' in condition (4).

Compare a related situation concerning the free and rational choices of human beings. Suppose that I face a choice between several alternatives, each of which is very good. For example, imagine that I can choose to attend medical school, to attend law school, or to attend art school, but that I can choose to do only one of these things. Suppose further that there is no morally overriding reason for me to choose any particular option. What should I do?

Let us suppose that in the end, I chose to attend art school. How might I explain why I made this decision? I will want to find a statement of the form 'I chose art school because—', where I can fill in the blank with a plausible reason. What constraints would we want to impose upon different ways of trying to complete this statement? At the very least, we would like the statement as a whole to be a true description of my reasons for choosing art school over the other alternatives.

There is a danger, though, that my explanation might work too well. If the explanation works too well, then it will seem impossible that I should have chosen medical school or law school instead. That would appear to rob me of my freedom, at least according to a libertarian conception of freedom.[9] For example, if I were to say that I chose to attend art school because I was pathologically afraid of both doctors and lawyers, then it would seem that I did not choose art school freely at all.

If my choice to attend art school is rational, it must be a reasonable response to the value of attending art school. But if my choice to attend art school is free, then there must be alternative options open to me. There is a vast literature on this topic, the problem of trying to explain how actions might be both rational and free at once.[10] I don't have anything new to say about this question, except to point out that the same question arises in an especially acute way in connection with the idea of answered prayer, since God's decisions are supposed to be both rational and free.

On the one hand, God's decisions are supposed to be rational because they are always made in light of a perfect grasp of whatever reasons or values are at stake in a situation.[11] The traditional doctrine of divine providence implies that God's actions in the world are not random, but instead based upon knowledge and love, guiding creation wisely in accordance with a good plan. At the very least, God's decisions with respect to prayers are rational in the sense that God answers prayers only for what is good (or at least not bad).

On the other hand, traditional theists typically suppose that God's decisions with respect to prayers must be free because creatures have no direct causal impact upon God and no way to compel God to act in any particular way. Some people have a rather magical view of the power of prayer according to which God is literally compelled to answer certain prayers, but this view is highly at odds with traditional theism.[12]

But if God's decisions with respect to prayers are both rational and free, then it is especially difficult to understand what it means to say that God answers a prayer. If I pray for something good to happen, then God already has a reason to bring it about, whether or not I pray for it, since it is a good thing. Suppose that I do in fact pray for something good and that God in fact brings about the thing in question. In order for God's bringing about this thing to count as *an answer to my prayer*, as noted above, it must be the case that God brought this about at least in part *because* I prayed for it. But what does this mean?

Let us suppose that, independently of my prayers, God has a number of reasons for bringing about the good thing in question. Now when I pray for this thing, God has an additional reason to bring it about, which I shall call reason x. When we say that God brings about the thing in question at least in part *because* of x (that is, because I prayed for it), we are saying something about the role that x plays among God's reasons for bringing about the thing in question. How central a role must x play in God's reasons for bringing about the thing in question in order for God's bringing it about to count as an answer to my prayer?

It is hard to be precise here, of course. Even in the case of human beings, where we feel more confident conceptually, it is hard to answer similar questions. For example, suppose that my neighbor asks me to remove some poison ivy from my fence that faces his yard, and imagine also that I have many reasons for doing this already. If I do decide to remove the poison ivy from the fence, what role must the reason provided by my neighbor's request play in my decision in order for my action to count as a *response* to my neighbor's request? There is the clear case where the neighbor's request plays no role at all (so that my action would not count as a response to the request), and the equally clear case where the neighbor's request plays a necessary role (so that my action would count as a response to the request). But in between these cases, so to speak, there are many unclear possibilities.

In what remains of this chapter, I shall develop in more detail the problem related to petitionary prayer just outlined, along with a few others. Thanks to the reasons account of answered prayer, it is possible to formulate and evaluate these problems with a degree of precision that was previously not possible. These problems are deep, perhaps even intractable, but I shall argue in the end that traditional theists should not find this result very troubling.[13]

3. THE DIVINE FREEDOM PROBLEM

If we consider more carefully the claim that God's decision whether or not to answer a prayer is free in the libertarian sense, then we run into a problem.

Imagine for the sake of the argument that someone asks God to bring about the occurrence of some event E. Suppose also that God has a number of good reasons for bringing about E already, and now that someone has prayed for E to occur, God has yet another reason for bringing about E.[14] To complete the story, let us imagine that God freely brings about the occurrence of E (in the libertarian sense of 'freely'). Could this qualify as a case of answered prayer?

Since God brings about E freely, God could have decided instead not to bring about E, in those very same circumstances, even though God had all the same reasons for bringing about E that God actually possesses.[15] But then how can the sum total of God's reasons for bringing about E possibly explain God's decision to bring about E? After all, those same reasons are compatible with God's choosing not to bring about E, so they do not explain why God chose to bring about E as opposed to choosing not to bring about E.[16] Since the sum total of God's reasons for bringing about E cannot explain why God chose to bring it about, neither can any subset of those reasons, including the offering of the prayer for E. So it is not the case that God brought about E at least in part because of the prayer, which implies that this is not a case of answered prayer after all. Let us call this 'the divine freedom problem' of petitionary prayer.

The divine freedom problem of petitionary prayer is a specific instance of the general problem of how reasons can possibly explain free action, and it clearly stems from a libertarian account of freedom. This problem does not arise for an important alternative picture of human action, according to which reasons are causes of action, and hence explain it in a very straightforward way.[17] Of course, there is considerable controversy (to say the least) over which kind of account of human action is the best one, over whether or not human beings are free in the libertarian sense. But traditional theists seem committed to the claim that God is free in just this sense. This is because of the traditional view that creation is free (as opposed to a kind of necessary emanation, of the sort described by Neoplatonists) and the obvious fact that nothing in the world could determine God's actions.[18] So the divine freedom problem is a serious problem for traditional theists who believe that God could answer petitionary prayers.[19]

4. THE DIVINE GOODNESS PROBLEM

Some traditional theists have held the view that God must always do what is best,[20] that God is obligated to do everything possible to maximize value in every situation.[21] If this were so, then of course God would be obligated to do anything for which anyone prays if such prayers happen to specify the maximum value available in a given situation. But in nearly all these cases,[22] God will be obligated to bring about those same states of affairs even if nobody prays for them,[23] which implies that God's bringing about those states of affairs would not qualify as answers to prayers, since the offering of prayer would not play an important enough role among God's reasons for bringing them about (according to the reasons account of answered prayer developed above).

Even if we set aside this highly stringent view of God's obligations, still one might wonder why God would not bring about something good in a given situation simply because nobody prayed for it.[24] It is helpful to view this question as identifying a version of the problem of evil. In response to the problem of evil, traditional theists often argue that particular evils are permitted by God in order to realize greater goods or to prevent worse evils. Defenders of the practice of petitionary prayer typically adopt this strategy as well (see below, sect. 6). But as I shall argue, the explanations of the necessity of petitionary prayer developed in the literature to date are completely unconvincing. Apart from the specific teachings of any particular religious tradition, which I shall not discuss here, there seems to be no reason to expect the God of traditional theism not to bring about some specific good just because no prayers were offered for it. But if God would have brought about the good things for which people prayed anyway, even if prayers had not been offered, then it follows from the reasons account that God's actions do not count as answers to those prayers, since the offering of the prayers cannot have played a significant enough role in God's decision. Let us call this 'the divine goodness problem' of petitionary prayer. Since traditional theism includes the claim that God is perfectly good (and perfectly loving), the divine goodness problem is a serious problem for traditional theists who believe that God could answer petitionary prayers.

5. The Reasons-Skeptical Problem

Given the complexity involved in saying that God answers a prayer, as indicated by the reasons account developed above, it seems impossible, apart from direct revelation, for any human being ever to know (or even be justified in believing) that any particular prayers have ever been answered. In order to see that this is so, suppose that every event is produced by God in some sense, as traditional theists have typically insisted.[25] Even if this is the case, apart from direct revelation, there is no way to have enough access to God's reasons for bringing things about to be able to distinguish between answered prayers, on the one hand, and events that God brought about for other reasons after prayers happened to have been offered, on the other hand.[26] And since no human being could possibly distinguish these things from each other, the only reasonable thing for human beings to do would be to withhold judgment on the matter. Let us call this the 'reasons-skeptical problem' of petitionary prayer.

Even in the case of so-called miraculous events, where one might think that there are good reasons for believing that God is the direct cause of some particular event, still one would have no reason to think that God had done those things *because of prayer*. In fact, the more impressive the miracle, and the more good that it accomplishes, the more likely that it would be just the kind of thing that God would have done anyway, whether or not anyone had prayed for it to occur.[27]

Exceptions to this general rule about miraculous events might include the cases discussed by Michael J. Murray[28] (Elijah's confrontation with the prophets of Baal in 1 Kings 18) and Thomas P. Flint[29] (the healing of the blind man by St Peter in Acts 3). In these cases, one could argue (as Flint does) that the offering of the prayer actually changes the circumstances in which God acts, and hence makes a difference by 'raising the stakes' in a situation, so to speak. But then God is responding in these cases to the change in the circumstances caused by the offering of the prayer (the raising of the stakes), rather than responding to the prayer per se. In other words, it is not the fact that *a prayer was offered for E* that explains why God brings about *E* in these cases; had a different kind of event (namely, one that did not involve prayer at all) changed the circumstances in just the same way by raising the stakes, then it would have given God the very same reasons for acting.

In addition, the unusual cases mentioned by Flint and Murray are clearly the exception rather than the rule. From the perspective of a traditional theist, the pattern exemplified in these cases is not a pattern that one should be encouraged to create on one's own. One could even argue that deliberately trying to raise the stakes in such situations is a way of trying to force God to act, or that it involves the kind of testing of God that is forbidden by the Judaeo/Christian/Islamic theistic religious traditions.[30] By contrast, in the typical cases in which traditional theists believe that their prayers have been answered, there is no convincing evidence that something miraculous has occurred, no good reason to think that the event in question would not have happened if no prayers had been offered, and most importantly, no way to discern what role prayers might have played in God's decisions (and hence no way to tell whether a given event is an answer to prayer or not).

A different version of the skeptical problem has been noted in the literature before, a version based on a counterfactual dependence account of answered prayer. This version of the problem is not quite as powerful as the reasons-skeptical version developed above (which emerges only after a reasons account of answered prayer has been identified). Even so, the force of this weaker skeptical problem has been underestimated. In a reply to David Basinger, Michael Murray states this problem clearly ('How could we ever know that this apparent answer to prayer would not have happened anyway, even if nobody had prayed for it?'), and then argues in reply that in the case of Elijah and the prophets of Baal, 'the indirect evidence makes it clear that the consumption of the sacrifice was a response by God to Elijah's petition'.[31] He adds that 'Many theists claim, similarly, that indirect evidence makes it plausible that particular events have occurred in response to their petitionary prayers. And while these judgments certainly will be false in some cases, there is no reason to think that they are always, or even often, unjustified' (Murray 2004: 265). Murray's empirical claim about the quality of evidence available to many theists is simply false. The typical person never has good 'indirect evidence' for answered prayer, let alone anything that remotely resembles the kind of evidence available in the case of Elijah and the prophets of Baal.

Murray also claims that 'God enlightens the mind of the petitioner to make certain features of the world salient (features related to the provision or failure thereof), and to see the reasons for the provision or its failure' (ibid. 249). But he provides no reason to think that God does this on a regular basis (or fails to do it when the prayers in question were not answered but God decided to bring about the events in question anyway). In other words, Murray seems to suggest that God enlightens the minds of petitioners just because something like that would be required in order for them to know that their petitions have been answered, but this is clearly ad hoc.[32]

All of this means that Murray's answer to the weaker skeptical problem is unsatisfactory. More importantly, there seems to be no way at all to answer the stronger reasons-skeptical problem of petitionary prayer, and this has important implications for the justifications of the practice of petitionary prayer offered in the literature to date.

6. IMPLICATIONS OF THE SKEPTICAL PROBLEM

Since it is impossible to know whether or not a given prayer has been answered, apart from direct revelation, many of the rational justifications for the practice of petitionary prayer offered in the literature collapse. For example, Murray argues that petitionary prayer keeps us from the idolatrous belief that we are self-sufficient. This is because God makes the provision of certain goods dependent on the offering of prayers, and being 'truly dependent on petitioning is what allows many, and maybe all, to "recognize God as the ultimate source of all the goods that we enjoy" in the first place' (ibid. 247). Like a father who gives his son an action figure only if he asks for it, God provides certain things for believers only if they ask for them (ibid. 246–7), and teaches us 'a number of things about [H]is own good nature and purposes in the world by responding one way or another to our petitions' (ibid. 249). In a similar vein, Isaac Choi claims that seeing some of our prayers 'clearly and objectively answered' can serve as a powerful reminder of God's reality, nature, and love (Choi 2003: 12).

But even when 'the antecedent probability of what we requested happening by chance is extremely low' (ibid. 12 n. 35), this does not provide good evidence for the conclusion that God has answered our prayers. This is because we are never in a position to say what the antecedent probability of a given event is when considered in the light of God's reasons and knowledge of a situation (since we do not have access to God's reasons or knowledge of a situation).[33] And so we cannot draw the lessons Murray and Choi describe from our experiences with any justification.[34]

One objection that might be offered in response to Murray's explanation of the necessity of petitionary prayer is that many people seem to flourish without offering any petitionary prayers at all (the so-called 'fat pagan' objection). By way of reply, Murray (2004: 253) says, 'All we can infer from the model I have offered is that there are some times when God makes provision dependent on petition, and in those particular cases, those who fail to pray will fail to receive what is dependent on petition. Nothing in the empirical evidence could show us that this never happens.' By way of reply, it only seems fair to note that nothing in the empirical evidence could show us that this ever does happen, either. This is because the empirical evidence is simply inadequate to justify a conclusion either way.

In fact, Richard Swinburne, a defender of the practice of petitionary prayer, actually claims that 'if God answered all prayers for the removal of bad states of affairs promptly and predictably, that would become evident', and this would be bad because it would eliminate the 'epistemic distance' between ourselves and God.[35] Swinburne (1998: 206) thinks that such distance is necessary in order for us to have a free choice between good and evil; otherwise, we would be like the child whose mother is watching, for whom the temptation to do wrong is 'overborne'.

'The more uncertainty there is about the existence of God, the more it is possible for us to be naturally good people who still have a free choice between right and wrong' (ibid. 207). Even if Swinburne is wrong about the necessity of epistemic distance for significant freedom, he echoes the point that the available evidence for answered prayer is ambiguous at best.

Swinburne defends petitionary prayer by arguing that 'If human responsibility is good, then this extension to it—of exerting influence on (though not of course compelling) God to change things [through petitionary prayer]—would surely also be good' (ibid. 115). But if it is impossible to know whether or not one's prayers are ever answered, then it seems unlikely that one is responsible (in any substantial sense) for the results of answered prayer. This is because in general, one's degree of responsibility for the obtaining of some state of affairs depends upon the degree to which one could foresee its obtaining, the degree to which one intended that it obtain as a result of one's actions, and the degree to which one's actions contributed causally to its obtaining.[36] So cases in which one person petitions another person to act freely in specific ways over time, especially when one does not know the outcome of such petitions, are cases in which one's responsibility for the obtaining of the state of affairs in question is dramatically diminished.[37]

Eleonore Stump, in the most widely discussed treatment of our question, argues that the practice of petitionary prayer keeps human beings from being either totally dominated or spoiled by God, and thus safeguards the divine/human friendship from one or another kind of using.[38] On the one hand, Stump claims that if God bestows certain goods only in response to petitionary prayers, then this will guard against unwelcome interference from God, which could produce an unbalanced friendship leading to a slavish or 'lackey-like' follower. By way of reply, it should be pointed out that if we don't know which goods God bestows upon us as a result of petitionary prayer (as opposed to those goods God bestows on us just because we need them, whether or not we ask), then we won't know whether or not God is 'respecting our boundaries', so to speak.[39]

On the other hand, with respect to the second danger, that of spoiling the creature, Stump (1979: 143) says the following about a prospective petitioner:

If he gets what he prayed for, he will be in a position to attribute his good fortune to God's doing and to be grateful to God for what God has given him. If we add the undeniable uncertainty of his getting what he prays for, then we will have safeguards against what I will call (for lack of a better phrase) overwhelming spoiling.

The problem with this suggestion, of course, is that if the petitioner does not know whether his prayers have been answered, he is lucky, or God was going to do these things anyway, then he will not be in a position to attribute his good fortune to answered prayer after all.[40]

All the attempts to provide a rational justification for the practice of petitionary prayer discussed above are undermined by the skeptical problem. But the remaining rational justifications in the literature are not above reproach for other reasons. For instance, in connection with the idea that petitionary prayer tends to guard against the idolatry of self-sufficiency, Murray (2004: 246) says that 'With each petition, the believer is made aware that she is directly dependent on God for her provisions in life.' It is worth noting that the same justification could be given for the practice of offering prayers of thanks, which face none of the problems discussed in this chapter (see sect. 7 for more on this). But as Choi points out, what Murray says about petitionary prayers would be true even if God never answered any of them, as long as people falsely believed that they were necessary and answered.[41] The same point applies to Murray's claims that God withholds certain goods until people pray for one another, thus forcing interdependence and unity among believers (ibid. 250) and providing them with a reason to share their needs with one another (ibid. 252).

Choi claims that God might not maximize the goodness in every human life in order to leave room for the improvement of our lives due to divine rewards and acts of human love. Efficacious petitionary prayers express praiseworthy attitudes, which God would naturally choose to reward (2003: 9–10).[42] Choi claims that '[petitionary] prayerlessness betrays a practical lack of faith and trust in God' (ibid. 11), but as we shall see below, this is not necessarily the case. And there are ways other than petitionary prayer to manifest praiseworthy attitudes.

Choi also claims that petitionary prayers provide us with a way to love those whom we cannot directly affect (ibid. 9–10). Ironically, C. S. Lewis points out that often people pray for others when they should be helping them instead.[43] But suppose that we confine our attention to prayers for those whom we cannot help ourselves. In this case, either there are others who can help those in need, or there are not. (1) If there are others who can help, then they should; but if they choose not to, is there any point in asking God to change their minds? If Choi thinks that there is a point in asking God to change their minds, then his main point is undercut, namely, the point that God does not maximize our well-being because this provides an opening for creatures to improve each other's lives through acts of love. After all, if God is willing to override my choices about whether or not to help in response to your prayers, then God is not taking seriously my choices about whether or not to improve the world. (2) Finally, if no people are in a position to help those in need, Choi has given us no reason to think that God would not provide for them, whether or not anyone asks for this. Here we run into the problem of divine goodness again (see above, sect. 4), and the problem of evil.

A more fundamental problem for Choi's position stems from the concepts of action and responsibility. Since God can freely decide not to answer any particular prayer, as noted above, it is not clear that we can describe answered prayers as acts of love performed by the petitioners. The offering of a petition might be an act of love performed by the petitioner, but the answering of the prayer would be an act of love performed by God, not by the petitioner. (If the offering of the petition is itself an act of love, then it is a good thing, but this will be true whether or not it is answered; see sect. 7 below for more on this.) Choi's point is that God 'leaves room' for us to make a difference in the lives of others, but it would be the answering, not the petitioning, that would make a difference in the world, and the petition does not cause the answering so long as God is free. Hence God should get the credit for the answered prayer, not the petitioner, which undercuts Choi's point that God leaves room for *creatures* to make a difference in the world.

7. HOW TRADITIONAL THEISTS SHOULD RESPOND

A reasons account of answered prayer seems to be the right kind of account, but it leads to very serious problems of petitionary prayer for traditional theists and undercuts all the extant defenses of the practice in the literature. Suppose that there are good reasons to believe that petitionary prayers are never answered, and that even if this is wrong, still it is impossible to know when prayers are answered. How should traditional theists respond to this conclusion? Several responses seem appropriate.[44]

First, consider the claim that one's relationship with God would be deficient in some way without answered prayers.[45] Why should this be so? What should matter here is not that God brings about good things for people in response to petitionary prayers, but rather that God loves them and provides for them, whether or not they ask for anything specifically. There is something inappropriately egocentric to insist that one be a cause (in some sense) of God's action in the world, rather than simply being grateful for God's provident care. Traditional theists believe that every good thing comes from God (ultimately, if not directly), and none of the problems outlined here with petitionary prayer applies to other kinds of prayers, such as prayers of thanksgiving.

In fact, contrary to what Choi says, one could argue that petitionary prayer reflects a lack of trust in God. Rather than trusting in God's love, power, and knowledge to care for everyone (unless there is a good reason not to do so—see the literature on the problem of evil), those offering petitionary prayers seem to think that God needs suggestions, reminders, or repeated badgering in order to act. As noted (see the discussion in n. 13 above), these things might be appropriate when dealing with fellow human beings, but surely an all-knowing, perfectly loving God needs no such prompting.

Dwelling on particular people and their needs is an expression of love and concern all by itself, whether or not it is done in the presence of God, so to speak, and whether or not it results in the offering of petitionary prayers. It would not be strange to find the heartfelt, thoughtful sympathy of an atheistic friend much more comforting than the petitionary prayers of an inattentive theistic friend, for example. Quite frequently we are unable to change the world, but a large part of being a good person is standing symbolically on the side of the good anyway.[46] Quite often the best we can do in a given situation is to express love and to identify symbolically with those in need. It is interesting to note that these things seem to be the main functions of the offering of petitionary prayers in public. These are very good things to do, even if prayers are not efficacious in the sense of moving God to act.[47]

For many people, petitionary prayer is an involuntary response in times of need, whether or not they believe that it will be efficacious, and traditional theists will probably find something appropriate about this (even if they believe that such prayers do not move God to act differently). So petitionary prayer is not pointless, even if it is not efficacious in the sense of moving God to act, since it serves various important functions. As a number of authors have suggested,[48] perhaps we should think of prayer in general terms not so much as the attempt to bring God's mind into line with our minds as the attempt to bring our minds into line with God's mind.

But it would be a mistake to assume that failing to pray in the petitionary way evinces a lack of concern for others. Instead, it could be the case that one does not petition God on behalf of a particular person's need simply because one knows all too well how pressing that need is, one knows that God sees this truth even more clearly than one does, one knows that God loves this person even more than one does, and one trusts that God will do what is best, whatever that might be. If this is right, then it may actually betray a lack of trust in God in some cases to pray for specific things to occur.

What should a traditional theist do who formerly believed in the efficacy of petitionary prayer, but now finds it pointless because of the sorts of arguments advanced in this chapter? Those who believe in the efficacy of petitionary prayer sometimes pray that God would take care of those for whom we have forgotten to pray. In a similar vein, those who find it difficult to pray in the petitionary way any longer might offer a conditional prayer to the effect that if they are wrong about the pointlessness of prayer, then would God do all those things for which they would have prayed had they continued to believe in the practice of petitionary prayer? If it turns out that the arguments of this chapter are mistaken and that petitionary prayer is efficacious after all, then why wouldn't God answer this particular prayer? Why would God punish a person, in effect, for having false beliefs about petitionary prayer, as long as they were based on (somewhat decent) arguments? Rather than taking God for granted, such a prayer would express faith in God's good will, confidence in God's providence, and trust in God's power.

Notes

For very helpful comments concerning earlier versions of this chapter, including many clever objections that I could not answer here, I wish to thank Thomas P. Flint, Michael Rea, Eleonore Stump, Michael Murray, Ronald L. Hall, Paul Draper, William Hasker, Kate Rogers, William Rowe, George Mavrodes, and participants in the 2006 Meeting of the Society for Philosophy of Religion in Charleston, South Carolina. Research toward the completion of this paper was supported by a course load reduction granted by Morehead State University, for which I am also grateful. Finally, it is worth noting that although I have argued here against the efficacy of petitionary prayer based on general considerations, I am also a practitioner of a particular theistic religious tradition that affirms it, so I look forward to future debate concerning these issues.

1. Of course, these questions would be interesting in their own right even if traditional theism turned out to be false.
2. This restriction renders my discussion rather limited and artificial, I admit, but a complete discussion would require something like a book-length treatment of the question.
3. For instance, see Swinburne 1998: 115; Flint 1998: 222, 226; Murray 2004: 243; and Basinger 2004: 255. The exception to the rule here is Flint (1998: 227 n. 22), who thinks that counterfactual dependence is probably not sufficient for answered prayer.
4. The structure of this counterexample is due to Harry Frankfurt's well-known attack on the so-called principle of alternate possibilities: see Frankfurt 1969.
5. We should draw the same conclusion in a case in which I prayed for strength, and the very act of praying for strength gave me strength all by itself.
6. As Michael Rea has pointed out to me, 'good' here must mean something like 'good, all things considered', as opposed to 'intrinsically good'.
7. Thomas P. Flint has pointed out to me that when I say that God 'brings about' something, as I do in condition (4), this should not be taken to imply that God directly causes the thing in question. Instead, my use of 'brings about' is intended to include what Plantinga (1974: 172–3) has called 'weak actualization'.
8. This means that we will need to appeal to that which Richard Swinburne (1979) has called 'personal explanation', or what others call 'folk-psychological explanation'. For a lively discussion of the difficulties facing folk-psychological explanations as applied to human beings, see Stich 1983.
9. According to a libertarian conception of freedom, an act is free only if nothing makes that action causally necessary at that time. For further discussion of this point, see Campbell 1957; Frankfurt 1969; Chisholm 1982; Fischer 1982; van Inwagen 1983; Flint 1988; Rowe 1991, 2004; and Davison 1994a, 1999a.
10. For a few contemporary examples, see Campbell 1957; Davidson 1963; Chisholm 1982; Fischer 1982; Dennett 1984; Kane 1985; Fischer and Ravizza 1998; and Wolf 1990.
11. I shall ignore here the question of whether or not God *creates* the values at stake in all situations (see Davison 1991a). I do not assume in this chapter that God is morally obligated to maximize the value in each situation; I shall say more about this below, in sect. 4.

12. See the discussions of this point in Philips 1981: ch. 6; Swinburne 1998: 115; and Flint 1998: 222; I say more about divine freedom in sect. 3 below.

13. In addition to the theoretical problems discussed below, there are two interesting practical puzzles that are worth noting that arise in connection with petitionary prayer. For instance, it is widely assumed that the better a thing would be, the more likely it is that God would answer prayers for its occurrence. But the reasons account of answered prayer suggests otherwise. For the better something would be, the stronger God's reasons are for bringing it about anyway, and hence the less likely it is that prayers played a significant role in God's decision. I call this 'the puzzle of increasing value'. Another practical puzzle has to do with what, exactly, a person should pray for. Defenders of petitionary prayer are quick to point out that God does not answer some prayers because answering them would not be good for us, despite appearances to the contrary (see Flint 1998: 217). Of course, it is often very difficult to know what the consequences of any particular event might be. Thinking about this tends to make one's prayers more and more general. More pressure in this direction comes from God's nature. Petitionary prayer sometimes gives the appearance of offering God advice about what to do, reminding God about a situation, or trying to explain to God why God should care about someone. All of these things would make sense if another human being were the object of such petitions, but God's complete knowledge of every situation and perfect love for everyone involved make them inappropriate. So the more clearly one thinks about the nature of God, the more general one's petitionary prayers become, and then the less clear it is whether or not one's prayers make a difference. I call this 'the puzzle of particularity'.

14. In this chapter, I shall speak as if God's decision process has stages that occur sequentially in time, but this is a dispensable convenience; without affecting the argument, we could imagine instead that God sees from eternity or knows by middle knowledge what a person will or would pray, and takes this into account when deciding what to do. For more on the notions of middle knowledge, providence, and the difficulties with this picture, see Flint 1988, 1998; Hasker 1989; Davison 1991*b*, 1999*b*, 2003, 2004, 2005.

15. For those who are fond of talking this way, if God acts freely in the actual world, then there is a possible world in which God does otherwise, and God's reasons and circumstances are the same in that possible world as they are in the actual world before the point of the decision to do otherwise.

16. Here I am appealing to something like the following principle: If an agent possesses reasons for acting R1, R2, ..., Rn, and the agent performs action A, and the agent could have performed action B in exactly the same circumstances, including the possession of all and only reasons R1, R2, ..., Rn, then the possession of reasons R1, R2, ..., Rn does not explain why the agent performed action A instead of action B.

17. See Davidson 1963; Goldman 1970; and Dretske 1988 for examples of this type of account. Of course, such accounts face difficulties of their own (see Davison 1994*a* for a discussion of Dretske's account, for example).

18. I say here that 'nothing in the world' could determine God's actions, but some theists are inclined to believe that God's actions are determined by God's own nature, thereby avoiding both a libertarian account of God's freedom and the view that God's actions are determined by something in the world. (Thanks to Kate Rogers for reminding me

of this fact.) This view implies that if a person prays for the right thing in the right circumstances, then given God's nature, God cannot refuse to answer the prayer. I find this conclusion to be highly at odds with traditional theism, but there is no doubt that the problems of petitionary prayer may force traditional theists to take a hard look at the nature of divine freedom. For more on this question, see the discussions mentioned in n. 8 and the detailed and provocative discussion of divine freedom in Rowe 2004.

19. Michael Rea has pointed out to me that there are several responses one could make to this argument: (*a*) libertarianism is false, in which case God needn't be free in the libertarian sense; (*b*) libertarianism is true, and the problems can be solved (even though we can't yet see how), in which case there's no special worry in the divine case. I can add two other possible replies to his list: (*c*) we can live with this problem in the human realm, but not with the puzzles it creates with respect to God and answered prayer; (*d*) traditional theists who believe (naturally enough) that God is free in the libertarian sense have inconsistent beliefs, but it's not clear what they should do about it. These are all interesting responses. For the record, I am not arguing here that there is a special problem for freedom and explanation in the divine case, just that there is a problem in the divine case, given the way that most traditional theists think about divine freedom, and that the reasons account enables us to appreciate it in a new way.

20. This section contains a refined version of the argument presented in Basinger 1983 and further refined in Basinger 2004.

21. Here I shall ignore the difference between saying that God must do what is best and saying that God is obligated to do what is best. Thanks to Michael Rea for reminding me of the difference.

22. I say that this is true in nearly all cases because Thomas P. Flint has pointed out that there are cases in which the very offering of the prayer changes the circumstances, and hence changes what would be the best outcome in a situation (see Flint 1998: 222). In these cases, though, God is responding to the change in the circumstances caused by the offering of the prayer, rather than responding to the offering of the prayer per se, and so they do not seem to be cases of answered prayer, either, according to the reasons account. (I shall say more about this kind of case below in sect. 5.)

23. As Basinger 2004: 260 ff. points out. Basinger develops what I have called the divine goodness problem of petitionary prayer in more detail than I do here, and in a slightly different direction, by discussing in detail several different views of divine obligations.

24. This line of thinking suggests that the divine goodness problem might lead to another practical problem for petitionary prayer for those who find it hard to believe that God would adopt this sort of policy; see n. 13 above for a discussion of other practical problems of prayer.

25. Traditional theists have insisted on this by embracing doctrines of divine creation, conservation, and concurrence with the operation of secondary causes; for a philosophical introduction to these doctrines, see the essays in Morris 1988.

26. This will be true given any plausible account of knowledge or justification, whether internalist or externalist. From an internalist point of view, human beings simply lack access to information about God's reasons for acting in specific circumstances, so nothing could justify our beliefs (however true) about answered prayer. From an externalist point of view, it seems completely implausible to suggest that there is a belief-forming process that is activated only when God answers prayers, but

not when God happens to bring about that for which a person prayed, but for independent reasons. For more on this, see the discussion below of Murray's reply to the weaker form of the skeptical problem and the helpful discussion in Lehrer 1990.

27. See the discussion of the puzzle of increasing value in n. 13 above.

28. See Murray 2004: 249.

29. See Flint 1998: 222.

30. It is worth noting that we are very suspicious of people who claim to be able to discern which prayers God will answer, and not just because it is hard in general to know what outcomes would be best in a given situation.

31. See Murray's response to Basinger 2004 Murray (2004: 264).

32. Since there is no way to know that God regularly enlightens the minds of petitioners when a prayer is answered (and fails to do so when the prayers in question were not answered but God decided to bring about the events in question anyway), one could always wonder whether one's belief that God had answered a prayer was true or justified. If God had enlightened one's mind, then it would be justified (but only according to an externalist conception of justification: see n. 26 above) and true. But if one had simply tried to explain to oneself what had happened after the offering of a prayer in a psychologically or spiritually satisfying fashion, even though God had not enlightened one's mind because God had brought about the event in question for independent reasons, then one's belief would be false and unjustified.

33. Of course, we cannot know the antecedent probability (given God's reasons and knowledge of a situation) of God's bringing about an event even if we do not pray for it; we also cannot know the antecedent probability of the same event's occurring if we pray for it (given God's reasons and knowledge of a situation). So we cannot fruitfully compare the two, which is what Choi's suggestion would require.

34. It is worth noting in passing that people actually draw all kinds of ridiculous conclusions about God on the basis of their experiences involving prayer. The point here is that none of these conclusions is justified.

35. Swinburne 1998: 118.

36. See Davison 1999a and 1994b ch. 5.

37. So if God really wants to extend human responsibility for the world, there must be a better way.

38. See Stump 1979.

39. If in fact this is important: see the reply to Stump in Hoffman 1985.

40. But if he attributes all good things to God, as a traditional theist should, then he will be thankful whether or not good things come in response to answered prayer. I shall say more about this below.

41. See Choi 2003. In practice, of course, people pray only for those things that lie beyond their immediate control; nobody prays that God would pass the salt, for instance.

42. See ibid. Lawrence Masek 2000: 274 ff. makes a similar point.

43. 'It's so much easier to pray for a bore than to go and see him': Lewis 1963: 66.

44. For another interpretation of petitionary prayer that does not require its efficacy, see the provocative and insightful discussion in Phillips 1981 esp. ch. 6.

45. Perhaps because it would degenerate into an 'impersonal deistic relationship', as Choi 2003: 12 says.

46. For more on this, see Adams 2002.
47. In fact, it seems to me that many people (perhaps even most of them?) actually offer petitionary prayers, even privately, in order to identify symbolically with those in need, not to move God to act. Nothing I have said in this chapter counts against this practice.
48. See Lewis 1963, for example.

REFERENCES

ADAMS, ROBERT M. (2002). *Finite and Infinite Goods*. Oxford: Oxford University Press.
BASINGER, DAVID (1983). 'Why Petition an Omnipotent, Omniscient, Wholly Good God?', in *Religious Studies* 19: 25–42.
——(2004). 'God Does Not Necessarily Respond to Prayer', in Michael L. Peterson (ed.), *Contemporary Debates in Philosophy of Religion*. Malden, Mass.: Blackwell, 255–64.
CAMPBELL, C. A. (1957). 'Has the Self Free-Will?', in *On Selfhood and Godhood*. London: George Allen & Unwin, 158–79.
CHISHOLM, RODERICK (1982). 'Freedom and Action', in Gary Watson (ed.), *Free Will*. Oxford: Oxford University Press, 24–35.
CHOI, ISAAC (2003). 'Is Petitionary Prayer Superfluous?', unpublished manuscript presented at the Eastern Division Meeting of the Society of Christian Philosophers, Asbury College, 5 December.
DAVIDSON, DONALD (1963). 'Actions, Reasons and Causes', *Journal of Philosophy* 60: 685–700; repr. in Donald Davidson (1980), *Essays on Actions and Events*. Oxford: Oxford University Press.
DAVISON, SCOTT A. (1991a). 'Could Abstract Objects Depend Upon God?', in *Religious Studies* 27 (Dec.), 485–97.
——(1991b). 'Foreknowledge, Middle Knowledge, and "Nearby" Worlds', *International Journal for Philosophy of Religion* 30/1 (Aug.), 29–44.
——(1994a). 'Dretske on the Metaphysics of Freedom', *Analysis* 54/2, NS 242 (Apr.), 115–23.
——(1994b). 'The Metaphysics of Moral Responsibility', unpublished doctoral dissertation, University of Notre Dame.
——(1999a). 'Moral Luck and the Flicker of Freedom', *American Philosophical Quarterly* 36/3 (July), 241–51.
——(1999b). 'Divine Providence and Human Freedom', in Michael J. Murray (ed.), *Reason for the Faith Within*. Grand Rapids: William B. Eerdmans.
——(2003). 'Divine Knowledge and Human Freedom', in Raymond Martin and Christopher Bernard (eds.), *God Matters: Readings in the Philosophy of Religion*. New York: Longman, 12–24.
——(2004). 'Craig on the Grounding Objection to Middle Knowledge', *Faith and Philosophy* 21/3 (July), 365–9.
——(2005). 'Prophecy', Edward N. Zalta (ed.), *The Stanford Encyclopedia of Philosophy (Summer Edition)*, <http://plato.stanford.edu/archives/sum2005/entries/prophecy/>, accessed 19 May 2008.

DENNETT, DANIEL C. (1984). *Elbow Room*. Cambridge, Mass.: MIT.

DRETSKE, FRED (1988). *Explaining Behavior: Reasons in a World of Causes*. Cambridge, Mass.: MIT.

FISCHER, JOHN MARTIN (1982). 'Responsibility and Control', *Journal of Philosophy* (Jan.): 24–40; repr. in John Martin Fischer (ed.), *Moral Responsibility*. Ithaca, NY: Cornell University Press, 1986, 174–90.

——— and RAVIZZA, MARK, SJ (1998). *Responsibility and Control: A Theory of Moral Responsibility*. Cambridge: Cambridge University Press.

FLINT, THOMAS P. (1988). 'Two Accounts of Providence', in Thomas V. Morris (ed.), *Divine and Human Action*. Ithaca, NY: Cornell University Press, 147–81.

——— (1998). *Divine Providence: The Molinist Account*. Ithaca, NY: Cornell University Press.

FRANKFURT, HARRY G. (1969). 'Alternative Possibilities and Moral Responsibility', *Journal of Philosophy* 66: 829–39; repr. in id., *The Importance of What We Care About*. Cambridge: Cambridge University Press, 1988, 1–10.

GOLDMAN, ALVIN (1970). *A Theory of Human Action*. Englewood Cliffs, NJ: Prentice-Hall.

HASKER, WILLIAM (1989). *God, Time and Knowledge*. Cornell University Press.

HOFFMAN, JOSHUA (1985). 'On Petitionary Prayer', *Faith and Philosophy* 2: 30–7.

KANE, ROBERT (1985). *Free Will and Values*. Albany, NY: State University of New York Press.

LEHRER, KEITH (1990). *Theory of Knowledge*. Boulder, Colo.: Westmont.

LEWIS, C. S. (1963). *Letters to Malcolm: Chiefly on Prayer*. New York: Harcourt Brace Jovanovich.

MASEK, LAWRENCE (2000). 'Petitionary Prayer to An Omnipotent and Omnibenevolent God', *American Catholic Philosophical Quarterly* 74: 273–83.

MORRIS, THOMAS V. (ed.) (1988). *Divine and Human Action*. Ithaca, NY: Cornell University Press.

MURRAY, MICHAEL J. (2004). 'God Responds to Prayer', in Michael L. Peterson (ed.), *Contemporary Debates in Philosophy of Religion*. Malden, Mass.: Blackwell, 242–54.

PHILLIPS, D. Z. (1981). *The Concept of Prayer*. New York: Seabury.

PLANTINGA, ALVIN (1974). *The Nature of Necessity*. Oxford: Oxford University Press.

ROWE, WILLIAM (1991). *Thomas Reid on Freedom and Morality*. Ithaca, NY: Cornell University Press.

——— (2004). *Can God Be Free?* Oxford: Oxford University Press.

STICH, STEPHEN (1983). *From Folk Psychology to Cognitive Science: The Case Against Belief*. Cambridge, Mass.: MIT.

STUMP, ELEONORE (1979). 'Petitionary Prayer', *American Philosophical Quarterly* 16 (Apr.), 81–91.

SWINBURNE, RICHARD (1979). *The Existence of God*. Oxford: Clarendon.

——— (1998). *Providence and the Problem of Evil*. Oxford: Oxford University Press.

WOLF, SUSAN (1990). *Freedom Within Reason*. New York: Oxford University Press.

VAN INWAGEN, PETER (1983). *An Essay on Free Will*. Oxford: Oxford University Press.

CHAPTER 14

MORALITY AND DIVINE AUTHORITY

MARK C. MURPHY

THE QUESTION FORMULATED

I will discuss morality and divine authority in the context of the question of whether God—that is, God's existence, nature, or activity—*explains* morality.[1] By way of introduction, let me make some clarifying remarks about what I will mean by 'God', 'morality', and 'explains'.

By 'God' I mean an absolutely perfect being. I will assume such a being to have the traditional divine perfections—necessity, aseity, omniscience, omnipotence, goodness, and freedom—and I will assume that this being is a creator, at least of every contingent being. When we say that God has some property or stands in some relation, sometimes we mean that any being that qualified as God has that property or stands in that relation; sometimes when we say that God has some property or stands in some relation, we mean that there is a being, whom we call 'God', who is thus qualified and who has that property or stands in that relation. I will reserve the expression 'fact about God' or 'theistic fact' for those facts whose obtaining we mean to assert when we speak of God in the second way; by 'fact about God' or 'theistic fact' I mean a fact that there is an omniscient (etc.) being who has that property or stands in that relation.

By 'morality' I mean the set of all of the valid norms of the form 'x is morally required to φ', where x ranges over human beings and φ over action-types, and where to be morally required is to be categorically reason-giving, overriding, and justifiable from an impartial point of view.[2] (I assume this set of norms is non-empty.) Some such norms may be universally quantified, and unqualified (e.g. *for all x, x is morally required to φ*); some such norms may be universally quantified, and qualified (e.g. *for all x, any x who is P is morally required to φ*); some such norms may be particular (e.g. *A [who is an x] is morally required to φ*). To be a *moral fact* is to be an obtaining state of affairs of the form 'x's being morally required to φ', whether of this universal or particular form. On this stipulative definition, then, assuming that they obtain, all the following states of affairs are moral facts: *everyone's being morally required not to kill the innocent*; *the well-off's being morally required to aid to the less-well-off*; and *Bob Dylan's being morally required not to break promises*.

I cannot give an adequate account of what it is for one fact to explain another. But when we ask whether God explains morality, we are asking whether there is an answer to the question 'Why is morality as it is?' and, if so, whether that answer includes facts about God. One addition that I can make to this ordinary under-standing is that the answer to this 'Why' question must appeal to some relationship between facts that is not observer-relative, that is, that is not dependent on one's mastery or failure of mastery of concept-use and that is not dependent on one's knowledge or ignorance of the relevant facts. This is also stipulative. One fairly common understanding of 'explains' is at least partly epistemic: to explain is, on this understanding, to give new information. But this more epistemic reading of 'explains' is parasitic on its metaphysical aspect: the way that explanations give new information is by making one aware of, or calling one's attention to, some relationship between facts that would hold independently of such awareness. It is that relationship between facts about God and facts about morality that I want to explore in this chapter.

So the question is whether God explains morality, understanding 'God', 'ex-plains', and 'morality' in these particular senses. It will be helpful to have a particular thesis to evaluate. Here it is:

Theistic Explanation of Morality (ThEM): For every moral fact, there is some fact (or facts) about God that explains it.

Defenses of this thesis might appeal to rather different sorts of relationship between moral and theistic facts, and I catalog some of those differences below. But here let me note a distinction between two broad classes of theistic explanation of morality. Suppose that we distinguish between *grounds* of moral requirements and their *validating conditions*.[3] This distinction between grounds and validating conditions cannot be spelled out in logical terms alone (for example, in terms of necessary or sufficient conditions); the distinction is, rather, that between a cause, or source, and the circumstances in which a cause can operate or a source can issue its product.[4]

Would-be defenders of ThEM might choose to support ThEM by holding that theistic facts are needed in order to explain how morality is grounded; alternatively, they might choose to support ThEM by holding that theistic facts provide for the validating conditions for moral norms. My discussion below focuses exclusively on how theistic facts might ground moral requirements, but philosophers have also followed this alternate route of appeal to theistic facts in order to offer validating conditions explanations for morality. For example: Kant holds that the condition for moral requirements to be binding on rational agents such as us, who also naturally aim at our own happiness, is that there exists a being who is capable of ensuring that virtue is proportioned to happiness. He also holds that a condition of our being capable of acting in according with the demands of morality—and this is important to validate moral requirements, as we cannot be bound to do what we are unable to do—is that we receive divine assistance.[5] This Kantian account is at least a partial theistic explanation of morality: God, on this view, makes the world safe for morality, makes the world a place in which moral norms can exert their due normative force. But I will be concerned here with God's explanatory role in the grounding of moral norms rather than in ensuring that their validating conditions obtain.

Explaining Moral Facts: Moral Subsumption

Our question is whether every moral fact is (or must be, or even can be) explained by facts about God. What, though, are the available strategies for explaining moral facts?

Consider the following moral fact, and how one might explain it. It is a fact that Mark Murphy is morally required to show up to teach his classes at Georgetown University. There is an obvious explanation for this fact. The obvious explanation is that people are morally required to do what they agree to do, and Mark Murphy has agreed to show up to teach his classes at Georgetown University.

This moral fact and its explanation are trivial. What is important is the structure of the explanation for moral facts suggested by the example. One way that we often explain a moral fact is by subsuming that moral fact under another moral fact of broader extension, together with a supplementary non-moral fact. The relevant relationship between the more particular moral fact to be explained and the more general moral fact that does the explaining is that of instantiation, in that the more particular moral fact is an *instance* of the more general fact: because Mark Murphy has made the agreement to show up to teach his classes, *Mark Murphy's being morally required to show up to teach his classes* is an instance of *Mark Murphy's being morally required to do what he has agreed to do.* Call this model of explanation of moral facts explanation by way of *moral subsumption.*[6]

I want to make three points about this model of explanation. The first is that one might well explain a number of moral facts by appeal to non-moral facts about God's existence, nature, or activity conjoined with a general moral fact about how persons are morally required to respond to God or to facts about God's existence, nature, or activity. One might claim that it is wrong to torture humans because it is wrong to express disrespect for what is an image of the divine perfection, humans are images of the divine perfection, and to torture expresses disrespect for humans. One might claim that it is wrong to ignore the plight of those undeservedly in need because God has commanded us to look after those undeservedly in need, and people are morally required to do what God commands. It is clear that in these cases, the requirements not to torture and to assist the needy are explained by appeal to non-moral facts about God (humans are images of God; God has given a certain command) that allows a more specific moral norm to be subsumed as an instance of a more general norm.

The second point is that this model of explanation is obviously intrinsically limited. If we can explain moral facts by appealing to more general moral facts and a non-moral fact regarding instantiation, then it is clear that there will remain some moral facts—at least one—that cannot be thus explained using this model of explanation. (I will consider in more detail the question of the extent to which moral facts can be explained by way of subsumption under the moral fact *people are morally required to obey God* later in this chapter.[7])

The third point is a conditional one. Suppose that we consider the set of moral facts that are explainable in this way. These are moral facts that can be subsumed under more general moral facts. It seems plain that even if a moral fact can be explained via moral subsumption without appeal to God's existence, nature, or activity, if it were the case that the general moral fact under which it is subsumed is explained by God's existence, nature, or activity, then the particular moral fact counts as being explained by God's existence, nature, or activity.[8] In the example above, the obtaining of *Mark Murphy's being morally required to teach classes* is explained by moral subsumption under the obtaining of the more general state of affairs *people's being morally required to honor their agreements.* There is no theistic appeal here, and one might say that it thus follows that there are at least some moral facts—for example, that Murphy is morally required to teach his classes— that are not explained in theistic terms. But given the conditional point above, we cannot conclude this. For if *people's being morally required to honor their agreements* is a state of affairs whose obtaining is explained by appeal to God's existence, nature, or activity, then the obtaining of the state of affairs *Mark Murphy's being morally required to teach his classes* should count as being theistically explained as well.

Explaining Moral Facts: The Brute and the Self-Explanatory

Let us turn, then, to those moral facts that are not explainable by way of moral subsumption. Suppose it is true that all these moral facts are theistically explained. If so, then ThEM will be true. For every moral fact explainable by way of moral subsumption is ultimately explained by way of some fact not explainable by moral subsumption. If all the facts not explainable by moral subsumption are theistically explained, and if the conditional point in the previous paragraph is correct, then ThEM will turn out to be true.

For each moral fact not explainable by way of moral subsumption, there are, prima facie, several possibilities with respect to its explanation. That moral fact might be simply brute, lacking any explanation. It could be self-explanatory. Or it could be explained by some other fact.

If a moral fact is a brute fact, there is nothing to say about why that moral state of affairs obtains. Obviously, in that case there will be no theistic explanation, and ThEM will be false. The notion that some moral facts are brute facts may seem perfectly respectable, so long as they are necessary. A brute contingent moral fact, by contrast, is anathema. It seems bizarre to think that a moral state of affairs could obtain in one world, fail to obtain in another world, yet there be no explanation for the difference. While brute necessary moral facts—one might hold, for example, that *those in a position to help ought to do something to relieve undeserved suffering* is simply a brute, necessary moral truth—are not anathema, they are on the surd side. If we are committed to the existence of moral facts, then we must accept brute moral facts, if no explanation of them is possible. But that is the last resort. We should look for explanations for these, and it is an open question whether the best such explanations will be theistic explanations.

Here is another option. One might claim that of the moral facts not explained via subsumption, some of them are self-explanatory. Alexander Pruss writes that a fact is self-explanatory if understanding the fact, and *that* it obtains, is sufficient for understanding *why* it obtains.[9] As I mentioned above, I want the notion of explanation here not to be observer-relative, and Pruss's definition seems to make it so. But this is easily handled. We can say that we are in a position to judge that some fact is self-explanatory if we are in a position to know, upon understanding some fact and that it obtains, why it obtains. Our understanding why something obtains upon knowing that it obtains is our basic test for the self-explanatory, though it is surely prone to err by failing to identify some facts as self-explanatory that really are.

One might think it obvious that if some of these moral facts are self-explanatory, then ThEM must be false: for if some of these moral facts are self-explained, then they are not explained by God's existence, nature, or activity, and that contradicts

ThEM. But there is at least an initially plausible way of bringing ThEM and the thesis that some moral facts are self-explanatory into consistency.

Here's a model for the consistency of ThEM and the self-explanatory character of some moral facts. Suppose that there is a single moral fact that explains all moral facts distinct from it. Suppose, for example, that the fact that people are morally required to obey God explains all other moral facts; for every other morally required act-type, it has its status as such in virtue of being commanded by God. Why are we morally required to refrain from telling lies? Because we are morally required to obey God, and God commanded us not to tell lies. And so forth.

One might plausibly make two claims about this moral fact. The first is that it is self-explanatory. If one grasps that the state of affairs *people's being morally required to obey God* obtains, then one is in a position to see why it obtains. James Rachels writes:

To bear the title 'God'...a being must have certain qualifications. He must, for example, be all-powerful and perfectly good in addition to being perfectly wise. And in the same vein, to apply the title 'God' to a being is to recognise him as one to be obeyed....And to recognise any being as God is to acknowledge that he has *unlimited* authority, and an unlimited claim on one's allegiance....That God is not to be judged, challenged, defied, or disobeyed, is at bottom a truth of logic.[10]

Rachels holds both that people are morally required to obey God is self-evident (its truth is immediately knowable a priori) and self-explanatory (why it is true is a matter of logic).

The second thing that one might claim about this moral fact is that it is also a theistic fact. It is a fact *about God*: God is such that people are morally required to obey him. This is not a mere rigged-up contingent fact, like God's being such that there are three paper clips on Murphy's desk, or even a rigged-up necessary fact, like God's being such that three is a prime number. This is a fact *about God*, one might claim, a fact about how people are to relate to him. And so, on this view, it is a fact about God's existence and nature, and thus qualifies as a theistic fact.

If the view that I have described so far is coherent, then we have a way to render ThEM at least consistent with the self-explanatory character of some moral facts. Both of the claims made here are hard to believe, though. It is hard to believe that the claim that God is to be obeyed is genuinely self-explanatory. It seems that one can grasp the state of affairs *people's being morally required to obey God* without thereby seeing why it obtains. For it is not clear why being a perfect creator involves created rational beings' being subject to a moral requirement of obedience; this needs further explanation.[11] Even if it *were* self-explanatory, it is not clear that it would count as a theistic fact. A theistic fact, as I am using the term, is a fact that involves God's existing; if a fact is a theistic fact, then its obtaining cannot be coherently asserted by an atheist. But this moral fact may not involve God's existing; it seems that the obtaining of this fact could be coherently asserted by an atheist. That God is to be obeyed entails that we are to render obedience to whatever being *qualifies as God*—to whatever being is the most perfect being possible. This moral fact could hold even without God's existing, and even though God does exist, that does not make this moral fact God's-existence-involving. (Indeed, Rachels uses this alleged *de dicto* logical truth about God to argue that there is no such being as God.)

As far as I can see, there is only one route of escape for one who wants to claim that *people are morally required to obey God* is a theistic fact. My argument has been that it does not follow from the moral requirement's telling us how to respond to God that it is a theistic fact. But there are other ways that one might argue for this being a theistic fact. If the property *being morally required* turns out to be itself a theistic property, then the moral fact *people are morally required to obey God* would be God's-existence-involving. But on this view the moral fact's being God's-existence-involving is not due to its being a fact about how we should respond *to God*, as opposed to how we should respond to each other, or ourselves, or dogs, or the environment. (I will discuss this account of moral properties in further detail below.) And even if it were to turn out that the best account of the property *being morally required* is that this property is a theistic property, that would do nothing to deal with the objection that the moral fact in question is not self-explanatory.

Theistic Explanations of Non-Subsumed Moral Facts

Let us put to the side for the moment the possibility of defending ThEM in terms of moral facts that are both theistic and self-explanatory. There are various ways to divide up the sorts of theistic explanations of moral facts that remain for consideration. One way to divide them up is by the sort of theistic facts included in the explanans: whether these theistic facts are facts about God's intrinsic nature, for example, or whether they are facts about God's free activity. Another way to distinguish them is by the sort of explanatory relationship that holds between the theistic and moral facts: whether the explanatory relationship is causal, for example, or perhaps constitutive. Another way to divide them up is by whether the explanatory relationship between theistic and moral facts is immediate or mediated by other sorts of facts.

Quinn's Account: Immediate Divine Causation

Here is one model of theistic explanation of morality that appeals to divine action. This is perhaps the simplest theistic account. For every moral fact, God causes that moral fact to obtain *ex nihilo*. Philip Quinn describes and defends such a view, on which God's bringing it about that one is morally obligated to φ occurs in a particularly robust way: the causal relationship between God's will and moral facts is total, exclusive, active, immediate, and necessary.[12]

Quinn offers an argument from divine sovereignty for this view.[13] The view of divine sovereignty that Quinn favors combines divine aseity with the dependence of non-divine fact on God's agency. (For Quinn, a fact is non-divine if it neither involves nor logically entails God's existence.) Quinn thinks that from this view ThEM follows—at least, ThEM follows if we exclude from the scope of ThEM all moral facts that involve or logically entail God's existence.[14] As we saw above, though, it is plausible that *no* non-subsumed moral facts involve or entail God's existence, at least not in virtue of their being about how one ought to respond to God. If the success of the argument from divine sovereignty does entail ThEM, then it is clear that the conclusion to be drawn is not only that ThEM is true, but that it is necessarily true: if divine sovereignty obtains only if all non-divine-facts depend on the exercise of God's causal powers, and God is necessarily sovereign, then ThEM is true necessarily.

It is important to note that Quinn's view does not entail the necessity or the contingency of non-subsumed moral facts. It might be thought that since such moral facts are, on this view, the result of God's free creative choices, such moral facts must be contingent. But it may be that God, though free, has a character such that God necessarily causes non-subsumed moral facts to obtain.[15] More plausible is the view that, even if non-subsumed moral facts are contingent, it is a necessary truth that if God creates human beings, then God causes certain moral facts to obtain. God's necessary love for the beings that he creates may well ensure that God freely wills the norms of morality to obtain that are the most loving.[16] If one doubts this, the likely source of the doubt would be that there is no set of moral norms that counts as *the most loving* norms that God could bring about.

What seems plausible about Quinn's view is that God's sovereignty entails that all non-divine-facts are ultimately to be explained by reference to the exercise of God's causal power. But it is hard to make sense out of Quinn's view that moral facts are made to obtain simply in virtue of an exercise of God's causal power. The relationship between moral facts and non-moral facts is, we tend to think, a *rational* relationship: if a non-moral fact contributes to making a moral fact obtain, it is in virtue of that non-moral fact's constituting the moral reason to perform a certain action, or in virtue of that non-moral fact's serving as an enabling condition for that reason, or in virtue of that non-moral fact's serving as a defeater-defeater for that reason.[17] But the explanatory relationship that Quinn posits between a non-moral fact (God's causal activity) and any moral fact is not a rational relationship; it is a merely causal relationship.

Perhaps those who would explain morality theistically would have reason to accept the strangeness of causation of moral facts *ex nihilo* if the doctrines of divine aseity and of dependence of the non-divine on the divine required it. But these doctrines do not require this view. For even if God's sovereignty entails that all non-divine facts are *ultimately* to be explained by reference to the exercise of God's causal power, Quinn's argument does not successfully show that the exercise of divine causal power is the *immediate* cause of the obtaining of non-subsumed moral facts.

Here is an analogy. Consider the question of the relationship between God's sovereignty and the physical fact that salt dissolves in water. There are some philosophers—'occasionalists'—who hold that it would be an affront to the divine sovereignty to hold that the fact that salt dissolves in water has any explanation in addition to that of the divine will's causing the dissolving.[18] Indeed, those defending this view would deny that there was any explanation of a *particular case* of salt's dissolving in water other than the divine will's causing that dissolving. But this view is a distinctly minority position, because to most philosophers it seems plain that it would not be contrary to divine sovereignty for God to operate in nature through secondary causes. It seems to be perfectly in keeping with the dependence of all creation on God that God could create a world in which there are beings that have, themselves, causal powers, and to which we can appeal in explaining physical facts. That salt dissolves in water is to be explained (in part) by the water's causal powers. This is not an affront to the divine sovereignty, so long as the water's having the causal powers that it has is somehow explained in theistic terms.[19]

Now, one might make the same case on behalf of theistic explanations of morality. One might hold, *pace* Quinn's specific account but nonetheless relying on the doctrine of divine sovereignty, that the divine will can explain morality while not immediately causing moral facts to obtain. The model for this would be: moral facts are explained by some other facts; and these other facts are themselves theistically explained.

Natural law theory: mediated theistic explanation

Here is an example of this sort of strategy. Consider the classic formulation of natural law ethics. According to natural law ethics, the fundamental norms of morality are necessarily true; one could not be a human being and fail to be bound by these norms.[20] The status of these norms as binding and as exhibiting their particular content is explained most immediately by reference to human nature. Human nature might be understood here in an Aristotelian way—as the set of distinctive potentialities the possession of which constitutes one's humanity[21]— or in a more Hobbesian way—as the set of innate drives that are characteristic of human beings.[22] In either case, the norms of morality are as they are due to facts about human nature. In asking why lying is wrong, it would be a mistake to bypass facts about human nature and go directly to God. For, on the theistic formulations of these views, it is by God's making human beings with the particular natures that they have that humans are morally required to act as they are.[23]

More than one detail of this account remains vague. What exactly is the relationship supposed to be between facts about human nature and moral facts? Surely it is not merely causal. The most promising idea, it seems to me, is that moral facts can be informatively identified with, that is, reduced to, certain facts about human nature. One might say, for example, that *being morally required* just is *being backed by reasons for (human) action (of a certain kind),* and *being a reason for (human) action* just is *being humanly good,* and *being humanly good* just is *being related (in a certain specific) way to human nature* (to the actualization of a human potentiality, as in the Aristotelian version, or to the satisfaction of an essential human desire, as in the Hobbesian version).

More important for our purposes is the relationship between facts about God and facts about human nature. If we take it that theistic facts are not to be invoked to explain the explanatory connection between the facts about human nature and moral facts, then there would be only one place to locate theistic explanation within a natural law view: in the existence of the nature, *human,* that entails the relevant moral facts.

How might God be responsible for the existence of the kind *human,* so that facts about God (God's making it the case that there is such a thing as *human*) can explain moral facts (e.g. *humans are morally required not to lie*) by way of the entailment from facts about human nature to moral facts? There are a variety of ways, some of them more interesting, some of them less interesting. If one holds the view that a kind cannot exist unless some members of that kind exist, then one can hold that it is simply God's creative act of bringing some humans into existence that explains why the kind *human* exists and exhibits God's role in explaining moral facts. How does God's activity explain why humans are morally required not to lie? Because *being human* explains *being morally required not to lie,* and without God's activity, there would be no humans, and so no such thing as *being human.* (Note well: this view is not the mere view that without God there would be no humans, and so no beings to which the moral norm *humans are morally required not to lie* can apply. This latter account is consistent with its being a moral fact that *humans are morally required not to lie,* even without there being any humans, and so God's role in creating humans would not be sufficient to support ThEM.)

This would do the job of vindicating ThEM, and of vindicating ThEM as a necessary truth, so long as we add that it is a necessary truth about any possible set of moral facts that it is explained by the kind to which the beings to whom those norms apply belong and that it is a necessary truth that no creaturely kind exists unless God brings about instances of that kind. But one can defend ThEM in terms of God's role in fixing kinds without holding that a creaturely kind does not exist unless God brings about instances of that kind. One might claim that a kind can exist without there being any instances of it, but only insofar as that kind is fixed by a divine idea—a particular creative possibility represented by the divine mind. *Human* is a certain creative possibility; there are no doubt other such possibilities involving created rational material beings. But if the kind is ontologically dependent on the divine mind, ThEM is still vindicated. For this view of the relationship between creaturely kinds and the divine ideas would suffice, in combination with the general natural law idea, to entail that all moral facts must be explained by facts about God.

But if either of these formulations of the natural law view is accepted, one might complain that while the letter of ThEM has been preserved, its spirit has been violated. One might have hoped that the way that facts about God explain morality has something *distinctive* about it, or that the connection between God's nature or activity and moral facts would be direct. Instead, on this particular formulation of the natural law account, facts about God explain the fact that humans are morally required not to lie in precisely the same way that facts about God explain the fact that water dissolves salt. God's role in the explanation goes only to accounting for the existence of the kinds (*human, water, salt*) in question.

There are ways to make God's role in explaining moral facts stronger without going so far as the normative occasionalism to which Quinn commits himself. One might argue, for example, that what is distinctive about the kind *human* (in comparison to the kind *salt* and the kind *water*)—its ability to ground explanations of moral facts—is due to some additional theistic explanation, not just some brute or self-explanatory facts about that nature. Recall that on the Aristotelian and Hobbesian varieties of natural law theory it is the role of proper actualization of a set of potentialities and necessary human desires (respectively) that fix the moral facts to be explained. One might claim that the status of some states of affairs as the proper actualization of beings of a certain type or the state of some states of affairs as the fulfillments of necessary human desires requires or permits distinctive theistic explanation.

Take the Aristotelian view first. One might claim that just as we appeal to the intentions of a minded being to explain what counts as the successful functioning of an artifact, we need to appeal to the intentions of a minded being to explain what counts as the proper actualization of the human being.

By contrast, on the Hobbesian view: one could say that what fills the role that God's 'maker's intentions' have in the Aristotelian view is the presence of *desire* in the human—so that there is a gap between the way humans are, and the way that they must be if they are to be fulfilled. What's more, some of these desires are *necessarily* possessed by humans, and central to their motivational structures. The special explanation of the moral in the Hobbesian scheme is to be located in God's making some creatures that have appetites, indeed appetites that are characteristic of members of that kind.[24]

The dispute between the sort of normative occasionalism defended by Quinn and the natural law view comes down to a dispute on whether ThEM should be defended by treating theistic facts as an unmediated or mediated explanans vis-à-vis moral facts. Quinn treats the explanatory relationship as unmediated causation, and understands the theistic facts that immediately cause moral facts as facts of the form 'God wills that A be morally required to φ.'[25] There are, however, other views on which the relationship between theistic and moral facts is unmediated, though the relationship is not a causal one.

Adams's Account: Unmediated Constitutive Explanation by Appeal to Divine Command

Consider, for example, the view defended by Robert M. Adams. On Adams's view, non-subsumed moral facts of the form 'any x who is P is morally obligated to φ' are explained by theistic facts of the form 'God commands all those who are P to φ.' The relationship between *God's commanding those who are P to φ* and *its being morally obligatory for those who are P to φ* is not a causal relationship, but a constitutive one: to be morally obligatory *just is* to be commanded by God. So, for each moral fact that one is morally required to φ, it can be explained by the fact that God commands one to φ and *being morally required to φ* just is *being commanded by God to φ*. This is a constitutive explanation of the moral fact.

Adams's reductive account would justify ThEM, and as a necessary truth: every moral fact must be theistically explained.[26] One might dispute this, claiming that on Adams's account, the moral fact that *being morally required to φ* just is *being commanded by God to φ* is not theistically explained, and so ThEM turns out false. But this claim is mistaken. That *being morally required to φ* just is *being commanded by God to φ* is not a moral fact, and so need not be theistically explained for ThEM to be true. It does not count as a moral fact because it does not affirm that any action has any moral status; one can be a complete moral nihilist, denying that any moral requirements exist, while also affirming that *being morally obligated to φ* just is *being commanded by God to φ*.

Adams's argument for the reduction of the morally obligatory to the divinely commanded is that the role of the obligatory—that is, the set of commonplaces about the obligatory that are recognized by competent users of that concept—is best filled by divine commands. By conceptual analysis alone we can know only that wrongness is a property of actions (and perhaps intentions and attitudes); that people are generally opposed to what they regard as wrong; that wrongness is a reason, perhaps a conclusive reason, for opposing an act; and that there are certain acts (for example, torture for fun) that are wrong. But given traditional theistic beliefs, the best candidate property to fill the role set by the concept of wrongness is that of *being contrary to (a loving) God's commands*. For that property is an objective property of actions. Further, given orthodox theistic views about the content of God's commands, this identification fits well with widespread pre-theoretical intuitions about wrongness; and given Christian views about human receptivity to divine communication and God's willingness to communicate both naturally and supernaturally, God's commands have a causal role in our acquisition of moral knowledge.[27] Adams also claims that it is part of the meaning of 'obligation' that obligations are social in character[28] and involve actually made demands by one party in the social relationship on another.[29] It is the fact that a demand is actually made that gives sense to the notion that one *has to* perform an action, rather than merely that it would be good, even the best, to do it.[30]

On Adams's view, as on the view of his fellow divine command theorist, John Hare, non-subsumed moral requirements can be contingent: even though the content of the divinely commanded is shaped by its being issued by a perfectly loving being, love does not yield a determinate set of commands, and so God's commands might well have been different.[31] But, again, their view on the explanation of moral requirements is consistent with the view that moral requirements are necessary, if one takes the divine nature to fix the commands that God gives to human beings.

There is a bit of a dilemma in the vicinity. It does seem on its face implausible that God's commands are entirely fixed, so that it is a necessary truth that, for each command God could give, given all of the facts about the natures of human beings and the environments in which we live, God must give precisely that command. Even if there are certain ways that the world could be such that, given that world, God can give only the precise set of commands that God gives, surely there is *some* looseness between God's commands and other facts about the world such that it is possible for God to give somewhat different commands while the world is otherwise the same. But it seems to me that if we acknowledge some divine freedom in commanding, we open the door to a powerful argument against the view that *being morally required* is identical with *being commanded by God*. Put the point this way. For every fact that it is morally required to φ, it seems deeply implausible that every fact not identical with (or including) its being morally required to φ could be the same yet it not be morally required to φ. For some fact of the form God's commanding φ-ing, it is extremely plausible that every fact not identical with (or including) that fact of God's commanding φ-ing could be the same yet God not command φ-ing. But, if so, then there is a tension in the thesis that its being morally required to φ is identical with God's commanding φ-ing: it is very plausible that its being morally required to φ supervenes on the set of facts each of which is neither identical with nor includes it; it is very plausible that there are some cases of God's commanding φ-ing that do not supervene on the set of facts each of which is neither identical with nor includes it. Of course, reductions often bring with them tensions of this sort; what needs to be asked is whether the pressure for reduction, and the other merits of the reduction, are sufficient to justify resolving the tension by rejecting our prior views either of the supervenience of the moral on the non-moral or of God's freedom in commanding.[32]

Zagzebski's Account: Unmediated Constitutive Explanation by Appeal to Divine Motivation

Consider, by contrast, the account offered by Linda Zagzebski. On her view, for an action to be morally required in given circumstances is for it to be an action the failure to perform which is contrary to a virtuous character; it is to be an action that necessarily, in those circumstances, the virtuous person performs.[33] But on Zagzebski's view, the standard for virtue is set by God; it is God's motivations that determine what count as good human motivations, and thus what count as human virtues.[34] The determination relation is not causal but constitutive: for a motivation to be good is for it to be the motivation that God would have in like circumstances. (This may strike one as a strange view, given the differences between God and human beings; Zagzebski points out that at least Christians may not be in a position to make this objection, since their view that God became human in Christ commits them to the view that in some cases we know fully well what God would do in certain circumstances of human life.[35])

Why think this? Like Adams's view, Zagzebski's begins with a set of claims that is not distinctively theistic: that in the construction of ethical theories we should begin not with concept-analysis but with cases, and in particular with exemplars of good persons.[36] Starting with clear cases of good persons, we can initially define good outcomes, acts, traits, and motivations in terms of what good persons would seek, want, and do. Such starting points are fully compatible with a philosophical inquiry into what *makes* someone a good person, just as starting our inquiry into tigers may rightly begin with paradigm cases of tigers and starting our inquiry into water may rightly begin with paradigm cases of water. But once we take these starting points and situate them within a framework of theistic belief, it is clear that our paradigm of good personhood is chosen, so to speak, for us; we cannot but think of God as an exemplar of a good person (unless one wants to deny God's personhood altogether), and we cannot think of God as simply one good person among others. God will have to be at the center of the view, and the best theory that places God at the center of the view, Zagzebski thinks, will make God's motivations central and defining of the good, and thus of moral requirement. All this turns out to generate non-subsumed moral requirements that are necessary, given (*a*) the necessity of the divine motivations, (*b*) the characterization of good human motivation in terms of divine motivation, and (*c*) the definition of obligation as what must be done by one who is properly motivated.

Zagzebski's account is, however, hard to accept. There are reasons to worry about the particular way that she appeals to exemplars to get the ball rolling on explaining moral properties; it seems to me that the sort of infallibility that she claims for our designation of certain persons as paradigms of goodness is simply incredible. She mentions Socrates, Buddha, and Jesus as exemplars, and she writes of exemplars of a natural kind N that 'Direct reference ensures that our semantic community cannot be radically mistaken about the members of the class of N';[37] 'we may be mistaken about some of them, but we cannot be mistaken about very many'.[38] Surely this cannot be right. It is epistemically possible, for example, that the Buddha actually had a hidden life that was sordid, that his motives were self-serving, that he was not a particularly admirable person. It is epistemically possible that Socrates was a jerk.[39] To put the point as uncontroversially as possible: if moral goodness is about motives, and even our own motives are very much hidden from us,[40] it hardly seems possible that we could claim for ourselves anything like incorrigibility about our exemplars. Perhaps we should distinguish real Buddha and real Socrates from idealized abstractions based upon them: our exemplars are Apparent-Buddha and Apparent-Socrates, and we thus avoid messy worries about the actual details of their lives. But not only does it seem obvious that we want to make this move because we have some criteria, implicit or explicit, to which the contrasting Real-Buddha and Real-Socrates might fail to measure up, but this move would undercut Zagzebski's idea that we learn about good motivation by observation of these exemplars.[41]

Put this to the side. More difficult to grasp is Zagzebski's account of the goodness of objects and states of affairs in terms of God's motivations. One might have some sympathy for the view that God's motivations fix the goodness of beautiful mountain ranges, the relieving of undeserved suffering, or the writing of crisp philosophical prose. What seems deeply objectionable, though, is that on Zagzebski's view even evaluative properties *of God* are fixed in this way: 'What about God's own thick properties? What does it mean to say that God is lovable if that does not mean deserving of love or having a property in advance that makes him lovable? It means that God loves himself, and his lovability is a constituent of his loving himself.'[42] The difficulty with this view is that it seems clear that whatever makes it the case that God's motivations are privileged with respect to the fixing of value is logically prior to those motivations fixing value; and surely what makes God thus privileged is to be understood in evaluative terms. Zagzebski's view requires us to give up one or the other of these two immensely plausible claims. And if we do end up saying that God's own goodness is not to be characterized in terms of divine motivations, then we leave open the door for explanations of moral facts that appeal directly to facts about God's goodness that do not involve divine motivations.

DIVINE AUTHORITY

I have been concerned thus far to see what sorts of strategies are promising ways to defend ThEM. The strategies that I have been discussing are global strategies, strategies to show that all non-subsumed moral facts possess a common theistic explanation. But there are ways to try to support ThEM, or to approach it, without employing a global strategy. One might try to defend the full or approximate truth of ThEM by appeal to specific moral facts, the application of which invariably requires a theistic fact. The most common such strategy is an appeal to God's status as legitimate commander—we humans are under a moral requirement to obey God, and so if God commands us to perform some action, then we are morally required to perform that action.[43]

I will not here undertake an investigation into the nature of divine commands, and how they can be given,[44] but I do want to consider the status of the putative moral fact that people are morally required to obey God. To take this to be a moral fact is to affirm the *divine authority principle* (DA)[45]—people are under a moral requirement to take God's commands as their guide to action. We are familiar with authority relationships outside a theistic content. It is commonly thought that parents are authorities over their children in this way: children are morally required to obey their parents, so that if I tell my son to help me to empty the dishwasher, then my son is morally required to empty the dishwasher, and the explanation includes the fact that I told him to. The difference between parental and divine authority is, we might say, in the scope (God's authority is supposed to extend to all created rational beings, and to a wider range of actions) and strength (the reasons for action given by God's commands are supposed to be weightier), but the formal features of the authority relationship are the same.

DA, the principle that God has rightful authority over us, can be employed in a number of ways—some more ambitious, some less ambitious—in one's overall account of how moral facts are to be explained. One might treat the fact that DA is true as a supreme and architectonic moral principle. On this view, which one might call *normative divine command theory*, that DA is the case is the sole non-subsumed moral fact, and so serves as that moral fact that explains every subsumed moral fact. For example, if it is true that one is morally required not to lie, the explanation is that people are morally required to obey God, and God has told us not to lie. But this is not the only way that one might appeal to DA. One might treat its obtaining as a supreme moral fact without holding that it is the sole non-subsumed moral fact. On this view, while there are moral facts that are not subsumed under the fact that DA obtains, DA is nevertheless superior to the other principles, either by qualifying them (for example, every distinct moral principle carries the rider 'unless God gives a command incompatible with this') or by being lexically ordered over them (that is, one's primary duty is to obey God; only once this is accomplished can one move on to the fulfillment of other moral principles). On this view, the principle that we are morally required to obey God controls the application of all other moral principles (and is not itself controlled by any of them), but does not ground the validity of those principles. On yet a third view, DA is not supreme; it is one principle among others. (One might find implausible this view, thinking that it would suggest that God could give a command that it would be permissible to disobey; and one might balk at that suggestion. But the allegedly untoward consequence does not at all follow: it may be that God necessarily would not give a command that requires violation of other moral principles.) On one version of this third view, DA is a moral principle that is not subsumed under a more fundamental moral principle or principles; on another version, it is so subsumed.[46]

There are two obvious points to be made here. The first is that, as I indicated earlier, even the strongest version of DA, on which DA is the sole non-subsumed moral principle, would not of itself establish ThEM. For it could be that DA lacks a theistic explanation—it could be that we do not need to resort to any theistic facts—facts about God's existence, nature, or activity—to explain why DA is true. The second is that the extent to which DA can explain the range of moral facts depends on where DA is placed within the system of moral facts. So when we turn, as we now will turn, to the question of whether we should hold that DA is true, we should also ask what these arguments for DA's truth would tell us about whether (1) DA is supreme and uniquely non-subsumed, or (2) it is supreme and non-subsumed, but not uniquely so, or (3) it is not supreme and non-subsumed, or (4) it is itself subsumed.

I am going to argue that, at present, we lack any good philosophical argument for the truth of DA, whether as a subsumed or non-subsumed principle. I will then ask what implications the failure of extant arguments for DA has for the objective of explaining some moral facts by appeal to DA.

There are three bases from which arguments for God's authority have been launched. One of these bases we have already encountered: a general account of how theistic facts are explanatorily related to moral facts. On such an account, one aims to show that given God's explanatory relationship to the moral order, it follows that God has authority over created rational beings. A second of these bases is an appeal to the divine nature. On such an account, one aims to show that given God's perfection, it follows that God is authoritative. A third is an appeal to widely held moral principles by which DA is subsumed. On such an account, one argues that given some correct moral principle or principles, alone or in conjunction with facts that hold across all possible worlds in which there are created rational beings, DA follows. But in my view no extant argument fitting within these schemas establishes the correctness of DA.[47]

Arguments from Morality's Dependence on God to Divine Authority

One might suppose that the affirmation of one of the views of God's relationship to morality discussed in the previous section would surely be sufficient to establish God's authority. If morality as a whole is dependent on God, one might think, then surely a fortiori God has authority over created rational beings. But this is a mistake.

Quinn's causation view does not entail DA, for example. Even if one holds that every moral state of affairs that obtains is caused to obtain by a free act of God's, that would not show that humans are morally required to obey God. God might, for example, have willed only the moral requirements *humans are morally required not to coerce one another* and *humans are morally required not to defraud one another* to obtain. If so, then there would have been no moral requirement to obey God; the fact that God tells someone to do something would not make any action morally required. Only if God were also to will *humans are morally required to obey God* would obedience be a required act. The same holds true of the natural law theories that place mediating natural facts as offering explanations of moral facts: that God is ultimately responsible for the moral requirements to which created rational beings are subject does not entail that those created rational beings are required to obey God.

More promising in the defense of DA would be a view like Adams's, on which the property *being morally required* just is the property *being commanded by God.* On this view, it follows that whatever is commanded by God is morally obligatory. But even putting to the side earlier objections to this view, we seem to fall short of a defense of a moral requirement of obedience. Success in performing all those actions that God has commanded one to perform does not require believing in God's existence. I might do what you tell me to do, and non-accidentally so, without believing that you exist or that you have commanded me to do anything. (My father may have told me always to finish my supper, and I may have long forgotten that he told me this; nevertheless, I might always finish my supper, and I might always finish it because my father gave me that command.) Indeed, this possibility is crucial for Adams, who wants to say that atheists can act well, and non-accidentally so, even while denying the existence of the facts that are strictly identical with facts concerning moral obligation.[48] But obedience to someone requires, at least if it is intelligible, belief in the existence of the person whom one is obeying. Obeying you (as opposed to simply acting consistently with your commands) requires my being guided by your commands *as your commands*, and so the mere identification of the morally obligatory with the divinely commanded is not enough to establish DA. One would have to identify *its being morally obligatory to φ* with *φ-ing's being constitutive of obedience to one of God's commands*, an identification that Adams declines to make.

Arguments from the Divine Nature to Divine Authority

An alternative to these arguments for divine authority is a direct appeal to the divine nature itself. Here is the idea. As we noted above, God is to be conceived as perfect. One might argue that it follows from God's status as a perfect being that God possesses authority over all created rational beings. The idea is plausible enough, but the difficulty is in making out the claim that God's perfection entails a moral requirement of obedience. None of the traditional divine perfections, either alone or in combination, provide the material for a successful argument that God is authoritative.

Consider *omniscience*. One might argue that if God is omniscient, then God knows all moral truths; and knowledge of these moral truths will be reflected in God's commands. We are morally required, then, to do what God tells us to do. But this argument fails. Even if God knows all moral truths and thus commands us to do only what is morally required, God's omniscience does not give us any reason to think that God's commands are themselves reasons to obey God; God's commands are indicators of what actions are independently morally required, actions whose status as moral requirements may be entirely independent of God's say-so.

Perfect moral goodness fails as a basis for an account of divine authority for similar reasons. Even if God is perfectly morally good, that does not give us any basis to suppose that God's commands give new reasons for action, only that God's commands are themselves morally good. Think of analogies with knowledgeable or morally good human beings. We want to imitate them, and to ask them for advice; but we don't take their knowledge or moral goodness to place us under an obligation to obey them.

Neither does *omnipotence* provide an argument for divine authority. Put to the side the fact that God's omnipotence ensures that God can threaten us with punishments for non-compliance, or rewards for compliance; such will not give us moral requirements to do God's will. On reflection, omnipotence is not a promising source of divine authority: for omnipotence is about what God can cause, and as we have seen, a merely causal account of God's relationship to morality is insufficient for divine authority.[49] There is no good argument from the traditional divine perfections to divine authority.[50]

Arguments from Other Moral Principles to Divine Authority

The arguments to DA from the general explanatory accounts of moral facts by theistic facts and from the divine perfection fail. One might, however, turn to arguments that hold that DA is an implication of some other moral requirement. Even if this strategy were fully successful, one would not be able to hold that DA is the sole non-subsumed moral requirement, or even that it is a non-subsumed moral requirement, for use of this sort of argument for DA entails that DA is a subsumed moral fact. But even if it is a subsumed moral fact, DA might be useful in explaining a variety of moral facts that might otherwise go unexplained. (If one believes, for example, that one is morally required to observe certain religious rituals, rituals that have their status as binding only from God's say-so, an appeal to DA, however DA is explained, might be very useful indeed.)

It turns out to be remarkably difficult, though, to find a moral principle with the relevant implications. Clearly, one cannot appeal to any authority-generating moral principle whose application conditions require a voluntary act on the part of the one subject to authority (for example, that one ought to keep one's promises), for such a principle cannot yield the universality of DA (that is, that all people are morally required to obey God). The most promising candidate principles are those that might be held to apply simply in virtue of God's creating and conserving rational beings; for, even if God creates contingently, the moral principles in question only govern possible worlds in which God creates such beings.

Some have held, for example, that created rational beings are God's handiwork, and so are divine *property*. Of the number of difficulties for this position, the pre-eminent is that, of the plausible rationales that we have for holding that being someone's handiwork establishes it the maker's property, none of them goes through in cases in which treating the handiwork as the maker's property necessarily involves an interference with another rational being's autonomy. The best case for holding that your making something gives you rightful title to it and its use is that if in making that thing you make others worse off in no way, including their freedom to act at their discretion, it would be an unjust deprivation of your freedom to be unable to make something for your own use and enjoyment. But claiming rightful title over a human being itself constitutes a deprivation of that human's freedom to act at his or her discretion. So on the best account of why making generates rightful title, God's making humans fails to explain God's rightful title over us.

Some have held, alternatively, that created rational beings are under a debt of *gratitude* to God for being made and conserved in being, and so one ought to repay this debt by yielding one's discretion over how to act to God. While some have argued that there is no such debt of gratitude to God, or that debts of gratitude never generate specific requirements of action, it seems that the bigger obstacle for this view is that even if the debt of gratitude owed to God must be repaid by yielding one's practical freedom to God, that does not entail that one is under divine authority; it entails at most that one ought to take steps to *place oneself* under divine authority. If I were presently under a massive debt of gratitude to you, it may well follow that I ought to give you many good things, things to which I presently have a right. But you do not come to have a right to them simply in virtue of my debt of gratitude. At most, my failure to give them to you shows me up as an ingrate; my failure does not itself trigger a transfer of ownership. Similarly, even if I owe an incalculable debt of gratitude to God, at most this would show that my failure to submit myself to God's authority marks me as an abominable ingrate; it does not of itself make God authoritative over me.

Should we conclude that DA is false, and so cannot be used to explain any other moral facts? Perhaps, but perhaps not. All these arguments for divine authority are top-down: they try to move from principles that are either more metaphysically or morally fundamental than DA to DA as an implication. One might, by contrast, take a more bottom-up approach. This would take DA to be a knowable truth, though not one as yet explained, whether through itself or by way of more fundamental metaphysical or moral principles.

One might, for example, just posit divine authority as a divine perfection. But this faces the immediate obstacle that authority requires someone over whom to be authoritative, and the existence of created rational beings is a contingent matter, a matter of God's discretion; but God possesses God's perfections necessarily. Even if one were to rig the perfection so that it is necessarily exhibited by God—God is *authoritative over whatever rational beings happen to exist*—so doing raises the question of such merely counterfactual perfections. One would think that such merely counterfactual perfections would be grounded in categorical ones. But, as we have seen, there are no successful arguments from categorical divine perfections to divine authority.

More promising would be the acceptance of the moral principle *people are morally required to obey God* without proof from more fundamental moral principles, or indeed by anything else. The philosophical task would be simply that of defining precisely the God/created rational being relationship, and defining precisely the scope of the authority that God is supposed to have, all the while guided (one might suppose) by the more stable considered judgments about the rightness of obedience to God's commands and about how the principle requiring us to obey God's commands relates to other moral principles. On this view, our belief in DA stands justified, if it does, by way of its being a clearly formulated principle that remains once we have reached reflective equilibrium.[51] To defend DA in this way requires us to take no stand on how DA is to be explained, whether DA is brute or self-explanatory or otherwise explained, and indeed, if we have nothing but this reflective equilibrium type argument for DA, we will be left with no adequate account of *why* DA is true, or whether there is an answer as to why DA is true.

This is less than we would hope for. But we should note that other attempts to provide top-down philosophical accounts of common authority relationships—in particular, the parent/child and state/citizen—have suffered failures similar to that with which I have charged the top-down arguments for divine authority.[52] It may well be that we are forced either reluctantly to accept the limited usefulness of these bottom-up accounts of authority or to reject, in a disturbingly wholesale way, the presence of these seemingly paradigmatic authority relationships.

Even if we are willing to accept DA on these terms, we have to concede that there is an explanatory gap that remains when we appeal to DA to explain other moral facts. Even if, for example, one thinks that such norms as *one is morally required to love one's enemies and pray for those who hate one* is a moral fact that can be explained only by way of God's command, the lack of an explanation for the truth of DA would leave any moral fact explained by DA inadequately accounted for. We would have to allow that we do not quite know why we must love our enemies and pray for those who hate us.

Notes

I am grateful to Mike Rea, Tom Flint, Trenton Merricks, Alex Pruss, Errol Pierre-Louis, Ryan Lupton, and Chuck Mackel for their comments on earlier drafts of this chapter.

1. I will not consider here the question of the relative merits of theistic and non-theistic explanations of morality.
2. This is no doubt stipulative and slides over important issues about the scope of morality's application to non-human beings (e.g. God, angels, Martians), the formal features that distinguish moral from other sorts of requirements, and the existence of non-deontic moral facts (that is, facts about moral goods rather than moral requirements), but it will serve our purposes to have a relatively clear and limited explanandum.
3. See, for a helpful discussion of this point in the context of Thomas Hobbes's theistic explanation of morality, Warrender 1957: 14–15.
4. A non-moral analogy: consider the event of the catching fire of a piece of paper. The distinction between the causal role of the lit match's being in contact with the paper and the causal role of the paper's not being damp corresponds to the difference between grounds of a moral requirement (what makes an act morally required) and its validating conditions (the circumstances in which those grounds are able to make that act morally required).
5. This is Kant's (1998) task in *Religion within the Boundaries of Mere Reason*; his account of the need for happiness to be proportioned to virtue, and of the necessity of theistic facts to make this possible, may also be found in the *Critique of Practical Reason* (1996*b*), 5. 114–32. These Kantian themes have been taken up both exegetically and in the service of a theistic account of ethics in the work of John Hare: see e.g. Hare 1996.
6. For a brief discussion of this model, see Murphy 2002*b*. Something like this account of explanation of moral norms has figured prominently in Mark Schroeder's (2005, 2007) work (on the explanation of reasons for action generally) in what he calls the 'Standard Model'.
7. See the 'Divine Authority' section below.
8. I am not appealing here to some general (and almost certainly) dubious claim about the transitivity of explanation in making this point. My point is specific to explanation via subsumption: since subsumption works as a mode of explanation by noting that some action can be an instance of a broader action type, if some fact explains the moral requirement to perform the broader action type, then that fact explains the moral requirement to perform the instances of it.
9. Pruss 2006: 123.
10. Rachels 1981: 43–4, emphasis in original.
11. Recall that on the conception of 'God' with which we are working, 'God' is simply to be understood as the most perfect being possible. Rachels's argument requires us to add to this that God has authority; it seems to me that it is not obvious that a perfect being has authority, and indeed we have reason to doubt it. See the 'Divine Authority' section below.
12. Quinn 1999: 54–5.
13. Quinn 1990, 1999: 63–5.
14. Quinn 1990: 293–5.

15. See Quinn 1999: 69–71, for thoughts in this direction.

16. For worries about this strategy, see Chandler 1985.

17. The fact of my promise can (partially) constitute a reason to pay you on Tuesday for a hamburger today; my being able to pay you on Tuesday can enable that reason to obtain; my having threatened you with a beating unless you release me from my promise can undercut the typical defeat of my reason that your releasing me from my promise would have.

18. See, for illuminating discussions of the pros and cons of occasionalism, Freddoso 1988 and Quinn 1988.

19. For accounts of God's role in the dissolving of the salt by the water alternative to that offered by the occasionalist, see Freddoso 1994.

20. For an overview, see Murphy 2002c.

21. See Aristotle (1985), *Nicomachean Ethics*, 1097b22–1098a22.

22. See Hobbes (1994), *Leviathan*, ch. vi para. 4.

23. I offer as an example of this Aristotelian approach an account on which it is God's relationship to the *agent's* nature that gives God a role in explaining moral facts. But one might have a *patient*-centered view, on which it is God's relationship to the natures of the entities to which the moral agent is responding that gives God that role. Or one could hold a combination of these views, on which morality is explained both by the nature of the agent and the nature of the entities to which he or she is responding; God's role in the explanation could involve both the natures of the agent responding and the entity to which the agent responds.

24. Talk of natural desires and natural law in Hobbes makes Hobbes sound a lot more like Aquinas and the predecessor natural law theorists than is customary. This isn't my fault; it's Hobbes's. *He's* the one who talks about natural desires and characterizes his own moral theory as a theory of the laws of nature, precepts that in themselves are rational but viewed in light of their giver are divine laws. See *Leviathan*, ch. xv para. 41.

25. At different points in his career Quinn held different views on this nature of the divine act that explains moral requirements. He originally held that the divine act that brings about the moral fact *A is morally required to* φ is God's commanding A to φ (Quinn 1979); later (Quinn 1990) he held that it is God's willing that it be morally obligatory for A to φ; later (Quinn 1999), he held that it is God's intending (antecedently) that A φ that causes the resultant obligation. (For the idea of antecedent intention of which Quinn was making use, see Murphy 1998.) But Quinn nevertheless continued to hold that the 'bringing about' relation between the theistic fact and the moral fact is an unmediated causal relationship. In my view this was a mistake: the view that the theistic explanans is God's antecedently intending that A φ fits better with a reductive account, on which an action's being morally required is identified with its being intended (antecedently) by God. For an account of the difficulties with Quinn's intention account, see Murphy 2002b.

26. Adams (1999: 281–2) does hold, though, that were there no God, or if God were not good, then something else (for example, the hypothetical intentions of an ideal observer) might fit the semantically indicated role of the morally obligatory.

27. Ibid. 257.

28. Ibid. 233.

29. Ibid. 245–6.

30. Ibid. 232.

31. Ibid. 255–6; see also Hare 2001: 66–75.

32. For a more complete version of this argument, see Murphy 2002a: 82–92. For responses, see Almeida 2004 and Wainwright 2005: 87–9.

33. Zagzebski 2004: 159–60.

34. Ibid. 129–220.

35. Ibid. 233, 237.

36. Ibid. 40–50.

37. Ibid. 51.

38. Ibid. 41.

39. I am persuaded by some remarks of Peter Geach's (1969: 118–19) that, at the very least, Socrates as portrayed in the *Euthyphro* is a not particularly admirable person.

40. As Kant (1996a) writes, 'In fact, it is absolutely impossible by means of experience to make out with complete certainty a single case in which the maxim of an action otherwise in conformity with duty rested simply on moral grounds and on the representation of one's duty.... [W]e like to flatter ourselves by falsely attributing to ourselves a nobler motive [than self-love], whereas in fact we can never, even by the most strenuous self-examination, get entirely behind our covert incentives, since, when moral worth is at issue, what counts is not actions, which one sees, but those inner principles of actions that one does not see' (*Groundwork for the Metaphysics of Morals*, 4. 407). Zagzebski might well deny that moral value is not concerned with actions, but given her emphasis on motivation as the ultimate explainer of value, Kant's point about the hiddenness of our motivations surely undercuts any pretense that we have any sort of infallibility about our moral exemplars merely from their being our exemplars.

41. Zagzebski 2004: 253.

42. Ibid. 225–6.

43. This is distinct from Adams's strategy, which is metaethical—he is arguing that the moral property of *being morally required* is itself the theistic property *being commanded by God*. The appeal to divine authority here is a normative strategy. It takes no stand on the nature of moral properties, holding only that the action-type *obeying God* exhibits the property *being morally required*.

44. For a discussion of how God commands, see Adams 1999: 262–70; for a more general account of God's performance of speech acts, see Wolterstorff 1995.

45. This is a relatively strong version of a divine authority principle. One might distinguish between one formulation of DA that requires one's actions to constitute *obedience* in order for the principle to be satisfied and another that requires one's actions simply to be *compatible* with God's commands in order for the principle to be satisfied: respectively, people are under a moral requirement to take God's commands as their guide to action and people are under a moral requirement to perform those actions that God tells them to perform. Both may plausibly be called authority principles, because both are such that God's say-so is a constituent part of any reason to perform an action grounded in that principle. Only the former, though, is such that in order to satisfy it one must act *under the description* 'doing what God says to do'.

46. Other permutations are possible, in which the principle that God is to be obeyed is superior to some but not all other moral principles; in which the principle that

God is to be obeyed is the source of some but not all important moral duties; and so forth.

47. What follows is argued in much more detail in Murphy 2002a.

48. Adams 1999: 355.

49. One might say that it diminishes God's power if God cannot place us under moral requirements by giving us commands. But it is no diminution of God's power to say that there are some things that God cannot do by way of doing other things—at least, that God cannot do some things by way of other things unless God has realized the further conditions that enable this connection to hold. It does not diminish God's power to say, and to say truly, that God can create stop signs by making octagonal red pieces of metal only if the world that God has made includes the social practice of having red octagonal pieces of metal as signs to stop. The point is that whether God's commands bring about moral requirements may depend on certain background conditions obtaining (for example, the existence of a distinct sort of rational being), background conditions that are up to God's discretion, the failure of which to obtain precludes God's commands from being moral requirements.

50. Given the failure of traditional divine perfections to provide the basis for an argument to divine authority, one might be tempted to posit authority as a divine perfection. See below for a discussion of this strategy.

51. 'Reflective equilibrium' is that condition in which our considered general and particular moral judgments form a coherent, mutually supportive whole; see Rawls 1999: 18–19.

52. For a skeptical treatment of parental authority, see Slote 1979; for such treatments of the authority of the state, see Simmons 1979; Raz 1979; and Green 1990.

REFERENCES

ADAMS, ROBERT M. (1999). *Finite and Infinite Goods*. Oxford: Oxford University Press.

ALMEIDA, MICHAEL J. (2004). 'Supervenience and Property-Identical Divine-Command Theory', *Religious Studies* 40: 323–33.

ARISTOTLE (1985). *Nicomachean Ethics*, trans. Terence Irwin. Indianapolis: Hackett.

CHANDLER, JOHN (1985). 'Divine Command Theories and the Appeal to Love', *American Philosophical Quarterly* 22: 231–9.

FREDDOSO, ALFRED J. (1988). 'Medieval Aristotelianism and the Case against Secondary Causation in Nature', in Thomas Morris (ed.), *Divine and Human Action*. Ithaca: Cornell University Press, 74–118.

——(1994). 'God's General Concurrence with Secondary Causes: Pitfalls and Prospects', *American Catholic Philosophical Quarterly* 68: 131–56.

GEACH, PETER (1969). 'The Moral Law and the Law of God', in *God and the Soul*. London: Routledge & Kegan Paul, 117–29.

GREEN, LESLIE (1990). *The Authority of the State*. Oxford: Oxford University Press.

HARE, JOHN E. (1996). *The Moral Gap*. Oxford: Oxford University Press.

——(2001). *God's Call*. Grand Rapids: Eerdmans.

HOBBES, THOMAS (1994). *Leviathan*, ed. Edwin Curley. Indianapolis: Hackett.

KANT, IMMANUEL (1996a [1785]). *Groundwork for the Metaphysics of Morals*, trans. Mary J. Gregor, in *Kant's Practical Philosophy*. Cambridge: Cambridge University Press.

—— (1996b [1788]). *Critique of Pure Reason*, trans. Mary J. Gregor, in *Kant's Practical Philosophy*. Cambridge: Cambridge University Press.

—— (1998 [1793]). *Religion with the Boundaries of Mere Reason*, trans. Allan Wood and George di Giovanni. Cambridge: Cambridge University Press.

MURPHY, MARK C. (1998). 'Divine Command, Divine Will, and Moral Obligation', *Faith and Philosophy* 15: 3–27.

—— (2002a). *An Essay on Divine Authority*. Ithaca: Cornell University Press.

—— (2002b). 'Theological Voluntarism', *Stanford Enyclopedia of Philosophy*, <http://plato. stanford.edu/entries/voluntarism-theological/>, accessed 20 May 2008.

—— (2002c). 'The Natural Law Tradition in Ethics', *The Stanford Encyclopedia of Philosophy*, <http://plato.stanford.edu/archives/win2002/entries/natural-law-ethics/>, accessed 20 May 2008.

PRUSS, ALEXANDER R. (2006). *The Principle of Sufficient Reason*. Cambridge: Cambridge University Press.

QUINN, PHILIP (1979). 'Divine Command Ethics: A Causal Theory', in Janine Marie Idziak (ed.), *Divine Command Morality*. New York: Edwin Mellen, 305–25.

—— (1988). 'Divine Conservation, Secondary Causes, and Occasionalism', in Thomas Morris (ed.), *Divine and Human Action*. Ithaca: Cornell University Press, 50–73.

—— (1990). 'An Argument for Divine Command Ethics', in Michael Beaty (ed.), *Christian Theism and the Problems of Philosophy*. Notre Dame: University of Notre Dame Press, 289–302.

—— (1999). 'Divine Command Theory', in Hugh LaFollette (ed.), *Guide to Ethical Theory*. Oxford: Blackwell, 53–73.

RACHELS, JAMES (1981). 'God and Human Attitudes', in Paul Helm (ed.), *Divine Commands and Morality*. Oxford: Oxford University Press.

RAWLS, JOHN (1999). *A Theory of Justice*, rev. edn. Stanford, Calif.: Harvard University Press.

RAZ, JOSEPH (1979). *The Authority of Law*. Oxford: Oxford University Press.

SCHROEDER, MARK (2005). 'Cudworth and Normative Explanations', *Journal of Ethics and Social Philosophy* 1.

—— (2007). 'The Humean Theory of Reasons', *Oxford Studies in Metaethics* 2: 195–219.

SIMMONS, A. JOHN (1979). *Moral Principles and Political Obligations*. Princeton: Princeton University Press.

SLOTE, MICHAEL (1979). 'Obedience and Illusions', in Onora O'Neill and William Ruddick (eds.), *Having Children*. Oxford: Oxford University Press.

WAINWRIGHT, WILLIAM A. (2005). *Religion and Morality*. Aldershot: Ashgate.

WARRENDER, HOWARD (1957). *The Political Philosophy of Hobbes: His Theory of Obligation*. Oxford: Oxford University Press.

WOLTERSTORFF, NICHOLAS (1995). *Divine Discourse*. Cambridge: Cambridge University Press.

ZAGZEBSKI, LINDA TRINKAUS (2004). *Divine Motivation Theory*. Cambridge: Cambridge University Press.

CHAPTER 15

✓ THE PROBLEM OF EVIL

PAUL DRAPER

INTRODUCTION

SUFFERING, immorality, and other evils generate a wide variety of practical, affective, and doxastic problems. Some of these problems can be stated in the form of a question and some of these questions are relevant to this handbook because they are *theological*—they are connected in some relevant way to God or to faith in God or to the metaphysical theory that God exists.

Practical problems of evil are concerned with what one ought to *do* in response to evil. They are theological when the issue is what actions one ought to perform, *in light of one's beliefs about God*, the assumption being that those beliefs should make a difference to how one responds to evil. If the question is whether or not one should (continue to) rely on or trust God, then this assumption is obviously true. It is also true, however, if the question is how best to oppose evils such as oppression or how best to alleviate evils such as suffering. One's beliefs about God can make a difference to how one answers such questions as these as well.

Affective problems of evil are concerned with whether the emotions one feels in response to evil are appropriate. They are theological when the issue is how one ought to respond emotionally to evil, *in light of one's beliefs about God*. Many theists have emotional responses to evil that appear to conflict with their beliefs about God. For example, evil may cause a believer to feel despair or hopelessness or anger toward God or abandoned by God, and it is hard to reconcile any of these feelings with the belief that an almighty God loves us. Even an issue as apparently unproblematic as how one should feel about the death of a loved one can become controversial if one really believes that the loved one is in 'a better place' and that one will be literally reunited with him or her after one's own death.

Both practical and affective problems of evil raise doxastic questions about evil. To determine what one ought to do or how one ought to feel in response to evil, one must first determine what one ought to believe, including what one ought to believe about God, in light of the evil in the world. It is important to notice, however, that there are many distinct doxastic problems of evil, because beliefs can possess or lack any of a variety of distinct merits. For example, a belief about God can be true or false, it can be probable or improbable (relative to the epistemic situations of its subject), it can result from properly or improperly functioning cognitive faculties, and its subject might be entitled to hold it or might instead hold it in violation of some moral or epistemic duty. When judging the significance of evil for belief in God, it is crucial that one be clear about exactly which of these (or other) doxastic merits is at issue.

In this chapter, I will focus on questions about evil that are both theological and doxastic, and more specifically *alethic*—i.e. questions about whether what we know about evil can be used to establish the falsity or probable falsity of the belief or proposition that God exists. Such a focus is natural for an agnostic (like me).[1] More generally, it is natural for anyone who is engaged in genuine inquiry about whether or not God exists. Such inquiry inevitably raises questions such as: does the evil in the world provide the resources for proving that God does not exist (e.g. because it can be shown to be logically incompatible with God's existence)? If not, does it nevertheless provide some evidence against God's existence (in the sense that it lowers the probability of God's existing)? If it does, then how strong is this evidence? And if this evidence is strong (in the sense that it decreases the ratio of the probability of theism to the probability of its denial many-fold), is it also significant (in the sense that it makes a large difference to the probability of theism being true)? Answers to these questions are no doubt relevant to many other doxastic problems of evil (and to affective and practical problems as well), but alethic problems of evil are not identical to any of those other problems. For example, no alethic problem is identical to the problem of whether or not the evil in the world renders belief in God irrational. After all, a false or probably false belief can be rational (in more than one distinct sense of that word); and a true or probably true belief can, of course, be irrational.

I will further narrow my focus by employing a specific concept of God. In particular, I will assume that to assert that God exists or that 'theism' is true is to assert that there exists a supernatural person who created the natural world and who is perfect in power ('omnipotent'), perfect in knowledge ('omniscient'), and perfect in moral goodness ('morally perfect'). This is obviously a narrow sense of the words 'God' and 'theism', but it is common in the philosophical literature.[2] The strategy I will use for investigating alethic problems of evil is also common: I will construct and evaluate a variety of 'arguments from evil' for the conclusion that God does not exist or that God's existence is improbable.

MT Arguments

At first glance, it may appear easy to construct a convincing argument from evil against theism. One obvious strategy is to formulate an argument of this very simple sort:

(1) If God exists, then e does not obtain.

(2) e obtains.

So,   (3) God does not exist.

Notice that any argument from evil of this sort will be deductively valid because it will have a valid argument form, namely, modus tollens. For this reason, I will call arguments from evil of this sort 'MT arguments'. Notice also that, so long as the variable e is replaced with some fact about evil that is *known* to obtain, an argument from evil of this sort will be sound if its first premise is true and it will be convincing if we have good reason to believe that its first premise is true. Since an 'evil' should be understood in discussions of arguments from evil to mean anything that is bad, including things that are bad because they imply the absence of something good, there are countless candidates to replace e. For example, e could be replaced by the fact that evil exists, or that suffering exists, or that undeserved suffering exists, or that horrific suffering exists, or that immorality exists, or that heinous immorality exists, or that some innocent children have been tortured, or that not every sentient being flourishes, or that some sentient beings flourish while most do not. Which replacement for e is chosen may affect the prospects for showing that the first premise of the resulting argument is true. The crucial question is whether this premise can be shown to be true for at least one suitable replacement of e.

It is far from obvious that the correct answer to this question is 'yes'. The first premise is a conditional statement. Assuming it is a material conditional, it is true if and only if it is not the case that both its antecedent is true and its consequent false. In other words, it is true if and only if it is false that both God exists and e obtains. But how can the falsity of the proposition 'God exists and e obtains' be established? One approach is to argue that the falsity of this proposition is entailed by the definition of the title 'God'. In other words, one might try to argue that the existence of a being qualified to bear the title 'God'—i.e. the existence of a loving supernatural person who is omnipotent, omniscient, and morally perfect—is logically incompatible with e's obtaining. To argue in this way would be to offer what philosophers have called a 'logical argument from evil' against theism. All other arguments from evil are called 'evidential arguments from evil'.

Although logical arguments from evil seemed promising to a number of philosophers in the 1950s and 1960s (e.g. J. L. Mackie 1955), they are rejected by the vast majority of contemporary philosophers of religion, for two reasons. First, some serious attempts have been made to demonstrate that the existence of evil and several other more specific facts about evil are logically compatible with God's existence. For example, Alvin Plantinga's (1974) influential 'Free Will Defense' persuaded many that it is logically possible that God exists, that God creates people with morally significant free will, and that some of those people make morally bad choices. If Plantinga is right that this is logically possible, then God's existence is logically compatible with the existence of evil and (more specifically) with the existence of moral evil. Plantinga also tried to extend the Free Will Defense to several other facts about evil. For example, he tried to show that theism is compatible with the *amount* of moral evil in the world, and he even appealed to the possibility of non-human persons who have free will (e.g. demons) in an attempt to show that theism is compatible with the existence of 'natural' evil (i.e. evil that does not result from *human* immorality). The appeal to demons may seem fanciful or even desperate, but one must keep in mind that Plantinga is responding to the *logical* argument from evil. If one's goal is only to prove logical compatibility, then it is legitimate to appeal to any possible state of affairs, no matter how unlikely.

There are, however, many replacements for e that no defense has shown to be compatible with theism. Thus, the unpopularity of logical arguments from evil cannot be explained solely by the success of the Free Will Defense or other defenses. A second, more fundamental and hence more important reason for the unpopularity of logical arguments from evil is that, even when some fact about evil cannot be shown to be compatible with theism, establishing an incompatibility is no less beyond our abilities (Pike 1963). Granted a God, being omnipotent and morally perfect, could eliminate any evils that he wanted to eliminate and would eliminate any evils that he had no good moral reason to permit; but all that follows from these claims is that a God would eliminate any evil that he had no good moral reason to permit. In order for a logical argument from evil to succeed, it is necessary to show that, for some known fact about evil, it is logically impossible for God to have a good moral reason to permit that fact to obtain. This, however, is precisely what most philosophers nowadays believe cannot be shown.

But why do they believe this? After all, when one examines the sorts of 'excuses' that human beings have for not eliminating evil, they all seem to involve imperfect power or imperfect knowledge. For example, human beings avoid blame for destructive tornadoes because they lack the power to prevent them. They avoid blame for not rescuing people lost at sea because they don't know their whereabouts. And, depending on the circumstances, they may avoid blame for evils they know about and have the power to eliminate, such as visits to the dentist, so long as those evils cause (or are caused by) greater goods such as healthy teeth. These sorts of excuses could not work for an omnipotent and omniscient being. This is obvious in the case of the first two types because they *explicitly* involve a lack of power or knowledge. But it is no less true about the third case, which *implicitly* involves a lack of power because an omnipotent being's power would not be limited by causal laws. For example, an omnipotent being would never need to use unpleasant dental procedures as a causal means of keeping someone's teeth healthy. Her merely willing that a person's teeth be healthy would suffice to make it so.

Still, it would be a mistake to jump to the conclusion that all good reasons for not eliminating evil involve some lack of power or knowledge. To understand why this would be a mistake, it is crucial to recognize that the inability to produce things that are logically impossible to produce, or to know statements that are logically impossible to know, does not count as a *lack* of power or a *lack* of knowledge. In other words, not even an omnipotent and omniscient being would have more power or more knowledge than it is logically possible for a being to have. Next, suppose that some good that is worth my suffering (perhaps it is even a good that benefits me) *logically implies* that I suffer (or at least that the objective chance of my suffering is not zero). For all we know or can prove, there could be such a good, even if it is beyond our ken. After all, even some goods we know about logically imply evils. For example, my showing fortitude in the face of pain logically implies that I feel pain and thus not even an omnipotent being could produce the good of my showing such fortitude without permitting the evil of my feeling pain. Of course, the good of my showing fortitude in the face of pain is probably not *worth* my feeling pain, especially since fortitude of other sorts does not require pain, but for all we know other goods not only logically imply my suffering but are also worth my suffering. Such goods would be known to an omniscient being even if they are unknown to us. Further, if there are such goods, then not even an omnipotent and omniscient being could produce them without allowing me to suffer and hence even an omnipotent and omniscient being might have a good moral reason to permit my suffering.[3]

One might object here that no good, no matter how great, could justify allowing such horrific evils as the torturing of innocent children. (The character Ivan in Fyodor Dostoevsky's *The Brothers Karamazov* is often interpreted to be making this claim.) Indeed, some philosophers (e.g. D. Z. Phillips 2004) seem to object to the whole notion of an 'outweighing' good. To be sure, this notion should be rejected if it implies that all value can be measured on a single numerical scale or if it presupposes a crude consequentialist understanding of morality. It need not be interpreted in this way, however. In fact, it is even compatible with the position that no good, no matter how great, 'outweighs' the harm done to an individual unless it benefits that individual. This last point is important because, for all we know, (1) there may exist goods far more valuable than any we can imagine, (2) these goods may logically imply the existence or risk of horrific evils, and (3) these goods may (if there is life after death) include among their beneficiaries the victims of horrific evils. If this possibility is taken seriously (and admittedly not all philosophers think it should be taken seriously or even that it is a *possibility*), then it is hard to be confident that the notion of an *outweighing* good breaks down in the face of horrific evil, especially given how imprecise and fallible our moral intuitions are. Therefore, since I believe this possibility should be taken seriously, I do not see how it is possible to construct a convincing logical argument from evil against theism, and for that reason the rest of the arguments from evil I discuss in this chapter will be evidential ones.[4]

Notice that not all MT arguments are logical arguments from evil. Consider, for example, the following two compound arguments.[5]

	(1)	No known goods justify God's permitting horrific suffering.
So,	(2)	No goods, whether known or not, justify God's permitting horrific suffering.
	(3)	God's existence entails that either some goods justify God's permitting horrific suffering or horrific suffering does not exist.
So,	(4)	If God exists, then horrific suffering does not exist.
	(5)	Horrific suffering exists.
So,	(6)	God does not exist.

	(1′)	Horrific suffering is appallingly bad (and the worse an evil is, the less likely it is that God would permit it).
	(2′)	God would be maximally empathetic (and the more empathetic a being is, the less likely it is that such a being would permit horrific suffering even if that being had a morally sufficient reason to do so).
	(3′)	Some goods that God would prima facie want to obtain, like the flourishing of all sentient beings, are incompatible with horrific suffering.
So,	(4)	If God exists, then horrific suffering does not exist.
	(5)	Horrific suffering exists.
So,	(6)	God does not exist.

Notice that these two compound arguments share steps 4–6, which is a standard MT argument from horrific suffering. Neither argument, however, defends the conditional premise of that MT argument by trying to show that its antecedent is a logically sufficient condition of its consequent.

In the first argument, this conditional follows deductively (necessarily) from steps 2 and 3, but step 2 is supposed to follow inductively from step 1. In other words, the truth of step 1 is supposed to make the truth of step 2 probable. This inductive inference is questionable. It involves reasoning from a sample of 'known goods' to a conclusion about all goods whether known or not. Obviously there is nothing wrong in principle with reasoning from samples to populations, but such inferences are correct only when one has good reason to believe that one's sample is representative of the population. One problem here is that we know so little about the population of all goods that it is hard to be confident that our sample of known goods is representative of that population (Alston 1991). A second problem is that any evidence we have that supports theism will ipso facto be evidence that our sample is biased and so may undermine the inference in question.

The second argument defends the conditional premise that if God exists then horrific suffering does not exist by giving reasons why a God would be unlikely to permit horrific suffering to exist. However, this strategy also fails because steps 1–3 are not by themselves good reasons to believe that 4 is true. To begin with, there might be strong evidence for God's existence. Any such evidence would, given the existence of horrific suffering, be strong evidence for the falsity of the statement that if God exists then horrific suffering does not exist. But even if no such evidence exists, giving reasons like the ones described above for believing that a God would be opposed to horrific suffering does not prove that the statement 'if God exists, then horrific suffering does not exist' is probably true. Instead, such reasons only show at most that the consequent of that conditional statement is antecedently very probable, given (i.e. 'conditional on') the truth of its antecedent. In short, instead of establishing the probability of a conditional, they establish only a conditional probability. And the former does not follow from the latter: from the fact that Q is antecedently probable given P, it does not follow that 'if P then Q' is probable.

This is a very easy mistake to make. Suppose, for example, that Detective Garcia is trying to locate a car and is certain that it is owned by either Smith or Jones. In her efforts to figure out which of the two is the owner, she discovers that the car was recently painted red. She then reasons:

	(1) Smith really likes green cars.
So,	(2) If Smith owns the car, then it was not recently painted red.
	(3) It was recently painted red.
So,	(4) Smith does not own the car.

The inference from 1 to 2 appears strong, but it is not. From the fact that Smith really likes green cars, it follows only that it is antecedently probable that the car would not have been painted red given that Smith owns it. It does not follow that the conditional statement 'if Smith owns the car, then it was not painted red' is probably true. To see why, suppose that Garcia also knows, not only that Jones really likes yellow cars but also that he was once struck by a red car and has had a strong aversion to red cars ever since. Then, even though it is antecedently likely that the car was not painted red given that Smith owns it, it is even more likely that it was not painted red given that Smith does not own it. This means that the fact that the car has recently been painted red is actually evidence that Smith is the owner! So from the fact that Smith really likes green cars it does not follow even inductively that, if Smith owns the car, then it was not recently painted red.

Similarly, from the fact that the non-existence of horrific suffering is antecedently likely given theism, it does not follow even inductively that, if God exists, then horrific suffering does not occur. To draw that conclusion, one would need to show, among other things, that the non-existence of horrific suffering is less likely on the assumption that God does not exist than it is on the assumption that God exists. And showing that is very difficult since, as I will explain in more detail later, it is far from clear what exactly one is assuming to be true when one assumes that the statement 'God exists' is false.

BAYESIAN ARGUMENTS FROM EVIL

Problems such as these make me doubt that a convincing MT argument from evil can be constructed. I'm much more optimistic about what I call 'Bayesian' arguments from evil. (I call them this because the structure of the reasoning in these arguments can be analyzed, made precise, and defended by appealing to a theorem of mathematical probability called 'Bayes' theorem'.) I'm more optimistic about these arguments for at least two reasons. First, they conclude only that, *other evidence held equal*, theism is very probably false and thus they do not presuppose without justification that there is no offsetting or even outweighing evidence in support of theism. Second, they avoid the problem faced by the second evidential MT argument discussed above by explicitly comparing the probability of certain facts about evil given theism to the probability of those facts given some relevant alternative hypothesis.

Bayesian arguments from evil (e.g. Draper 1989) have the following structure:

(1) We know that e obtains.
(2) e's obtaining is antecedently many times more probable given some alternative hypothesis h to theism than it is given theism.[6]

So, (3) e's obtaining is strong evidence favoring h over theism (i.e. our knowledge that e obtains increases the ratio of the probability of h to the probability of theism many-fold).

(4) h is at least as plausible as theism (i.e. h is at least as probable as theism independent of all evidence for and against theism and h, or at least we have no good reason to believe otherwise).

So, (5) Other evidence held equal, theism is very probably false.

The inferences in arguments of this sort are not as uncontroversial as the inference in an MT argument. However, Bayes' theorem supports the inference from steps 1 and 2 to step 3 so long as the claim that e's obtaining is *strong* evidence favoring h over theism is understood to mean that our knowledge that e obtains increases the ratio of the probability of *h* to the probability of theism *many-fold*. Notice that the only way that a Bayesian argument could have a false conclusion (step 5) despite having a true sub-conclusion (step 3) is if theism were more probable than the alternative hypothesis *h apart from considerations of evidence*. Step 4 of the argument, however, states that this is not the case, that in fact *h* is at least as 'plausible' as theism. Therefore, step 5 follows from steps 3 and 4: in the absence of additional evidence besides *e* that *favors* theism over *h*, theism is *very* probably false. Notice that it also follows that in the absence of additional evidence besides *e* that *strongly* favors theism over *h*, theism is *probably* false.

I should mention also that the word 'antecedently' in the second premise of Bayesian arguments is crucial. What this means is that the probabilities being compared are not 'all things considered' probabilities. Instead, an abstraction is being made. Premise 2 claims that, *independent of the observations and testimony upon which our knowledge specifically of e is based, e* is much more probable given *h* than it is given theism. When assessing the probabilities in the second premise of a Bayesian argument, however, one should take into account most of what one knows, including that we live in a complex physical universe containing a variety of living things, some of which are conscious beings, some of which are self-aware beings, and some of which are moral agents. Some philosophers (like me) believe that at least some of these known facts are evidence strongly favoring theism over competing hypotheses. Even if that is so, it is not relevant to the evaluation of premise 2 of the argument, but instead is taken into account by the clause 'other evidence held equal' in the conclusion of the argument, which is to say that the conclusion of a Bayesian argument from evil is compatible with the claim that, on the *total* evidence, theism is probably true.

Like MT arguments, Bayesian arguments from evil vary depending on which facts about evil are used to replace the variable *e*. Unlike MT arguments, however, Bayesian arguments also vary because different hypotheses are chosen to replace the variable *h*. One natural choice is, of course, atheism. Consider, then, the following Bayesian argument from evil:

     (1) We know that horrific suffering exists.
     (2) The existence of horrific suffering is antecedently many times more probable on the assumption that God does not exist (atheism) than it is on the assumption that God exists (theism).
So,   (3) The existence of horrific suffering is strong evidence favoring atheism over theism.
     (4) Atheism is at least as plausible as theism.
So,   (5) Other evidence held equal, theism is very probably false.

This argument appears to be very convincing, but it does have one major flaw. Its second premise is not obviously true and it is hard to see how one could successfully argue for its truth.

Good reasons can, I believe, be given for believing that horrific suffering is unlikely given theism, but it is difficult to show that horrific suffering is any less unlikely given atheism. This is difficult to show because the probability of horrific suffering given atheism depends on what is likely to be true on the assumption that theism is false. For example, if theism is false, then naturalism might be true. Or perhaps panentheism is true. Or maybe pantheism or polytheism. Indeed, if theism is false, then isn't there a good chance that what is true is some non-theistic form of supernaturalism that can't even be understood by human beings because of their cognitive limitations? Some theists might think so. The point is that, even if we could agree on a list of serious possibilities and restrict our attention to those (estimating the probability of horrific suffering given atheism by taking a probability weighted average of the probability of horrific suffering on each of those possibilities), the calculation of the probability of horrific suffering given atheism would be prohibitively difficult.

William Rowe, whose 1996 argument from evil explicitly appeals to Bayes' theorem and uses atheism as the alternative to theism, ingeniously tries to circumvent this problem by using an evidence statement that is entailed by atheism and hence has a probability of one given atheism. Consider, for example, this evidence statement:

(R) For all goods g that we know of, g does not justify God in permitting horrific suffering.

Rowe's strategy yields the following Bayesian argument:

(1) We know that R.

(2) R is antecedently many times more probable on the assumption that God does not exist (atheism) than it is on the assumption that God exists (theism).

So,   (3) R reports strong evidence favoring atheism over theism.

(4) Atheism is at least as plausible as theism.

So,   (5) Other evidence held equal, theism is very probably false.

Since a good can justify God's permitting horrific suffering only if God exists, atheism entails R and hence the probability of R given atheism is 1, which is, of course, greater than the probability of R given theism.

This argument faces two problems, however. The first is that, while R is obviously more probable on atheism than on theism, it is not clear that it is much (i.e. many times) more probable. Given theism and the existence of horrific suffering, perhaps it is not all that surprising that the goods that justify God's permitting horrific suffering are unknown to us. In any case, additional arguments would be needed to prove otherwise. If it cannot be shown that the probability of R given atheism is at least one order of magnitude greater than the probability of R given theism, then R is only relatively weak evidence for atheism and hence of little significance. The second problem is more serious in the sense that a solution seems impossible.

This problem was first clearly identified by Richard Otte (2003). Unfortunately, the technical nature of Otte's point has resulted in the importance of his paper going largely unnoticed. I will briefly reconstruct Otte's reasoning here. Readers with no background in confirmation theory may wish to skip the next two paragraphs.

Although Otte himself does not put it exactly this way, the problem he identified is that the evidence statement R very subtly understates what we know about the relationship of goods we know of to horrific suffering. This makes it appear that there is a stronger case against theism based on 'inscrutable evils' than there really is. To see why, compare R with

> (R*) For all goods g that we know of, either God exists and g does not justify God in permitting horrific suffering, or God does not exist and, if God were to exist, then g would not justify God in permitting horrific suffering.

R* entails R but is clearly not entailed by R since, unlike R, R* is not entailed by atheism. Further, our knowledge that R is true is based (at least in this context), not on any alleged knowledge that God does not exist but rather on the knowledge that R* is true.[7] The crucial point is that, while the understated evidence R is more probable on atheism than on theism, it is far from clear that the fully stated evidence R* is (and even less clear that it is *much* more probable on atheism than on theism). The mistake in reasoning here is essentially the same (though it is much harder to detect and is not intentional) as the mistake a prosecutor makes when he points out to a jury that a defendant accused of murder purchased a gun shortly before the victim was shot to death, neglecting to mention that the gun in question is a stun gun.

To appreciate this analogy, notice that the evidential argument from R is based on the fact that R is entailed by atheism and thus $P(R/\sim T) = 1 > P(R/T)$. (Stated in English, this says that the probability of R given atheism equals one, which is greater than the probability of R given theism.) But given that theism is true, R can't be true unless R* is; while given that atheism is true, R can be true without R* being true. This means that, given theism and R, R* is certain, while given atheism and R, R* is not certain: $P(R*/T\&R) = 1 > P(R*/\sim T\&R)$. Thus, relative to R, R* is evidence *for* theism! (Compare: the fact that the defendant bought a gun is more likely on the assumption that he killed the victim, but given that he did buy a gun, it is more likely that it is a stun gun given that he did not kill the victim.) It follows that the argument from R could be repaired only if it could be shown that $P(R*/\sim T\&R) > P(R/T)$, from which it would follow that the fully stated evidence R* is more probable on atheism than on theism—i.e. that $P(R*/\sim T) > P(R*/T)$. [This would follow because R* entails R and so is logically equivalent to R&R*, which implies that, for any hypothesis h, $P(R*/h) = P(R\&R*/h) = P(R/h) \times P(R*/R\&h)$.] Indeed, to avoid the additional objection that we are dealing only with relatively weak evidence here, what really needs to be shown is that $P(R*/\sim T\&R) \gg P(R/T)$ and hence that $P(R*/\sim T) \gg P(R*/T)$, where the symbol '$\gg$' means 'is many times greater than'. But showing that P(R*/∼T&R) is many times greater than or even that it is greater than P(R/T) is no easy task since, as I pointed out earlier, it is far from clear what would be true on the assumption that theism is false, and thus it is very hard to see how any precise calculation of P(R*/∼T&R) can be made. So if we replace R with R*, then we are back to the same problem that the argument from R was supposed to solve. And if we don't replace R with R*, then we achieve success only by misleadingly understating the relevant evidence. Either way, we don't have a powerful evidential argument from evil against theism.

I submit, then, that the best way to formulate a Bayesian argument from evil is to use a specific alternative hypothesis to theism instead of the general hypothesis that theism is false. While doing so will make the third premise of the argument (step 4) harder to defend, it will make the second premise much easier to defend. Not any more specific alternative will do, of course, even if it renders premise 2 true. For if it is too specific (e.g. if one simply builds the facts about evil mentioned in premise 1 into the hypothesis), then premise 4 will be either false or indefensible. Thus, choosing the correct hypothesis is crucial. One promising candidate is the 'hypothesis of indifference' or 'HI' for short (Draper 1989), which states that neither the nature nor the condition of sentient beings on earth is the result of actions performed by benevolent or malevolent non-human persons. (I will argue later that this hypothesis is more plausible than theism.) Now let 'O' stand for a statement reporting what we know about the pain and pleasure in the world. Using HI as the alternative hypothesis to theism and O as the evidence statement yields the following Bayesian argument from evil:

> (1) We know that O.
> (2) O is antecedently many times more probable on the assumption that HI is true than it is on the assumption that theism is true.
>
> So, (3) O is strong evidence favoring HI over theism.
>
> (4) HI is at least as plausible as theism.
>
> So, (5) Other evidence held equal, theism is very probably false.

This argument is similar in two important ways to the argument formulated by the character Philo in Part 11 of David Hume's *Dialogues Concerning Natural Religion* (1779).[8] First, Philo also compares theism to a sort of 'indifference hypothesis' (namely, that the causes of the universe are neither benevolent nor malevolent). Second, like O, Philo's evidence statement mentions not just pain, but also pleasure. This is an important insight on Hume's part. Logical arguments from evil can ignore the good in the world (as Philo emphasizes in Part 10 of the *Dialogues*), but evidential arguments from evil cannot. Pointing out that various facts about pain are evidence against theism is of little significance if parallel facts about pleasure are equally strong evidence for theism. Of course, there are other goods and evils besides pleasure and pain, but facts about those goods and evils are part of the evidence that is being 'held equal' by the argument.

Most of my 1989 article is devoted to defending premise 2 of this argument. Very roughly, I first make a prima facie case for premise 2 by arguing that we have much more reason on HI than we have on theism to expect that pain and pleasure will play the biological roles they do. After all, on HI, the fact that other parts of organic systems systematically promote survival and reproduction supports the claim reported by O that pain and pleasure will do the same. But on the assumption that theism is true, the moral significance of pain and pleasure undermines this support. On theism, it would not be surprising at all if pain and pleasure played a fundamentally moral role in the world without also playing the same biological roles that other parts of organic systems play. Further, even assuming that God would have a good moral reason to use pain and pleasure to promote the biological goals of survival and reproduction, what we know about biologically gratuitous pain and pleasure (e.g. that it includes horrific suffering and does not include an abundance of pleasure) is also more likely on HI than it is on theism.

I then turn this prima facie case for premise 2 into an ultima facie one by arguing for two further claims. The first is that, contrary to what the theodicist would have us believe, the known moral roles played by pain and pleasure in the world do not significantly raise the probability of O given theism. They may raise the probability of certain individual facts reported by O (e.g. the fact that suffering sometimes leads to improved moral character), but only by making other facts reported by O even more surprising (e.g. the fact that suffering is often demoralizing). The second claim is that, contrary to what the skeptical theist would have us believe, the possibility of God having moral reasons *unknown* to us to permit O does not undermine my case for premise 2, because God's having reasons to permit O that are unknown to us is no more likely antecedently than God's having reasons to *prevent* O that are unknown to us.

Of course, the skeptical theist could respond that the possibility of unknown justifying goods is not just supposed to defeat a prima facie case for premise 2, but instead prove that there is no such case to be defeated—that O, for example, is not even prima facie more probable on HI than on theism because it has no discernible probability on theism. In defense of this response, skeptical theists might assert that O has a discernible probability on theism only if the probability that a God would have a good reason to permit O is discernible. They might then argue that we are in no position to judge how likely or unlikely it is that a God would have a good reason to permit O. One problem (from a theistic perspective) with this response, however, is that it undermines evidential arguments in support of theism. Another more fundamental problem is that it ignores the role that background knowledge plays in conferring differential probabilities on O given various hypotheses. In addition, it assumes incorrectly that any probability that would, *if known*, affect a second probability must actually be known in order for that second probability to be known. If that assumption were true, skepticism about all non-trivial probability judgments would follow.[9]

Turning now to premise 4,[10] it is important to realize that philosophers do not agree on how such a premise should be interpreted in the context of a Bayesian argument. Some philosophers believe that plausibility judgments are purely subjective. We just find ourselves taking some hypotheses seriously while dismissing others out of hand. The former we judge worthy of being tested by evidence, while the latter we ignore. If this is correct, then a Bayesian argument from evil like the one being considered may still be sound relative to the epistemic situations of those who take HI seriously (which I suspect includes most contemporary philosophers, including many philosophers who are theists), while it won't be sound relative to the epistemic situations of others for whom HI is not a live option.

Other philosophers believe that plausibility judgments are objective (or at least are subject to substantial objective constraints). For example, my own view is that the plausibility of a hypothesis should be equated with its intrinsic (epistemic) probability—the probability it has simply by virtue of what it asserts and what we know about the world by means of rational intuition. The intrinsic probability of a hypothesis depends on its coherence (in the sense of the degree to which the various statements it entails evidentially support one another[11]) and its modesty (in the sense of the degree to which it is narrow in scope and lacks specificity). If plausibility is a function of coherence and modesty, then HI is at least as plausible as theism, because HI is no less coherent than theism, and it is considerably more modest.

Allow me to explain the latter point. The degree of modesty of a hypothesis depends on how little that hypothesis purports to tell us about the world that we do not already know by rational intuition. Relative to certain practical goals, a lack of modesty is often a virtue; but relative to the goal of truth, it is a vice. For the more that a hypothesis asserts that (for all we know by rational intuition) *might be* false, the more likely it is (prior to considering evidence) to assert something that *is* false, and hence, in the absence of evidence, the less likely it is to be true. HI is clearly more modest than theism. It is compatible with metaphysical naturalism (i.e. with the view that there are no 'supernatural' entities, no entities that can affect natural entities despite not being natural themselves), as well as with a variety of supernaturalist hypotheses. Theism, on the other hand, claims not only that all natural entities possess (proximate or remote) supernatural causes, but also that they depend for their existence on a single ultimate supernatural cause, and further that this cause is a person, and even more specifically an omnipotent, omniscient, and morally perfect person. Because of the great specificity of these claims, it is fairly safe to conclude that HI is considerably more plausible than theism and it is very safe to conclude that premise 4 is true—that HI is at least as plausible as theism. One might object that some theists maintain that God *necessarily* exists, but that won't make theism any less specific and thus won't raise the intrinsic probability of theism because we don't know by rational intuition that God's existence is necessary. In other words, even if God's existence is necessary, we can't just 'see' the necessity of the proposition 'God exists' in the way we can see the necessity of 'all dogs are dogs' and '2 + 2 = 4'.

OBJECTIONS TO BAYESIAN ARGUMENTS
FROM EVIL

In spite of their advantages over MT arguments, Bayesian arguments from evil have been challenged in several different ways. I will devote the remainder of this chapter to discussing some of the most common or important of these challenges.

One popular challenge concerns Bayesian arguments that use naturalism as the alternative hypothesis to theism. According to this challenge, evil can't be more probable on naturalism than on theism because nothing is evil (or good) if naturalism is true. Defenders of Bayesian arguments have two replies available to them. The first is to argue that naturalism does not rule out the existence of genuine evil—i.e. that some entities are bad, even on the assumption that naturalism is true. The second is to use an evidence statement that makes no value judgments; for example, it might simply describe the suffering in the world without either affirming or denying that suffering is bad. Such a statement could very well be antecedently more probable on naturalism than on theism. For while the facts reported by such an evidence statement might be unsurprising on naturalism whether or not suffering has negative value, they might be surprising on theism precisely because suffering would be objectively bad on the assumption that theism is true.

A second objection to Bayesian arguments is that facts about suffering must be more likely on theism than on any plausible alternative to theism because suffering cannot exist unless sentient beings exist and the existence of sentient beings is more likely given theism than it is given any plausible alternative to theism. This objection fails for two reasons. First, it overlooks the fact that, typically, knowledge of the existence of sentient beings would be part of the epistemic situation relative to which the probability judgments in a Bayesian argument from evil are made (and so would be part of the 'other evidence held equal' mentioned in the conclusion of the argument). Second, even in the case of a Bayesian argument that included the existence of sentient beings in its evidence statement, the inference in this objection would be incorrect. For example, suppose that the evidence statement in some Bayesian argument were 'sentient beings exist and sometimes suffer horrifically'. It doesn't follow from the (alleged) fact that the existence of sentient beings is more likely on theism than on some alternative hypothesis h that the existence of sentient beings that suffer horrifically is *not* more likely or even much more likely on h than on theism.

A third objection to Bayesian arguments from evil is that they compare some atheistic hypothesis such as naturalism or HI to 'generic' or 'mere' theism rather than to a sectarian theistic hypothesis such as Christian theism or Jewish theism or Muslim theism. Thus, while they may create epistemic problems for generic theists (i.e. for theists who do not accept any specific revealed religion), they do not create any epistemic problems for Christian or Jewish or Muslim theists, especially since the evidence statements to which Bayesian arguments typically appeal are entailed by (and thus antecedently certain on) these sectarian theistic hypotheses (Otte 2004). The short answer to this objection is that sectarian theistic hypotheses entail theism and thus can't be more probable than theism.[12] Thus, any reason to believe that theism is improbable is also a reason to believe that Christian or Jewish or Muslim theism is improbable. Moreover, just because an evidence statement e is more probable on, say, Christian theism than on, say, naturalism, it doesn't follow that there is a good Bayesian argument from e against naturalism. For building e into a theistic hypothesis (e.g. by adding Bible stories about suffering and other evils to one's theistic hypothesis) will make that hypothesis very specific (immodest) and so much less probable intrinsically than a hypothesis such as naturalism. Further, the fact that the second premise of a Bayesian argument would be false if theism is replaced with 'Christian theism' in the argument is irrelevant. The failure of the revised argument does not imply that the original argument is not sound.

This is not to deny, however, that other religious (or non-religious) beliefs may be relevant to the issue of whether the second premise of a Bayesian argument from evil is true or false. Indeed, religious or ethical or metaphysical or epistemological beliefs could potentially raise $P(e/T)$—i.e. the antecedent probability of the evidence statement e given theism. To determine if they do, one should apply this 'weighted average principle':

$$P(e/T) = P(B/T) \times P(e/T\&B) + P(\sim B/T) \times P(e/T\&\sim B).$$

The idea here is that, if B is, for example, some Christian belief, then $P(e/T)$ will be an average of $P(e/T\&B)$ and $P(e/T\&\sim B)$. What makes it an average is the fact that $P(B) + P(\sim B) = 1$. But it is not necessarily a straight average because $P(B/T)$ and $P(\sim B/T)$ may not each equal $\frac{1}{2}$. Thus, for example, if $P(B/T) = \frac{2}{3}$ and $P(\sim B/T) = \frac{1}{3}$, then $P(e/T\&B)$ is given twice as much weight as $P(e/T\&\sim B)$ in calculating the average.

Consider, for example, the belief that there is life after death ('L' for short). Suppose that $P(L/T)$ were very high and also that $P(O/L\&T)$ were much greater than $P(O/HI)$. Then the second premise of my evidential argument from evil would be false, because $P(O/T) = P(L/T) \times P(O/L\&T) + P(\sim L/T) \times P(O/\sim L\&T)$. Of course, while I do believe that $P(L/T)$ is high, I don't believe for a moment that $P(O/L\&T)$ is much greater than $P(O/HI)$. The hypothesis that we will survive death explains very little of what we know about pain and pleasure. The point I want to make here, however, is that there is a precise method for evaluating the relevance of other religious and non-religious beliefs to Bayesian arguments from evil. The same method should be used to evaluate how successful various theodicies or defenses are in undermining (the second premise of) a Bayesian argument from evil.

The last objection to Bayesian arguments that I will consider, one raised by Alvin Plantinga (1996, 2000, 2007), is that Bayesian arguments from evil are insignificant, even if they are sound, because there is overwhelming non-propositional (or propositional) evidence favoring theism over atheism.[13] If it were obvious that such other evidence exists (or even if it were obvious to all theists that this other evidence exists), then this objection might be more convincing. Clearly, however, this is not obvious, even to theists. Many theists (let alone atheists and agnostics) reject the natural theologian's position that there is overwhelmingly strong propositional evidence for God's existence, and many theists reject Plantinga's position that there is very strong non-propositional evidence for beliefs about God. Concerning the latter, Plantinga himself emphasizes that he cannot prove his position; his goal is just to show that the existence of such evidence is epistemically possible and that, *if* (Christian) theism is true, then it is likely that many theists *know* that God exists because of such evidence. I find even this modest claim hard to accept. Even if God exists, the behavior of most theists in a variety of circumstances suggests that they lack the sort of deep confidence in their beliefs about God that would be necessary for genuine knowledge. Many don't even claim to have such knowledge, and many who do claim to have such knowledge betray their deep uncertainty by undermining that claim with qualifications (e.g. 'I know in my heart not my head') or by behaving in a variety of other ways (e.g. feeling terror in the face of imminent death) that would be inappropriate or surprising for someone who truly had such knowledge.

There are, in my opinion, additional problems with Plantinga's sophisticated form of apologetics,[14] but I have no space in this chapter to discuss them. Instead, let's suppose that I am wrong about all this. Let's suppose that it is perfectly reasonable for most theists to be unmoved by Bayesian arguments from evil because they possess overwhelming non-propositional evidence in support of theism. Even supposing all that, it still does not follow that Bayesian arguments from evil are insignificant. It does follow that they are of no interest to *Plantinga*, because he is interested primarily in the question of whether what we know about evil threatens the rationality or (external) warrant of 'most' theists or perhaps most traditional Christian theists. Plantinga's mistake, however, is to assume that the significance of an argument from evil depends on its proving that most theistic belief is irrational or unwarranted. In other words, he assumes incorrectly that the significance of alethic problems of evil derives solely from their relationship to other doxastic problems of evil. The reason that this is a mistake (a mistake also made in Draper 1991) is that there are many people who, like me, don't believe they already *know* that God exists (or that God doesn't exist), and for that reason believe that it is appropriate and important to engage, not in apologetics, but in genuine inquiry designed to determine, to the best of their ability, whether or not God exists. Included here are agnostics as well as theists and atheists who have doubts about God's existence or non-existence. These skeptical souls have little choice but to do their best objectively to assess the available evidence. Thus, for them, the fact that O or some other statement about evil reports strong evidence favoring HI (or some other serious alternative to theism) over theism is of great significance. For them, a Bayesian argument from evil, if sound, is very important indeed. Notice also that for them, indeed for anyone who *doubts* that God exists, it doesn't help to be told by Plantinga that, *if* God does exist, then some or even most theists probably know he does!

Notes

For helpful comments on earlier drafts of this chapter, I am grateful to Tom Flint, Mike Rea, and William Rowe. I am also indebted to various members of the philosophy department at the University of Georgia, where I presented a draft of most of the paper as part of their Kleiner Lecture Series.

1. No doubt the most important problems of evil are practical, but since I do not believe in God, those problems are not, for me, theological and thus are not relevant to this volume.
2. For a defense of this choice, see Swinburne 2004, ch. 5.
3. I am indebted to Nelson Pike for most of the points in this and the preceding paragraph.
4. The previous seven paragraphs, as well as some of the points I make in the remainder of this section and the next, also appear in Draper 2007.
5. The first of these arguments is similar to William Rowe's (1979, 1986) early evidential arguments from evil, and the second is similar to J. L. Schellenberg's (2000) evidential argument from evil. I do not wish to claim, however, that these two arguments do justice to Rowe's and Schellenberg's sophisticated arguments from evil. Although I hope that my criticisms of these two arguments will suggest strategies that could be used successfully to refute Rowe's and Schellenberg's arguments, proving that is beyond the scope of this chapter.
6. One might wonder why I require of a Bayesian argument from evil that e's obtaining be *many times* more probable on the alternative hypothesis than on theism. After all, if this phrase were deleted from premise 2, it would still follow from the premises of a Bayesian argument from evil that, other evidence held equal, theism is probably false (though it would no longer follow that, other evidence held equal, theism is *very* probably false). My reason for restricting the class of Bayesian arguments in this way is that very many facts are slightly more or less probable on various alternatives to theism than they are on theism. So Bayesian arguments from evil that don't meet this higher standard are of little or no significance.
7. In claiming that we know that R* is true, I assume here that none of the attempts that have been made to explain horrific suffering in terms of theism has succeeded. If this assumption is incorrect, then horrific suffering should be replaced with some

other sort of evil or, following Rowe, some particular evil for which the corresponding assumption is correct.

8. See Draper 2004 for a description of important differences between Philo's evidential argument from evil and my own.

9. For a detailed defense of skeptical theism, see Bergmann's Ch. 17 in this volume. For a detailed defense of my argument from evil against skeptical theism, see Draper 1996.

10. I do not defend or even explicitly state premise 4 of the argument in my 1989 article. It is implicit in my requirement in that paper that HI be a 'serious' alternative to theism.

11. Consider the following two statements: (1) 'ball #1 is red and ball #2 is red' and (2) 'ball #1 is red and ball #2 is green'. These two statements are equally specific, but the first is intrinsically more probable than the second because it is more coherent.

12. For a much longer answer, see Draper 2004.

13. Plantinga appears to reject the reasoning in Bayesian arguments from evil, but many of the examples he uses to challenge that reasoning involve alternative hypotheses that, unlike HI, are far less plausible than the hypothesis to which they are being compared. And the rest of his examples involve hypotheses that, unlike theism, are *obviously* supported by overwhelming propositional or non-propositional evidence. Since a Bayesian argument from evil could be sound even if there were such overwhelming counterevidence in support of theism, I take the point of these examples to be to challenge the significance instead of the soundness of Bayesian arguments from evil.

14. See e.g. Sennett 1998. Sennett argues convincingly that, in order for a class of beliefs (e.g. memory beliefs or beliefs about God) to be directly justified, giving beliefs of that sort prima facie credence in the appropriate circumstances must be unavoidable, practically speaking. If this appealing criterion of 'proper basicality' is correct, then beliefs about God, unlike memory beliefs, are not directly justified or warranted by non-propositional evidence.

REFERENCES

ALSTON, W. (1991). 'The Inductive Argument from Evil and the Human Cognitive Condition', *Philosophical Perspectives* 5: 29–67.

DRAPER, P. (1989). 'Pain and Pleasure: An Evidential Problem for Theists', *Noûs* 23: 331–50.

—— (1991). 'Evil and the Proper Basicality of Belief in God', *Faith and Philosophy* 8: 135–47.

—— (1996). 'The Skeptical Theist', in Daniel Howard-Snyder (ed.), *The Evidential Argument from Evil*. Bloomington: Indiana University Press, 175–92.

—— (2004). 'More Pain and Pleasure: A Reply to Otte', in Peter van Inwagen (ed.), *Christian Faith and the Problem of Evil*. Grand Rapids: Eerdmans, 41–54.

—— (2007). 'The Argument from Evil', in Paul Copan and Chad Meister (eds.), *Philosophy of Religion: Classic and Contemporary Issues*. Oxford: Blackwell.

MACKIE, J. L. (1955). 'Evil and Omnipotence', *Mind* 64: 200–12.

OTTE, R. (2003). 'Rowe's Probabilistic Argument from Evil', *Faith and Philosophy* 19: 147–71.

—— (2004). 'Probability and Draper's Evidential Argument from Evil', in Peter van Inwagen (ed.), *Christian Faith and the Problem of Evil*. Grand Rapids: Eerdmans, 26–40.

PHILLIPS, D. Z. (2004). *The Problem of Evil and the Problem of God*. London: SCM.

PIKE, N. (1963). 'Hume on Evil', *Philosophical Review* 72: 180–97.

PLANTINGA, A. (1974). *The Nature of Necessity*. Oxford: Clarendon.

—— (1996). 'On Being Evidentially Challenged', in Daniel Howard-Snyder (ed.), *The Evidential Argument from Evil*. Bloomington: Indiana University Press, 244–61.

—— (2000). *Warranted Christian Belief*. Oxford: Oxford University Press.

—— (2007). 'Objections to Draper's Argument from Evil', in Paul Draper (ed.), *God or Blind Nature? Philosophers Debate the Evidence*, <www.infidels.org/library/modern/debates/great-debate.html>.

ROWE, W. L. (1979). 'The Problem of Evil and Some Varieties of Atheism', *American Philosophical Quarterly* 16: 335–41.

—— (1986). 'The Empirical Argument from Evil', in R. Audi and W. J. Wainwright (eds.), *Rationality, Religious Belief, and Moral Commitment*. Ithaca: Cornell University Press.

—— (1996). 'The Evidential Argument from Evil: A Second Look', in D. Howard-Snyder (ed.), *The Evidential Argument From Evil*. Bloomington: Indiana University Press, 262–85.

SCHELLENBERG, J. L. (2000). 'Stalemate and Strategy: Rethinking the Evidential Argument from Evil', *American Philosophical Quarterly* 37: 405–19.

SENNETT, J. F. (1998). 'Direct Justification and Universal Sanction', *Journal of Philosophical Research* 23: 257–87.

SWINBURNE, R. (2004). *The Existence of God*, 2nd edn. Oxford: Clarendon.

CHAPTER 16

THEODICY

MICHAEL J. MURRAY

INTRODUCTION

DURING a recent visit to Germany, Pope Benedict XVI visited the Nazi death camp at Auschwitz. While surveying the memorial to the nearly 1.5 million victims, he found himself at a loss for words of explanation or consolation: 'In this place, words fail. In the end, there can only be dread silence—a silence which is itself a heartfelt cry to God ... How could you tolerate all this?' *Washington Post* columnist Richard Cohen commented as follows:

Religious people can wrestle with the Pope's remarks. What does it mean that God was silent? That he approved? That he liked what he saw? That he didn't give a damn? You tell me. And what does it mean that he could 'tolerate all this'? That the Nazis were OK by him? That even the murder of Catholic clergy was no cause of intercession? I am at a loss to explain this. I cannot believe in such a God. (Cohen 2006: A10)

Theists and atheists alike seem to agree that evil does indeed count against the existence of God. And it is not merely the vast *quantities* of evil that stagger belief. In addition, it seems that the *types* and *distribution* of evil fit poorly with the claim that the world is providentially directed by an all-good, all-powerful creator. While we might admit that a comprehensive divine plan for the universe could be expected to include some evil, how can we be expected to accept that senseless torture, degrading sexual abuse, catastrophic tsunamis, and so on are also components of such a plan? And what is more, how can theists explain the fact that the distribution of evil seems almost entirely random? Vice and suffering on the one hand, and virtue and happiness on the other, do not seem proportional in this life, a fact acknowledged by religious believers and atheists alike. In the words of the Hebrew prophet Jeremiah: 'You are always righteous, O LORD, when I bring a case before you. Yet I would speak with you about your justice: Why does the way of the wicked prosper? Why do all the faithless live at ease?' (Jer. 12: 3). Needless to say, the pattern of evil we find in the world does not exactly fit our initial expectations of what a world would look like if theism were true.

Since the dawn of religious thought, religious believers have wrestled with how to explain God's permission of evil. During the last three centuries, theistic attempts to explain evil have been labeled 'theodicies'. The word springs from a title of a book written in 1710 by the German Lutheran philosopher Gottfried Leibniz (1988). Leibniz coined the word 'theodicy' from two Greek words which mean, respectively, 'God' and 'justice', and the book aims to offer a comprehensive explanation of how it is that God's justice can be vindicated in the face of the apparent quantity, types, and distribution of evil that we find around us.

From Leibniz's time until the mid-1970s, the word 'theodicy' was used to describe attempts of this sort to explain God's permission of evil. Since the mid-1970s however, the word has taken on a more refined sense among philosophers of religion, a change that can be attributed to Alvin Plantinga's book *God, Freedom and Evil* (1974). In this work, Plantinga distinguishes between two types of explanations of evil that theists might construct. The first type is offered in response to arguments that the coexistence of God and evil is impossible. Explanations of this sort, which Plantinga calls 'defenses', need only show the *logical compatibility* of God and evil. The second type aims to provide plausible and perhaps even likely-to-be-true explanations of evil, explanations that show that the existence of evil is not unlikely given the existence of God (or perhaps given the existence of God and some additional plausible and/or likely-to-be-true claims). Plantinga labeled explanations of this latter sort 'theodicies' (ibid. 27–8). Plantinga's distinction has left a lasting mark on the field and indeed, in the contemporary literature, philosophers of religion use the term 'theodicy' in this narrower sense, and it is in this sense that it will be addressed in this chapter.

RECENT DETERRENTS TO THEODICY

While philosophers and theologians have constructed and defended explanations for God's permission of evil through the centuries, two recent developments in philosophy of religion have made the enterprise of theodicy less appealing to some. First, some philosophers have argued that there is something distasteful, prideful, or arrogant about any attempt to explain how or why God would permit evil. Those who find it distasteful think that such explanations serve either to blind us to the genuine horror that evil represents, or perhaps to console us (or, worse, induce a Stoic resolve) in a way that deflates our enthusiasm for opposing it (Tilley 1991).

These critics may be right that attempting to explain evil sometimes has this effect on us. However, it is also true that it should not have this effect. The reason for this is the (obvious) fact that attempts to explain evil, even if they succeed, do not make evil any less real or urgent. The patient whose hand is amputated due to an incurable gangrenous infection might understand that the loss was required in order to save his life. Yet explaining why such an evil was unavoidable does not serve to diminish his suffering or his loss. By attempting to explain evil, the theist is not, or ought not be, attempting to 'explain it away' (Stump forthcoming).

Likewise, critics are right that explanations of evil are sometimes offered in a spirit of pride and arrogance. One need only consult the news media after a tragic flood, famine, or epidemic to find religious believers who are quick to catalogue the sins of the victims that are to blame. This sort of pontificating often betrays a disgraceful spirit of moral superiority and indifference to human suffering. Yet theists who shy away from *any* attempt to explain evil are themselves forced to confront the fact that sacred writings in the major theistic traditions often provide the very sort of explanation these critics find unpalatable. Although some sacred texts, the Hebrew Bible's book of Job for example, adopt a more skeptical stance toward the human endeavor to understand evil, the very same Hebrew Bible explains the plagues visited on Egypt in advance of the Exodus as arising from Pharaoh's 'hardness of heart'. Similarly, for Christians, the Passion of Christ is portrayed as an evil necessary for bringing about the greater good of restoring humanity to communion with God.

The second challenge arises from the increasing popularity of a view with the unfortunate label of 'skeptical theism'. Skeptical theists note that explanations of God's permission of evil typically aim to show how certain types of evil are unavoidable preconditions for, or by-products of, outweighing goods. As a result, insofar as we want to explain the evil in our world, we must be well positioned to know what goods God wants to bring about in the world, and how the evils that we find are connected with getting them. Therein lies the problem. For according to skeptical theists, we labor under two liabilities that make such explanations either very difficult or impossible. First, given the immensity of divine goodness and the finitude of our human cognitive and moral faculties, it seems likely that there are some (and perhaps many) types of good with which we are not in any way acquainted. If we do not even know what the relevant goods are that evils are supposed to secure, our attempts to make judgments about whether or not God has good reason for permitting evil are futile. To be clear, one can defend skeptical theism without shying away from engaging in the task of theodicy. Yet there is nonetheless a natural tendency to think that the stance of the skeptical theist makes the prospects for a successful theodicy look grim.

Second, even if we believe ourselves to be acquainted with the relevant goods, there is good reason to think that we would be unable to grasp whether or not particular evils play a role in bringing about such goods. To know that they do, I would have to see how the evils I encounter might be connected with outweighing goods in ways that render the evil justifiable. But how could I know what sorts of ultimate good ends might be accomplished by the permission of this or that token instance or type of evil? Some evils might be necessary conditions for outweighing goods not realized for hundreds or thousands of years. Absent omniscience, I simply cannot have any good grasp of which events are necessary conditions for which other events distant in time and space. This should leave us with a healthy dose of uncertainty about our ability to make judgments about the connections between evils and outweighing goods.[1]

There is nothing about skeptical theism that *requires* that we abandon the task of theodicy. However, there are two reasons that skeptical theism might serve to diminish our enthusiasm for it. First, theists who are inclined to rely on skeptical theism as a way of resisting the seemingly potent argument for atheism that arises from evil might demur when it comes to the task of constructing theodicies insofar as they think that the only reason to construct and defend such explanations is to turn back this argument. Second, if the skeptical theist is right, we are, for all we know, in a very poor position to reconstruct the reasons that God might have for permitting evil. As a result, attempts to piece together such explanations might leave us either empty-handed or in serious error. That realization too can be a deterrent to the task of theodicy.

However, the specter of skeptical theism should not have the deterrent effect it sometimes seems to have. As we saw earlier, evil raises concerns for the theist that have nothing to do with the argument for atheism from evil. Thus, even if skeptical theism undermines that argument, explaining evil can still be a useful enterprise. Further, though the considerations raised by skeptical theists might lead us to doubt that we can explain God's permission of evil, theists will need to balance this against the fact that the major theistic traditions are often quite forthright in offering explanations for evil. In this way, these theistic traditions are committed to the idea that one can and does know some of the actual reasons that God permits some evils.

STANDARDS FOR A SUCCESSFUL THEODICY

God is justified in permitting an evil only if he has a morally sufficient reason for doing so, and theodicies are attempts to spell out such reasons. According to most theists, a reason counts as morally sufficient when the evil permitted is connected with a greater good in a way that meets the following three conditions:[2]

(A) The Necessity Condition: The good secured by the permission of the evil, E, would not have been secured without permitting either E or some other evils morally equivalent to or worse than E.

(B) The Outweighing Condition: The good secured by the permission of the evil is sufficiently outweighing.

(C) The Rights Condition: It is within the rights of the one permitting the evil to permit it at all.

Let's consider these conditions in turn. No one thinks a surgeon is evil in causing you to endure the pain and suffering of surgery when that surgery is a *necessary condition* for saving your life. However, you would be rightly indignant if a surgeon tells you, after the surgery, that you could just as easily have been cured by taking a pill that is equally effective and has no side-effects. If the pain and suffering of surgery were not necessary to secure the good result (saving your life), we would conclude that this surgeon is a greedy moral monster. Likewise, if God permits an evil to occur, it must be because the good that is in fact connected with it would not have been secured at a 'lower price' (i.e. with less evil).

Note that the Necessity Condition requires that the goods in question would not have been obtained without allowing either the evil in question *or* some other evil that is as bad or worse. This is important when thinking about theodicy because it means that evils can be connected with outweighing goods in ways that will sometimes be far from transparent. Consider this thought experiment: imagine that all creatable worlds can be rank ordered with respect to goodness. Further imagine that on this ordering, two worlds tie for the title of best world. Finally, imagine that these worlds are identical except that World 1 contains Smith dying in a tragic auto accident, while World 2 contains Jones dying in a tragic car accident. If God were to arbitrarily choose to create World 1, those looking for an explanation for the evil of Smith's death would likely never imagine that the reason for it is that it (or an equally bad evil) is a necessary by-product of creating the best world. But this would indeed be the explanation. Because of considerations like this, theists and atheists alike are forced to admit that there might be evils that God permits for very good reasons, but where those reasons will be opaque to those of us who aren't omniscient.

Not all theists accept the Necessity Condition as a requirement for theodicy. While critics of this condition cite various motivations for their opposition, the most important criticism of it is found in the work of defenders of open theism. Open theism is a cluster of theological doctrines that includes the denial that God does or can have detailed foreknowledge concerning certain types of future events. Some open theists argue that such foreknowledge is impossible because God is bound in the present time in a way that precludes such knowledge. Others argue that it is impossible because no being, God included, can have knowledge concerning future events that are not determined by current events, including free choices and perhaps certain natural events as well. As a result, open theists argue that at least some future events are unpredictable and, as a result, that there is nothing God can do to prevent their particular occurrence (Hasker 2004).[3] God permits some evil, then, not because it is a foreseen and necessary condition for some greater good, but rather because God 'didn't see it coming'. Because of this, God could not, in creating, have any way to ensure or know that the goods secured by permitting the evils the world contains would not have been secured at the cost of less evil, and so the Necessity Condition need not be met after all.

However, open theists do not adopt this unusual explanation for evil merely because they take it to follow from certain ways of thinking about divine foreknowledge or God's relationship to time. Rather, open theists argue that this explanation of evil is more theologically palatable. Many of them find it hard to believe that God would create a world knowing that it would contain such evils as the Holocaust or the tsumani disaster in Bande Aceh. But if God lacks foreknowledge with respect to such evils, he could not have prevented them and is thus not culpable for allowing them. Open theists regard explaining some evils in this way as theologically superior to explanations that suppose that God knew that such events were going to occur, and simply chose not to intervene to prevent them.

Open theists are right to claim that if God lacks foreknowledge there will be some evils that God cannot prevent. However, it is not obvious that this will solve the problems they take it to solve, for three reasons. First, it is not at all clear that God's inability to know that certain events will occur renders God any less responsible for their occurrence. On open theism, God does not, and cannot, know that Adam would sin if created by God. But God knows that Adam *can* sin. Indeed, on open theism, when God creates, he knowingly leaves open the possibility that Adam will sin, that Holocausts (or worse) will occur, and that tsunamis will wipe out hundreds of thousands (or more). Since there is no good reason to think that God will be able to calculate the probabilities of such evils occurring before creating, God might often be utterly in the dark about the likelihood that events like these will occur. This might leave God blissfully ignorant of the actual evils that the future contains; but it also casts God as objectionably reckless. If the evils that occur in our world result from this sort of divine recklessness, God is hardly off the hook for the evils that subsequently occur.

Second, since God cannot foresee the future, he leaves the door open, when creating, to the possibility that that world will ultimately turn out to be filled with free creatures who willfully despise God and scorn their neighbors. As a result, open theists are not entitled to claim—though they often do—that God can create with sufficient confidence that things will not ultimately come to ruin. In addition, given God's lack of foresight, there are two possible outcomes that might arise in a world with free creatures, either of which should provide sufficient reason for God to refrain from creating at all. First, if the world might come to ruin as described, then it might come to have evils that are not outweighed by the goods the world contains. Second, if God cannot foresee how creatures will freely choose, those creatures might choose to do things that it is not within God's rights to permit. In either case, it would be impermissible for God to risk creating at all.

Finally, even if it is true that there are some evils that God cannot prevent because they cannot be foreseen, there are other evils that God can foresee and yet still permits, even on open theism. Because of this, the open theist's explanation of evil has less vindicating power than one might have initially thought. Elsewhere, Michael Rea and I have expressed this worry as follows:

Why is it repugnant to think that God *knew* millions of years ago that many would suffer at the hands of Hitler but chose to permit that suffering anyway, but not repugnant to think that God knew in (say) 1941 that many (more) would suffer at the hands of Hitler but chose to permit that suffering anyway? In short, the Openist view, like its rivals, is committed to acknowledging the existence of preventable suffering that was both foreseen and permitted by God. Given this, it is hard to see why the limitations on God's foresight imposed by the Openist view should be regarded as especially advantageous.   (Murray and Rea 2007)[4]

Open theism thus seems to provide less help in reconciling theism and the existence of evil in the world than we might have initially supposed.

The Outweighing Condition stipulates that the greater good in question is 'sufficiently outweighing'. Why not rather stipulate that the greater good merely be 'outweighing'? The answer is that gaining an extra measure of overall goodness might sometimes require allowing a substantial additional quantity of evil, and that substantial quantity might well make the overall greater balance of good over evil not worth the price. This is important since it shows us why explanations for evil should seek to explain not only how evil is a necessary condition for some outweighing good, but also why it would not be better to have neither the evil nor the good that it spawns. For example, creating creatures with free choice may yield a world in which the good that results ultimately outweighs the moral evil. But given the vast quantity of permitted moral evil required to get those goods, some might conclude that a world with no free creatures is, all things considered, to be preferred.

The Rights Condition is necessary since there may be occasions on which one being can permit evils in the service of securing greater goods, but where the absence of a right to do so would render such permission immoral. If a stranger wants to take the life of my son in order to use his two kidneys to save the lives of her two children, I have no right to give my child to this stranger, even if we agree that saving two lives is better than saving one.[5]

Does the Rights Condition place any substantive constraints on theodicy? Some philosophers have argued that it does. In particular, many theists argue that God cannot properly permit an evil unless the following condition is satisfied: when there are innocent victims of evil, those evils must not only be necessary conditions for outweighing goods generally, they must also be necessary conditions for outweighing goods *for the victim*. Eleonore Stump (1985: 58) puts the point this way, 'if a good God allows evil, it can only be because the evil in question produces a benefit *for the sufferer* and one that God could not produce without the suffering'.[6] We might characterize the underlying principle here as follows:

> (P) For any innocent person S, God has the right to allow S to suffer only if there's some outweighing good that S wouldn't enjoy if God didn't allow S so to suffer.

The motivation behind this requirement is similar to the motivation behind Kant's categorical imperative. If God were to allow someone to be victimized by evil only for the sake of securing global goods or goods for other persons, then the victim would have been used as a mere means. But using persons merely as means is morally impermissible for God or anyone else. As a result, an adequate theodicy would have to show not only that the evils that occur are necessary for outweighing goods, but also how the victims of the evil are directly and properly compensated for their role in the overall scheme.

What should we think of (P)? While it initially seems to be a fairly non-controversial application of Kant's principle, critics have noted some crucial difficulties. First, if (P) were true, it would seem to provide us with a powerful argument against some basic principles of ordinary morality. Ordinary morality dictates that when I see an innocent sufferer it is morally good for me to intervene to stop the suffering. However, if (P) is true, in stopping the suffering I am ultimately depriving the sufferer of a greater good. Thus, by intervening to help the victim, I ultimately cause her harm. Any principle that wars with ordinary morality in this way must surely be false (Jordan 2004).

Others have argued instead that the principle applies only under conditions that make it inapplicable to God. For example, one person (X) can justly allow another person (Y) to suffer even when the suffering does not yield a net benefit for Y, under the following conditions: (a) X is in a position of lawful authority over Y and any others who stand to gain or lose from Y's suffering; (b) X is responsible for the welfare of Y and these others; (c) the good to be gained by allowing Y to suffer substantially outweighs the suffering experienced by Y; and (d) there is no other way to obtain the goods produced by allowing Y's suffering without permitting some situation in which the overall balance of goods and evils is worse. For example, the state might be permitted to quarantine a patient with a virulent and incurable disease, perhaps without the benefit of even being able to receive medical treatment, in order to protect other citizens from contracting the disease. Since God has lawful authority over us that exceeds the authority of the state, and since God is responsible for the well-being of the entirety of his creation, God too might be in a rightful position to allow there to be uncompensated victims of suffering if that were necessary for securing certain outweighing goods (van Inwagen 1995: 121).[7]

In addition to satisfying the three conditions set out above, there are epistemic conditions that an explanation must satisfy to count as a theodicy. Above we characterized a theodicy as an explanation aimed at showing why the existence of evil is not unlikely given the existence of God. In order to show this, a theodicy will have to undermine the claim—a claim that seems obvious to us when we first think about evil—that the existence of evil just *does* seem unlikely if indeed there is a God who is wholly good, knowledgeable, and powerful. What does a theodicy need to look like in order to play this role?

David Lewis claims that we need to develop 'hypotheses that are at least somewhat plausible, at least to the [theist]' (Lewis 1993: 152) which show how evil does or can provide a necessary means for certain goods. However, the standard of requiring 'somewhat plausible' hypotheses is too high. We can see this by considering an example. My colleague tells me he is going to Miami today. Later today I get a call from a friend in the Midwest telling me that he saw my colleague having dinner that evening in a swanky Detroit restaurant. Should I conclude that my colleague lied to me? Not necessarily. Maybe he took a flight that connected through Detroit and, due to bad weather, was left stuck there for the night. Is that explanation *plausible*? No. It's *possible*. But note: I don't really have any reason to believe it at all. And, of course, I don't have any reason to disbelieve it either. Still, the explanation (*a*) would be a good explanation if it's true and (*b*) is not ruled out or even unlikely given the other things I believe. Because of this, an explanation of this sort is sufficient to preserve my belief in the integrity of my colleague even in the face of evidence that might be taken to show that he is a liar.

Theodicies should be judged sufficient when they meet a similar standard. Even when the theist is unaware of *plausible* explanations for evil, there might be a variety of reasons that are true for all she knows, not rendered unlikely given the other things she believes, and are such that if they were true, they would constitute good explanations for evil (that is, they would be consistent with theism and would explain why the types of evil in question would be necessary for securing outweighing goods). The theodicies we will consider in this chapter should and do aim to meet this standard.

The Punishment Theodicy

Christians, Jews, Muslims, theistic Hindus, and numerous other theistic religious believers have affirmed that some evil is to be explained as a result of divine punishment for human wrongdoing.

Successful theodicies must show that the evils they treat are connected to securing outweighing goods. Thus in this case we ought to ask: is it reasonable to think that evils of divine punishment secure greater goods? Answering that question depends on what punishment is supposed to be good for. Defenders of the punishment theodicy have argued that punishment can be good for one (or more) of four things: *rehabilitation, deterrence, societal protection*, and *retribution*.

The first three goods of punishment describe good consequences for the wrongdoer or other human agents. In the case of rehabilitation, the result is that the wrongdoer herself learns the wrongness of her action and no longer performs the bad action. The third-century Christian thinker Origen of Alexandria summarized this benefit of punishment along such lines: 'But our chastisement by Providence has been that of children by a teacher or father. God does not take vengeance, which is the requital of evil for evil, but he chastises for the benefit of the chastised' (Bettenson 1956: 257). The goods of *deterrence* or *societal protection* instead benefit those around the wrongdoer. In the case of deterrence, the punishment inflicted on the wrongdoer either acts as a disincentive for others tempted to commit evil actions or leads others to reform their behavior. Protection of society can be secured if the punishment makes the wrongdoer unable to carry out further wrong acts. Such punishment either brings about a physical or psychological disability or, in capital punishment, the death of the wrongdoer.

The fourth and most controversial good of punishment is the good of retribution. Many theistic traditions defend the notion that when someone commits a wrong they merit a punishment which exacts a cost that goes above and beyond mere recompense. If I steal two hundred dollars from the bank and am caught, I am expected to repay what I stole. But merely having to give back the money is not enough. I committed a wrong, and this obligates me to do something more than merely offer recompense—I must, for example, pay a fine or spend time in jail. According to retributivists, this additional cost is due simply as the penalty I have earned for the wrong I have done. Exacting the additional penalty constitutes retribution. St Thomas Aquinas argues that retribution is an important aspect of divine punishment because it is a necessary condition for maintaining justice in the universe: 'Nevertheless the order of justice belongs to the order of the universe; and this requires that penalty should be dealt out to sinners. And so God is the author of the evil which is penalty, but not of the evil which is fault' (St Thomas 1981: I q. 49 a. 2). Since divine punishment could potentially serve to bring about any of these goods, some evil might be justified as divine punishment.

Natural Consequence Theodicy

The Punishment Theodicy shows how some evil (the punishment) can be an indirect result of morally bad choices. Sometimes, however, bad moral choices lead to bad consequences directly. If I choose to spend my life indulging my every desire, seeking out sensual pleasure at every turn, and having no concern for the well-being of others, I may end up fat, lazy, and alone. Those consequences would be bad, but they are not the result of divine punishments. Instead, these evils are the natural consequences of immoral choosing. Leibniz put the point this way:

The most usual aim of punishment is amendment; but it is not the sole aim, nor that which God always intends. . . . Original sin, which disposes men towards evil, is not merely a penalty for the first sin; it is a natural consequence thereof. . . . It is like drunkenness, which is a penalty for excess in drinking and is at the same time a natural consequence that easily leads to new sins.   (Leibniz 1988: 200)

It is reasonable to think that a world designed by God would be one in which choosing badly would sometimes turn out to be bad for us. God might be able to use the bad consequences that arise from bad choosing as a tool for helping us to learn how to live lives of moral uprightness in loving communion with God and our fellow human beings. Recognizing the poverty of a life lived in immorality and out of communion with God and our fellows might be the only way of moving us to change our ways freely. In this way, allowing wrongdoing to have bad natural consequences brings about an outweighing good. Peter van Inwagen defends this view as follows.

God's plan of Atonement . . . is to make us *dissatisfied* with our state of separation from Him; and not by miraculously altering our values or by subjecting us to illusion or by causing us suffering that has no natural connection with our separation, but simply by allowing us to 'live with' the natural consequences of this separation, and by making it as difficult as possible for us to delude ourselves about the kind of world we live in: a hideous world, much of whose hideousness is quite plainly traceable to the inability of human beings to govern themselves or to order their own lives.   (van Inwagen 1995: 110)

Punishment and Natural Consequence theodicies can only go so far, however. First, it seems clear that many evils that occur cannot be explained as divine punishment or natural consequences for moral wrongdoing, most notably evils experienced by those who are innocent, such as infants or non-human animals. Second, on the punishment theodicy, the evils that result from punishment are necessary in order to restore justice in the cosmic order or to generate certain consequences for the wrongdoer or other human agents. Such things might be good, but their goodness only makes sense because there was some prior wrongdoing on the part of free creatures. If those free creatures never did wrong, there would be no need for punishment in the first place. As a result, the punishment theodicy needs to be supplemented with another theodicy that explains why God would permit moral evil in the first place.

The Free Will Theodicy

Philosophers addressing the topic of theodicy typically divide the types of evil that our world contains into two broad categories: moral evil and natural evil. Moral evil is evil that results from free creatures using their freedom in morally blameworthy ways. Natural evil is evil that does not directly involve blameworthy creaturely action. The most commonly invoked theodicy for moral evil is the Free Will Theodicy.

Theists and atheists alike largely agree that creating a universe would count as a good, and that it would further count as good if the universe God creates were to contain creatures capable of making free choices. Such creatures can enjoy the very great good of making free and autonomous choices. Furthermore, such creatures are capable of producing moral good in the world, engaging in relationships of love and friendship, displaying genuine charity and courage, and so on. Yet free creatures of that sort necessarily have the ability to choose to do evil. And if those creatures are genuinely free in making their choices, they cannot be determined to choose only the good.

Now let's imagine that God is faced with the prospect of creating a universe. Wanting to fill the creation with the greatest types of good, God decides to create a world containing a number of creatures with free choice. Can God create a world with such freely choosing creatures who never choose to do wrong? Maybe or maybe not. We just don't know. When God considers all the possible universes he can create with free creatures in them, it just might turn out that in every one of them, at least one of the creatures (or perhaps even every one of the creatures) in them chooses to do wrong. And if that's right, then God cannot create a world that contains the good of free choice but that also has no evil in it. In this case, putting up with moral evil is the price God in fact must pay in order to get a universe with the very great good of creatures with free choice.[8]

This theodicy provides us with an explanation of why a universe with free creatures might contain morally evil choices. However, critics have pointed out that this does *not*, all by itself, explain why those evil choices must issue in (further) evil results. There is, after all, a distinction between the moral evil of making a morally bad choice, and the moral evil that *results from* that bad choice. It might be reasonable to hold that the reality of free choice makes it inevitable that there will be some *bad moral choices*. But couldn't God allow free choices, bad choices among them, without allowing those bad choices to have further bad consequences? It might be good for me to have the ability to make a free choice to run out of the restaurant before I pay my bill. But couldn't God safeguard the restaurant owner from harm by miraculously making money appear on the table in an amount equal to the cost of my meal (with a generous tip to boot)? It might be good for me to be able to choose to run over your mailbox in anger. But couldn't God make the mailbox post magically elastic so that shortly after I drive away—content that I smashed it—the mailbox springs back upright without a scratch?

Some philosophers have argued that while it is a good thing to allow creatures to have free choice, it is a bad thing to allow those free choices to cause harm or injury to others. Instead, they argue, God should put us all in a virtual 'playpen' in which choices can be made without any real harm to others being caused. Good choices could be made, and the good consequences that follow from them allowed. But bad choices, while not prevented altogether, would be prevented from causing additional damage. Couldn't God simply block such negative consequences? (Lewis 1993).

The first question to ask here is: What would it look like if God were to do so? I intend to pull the trigger to shoot you but suddenly find that my finger is paralyzed, or ... I intend to steal the car but when I rear back to throw the brick at the car window to gain entry, I suddenly fall asleep. Would this suffice? In one sense it would. Were the world so configured, I would not be able to bring about any evil beyond my evil choices. Unfortunately, the result of such an arrangement is that, before long, I would not be able to make evil choices either. The reason for this is that my experience will make it clear to me that doing evil is in fact impossible. We can see this by considering an example. When I was 5 years old, I and a few friends decided that we would jump from a concrete wall and fly. After twenty minutes of consistent failure and sore fannies, we could see that flying was not in our future. To the best of my knowledge, no one in that group has since been tempted to fly off a concrete wall. Indeed, I suspect none of my kindergarten companions *could now even form the intention* to fly off the wall. They know by their experience that doing so is as impossible as leaping to the moon or swallowing the ocean. If God were simply to block the evil consequences as the virtual playpen scenario advocates, choosing evil would be no more possible for us than choosing to fly is for us in the actual world.[9]

As a result, for there to be a playpen world that preserves our ability to choose and intend to do evil, God would need to block the consequences of our evil choices *while at the same time* giving us the illusion that the evil action we intended was indeed carried out. There is real moral evil in such a world, since the choice itself is a morally evil one. But there is *less* overall evil since the evil consequences are never realized and, perhaps best of all, no one except the evildoer is ever harmed by those evil choices. Wouldn't this souped-up virtual playpen be preferable to the actual world?

There are good reasons to think that the playpen so described is impossible, as I will show below. However, if the critic thinks that such a world were possible, that critic would have to confront this question: how do we know that we are not in fact in such a world? If we are, the prospect of such a playpen does not count as an objection to the Free Will theodicy but rather an articulation of it! Leaving that possibility aside, one might object that the playpen world casts God objectionably in the role of a deceiver since he would be leading the murderer or the car thief to believe that they have murdered someone or stolen a car, when in fact they have merely elected to do so (and been subjected to an illusion that they have actually done so). But if such deception is the only way to allow the possibility of evil-choosing-freedom without allowing harm to others, perhaps the deception is *itself* an evil necessary for this outweighing good.

There are good reasons, however, to think that virtual playpens would quickly degenerate into semi-solipsistic, causally isolated worlds. This is the case because it would be impossible for free creatures to remain in genuine contact with one another after an extended period of making evil choices with these illusory consequences. Were I to be in the playpen, I would be unable to apologize to someone for harming them, or to receive apologies from those who (think that they) harmed me. I would be unable to see someone wearing a watch or driving a car that I think I stole from them. And so on. In the playpen I would have to become increasingly blind to the way the world really is. In order to keep all these illusions working, I would be withdrawn deeper and deeper into a solipsistic world until I became disconnected from the real world entirely. But such an arrangement also serves to eliminate the possibility of engaging in relationships of love and friendship with others, thus undermining what is perhaps the central good that freedom makes possible.

Thus, even if playpen worlds were free of these liabilities, there are good reasons to think such a world would be worse than the sort of world we actually find ourselves in. While such a world would be better in the sense that the evil consequences of our immoral choices would be thwarted, something else is missing from such a world—and it is part, perhaps the largest part, of what makes freedom valuable in the first place. What is good about free choice is not simply that I have the ability to choose among a list of items on a mental menu. Rather, what is good is that I have the ability to exercise my powers in my environment *by means of my choices*. I have the capacity to *choose* to show love to my spouse or my child *and to do it*. I have the ability to *choose* to sacrifice for the sake of my friend, *and to do it*. Being able to choose is a great good. Being able to effect states of affairs in the world in virtue of our choices is even better.

The Free Will Theodicy thus seems to provide at least a possible explanation for the fact that God allows a world in which creatures can make evil moral choices and in which those choices can sometimes issue in bad consequences. But like Punishment Theodicies, Free Will Theodicies are not comprehensive. Even if these considerations sufficed to explain moral evil, they don't seem to offer us any explanations for natural evil.

The Natural Law Theodicy

Free Will Theodicies focus on explaining evil as a consequence or result of creaturely free choice. Yet this is not the only way that freedom might be connected with the permission of evil. A number of conditions must be in place for free creatures to be able to exercise their freedom. We have, in fact, seen an example of this already. Above I told the story of my youthful attempts at flying. Those attempts failed, of course, and as a result I no longer attempt to fly, and, in fact, I doubt I could even form the intention to fly because of those experiences. Because the world would not cooperate with my intentions back then, I am no longer free to try to act in that way.

What this shows us is that in order for us to be free in a certain domain of action, the world needs to cooperate with our choice-making. If the world proves wholly unresponsive to certain choices I make (to fly unaided, for example), I will lose the freedom to choose such things. What is required for the world to 'cooperate' with my choices in the needed way? At least one thing that is required is that the environment around me be governed by regular, orderly laws of nature. The reason for this is that in most cases, I act by moving my body in certain ways and, in turn, affecting the world in certain ways. When I want to tell my daughter a story, for example, I move my mouth in ways that make sounds that communicate a story, and so on. If the environment around me were not regular and lawlike, I couldn't do such things, since I wouldn't know how to intend to bring them about.

We can see this by considering a chaotic world in which there are no stable and reliable laws of nature. In this world, vibrating my vocal cords would sometimes cause air to move in such a way that I make sounds, and sometimes it wouldn't. If the world were chaotic in this way, I would never come to discover a connection between vibrating my vocal cords and making sounds that allow me to tell a story. If I had a desire to tell a story, I wouldn't have any idea how to go about doing it, since the chaotic world has failed to cooperate in ways that allow me to do it reliably. As a result, it seems that I could have desires to do all sorts of things, but that I would never *actually choose* to do them because I would have no idea how to do so (Mawson 2004; Reichenbach 1982: 103–4).

Any world in which there are going to be free creatures capable of carrying out free actions with consequences beyond their own skin must then be a world that operates according to regular, orderly laws of nature. And this can lead to problems. The very same laws of momentum that allow me to use a hammer to drive a nail, can cause that hammer to smash my thumb. The very same laws that allow me to tell stories by vibrating air with my vocal cords, allow tornadoes to knock down houses. And so on. In a world governed by regular, orderly natural laws, it is possible for these laws to conspire to intersect with the interests of creatures to cause them harm. When they do so, natural evil will be the result.

There are two serious objections that Natural Law Theodicies need to confront. First, one might wonder why God did not create a world with better laws that yield less natural evil. After all, would the world have been any worse if the laws were set up that did not allow viruses to occur? Second, aren't there plenty of cases of natural evil that could be eliminated without undermining the regularity of the laws of nature to such an extent that our freedom would be disabled? Would preventing one major hurricane undermine the possibility of my exercising my free will? If not, shouldn't God prevent one or two (or ten) more hurricanes? Let's consider these in turn.

Could the laws of nature have been configured to yield a world that has a substantially better overall balance of good than our world? To show that such a better world is possible, we would need to describe a regular, lawlike world that (*a*) contains goodness of the sorts (either the same sorts or equivalent or better sorts) and amounts found in the actual world and which (*b*) contains substantially less natural evil than the actual world. There are two problems with trying to offer such a description. First, there is good reason to think that there is not much wiggle room in the way the laws and constants of the world are structured. One fairly recent discovery of scientists is that the cosmos seems to be balanced on a razor's edge in such a way that were the laws and constants that govern its activity slightly different, the cosmos would be unable to sustain intelligent life (Barr 2003: 118–38). This provides us with some good reason to suppose that if the universe is going to be capable of supporting life, it will have to be governed by laws and constants similar to those we find in the actual world.[10] Second, even if a better set of laws could be specified, it is doubtful that we could know this. Knowing such a thing would require knowing how changes we propose to certain laws and constants would impact not only the natural evils we are trying to prevent, but other laws of nature and the goods and evils that arise from their mutual interactions. It is unreasonable to think we could unscramble such things and thus unreasonable to think that the laws might be changed to yield a better world with less natural evil.

The second objection is more formidable. If lawlike regularity in the world exists for the purpose of allowing free creatures to use their free choice, then any natural evils that could be eliminated without eliminating that good result would be gratuitous. And yet it seems that there are many such evils. Even if God could not prevent all such evils by systematically altering the laws that hold in our universe, he could at least eliminate many by miraculous intervention. The evils of kidney stones or ingrown toenails seem good candidates for such elimination.

The theist might respond that God already does miraculously intervene to prevent some such evils. This answer is not sufficient, however, since the critic wants to know why *even more* such evils are not prevented. The only answer available to the theist is that natural evils serve as necessary conditions for some good ends. One of those is the good of allowing free creatures to exercise their freedom. But there must be others. Thus, while the regularity and lawlikeness that allows for natural evil serves to make the good of free choice possible, it makes other goods available as well, and it is those goods that explain why some of the apparently gratuitous natural evils we find around us are not gratuitous after all. What this shows us is that the Natural Law Theodicy will not be able to provide a comprehensive explanation for natural evil.

Soul-Making Theodicies

The theodicies considered so far all regard evil as a consequence of free choice or of necessary preconditions for free choice. Other theodicies treat evil as a necessary condition for goods of other sorts. For example, many theistic traditions regard the earthly life as an arena in which people make choices for the purpose of cultivating moral and spiritual growth. If the world were filled with perpetual pleasure and satisfaction we would never experience the growth that can come only from real suffering, hardship, and defeat. As a result, some theists propose that God allows for evil in the world to allow us to cultivate virtues of outweighing goodness that could not otherwise be cultivated.

It is easy to think of some such virtues. I could not become charitable unless there were cases of someone in need. I could not become courageous unless there were real dangers to be confronted. And so on. More than that, I could not become a lover or a friend unless the possibility of losing that love or friendship made it possible for both me and the beloved or the friend to lose something of great value. All these cases highlight the fact that one of the important goods in our world is that it provides an arena for *soul-making* or character building. And this important good requires that the universe contain some evil.

This theodicy, pioneered by the second-century Christian thinker Irenaeus (Irenaeus 2001) and resurrected in the twentieth century by philosopher John Hick, stipulates that four conditions must be in place for soul-making to occur. First, there must be creatures capable of choosing between good and evil. Second, those creatures must be placed in an environment that allows free choices to be carried out. Third, the environment must contain challenges to one's character of a sort that allows for both virtuous and vicious responses. And finally, creatures must have sufficient opportunities to respond to make character building possible (Hick 1977).

Soul-making theodicies must confront a couple of important objections, the more important of which is that many sorts of moral and spiritual growth envisioned in soul-making scenarios require only that there be *apparent* evils in the world. For me to develop the virtues of charity and courage there need not be any *actual* need or *actual* peril, it only needs to seem to me that there is. Once again, such a world as the virtual playpen described earlier would seem to be sufficient; as long as it seems to me as if I lived in a world filled with evil, soul-making can occur, and without the cost of my having to confront any *actual* suffering or danger. Wouldn't such a world be preferable? Some theists have argued that it would not. Daniel-Howard Snyder thus argues as follows:

However, if God were to set up a world in which there was only illusory evil to which we could respond in the formation of our character, something of immense value would be missing. No one would in fact help anybody else; and no one would be helped. No one would in fact be compassionate and sympathetic to another; and no one would receive compassion and sympathy. . . . No one would in fact generously give of their time, their talents or their money to the poor; and no one would receive generosity from another. In short, if every opportunity for a virtuous response were directed at illusory evils, each of us would live in our own little 'world,' worlds devoid of any genuine interaction and personal relationships.

(Howard-Snyder 1999: 99)

While some evils might be avoided in such a world, the cost of avoiding them would be the elimination of many of those aspects of the world that we take to be the most valuable: our interactions of love and friendship with others.

Theodicies of Animal Suffering

Some philosophers have recently argued that one distinctive sort of evil is especially troublesome and difficult to explain: non-human animal suffering (or 'animal suffering' for short). Animal suffering is problematic not only because there are more animals than humans, and because animals have been around for so much longer than humans, but because, if Darwinian naturalism is right, animal suffering, pain, and death, seem to be among the very instruments of creation. In light of the evolutionary carnage, philosopher Philip Kitcher (2005: 268) finds it incredible that theists can sustain belief in an all-wise, benevolent creator:

[Were we to imagine] a human analogue peering down over a miniaturized version of this arrangement—peering down over his creation—it's hard to equip the face with a kindly expression. Conversely, it's natural to adapt Alfonso X's famous remark about the convolutions of Ptolemaic astronomy: had a benevolent creator proposed to use evolution under natural selection as a means for attaining his purposes, we could have given him useful advice.

Animal suffering is all the more vexing when we realize that the theodicies considered so far do not offer much help in explaining it. Even if some of the explanations take us some way towards explaining the reality of animal suffering (some animal suffering is caused by the evil free choices of humans, for example), most of it is still entirely unexplained. In general, there are two facts about animal suffering that seem to make it especially resistant to explanation using traditional theodicies. First, most animal suffering predates the advent of human beings. As a result, any theodicy that aims to explain evil as a consequence or precondition of human free choice, soul-making, and the like is going to struggle to explain animal suffering. Second, there does not seem to be any reason on the earlier described theodicies that God would have to create animals capable of experiencing pain and suffering in the first place. If a world with natural regularities is one in which organisms might sometimes become innocent victims of the forces of nature, it might be better, all things considered, not to outfit non-human animals with the tools that allow them to experience pain and suffering in the first place.

The problem raised by animal suffering was of some concern to philosophers and theologians in the late nineteenth century, but interest in the topic seems to have waned from that time until quite recently. If there is to be a successful theodicy of animal suffering, it will have to follow one of the following outlines.

First, some theists have tried to account for the reality of animal pain and suffering not as a result of the misuse of human free choice but rather as a result of the misuse of the free choice of non-human free creatures. There is a long tradition in western theism of supposing the existence of creatures (demons, for example) with free choice whose existence predates human existence. If such beings did or do exist, they might perhaps have had powers sufficient to steer evolutionary history in a way that allowed for non-human animals to have the capacity to experience pain and suffering, as well as to inflict actual pain and suffering on them (Boyd 2001).

Second, some theodicies claim that, for all we know, animals do not have the necessary mental equipment to experience pain and suffering, or to experience it in a way that is morally relevant. Descartes, for example, argued that animals were merely complex machines displaying behaviors that make it appear that they are in pain. Some recent philosophers have argued that pain and suffering are possible only for organisms that are able to have a 'second-order' awareness of their first-order mental states. Human beings have such advanced mental capacities. However, second-order awareness requires a good deal of neural and cognitive complexity, and it is not clear that animals have what is needed to experience such second-order awareness (Murray and Ross 2006).

Third, some theodicies claim that nervous systems that produce pain and suffering are necessary for embodied organisms to be able to avoid harm and preserve their bodily integrity. While there are many ways in which our nervous systems could signal that our bodily integrity is in jeopardy, there is some experimental evidence that only signals that are 'qualitatively unpleasant' will cause organisms to behave in ways that are necessary to avoid injury (Eccles 1980; Murray 2008: ch. 4).

Finally, some theodicies of animal suffering contend that animals with minds capable of experiencing pain and suffering are necessary evolutionary precursors for organisms with the special cognitive skills of human beings—skills that, for example, make possible free choice and moral responsibility. Of course, explanations of this sort seem to make animals mere by-products on the evolutionary step-ladder leading to human beings, making one wonder whether there is some good explanation for why God had to employ such precursors in the first place. One answer might be found in the claim, defended most famously by the French philosopher Nicholas Malebranche, that a world is better insofar as the complexity in that world results from the regular, orderly operation of divinely ordained laws of nature (Malebranche 1958–84: ix. 1085). If one finds such a position plausible, one might argue that the only way to get such beings as us into creation via lawlike processes is to allow our universe to unfold in much the way that it did: evolving from an initial singularity to later stages in which there are highly concentrated pockets of privileged order (such as is found on our own planet, and perhaps others as well). Animals would then be necessary stages in the development of this lawlike universe, leading to such organisms as us as well as perhaps organisms of even greater complexity and worth in the future.

Notes

1. For a robust defense of skeptical theism see Michael Bergmann 2001: 278–96, as well as his 'Skeptical Theism and the Problem of Evil', Ch. 17 in this volume. For a recent critique of skeptical theism see Almeida and Oppy 2003.

2. Adapted from Swinburne 1998.

3. God could, of course, prevent any token instance of an unpredictable event by simply annihilating the entirety of creation. The point here is that there is nothing God could do to prevent specific unpredictable events from occurring while leaving the created order intact.

4. A similar point has been made by Edward Wierenga (1997).

5. The example is a modification of one used by Swinburne (1998: 11). Of course one might not agree that saving the lives of two persons through killing a third, innocent person is an outweighing good. But none of this matters for the general point that there are conditions where one is not morally permitted to allow the occurrence of preventable evils the permission of which is necessary to secure outweighing goods.

6. Emphasis mine. Similar views have been defended by Adams, 1999: 29–31; William Rowe, 'The Empirical Argument from Evil', in Audi and Wainwright (eds.) 1986: 244–5; Eleonore Stump, 'Providence and the Problem of Evil', in Flint (ed.) 1990: 65–8; and Michael Tooley, 'The Argument from Evil', in Tomberlin (ed.) 1991: 110–11.

7. Finally, Sorensen and Boorse 1988 argue that the principle is false on other grounds. Consider the following: a boulder is bouncing down an embankment towards me. If I duck, the boulder will miss me, but hit you (who happens, unfortunately, to be standing right behind me). If I do not duck, I will be crushed and you will be spared. Surely, they claim, it is morally permissible for me to duck. But in that case, (B) is false. Some might object, of course, that authentic neighbor love entails that one not duck after all. If so, this objection will miss the mark.

8. Such an explanation for evil is worked out in detail as a defense (rather than a theodicy) in Plantinga 1972.

9. Both volume editors have remarked that in such a world one could nonetheless continue to fantasize about visiting harm on others, or at least hope that harm would be visited on them. While neither of these involve full fledged intentional action, they are still reasonably seen as being produced or sustained by our free choices. I take the first to be unlikely since such an environment lacks necessary conditions for allowing me to form the belief that I can in fact cause such a thing as harm in the first place. Nothing on the account I have described here would preclude the second. However, it is not clear that mere wishing ill on others counts as free or voluntary.

10. One might object that, while it might not be possible to have a world that sustains life and preserves the other's goods dependent on lawlike regularity without allowing the possibility of natural evil that causes injury, injury and injury avoidance need not involve the qualitatively unpleasant sensations of pain. This objection is addressed in detail in Murray 2008: ch. 4.

References

ADAMS, MARILYN MCCORD (1999). *Horrendous Evils and the Goodness of God*. Ithaca: Cornell University Press.

ALMEIDA, MICHAEL, and OPPY, GRAHAM (2003). 'Skeptical Theism and Evidential Arguments from Evil', *Australasian Journal of Philosophy* 81: 496–516.

AUDI, ROBERT, and WAINWRIGHT, WILLIAM J. (eds.) 1986. *Rationality, Religious Belief, and Moral Commitment*. Ithaca: Cornell University Press.

BARR, STEPHEN M. (2003). *Modern Physics and Ancient Faith*. Notre Dame: Notre Dame University Press.

BERGMANN, MICHAEL (2001). 'Skeptical Theism and Rowe's New Evidential Argument from Evil', *Noûs* 35: 278–96.

BETTENSON H. (1956). *The Early Christian Fathers*. Oxford: Oxford University Press.

BOYD, GREGORY A. (2001). *Satan and the Problem of Evil: Constructing a Trinitarian Warfare Theodicy*. Downers Grove: Inter-Varsity Press.

COHEN, RICHARD (2006). 'Whose Silence', *Lancaster Intelligencer Journal*, 6 June 2006, A10.

ECCLES, SIR JOHN (1990). *The Human Psyche*. New York: Springer-Verlag.

FLINT, T. (ed.) (1990). *Christian Philosophy*. Notre Dame: University of Notre Dame Press.

HASKER, WILLIAM (2004). *Providence, Evil, and the Openness of God*. New York: Routledge.

HICK, JOHN (1977). *Evil and the God of Love*. New York: Macmillan.

HOWARD-SNYDER, DANIEL (1999). 'God, Evil, and Suffering', in Michael Murray (ed.), *Reason for the Hope Within*. Grand Rapids: Eerdmans.

IRENAEUS (2001). 'Against Heresies', in *The Apostolic Fathers with Justin Martyr and Irenaeus*, The Ante-Nicene Fathers. Grand Rapids: Eerdmans.

JORDAN, JEFF (2004). 'Divine Love and Human Suffering', *International Journal for Philosophy of Religion* 56: 169–78.

KITCHER, PHILIP (2005). 'The Many-Sided Conflict Between Science and Religion', in William E. Mann (ed.) *The Blackwell Guide to the Philosophy of Religion*. Malden: Blackwell.

LEIBNIZ, GOTTFRIED (1988). *Theodicy*, trans. E. M. Huggard. La Salle: Open Court.

LEWIS, DAVID (1993). 'Evil for Freedom's Sake', *Philosophical Papers* 22: 152.

MALEBRANCHE (1958–84). 'Abrégé du traité de la nature et de la grace', in A. Robinet (ed.), *Œuvres complètes de Malebranche*, 20 vols. Paris: J. Vrin.

MAWSON, T. J. (2004). 'The Possibility of a Free-Will Defense for the Problem of Natural Evil', *Religious Studies* 40: 23–42.

MURRAY, MICHAEL J. (2008). *Nature Red in Tooth and Claw*. Oxford: Oxford University Press.

——and ROSS, GLENN (2006). 'Neo-Cartesian Theodicies of Animal Suffering', *Faith and Philosophy* 23: 169–90.

——and REA, MICHAEL (2007). Introduction to Philosophy of Religion. Cambridge: Cambridge University Press.

PLANTINGA, ALVIN (1974). *God, Freedom and Evil*. Grand Rapids: Eerdmans.

REICHENBACH, BRUCE (1982). *Evil and a Good God*. New York: Fordham University Press.

SORENSON, ROY, and BOORSE, CHRISTOPHER (1988). 'Ducking Harm', *Journal of Philosophy* 85: 115–34.

STUMP, ELEONORE (1985). 'The Problem of Evil', *Faith and Philosophy* 2.

—— (forthcoming), *Wandering in the Darkness.*

SWINBURNE, RICHARD (1998). *Providence and the Problem of Evil.* Oxford: Oxford University Press.

THOMAS, AQUINAS, ST (1981). *Summa theologiae.* Wheaton: Christian Classics.

TILLEY, TERRENCE (1991). *The Evils of Theodicy.* Washington: Georgetown University Press.

TOMBERLIN, J. (ed.) (1991). *Philosophical Perspectives 5. Philosophy of Religion.* Atascadero: Ridgeview.

WIERENGA, EDWARD (1997). 'Review of: *The Openness of God* by Clark Pinnock et al.', *Faith and Philosophy* 14: 248–52.

....

SKEPTICAL THEISM AND THE PROBLEM OF EVIL

....

MICHAEL BERGMANN

IN philosophy of religion, some moves—like appealing to evil to support atheism or appealing to the appearance of design in nature to support theism—are very natural. They occur easily to non-philosophers in their reflective moments. Others (e.g. the ontological argument) are moves only a philosopher would think of. The skeptical theist's signature move is a very natural one. To see this, consider what would happen if you were addressing some freshman college students in an introductory philosophy class and you presented them with the following argument from evil:

(1) There are some evils that are such that humans can't think of any God-justifying reason for permitting them.[1]
(2) So probably there aren't any God-justifying reasons for permitting those evils.
(3) If God existed, he wouldn't permit these evils if there were no God-justifying reason for permitting them.
(4) Therefore, probably God does not exist.

If you asked them what they think of the argument, it's almost a certainty that someone in the class would point out that the inference from (1) to (2) doesn't seem persuasive: the fact that humans can't think of any God-justifying reason for permitting an evil, doesn't make it likely that there are no such reasons; this is because if God existed, God's mind would be far greater than our minds, so it wouldn't be surprising if God had reasons we weren't able to think of. This very natural sort of response is precisely the move the skeptical theist is known for.

Some say the term 'skeptical theism' is a bad name for the view under consideration here. The main complaint is that one needn't be a theist to object to the above argument in the way skeptical theists do.[2] I agree that one needn't be a theist to object to the above argument in the way skeptical theists do. But I don't think that makes 'skeptical theism' a bad name for the view. Skeptical theism has both a skeptical component and a theistic component. The theistic component is just theism, the view that there exists an omnipotent, omniscient, wholly good, eternal person—i.e. a perfect being of the sort endorsed by the western monotheisms. The skeptical component advocates skepticism about the realm of potentially God-justifying reasons—a degree of skepticism that leads to a denial of the cogency of such noseeum inferences as the one above from (1) to (2). (Wykstra 1996: 126 calls this a 'noseeum inference' because it says that since we don't see 'um, they probably ain't there.) And although non-theists won't endorse skeptical theism given its *theistic* component, many think that non-theists should—and some do—endorse its *skeptical* component, which is why they can agree with the objection in the previous paragraph. Moreover, it makes perfect sense that those who first made popular this sort of move in response to the above argument from evil were called 'skeptical theists': they were, after all, theists; and their advocacy of skepticism about certain matters relevant to God's ways was a striking feature of their view. It was only natural, then, to call the view they espoused 'skeptical theism'.

For our purposes here, what's most interesting about skeptical theism is its skeptical component. When skeptical theists use that skeptical component in responding to arguments from evil, they think it is reasonable for their non-theistic interlocutors to accept that skeptical component, even if they don't expect them to accept their theism. It is that skeptical component that will be the focus of this chapter. In the first section, I will explain more precisely what the skeptical theist's skepticism amounts to and how it is used in response to various sorts of arguments from evil. Then, in sect. II, I will consider and respond to objections to skeptical theism. One thing we'll find is that just as there are non-theists who accept the skeptical theist's skepticism, so also there are theists who reject it.

I. The Skeptical Theist's Skepticism

The skeptical theist's skepticism applies to the realm of God-justifying reasons. (What exactly is required for something to count as a God-justifying reason? Here's a very natural proposal that can serve as a first approximation: a good state of affairs G—which might just be the prevention of some bad state of affairs E*—is a God-justifying reason for permitting an evil E if and only if (1) G's goodness outweighs E's badness and (2) G couldn't be obtained without permitting E or something as bad or worse.[3]) Skepticism about the realm of God-justifying reasons leads many theists as well as some non-theists to reject noseeum inferences such as the one from (1) to (2), which Howard-Snyder (1996a: 291) calls 'the inference from inscrutable to pointless evil'. In this section, I want to address three questions: what exactly is involved in this skepticism? What motivates it? To which arguments from evil does the skeptical theist's skepticism apply?

A. What's Involved in the Skeptical Theist's Skepticism and What Motivates It?

The skeptical theist's skepticism[4] is, I believe, best explained as an endorsement of some skeptical theses, among which these three are prominent:

(ST1) We have no good reason for thinking that the possible goods we know of are representative of the possible goods there are.

(ST2) We have no good reason for thinking that the possible evils we know of are representative of the possible evils there are.

(ST3) We have no good reason for thinking that the entailment relations we know of between possible goods and the permission of possible evils are representative of the entailment relations there are between possible goods and the permission of possible evils.[5]

Three clarificatory remarks are in order.

First, as William Rowe (1996: 264) emphasizes, possible goods are abstracta—good states of affairs that could obtain. Thus, if we set aside concerns about God being a necessary being if he exists at all, atheists can agree that the beatific vision is a possible good, despite the fact that they think it isn't an actual good since it entails God's existence. Likewise, possible evils are bad states of affairs that could obtain. And, of course, among the possible goods and evils are actual goods and evils as well as merely possible ones.

Second, one might wonder why there is a focus in (ST1)–(ST3) on *possible* goods and evils instead of on *actual* goods and evils (i.e. possible good and evil states of affairs that obtain). In the case of evils, this isn't difficult to understand. God might permit an evil E in order to *prevent* a worse evil E* which will obtain if E isn't permitted. Here there is clearly no need for E* to be an actual evil. As for goods, it's true that in order for God's aim of obtaining G to be of use in actually justifying his permission of E, G must *eventually* be actual. But it doesn't need to be currently actual. It may currently be merely possible and it may become actual only as a result of permitting E, perhaps long after E is permitted. Moreover, if one's goal is simply to respond to arguments from evil such as the one mentioned at the beginning of this chapter (a goal an agnostic and theist might share), there's no need to defend the claim that God *does* exist or that there in fact *is* a God-justifying reason for permitting the evils mentioned. It's enough that we lack any good reason or justifying ground for thinking it's likely that there isn't such a God-justifying reason. Hence, considerations having to do with possible goods that we have no good reason to think are unlikely to be actual (now or in the future) are relevant in addressing such arguments—even if those goods are in fact *merely* possible.

Third, a sample of Xs can be representative of all Xs relative to one property but not another. For example, a sample of humans can be representative of all humans relative to the property of *having a lung* while at the same time not being representative of all humans relative to the property of *being a Russian*. To say a sample of Xs is representative of all Xs relative to a property F is just to say that if n/m of the Xs in the sample have property F, then approximately n/m of all Xs have F. In (ST1)–(ST3), what we are interested in is whether our sample of possible goods, possible evils, and entailment relations between them (i.e. the possible goods, evils, and relevant entailments we know of) is representative of all possible goods, possible evils, and entailment relations there are *relative to the property of figuring in a (potentially) God-justifying reason for permitting the inscrutable evils we see around us.*[6] Although that property is not explicitly mentioned in (ST1)–(ST3), it is representativeness relative to that property that (ST1)–(ST3) are speaking of.

Thus, the skeptical theist's skepticism affirms certain limitations to our knowledge with respect to the realms of value and modality. The claim isn't that we know nothing about those realms. I can confess to being in the dark about which of two proposed courses of action will have the best overall consequences without thereby admitting complete skepticism about value. And I can confess that I don't know whether simple mathematical truths entail Goldbach's conjecture without admitting to complete modal ignorance. Likewise, endorsing the limitations mentioned in (ST1)–(ST3) isn't an acknowledgment of complete skepticism about value and modality. As we'll see below in sect. II, objectors to skeptical theism often argue that the skeptical theists' skepticism *commits them* to further unpalatable skepticism. But we should recognize up front that the skeptical theist intends to affirm only a modest form of skepticism.

What, exactly, is the upshot of (ST1)–(ST3)? Suppose we've thought long and hard about what God-justifying reason there might be for permitting the following horrific evils, which are commonly used as examples in the literature:

(E1) the evil of a fawn trapped in a forest fire and undergoing several days of terrible agony before dying.

(E2) the evil of a 5-year-old girl being raped, beaten, and murdered by strangulation.

Such thinking will typically involve considering various possible goods and evils and the conditions of their realization—e.g. whether permitting (E1) and (E2) is necessary for obtaining some outweighing possible good or for avoiding the obtaining of some worse possible evil. Now suppose we fail to come up with anything that we think is a God-justifying reason for permitting, say, (E2). That is, suppose that both of the following are true:

> (a) none of the possible goods we know of that outweigh (E2) stand in entailment relations we know of to (E2) such that obtaining those goods would justify permitting (E2);
> (b) none of the possible evils we know of that are worse than (E2) stand in entailment relations we know of to (E2) such that preventing the obtaining of those evils would justify permitting (E2).

If we recognize the truth of (ST3), then it seems we can't infer from (a) and (b) that it's false or even unlikely that permitting (E2) (or something as bad or worse) is required—by entailment relations we *don't* know of—for the obtaining of outweighing possible goods we *know* of or the prevention of worse possible evils we *know* of. We are simply in the dark about whether there are such entailment relations between the possible goods and evils we know of.[7] And if we recognize the truth of (ST1) and (ST2), then it seems we can't infer from (a) and (b) that it's false or even unlikely that permitting (E2) (or something as bad) is required for the obtaining of outweighing possible goods we *don't* know of or for the prevention of worse possible evils we *don't* know of. We are simply in the dark about whether there are goods and evils we don't know of that could feature in a God-justifying reason for permitting (E2). Thus, (ST3) keeps us from using (a) and (b) to conclude that it's false or even unlikely that:

> (c) the possible goods or evils *we know of* feature in a God-justifying reason for permitting (E2).

And (ST1) and (ST2) together keep us from using (a) and (b) to conclude that it's false or even unlikely that:

> (d) the possible goods or evils *we don't know of* feature in a God-justifying reason for permitting E2.

In short, (ST1)–(ST3) tell us that we can't use our failure to think of a God-justifying reason for permitting the horrendous evil (E2) to conclude that it's unlikely that there is such a reason—either among known goods and evils or among unknown goods and evils.[8]

Analogies are often used to support and drive home the skeptical theist's point. We can't use our failure to see any insects in the garage (when taking a look from the street) to conclude that it's unlikely that there are any insects in the garage. We can't use our failure to discover any rational agents on other planets to conclude that it's unlikely that there are some on some other planet. We can't (if we're chess novices) use our failure to detect a good reason for a particular chess move made by a world champion chess player to conclude that it's unlikely that there is any good reason for that chess move. Likewise, say skeptical theists, we can't use our failure to discern any God-justifying reason for permitting (E2) to conclude that it's unlikely that there is any God-justifying reason for permitting (E2). There's nothing unreasonable or excessive about the skepticism involved in the cases of the insects, extraterrestrial life, or chess champion. Skepticism in those cases doesn't seem to force us to accept other more extreme and unpalatable sorts of skepticism. Likewise, says the skeptical theist, there's nothing unreasonable or excessive about the skepticism involved in the case of God-justifying reasons for permitting (E2).

Are these good analogies? Are we really that ignorant about possible goods, possible evils, and possible entailment relations between them? Notice that (ST1)–(ST3) don't deny there are many possible goods, evils, and entailment relations between them that we know of. So the claim isn't that we know very little about these things. Rather, the claim is just that we have no good reason to think that what we know of these things is representative of what there is to know about them. We've no reason to deny that what we know about possible goods, evils, and entailments between them is a very small (percentage-wise) and unrepresentative sample of these things—unrepresentative with respect to the property of *figuring in a (potentially) God-justifying reason for permitting the evils we see around us*. But if we have no such reason, then we are seriously in the dark about whether the possible goods, evils, and entailments between them are likely to contain the makings of a potentially God-justifying reason to permit (E2). And this, says the skeptical theist, makes the analogies in the previous paragraph seem like good ones.

(ST1) and (ST2) suggest that we don't have good reason to deny that there is, among the *unknown* goods and evils, a God-justifying reason for permitting (E2). (ST3), on the other hand, suggests that we don't have good reason to deny that there is, among the *known* goods and evils, a God-justifying reason for permitting (E2). There's another skeptical thesis, the import of which is similar to (ST3)'s:

> (ST4) We have no good reason for thinking that the total moral value or disvalue we perceive in certain complex states of affairs accurately reflects the total moral value or disvalue they really have.[9]

The question raised here is: in comparing some of the very complex goods and evils we know of that are unrelated to the concerns of everyday life, why think we are able to grasp them sufficiently to make the value comparisons needed to determine whether securing or preventing them could justify the permission of the evils around us? If we can't grasp them sufficiently to make such value comparisons, then our failure to think of a God-justifying reason for permitting some evil might be due to our failure to recognize that some good we know of outweighs (or that some evil we know of is worse than) the evil in question. Less emphasis is placed on (ST4) in the literature and it's not needed to make the skeptical theist's point. But it's worth mentioning (ST4) as an additional consideration that supports the lesson taught by (ST3)—namely, that there may be a God-justifying reason for permitting (E1) and (E2) among the goods and evils we know of. Using van Inwagen's terminology, (ST4) expresses skepticism about our grasp of the intrinsic value (or, as Alston puts it, the nature) of at least some of the goods and evils we know of while (ST3) expresses skepticism about our grasp of the extrinsic value (or, as Alston puts it, the conditions of realization) of the goods and evils we know of.[10]

Three further clarificatory points are worth mentioning here. First, the skepticism encouraged by (ST1)–(ST4) seems to be focused on our ability to make informed judgments about how considerations of consequences would (if God existed) factor into God's decisions about what is the best thing to do. (ST1)–(ST4) have to do with our knowledge and understanding of the realm of possible goods and evils—including our knowledge and understanding of the entailment and comparative value relations that hold between possible goods and evils. An appreciation of these relations is important when considering what the consequences are of bringing about or preventing a good or of preventing or permitting an evil. However, the fact that (ST1)–(ST4) are relevant to considering such consequences doesn't in any way take for granted the truth of consequentialist ethical theories. For it may be that consequentialist ethical theories are false (because, say, we have absolute duties that bind us regardless of the consequences), but that very often, moral agents should be guided in their moral deliberations by considerations of consequences. This is because very often the right thing to do is to try to bring about what seems best for those we love, so long as doing so involves no violation of duties. Thus, non-consequentialist ethical theories have no trouble allowing for considerations of consequences to play a role in moral decision-making.

The second clarificatory point is that there's a difference between (a) describing a potentially God-justifying reason X and then announcing that we have no good reason to think it's unlikely that X itself *is* the God-justifying reason God has for permitting some evil such as (E1) or (E2) and (b) simply pointing out that, in light of (ST1)–(ST4), we have no good reason to think it unlikely that there is some God-justifying reason God has for permitting such an evil. Although some skeptical theists (e.g. Alston 1991 and van Inwagen 1991) sometimes aim to do (a), it's a mistake to think (as some philosophers seem to) that (b) by itself—without any effort to do (a)—is insufficient for defending the skeptical theist's skepticism. So long as we have reason to endorse (ST1)–(ST4) and we can see that they do in fact imply that we aren't justified in thinking it's unlikely that there are God-justifying reasons for permitting the horrific evils we see around us, doing (a) is unnecessary for making the skeptical theist's case.

Third, it's important to realize that the skeptical theist's skepticism does nothing to show that theism is likely to be true or reasonable to believe. But, so far as I know, no theist has claimed otherwise. Instead, skeptical theists claim that the skeptical theist's skepticism undermines certain arguments from evil for atheism, showing that such arguments don't make it reasonable to reject theism. Which arguments from evil does it undermine? Let's consider that question next.

B. To Which Arguments from Evil Does the Skeptical Theist's Skepticism Apply?

There are many different arguments from evil. For some it's pretty clear that the skeptical theist's skepticism applies whereas for others it's controversial whether it applies.[11] (Whether there are some arguments from evil to which it clearly doesn't apply is a question I won't address in this chapter.) Let's begin by looking at three arguments—all by William Rowe—to which the skeptical theist's skepticism seems quite clearly to apply.

It's easy to see how (ST1)–(ST4) apply to the following argument, similar to the one given in the opening paragraph of this chapter:

(A1) We can't think of any God-justifying reasons for permitting (E1) and (E2).[12]

(A2) So probably there aren't any God-justifying reasons for permitting (E1) and (E2).

(A3) If an omnipotent, omniscient, perfectly good being existed, it wouldn't permit any evils unless it had a God-justifying reason for permitting them.

(A4) Therefore, probably there is no omnipotent, omniscient, perfectly good being.

This is basically how Rowe's 1979 argument from evil goes. The skeptical theist's skepticism straightforwardly challenges the inference from (A1) to (A2). The fact that we can't think of any God-justifying reasons for permitting (E1) and (E2) doesn't make it probable that there aren't any—any more than the fact that we can't see any insects in the garage (from our vantage point standing in the street) makes it probable that there aren't any insects in the garage.

Rowe proposed a slightly different argument from evil in later papers (see his 1988 and 1991):

(P) No good we know of justifies an omnipotent, omniscient, perfectly good being in permitting (E1) and (E2);

therefore [it's probable that],

(Q) no good at all justifies an omnipotent, omniscient, perfectly good being in permitting (E1) and (E2);

therefore [it's probable that],

($\sim$G) there is no omnipotent, omniscient, perfectly good being.[13]

This attempt by Rowe to improve the 1979 argument has been viewed by skeptical theists as a change for the worse. For now we have two problems. First, the inference from (P) to the likelihood of (Q) seems faulty given (ST1) and (ST2). Even if we could be sure that no *known* goods figure in God-justifying reasons for (E1) and (E2), this tells us nothing about whether there are *unknown* goods and evils that could figure in God-justifying reasons for (E1) and (E2) (since—as (ST1) and (ST2) tell us—we've no reason to think the goods and evils we know of are representative of the goods and evils there are). But second, (ST3) and (ST4) imply that we have no good reason to believe (P). As I noted in sect. IA, (ST3) and (ST4) emphasize that we have an inadequate grasp of the extrinsic and intrinsic value of some known goods. In light of this, we are simply in the dark about whether there is a God-justifying reason for (E1) and (E2) among the goods we know of. For both these reasons, this second argument from Rowe also fails by the skeptical theist's lights.[14]

A third argument by Rowe, proposed specifically to avoid the skeptical theist's skepticism, nevertheless also falls prey to it.[15] Instead of arguing from (P) to (Q) and then from (Q) to (~G), as in the previous argument, this time Rowe argues directly from (P) to (~G). We needn't examine any further how this argument goes in order to see that (ST3) and (ST4) imply (as I noted in the previous paragraph) that we have no good reason to believe (P). This is enough by itself to make this argument unacceptable from the skeptical theist's perspective.[16]

Let's turn next to two arguments whose proponents view them as not being targeted by the skeptical theist's skepticism, but which are, arguably, targeted by it nonetheless. The first of these, touched on by Rowe and developed at length by John Schellenberg, is the argument from divine hiddenness:

(B1) If God exists and is unsurpassably loving, then for any human subject H and time t, if H is at t capable of relating personally to God, H at t believes that God exists, unless H is culpably in a contrary position at t.[17]

(B2) There is a human subject H and a time t such that H is at t capable of relating personally to God, H is not culpably in a contrary position at t, and yet H at t fails to believe that God exists.[18]

(B3) Therefore, God does not exist.

Does the skeptical theist's skepticism raise any difficulties for this argument? Here's a way in which it might: (B1) is false if there are God-justifying reasons to permit a period of divine hiddenness (that's what I'll call a period of time during which a human, who is capable of relating personally to God and is not culpably in a contrary position, fails to believe in God). For if there were such reasons, then, if God existed, he would permit periods of divine hiddenness, contrary to what (B1) says. After all, God, being perfectly loving, would want what is best for his creatures. So long as it isn't intrinsically wrong to permit a period of divine hiddenness regardless of the benefits it might produce (and there seems to be no good reason for thinking this is the case), God would do so if doing so would bring about a greater good or prevent a worse evil. But (ST1)–(ST4) suggest that we're simply in the dark about whether (and how likely it is that) there are any God-justifying reasons for permitting a period of divine hiddenness. Thus, since we know that the existence of a (potentially) God-justifying reason for permitting divine hiddenness entails the falsity of (B1), and we are in the dark about the truth and the likelihood of the claim that there exists such a reason, it follows that we are likewise in the dark about the truth and likelihood of (B1).

The second argument from evil I want to look at whose vulnerability to the skeptical theist's skepticism is controversial is proposed by Paul Draper. Let 'T' be theism. Let 'HI' be the Hypothesis of Indifference—i.e. the hypothesis that neither the nature nor the condition of sentient beings on earth is due to the malevolent or benevolent actions of any non-human person. And let 'O' report what we know about the kinds, amounts, and distribution of pain and pleasure in the world. Using these abbreviations, Draper argues as follows:

(C1) O is known to be true.
(C2) HI is at least as probable intrinsically as T.
(C3) $Pr(O/HI) >! Pr(O/T)$.[19]
(C4) Therefore, other evidence held equal, T is very probably false.[20]

How might the skeptical theist's skepticism apply to this argument? Well, in order sensibly to assert (C3), we'd have to have some idea what $Pr(O/T)$ is—at the very least, we'd have to know that it's not quite high, since if $Pr(O/T)$ *is* high, (C3) is false. But it seems that $Pr(O/T)$ depends on what the likelihood is of there being a God-justifying reason for permitting the evil state of affairs described in O (i.e. if the latter is quite high, so is the former; and if the latter is quite low, so is the former). And, according to (ST1)–(ST4), we're in the dark about whether—and how likely it is—that there is such a reason. This means we're in the dark about whether that likelihood is quite high. Thus, since (1) we know that the high probability of the existence of a (potentially) God-justifying reason for permitting the evils described in O entails that $Pr(O/T)$ is high (making (C3) false) and (2) we are in the dark about whether it's highly likely that there exists such a God-justifying reason, it follows that we are likewise in the dark about the truth and likelihood of (C3).

As I've already indicated, Schellenberg and Draper object to the charge that the skeptical theist's skepticism applies to their arguments from evil.[21] As I understand them, they each offer this sort of reply: 'It's true that we know that my premise implies that it's unlikely for there to be a God-justifying reason for permitting the evil I'm focusing on. But I've given reasons for my premise. From all this it follows that these reasons for my premise double as reasons for thinking it's unlikely for there to be a God-justifying reason for permitting the evil I'm focusing on. Hence we have a reason for thinking it's unlikely for there to be such a reason, even if (ST1)–(ST4) are true.'[22]

Is this reply adequate? Can the reasons Draper and Schellenberg give for their premises successfully be used to show that it's unlikely for there to be a

God-justifying reason for permitting the evils in question? The evils they focus on are these:

(E3) the evil of there being a period of time during which a human who is capable of relating personally to God and is not culpably in a contrary position, fails to believe in God.

(E4) the evil of there being the distribution of pain and pleasure that we know there is in the world.

It's clear that there are evils worse than (E3) (e.g. that human never experiencing the beatific vision; if God were forced to inflict one or the other on a beloved creature, he would inflict (E3)). And it's clear that there are goods that outweigh (E3) (e.g. that human experiencing the beatific vision; if God wanted one of his creatures to experience the beatific vision and could do so only by permitting that creature to undergo (E3), he would permit it). The same points apply to (E4). But could an omnipotent being be *forced* to permit (E3) or (E4) or something as bad, in order to obtain some outweighing good? (ST3) suggests we are seriously in the dark about the answer to this question. Insofar as we have no reasons for thinking the entailments we know of between possible goods and evils are representative of the entailments there are between goods and evils, we simply aren't in a position to comment in an informed way about how likely it is that an omnipotent being would be forced to permit (E3) or (E4) or something as bad, in order to obtain some outweighing good. What do Schellenberg and Draper have to say about this? What reasons do they give for thinking it's false or unlikely that God would permit (E3) or (E4) that might possibly double as reasons to think it is unlikely or false that any outweighing possible good entails the permission of (E3) or (E4) or something as bad?

As I read them, they point, ultimately, to two main reasons for thinking it's false or unlikely that God (if he exists) would permit (E3) or (E4): God's perfect love and God's infinite resourcefulness.[23] But I don't quite see how either of these is at all relevant to whether any outweighing possible good entails the permission of (E3) or (E4) or something as bad. Suppose that God, if he exists, deeply loves all humans and places an exceedingly high value on having a relationship with them. What does that imply about whether some outweighing possible good entails the permission of (E3) or (E4) or something as bad? Nothing much as far as I can see. Whether some outweighing possible good entails the permission of (E3) or (E4) or something as bad is a necessary truth that doesn't seem to be relevant to whether God loves us deeply and wants a relationship with us. Likewise, suppose—as also seems plausible—that God, if he exists, has the infinite resourcefulness implied by omniscience and omnipotence. Does that suggest that no outweighing possible good entails the permission of (E3) or (E4) or something as bad? Again, I can't see how. It's widely accepted that omnipotence doesn't imply the ability to actualize what is metaphysically impossible. This means that if some outweighing possible good does entail the permission of (E3) (or something as bad), God wouldn't be able to do anything about that.

Can one sensibly appeal to God's perfect love and infinite resourcefulness to support the claim that God is unlikely to permit (E3) or (E4) and then use that result to support the further claim that no outweighing possible good entails the permission of (E3) or (E4) or something as bad? No. Once we see that God's perfect love and infinite resourcefulness don't support the conclusion that no outweighing possible good entails the permission of (E3) or (E4) or something as bad, we thereby see that there's also no reason to think they support the claim that God is unlikely to permit (E3) and (E4).

There is, however, a way in which Draper's argument has an advantage over Schellenberg's. For, given that Draper's argument focuses on comparing probabilities, he can offer the following reply (suggested by the work of Mark Bernstein[24]): 'I can grant the skeptical theist's point that I'm in the dark about Pr(O/T). But consider what we should do when deciding between inconsistent claims X and Y if we know that Pr(P/X) is high and we're completely in the dark about Pr(P/Y)—where P is some piece of evidence we have. For example, suppose we know that P, where that is the claim that the ball recently pulled out of one of two nearby urns is white. And suppose that X is the claim that the ball was randomly pulled out of the left urn and Y is the claim that the ball was randomly pulled out of the right urn. Let's say you know that the strong majority of the balls in the left urn are white and, therefore, that Pr(P/X) is high. And let's say you have no idea what Pr(P/Y) is—you have no idea whether all the balls in the right urn are white or none of them are or some fraction between 0 and 1 are white. Now, if you are offered a bet of one million dollars to identify correctly which urn the white ball was drawn from, the reasonable thing for you to do is to say X is true (i.e. that the ball came from the left urn). This shows that when you are comparing a known high probability with an unknown probability, it's reasonable to think that the unknown probability is lower than the known high probability. Thus, (C3) from Draper's argument is true even if we don't know what the value of Pr(O/T) is.'

This reply is effective if we can reasonably use the Principle of Indifference to conclude that, if the likelihood of Pr(O/T) is unknown, then the likelihood that Pr(O/T) is less than 0.5 is 0.5, and the likelihood that it is higher than 0.9 is 0.1, and the likelihood that it is between 0.11 and 0.12 is about 0.01, and so on. But suppose it's not reasonable to use the Principle of Indifference in that way in this case. Suppose instead it's reasonable to conclude, based on (ST1)–(ST4), that we have no idea what the likelihood is that Pr(O/T) is, say, higher than 0.99. Suppose the likelihood that Pr(O/T) is higher than 0.99 might be 0 or 1 or anything in between; contrary to what the Principle of Indifference suggests, we just don't know how likely it is that Pr(O/T) is higher than 0.99. Then the reply in the previous paragraph—which seems to assume that Pr(O/T) is more likely to be lower than a high probability than it is to be higher than that high probability—fails. From the failure of this reply (given the suppositions noted in this paragraph) we may conclude that *if* the skeptical theist's skepticism can reasonably be combined with rejecting the use to which the Principle of Indifference was put in the reply inspired by Bernstein in the previous paragraph, *then* the skeptical theist's skepticism causes trouble for Draper's argument.[25] I won't undertake here to discuss the antecedent of that conditional except to say that I myself don't find it implausible.[26]

II. Objections to the Skeptical Theist's Skepticism

I will consider two sorts of objections to the skeptical theist's skepticism. The first argues (1) that for some horrific evils there *appear* not to be any God-justifying reasons to permit them and (2) that this fact counts as a prima facie reason for thinking there *are* no God-justifying reasons to permit them—a prima facie reason that is not overridden by the considerations the skeptical theist highlights. The second sort of objection comes in several versions. The basic idea of each version is that by endorsing the skeptical theist's skepticism, one is committed to some other unpalatable form of skepticism (such as skepticism about the past or the external world or moral reasoning). The obvious implication is that, given that we should reject the unpalatable skepticism, we should reject the skeptical theist's skepticism too. In what follows, I'll consider and respond to both sorts of objection.

A. Objection One: The Appearance of No God-Justifying Reasons

Swinburne's objection to the skeptical theist's skepticism depends on three points. First he argues that, in the absence of any God-justifying reason we can think of for permitting horrific evils such as (E1) and (E2), *it appears that* there is no God-justifying reason for permitting them. Second, he notes that the Principle of Credulity tells us that, other things being equal, it's rational to believe that things are as they appear. Third, although the skeptical theist is right that things may be better than they appear (since there may be some unknown greater good that is secured by permitting the evil in question and that itself brings about no greater evil), we should also recognize that things might be worse than they appear (since there may be some unknown greater evil that is produced by the evil in question and that doesn't itself bring about any greater good); and since it's just as likely that things are worse than they appear as it is that they're better than they appear, we should conclude that things are probably as bad as they appear. Based on the first two points, Swinburne concludes that if we can't think of any God-justifying reason for permitting (E1) and (E2), then, other things being equal, this makes it reasonable for us to conclude that probably there is no such reason.[27] And based on the third point, Swinburne concludes that although the skeptical theist is right to point out that God may have reasons we are ignorant of, this does nothing to change the conclusion derived from the first two points.[28]

The main problem with Swinburne's objection to the skeptical theist's skepticism is that the skeptical theist thinks there is good reason not to grant his first point that *it appears that* there is no God-justifying reason for permitting evils such as (E1) and (E2). According to (ST1)–(ST4), it *doesn't* appear that there is no God-justifying reason for permitting for (E1) and (E2). Nor does it appear that there is such a reason. Nor does it appear likely that there is. Nor does it appear likely that there isn't. Rather, we just don't know how likely it is that there is a God-justifying reason for permitting evils such as (E1) and (E2). To see this, notice the difference between saying 'it appears that there are no Fs' and saying 'it doesn't appear that there are Fs'. If, while standing in a friend's garage that is normal in size and uncluttered, you look around and can't see an automobile in it, then it's reasonable for you to conclude both that *it doesn't appear that there is an automobile in the garage* and that *it appears that there is no automobile in the garage*. But suppose instead you are standing on the street and, upon looking into a rather cluttered garage, you fail to see any fleas. Then, although it's rational for you to conclude that *it doesn't appear (to you upon looking from the street) that there are fleas in the garage*, it's not rational to conclude that *it appears that there are no fleas in the garage*. According to (ST1)–(ST4), we've no good reason to deny that God-justifying reasons for permitting (E1) and (E2) sought for from our vantage point (apart from divine revelation) are like fleas in a cluttered garage viewed from the street. Hence, we can't reasonably conclude, as Swinburne does, that *it appears that there is no God-justifying reason for permitting evils such as (E1) and (E2)*. At best we can reasonably conclude that *it doesn't appear (to us) that there is a God-justifying reason for permitting (E1) and (E2)*. But of course that can't be used in conjunction with Swinburne's Principle of Credulity to get him the conclusion he's after in responding to the skeptical theist's skepticism. For if it could, then we could use a Swinburne-like response to conclude, on the basis of our failure to see any fleas in the garage when looking from the street, that there probably aren't any in the garage.

Thus, Swinburne misconstrues the skeptical theist's response. He thinks the skeptical theist's aim is to show that the likelihood of some evil or other on theism might for all we know be higher than it initially appears. And he replies that similar remarks show that it might for all we know be lower than it initially appears. And he replies that similar remarks show that it might for all we know be higher than it initially appears. Since, according to him, it's just as likely to be higher than it initially appears as it is to be lower than it initially appears, it's reasonable to go with initial appearances. But in fact, the skeptical theist's response is that we aren't justified in thinking the probability judgment initially appears the way Swinburne says it appears. Clear thinking and reflection on (ST1)–(ST4) reveal that there's no particular value or range (short of the range between 0 and 1) that the probability in question appears to be.[29]

Swinburne's (1998: 23) response to the remarks in the previous paragraph is as follows:[30]

And if our understanding of possible reasons why anyone might allow suffering to occur provides us with no reason for supposing that a good God might allow certain suffering, we ought to believe that there is no God—unless we have a contrary reason. Just reflect on some of the horrors that we read about in our newspapers and history books: the prolonged cruelty of parents to lonely children, the torture of the innocent, the long-drawn-out acute physical pain of some disease, and so on. If we cannot see all that as a reason for believing that there is no all-good and all-powerful being, when we cannot think of any reason why such a being should allow it all to happen, there really is something deeply wrong with *us*. We have lost our sensitivity to the good.

In short, if we don't conclude, upon our failure to think of any God-justifying reason for permitting evils like (E1) and (E2), that (other things being equal) there probably is no God, we have lost our sensitivity to the good.[31] I find this extremely unpersuasive. What I grant is that if we can't see that a good God would, other things being equal, want to prevent horrific evils, then it seems we have lost our sensitivity to the good. When we see or learn of utterly horrific suffering, the sensible and appropriate response is to be extremely upset that it has occurred and, with deep feeling, to think 'There had better be a good reason for God, if he exists, to permit that suffering; if there isn't, then there is no perfectly good God.'

But although it's extremely common, it's not reasonable, given (ST1)–(ST4), to go on from there to think that it's *unlikely* that there is a God-justifying reason for permitting such suffering (and, hence, unlikely that God exists). For the only basis we have for that conclusion is our own inability to think of any such reason. Suppose I'm considering possible goods, possible evils, and possible entailment relations between them with the aim of discovering a (potentially) God-justifying reason for permitting (E1) and (E2). If I accept (ST1)–(ST4), then my failure, upon engaging in such a search, to discover any God-justifying reason for permitting (E1) and (E2) won't lead me to conclude that there is no such reason. In refraining from drawing that conclusion, I'll be just as rational as the person who refrains from concluding there are no fleas in the garage on the basis of a failure to see any when looking from the street. Does the fact that I refrain under these conditions from concluding that there are no God-justifying reasons for permitting (E1) and (E2) (or even that it's unlikely that there are any such reasons) demonstrate that I've lost my sensitivity to the good? Hardly. It demonstrates only that I don't want to jump inappropriately to unfounded conclusions (about fleas in the garage or about God-justifying reasons). But if it's reasonable for me to refrain from concluding that it's false or unlikely that there are God-justifying reasons for permitting (E1) and (E2) (on the basis of my failure to discover any such reasons), then it's also reasonable for me to refrain from concluding on that basis that it's false or unlikely that God exists. Such reasonable thinking does nothing to suggest any insensitivity to the good.

B. Objection Two: Commitment to Unpalatable Skepticism

This second type of objection to skeptical theism seems to be the most common, though (as I've already noted) it comes in different forms, depending on what sort of unpalatable skepticism it focuses on. I'll briefly consider four forms of this objection.

B.1. Skepticism about Certain Theistic Arguments

The first charge of skeptical commitment is the charge that if one endorses the skeptical theist's skepticism, one can't consistently endorse certain arguments for theism.[32] In particular, some arguments for God's existence based on identifying something as an all-things-considered good—even in light of its consequences—will be undermined by the skeptical theist's skepticism. So, for example, if the order one sees in the natural world or the joy one witnesses in people's lives is identified as reason to think that there is a good being who is the cause of such things, one is failing to take into account the lessons of (ST1)–(ST4). Given our cognitive limitations, we simply don't know what evils might be entailed by those good things and this prevents us from being able to conclude that they are all-things-considered goods that an omnibenevolent being would bring about.

The skeptical theist's response to this charge should, I think, be to accept it. We aren't able to determine whether something is an all-things-considered good simply by noticing how good it is since we don't know what it might bring in its wake. Of course, perhaps there are other ways of learning something is an all-things-considered good. Maybe divine revelation is such a way. But given that theists don't seem to be able to arrange for divine revelation to be passed on to non-theists, this way of learning something is an all-things-considered good won't be of much help in offering a theistic argument that will be persuasive to a non-theist. We needn't conclude from this that the skeptical theist's skepticism is inconsistent with *every* way of arguing for the existence of a good God (just as we needn't conclude it is inconsistent with every atheistic argument). But there's no doubt that some theistic arguments collapse under pressure from (ST1)–(ST4).

B.2. Skeptical Theism No Matter How Much Evil There Is

The second charge of skeptical commitment is the charge that skeptical theists are forced to admit that, no matter how much suffering or evil we witness, we cannot reasonably conclude that God wouldn't permit it. As Rowe puts it, even 'if human life were *nothing more than a series of agonizing moments from birth to death*, [the skeptical theists'] position would still require them to say that we cannot reasonably infer that it is even likely that God does not exist'.[33] But since this is an absurd conclusion, Rowe argues, the skeptical theist's skepticism, which forces her to this absurd conclusion, must also be mistaken.

This charge does not stick. It's true that, given (ST1)–(ST4), we can't determine *merely by trying to consider the consequences of goods and evils* whether a certain amount or kind of suffering is such that there couldn't be a God-justifying reason to permit it. But there are other ways of determining this that don't rely on considerations of consequences. Tooley has proposed, as a premise in one of his arguments from evil, the principle that God would permit horrific suffering only for the benefit of the sufferer.[34] I don't find that particular moral principle plausible.[35] But there are others like it that seem more promising. Swinburne (1998: 229–36) argues that a perfectly good God would not permit suffering unless the sufferer's life is on the whole a good one (notice that this is a weaker requirement than Tooley's according to which the reason the suffering is permitted must be to benefit the sufferer). It's true that Swinburne is no friend of skeptical theism, but I see no reason why those endorsing the skeptical theist's skepticism couldn't consistently accept this principle Swinburne proposes (since we can see the truth of such general principles even if we can't see what all the consequences of the goods and evils we know of are). And by accepting this principle, skeptical theists would have reason to say that a good God would not permit a human life to be literally *nothing more* than a series of agonizing moments from birth to death.

B.3. Skepticism about the Past and the External World

According to a third charge, those who endorse the skeptical theist's skepticism are committed to skepticism about the external world and the past. The idea is basically that, given (ST1)–(ST4), I have no idea whether there is a God-justifying reason to permit or to arrange for the following bad states of affairs to obtain:

(E5) My being a bodiless victim of an evil demon who deceives me into thinking there's an external physical world when in fact there is not.

(E6) My being deceived by an evil demon into believing that I and the physical universe have been around for years when in fact I and the physical universe came into existence five minutes ago (me with false memories, the physical universe with the misleading appearance of being old).

Given this, the objector concludes that if I endorse the skeptical theist's skepticism, I should likewise endorse skepticism about the external world and about the past.

The skeptical theist's reply is to note that our way of knowing that (E5) and (E6) aren't actual is *not* by considering possible goods, possible evils, and entailments between them—seeing that these provide no God-justifying reason to permit the obtaining of (E5) and (E6) and concluding that, since God exists, (E5) and (E6) must not be actual.[36] Not at all. Rather, we have some independent way of knowing that (E5) and (E6) aren't actual and we can conclude, from the fact that they aren't actual, that if God exists, he has no good reason to arrange for them to be actual. This way of knowing something about God's reasons is consistent with (ST1)–(ST4). (What is the independent way—i.e. independent of considering possible God-justifying reasons for permitting (E5) and (E6)—in which we know (E5) and (E6) aren't actual? Epistemologists offer many different answers to this question. This isn't the place to explore these answers. But it's widely held, by theists and non-theists, that we have some independent way of knowing that (E5) and (E6) aren't actual.[37])

Why can't the proponent of the argument from evil make the same sort of move? Why can't she say that we know independently that there's no God-justifying reason for permitting evils such as (E1) and (E2)—not by surveying possible goods, possible evils, and entailments between them but in some other way? That's certainly a strategy worth considering. But what we need is some plausible suggestion of what that independent way of knowing might be. And in the case of the arguments from evil we've been considering, no such suggestion is forthcoming. It's not plausible to claim that we know independently that such a supremely loving and resourceful being as God is likely to prevent evils such as (E1) and (E2) (or (E3) and (E4) mentioned above in connection with Draper and Schellenberg). What we seem to know independently is that a perfect being definitely wouldn't permit (E1)–(E4) without a God-justifying reason for doing so. But this doesn't enable us to know independently that God is likely to prevent (E1)–(E4), not unless we have some independent way of knowing that *it is unlikely for there to be a God-justifying reason for permitting those evils*. But plausible suggestions of independent ways of knowing *that*—ways that don't rely on our failure to think of any such reasons upon considering possible goods, possible evils, and entailments between them—are in short supply.

B.4. Skepticism about Morality

Perhaps the most common and influential charge of skeptical commitment lodged against skeptical theists is the one that says that, by endorsing the skeptical theist's skepticism, we are forced into an appalling sort of skepticism about the morality of various actions. For example, the skeptical theist's skepticism tells us that we have no good reason to think that the horrific rape and murder of a small child won't bring about some outweighing greater good. Given this, why should we think it's good to prevent such horrific suffering if we are easily able to do so? According to this sort of objector, considerations like these suggest that consistency requires the skeptical theist to be skeptical about whether it's right to prevent such horrific suffering when we easily can. But skepticism about such moral issues as these is both appalling and implausible. Hence, the skeptical theist's skepticism, which supposedly leads to this unpalatable moral skepticism, should be rejected.[38]

By way of response, those (theists and non-theists) who accept the skeptical theist's skepticism can offer the following proposals about how we make moral decisions. First, it is very often important in making moral decisions that we consider the consequences of our actions—the good and the harm that we think will result from our choices. We can acknowledge this while at the same time recognizing that we may have some duties that constrain our behavior independently of the consequences of our actions. (So, as already noted at the end of sect. I.A, recognizing the importance of considering consequences doesn't commit us to a consequentialist moral theory.) Second, in cases where it *is* important for us to be guided by considerations of possible good and bad consequences of our actions, we aren't morally bound to do what *in fact* has the overall best consequences (since we typically can't determine that). What is relevant are the likely consequences we have some reason to be confident about after a reasonable amount of time and effort aimed at identifying the expected results of our behavior. If, after such consideration, a particular course of action seems clearly to maximize the good (or minimize the bad) among the consequences we're able to identify and we non-culpably and reasonably take ourselves to have no overriding consequence-independent obligation to refrain from that action, then that action is a morally appropriate one for us to perform. Third, God's moral decision-making can be viewed as analogous to our own as it was just described. God too will seek to bring about the best consequences except in cases where what morality requires is not dependent on consequences. And, in those cases where consequences of an action matter, God too will put the right amount of effort and time into determining what the best consequences are. (Of course, in God's case, this might require no time and not much effort; and, unlike in our case, what God *thinks* is the action with the best consequences *is* the action with the best consequences.[39]) Fourth, when considering whether to permit someone to suffer in order to bring about some outweighing good, it matters tremendously what one's relationship is to the one permitted to suffer. It may be morally appropriate for me to allow or even bring about certain minor sorts of suffering in my own child for her good whereas similar treatment of some stranger's child would be morally inappropriate. Likewise, it may be morally appropriate for your loving and omniscient creator to permit you to experience preventable horrific suffering in order to achieve some good whereas it wouldn't be morally appropriate for another human to do so.

In light of the four considerations from the previous paragraph, the 'moral skepticism' objection to skeptical theism seems to lose its force. The fact that we're in the dark about whether there are reasons that would justify *a perfect being* in permitting easily preventable horrific suffering doesn't give us a reason to doubt that *we* ought to prevent easily preventable horrific suffering when, even after taking a reasonable amount of time and effort, we can think of no outweighing goods that will be achieved by our permitting it. For we are reasonable and moral to base our decision on the likely consequences we know of and ignore the far-off ones we're ignorant of (only the most committed actual-consequence consequentialist would think otherwise). Moreover, in the case of preventing easily preventable horrific suffering, we know we have a prima facie duty to prevent great harm to others when this is easy for us to do and that this gives us a strong prima facie reason to prevent the suffering. If after a reasonable amount of time and effort we can't think of any negative consequence of such suffering-prevention that might outweigh its obvious goodness, then we ought to prevent the suffering we have strong prima facie reason to prevent—even though we don't know the long-term consequences of such prevention (again, only a diehard actual-consequence consequentialist would think otherwise). And even if we knew that the overall consequences that would result from permitting the easily preventable horrific suffering would be good, it's not at all clear that we have the sort of relationship with the sufferer (e.g. we aren't the sufferer's loving creator) that makes it appropriate to permit the person's horrific suffering for the sake of some greater good.

Derk Pereboom has responded on behalf of the 'moral skepticism' objection by arguing that skeptical theists have a reason for thinking they shouldn't intervene to prevent easily preventable horrific suffering. Pereboom makes his case by comparing two scenarios.[40] In the first, Jack (a nurse) knows that morphine will ease the suffering of the patients in the clinic in which he assists doctors. But he's noticed that in his experience, the doctors never give morphine to the bone cancer patients though they give it to other patients. He has no idea why this hasn't been done (at least not when he's been watching) or whether they've given morphine to bone cancer patients in the past. On a day when the doctors are unable to make it into work, he has the opportunity to relieve the suffering of bone cancer patients. But (says Pereboom) Jack clearly has some significant moral reason not to give the patients morphine. In the second scenario, Sue is a doctor who has (rationally) become a skeptical theist. She sees that God has for millennia let people suffer from a disease X. But a cure has just been developed and she has an opportunity to administer it. It seems (says Pereboom) that just as Jack has a significant moral reason not to give the patients morphine, so also Sue has a parallel reason not to administer the cure for disease X.

The problem with this response by Pereboom is that the most we should suspect (based on noticing that the disease has progressed in humans unchecked for millennia) is that a person with a relationship to humans such as the one God has with them has a reason not to administer the cure. In Jack's case, he knows that he has to the patients a relationship sufficiently like the relationship the doctors have—i.e. a human caregiver—so he knows that if the doctors have a right to withhold the morphine for some greater good, he does too. But it's clear to Sue that she doesn't have a relationship to other humans that is like that of a loving creator to his creatures. She thinks she does not have the right to let them suffer terribly for their moral development, say, even though God does have that right in light of his relationship with them. So although Jack has a good reason to hesitate rather than relieve the suffering of the bone cancer patients, Sue does not have such a reason to hesitate rather than administer the cure for disease X. Thus, the 'moral skepticism' objection to skeptical theism—like the other objections I've considered in sect. II—does not succeed.

NOTES

My thanks to Paul Draper, Tom Flint, Patrick Kain, Trenton Merricks, Michael Rea, William Rowe, and Chris Tucker for helpful comments on earlier drafts.

1. A God-justifying reason for permitting an evil E is, as you might guess, a reason for permitting E that would justify God, if God existed, in permitting E.

2. Draper (unpublished) and Howard-Snyder (forthcoming) both express this sort of concern, though Draper confesses there to being the one to introduce the terminology in print in his 1996.

3. Unfortunately, that first approximation needs some tweaking. For starters, as Plantinga 1967: 120 points out, G's possessing the two features noted won't guarantee that the aim of obtaining G can be used to justify God in permitting E. Suppose, for example, that G is a conjunctive good (G*&E). It may be that because G* is so good, the goodness of (G*&E), outweighs the badness of E. And clearly (G*&E) entails E. So the conjunctive good (G*&E) has the two features noted above. But this doesn't guarantee that the aim of obtaining (G*&E) would justify God in permitting E. For suppose that G* doesn't entail E and that G*'s goodness is greater than the goodness of the conjunctive good (G*&E). In that case, it seems God could have done better by obtaining G* instead of the conjunctive good (G*&E) and that he could do so without permitting E. Rowe (1979: 10) and Plantinga (1967: 121) suggest ways to handle this difficulty. The basic idea is to say that if G is to justify God in permitting E, then, in addition to satisfying the two conditions identified above in the text, it must also be the case that (3) there is no distinct good G* that is as good or better than G and could be obtained without permitting E (or something as bad or worse).

   Another complication that needs to be mentioned has to do with the Molinist view that there are counterfactuals of freedom that are true of individual creaturely essences even before those essences are instantiated as free creatures. According to this view, the truth of these counterfactuals of freedom is contingent. Moreover, on one plausible notion of freedom, God (if he exists) wouldn't have control over their truth, despite their contingency. So—in addition to necessary truths having to do with entailment relations between possible goods and possible evils—there might be these contingent truths that place additional constraints on what God can bring about. (For an account of how such truths might place constraints on what God can do, see Plantinga 1974: ch. 9. For a defense of the view that there are true counterfactuals of freedom, see Flint 1998.) To deal with these concerns about counterfactuals of freedom that might place limitations on what God (if he exists) is able to bring about, we need to say something about how to interpret the 'couldn't' in clause (2) and the 'could' in clause (3). To say 'G couldn't be obtained without permitting E' is to say that God (if he exists) is not able to bring about G without permitting E—either because G's obtaining entails the permission of E or because G's obtaining *together with the counterfactuals of freedom that are contingently true of individual creaturely essences* entails the permission of E. Likewise, to say 'G* could be obtained without permitting E' is to say that God (if he exists) is able to obtain G* without permitting E—because it's the case both that G*'s obtaining doesn't entail the permission of E and that G's obtaining *together with the counterfactuals of freedom that are contingently true of individual creaturely essences* doesn't entail the permission of E.

For simplicity's sake, I will continue to focus in the main text only on clauses (1) and (2) mentioned there. But clause (3) should also be understood as being required and the interpretation of clauses (2) and (3) mentioned at the end of the previous paragraph in this note should also be assumed.

4. Probably the best place to start in getting a feel for the skeptical theist's position is William Alston's 1991. Peter van Inwagen's 1991 is also a good resource for this purpose. Wykstra's 1984 is a classic for contemporary skeptical theists (and their opponents), though he focuses on formulating a general epistemic principle (for when we are entitled to claim 'it appears that p') instead of on explaining and defending the rationale behind the skeptical theist's views as Alston does.

5. These are from Bergmann 2001.

6. The inscrutable evils we see around us are those that many thoughtful atheists and theists agree are ones for which we can't think of a God-justifying reason.

7. As I mentioned in n. 3, the Molinist view that there are true counterfactuals of freedom reminds us that—in addition to necessary truths having to do with entailment relations between possible goods and possible evils—there may be some contingent truths that place additional constraints on what God can bring about. It's worth noting here that if that Molinist view is true, we've no reason to think that what we in fact know about these contingent truths for all creaturely essences—instantiated and uninstantiated—is representative of what there is to know about them (again, I have in mind representativeness relative to the property of their figuring in a potentially God-justifying reason for permitting the inscrutable evils we see around us).

8. It may not be true, as a general rule, that an inference from a sample is justified only if the person making the inference explicitly believes that the sample is representative. But justification for such inferences *does* require that it's false that the person making the inference does or should disbelieve or (due to uncertainty) withhold the proposition that the sample in question is representative (in the relevant respect). And those who recognize the truth of (ST1)–(ST3) *should*, it seems, withhold (due to uncertainty) the propositions about the representativeness of the samples there mentioned.

9. This is how John Beaudoin formulates this skeptical thesis, which is reflected in the work of Alston (1996: 324), Howard-Snyder (1996a: 302–3), and van Inwagen (1991: 161–2). See Beaudoin 2005: 50.

10. See Alston 1996: 325 and van Inwagen 1991: 162–3.

11. To say it applies to an argument isn't to say it's right. Rather, it's to say that if the skeptical theist's skepticism is right, then these arguments fail.

12. (E1) and (E2) are the evils of the horrific deaths of the fawn and the 5-year-old girl, both mentioned earlier in this chapter.

13. This summary of the argument given in his 1988 and 1991 is from Rowe 1996: 262–3.

14. And by Rowe's lights too, it seems. See ibid. 267 where he says that he thinks 'this argument is, at best, a weak argument' and he proposes 'to abandon this argument altogether'.

15. This argument is proposed in Rowe 1996.

16. See Alston 1996: 323–5; Bergmann 2001: 294 n. 9; Howard-Snyder 1996a: 295; and Plantinga 1998: 534 for this objection to P. See Plantinga 1998 and Bergmann 2001 for further objections to this third argument by Rowe; and see Rowe 1998, 2001 for his replies.

17. In Schellenberg (2002: 51) this proposition is called 'P2'.

18. To culpably be in a contrary position involves one's own free choice: 'whether it is the free choice to ignore a God we are aware of, or to take steps to remove that awareness, and so to remove ourselves from that place where we are in a position to relate personally to God' (ibid. 42–3).

19. $\Pr(X/Y) >! \Pr(X/Z)$ says that the probability of X given Y is *much* greater than the probability of X given Z.

20. He gives the argument this formulation in Draper 2004: 45 n. 6. He defends something like this argument in Draper 1989.

21. See Schellenberg 1996 and Draper 1996, both of which make it clear that they would like to avoid conflict with the skeptical theist's skepticism—presumably because they think there is some merit to that skepticism.

22. Draper has made this sort of point to me in email correspondence in July 2006. See also Schellenberg 1996: 456–9.

23. See Draper 1989: 17–18 and Schellenberg 2002: 42–52.

24. See Bernstein 1998: 155–6.

25. I should note that Bernstein himself makes no explicit appeal to the Principle of Indifference in laying out his objection, but I think that is what's lurking behind his reasoning.

26. Consider the following comment by Hájek (2003: sect. 3.1) on how philosophers think about applications of the Principle of Indifference: 'This brings us to one of the chief points of controversy regarding the classical interpretation. Critics accuse the principle of indifference of extracting information from ignorance. Proponents reply that it rather codifies the way in which such ignorance should be epistemically managed—for anything other than an equal assignment of probabilities would represent the possession of some knowledge. Critics counter-reply that in a state of complete ignorance, it is better to assign vague probabilities (perhaps vague over the entire [0, 1] interval), or to eschew the assignment of probabilities altogether.' One further possibility to consider is that—because of differences in the amount or degree of ignorance in particular cases—the Principle of Indifference may be sensibly

applied in some cases of ignorance whereas eschewing the assignment of probabilities altogether may be appropriate in other cases (and the latter approach may be best in the cases discussed by skeptical theists).

27. As becomes clear in his 1998, Swinburne himself thinks we *can* think of God-justifying reasons for permitting evils such as (E1) and (E2) so he doesn't endorse the atheist's argument.

28. These three points come out in Swinburne 1998: 20–8.

29. Remarks similar to those I've made in these last few paragraphs apply to what William Hasker 2004—another theist who rejects skeptical theism—says.

30. In correspondence, Swinburne pointed me to these remarks of his when I mentioned to him the points raised in the previous paragraph.

31. Gale 1996: 214 says something similar.

32. See e.g. Wilks 2004: 317–18.

33. Rowe 2001: 298.

34. From this he concludes that God would not permit animals to suffer lonely, horrific deaths since, he thinks, they cannot benefit from them. See Tooley 1991: 111. Stump 1985, 1990 also endorses a principle like this, though, unlike Tooley, she maintains it while defending theism against arguments from evil rather than using it to argue for atheism.

35. See van Inwagen 1988: 121–2 and Swinburne 1998: 223–36 for some reasons to doubt it.

36. See Beaudoin 2005: 45 and Bergmann 2001: 295 n. 27.

37. My own account of how we know (E5) and (E6) aren't actual is discussed in Bergmann 2006: 206–11.

38. This charge is developed in a number of places. See Almeida and Oppy 2003; Pereboom 2004; Hasker 2004; Russell 1996; and Tooley 1991. For replies to this line of reasoning see Bergmann 2001; Bergmann and Rea 2005; and Howard-Snyder forthcoming.

39. Or at least this is so if we assume the falsity of the open theist's conception of God.

40. See Pereboom 2004: 164–5.

REFERENCES

ALMEIDA, MICHAEL, and OPPY, GRAHAM (2003). 'Sceptical Theism and Evidential Arguments from Evil'. *Australasian Journal of Philosophy* 81: 496–516.

ALSTON, WILLIAM (1991). 'The Inductive Argument from Evil and the Human Cognitive Condition', *Philosophical Perspectives* 5: 29–67; repr. in Howard-Snyder 1996*b*: 97–125. Page references are to the reprint.

—— (1996). 'Some (Temporarily) Final Thoughts on Evidential Arguments from Evil', in Howard-Snyder 1996*b*: 311–32.

BEAUDOIN, JOHN (2005). 'Skepticism and the Skeptical Theist', *Faith and Philosophy* 22: 42–56.

BERGMANN, MICHAEL (2001). 'Skeptical Theism and Rowe's New Evidential Argument from Evil', *Noûs* 35: 278–96.

—— (2006). *Justification without Awareness*. Oxford: Oxford University Press.

——and REA, MICHAEL (2005). 'In Defence of Sceptical Theism: A Reply to Almeida and Oppy', *American Philosophical Quarterly* 83: 241–51.

BERNSTEIN, MARK (1998). 'Explaining Evil', *Religious Studies* 34: 151–63.

DRAPER, PAUL (1989). 'Pain and Pleasure: An Evidential Problem for Theists', *Noûs* 23: 331–50; repr. in Howard-Snyder 1996b: 12–29. Page references are to the reprint.

——(1996). 'The Skeptical Theist', in Howard-Snyder 1996b: 175–92.

DRAPER, PAUL (2004). 'More Pain and Pleasure: A Reply to Otte', in Peter van Inwagen (ed.), *Christian Faith and the Problem of Evil*. Grand Rapids: William B. Eerdmans, 41–54.

——(unpublished). 'Partisanship and Inquiry in Philosophy of Religion', presented as an invited symposium paper at the Central Division Meeting of the American Philosophical Association in Chicago, April 2006.

FLINT, THOMAS (1998). *Divine Providence: The Molinist Account*. Ithaca: Cornell University Press.

GALE, RICHARD (1996). 'Some Difficulties in Theistic Treatments of Evil', in Howard-Snyder 1996b: 206–18.

HÁJEK, ALAN (2003). 'Interpretations of Probability', in Edward N. Zalta (ed.), *The Stanford Encyclopedia of Philosophy (Summer Edition)*, <http://plato.stanford.edu/archives/sum2003/entries/probability-interpret/>, accessed 22 May 2008.

HASKER, WILLIAM (2004). 'The Sceptical Solution to the Problem of Evil', in William Hasker, *Providence, Evil, and the Openness of God*. London: Routledge, 43–57.

HOWARD-SNYDER, DANIEL (ed.), (1996a). 'The Argument from Inscrutable Evil', in Howard-Snyder 1996b: 286–310.

——(1996b). *The Evidential Argument from Evil*. Bloomington: Indiana University Press.

——(forthcoming). 'Does Skepticism about Arguments from Evil Lead to Moral Skepticism?' *Oxford Studies in Philosophy of Religion*.

PEREBOOM, DERK (2004). 'The Problem of Evil', in William Mann (ed.), *The Blackwell Guide to the Philosophy of Religion*. Oxford: Blackwell, 148–70.

PLANTINGA, ALVIN (1967). *God and Other Minds*. Ithaca, NY: Cornell University Press.

——(1974). *The Nature of Necessity*. Oxford: Oxford University Press.

——(1998). 'Degenerate Evidence and Rowe's New Evidential Argument from Evil', *Noûs* 32: 532–44.

ROWE, WILLIAM (1979). 'The Problem of Evil and Some Varieties of Atheism', *American Philosophical Quarterly* 16: 225–41; repr. in Howard-Snyder 1996b: 1–11. Page references are to the reprint.

——(1988). 'Evil and Theodicy', *Philosophical Topics*. 16: 119–32.

——(1991). 'Ruminations about Evil', *Philosophical Perspectives* 5: 69–88.

——(1996). 'The Evidential Argument from Evil: A Second Look', in Howard-Snyder 1996b: 262–85.

——(1998). 'Reply to Plantinga', *Noûs* 32: 545–52.

——(2001). 'Skeptical Theism: A Response to Bergmann', *Noûs* 35: 297–303.

RUSSELL, BRUCE (1996). 'Defenseless', in Howard-Snyder 1996b: 193–205.

SCHELLENBERG, JOHN (1996). 'Response to Howard-Snyder', *Canadian Journal of Philosophy* 26: 455–62.

——(2002). 'What the Hiddenness of God Reveals: A Collaborative Discussion', in Daniel Howard-Snyder and Paul Moser (eds.), *Divine Hiddenness: New Essays*. New York: Cambridge University Press, 33–61.

STUMP, ELEONORE (1985). 'The Problem of Evil', *Faith and Philosophy* 2: 392–423.

—— (1990). 'Providence and the Problem of Evil', in Thomas Flint (ed.), *Christian Philoso-phy*. Notre Dame: University of Notre Dame Press.

SWINBURNE, RICHARD (1998). *Providence and the Problem of Evil*. Oxford: Oxford University Press.

TOOLEY, MICHAEL (1991). 'The Argument from Evil', *Philosophical Perspectives* 5: 89–134.

VAN INWAGEN, PETER (1988). 'The Magnitude, Duration, and Distribution of Evil', *Philo-sophical Topics* 16: 161–87. Reprinted in Peter van Inwagen, *God, Knowledge, and Mystery*. Ithaca: Cornell University Press, 96–122. Page references are to the reprint.

—— (1991). 'The Problem of Evil, the Problem of Air, and the Problem of Silence', *Philo-sophical Perspectives* 5: 135–65; repr. in Howard-Snyder 1996b: 151–74. Page references are to the reprint.

WILKS, IAN (2004). 'The Structure of the Contemporary Debate on the Problem of Evil', *Religious Studies* 40: 307–21.

WYKSTRA, STEPHEN (1984). 'The Human Obstacle to Evidential Arguments from Suffering: On Avoiding the Evils of "Appearance" ', *International Journal for Philosophy of Religion* 16: 73–94.

—— (1996). 'Rowe's Noseeum Arguments from Evil', in Howard-Snyder 1996b: 126–50.

PART IV

TOPICS IN CHRISTIAN PHILOSOPHICAL THEOLOGY

CHAPTER 18

THE TRINITY

MICHAEL C. REA

ONE of the central mysteries of the Christian faith concerns the tri-unity of God. According to traditional Christian doctrine, God is *three persons* who are somehow *consubstantial*—one in substance. The persons are the Father, the Son, and the Holy Spirit. Each person possesses all the traditional divine attributes—omnipotence, omniscience, perfect goodness, eternality, and so on. And yet (in the words of the Athanasian Creed), 'they are not three eternals, but there is one eternal ... there are not three almighties, but there is one almighty ... there are not three Gods, but there is one God.'[1] But what does all of this really mean? And how could it possibly be true?

In addressing these two very general questions, there are several more specific issues on which we might try to focus. One is interpretative: how were the central terms in the doctrine—terms such as *person*, *substance*, and *consubstantial*—understood when the doctrine was first formulated, and how have they evolved throughout the history of the doctrine? Another is more straightforwardly philosophical: how could three distinct persons (in any reasonable sense of that term) be consubstantial in a way that would make them countable as *one God*? These questions are not wholly distinct from one another, and there are many others in the neighborhood that are also worth pursuing. But the one on which I will focus is the second. More exactly, I'll explore various attempts to show that the central statements in the doctrine, under some intelligible and orthodox interpretation, do not imply a contradiction. Along the way, I'll touch a bit on the first question, but for the most part it will be set aside.[2]

The question that concerns us here is commonly referred to by philosophers as 'the logical problem of the Trinity' and by theologians as 'the threeness–oneness problem'. The goal of the first section of this chapter is to explain in some detail just what the problem is supposed to be. I'll begin by stating the central theses of the doctrine of the Trinity. Then I will formulate the logical problem of the Trinity and lay out the constraints that a solution must satisfy in order to preserve an orthodox understanding of the doctrine. In the next section, I will briefly sketch a few of the most important solutions to the problem. Finally, in sect. 3, I'll present my own view of the Trinity and argue that it has both better historical pedigree and better prospects for solving the problem of the Trinity than the rival views presented in sect. 2.

1. THE PROBLEM OF THE TRINITY

The two creeds to which contemporary Christians typically look for 'official' expressions of Trinitarian doctrine are the Nicene-Constantinopolitan Creed of 380/1 and the Athanasian Creed (c.500). The fourth and fifth centuries witnessed a great deal of philosophical reflection and controversy over the doctrine of the Trinity, and the language of these two creeds is in large part a product of that discussion.[3] The former creed is a revised and expanded version of the Creed of Nicaea, which was produced by the First Nicene Council in AD 325. (Nowadays the Nicene-Constantinopolitan Creed is typically called just the 'Nicene Creed'. I'll follow this usage.) Like its predecessor, the Nicene Creed was written in Greek and subsequently translated into Latin. It includes the following words:

We believe in one God, the Father, almighty, maker of heaven and earth, of all things visible and invisible; And in one Lord Jesus Christ, the only-begotten Son of God, begotten from the Father before all ages, light from light, true God from true God, begotten not made, of one substance [homoousion] with the Father...And in the Holy Spirit, the Lord and life-giver, Who proceeds from the Father, Who with the Father and the Son is together worshipped and together glorified, Who spoke through the prophets.

(Schwartz 1914: 244–50; quoted in Kelly 1972: 297–8)

I have highlighted the Greek term 'homoousion' (ὁμοόυσιον) because that term—the term we translate as 'consubstantial' or 'of the same essence' or 'of one substance'— was at the center of some of the most important fourth-century debates about the doctrine of the Trinity.

The Athanasian Creed—named after, but not written by, the famous fourth-century defender of Nicene orthodoxy, Athanasius—was written in Latin, and includes the following statements:

Now this is the catholic faith, that we worship one God in Trinity, and the Trinity in unity, without either confusing the persons or dividing the substance. For the Father's person is one, the Son's another, the Holy Spirit's another; but the Godhead of the Father, the Son, and the Holy Spirit is one, their glory equal, their majesty co-eternal. Such as the Father is, such is the Son, such also the Holy Spirit. . . . Thus the Father is God, the Son God, and the Holy Spirit God; and yet there are not three Gods, but there is one God. Thus the Father is Lord, the Son Lord, the Holy Spirit Lord; and yet there are not three Lords but there is one Lord. . . . Because just as we are obliged by Christian truth to acknowledge each person separately both God and Lord, so we are forbidden by the catholic religion to speak of three Gods or Lords.   (Kelly 1964: 17–20, repr. in Leith 1972: 705)

The Athanasian Creed is widely regarded as manifesting a bias toward 'Latin' theories of the Trinity (see sect. 2 below).

In the two passages just quoted, we have the three central tenets of the doctrine:[4]

(T1) There is exactly one God, the Father almighty.[5]
(T2) Father, Son, and Holy Spirit are not identical.
(T3) Father, Son, and Holy Spirit are consubstantial.

Each creed includes each of these tenets, if not explicitly, then by implication. The Nicene Creed affirms (T1) in its first line (though the 'exactly' is only implied). It also explicitly affirms the Father–Son components of (T2) and (T3). The distinctness and consubstantiality of the Spirit are implicit in the remark that the Holy Spirit is 'together worshipped and together glorified' with the Father and the Son. Moreover, they are explicitly affirmed in the Synodical Letter written in 382 by the same council that produced the Nicene Creed.[6] The Athanasian Creed enjoins us not to confound the persons or divide the substance, thus committing to (T2) and (T3). It also affirms (T1): we worship *one* God, and the Father is God. To be sure, it says a lot more than this (for example, it says that the Son is God too); but the more that it says is pretty clearly just a listing of some of the logical consequences of the conjunction of (T1) and (T3).

The logical problem of the Trinity is just the fact that (T1)–(T3) appear to be mutually inconsistent. There are various ways of trying to demonstrate the inconsistency, but the one I favor focuses on the (apparent) meaning of *consubstantiality*. To say that x and y are consubstantial, or of the same substance is, it seems, just to say that x and y share a common nature—i.e. they are members of *one and the same kind*. To say that *two* divine beings are consubstantial, then, would be to say that the two beings in question are *identical with respect to their divinity*: neither is subordinate to the other; they are not divine in different ways; and if one is a God, then the other one is too. (Note, by the way, that 'God' functions in (T1) above as a kind-term, like *man*, and not as a name, like *Fred*. Thus, though it looks a bit odd, it makes perfect sense to speak of the Father as *a* God. If 'God' were functioning as a name, then (T1) would be saying something very much like 'There is exactly one YHWH,' which isn't so much a monotheistic claim as a rather strange way of asserting the existence of YHWH.)

Given all this, the logical problem of the Trinity can be expressed as follows:

(LPT1) There is exactly one God, the Father Almighty. (From (T1))

(LPT2) The Father is a God. (From (LPT1))

(LPT3) The Son is consubstantial with but not identical to the Father. (From (T2) and (T3))

(LPT4) If there are x and y such that x is a God, x is not identical to y, and y is consubstantial with x, then it is not the case that there is exactly one God. (Premise)

(LPT5) Therefore: It is not the case that there is exactly one God. (From (LPT2), (LPT3), (LPT4))

***Contradiction

The only way out of the contradiction is either to give up one of the tenets of the doctrine of the Trinity or to give up (LPT4).

At this juncture, some will wonder why Christians don't just give up on one of the tenets of the doctrine of the Trinity. After all, the doctrine isn't *explicitly* taught in the Christian Scriptures, and the precise language in which it is expressed wasn't settled until the fourth century.[7] So why not just abandon (say) (T2) or (T3)? What reasons are there for accepting traditional Trinitarian doctrine?

Some have argued that the doctrine of the Trinity (or something like it) can be established via a priori argument.[8] But the main reason Christians take themselves to be committed to (T1)–(T3) is that they seem to be implied both by Christian practice and by central claims in the Christian Scriptures.[9] For example, both the Old and New Testaments make it clear that there is only one being who deserves worship and who deserves such titles as 'God Almighty' or 'the one *true* God'; and Jesus refers to this being as 'our heavenly Father'.[10] Hence (T1). Moreover, though Jesus says things such as 'I and the Father are one,' it is clear that, from the point of view of the New Testament, Jesus (the Son) and the Father are distinct.[11] Jesus prays to the Father; claims to submit to the Father's will; is blessed by the Father; and so on. Likewise, the Holy Spirit is distinct from the Father and Son: the Spirit is sent by the Son and is said to intercede for us with the Father. Hence (T2). And yet the New Testament advocates worshipping Jesus (the Son) and the Holy Spirit;[12] we find Jesus saying such things as, 'Anyone who has seen me has seen the Father'; and we find the apostle Peter saying (of someone who has lied to the Holy Spirit), 'You have not lied to men, but to God.'[13] In short, there is pressure to say that the Son and Spirit are divine—and not in some derivative, or degenerate sense, but *truly* divine, like the Father. The only clear way to say this without contradicting (T1), however, is to say that the Son and the Spirit are consubstantial with the Father: the divinity of the Father, which *is* the 'substance' of the Father (more on this later), is no different from the divinity of the Son. Hence (T3).[14]

Thus we return to the challenge of unpacking the notion of consubstantiality in a way that enables us to reject (LPT4) without incoherence or heterodoxy. The next two sections will be devoted to this task; but first let me say a bit about the boundaries of orthodoxy. Broadly speaking, there are three main 'errors' that the church has condemned with respect to the doctrine of the Trinity: subordination-ism, modalism, and polytheism. The task, then, is to explicate the doctrine in a way that avoids these errors. I'll discuss each in turn.

Subordinationism is the view that neither the Son nor the Spirit is truly and fully divine. Either they are not divine at all, or their divinity is somehow subordinate to that of the Father. They are gods of a sort, but lesser gods. Subordinationism is ruled out by such language as 'true God from true God' or, more explicitly, 'the Father is God, the Son is God, and the Holy Spirit is God'.

Modalism is the view that the Father, Son, and Holy Spirit are merely different *aspects* or *manifestations* of God—different *modes of appearance* by which God makes himself known. If modalism were true, then the terms 'Father', 'Son', and 'Holy Spirit' would be analogous to terms such as 'Superman' and 'Clark Kent'. The substance called 'Superman' is strictly identical to the substance called 'Clark Kent'. But there is, nevertheless, a distinction to be drawn. The Superman-disguise is different from the Clark-Kent-disguise; and so it makes perfect sense to say that Superman and Clark Kent are *different* manifestations of Kal El (the Kryptonian who *is* both Superman and Clark Kent), or different modes in which Kal El appears. If modalism is true, then precisely the same sort of thing can be said about the terms 'God the Father', 'God the Son', and 'God the Holy Spirit'. Insofar as they are distinct, Father, Son, and Holy Spirit do not fall into the category of substance; rather, they fall into the category of 'aspect' or 'property'.

Polytheism is harder to characterize. According to standard dictionary defin-itions, 'polytheism' is the view that there are many gods, and a 'god' is any divine being. Given that Father, Son, and Holy Spirit are divine, these definitions plus (T2) imply polytheism. Father, Son, and Holy Spirit are three divine beings; so they are three gods; so polytheism is true. If this is right, and if (T1) and (T3) are together meant to rule out polytheism, then the doctrine of the Trinity is incoherent. But, of course, it can't be a simple matter of dictionary-definition that sinks the doctrine of the Trinity. The standard definitions require nuance. But how shall we modify them? I suggest the following:

x is a god $=_{df}$ x is a divine substance.
polytheism = the view that there is more than one divine substance.

I won't insist on these definitions here, though. For present purposes, I'll leave the terms officially undefined and invite readers simply to consult their own intuitions about polytheism in making decisions about whether various models of the Trinity have managed to avoid it.

2. SOLVING THE PROBLEM

In this section, I want to lay out some of the main strategies for solving the problem of the Trinity. Since the end of the nineteenth century, it has been common to divide the landscape of views into two camps: *Latin* (or *Western*) *Trinitarianism* (LT) and *Greek* (or *Eastern*) *Trinitarianism* (GT).[15] Those who divide the territory this way tell roughly the following story about their classificatory scheme: the Latin tradition traces its historical roots through the western church. It is epitomized in the work of such theologians as St Augustine and St Thomas Aquinas; it takes the unity of the Godhead as given and seeks to explain the plurality in God (rather than vice versa); and those in the tradition tend to gravitate toward psychological analogies. The Greek tradition, on the other hand, traces its roots through the eastern church; it is epitomized in the work of the Cappadocian Fathers; it takes the plurality of the divine persons as given and seeks to explain their unity; and those in the tradition tend to favor social analogies.[16] (GT is commonly identified with 'social trinitarianism', discussed below.)

In recent years, the standard way of dividing the territory has come under heavy attack, and I am inclined to reject it as well.[17] Moreover, as we'll see shortly, there is a lot more at stake in making a decision about the standard story than the viability of a mere heuristic device for classifying views about the Trinity. For purposes of a handbook chapter, however, it seems prudent to start by presupposing the standard classificatory scheme, present some of the main views that fall under each heading, and only later subject the standard scheme to criticism. So that is how I shall proceed.

In the two main parts of this section, I'll present some of the more well-known LT and GT models of the Trinity. Though each of these models is intended to guide us toward a solution to the logical problem of the Trinity, we'll see that all of them fall short. Moreover, I'll argue that the most popular contemporary view, social trinitarianism, depends heavily for its plausibility upon one of the central claims involved in the LT–GT classificatory scheme: namely, the claim that the Greek tradition, starting with the Cappadocian Fathers, favored 'social analogies' as ways of explicating the doctrine of the Trinity. This done, I'll go on in sect. 3 to present my own view of the Trinity—a version of the so-called 'Relative Identity' solution (which I'll also save for discussion in sect. 3) that transcends the alleged LT–GT divide. I'll also present alternative readings of Augustine and the Cappadocian Fathers that identify their views as ancestors of mine. Ultimately, my conclusion will be that, of all the models considered herein, the view defended in sect. 3 has the best claim to being orthodox and in accord with the views of the earliest defenders of the Creed of Nicaea.

2.1 Latin Trinitarianism

In *On the Trinity*, St Augustine provides several different analogies, or 'images' of the Trinity. According to one analogy, Father, Son, and Holy Spirit are like the mind, its understanding of itself, and its love for itself.[18] Another—his preferred analogy—compares Father, Son, and Holy Spirit with the mind's memory of itself, the mind's understanding of itself, and the act(s) of will whereby the mind obtains self-understanding from its own memory of itself and delights in and makes use of what it remembers and understands.[19] The usual glosses on these psychological models emphasize two points (not always discussed together, or connected very clearly): (1) The Son and the Spirit in the first analogy, and the Father as well in the second, are being compared to distinct faculties of the mind, or to distinct ways in which the mind operates. (2) Both analogies indicate that the difference between at least two of the persons is fundamentally a *relational* difference: the persons are at least roughly analogous to different ways in which a subject might be related to itself, or different ways in which the mind relates to objects of thought in general.[20]

As noted above, psychological models of the Trinity are common in the work of thinkers falling under the LT classification. So too is the idea that differences among persons are akin to differences among reflexive relations. Indeed, according to Richard Cross (2002a: 287), the 'vast consensus in the West' is that 'the *only* distinguishing features among the persons are their relations—that, in the standard terminology, they are subsistent relations'. The view that the persons are subsistent relations is a development of the Augustinian models,[21] and it is most notably associated with the name of St Thomas Aquinas. According to Aquinas,

Distinction in God arises only through relations of origin. . . . But a relation in God is not like an accident inherent in a subject, but is the divine essence itself. So it is subsistent just as the divine essence is subsistent. Just as, therefore, the Godhead is God, so the divine paternity is God the Father, who is a divine person. Therefore, 'divine person' signifies a relation as subsistent.   (*Summa Theologiae* I q. 29 a. 4 c, quoted and translated in Cross 2002: 286)

What exactly it would mean for a relation to subsist, however, is open to interpretation.

The usual objection to the views of Augustine and Aquinas (based on the characterizations just offered) is that they slip into modalism. Granted, Augustine and Aquinas both succeed in drawing distinctions among the persons of the Trinity. But in doing so, they seem to locate the persons in the wrong category. On some interpretations, the Augustinian view suggests that the persons are to be identified with cognitive faculties, or mental modes of operation, both of which are clearly mere *aspects* of a mind. But even on somewhat more careful interpretations, the Augustinian view at least suggests that the persons are to be identified with relations. And the Thomistic view is explicit on that score. But relations are commonly construed as properties of a certain kind (*polyadic properties,* to be specific) rather than as substances.[22] But if neither Father, Son, nor Holy Spirit is a substance—if they are mere properties—then modalism is true.

Aquinas, at least, tries to locate the persons in the right category by calling them 'subsistent' relations. But contemporary writers typically respond to this idea with bafflement. What, really, could it mean for a relation to subsist? Not having an answer, they then proceed to object that Aquinas has simply identified the divine persons with *relations,* which brings us back to modalism.[23]

Similar problems beset contemporary psychological analogies, most of which can also be classified under the LT heading. For example, Thomas V. Morris suggests (without affirming) that the Trinity might be modeled on the different personalities of a patient suffering from multiple personality disorder.[24] Trenton Merricks, on the other hand, suggests that the persons might be thought of on analogy with the distinct 'centers of consciousness' that seem to be associated with the two hemispheres of a human brain. (In experimental situations, commissurotomy patients—people who have undergone a surgical procedure that severs the bundle of nerves that allows the two hemispheres of the brain to communicate with one another—show behavior that seems to indicate that their consciousness is divided, as if there is a separate stream of thought associated with each hemisphere.) There is some pressure to classify these models under the GT heading instead; for, as we'll shortly see, the standard lore about GT is that it is wedded to 'social models', which, allegedly in contrast to Latin views, regard the persons of the Trinity as distinct psychological subjects. My own inclination, though, is to think that neither of them compares the persons of the Trinity with *distinct* psychological subjects. Rather, each compares the Trinity as a whole with a *fragmented* psychological subject. The personalities of someone with multiple personalities are not substances; they are aspects of a substance. Plausibly, the same is true of the distinct 'centers of consciousness' that are elicited as a result of commissurotomy.[25] Thus, again, modalism looms.

The final version of LT that I want to consider is Brian Leftow's (2004).[26] Leftow regards his view as an instance of LT because it 'begin[s] from the oneness of God' (ibid. 304). On his view, the persons of the Trinity might be thought of as analogous to a time traveler who appears thrice located at a single time. He offers us the example of Jane, a Rockette who is scheduled to dance in a chorus line but, at the last minute, discovers that two of her partners have failed to show up. Jane goes on stage and dances her part, then later enters a time machine (twice) so that she can (twice) go on stage with herself and dance the leftmost and rightmost parts as well. According to Leftow, there is a very clear sense in which this part of the chorus line contains three of something; and yet there is just one substance (Jane) in that part.

Is the view adequate? It is hard to tell, because Leftow's presentation is imprecise at a crucial juncture. Consider Jane's part of the chorus-line, and suppose we use

the labels, 'L', 'M', and 'R' to refer to the occupants of the three positions in that part of the line. Now, let us ask what the relations are between L, M, and R. Upon reflection, we face a problem: it is not at all clear what we mean by *the occupants of the three positions*. One might think that there is just *one* occupant, Jane, multiply located in three positions. In that case, 'L', 'M', and 'R' are all just names for Jane; and the relation between L, M, and R is identity:

Case 1: L = M = R = Jane

Alternatively, we might think that what the names 'L', 'M', and 'R' refer to are *three* distinct events in the life of Jane. In that case, there are, after all, three Rockettes, and each Rockette is an event:

Case 2: L = the leftmost dancing event; M = the middle dancing event; R = the rightmost dancing event; and L ≠ M ≠ R

Which case does Leftow have in mind? Unfortunately, it looks as if he has *both* in mind. He writes:

If (as I believe) Jane has no temporal parts, then not just a temporal part of Jane, but Jane as a whole, appears at each point in the chorus line, and what the line contains many of are segments or episodes of Jane's life-events. This may sound odd. After all, Rockettes dance. Events do not. But what you see are many dancings of one substance. What makes the line a line is the fact that these many events go on in it, in a particular set of relations. *Each Rockette is Jane.* But in *these many events*, Jane is there many times over.   (ibid. 308, emphasis mine)

The quoted passage says that 'what there are many of' is events; and it speaks of *Rockettes* in the plural. Thus, Case 2 looks like the correct interpretation. On the other hand, *each Rockette is Jane*. Thus, Case 1 looks like the correct interpretation. But it is impossible for *both* interpretations to be correct. So it is hard to know what to make of what Leftow is saying here.

Elsewhere, however, he says a bit more. 'Perhaps,' he says, 'the triune Persons are event-based persons founded on a generating substance, God' (2007: 373–4). An event-based person is, roughly, a person whose existence is constituted by the occurrence of an event: what it is for the person to exist is for that event to occur in a particular substance (ibid. 367–8). In the case of Jane, then, L, M, and R are presumably supposed to be analogous to event-based persons. Jane (the generating substance) *exists in* each of the three, as Leftow says at the end of the quoted passage above; but she is not strictly identical to any of the three. Likewise, God exists in each of the event-based persons that together constitute the Trinity.

If we take Leftow (2007) as definitive, then we have clarity on the relation between L, M, R, and Jane: all are distinct. But it is still hard to see how the view sheds light on the Trinity. Are L, M, and R consubstantial? It is hard to tell. They are events (or event-based things) involving a common substance; but that doesn't guarantee consubstantiality. Suppose I paint a wall red. We then have two events: the wall's becoming wet and the wall's becoming red. But these two events are not consubstantial, for they are not substances that share a common nature. Indeed, they're not substances at all; and even if they were, what they share isn't a *nature*. So too, apparently, in the case of L, M, and R. Of course, Leftow might have more to say on the subject; but until more *is* said, it is, again, hard to know what to make of the view.[27]

The reader will have noticed by now that, though I have offered several analogies under the heading of LT, I have *not* yet said how, exactly, any of the models solves the problem of the Trinity. The reason is simple: They don't—at least not as they have been interpreted here. The reason they don't is that, though they offer 'senses' in which God is both three and one, they do not explain how it is that *numerically distinct consubstantial* beings count as one God. Leftow's model aside, the distinct items in so-called Latin models *as they are interpreted here* are pretty clearly not consubstantial. Indeed, they are not substantial at all. And, as we have seen, Leftow's model is problematic for other reasons. This defect is not shared by GT models, which provide straightforward reasons for rejecting (LPT4), grounded in a clear account of the consubstantiality of the persons (they are consubstantial by virtue of being members of a common kind) and varying analogies aimed at explaining why we cannot conclude (as (LPT4) effectively does) that distinct consubstantial divine beings would count as more than one God. But these models have other problems, as we shall now see.

2.2 Greek Trinitarianism

In the contemporary literature on the doctrine of the Trinity, there is a family of views that falls under the label 'social trinitarianism' (ST).[28] Taking the LT-GT classification scheme for granted, ST is normally regarded as co-extensive with GT. What set the Cappadocian Fathers apart from the LT tradition, according to the common lore, was precisely their endorsement of ST; and contemporary versions of ST are basically just contemporary developments in the GT tradition. Owing in large part to misunderstandings that lead people to think of LT models as modalistic, ST models of the Trinity tend to be more popular in the contemporary literature. Critics, however, charge ST with polytheism (for reasons I shall explain shortly). This brings to light the fundamental import of the LT-GT classification scheme, and of recent criticisms of it. The Cappadocian Fathers are universally acknowledged to have played a vital role in the earliest defenses and interpretations of the creed of Nicaea. They are among those who helped to *define* orthodoxy; so it would be surprising, to say the least, if whatever view they held turned out to be heretical. In short, saying 'The Cappadocian Fathers endorsed model M' is, if true, nearly decisive as a response to charges that model M is polytheistic or otherwise heretical. Hence the importance of the contemporary claim that there is such a thing as GT which (1) is found in the work of the Cappadocian Fathers and other key eastern theologians, and (2) differs from LT by taking plurality rather than unity as its starting point, as evidenced by their endorsement of ST models. Historical challenges to the viability of the LT-GT classification scheme take issue with each of these points. They deny that the Cappadocians endorsed ST; they deny that there is reason to think that the Cappadocians took different 'starting points' from key Latin theologians such as St Augustine; and they deny that there is any such thing as GT or LT as they are commonly conceived.[29] If the challenges are right, then contemporary criticisms of ST are suddenly *much* more forceful; for not only does ST *lose* the backing of the Cappadocians that is so vital to warding off those criticisms, but some other view—whatever view the Cappadocians *actually* endorsed—acquires their backing.

In the next section, I will present a view that I take to be a contemporary development of what was *held in common* by (at least) Augustine and the Cappadocian Fathers. But for now, I want to focus on explaining what ST is and why it is inadequate as a way of understanding the Trinity.

Contemporary social trinitarians have not been especially clear about what the central tenets of their view are supposed to be. Neither have their critics. First and foremost, ST theories are identified by their reliance on analogies that compare the persons of the Trinity to things that are numerically distinct but share a common nature—usually rational creatures of some sort, like human beings. These are called 'social analogies' because many of them (though not all) at least imply, if not explicitly state, that the unity among the divine persons is some sort of social unity: God is like a family, or a perfectly unified community of rulers, or whatever. This suggests that ST might fruitfully be characterized as committed to the following central tenets:

1. Father, Son, and Holy Spirit are not numerically the same substance. Rather, the persons of the Trinity are consubstantial only in the sense that they share a common nature; and the sharing is to be understood straightforwardly on analogy with the way in which three human beings share a common nature.

2. Monotheism does not imply that there is exactly one divine substance. Rather, it implies at most only that *all divine substances*—all gods, in the ordinary sense of the term 'god'—stand in some particular relation R to one another, a relation other than *being the same divine substance*.

3. The persons of the Trinity stand to one another in the relation R that is required for monotheism to be true.

Different versions of ST might then be distinguished in accord with differences over what relation R amounts to.

There are many candidates in the literature for being monotheism-securing relations, but the most popular are the following:

(*a*) Being parts of a whole that is itself divine.

(*b*) Being the only members of the only divine kind.

(*c*) Being the only members of the community that rules the cosmos.

(*d*) Being the only members of a divine family.

(*e*) Being necessarily mutually interdependent, so that none can exist without the others.

(*f*) Enjoying perfect love and harmony of will with one another, unlike the members of pagan pantheons.

Most social trinitarians in fact opt for a combination of these, and most (but not all) of the combinations include at least (*a*), (*b*), and (*c*). So, for example, Richard Swinburne (1994) focuses on the fact that YHWH is a composite individual or society whose parts or members stand in the relations identified in (*e*) and (*f*).[30] But, of course, he wouldn't deny that they stand in (*b*) and (*c*) as well. J. P. Moreland and William Lane Craig (2003) focus primarily on (*a*). On their view, YHWH is composed of the Persons in a sense analogous to the way in which the three-headed dog Cerberus, guardian of the underworld in Greek mythology, might be thought to be composed of three 'centers of consciousness' (ibid. 593). On their view, the three conscious parts of Cerberus are not *dogs*; there is only one dog—Cerberus. But the centers of consciousness are canine, just as any other part of Cerberus is (derivatively) canine. One dog, then; three derivatively canine individuals. Likewise in the Trinity: one God; three derivatively divine individuals. Monotheism is thus secured by the fact that the Persons are parts of a single fully divine being. Cornelius Plantinga Jr. (1989: 31), on the other hand, argues that social Trinitarians may 'cling to respectability as monotheists' simply by affirming that the persons are related in the ways described by (*b*), (*c*), and (*d*). His idea seems to be that monotheism is true, no matter how many gods there are, so long as all gods derive their divinity from one source, or share a single divine nature (as we humans share a single human nature), or are joined together as a divine family, monarchy, or community. There are other suggestions in the literature; but they tend to run along very similar lines.

A standard criticism of social trinitarianism is that these (re-)characterizations of monotheism are implausible. Those lodging the criticism typically do so in one of two ways. Some try to argue that statements in the Nicene and Athanasian Creeds that are commonly taken to rule out polytheism also speak against social trinitarianism.[31] But from the point of view of those who accept the standard LT-GT distinction, there are two strikes against this objection. First, the Athanasian Creed was written in Latin and incorporates language from Augustine. So it can be dismissed as an LT treatise—one which we would antecedently expect to reflect an anti-ST bias. Second, the chief *defenders* of the creed of Nicaea were themselves social trinitarians (according to the common lore); so the claim that ST violates *that* creed is simply not credible. So, at this stage anyway, the credal objection is indecisive. Others object to ST on the grounds that it is not plausible to think that (say) Greek polytheism would become monotheistic if only we added that Zeus and the other gods enjoyed perfect love, harmony, and mutual interdependence with one another; nor would it seem to help if we were to pare the pantheon down to a single divine family that rules the cosmos.[32] I think that this objection *is* intuitively decisive against the suggestion that the relations described in (*b*), (*c*), (*d*), (*e*), or (*f*), singly or in combination, could possibly secure monotheism. But it has no implications for the more popular suggestion that Christianity is monotheistic because (*a*) the persons are *parts* of the one and only fully divine being. Moreover, it has the awkward implication that, if the Cappadocians really were social trinitarians, then they were polytheists after all. To close the case against ST, then, two tasks must be accomplished: (1) part–whole models must be shown to be problematic; (2) one must either explain how the Cappadocians managed inadvertently to fall into one of the very errors they were most concerned to avoid, or one must show that the Cappadocians really were not social trinitarians.[33]

Various objections against part–whole trinitarianism are already present in the literature.[34] Rather than summarize those, however, I want here to present a new one.[35] I will take as my target the version of part–whole trinitarianism developed by J. P. Moreland and William Lane Craig (2003). I do this because theirs is the most developed version of part–whole trinitarianism currently available, but I think that substantially the same objection could be raised against any version.

As I have already noted, Moreland and Craig compare God to the mythical dog Cerberus and the persons to Cerberus's three heads (or, better, the souls that might be embodied in those heads). So, on their view, the divine persons—all of them—are parts of God. For obvious reasons, however, Moreland and Craig want to preserve the view that God is divine while denying that that God is a *fourth* divine thing on a par with the persons. Thus, they distinguish two kinds of divinity: the *full* divine nature, which is possessed by God and implies tri-unity; and a *derivative* divine nature, possessed by each person. The distinction is analogous to the (allegedly) two ways in which something might be said to be feline: something can be feline by being a cat; or something can be feline in a derivative way by being part of a cat. Moreover, the making of this sort of distinction is implicit in every version of part–whole trinitarianism of which I am aware. Nobody wants to be pressed into affirming a quaternity in God; thus the composite is always treated, at least implicitly, as a different kind of thing from the parts—a non-person composed of persons, or a group-mind composed of single minds, etc. So much for the view itself.

But now we face two problems, both devastating: first, Moreland and Craig cannot affirm the opening line of the Nicene creed: 'We believe in one God, the Father, almighty.' For, on their view, God is a fundamentally different thing from the Father.[36] Moreover, they cannot affirm the crucial *homoousion* clause in the same creed unless they reject the idea that there is exactly one divine nature—an idea that the Cappadocians and (so far as I am aware) every other major interpreter and defender of the creed of Nicaea in the fourth and fifth centuries were in agreement about. Here is why: the only viable interpretations of the credal claim that the Son is *homoousion* with the Father have it that the Son is either numerically the same substance as the Father or of the same nature as the Father. (Natures were also referred to as 'substances'; hence, being consubstantial with something might just mean having the same nature.) The former, of course, they reject. The latter they accept; but in accepting it, they posit, effectively, two divine natures—one 'genuine', possessed only by God; the other derivative, but still divine, possessed by the two persons. Of course, they could deny that the derivative nature is a divine nature. But in so doing, they seem to strip the persons of their divinity, which would conflict with other parts of the Nicene and Constantinopolitan creeds. If all this is right, then, part–whole trinitarianism is in serious trouble, at least if its proponents intend (as Moreland and Craig do) to be offering a view that respects Nicene orthodoxy.

But now what of the Cappadocian Fathers? The initial justification for treating the Cappadocian Fathers as social trinitarians comes primarily from their own apparent employment of social analogies.[37] Under the usual interpretation, the Cappadocian view was that, 'just as Peter, Paul, and Barnabas are each man, so the Father is God, the Son is God, and the Holy Spirit is God' (Plantinga 1986: 329–30). In short: the persons of the Trinity are 'of the same substance' only in the sense that they share a common nature; and the sharing is to be understood straightforwardly on analogy with the way in which three men share a common nature.

As I have already indicated, however, this way of interpreting the Cappadocian Fathers has, of late, come under heavy criticism. Space will not permit me to present the exegetical case against the standard interpretation; but in the next section, after laying out the view that I call Constitution Trinitarianism, I will present reasons for thinking that the Cappadocians were actually gesturing toward that view rather than toward ST. If this is right, then one of the most important reasons for accepting ST is undermined.

3. THE CONSTITUTION MODEL

I turn now to the model that I prefer.[38]

Let me begin here by identifying a general strategy for solving the problem of the Trinity that I have so far omitted from our discussion: the Relative Identity strategy.[39] The problem, as I have characterized it, is generated by the conjunction of the following premise (from sect. 1 above) with the central tenets of trinitarian doctrine:

(LPT4) If there are x and y such that x is a God, x is not identical to y, and y is consubstantial with x, then it is not the case that there is exactly one God. (Premise)

But (LPT4) is true only if the following principle is also true:

(P1) Necessarily, if x and y are not identical, then x and y are not numerically the same substance.

If (P1) is false, then (LPT4) simply ignores the possibility that x and y are distinct but (perhaps by virtue of their consubstantiality) *one and the same* God. In other words, (LPT4) presupposes that it is impossible for an object a and an object b to be numerically the same F without being absolutely identical. Give up that presupposition, and the argument that depends on (LPT4) fails.

But how can we reject (P1)? The way to do it is to endorse the doctrine of *relative identity*. There is a weak version of this doctrine, and a strong version. The weak version says:

(RI1) States of affairs of the following sort are possible: x is an F, y is an F, x is a G, y is a G, x is the same F as y, but x is not the same G as y.

The strong version is just the weak version plus (RI2):

(RI2) Either absolute (classical) identity does not exist, or statements of the form '$x = y$' are to be analyzed in terms of statements of the form 'x is the same F as y' rather than the other way around.

RI2 is not needed for solving the problem of the Trinity; but some philosophers—notably, Peter Geach—endorse it for other reasons, and it serves as independent motivation for RI1.[40]

Defenders of the relative identity solution have mostly occupied themselves with working out the *logic* of relative identity in an effort to show that the doctrine of relative identity itself is coherent, and to show that the doctrine of the Trinity can be stated in a way that is *provably* consistent given the assumption of relative identity.[41] (What I have done here falls short of the latter goal. I have shown how accepting (RI1) enables one to rebut a single argument for the *inconsistency* of the doctrine of the Trinity; but I have not shown that *every* argument against the consistency of the doctrine as I have stated it must fail.)

Despite the efforts of its defenders, however, the relative identity solution has remained rather unpopular. (RI2) in particular is widely rejected as implausible; and I have argued elsewhere (Rea 2003) that invoking it in a solution to the problem of the Trinity implies that the difference between the persons is theory-dependent, and so merely conceptual. But without (RI2), (RI1) is (at first glance, anyway) unintelligible. The reason is simple: sameness statements are naturally interpreted as identity statements. So, the claim that '*x* and *y* are the same F' seems logically equivalent to the claim that '*x* is an F, *y* is an F, and *x* = *y*'. (RI1) is inconsistent with this analysis of sameness statements. But on its own, it doesn't supply any *replacement* for that analysis. Thus, it renders sameness claims utterly mysterious. Appealing to (RI1) without a supplemental story as a way of solving the problem of the Trinity, then, simply replaces one mystery with another. That is hardly progress.

The constitution view supplies the relevant supplemental story. The story begins with an example: an artistic building contractor fashions a marble statue that is to be used as a pillar in the building he is constructing. So he has made a statue; he also has made a pillar. It would be strange to say that he has made *two* material objects that are simply located in exactly the same spot at the same time (though many philosophers do *in fact* say such a thing). What we are inclined to say is that the statue and the pillar are one and the same material object, not two. And yet they are *distinct*. Surface erosion will destroy the statue without destroying the pillar. Internal corruption that preserves the surface but undermines the statue's capacity to support the weight of a building will destroy the pillar but (if the statue is removed from its position as a load-bearing structure) will not destroy the statue. Thus, what we want to say is that the statue and the pillar are the *same material object*, even though they are *not identical*. If we do say this, we commit ourselves to (RI1). But we can make (RI1) intelligible by adding that all it means to say that two things are the same material object at a time is that those two things share all the same physical matter at that time.

Let us flesh out the story just a bit further. Aristotle maintained that every material object is a compound of *matter* and *form*. The form might be thought of as a complex organizational property—not a mere shape, as the term suggests in English, but something much richer. For Aristotle, the form of a thing was its *nature*; and forms, like concrete things (though not in exactly the same sense), count as substances. Thus, on his view, St Peter would be a compound whose constituents were some matter and the form, *humanity*, or *human nature*. St Paul would be a compound whose constituents were that *same* form, but *different* matter.[42] Peter and Paul would thus be 'of one substance' on the Aristotelian view; though (unlike Gregory of Nyssa) Aristotle would not have spoken of Peter and Paul as being numerically the same man, nor would he have regarded them as numerically the same substance. With some minor modifications (plus the non-Aristotelian assumption that statues and pillars are substances, just like men are) Aristotle's view *would* permit us to say that the statue and the pillar are numerically the same substance, even though they would not be 'of the same substance' since they would not share the same form, or nature. They would be numerically the same substance, one material object, but distinct matter-form compounds. They would be the same without being identical.

In the case of our statue, then, we have *two* complex properties—*being a statue* and *being a pillar*—both had by the same underlying subject, some undifferentiated matter.[43] This gives us two compounds, a statue and a pillar. Each is *a* substance. Thus, the statue and the pillar are emphatically *not* mere aspects of a common substance. They are not properties or relations or anything of the sort. Furthermore, each is distinct from the other. But they are, nevertheless, the *same* substance. Note too that the underlying matter is *not* a substance, since it is not a matter-form compound. But even if it were, it would not be a *fourth* substance—it would be the *same* substance as the statue and the pillar (by virtue of sharing all its matter in common with them). Nor (obviously) would it be a third compound. Hence, there is just one substance and two compounds.

You might think that if there is just one substance, then we ought to be able to ask whether *it*—the one substance—is essentially a mere statue or essentially a mere pillar (or perhaps essentially a statue-pillar). But this thought is incorrect. On the present view, terms such as 'it' and 'the one substance' are ambiguous: they might refer to the statue, or they might refer to the pillar. For, again, statue and pillar are distinct, though not distinct *substances*.

You might think that if there are three matter-form compounds, then there are three 'primary substances' but only one 'secondary substance' (where a primary substance is a concrete particular, like a human being, and a secondary substance is a nature, or form). But this is also incorrect. On the view I am defending, if x and y share the same matter in common, and x is a primary substance and y is a primary substance, then x and y are the *same* primary substance, despite being different matter-form compounds.[44]

By now the relevance of all this to the Trinity should be clear: almost everything that I just said about the statue and pillar could likewise be said about the divine persons. In the case of the divine persons, we have three properties—*being the Father, being the Son,* and *being the Spirit*; or, perhaps, *being Unbegotten, being Begotten,* and *Proceeding*—all had by something that plays the role of matter. (It can't *really* be matter, since God is immaterial. Suppose, then, that it is *the divine substance,* whatever that is, that plays the role of matter.)[45] Each divine person is *a* substance; thus, they are not mere aspects of a common substance. Furthermore, each is distinct from the other. (So modalism is avoided and (T2) is preserved.) But they are nevertheless the *same* substance. (Hence (T3).) Thus, there is just one divine substance, and so the view allows us to say, along with the creed, 'We believe in one God, the Father, almighty...and in one Lord Jesus Christ...begotten, not made, being of one substance with the Father.' Since Father, Son, and Holy Spirit count, on this view, as numerically the same substance *despite their distinctness*, (LPT4) is false, and the problem of the Trinity is solved.

So far so good; but there is one loose end that remains to be tied. What is it that plays the role of matter in the Trinity? And is it a substance itself? Here I want to offer only a *partial* view that might be developed in a variety of different ways. What plays the role of matter in the Trinity is *the divine nature*; and the divine nature *is* a substance. It is not a fourth substance, for reasons already discussed; nor is it a fourth person (since it is not a compound of 'matter' plus a person-defining-property). But it is a substance, since (again, taking cues from Aristotle) *natures* are substances. What I don't want to take a position on here is the question of what, exactly, a nature is. Is it concrete or abstract? Is it particular or universal? Is it a property or something else? These questions I will not answer. I think that they must be answered in a way that allows the divine persons to be concrete particular non-properties; but I think that there are various ways of answering these questions that are compatible with that view.

This completes my presentation of the constitution view. We are now in a position to see how the view connects with the views of fourth- and fifth-century defenders of Nicaea. At the heart of the constitution view is the idea that the divine persons are compounds whose constituents are a shared divine nature, which plays the role of Aristotelian matter, and a person-defining property (like *being the Son*, or *being Begotten*) that plays the role of form. But this is almost *exactly* the view that Richard Cross identifies as the fundamental point of agreement between eastern and western views of the Trinity. According to Cross, east and west agreed that (*a*) the divine nature is a property, and (*b*) one and the same divine nature is a constituent of each of the divine persons—i.e. it is the point at which they overlap.[46]

So far so good; but mere overlap is not sufficient to suggest the constitution model. For if nature-sharing is a kind of overlap (as it seems to be for the Cappadocians, at least),[47] then two men overlap on a constituent as well. But, of course, they don't constitute one another. In order to attribute something like a constitution model to Augustine and the Cappadocians, we would have to show that their view posited not only overlap among the persons but a kind of overlap that guaranteed the sort of *absence of separation* that we find in objects (like the statue and the pillar) that constitute one another. Encouragingly, Michel Barnes insists that this idea was as crucial to both east and west as Cross thinks the idea of overlap was. Thus, he writes (speaking of both Augustine and the Cappadocians), 'the most fundamental conception and articulation in "Nicene" Trinitarian theology of the 380s of the unity among the Three is the understanding that *any action of any member of the Trinity is an action of the three inseparably*' (Barnes in Davis, Kendall, and O'Collins (eds.), 1999: 156, emphasis in original).[48] Moreover, as we'll see, both Augustine and the Cappadocians endorsed models that reinforce this reading and the Cappadocians, at least, rejected models that conflict with it.

Let us return again (for starters) to Augustine's favored analogy: self-memory, self-understanding, and self-directed willing. At the end of Book 10 of *On the Trinity*, after introducing the favored analogy, Augustine raises some concerns and then says that the 'discussion demands a new beginning'. In Book 11, he opens with two new analogies, the first of which compares the divine persons with an *external body*, *vision of the body*, and the *attention of mind* that joins these two. If Augustine's goal really were to model the Trinity on different faculties or modes of operation for the human mind, returning to an analogy like this would be bizarre. For, after all, an external body has nothing essentially to do with the mind of one who beholds it. But, of course, this isn't really Augustine's goal at all. The key to understanding this is to attend carefully to the theory of vision that gets presented along with the analogy. For Augustine, vision involves a kind of reproduction in the viewer of the nature or form of the thing viewed.[49] So when an external body is seen, the form of that body is present both in the body and in the visual faculty of the viewer. Moreover, he seems to think that, in *directing* vision toward the external body and *retaining* the image of it in the visual faculty, the will takes on the same nature as well—just as 'the little body of a chameleon [varies] with ready change, according to the colors which it sees'.[50] Once we see this, however, the point of the new analogy becomes clear. The case at hand is one in which three *very* different items are unified by virtue of a kind of overlap: they have (in a way) the very same nature present in them.

Of course, the analogy is imperfect; for, among other things, the external body's nature is present in it in a way different from the way in which it is present in the viewer's visual faculty or will. Augustine therefore offers another analogy to correct this defect; but, in the end, the best analogy is the one that I have called 'the favored analogy'. It is the best because, in that analogy, *one and the same substance* is present in three distinct things which are distinguished from one another only by their relations to that one substance. The things in question are not faculties or modes of operation. They are, rather, concrete events, each of which is, in effect, a complex whose constituents are a substance and a reflexive relation: *the mind remembering itself, the mind understanding itself*, and *the mind willing itself*. These events are not identical; and, as events, they are at least closer to the category of substance than to the category of property or aspect. Moreover, since it is the mind itself that is the common constituent in each complex, and since it is the mind that is *doing* the self-remembering, self-understanding, self-willing, the view strongly suggests the sort of absence of separation that one finds in the constitution view; and it even suggests shared agency among the persons.

What of the Cappadocians? The Cappadocians clearly thought of consubstantiality as the *sharing of a nature*—on this I think there is no substantive disagreement. Moreover, it seems clear that they thought of nature-sharing as the sharing of a common constituent. Gregory of Nyssa claims (in *On Not Three Gods: To Ablabius*) that 'the man in [a group of men] is one' (Schaff & Wace 1900/1999: v. 332). Likewise, in his *Fifth Theological Oration: On the Holy Spirit*, Gregory Nazianzen says that 'the Godhead [or divine nature] is One', and he speaks of the Persons as those 'in Whom the Godhead dwells', which suggests that the Godhead—i.e. the divine nature—is a common constituent of the three (ibid. vii. 322). Moreover, in the following passage he seems to indicate outright that the relation between the persons involves overlap on a common nature and differentiation by three properties:

the very fact of being Unbegotten or Begotten, or Proceeding has given the name of Father to the First, of the Son to the Second, and [to] the Third . . . of the Holy Ghost, that the distinction of the Three Persons may be preserved in the one nature and dignity of the Godhead. . . . The Three are One in Godhead, and the One three in properties.

(Fifth Theological Oration, IX, ibid. 320)

But what of inseparability? I said earlier that not only do the Cappadocians affirm models that posit the inseparability of the persons, but they reject models that conflict with it. Thus, though Gregory Nazianzen acknowledges that Adam, Eve, and Seth are consubstantial, he goes on to make it very explicit that his point in saying that they are is *only* to show that distinct things can be consubstantial, *not* to embrace what would now be called a social analogy:

were not [Adam, Eve, and Seth] consubstantial? Of course they were. Well then, here it is an acknowledged fact that different persons may have the same substance. I say this, not that I would attribute creation or fraction or any property of body to the Godhead . . . but that I may contemplate in these, as on a stage, things which are objects of thought alone. For it is not possible to trace out any image exactly to the whole extent of the truth.

(Fifth Theological Oration, XI, ibid. 321)

Elsewhere, he is even clearer about the importance of inseparability, and the inadequacy of the analogy with three human beings:

To us there is One God, for the Godhead is One . . . For one [Person] is not more and another less God; nor is One before and another after; nor are They divided in will or parted in power; nor can you find here any of the qualities of divisible things; but the Godhead is, to speak concisely, undivided in separate Persons. . . . [D]o not the Greeks also believe in one Godhead, as their more advanced philosophers declare? And with us, Humanity is one, namely the entire race; but yet they have many gods, not One, just as there are many men. But in this case the common nature has a unity which is only conceivable in thought; and the individuals are parted from one another very far indeed, both by time and by dispositions and by power. For we are not only compound beings, but contrasted beings, both with one another and with ourselves; nor do we remain entirely the same [over time].

(Fifth Theological Oration XIV, XV, ibid. 322)

As I see it, the upshot of these passages is that the analogy with three humans breaks down at *precisely* the point where the social model and the constitution model differ. Three humans are *separated* in matter, time, space, and agency; the three Persons are not.

There are other indications in both Gregory of Nyssa and Gregory Nazianzus that their view of the Trinity was along the lines of the constitution model.[51] I want to close, however, by dismissing an argument for the claim that they *rejected* the constitution model. In *Epistle 52*, Basil of Caesarea writes:

For they maintained that the homoousion set forth the idea both of essence and of what is derived from it, so that the essence, when divided, confers the title of co-essential on the parts into which it is divided. This explanation has some reason in the case of bronze and coins made therefrom, but in the case of God the Father and God the Son there is no question of substance anterior or even underlying both; the mere thought and utterance of such a thing is the last extravagance of impiety.   (ibid. viii. 155)

Commenting on this passage, William Lane Craig (2005: 80) takes Basil to be 'vehemently' rejecting constitution models outright. But this seems to me to be exactly the wrong interpretation. Though constitution theorists would certainly want to say of each coin that it is constituted by a piece of bronze, *Basil is not here considering a case in which multiple bronze items constitute one another.* Indeed, what Craig does not recognize is that the coins in this example are consubstantial (if at all) in the way that Father, Son, and Holy Spirit would be on the *social trinitarian* view. So, if any contemporary model is being rejected, it is that one (the one Craig himself favors) and not the constitution view. Moreover, what is at issue for Basil here is *just* the question whether there is an anterior substance underlying the Persons. But the constitution model is not committed to an anterior substance. An anterior substance would be one that is *prior to* and *not the same substance as* the persons. But, on the constitution view, the divine nature is neither.

If the foregoing is right, then, the Cappadocians did not in fact favor anything like social trinitarianism; rather, their view was much more in line with constitution trinitarianism. Likewise, Augustine did not favor the modalistic-sounding view that was attributed to him in sect. 2.1; rather, he too was defending a view in line with the constitution view. This is substantial support; and, to my mind, the constitution view wins out on purely intuitive grounds as well.

Notes

I am grateful to Jeff Brower and Tom Flint for very helpful comments on an earlier draft of this chapter.

1. *Quicumque vult* (The Athanasian Creed); trans. Jeffrey Brower, quoted from Brower and Rea 2005a: 488.

2. The most important and illuminating contemporary literature aimed at sorting out these difficulties has been written by theologians working in the field of Patristic studies. For a start into this literature, the following sources are especially useful: Ayres

2004; Barnes 1998; Coakley 1999; Coakley (ed.) 2003; Stead 1977; Turcescu 2005; and Wolfson 1964.

3. For details on the relevant controversies, see especially Ayres 2004.

4. It is more common nowadays to claim that the central tenets of the doctrine are these three: (1) there is exactly one God; (2) the Father is not the Son, the Son is not the Spirit, and the Father is not the Spirit; and (3) the Father is God, the Son is God, and the Spirit is God. This way of characterizing the doctrine more closely follows the Athanasian Creed. But the language of (3) is less clear than the language of (T3) above (due to the fact that the predicate 'is God' can be, and has been, assigned a variety of different meanings). Just as importantly, this formulation obscures the centrality of the notion of *consubstantiality* in the doctrine—the very notion that lay at the center of some of the most important controversies surrounding the First Nicene Council. My own formulation of the doctrine is more in accord with formulations found, for example, in the systematic theologies of Berkhof (1938/1996) and Hodge (1873).

5. I take this straight from the first line of the Nicene Creed. The first line can be translated in ways different from what I have reproduced here; but every credible way of translating it strongly suggests that the Father is somehow the *same* as God.

6. Kelly 1972: 340–1; Schaff and Wace 1900/1999: xiv. 189.

7. The common story is that it was settled in 325 and then challenged by Arian rebels. Lewis Ayres (2004) and Michel Barnes (1998) tell a different story, however—one according to which the language wasn't entirely settled in 325, but rather later in 380/1.

8. The best-known argument along these lines is one that is at least latent in the thought of a variety of medieval theologians, explicit in the work of Richard of St Victor, and developed in detail most recently by Richard Swinburne 1994: ch. 8.

9. As the fourth-century defenders of Nicaea were at pains to show. See, for starters, Athanasius's 'Defence of the Nicene Council' in Schaff and Wace 1900/1999: iv.

10. See e.g. Exod. 20: 3–5; Isa. 42: 8; Matt. 5: 9–13, 7: 21; and John 2: 16.

11. Compare John 10: 30; Matt. 24: 36; Luke 22: 42; and John 1: 14, 18.

12. e.g. Phil. 2: 10–11.

13. John 14: 9; Acts 5: 3–4 (NIV).

14. Obviously the discussion here is highly compressed. For a fuller discussion of the biblical case for the doctrine, see (e.g.) O'Collins 1999: chs. 1–4.

15. According to Michel Barnes, what I am calling the 'standard' classificatory scheme takes its cues from the work of the nineteenth-century theologian, Theodore de Régnon (1892–8). (Though Ayres notes that de Régnon's own classificatory scheme wasn't so much a division between Greek and Latin models as between patristic and scholastic models. See Ayres 2004: 302 ff.) Barnes subjects de Régnon's scheme and its relatives to trenchant criticism in Barnes 1995a, b.

16. Cf. e.g. Brown 1985; Cary 1995; Cross 2002; LaCugna 1986, 1991; and Placher 1983: 79.

17. See e.g. Ayres 2004; Barnes 1995a, b, 1998; Cary 1995; Coakley 1999; and Cross 2002. The idea isn't that there is no difference whatsoever between eastern and western, or Latin and Greek, conceptions of the Trinity, but that the differences aren't nearly as sharp as they are commonly construed, that they aren't aptly characterized as

differences over 'starting points' or as a fundamental difference in attitudes toward 'social' and 'psychological' analogies.

18. *On the Trinity*, Bk. 9 chs. 3 ff.; Schaff and Wace 1887/1999: 127 ff.

19. *On the Trinity*, Bk. 10 chs. 10–12 and Bk. 15 ch. 3; Schaff and Wace 1887/1999: iii. 140–3, 200–2. He characterizes the latter analogy as a 'more subtle' treatment of the matter than the former.

20. Cf. Brown 1985: ch. 7; LaCugna 1991: ch. 3; O'Collins 1999: ch. 7; Richardson 1955.

21. Moreland and Craig 2003: 585 say that Aquinas 'pushes the Augustinian analogy to its apparent limit'. But this makes it sound as if the 'subsistent relations view' isn't present in Augustine. I myself don't mean to suggest that, however. All I mean to suggest is that it is not explicit in Augustine.

22. A *polyadic* property is one that applies to several things together. A property such as *being loved* is monadic: it applies to a single subject (even if there are many subjects to which it applies). Relations such as — *loves* —, or — *thinks that* — *is* —, are polyadic. The former applies to a pair, the latter to a triad. Note, however, that, though it is nowadays common to treat relations as polyadic properties (as e.g. in van Inwagen 2004), Jeff Brower argues that medieval philosophers did not treat them as such. See Brower 2001 and 2005.

23. I think that the objection can be met, and that the way to do it is to develop Aquinas's view along the lines of the view described in sect. 3. But I won't attempt to do that here.

24. Morris 1991: ch. 9.

25. Admittedly, though, one might think of them as distinct (subsistent) minds or souls, embodied in or emergent upon the same material substance. If we think of them this way, then, as Jeff Brower and I note elsewhere (Brower and Rea 2005*b*) polytheism looms, rather than modalism. Whether the view actually falls into polytheism, however, depends entirely upon whether the relevant 'centers of consciousness' are in any sense *the same substance*. On this question, Merricks is silent.

26. See also Leftow 2007.

27. Thanks to Brian Leftow for helpful correspondence about his view. Naturally, if I have him wrong here, that is my fault and not his. My own view is that Leftow's view can be made workable by developing it in the direction of the constitution view, described in sect. 3. But I won't attempt that here.

28. Proponents of the ST strategy include Timothy Bartel (1993, 1994); David Brown (1985, 1989); Peter Forrest (1998); C. Stephen Layman (1988); J. P. Moreland and William Lane Craig (2003); Cornelius Plantinga, Jr. (1986, 1988, 1989); Richard Swinburne (1994); Edward Wierenga (2004); and C. J. F. Williams (1994). Hasker (1970) *claims* to endorse ST; but some of what he says seems more in line with the constitution view (see esp. pp. 27–30). According to Richard Swinburne, the 'most influential modern statement of social Trinitarianism' is Moltmann 1981.

29. See n. 17 for references.

30. Cf. Swinburne 1994: 181.

31. See esp. Brower 2004*a*; Clark 1996; Feser 1997; and Leftow 1999.

32. See esp. Leftow 1999 and Merricks 2006.

33. Or one might just try to sink it with the weight of other objections. And there *are* other objections in the literature—see e.g. Tuggy 2003, 2004. My own view, though, is

that even after these further objections have been piled on, the cumulative case is not dialectically strong enough apart from the two further tasks just mentioned.

34. See e.g. Howard-Snyder 2003; Leftow 1999; Rea 2006; and Tuggy 2003.

35. My objection bears some similarity to objections based on the Athanasian Creed raised by Jeffrey Brower (2004a) against Wierenga's (2004) social trinitarian view.

36. Dale Tuggy (2003 and esp. 2004) presses roughly this point against all versions of ST. Part–whole trintiarians *could* respond by saying that the Son and Spirit are parts of the Father (who is also a person). But in that event, their doctrine of two kinds of divinity (full and derivative) would commit them to denying that the Son and the Spirit (who would still be derivatively divine) have the same nature as the Father (who alone would have the full divine nature). Thus, they would run into direct conflict with the requirement that the Son be *of the same substance* with the Father.

37. Plantinga 1986, 1988, and 1989 provide representative examples.

38. See Brower and Rea 2005a, b. See also Brower 2004b.

39. Proponents of this strategy include G. E. M. Anscombe and P. T. Geach (1963: esp. 118–20); James Cain (1989); A. P. Martinich (1978, 1979); and Peter van Inwagen (1988, 2003). I count myself as both a critic and a proponent, since I reject one way of deploying the strategy but endorse another. (See Rea 2003; Brower and Rea 2005a, b). For other criticism, see Bartel 1988; Cartwright 1987; Merricks 2006; and Tuggy 2003.

40. See e.g. Geach 1967, 1980: sects. 30, 34, 110.

41. See esp. van Inwagen 1988, 2003.

42. There's controversy in the literature on Aristotle over whether distinct human beings really share *numerically the same* form or not. Here I assume that they do; but since I feel no special burden to follow Aristotle on that point, nothing really depends on the assumption.

43. Or, if you like, a *lump* of matter. See Brower and Rea 2005a: 504 n. 10 for discussion.

44. Cf. Cary 1992: 381.

45. One might want to say that it is the Father who plays the role of underlier, that the Son is a compound of the Father and the property *being Begotten*, and that the Spirit is a compound of the Father (or the Son) and the property of *Proceeding*. This view is suggested by passages in Augustine, and was first brought to my attention by Anne Peterson. I take it as a variation on the present theme, rather than a genuine rival to the view I am defending.

46. Cross 2002a: 284. See also Cary 1992.

47. On Gregory of Nyssa's view of universals, see Cross 2002b.

48. I want to avoid views that rule out shared agency; but I don't myself want to commit to it. For, of course, it raises serious questions. The Son prays to the Father. Does the Father do so as well? Proponents of shared agency will say 'yes, but not in the same way.' (See e.g. Hasker 1970: 29.) Trying to make good sense of this response, however, would require another paper.

49. *On the Trinity* Bk. 11 ch. 2; in Schaff and Wace 1887/1999: iii. 145–6.

50. Ibid. ch. 5; in Schaff and Wace 1887/1999: iii. 146–7.

51. See e.g. Gregory Nazianzen's analogy of three suns in his *Fifth Theological Oration*, ch. 14, and the rainbow analogy in Basil of Caesarea's *Epistle 38* (generally regarded as having been written by Gregory of Nyssa rather than by Basil).

REFERENCES

ANSCOMBE, G. E. M., and GEACH, P. T. (1963). *Three Philosophers*. Ithaca: Cornell University Press.

AYRES, LEWIS (2004). *Nicaea and its Legacy: An Approach to Fourth-Century Trinitarian Theology*. New York: Oxford University Press.

BARNES, MICHEL RENÉ (1995*a*). 'Augustine in Contemporary Trinitarian Theology', *Theological Studies* 56: 237–50.

—— (1995*b*). 'De Regnon Reconsidered', *Augustinian Studies* 26: 51–80.

—— (1998). 'The Fourth Century as Trinitarian Canon', in Lewis Ayres and Gareth Jones (eds.), *Christian Origins: Theology, Rhetoric, and Community*. London: Routledge, 47–67.

—— (1999). 'Rereading Augustine's Theology of the Trinity', in Davis, Kendall, and O'Collins (eds.) (1999: 145–76).

BARTEL, TIMOTHY (1988). 'The Plight of the Relative Trinitarian', *Religious Studies* 24: 129–55.

—— (1993). 'Could There Be More Than One Almighty?' *Religious Studies* 29: 465–95.

—— (1994). 'Could There Be More Than One Lord?' *Faith and Philosophy* 11: 357–78.

BERKHOF, LOUIS (1938/96). *Systematic Theology: New Combined Edition*. Grand Rapids: Wm. B. Eerdmanns.

BROWER, JEFFREY (2001). 'Relations without Polyadic Properties: Albert the Great on the Nature and Ontological Status of Relations', *Archiv fur Geschichte der Philosophie* 83: 225–57.

—— (2004*a*). 'The Problem with Social Trinitarianism: A Reply to Wierenga', *Faith and Philosophy* 21: 295–303.

—— (2004*b*). 'Abelard on the Trinity', in J. E. Brower and K. Guilfoy (eds.), in *The Cambridge Companion to Abelard* (Cambridge: Cambridge University Press), 223–57.

—— (2005). 'Medieval Theories of Relations', *Stanford Encyclopedia of Philosophy*, <http://plato.stanford.edu/entries/relations-medieval/#3.3>, accessed 27 May 2008.

—— and REA, MICHAEL (2005*a*). 'Material Constitution and the Trinity', *Faith and Philosophy* 22: 487–505.

—— (2005*b*). 'Understanding the Trinity', *Logos* 8: 145–57.

BROWN, DAVID (1985). *The Divine Trinity*. La Salle: Open Court.

—— (1989). 'Trinitarian Personhood and Individuality', in Feenstra and Plantinga (1989: 48–78).

CAIN, JAMES (1989). 'The Doctrine of the Trinity and the Logic of Relative Identity', *Religious Studies* 25: 141–52.

CARTWRIGHT, RICHARD (1987). 'On the Logical Problem of the Trinity', in id., *Philosophical Essays*. Cambridge, Mass.: MIT, 187–200.

CARY, PHILIP (1992). 'On Behalf of Classical Trinitarianism: A Critique of Rahner on the Trinity', *Thomist* 56: 365–404.

—— (1995). 'Historical Perspectives on Trinitarian Doctrine', *Religious and Theological Studies Fellowship Bulletin*, Nov/Dec, <http://www.scribd.com/doc/2385279/Historical-Perspectives-on-Trinitarian-Doctrine-by-Phillip-Cary>, accessed 27 May 2008.

CLARK, KELLY JAMES (1996). 'Trinity or Tritheism?', *Religious Studies* 32: 463–76.

COAKLEY, SARAH (1999). ' "Persons" and the "Social" Doctrine of the Trinity: A Critique of Current Analytic Discussion', in Davis, Kendall, and O'Collins (eds.), *The Trinity*, 123–44.

—— (ed.) (2003). *Re-thinking Gregory of Nyssa*. Oxford: Blackwell.

CRAIG, WILLIAM LANE (2005). 'Does the Problem of Material Constitution Illuminate the Doctrine of the Trinity?', *Faith and Philosophy* 22: 77–86.

CROSS, RICHARD (2002*a*). 'Two Models of the Trinity?', *Heythrop Journal* 43: 275–94.

—— (2002*b*). 'Gregory of Nyssa on Universals', *Vigiliae Christianae* 56: 372–410.

DAVIS, STEPHEN T., KENDALL, DANIEL, and O'COLLINS, GERALD (eds.) (1999). *The Trinity*. New York: Oxford University Press.

DE RÉGNON, THEODORE (1892–8). *Études de théologie positive sur la Sainte Trinité*, 4 vols. Paris: Victor Retaux.

FEENSTRA, RONALD, and PLANTINGA, CORNELIUS, JR. (eds.) (1989). *Trinity, Incarnation, and Atonement*. Notre Dame: University of Notre Dame Press.

FESER, EDWARD (1997). 'Swinburne's Tritheism', *International Journal for Philosophy of Religion* 42: 175–84.

FORREST, PETER (1998). 'Divine Fission: A New Way of Moderating Social Trinitarianism', *Religious Studies* 34: 281–97.

GEACH, PETER (1967). 'Identity', *Review of Metaphysics* 21: 3–12. Repr. in *Logic Matters*. Berkeley: University of California Press, 1972.

—— (1980). *Reference and Generality*, 3rd edn. Ithaca: Cornell University Press.

HASKER, WILLIAM (1970). 'Tri-Unity', *Journal of Religion* 50: 1–32.

HODGE, CHARLES (1873). *Systematic Theology*. New York: Scribner, Armstrong, i.

HOWARD-SNYDER, DANIEL (2003). 'Trinity Monotheism', *Philosophia Christi* 5: 375–403.

KELLY, J. N. D. (trans.) (1964). *The Athanasian Creed*. London: Adam & Charles Black.

—— (1972). *Early Christian Creeds*, 3rd edn. New York: Longman.

LACUGNA, CATHERINE MOWRY (1986). 'Philosophers and Theologians on the Trinity', *Modern Theology* 2: 169–81.

—— (1991). *God For Us: The Trinity and Christian Life*. San Francisco: Harper San Francisco.

LAYMAN, C. STEPHEN (1988). 'Tritheism and the Trinity', *Faith and Philosophy* 5: 291–8.

LEFTOW, BRIAN (1999). 'Anti Social Trinitarianism', in Davis, Kendall, and O'Collins, *The Trinity*, 203–49.

—— (2004). 'A Latin Trinity', *Faith and Philosophy* 21: 304–33.

—— (2007). 'Modes without Modalism', in P. van Inwagen and D. Zimmerman (eds.), *Persons: Human and Divine*. Oxford: Oxford University Press, 357–75.

LEITH, JOHN H. (ed.) (1982). *Creeds of the Churches*, 3rd edn. Louisville, Ky.: John Knox.

MARTINICH, A. P. (1978). 'Identity and Trinity', *Journal of Religion* 58: 169–81.

—— (1979). 'God, Emperor, and Relative Identity', *Franciscan Studies* 39: 180–91.

MERRICKS, TRENTON (2006). 'Split Brains and the Godhead', in Thomas Crisp et al. (eds.), *Knowledge and Reality: Essays in Honor of Alvin Plantinga*. Dordrecht: Kluwer.

MOLTMANN, JÜRGEN (1981). *The Trinity and the Kingdom: The Doctrine of God*, trans. Margaret Kohl. San Francisco: Harper San Francisco.

MORELAND, J. P., and CRAIG, WILLIAM LANE (2003). *Philosophical Foundations for a Christian Worldview*. Downers Grove: InterVarsity Press.

MORRIS, THOMAS V. (1991). *Our Idea of God*. Downers Grove: InterVarsity Press.

O'COLLINS, GERALD (1999). *The Tripersonal God*. Mahwah: Paulist Press.

PLACHER, WILLIAM (1983). *A History of Christian Theology*. Philadelphia: Westminster.

PLANTINGA, CORNELIUS, JR. (1986). 'Gregory of Nyssa and the Social Analogy of the Trinity', *Thomist* 50: 325–52.

—— (1988). 'The Threeness/Oneness Problem of the Trinity', *Calvin Theological Journal* 23: 37–53.

—— (1989). 'Social Trinity and Tritheism', in Feenstra and Plantinga, *Trinity, Incarnation, and Atonement*, 21–47.

REA, MICHAEL (2003). 'Relative Identity and the Doctrine of the Trinity', *Philosophia Christi* 5: 431–46.

—— (2006). 'Polytheism and Christian Belief', *Journal of Theological Studies* 57: 133–48.

RICHARDSON, CYRIL (1955). 'The Enigma of the Trinity', in Roy Battenhouse (ed.), *Companion to the Study of St. Augustine*. New York: Oxford University Press, 235–56.

SCHAFF, PHILIP, and WACE, HENRY (1887/1999). *Nicene and Post-Nicene Fathers, First Series*, 14 volumes. Peabody: Hendrickson.

—— —— (1900/1999). *Nicene and Post-Nicene Fathers, Second Series*, 14 volumes. Peabody: Hendrickson.

SCHWARTZ, E. (ed.) (1914). *Acta Conciliorum Oecumenicorum* (Berlin: W. de Gruyter).

STEAD, CHRISTOPHER (1977). *Divine Substance*. New York: Oxford University Press.

SWINBURNE, RICHARD (1994). *The Christian God*. Oxford: Clarendon.

TUGGY, DALE (2003). 'The Unfinished Business of Trinitarian Theorizing', *Religious Studies* 39: 165–83.

—— (2004). 'Divine Deception, Identity, and Social Trinitarianism', *Religious Studies* 40: 269–87.

TURCESCU, LUCIAN (2005). *Gregory of Nyssa and the Concept of Divine Persons*. New York: Oxford University Press.

VAN INWAGEN, PETER (1988). 'And Yet They Are Not Three Gods But One God', in Thomas Morris (ed.), *Philosophy and the Christian Faith*. Notre Dame: University of Notre Dame Press, 241–78.

—— (2003). 'Three Persons in One Being: On Attempts to Show that the Doctrine of the Trinity is Self-Contradictory', in Melville Stewart (ed.), *The Holy Trinity*. Dordrecht: Kluwer, 83–97.

—— (2004). 'A Theory of Properties', *Oxford Studies in Metaphysics* 1: 107–38.

WIERENGA, EDWARD (2004). 'Trinity and Polytheism', *Faith and Philosophy* 21: 281–94.

WILLIAMS, C. J. F. (1994). 'Neither Confounding the Persons nor Dividing the Substance', in Alan Padgett (ed.), *Reason and the Christian Religion: Essays in Honor of Richard Swinburne*. Oxford: Clarendon, 227–43.

WOLFSON, H. A. (1964). *The Philosophy of the Church Fathers*, i. *Faith, Trinity, Incarnation*. Cambridge: Harvard University Press.

CHAPTER 19

ORIGINAL SIN AND ATONEMENT

OLIVER D. CRISP

THE atonement is one of the central and defining doctrines of Christian theology. Yet the nature of the atonement—how it is that Christ's life and death on the cross actually atone for human sin—remains a theological conundrum. Over the centuries a number of different theories of the atonement have been proposed that attempt to make sense of the biblical data and offer an account of the nature of the atonement. But none has won universal support. This chapter offers a new argument for an old theory of the atonement, namely, penal substitution. This is called for because it seems to me that traditional arguments for penal substitution (though not the doctrine itself) face several serious difficulties that have led a number of theologians, past and present, to reject or amend the doctrine. If my argument is correct, then some of the most serious problems facing traditional arguments for penal substitution can be circumvented.

We shall proceed as follows. First I shall set out the theological context for the argument. This involves giving some account of alternative theories of the atonement in the tradition, and why penal substitution might be thought a particularly appealing way of thinking about the atonement. Then I shall set forth an argument for a version of penal substitution that involves the application of an idea found in some Augustinian accounts of the transmission of sin from Adam to his progeny. At the end of this exposition, I offer some brief comments on the metaphysics undergirding the theology of this argument. In a final section, several theological and philosophical objections to this reasoning are discussed.

CONTEXT: SOME THEORIES OF ATONEMENT

Systematic theologies usually include a discussion of a number of different accounts of the atonement found in the Christian tradition. Although different taxonomies could be offered, I shall discuss the following: the ransom theory; the satisfaction theory; the moral exemplar theory; and penal substitution. These are not all the theories of atonement one can find in the Christian tradition. But they are arguably the most influential.[1]

Some version of the ransom theory is often thought to be the majority view in the Patristic period of the church. It is certainly not the view of all the Fathers, but it is reflected in the work of a number of patristic authors.[2] The story informing some historic versions of this theory runs like this: through sinning against God, human beings have sold themselves into slavery to the Devil. God, not wishing to see humanity remain in this benighted situation, deigns to bring about the means by which human beings can be emancipated from their vitiated moral condition and indentured state. This involves the incarnation and work of Christ, who hoodwinks the Devil into bringing about his death on the cross. Instead of destroying Christ, this act actually enables Christ to pay the ransom price required to liberate human beings. Thus, the work of Christ achieves two interconnected goals: to break the hold evil (in the person of Satan) has over human beings, and to enable human beings to be reconciled with God.

The ransom theory (expressed in the sort of story just given) was dusted down in the mid-twentieth century by the Scandinavian theologian Gustaf Aulén, whose book *Christus Victor* claimed that the ransom model was the 'classic' view of the atonement, which had been overlaid by centuries of theological accretions.[3] He maintains that this classic view is superior to later accounts of the work of Christ and should be preferred to other ways of thinking about the atonement. Aulén's work has been widely discussed, particularly amongst systematic theologians. But it is not without problems.

One concern with Aulén's work is that it is not obvious that the ransom view is *the* 'classic' account of the atonement, or the best or most comprehensive way of thinking about the nature of atonement. That would have to be argued for. Even if the ransom view is the majority position amongst the Fathers, this does not automatically give it a privileged status above other theories of the atonement. The venerable pedigree of a given theory is not, after all, a cast-iron guarantee of its being the best explanation of the data. A second problem is that the ransom theory involves a rather naive account of the relationship between the Fall, human sin, and enslavement to the Devil, with unpleasant overtones of God being implicated in an act of deception. That said, the conceptual hard core of the doctrine is that Christ's work is remedial, being the price required to 'purchase' or 'buy back' some number of fallen humanity enslaved to evil. It is perfectly feasible to set out such a doctrine without the paraphernalia of the story about deceiving the Devil. Then, Christ's work would bring about the reconciliation of some number of fallen humanity, including their release from the power of evil—the language about the personification of evil having been removed. This would have the advantage of divesting the theory of the unwelcome consequence of God's involvement in deception. However, if the core of the theory can be stated without the need for personified evil, to whom is the ransom price of Christ's work paid? It might be possible to 'amend' the theory in the direction of a satisfaction account of the atonement at this point. In which case God, whose moral governance has been impugned by human sin (let us say), requires the 'ransom' as the price for human wickedness. Taken in this way, Christ's work is not so much a question of paying the ransom demand of the Devil as paying the price demanded by the divine moral law for human sin. This moral demand might be thought a 'ransom' in a loose, non-philosophical sense, since it involves payment of a price set in order to bring about the reconciliation of some number of fallen human beings. But it is not a ransom in the sense of a payment made to a diabolical entity that has enslaved humanity.

But it may be simpler to put to one side those aspects of this theory that are objectionable, and search for an atonement theory able to account for what is helpful in this understanding of the work of Christ. I suggest there are good theological reasons for pursuing such an alternative. For one thing, New Testament references to the payment of a ransom (e.g. the Greek word *lutron* used in Matt. 20: 28 and the parallel in Mark 10: 45) do not require a ransom theory of atonement to be rendered plausible or consistent with other things in Scripture. In the context of these passages, the idea of ransom has to do with saving fallen humans ('the many') from a condition of oppression through an act of self-sacrifice. In fact, there are no biblical grounds for thinking God enters into some unholy pact with the Devil over the enslavement and ransom of humanity. Moreover, satisfaction or penal substitution theories of atonement can make sense of this biblical idea of ransom, along the lines of Christ's work being able to 'buy back' some number of fallen humanity from the moral consequences of sin, without the unhelpful elements of the ransom theory.[4]

This brings us to the satisfaction theory, elements of which we have already segued into the ransom account. Satisfaction is a theory that is given its first systematic exposition in St Anselm of Canterbury's magisterial *Cur Deus Homo* (Why The God-Man). Famously, St Anselm's version of satisfaction theory is set up *remoto christo*—that is, setting aside the incarnation and reasoning simply on the basis of more general theological claims to the necessity of the incarnation of a God-Man for atonement to be made. St Anselm thinks that the nature of God is such that he *requires* satisfaction for sin committed against him. God cannot set aside satisfaction without in some way compromising his own perfect character, which is impossible. Because human sin is committed against a being of infinite worth and honour (i.e. God), it generates a correspondingly infinite demerit that no finite human being can annul, even if he or she were without sin.[5] And any putative redeemer would have to be without sin because only then would such a person be in a position to perform an act of supererogation, that is, an act that is non-obligatory and generates a merit sufficient to atone for human sin (i.e. a merit of infinite worth). Any sinful human would be incapable of producing such an act since he or she is already infinitely indebted to God on account of his or her sinful condition. And any sinless human would still be incapable of producing a supererogatory act of sufficient merit to balance off the sin of all humanity, since no mere human moral action generates an infinite merit that can be applied to all humanity. Although he does not make this explicit, the logic of St Anselm's position means that some other creature, e.g. a sinless angel, cannot act on behalf of human beings in this regard—nor could an angel generate an act of sufficient merit to balance off human sin, since angels cannot perform acts that have an infinite merit, on account of being finite creatures.[6] In fact, reasons St Anselm, only God is capable of producing a supererogatory act that would be of sufficient merit to offer satisfaction for human sin. But since one of the stipulations for satisfaction according to St Anselm is that a human being acts on behalf of other human beings in atonement,[7] only a being that is at-one-and-the-same-time both fully divine and fully human can provide satisfaction for (human) sin. Hence, St Anselm arrives at the conclusion that only the God-Man can perform an act of supererogation that has the worth requisite to provide satisfaction; God must become human in order to atone for human sin.

On the Anselmian account, the mechanism for atonement has to do with the God-Man performing some infinitely meritorious act that may be used as a merit sufficient to balance out the demerit of human sin. Christ performs such an act in his atonement, offering the merit to God on behalf of fallen human beings. His meritorious act is performed in order to satisfy the moral law to which fallen humans are, as it were, 'indebted'. But it is no part of this theory that the God-Man take upon himself the penal consequences of human sin, standing in the place of fallen humans as a penal substitute, as with the penal substitutionary theory of atonement. The soubriquet 'the commercial theory of atonement' by which the Anselmian view is known in some older textbooks of theology underlines the transactional character of the Anselmian satisfaction theory.

Recently, Richard Swinburne has defended a modified version of satisfaction theory, without St Anselm's commitment to the notion that God *requires* satisfaction for sin, commitment to the moral claim that sin is infinitely heinous, or the idea that Christ's atonement must be strictly equivalent in value to the sin committed against God.[8] He speaks of his theory in terms of the biblical idea of sacrifice, which he regards as the most helpful way of conceiving of the work of Christ found in Scripture, namely, Christ offering himself up as a sacrifice for human sin. But in Swinburne's hands this notion of sacrifice is construed in a way that is consistent with a version of satisfaction. Christ offers up some supererogatory act of sacrifice to God, and fallen human beings are able to somehow 'access' that work in order to bring about their own redemption. In some respects, this echoes the more moderate version of satisfaction theory advocated by St Thomas Aquinas, according to which Christ's satisfaction for sin is a most fitting means of atonement, but not necessarily the only one possible, all things considered. That said, St Thomas does suggest that the atonement is consequentially necessary in some sense, that is, necessary as a consequence of God ordaining to bring about the sort of world he did, with human beings who would sin and require salvation.[9] Swinburne distances himself from this language about the consequential necessity of atonement, and several other aspects of the Thomist understanding of Christ's work in his own account of Christ's work.

The concept of atonement used to do much of the work in Swinburne's theory includes four distinct components: repentance, apology, reparation, and penance. Humans are able to repent and apologize to God for their sin. But they are not able to offer adequate reparation or penance—God must arrange this. Swinburne thinks that 'the way in which we humans can use Christ's life and death as a means of removing sin is by offering it as our reparation and penance. To do so, we must join to it our feeble repentance and halting words of apology.'[10] He concedes that God may set aside satisfaction and simply forgive sin. But God has good reason not to do this. Human beings need to understand the moral seriousness of their sins, just as children need to be corrected when they have gone astray. And it is permissible for God to bring about some supererogatory act of satisfaction through the work of Christ, though there is no necessity for God to do so, all things considered. If we think of Swinburne's theory as a moderate version of satisfaction as I am suggesting, then it looks like the hard core of satisfaction theories has to do with the issue of God's honour and/or moral law being satisfied by some act of supererogation which is performed by the God-Man, and to which we join our own act of penitence. Whether Christ's act is a requirement for satisfaction, what moral value it must have (if it must have a particular moral value at all) and in what sense it is necessary all things considered, if it is necessary at all, appear to be matters that not all satisfaction theorists agree upon.

To my mind, the satisfaction theory of atonement is less attractive than penal substitution—though only marginally less attractive—for reasons that will become apparent presently. In any case, what I am calling the 'hard core' of satisfaction theories can be assimilated by theories of penal substitution, though the exact mechanism by which atonement is brought about differs between the two theories.[11] However, if it transpires that some of the more controversial aspects of penal substitution are indefensible (e.g. the claim that culpability for my sin can be transferred to Christ), some version of the satisfaction theory may be able to succeed where penal substitution fails.

We come to the moral exemplar theory, the first clear statement of which is often thought to be traceable to elements of Abelard's theory of atonement, written at least in part in response to St Anselm's work. However, caution needs to be exercised in evaluating this claim, often repeated in textbooks of Christian theology. Recently, Philip Quinn has challenged the idea that Abelard's account of the atonement is reducible to something like the idea that Christ is merely a moral example whose work we should emulate, and whose act of love in the atonement ought to stimulate in us a reciprocal response of love to God.[12] Whether or not Abelard's medieval theory has elements that sound at times like an embryonic version of a moral exemplar theory, it is certainly true that the moral exemplar theory enjoyed a vogue in early modern theology with the advent of Socinianism, which, in the work of Faustus Socinus, sought to overthrow the arguments of advocates of penal substitution and satisfaction theories of atonement.[13] Interest in this theory continued in nineteenth-century liberal theology. A modern version of this sort of view can be found in the work of the British philosopher of religion, John Hick.[14] As part of his bid to provide a religiously pluralist account of Christology, he argues that Christ's work must be seen primarily in terms of a moral example of self-sacrificial love, and what, following F. D. E. Schleiermacher, we might call 'God-consciousness'. There is no satisfaction brought about by the work of Christ, on this view, since no such satisfaction is necessary. Indeed, one persistent objection to this sort of account of the work of Christ is that it is not really a theory of atonement at all, since the logic of this view is that nothing is atoned for. On Hick's version of the theory, human sin is really a matter which, though not trivial, may be forgiven without any reparation being exacted as satisfaction. But even if this view does not necessarily trivialize sin, it does raise a rather serious problem about the moral cost involved in the incarnation and death of Christ. One is left wondering why God could not have provided the requisite moral example for human beings to emulate without such terrible cost to himself.

This is not to deny that Christ's atonement is a moral example and act of love. The question is whether the work of Christ is *reducible* to these elements. In my view it is not. As I have just indicated, something more needs to be said about the nature of Christ's work in order for it to be a work of atonement, although Christ's work certainly includes the components of the moral exemplar theory. Here much depends on the theory of punishment one adopts. Defenders of the moral exemplar theory reject the idea that retribution—where there must be a moral 'fit' between crime and punishment—is part of the theory of punishment that informs the work of Christ. God is not 'wroth with sin'; he is not bound to punish; in fact, in some versions of this theory he is bound not to punish, but to forgive sin. All of which is in stark contrast to the other theories of atonement canvassed here, which in various ways include retributive punishment as a constituent of divine distributive justice.[15]

The final theory of atonement we shall consider is penal substitution. I take it that penal substitution is that family of views of the atonement according to which Christ's atoning work on the cross consists in his acting as a penal substitute, taking upon himself the penal consequences of my sin and being punished for that sin in place of the sinner. As I have already intimated, this atonement theory is able to incorporate the core ideas of the other theories we have discussed, whilst offering a different understanding of the nature of the atonement.[16] Hence, the advocate of penal substitution can agree that Christ's work is remedial, as per the ransom theory. It also includes the concept of satisfaction (of divine moral law). And, in common with moral exemplar, satisfaction, and ransom theories, defenders of penal substitution may speak of Christ's work as providing a moral example in life and death of obedience to the will of God that Christians ought to emulate.

In the theological literature, the relation between Christ's penal substitution for the sinner and the sinner's sin and/or guilt is usually (though not always) made sense of according to what I shall call a *forensic fiction*.[17] God treats Christ as if he is guilty of the sin of fallen human beings, and 'punishes' him accordingly, bringing about his death on the cross, which is a suitable act of atonement. God also treats the sinner as if she was sinless in view of Christ's work on the cross, provided the sinner appropriates that work for herself. (Quite how that is done is beyond the scope of this chapter.) The important thing to see here is that on this forensic fiction account of penal substitution, the innocent Christ really is treated as if he were the guilty sinner, though he is not. And God really does punish the innocent in the place of the guilty. Christ is said to 'represent' the sinner in his act of atonement.

There are, as David Lewis points out, definite analogues to penal substitution in human systems of justice, and in many ways we humans are in two minds about penal substitution, irrespective of whether or not we believe in its theological application.[18] We allow it under certain conditions for certain sorts of crime where the penal consequences of the crime committed are pecuniary in nature. But we do not allow it when the crime is, say, first-degree murder. In that case, the penal consequences of the crime committed have to be met by the one guilty of the crime and we would consider it unjust if a substitute were to serve the punishment in place of the perpetrator. Cases of crimes where the penal consequences involved are pecuniary, or monetary, need not be trivial. They can be very serious crimes such as large-scale fraud, which carry with them crippling financial consequences for the person convicted of that crime. In such circumstances what is important is that the fine is paid, not that the perpetrator pays it. Someone generous enough might pay the full penalty on behalf of the fraudster, if they had the financial wherewithal. The law would be satisfied, even though the perpetrator of the crime has not actually paid the penal consequence set out by the law—a substitute has done so instead. But importantly, we find no examples of legislation allowing substitution when the crime is a serious felony, such as murder. In such cases, the one guilty must meet the penal consequences of that crime, and we would consider it a terrible miscarriage of justice were a substitute punished in place of the perpetrator.

Hence, there are circumstances in which penal substitution in human jurisprudence is deemed appropriate, while there are others—perhaps more precise analogues to our situation as condemned sinners before God—where, it seems, it is not. What the defender of the theological application of penal substitution needs is some reason for thinking that it is just for God to punish Christ in place of the sinner. We need to know why the theological application of the doctrine is morally permissible, as with the case of pecuniary penal substitution, outlined by Lewis. For, whatever else the defender of penal substitution says, unlike pecuniary penal substitution, it certainly *looks* unjust that Christ, an innocent individual, should be punished in place of me, a sinful individual. This concern goes all the way back to the Socinians of the immediate post-Reformation period, and can still be heard today.[19]

REALIST PENAL SUBSTITUTION:
THE ARGUMENT

Nevertheless, I think an argument for penal substitution can be had, which gets around these difficulties. It is to that argument we now turn. A central plank of the reasoning I will set forth involves appropriating a theological concept called Augustinian realism, deriving from St Augustine of Hippo's work on original sin.[20] Advocates of this view claim that original sin includes both the state of moral corruption with which all humanity post-Adam are born, which inevitably leads humans into acts of sin, and the culpability aspect of guilt that accrues to Adam's first sin.[21] Both the moral corruption engendered by Adam's primal sin and the culpability aspect of his guilt is transferred, on this way of thinking, from Adam to his progeny. This transfer of Adam's sin and guilt to me is just provided God somehow organizes things such that Adam and his posterity are one metaphysical entity so that what the first part of that entity does has moral implications for later parts of the same entity.[22] Hence, Adam's sin and guilt on this view is (somehow) *really* mine. For this reason, the view is called Augustinian *realism*.

A number of theologians who have defended robust accounts of original sin including the concept of original guilt have thought that it makes much more sense to conceive of the transmission of original sin as a question of God imputing Adam's sin and guilt to me, treating me as if I was originally sinful and guilty of Adam's sin, though I am not, strictly speaking (which is, of course, another instance of a theological forensic fiction). But defenders of Augustinian realism usually object that treating someone *as if* they are guilty of a crime is not the same as their being guilty of that crime. Moreover, being held culpable for the crime of another, especially another that is removed in time and space from me, and whose course of action I did not and could not have approved or otherwise endorsed, is monumentally unjust. Thus, if God imputes the sin and guilt of Adam to me, he acts unjustly. But God cannot act unjustly. Scripture states that God does transmit the sin and guilt of Adam to his progeny (Rom. 5: 12–19). So there must be some other account of this transmission that does not have the morally unpalatable consequence of God imputing Adam's sin and guilt to me. And Augustinian realism is such an explanation.[23] St Augustine does not put it quite like that, but there are certainly later Augustinian realists who do think in these terms.[24]

The central Augustinian realist notion that Adam and his progeny are somehow metaphysically united so that original sin may be justly transmitted from Adam to his posterity is often conflated with a particular theory about the manner of such transmission. But Augustinian realism is not a thesis that requires a particular account of the exact mechanism by which this transmission occurs. It is simply the theological notion that such an arrangement obtains between Adam and his progeny. How such a metaphysical arrangement obtains is not the same issue as that it obtains (if it does obtain). Some Augustinian realists claim that the mechanism by which this arrangement obtains involves traducianism. Individual souls are produced by fission or parturition, being generated by the soul of one or both parents as part of the process of natural generation. The parent souls are produced in the same fashion from their parents, and so on, going all the way back through the generations to the first human pair. In which case, my soul is literally, though mediately, a chip off the old (Adamic) block; my soul was part of the soul of Adam when he sinned prior to its being 'individualized', so to speak, through a process of fission or parturition down through the generations from Adam to me.[25] According to the traducian, it is just for God to punish me for Adam's sin since my soul was part of Adam's soul when it sinned. But an Augustinian realist need not be a traducian, although, as a matter of historical fact, most have been. That is, an Augustinian realist need not be committed to a particular theory of *how* God brings about the distinction between Adam and his progeny whilst still making the idea of original unity plausible, in order for sin to be justly transmitted from one human being to the other.

Let us now attempt to apply this theological 'realist' thesis about the union of Adam and his progeny in the transmission of original sin to the atonement in order to help make sense of the union between Christ and those human beings he saves through his work. In so doing I shall not be concerned with expounding Augustine or his followers, but merely with trying to make sense of a particular construal of Augustinian realism, and its application to the work of Christ. This construal avoids the traducian version of Augustinian realism and opts instead for a different, four-dimensionalist account of the 'realist' transmission of sin.

We begin with the idea that Adam and his progeny are (somehow) one metaphysical entity such that God may justly pass on the moral consequences of Adam's sin to his heirs because they are all members of one persisting entity, or object, that we might call *Fallen Humanity*. To be clear, this object is composed only of Adam and his progeny all of whom are 'parts'[26] or phases in the life of the whole entity. On the sort of view of Fallen Humanity I have in mind, if the first 'part' of the object sins, later 'parts' of the same object (including all of humanity after Adam) have a vitiated moral nature as a result of the action of Adam. It is rather like an acorn that is infected with some disease that then affects all the later stages in the life of the sapling and tree into which it grows.[27]

Of course, it does not follow that just because Adam and his progeny are 'parts' of one persisting object, Adam's progeny share the same morally vitiated condition as Adam. Nor does it follow that just because an acorn is infected with some disease all the later stages in the life of the tree into which it grows are affected by this disease. Some diseases might only affect the first phase of the life of the tree, rather than all phases of its life. But the sort of reasoning I have in mind is offered as a possible explanation of how original sin is transmitted from one generation to the next from some first human parents. It is true that later phases of the life of a persisting entity may not be affected by what happens in an earlier phase of the same life. But the Augustinian realist story is concerned to make sense of the claim that just such an arrangement does obtain in the case of Adam and his progeny. All that needs to be granted here is that it is possible for a given entity to have phases of its life that are affected by earlier phases of its life, and that all phases of the life of a given persisting entity may be affected by what happens to one of the first 'parts' or phases of that entity. This seems plausible just as it seems plausible to think that an infected acorn may grow into a tree that is diseased in every subsequent phase of its existence. And this fits with the Augustinian realist story of original sin I am drawing upon.[28]

Still, even if there are diseases that affect the life of the tree in all its phases, the disease afflicting the life of the mature oak is not necessarily the same as the disease affecting the life of the sapling, or the acorn. But suppose it is the same disease introduced to the acorn that affects all the later phases of the life of the oak into which it grows. Is the corruption affecting the oak the same as the corruption affecting the acorn? Much depends here on the ontology one adopts. If one thinks persisting objects are wholly present at each moment of their existence, then one might think that this is the same disease. But if one thinks that the acorn and oak are different temporal parts of one perduring four-dimensional whole object, then one has a reason for thinking the disease affecting the oak is not numerically the same as that affecting the acorn. For presumably any disease persisting through time has temporal parts just as the tree it infects has. And the temporal parts of a given thing are said to be numerically distinct. So the fact that on this way of thinking the oak tree does not have numerically the same disease as the sapling does not pose any particular problem that defenders of temporal parts are not already familiar with.

Temporal parts theorists sometimes speak of 'tokens' possessed by individual temporal parts of an object, and the property possessed by a whole object. On this way of thinking, the guilt-token of the temporal part of Trevor existing now is numerically distinct from the guilt-token of Trevor existing a moment ago. Yet both are tokens of the guilt of Trevor, the four-dimensional entity who has these temporal parts. The Augustinian realist can claim that the original sin (and guilt) Trevor has transmitted to him from the first human is like the example of the guilt-token later temporal parts of Trevor share with earlier temporal parts of Trevor. God arranges things such that Adam and his progeny are a four-dimensional entity to whom such moral-tokens can be attributed, and the morally vitiated condition Adam post-Fall incurs is one that is transmitted to all later phases of the life of this entity, Fallen Humanity.

But this may not be the only metaphysical story consistent with Augustinian realism. Perhaps one can say both that objects that persist through time are normally wholly present at each moment of their existence, and that in the case of the transmission of original sin the human species propagates sin through natural generation. Construed along the lines of traducianism, this means that I have Adam's sin and guilt because my soul is either a fraction of the soul Adam possessed (if souls are generated through fission) or the product of the soul of at least one of my parents, going all the way back to Adam (if souls are parturient). Though 'individualized' or otherwise brought about through natural generation, I retain the property of original sin that has been passed on to me, as would be the case with inherited physical diseases. The important difference between inherited disease and original sin, on this way of thinking, is that my soul was present when Adam sinned as part of the 'unindividualized' soul that Adam possessed. Or, perhaps, the 'seed' of my soul was present in the soul of Adam, if souls are parturient rather than fissiparous (compare Heb. 7: 10). So I am guilty of Adam's sin on account of possessing a fraction of Adam's soul or 'seed' thereof that is now 'individualized' through soul-fission or parturition. But it seems consistent with this theological account of the manner by which sin is transmitted to say that persisting objects are wholly present at each moment of their existence. If this is right, then an Augustinian realist account of the transmission of original sin can be underpinned by more than one metaphysical account of persisting objects, depending on what the Augustinian realist thinks about the mechanism by which sin is transmitted.

This reasoning about an Augustinian realist account of the doctrine of original sin can be applied, the relevant changes having been made, to Christ and those for whose sins he came to atone—call them, with a nod to the tradition, the elect. Consider the possibility that Christ and the elect together compose one metaphysical entity that persists through time, just as, on the Augustinian realist way of thinking, Adam and his progeny do. This object we shall dub *Redeemed Humanity*. Christ is in some sense the first member of this entity, and the elect are subsequent members.

But here the analogy between Adam and Christ begins to break down. For, according to the Augustinian realist account of the transmission of sin, Adam as the first human can affect the moral condition of all subsequent humans in a way that some later human being could not (because some earlier humans would already have perished, or be beyond the influence of this later person, or could not be in possession of the whole 'unindividualized' soul that Adam had, or whatever). However, Christ's influence cannot just follow the arrow of time, moving from the moment his atonement is complete to include all those who are elect that exist after that time. Were this the case, then we would have no reason to think that anyone who lived temporally prior to Christ's act of atonement was amongst the elect. But, of course, Scripture says otherwise, with Hebrews 11 recounting a great cloud of witnesses for the faith in the Old Testament, and Paul in 1 Corinthians 10 speaking of the presence of Christ with the children of Israel wandering in the desert, that drank from the rock (at Meribah) that was Christ. So, a realist account of the atonement must also be able to include within the ambit of salvation those of the elect who lived prior to Christ.

One way of making sense of this[29] would involve co-opting Karl Barth's doctrine of election, or something very like it, as found in *Church Dogmatics* ii pt. 2.[30] According to Barth, Christ is the Elect One and all those for whom Christ's work atones are somehow derivatively elect 'in' Christ (which, for present purposes, we shall take to be functionally equivalent to Redeemed Humanity). This solves the problem of those who are derivatively elect and die before Christ by making Christ the 'first' amongst the elect, or, perhaps better, the agent through whom election is derived. He would not be temporally first amongst all the derivatively elect as Adam, on the Augustinian realist account, must be temporally the first human being for his sin to affect *all* those living after him. Instead, he would be somehow 'logically' or 'metaphysically' prior to the derivatively elect, whose derivative election depends, in some proleptic sense, on Christ's work as the Elect One. A 'realist' version of a Barth-like doctrine of election would also go some way towards explaining the relation between Christ and the derivatively elect, that is, Redeemed Humanity. They are all somehow members of one metaphysical entity with Christ being metaphysically 'prior', as it were, to those elect-in-Christ. Each of the derivatively elect is a part of a larger whole, including Christ. But—and here the Augustinian realism comes to the fore—the punishment due for the sin of the derivatively elect is transferred to Christ, or to that 'part' of Christ on the cross such that he really does take upon himself the penal consequences of sin for humanity. Although he is not the one who has sinned, or the part of the mass of Redeemed Humanity that has sinned, because he is a member of this larger entity, he may pay the consequences of the sin of other members of the same entity, by which I mean the derivatively elect, like you and me.

Conversely, the atoning work of Christ means that the derivatively elect are really united with Christ as 'parts' of one whole entity (Redeemed Humanity). Notice that there is no 'imputation' involved in this process, no forensic fiction, whereby God treats Christ as if he were the sinner for the purpose of bringing about atonement, as with many traditional accounts of penal substitution. The transference of the punishment for sin from fallen humanity to Christ, and the union of those self-same humans with Christ are two aspects of Christ's atoning work that involve a real union between Christ and the human beings concerned. And, plausibly, this Barth-like doctrine of election could be conjoined with a construal of the nature of the atonement as an act of penal substitution.[31] If what has been said so far sketches out how a Barth-like doctrine could tell an internally consistent story about the way in which the punishment due for human sin is transferred to Christ and how sinful human beings may be united to Christ in virtue of his act of atonement such that the nature of Christ's atonement is realist, then what remains to be explained is the manner in which his work brings about atonement.

The explanation goes like this. At the cross Christ has transferred to him the penal consequences of the sin of the derivatively elect—that is, the derivatively elect members of Redeemed Humanity. At that moment, he takes the penal consequences for which they are guilty, as one 'part' of the larger metaphysical whole. As a result he suffers for that sin. Having made atonement by expiating human sin in his own person, the members of Redeemed Humanity for whose sin he has atoned are reconciled to God.

A variation on this Barth-like version of realist penal substitution that involves a more traditional Reformed account of election could be applied just as well (nor do I suppose these are the only two ways of construing this doctrine[32]). As with the Barth-like version of the doctrine, the key problem is accounting for those amongst Redeemed Humanity who die prior to Christ's atoning act. A distinction must be maintained between the natural union of Adam and his progeny, in which Adam had to be the first human being in order that his sin might be transferred to the rest of humanity, and the forensic union of Christ and the elect. The forensic nature of the atonement does not require that Christ is chronologically the first human of a new, elect humanity. All it requires is that somehow his atonement is the catalyst by which human sin is atoned for. In this respect, as before, he is metaphysically or logically 'prior' to the other parts of Redeemed Humanity, although many of those who make up Redeemed Humanity live chronologically prior to Christ.

The manner of atonement on this more traditional Reformed account is as follows. Christ on the cross has transferred to him the penal consequences for the sin of the rest of Redeemed Humanity, and he atones for their sin on the cross. As a consequence of this act, the members of Redeemed Humanity other than Christ, including all those who lived and died prior to the atonement, are reconciled to God.[33] The important difference between Christ and the elect and Adam and his progeny on this view is that because the relation between Christ on the cross and the elect is a forensic one, Christ is not a 'part' of Redeemed Humanity that is guilty of sin. He is innocent. But he is able to take upon himself the penal consequences of the sin of the elect because he is a part of the same object.[34]

So, we have at least two ways in which an Augustinian realist account of the atonement could be set forth, namely, the Barthian and the traditional Reformed versions of the doctrine. Note that although both the Barthian and more traditional, Reformed realist versions of penal substitution require that the penal consequences of the sin of the elect is transferred to Christ, they avoid the moral problems besetting other, standard arguments for penal substitution that require only that Christ acts on behalf of sinful humans as their representative. This is usually called *representationalism*, and it is this argument that requires a forensic fiction in order to make good on the act of atonement. It is this that has generated so much of the difficulties facing apologists for penal substitution. This problem is not so much overcome as circumvented by the realist accounts of penal substitution offered here, because Christ's act of atonement is not merely representationalist; he really takes upon himself the penal consequences for human sin. This does not mean that the other members of Redeemed Humanity are no longer guilty of sinning. As many classical theologians have noted, there is a difference between *being the one guilty of committing a sin*, and *being the one whose guilt requires punishment for that sin*. My sin can be atoned for. Yet I remain the one who committed that sin. It is just that the penal consequences of it have been dealt with so that I am no longer liable to punishment for that sin. (The same is true according to representationalism, of course, *mutatis mutandis*.) But according to the realist doctrine, these penal consequences of sin are transferable to Christ because he and I are members of one metaphysical whole, Redeemed Humanity.

Earlier, in outlining Augustinian realism, I pointed out that the central theological thesis of this theory is consistent with more than one metaphysical story concerning the mechanism by which God transmits original sin from Adam to his progeny. But it is difficult to see how the same could be true of the several realist accounts of atonement just offered. For it looks like the advocate of a version of 'realist' penal substitution is committed to some metaphysical story that includes a four-dimensionalist ontology, since, as I have set out the argument above, both Fallen Humanity and Redeemed Humanity are, in some sense, four-dimensional entities. But there are different ways in which one could extrapolate a four-dimensional ontology.[35] All I have said thus far concerning the 'realist' component of realist penal substitution commits its advocates to this sort of ontology. But there is still plenty of scope to argue over how one makes sense of that ontology, and in particular, how it is that the 'parts' or phases in the life of Fallen and Redeemed Humanity are related to one another, and to the four-dimensional entity as a whole.

Objections

Now this, I will admit, is strong mead that may be difficult to swallow. But then, the problems of the transmission of Adam's sin (and guilt) and of the transmission of the penal consequences of my sin to Christ are theological difficulties at the heart of the Christian faith that many of the greatest minds in Christendom have struggled to overcome. What I am suggesting is novel in some respects, although not without precedent (Tobias Crisp, John Owen, and even Eusebius of Caeserea use realist-sounding language of the atonement at times).[36] But even if there have been a small number of theologians in the past willing to consider something approaching a realist doctrine of the atonement, or who have made much of the language of 'mystical union' between Christ and the believer via the atonement, no one, to my knowledge, has mounted this sort of argument for the conclusion that penal substitution is just.

One problem with this is that many Christian thinkers are somewhat suspicious of theological novelty because any articulation of a particular doctrine must conform to Scripture and the tradition. I do not think the doctrine just outlined is contrary to Scripture. In fact, it seems to me to make good sense of Isa. 53: 6, Rom. 5: 12–19, and 2 Cor. 5: 21 in particular, where union with Christ and the notion of Christ 'becoming sin for us' are stressed. But it is true to say that this is not a traditional argument and that may be a problem. However, if this realist doctrine makes better sense of the theological version of penal substitution by offering a different metaphysical underpinning for that doctrine that avoids certain problems that beset traditional accounts of the doctrine, then I think it is worthy of serious consideration. After all, our understanding of the truth of the Gospel is sometimes mistaken. And, though I have not argued for this here, it seems to me that penal substitution is an important component of a true account of what Scripture teaches concerning the atonement.

In addition to such theological concerns, there are objections of a more philosophical nature that could be raised. One of the most pressing concerns how an apparently gerrymandered object such as Redeemed Humanity can possess moral properties, such as 'being sinful' or 'having temporal parts that are sinful'. It makes sense to think that you or I can be thought of like this because we are recognizably objects that persist through time (whatever that means). But Redeemed Humanity is not like that. It is an object cobbled together from 'real' persisting or perduring objects, that is, human persons, which seems to lack the integrity and personhood requisite to have such moral properties.

One line of response might be to query whether Fallen and Redeemed Humanity really are the subjects of moral properties, like persons. 'Being sinful' looks like a moral property, and one that does not apply to Fallen or Redeemed Humanity as a four-dimensional entity. But is, say, 'having temporal parts that are sinful' the sort of property that requires the entity of which it is predicated to be a moral subject? Not obviously. I suggest that Fallen Humanity does not have any moral properties that would require it to be a moral subject, like a person. Though Fallen Humanity is a real object, according to the Barth-like and traditional Reformed versions of realist penal substitution, it is not a person, nor a moral subject. Some of its members have moral properties. But it does not have moral properties that are predicated of it over and above the moral properties of some of its members. And the same is true, *mutatis mutandis*, for Redeemed Humanity.

Still, if this means that some members of Fallen Humanity and Redeemed Humanity have moral properties, this might be problematic. Earlier, in explaining how an advocate of Augustinian realism might appropriate a temporal parts construal of a four-dimensionalist ontology, I said perdurantists maintain that moral properties apply to certain sorts of 4-D wholes, like persons, the temporal parts of which have tokens of moral properties. Perhaps this component of a temporal parts doctrine can be applied here as well. Assume Fallen Humanity and Redeemed Humanity are objects that have temporal parts. Some of the temporal parts of these objects are themselves parts of other entities, distinct human agents that are themselves 4-D perduring objects that are moral subjects, whose temporal parts may only have tokens of moral properties. Now, Fallen and Redeemed Humanity have human agents as temporal parts—or, perhaps better, as phases (the term 'stages' having already been co-opted by another sort of four-dimensionalist, about which more in a moment). But from this it does not necessarily follow that Fallen or Redeemed Humanity as an object has properties that only a moral subject may.

There is another way of understanding a four-dimensionalist ontology that is also of help to the theologian in making sense of the transference of sin from Adam to his progeny, and of righteousness from Christ to his elect. This is stage theory.[37] According to the stage theorist, what we have been calling the temporal parts of 4-D wholes—but what they call 'stages' of 4-D entities—*do* have moral properties and it *does* make sense to say 'this stage of a 4-D agent is guilty of sinning at t_n'. Stage theorists need not posit such entities as Fallen and Redeemed Humanity either. They can tell a story according to which God treats certain stages as one persisting (i.e. exduring) entity, or 'makes' this the metaphysical truth of the matter. Or, perhaps there are certain immanent causal relations between stages of Adam up to his moment of original sin and all his progeny, on the one hand, and of Christ on the cross and all the elect, on the other, which corresponds to what I have been calling Fallen and Redeemed Humanity, respectively. But the argument I have offered thus far, which depends on the sort of organic connection between Adam and his progeny and Christ and his elect spoken of by a number of theologians, is not quite the same as this. Perhaps a stage-theoretic account of original sin and union with Christ is preferable to the perdurantist story. For present purposes three issues need to be made clear: that the 4-D ontology assumed in the foregoing argument for realist penal substitution can be construed in at least two ways, namely, a doctrine of temporal-parts or stage theory; that the temporal-parts construal of Fallen and Redeemed Humanity need not end up requiring that these two 4-D objects are moral agents of some kind; and that one could take a stage-theoretic account rather than a temporal-parts account of these things, making use of the same ontology understood rather differently. Either way, the problem of attributing moral properties to 'gerrymandered' 4-D wholes may be avoided.

I have already hinted that the 4-D ontology (however this is construed) might be thought to depend on a divine conventionalism, which seems consistent with Scriptures such as Rom. 9, Mal. 1, and other biblical passages that suggest there is no partiality with God, even that God's choice does not depend on creaturely actions (e.g. 2 Chron. 19: 7; Job 34: 19; Luke 20: 21; Gal. 2: 6; Col. 3: 25, etc.). But then it looks as though divine convention is doing all the work, which is yet another sort of philosophical objection to a realist penal substitution argument conjoined with some doctrine of divine conventionalism with respect to God bringing about certain 4-D objects. In fact, there are two parts to this objection, which might be put like this: Couldn't God bring about something like realist penal substitution, or an Augustinian realist account of the transfer of original sin from Adam to his progeny, by divine convention and without a doctrine of temporal parts or stage theory? And couldn't something much more like the commonsense view I mentioned earlier have purchase here if God simply ordains that a realist penal substitution, and/or a realist account of the transfer of original sin, obtains?

We have already answered the first of these questions in the affirmative: there are several ways of construing the 4-D ontology that underpins the versions of realist penal substitution we have set forth. The argument will need to be tweaked, depending on which construal of this ontology one opts for. But I am much more dubious about using a different ontology to make sense of realist penal substitution, such as that presupposed by the commonsense position, according to which persisting objects are wholly present at each moment of their existence. The obvious way forward for a commonsense way of thinking about these things is to say that God imputes Adam's sin to me, and my sin to Christ. But, it should be clear that such a way of thinking about these matters is mired in real moral difficulties, having to do with the very idea of imputing sin from one person to another, which implies a sort of moral and/or legal fiction that appears unjust. If it is said that divine conventionalism means God may treat any two persons or their parts as related in certain sorts of ways—even certain sorts of moral ways—as he sees fit, this seems to me divine conventionalism run amok. It is no part of the version of penal substitution outlined thus far that there are no morally relevant similarities between the temporal parts that make up Fallen or Redeemed Humanity. Nor is it any part of this doctrine that God may simply gerrymander temporal parts willy-nilly. For I suppose that God acts in accordance with his divine character, doing that which seems to him most fitting.

There is much more to be said about the atonement. What I have set out here is one theological story that connects the atonement with the doctrine of original sin in a way that involves a somewhat novel use of Augustinian realism, but remains faithful, I think, to those passages in Scripture wherein the union between Adam and his progeny on the one hand, and Christ and his elect on the other, are treated.

I have tried to indicate some of its virtues, not the least of which is that on this view we can say with the Apostle that, 'as by one man's disobedience many were *made* sinners, so also by one man's obedience many will be *made* righteous' (Rom. 5: 19).

Notes

My thanks to Gavin D'Costa, Tom Flint, Paul Helm, Daniel Hill, Joseph Jedwab, Brian Leftow, Mike Rea, Bill Schweitzer and Richard Swinburne for their comments on or concerning the argument of previous drafts of this chapter. Thanks too to the members of the Systematic Theology Seminar in the Faculty of Divinity, Cambridge University, The Joseph Butler Society, Oriel College, Oxford, and the Theology Seminar at St, Mary's College, University of St Andrews, where earlier versions of the latter part of this chapter were read in 2007.

1. I have dealt with two other views of the atonement elsewhere, namely, the governmental and the idea of Christ's vicarious humanity (stemming from the work of the nineteenth-century Scottish theologian John McLeod Campbell). Interested readers should consult Crisp 2008 and 2007*b* respectively. There has been renewed interest in discussion of the atonement as essentially a sacrifice amongst contemporary systematic theologians. There have also been a number of recent revisionist accounts of the atonement, which I will not enter into here. For discussion, see Fiddes 2007.

2. St Gregory of Nyssa's *Great Catechism* epitomizes the ransom view amongst the Patristic authors, whereas parts of St Athanasius' *On the Incarnation*, especially chs. 2 and 4, sound much more like a primitive satisfaction account of the atonement. For a standard historical discussion of the development of atonement doctrine, see Franks 1962.

3. Aulén 1931.

4. Other atonement theories may also offer a way of making sense of the biblical material on ransom, e.g. the governmental theory of atonement. I am not suggesting satisfaction or penal substitution theories are the only plausible alternatives.

5. This does have the apparently counterintuitive consequence that all sin entails an infinite demerit, which appears to make all sin equal for the purposes of culpability. There are possible responses to this problem, but it would take us too far from the main argument to discuss them. See e.g. Crisp 2003 and the literature cited there.

6. Like St Augustine of Hippo, St Anselm does think that one motivation for the redemption of fallen human beings is that their number make up the number of angels that fell with the Devil. See *Cur Deus Homo* 1. 16–18 in St Anselm 1998.

7. 'But the obligation rests with man, and no one else, to make the payment referred to. Otherwise mankind is not making recompense.' *Cur Deus Homo* 2. 6. Cf. 2. 7 in St Anselm 1998: 320–1.

8. Swinburne 1989.

9. Aquinas 1948, III q. 46. a. 1–4.

10. Swinburne 1989: 161.

11. One recent attempt to include aspects of Swinburne's account in a moderate doctrine of penal substitution can be found in Porter 2004.

12. Quinn 1993. See also Bynum 2004.

13. Franks 1962: 366 says that for Faustus Socinus, 'the death of Christ operates to redeem us in so far as it is an example of obedience, leads us to trust God, and gives us hope of deliverance from punishment'. The major work on the atonement by Faustus Socinus is *De Jesu Christo Servatore* (1594). A recent historical-theological reassessment of Socinus' importance can be found in Gomes 1993.

14. Hick 1993: 112–33. Another influential modern theological statement of the moral exemplar view *sans* commitment to religious pluralism can be found in Rashdall 1919.

15. Swinburne's theory means God could set aside divine retribution, though he does not. But saying God may not exact some reparation or satisfaction from humanity for human sin is not the same as saying God cannot exact some reparation or satisfaction from humanity because the very idea that God would act in this way is somehow immoral, or beneath the divine dignity. Those moral exemplarists that make this latter claim seem to be committed to a very different understanding of divine justice, according to which Christ's work is about reconciliation, but not atonement.

16. This is not a novel idea. In the modern literature it is discussed in Packer 1999.

17. Murray 1959 offers a classic treatment of this. The nineteenth-century Presbyterian theologian Charles Hodge has an idiosyncratic version of the forensic fictional view that is noteworthy. See Hodge 1940.

18. See Lewis 1997.

19. Thus Vincent Brümmer 2005: 75 'a theory of penal substitution strikes many of us today as highly immoral since it claims that God punishes the innocent for the transgressions of the guilty'.

20. St Augustine seems to think that all humanity was somehow 'seminally present' in Adam. See Augustine 1972, 13. 14. For a theological recapitulation of this view, see Berkhof 1939: 241–2.

21. A number of Augustinians distinguish between that aspect of guilt which is non-transferable, i.e. 'that *Trevor* was the one guilty of stabbing Dean' and the aspect of guilt that is transferable, having to do with liability to punishment. As we shall see in a moment, the punishment for a crime might be transferred to a penal substitute, though the person who committed the crime is still the one guilty of perpetrating the crime.

22. In fact, as we shall see, one construal of Augustinian realism is stronger than this. On this stronger view, the transfer of Adam's sin and guilt to me is just provided God somehow organizes things such that Adam and his posterity are one metaphysical entity *at the moment of primal sin*, and only thereafter differentiated into distinct human natures.

23. The idea that God imputes Adamic sin and/or guilt to Adam's progeny is found in much, though not all, Reformed theology. 'Realism' is a somewhat plastic term, having a variety of different applications in the current philosophical literature. But, as I indicate here, Augustinian realism uses the term in a rather different way from current analytical discussions about realism vs. anti-realism.

24. A robust defence of the imputation view can be found in Murray 1959. An example of the Augustinian realist view can be found in Shedd 2003: 434–82, 557–64, 630–1.

25. I take it that traducians deny a doctrine of the simplicity of souls, according to which souls are, as Chisholm puts it, 'simple substances', that is, without more basic parts from which they are composed. See Chisholm 1991.

26. I place 'parts' in parentheses here and in what follows because at this stage of the argument I am not concerned to assimilate the particular theological story concerning a realist account of penal substitution with the doctrine of temporal parts, which I take to be a particular metaphysical account of perduring objects. A doctrine of temporal parts is one possible means of underpinning this theological story. But it is not the only means—a matter to which we shall return.

27. Strictly speaking, Fallen Humanity has parts that are not 'fallen', since Adam prior to his primal sin was unfallen, and Christ does not possess a 'fallen' human nature (i.e. a human nature that has original sin), though he is a 'Son of Adam'. So it seems that possession of original sin is a contingent property of almost all the 'parts' or phases of the life of Fallen Humanity. Alternatively, Fallen Humanity comprises the phase of Adam's life from his primal sin onwards and all other humans born after Adam, except Christ, whose human nature is miraculously preserved from being tainted with original sin.

28. Advocates of Augustinian realism often point to Heb. 7: 9–10 as evidence that Levi was (somehow) in the loins of Abraham when Abraham paid a tithe to Melchizedek. But it seems to be consistent with other passages of Scripture too, including Rom. 5: 12–19 and 1 Cor. 15: 22.

29. Another way of making sense of this would involve using a doctrine of backwards causation. Then, Christ's work could backwardsly cause the election of those who lived before him. But I do not really understand backwards causation, and it is a controversial idea anyway. So I shall not pursue this possibility here.

30. Barth 1957–69.

31. Given that this doctrine is only *inspired* by Barth's account rather than being an exposition of it, it does not matter whether it tracks all that Barth himself believed about election and atonement. What matters is that these notions can be fitted together into a coherent whole.

32. It may be possible to construct a version of realist penal substitution that factors in a doctrine of traducianism. Then Christ has a fraction of Adam's soul that is miraculously cleansed at the moment it is individualized, so to speak. But I shall not outline such a view here, since I am dubious about traducianism.

33. And lest we forget, the problem of Christ being temporally subsequent to some of the elect is a problem common to all accounts of Christ's work that suppose Christ's death is an atonement for sin. He lives before some of his elect, and after others, but somehow his death has consequences for all the elect existing at many different moments in time, before and after Christ.

34. This could be taken in a more radically 'realist' direction where Christ is really united with sinners, and really becomes guilty for their sin. Then justice is truly being carried out at the cross, exacting punishment for one guilty of the sin of other temporal parts of the same Redeemed Humanity, not wrongfully afflicting the innocent. But this radically 'realist' doctrine does also have the unwelcome consequence that Christ is truly guilty of sin. And that seems theologically untenable. So I shall not pursue this option here.

35. I suppose one could offer a 'fictionalist' account of Fallen and Redeemed Humanity, according to which these entities are not real but fictional, or entities that are in some sense merely conventional. But it is difficult to see how this would be an improvement on those forensic fiction accounts of the atonement according to which Christ

represents me, and is treated as if he is the one culpable for my sin though he is not, strictly speaking.

36. See Crisp 2007a: 102 n. 7 for references.

37. For an excellent treatment of this, see Rea 2007.

REFERENCES

ST ANSELM OF CANTERBURY (1998). *St Anselm of Canterbury, The Major Works*, ed. Brian Davies and Gillian Evans. Oxford: Oxford University Press.

AQUINAS, ST THOMAS (1948) [1911]. *Summa Theologica*, trans. Fathers of the English Dominican Province. IIa IIae qq. 149–89; IIIa qq. 1–73. New York: Benziger Brothers, iv.

ST AUGUSTINE OF HIPPO (1972). *City of God*, trans. Henry Bettenson, Introduction by John O'Meara. Harmondsworth: Penguin Books.

AULÉN, GUSTAV (1931). *Christus Victor*. London: SPCK.

BARTH, KARL (1957). *Church Dogmatics*, ed. G. W. Bromiley and T. F. Torrance. Edinburgh: T&T Clark, ii pt. 2.

BERKHOF, LOUIS (1939). *Systematic Theology*. Edinburgh: Banner of Truth.

BRÜMMER, VINCENT (2005). *Atonement, Christology and The Trinity, Making Sense of Christian Doctrine*. Aldershot: Ashgate.

BYNUM, CAROLINE WALKER (2004). 'The Power in the Blood: Sacrifice, Satisfaction, and Substitution in Late Medieval Soteriology', in Stephen T. Davis, Daniel Kendall, and Gerald O'Collins (eds.), *The Redemption*. Oxford: Oxford University Press, 177–86.

CHISHOLM, RODERICK M. (1991). 'On the Simplicity of the Soul', in James Tomberlin (ed.), *Philosophical Perspectives* v. *Philosophy of Religion (1991)*. Atascadero: Ridgeview, 167–81.

CRISP, OLIVER D. (2007a). *An American Augustinian: Sin and Salvation in the Dogmatic Theology of William G. T. Shedd*. Milton Keynes: Paternoster; Eugene, Ore.: Wipf & Stock.

—— (2003). 'Divine Retribution: A Defence', in *Sophia* 42: 35–52.

—— (2007b). 'Non-penal Substitution', in *International Journal of Systematic Theology* 9: 415–33.

—— (2008). 'Penal Non-Substitution', in *Journal of Theological Studies* NS 59: 140–68.

FIDDES, PAUL F. (2007). 'Salvation', in John Webster, Kathryn Tanner, and Iain Torrance (eds.), *The Oxford Handbook of Systematic Theology*. Oxford: Oxford University Press, 176–96.

FRANKS, R. S. (1962) [1918]. *The Work of Christ*. Edinburgh: Thomas Nelson & Sons.

GOMES, ALAN W. (1993). '*De Jesu Christo Servatore*: Faustus Socinus on the Satisfaction of Christ', in *Westminster Theological Journal* 55: 209–31.

HICK, JOHN (1993). *The Metaphor of God Incarnate, Christology in a Pluralistic Age*. Louisville: Westminster John Knox.

HODGE, CHARLES (1940) [1871]. *Systematic Theology*, ii. *Anthropology*. Grand Rapids: Eerdmans.

LEWIS, DAVID (1997). 'Do We Believe in Penal Substitution?', in *Philosophical Papers* 26: 203–9.

MURRAY, JOHN (1959). *The Imputation of Adam's Sin*. Grand Rapids: Eerdmans.

PACKER, JAMES I. (1999). 'The Logic of Penal Substitution', in *The J. I. Packer Collection*, ed. Alister McGrath. Downers Grove, Ill.: IVP.

PORTER, STEVEN (2004). 'Swinburnian Atonement and the Doctrine of Penal Substitution', in *Faith and Philosophy* 21: 238–9.

QUINN, PHILIP L. (1993). 'Abelard on Atonement: "Nothing Unintelligible, Arbitrary, Illogical, or Immoral about it"', in Eleonore Stump (ed.), *Reasoned Faith*. Ithaca, NY: Cornell University Press, 281–300.

RASHDALL, HASTINGS (1919). *The Idea of Atonement in Christian Theology*. London: Macmillan.

REA, MICHAEL C. (2007). 'The Metaphysics of Original Sin', in Peter van Inwagen and Dean Zimmerman (eds.), *Persons: Human and Divine*. Oxford: Oxford University Press, 319–56.

SHEDD, WILLIAM G. T. (2003). *Dogmatic Theology, Third Edition*, ed. Alan W. Gomes. Phillipsburg, NJ: Presbyterian & Reformed.

SWINBURNE, RICHARD (1989). *Responsibility and Atonement*. Oxford: Oxford University Press.

CHAPTER 20

THE INCARNATION

RICHARD CROSS

THE Christian doctrine of the Incarnation maintains that the second person of the Trinity became a human being, retaining all attributes necessary for being divine and gaining all attributes necessary for being human. As usually understood, the doctrine involves the claim that the second person of the Trinity is the subject of the attributes of Jesus Christ, the first-century Jew whose deeds are reported in various ways in the New Testament. For most theologians, this requires the further claim that the second person of the Trinity is *identical* with Jesus Christ. It certainly seems to have been taken as such by the Council of Chalcedon (451 CE), generally understood to be the standard for orthodox teaching on the matter. The Council teaches that

one and the same Christ, Son, Lord, only-begotten, [is] acknowledged in two natures which undergo no confusion, no change, no division, no separation;...the property of both natures is preserved and comes together into a single person and single subsistent being (*hypostasis*); he is not parted or divided into two persons, but is one and the same only-begotten Son, God, Word, Lord Jesus Christ.   (N. P. Tanner 1990: i. 86*)

The view of Chalcedon, then, is that one and the same person—the second person of the Trinity (the 'Word', identical with the 'Lord Jesus Christ', according to the final list of Christological titles)—exists 'in two natures', divine and human.[1] One of the views that the Council opposes is that known as Nestorianism, according to which there are somehow two distinct subjects in Christ—one divine, and one human. The point of rejecting this view is to ensure that the divine person—the second person of the Trinity—is the subject not only of divine but also of human attributes or properties. Now, the Council does not define its terms, and some recent theological commentators maintain that it gives no more than particular syntactic rules governing the use of the terms 'person' and 'nature'. But it seems to me—as it has seemed to most recent philosophical commentators—that the linguistic rules are secondary to some apparently substantive metaphysical claims: namely, that there is some divine subject of properties—the second person of the Trinity—that gains human properties (a human nature). Clearly, the metaphysics leaves open just what a nature is—for example, a universal or a particular—and as we shall see, this issue crops up in a number of recent discussions too.

As thus put, the doctrine raises a series of issues of general interest to philosophers: for example, questions of the relation between individuals and their individual-essential and kind-essential natures, and of identity across time. But the fundamental philosophical problem specific to the doctrine is this: how is it that one and the same thing could be both divine (and thus, on the face of it, necessary, and necessarily omniscient, omnipotent, eternal, immutable, impassible, and impeccable) and human (and thus, on the face of it, have the complements of all these properties). Most of the philosophical effort devoted to the specifics of the doctrine has centered on this issue, and I shall concentrate on it below. In addition to this array of topics, there are a number of other potential problems with the doctrine. Some of these were nicely focused in a book that in effect kick-started the modern Christological debate. Thirty years ago a group of British philosophers and theologians published *The Myth of God Incarnate* (Hick (ed.) 1977) in which they outlined a series of objections to the orthodox doctrine of the Incarnation: in particular, the coherence objection just mentioned, and in addition worries about the particularity of the Incarnation (given the vastness of the universe), and concerns about the lack of—or impossibility of—evidence for the Incarnation. But I shall focus here on the coherence objection, as indicated.[2]

I have mentioned the Council of Chalcedon as a formative event in the history of the doctrine. Recent work in the history of Christian doctrine has tended to emphasize the open-endedness of Chalcedon, and its (historical) failure to reach any kind of resolution of the various Christological controversies of the early- to mid-fifth century. Philosophers of religion often (though not always) pass over the equally important developments at the Third Council of Constantinople (680–1 CE). Chalcedon teaches that Christ has all the properties necessary for being divine, and all the properties necessary for being human. Constantinople III clarifies that these properties must include both divine causal powers (energy and will) and human causal powers (energy and will). The point might sound obvious, but anyone who wants to associate causal power—or mind, for that matter—with personal identity might find it difficult to assert the existence of two irreducibly distinct varieties of such power in one person, or two irreducibly distinct minds in one person. As we shall see, the kinds of position defended at Constantinople III are central to at least one very important development in modern philosophical Christology—the insight that Christ must in some sense have two minds.

Before considering in detail the approach to the coherence problem adopted by philosophers of religion in the analytic tradition, it is worth considering a suggestion made by certain philosophically inclined theologians who, while they would not count themselves as part of this philosophical tradition, nevertheless have some sympathy for it and adopt approaches that are on occasion analogous to it. I have in mind the suggestion made by thinkers such as Herbert McCabe, Kathryn Tanner, and David Burrell, that the whole project of thinking of the issue in terms of a problem about contradictory properties is misconceived. The two natures, divine and human, are not competing for existence in the same 'logical world' (McCabe 1987: 57); giving an account of the metaphysics of the Incarnation is not a case of practising a 'zero-sum game' (Burrell 2004: 469). Thus Kathryn Tanner (2001: 11): 'Because divinity is not a kind, God is not bound by apparent contrasts between divine and creaturely qualities; God is thereby free to enter into intimate community with us, without loss to the divine nature.' Why is this? Tanner (ibid. 15) explains by means of an example: 'Divine omniscience is not something like human knowledge, just better, minus the ignorance or the limitations of finitude.' Presumably the point is that the divine attributes are such that they are neither contradictories nor contraries of the relevant human attributes. The problem with this is fundamentally one of plausibility: whatever divine omniscience amounts to, for example, it is hard to see how it can be compatible with the kinds of ignorance that Jesus exhibited on earth. Neither does a mere appeal to God's (allegedly) not belonging to a kind sufficiently secure the conclusion that his attributes are such that they fail to be the contraries of corresponding creaturely attributes— indeed, if they fail to be the contraries of corresponding creaturely attributes, we might reasonably wonder whether there is such a thing as divine transcendence, or, alternatively, whether our doctrine of God is not so mysterious as to amount to nothing much at all.

Still, there is a substantive point here. We do not know—and certainly do not know in advance of the doctrine of the Incarnation—what the complete list of divine and human essential attributes consists in. So we do not know in advance whether or not the list contains contradictory pairs. So the agnostic strategy just outlined could underlie at least two possible approaches to the doctrine that have proved popular in recent debate, one of which uses the doctrine to restrict the list of kind-essential human attributes, the other of which uses the doctrine to restrict the list of kind-essential divine attributes—both discussed in sect. 4 below. Of course, it would be just as possible to combine these two strategies in some shape or form, and I shall argue below that this may well turn out to be the best way forward. In what follows, then, I shall try to outline very briefly the most important recent attempts by philosophers of religion to deal with the fundamental Christological problem that I have identified here, and to come to some kind of assessment of the value of each attempt.

1. Reduplication and Adverbial Modifiers

The Council of Chalcedon suggests one way of dealing with putative contradictions. It claims of Christ that he was 'begotten before the ages from the Father as regards his divinity (*kata tēn theotēta/secundum divinitatem*), and in the last days the same for us and for our salvation from Mary the virgin God-bearer (*theotokou*) as regards his humanity (*kata tēn anthrōpotēta/secundum humanitatem*)' (N. P. Tanner 1990: i. 86*). This suggests that we can defuse the problem by dividing potentially contradictory properties into two groups, associating one with the divine nature, and the other with the human nature. There are various ways of signalling gramatically the kind of adverbial modification suggested by Chalcedon. I shall talk of qua-qualifiers: thus 'S qua N is F.' Thomas Senor has recently summarized the three possible construals of such adverbial modifiers known in the tradition, and I shall add a couple more as well in this section and the next.

The first is the one that the medieval theologians knew as the 'reduplicative' analysis (see Cross 2002: 193–5). On the reduplicative analysis, 'S qua N is F' should be understood as ' "In virtue of being N, S is F" ' (Senor 2002: 229). This understanding, as the medievals noticed, does nothing to help deal with putative contradictions:

> Sentences of the form 'in virtue of N, S is F' entail sentences of the form 'S is F.' So 'In virtue of being divine, Christ is omnipotent' entails 'Christ is omnipotent'; and 'In virtue of being human, Christ is not omnipotent' entails 'Christ is not omnipotent.' ... Hence, understanding reduplicative sentences like this will not help defend orthodoxy because in the end we will still be left with *simpliciter* properties and the contradictions they promote.
>
> (ibid.)

Thomas Morris clarifies:

> Consider any conjunctive reduplicative proposition of the form '*x* as *A* is *N* and *x* as *B* is not *N*.' If the subjects of both conjuncts are the same and the substituends of *N* are univocal across the conjunction, then as long as (1) the reduplication predicates being *A* of *x* and predicates being *B* of *x*, and (2) being *N* is entailed by being *A*, and not being *N* is entailed by being *B*, then the reduplicative form of predication accomplishes nothing except for muddying the waters, since in the end the contradiction stands of *x* being characterized as both *N* and not *N*.   (Morris 1986: 48–9)

In fact, this is not the only form of reduplication that is possible. Douglas K. Blount has objected to Senor's attempt to dismiss reduplication by noting that the 'in virtue of' analysis is not appropriate for some cases that seem very close to those that Senor considers. For example,

> When one claims that
> Jesus Christ qua man read in the synagogue before Jesus Christ qua man carried his cross,

One typically does not mean to be claiming that

> Jesus Christ *in virtue of* being human read in the synagogue before Jesus Christ *in virtue of* being human carried his cross.   (Blount 2002: 239, original emphasis)

This is clearly true, at least if we understand the 'in virtue of' locution to state a sufficient condition, and shows that not all cases can be analyzed in just the same way. Still, even in these cases the reduplication provides some sort of explanation for the truth of the predication—as in the more standard reduplicative case considered first. In fact, the reduplication here seems to signal something like an INUS condition: an *i*nsufficient but *n*ecessary member of a set of *u*nnecessary but jointly *s*ufficient conditions (hence 'INUS'). Christ's being human is an INUS condition for his reading in the synagogue, and for his carrying the cross. But he still read in the synagogue, and carried his cross. So this secondary sort of reduplicative sentence does not provide a way to prevent the ascription of the predicates to their subjects *simpliciter*; thus it does not prevent one and the same person being characterized in contradictory ways.

Marilyn McCord Adams has recently argued in a similar way, proposing what is in effect a further variant on the reduplicative strategy. Because Christ's human nature is non-essential to him, we can claim that Christ has *simpliciter* all the attributes of deity, but that he has human attributes only in a qualified way. So Christ is *simpliciter* omniscient, and limited in knowledge qua human; this is sufficient to circumvent the putative contradiction. According to Adams (2006: 135–6), the relevant attributes are the same as in their usual contexts; but the way in which the human attributes are possessed is different in the case of Christ from that of all other human beings. According to Adams, 'qua' here means 'by virtue of'; but 'by virtue of' is ambiguous, and in these cases 'N is the nature by virtue of which x is F because N entails the real possibility of F' (ibid. 136–7). Still, this strategy alone does not seem sufficient to block the alleged contradiction, since the obvious Christological problem is not just that Christ is possibly ignorant or mistaken, but that he is *actually* ignorant or mistaken; 'qua' must amount to more than just a modal qualification of the kind proposed by Adams. In any case, essential omniscience is incompatible with even possible ignorance.

On Senor's second way of understanding qua-propositions, we should take the qua-clause

> to be imbedded in the grammatical subject of the sentence. We can make this clear by appropriately placing hyphens. 'Qua N, S is F' becomes 'S-qua-N is F.' The properties of omnipotence and non-omnipotence [for example] are predicated *simpliciter*, but contradiction is avoided because the properties are predicated of different subjects, i.e., Christ-qua-God and Christ-qua-human.   (Senor 2002: 229–30)

Senor comments that the cogency of this grammatical analysis seems to presuppose the Nestorian claim that there are two real subjects in Christ (ibid. 230). This may be a little quick. For the medieval theologians, the kind of analysis that Senor is describing was known as the 'specificative' analysis, and they usually took it as a mark of *synecdoche*—ascribing to a whole a property of a part of that whole (see Cross 2002: 195–203). As far as I can see the cogency of this analysis does require some theological commitments: namely that we adopt a mereological account of the person of Christ, or something that draws on a close analogy to such accounts. I return to this in sect. 3 below, where I shall try to judge whether or not such mereological Christologies are *eo ipso* Nestorian.

On a third way of understanding qua-sentences proposed by Senor, also known to the medievals (see ibid. 203–4), we should understand

'S qua N is F' as ' "S is F-qua-N." That is, the qua-clause gets packed into the predication in such a way as to form as single, non-compositional, simple property. The F-entailment is blocked here because the properties being ascribed bear no non-trivial logical relation to each other' (Senor 2002, 230).

Of course, coherence here comes at a price: specifically, considerable agnosticism about what we mean when we make Christological (and other) claims. For take the locutions 'incorporeal-qua-God' and 'corporeal-qua-man'. Is incorporeality-qua-God a determinate of incorporeality, and corporeality-qua-man a determinate of corporeality? If so, then we simply have another variant of reduplication properly so called, and the entailment to a contradiction will go through. If not, then it is not clear what the attributes are supposed to be. We could claim that our agnosticism extends only as far as the divine attributes, and adopt a strategy similar to that proposed by Kathryn Tanner in the discussion cited at the beginning of this chapter. We could claim, for example, that Christ is corporeal-*simpliciter*, and incorporeal-qua-God, where 'incorporeal-qua-God' picks out the unknown attribute that is God's incorporeality. But we need to understand what we are committing ourselves to if we adopt this approach: if being incorporeal-qua-God is compatible with being corporeal, we really have *no* idea what 'incorporeal-qua-God' means. And the more attributes we add to the list, the less we will be able to talk meaningfully about God at all. And I do not think that many theologians would want to make such a strong claim, even at the price of preserving some kind of formal coherence to Christological formulations.

2. RELATIVE IDENTITY SOLUTIONS

One way of utilizing these qua-qualifications is by appealing to the notion of *relative* identity in this context. Adherents of relative identity claim that identity is 'sortal relative', such that

'*a* and *b* could be the same *F* but not the same *G* (where "*F*" and "*G*" stand in for sortal terms, or general count nouns with associated criteria for individuation and reidentification)' (Morris 1986: 28).

Peter van Inwagen, for example, has argued that the doctrine of the Incarnation can be shown to be 'free from formal contradiction' (van Inwagen 1994: 225) if we adopt such an account, such that two distinct beings could be the same person (ibid. 217). Equally, the position allows for one being to be (e.g.) human and the other non-human without contradiction, and one being to be (e.g.) passible and the other impassible without contradiction, while yet allowing both beings to be one and the same person (ibid. 221–3). This is a version of the specificative analysis outlined in the previous section, since it treats the two beings in Christ as subjects distinct from each other, though not from the divine person with which each severally is identical. But unlike that analysis, it does not rely on a mereological account of the Incarnation, since the two beings postulated to be the same person in van Inwagen's account are not *parts* of that person. Rather, each being is severally the same person as the second person of the Trinity and as Jesus of Nazareth (ibid. 217–18).[3]

There are various ways in which this kind of approach can have some appeal. For example, it could do so if we were to adopt some more wide-ranging anti-realism: if we were to adopt, for example, the view that there are no theory-independent facts about the natures of things, or the distinctions of one thing from another. Many, though not all, theologians find such anti-realism at the very least counterintuitive, and in any case some anti-realists would be more than happy to deny relative identity: relative to each theory about how to cut up the world, identity remains absolute. In fact, van Inwagen's own working out of the doctrine along these lines does not involve making any explicitly anti-realist claims. What it does involve is accepting a logic of relative identity that lacks a rule permitting inferences that conform to the principle of the indiscernibility of identicals. The logic thus licences the use of premises that can violate the principle of the indiscernibility of identicals: something that most philosophers would be reluctant to accept. So van Inwagen's approach is ultimately of very limited appeal. And as he himself notes, even if we accept his account, much work would be left to be done: 'I [do] not claim to have penetrated the mystery of the Incarnation, but at most to have shown that that doctrine can be stated without formal contradiction' (ibid. 202). The interest of the logic turns out to be restricted to its application—and the philosophical price would be felt by many to be too high.

3. PARTS AND PROPERTIES

We often talk of things having the same features as each other—of two or more things sharing certain features. And we usually talk not merely of things *having* such-and-such features, but of *being* such-and-such. In such contexts, we are likely to claim that we are committed to there being *properties* of things, whatever those properties be. In more technical jargon, we claim that these properties are instantiated or exemplified. For some philosophers, properties are universals, shared by the various particulars that exemplify them. On this view, to explain the truth of a conjunction such as 'Socrates is white and Plato is white' we need to posit some entity, *whiteness*, in some sense the same (usually *numerically* the same) in both Socrates and Plato. Other philosophers hold that the properties are as particular as the things of which they are properties—that they are analogous to parts, but parts of a very abstract kind. These 'thin' parts nowadays usually go under the designation of 'tropes'. Still other philosophers think that properties are merely linguistic items, things that can be predicated of, or said of, particulars. Whatever our view of properties, we should in this context make a distinction between properties and substances. Substances are concrete objects, with causal powers; properties are abstract, and lack such powers. They do not interact with other things in the world in the way that substances do (though some of them could of course *be* the causal powers of substances).

Some thinkers claim that all properties are parts of substances. But whatever we think about this, it is more important for our purposes here that some parts of substances are not properties but rather (themselves) substances.[4] For there are some Christologies that explicitly rest on the claim that the two natures could count as parts rather than properties—and thus as (in some sense) substances (rather than properties: concrete, not abstract, items). Setting aside for a moment the distinction between substances and parts, the relevance of the universal property/particular property distinction to the doctrine of the Incarnation is well known. Richard Swinburne, for instance, claims that we should think of a nature—or at least the human nature—as some kind of universal, on pain of Christological incoherence. An individual nature

'would be the essential core of the individual—what made him who he is—and could not be possessed temporarily or accidentally by anyone else. Christ therefore could not have an individual human nature. His human nature must be universal, in no way peculiar to Christ—it is just a set of properties which he acquires' (Swinburne 1994: 212–13; see too Williams 1967).

Now, one obvious way of thinking of the Incarnation is to think of the two natures not as properties but as (concrete) parts of the divine person. Making such a move involves denying Swinburne's claim that an individual nature is in every case the 'essential core of the individual'. This strategy was adopted by, for example, many of the medieval theologians (for some of the ways in which they blocked Swinburne's inference, see Cross 2002: 246–309). Indeed, talk of parts in the Christological context is initially quite appealing as a way of dealing with putative contradictions, since the different properties can be attributed to the different parts or substances that (on a mereological analysis) the two natures are. As I mentioned above, the usual way of understanding the specificative sense of 'qua' is mereologically, and in line with this we can assert that the two natures are parts of the whole person, and ascribe the relevant properties to the person by 'piggy-backing': the properties piggy-back from the parts to the whole.

Eleonore Stump has developed this view with considerable sophistication, starting from some common-sense assumptions: 'On the [specificative] strategy, the attributes that are incompatible with each other are also segregated from each other in the incarnate Christ in virtue of inhering in different natures of his' (Stump 2003: 412). On this view, not only are the natures in some sense real constituents of a person, but also they are themselves the subjects of properties—and thus in some sense substances. It is in virtue of a property's inherence in a nature that it can inhere in a person. As Stump notes,

there is a distinction between a property a whole has in its own right and a property it has in virtue of having a constituent that has that property in its own right; it is possible for a whole to 'borrow' a property from one of its constituents. This distinction between ways in which a whole can have a property gives us one helpful manner in which to analyze locutions of the form *x qua* A *is* N. In such a locution, the property of being N is predicated of *x*, but it is predicated of *x* just in virtue of the fact that *x* has a constituent C which has the property of being N in its own right.   (ibid.)

In the case of the Incarnation, then, we can think of the two natures, divine and human, as somehow or other parts of the incarnate second person of the Trinity. This mereological account is not Nestorian. On the one hand, it does not preclude some kind of duplication of different properties of the same basic kind (two wills, or two minds, for example—something I return to below). On the other, it also allows that all properties are properties of the person, and thus avoids positing a complete duality of ultimate subjects in Christ. Clearly, not every kind of constituent and every kind of property can allow piggy-backing of properties in the right kind of way. (Consider quantitative predicates.) But this is perhaps not surprising: different properties have different natures, which might interact differently with the part–whole relation.

There seems to be a problem with Stump's proposal nevertheless. If we deny that an individual nature is the 'essential core' of a person, it is perhaps easy enough to see how the human nature could be a concrete particular part of a divine person. But it is harder to see how the divine nature could be such a concrete part. The divine nature or divinity, in standard Christian orthodoxy, is supposed to be shared somehow by the divine persons, such that in virtue of their possession of divinity, each person is said to be divine. It will thus be more like a property than like a part, at least in the kinds of sense outlined above. For it is hard to see how any such shared object could be a concrete part: we usually think of such shared objects, those in virtue of which something is said to be such-and-such, as paradigm cases of abstract objects. Suppose that the divine nature is a concrete substance, and suppose we claim that (for example) this substance is impassible. On the Christological solution I am now considering, the divine nature is an impassible substance, while a divine person (at least the second person of the Trinity) turns out to be a passible substance, since he borrows passibility from his human substance. But in this case, what is it in general for a divine person to have a divine nature? Is it perhaps for the person to 'borrow' divinity, and (for example) impassibility, from the nature? This is certainly suggested by the Christological application. But this makes it look as though there are four *concrete* objects in God (the three divine persons and the concrete divine substance), something that would take considerable effort to defend from charges of quaternitarianism.

One way of developing the insight that the divine essence is a concrete object is by maintaining that the relation between the divine essence and the divine persons is some kind of *inclusion* relation: the divine essence is *more* than any one person. For example, suppose that each person is a sphere of consciousness of one divine substance. But the substance is not, on this view, a *part* of the person (as it would need to be on Stump's understanding); if anything, the mereological relationship would go the other way round.

It is important to keep in mind here that the whole Christ is, on the Chalcedonian definition as I am reading it, *identical* with the second person of the Trinity. Before the Incarnation, this person comprises the divine essence along with whatever property distinguishes the person from the other two divine persons—standardly, filiation: the relation of being generated/begotten. After the Incarnation, this person comprises the divine essence, personal property, and human nature. This identity claim is important from an orthodox point of view, but it seems to be denied in a significant recent mereological account of the Incarnation. According to Brian Leftow, Christ is a whole whose parts are the second person of the Trinity, a human body, and a human soul. This avoids the problem that I identified above in Stump's proposal—namely, the difficulty of seeing how the divine *nature* could be a concrete part of anything. Here, the divine *person* is a concrete part of Christ. Leftow identifies Christ as a whole whose parts are those outlined because he believes that by so doing he can make full use of qua-qualifiers: we can ascribe divine and human attributes to Christ because Christ is a whole made up of the divine person and a human body and soul (Leftow 2002: 288–9).

Leftow is clearly right to think that his view allows full use of qua-qualifiers, but his way of construing the part–whole relationship seems nevertheless to engender certain Christological difficulties. In particular, on his proposal it is hard to see how the second person of the Trinity could be the subject of human attributes. We can see this by considering a close relation to Leftow's view found in the early church, namely the view of Nestorius's (explicitly condemned at the Council of Ephesus in 431 CE) that we should hold not that Mary was the mother of God (*theotokos*), but rather that she was the mother of Christ (*Christotokos*). The claim that Mary was mother of Christ is true, according to Nestorius, in virtue of the fact that Mary was the mother of the man Jesus who, along with the second person of the Trinity, constituted Christ, such that the second person of the Trinity is a *part* of Christ, not *identical* with him. The problem here, identified by Nestorius's main orthodox opponent, Cyril of Alexandria, is that the second person of the Trinity is not himself the subject of human attributes. (Hence Mary is not his mother.) I conclude that Leftow's impressive strategy avoids the problems of contradiction only at too high a price—the danger of a Nestorian denial that the Son of God (as opposed to the whole of which he is a part) is human, or has human attributes, at all.

Underlying Leftow's account is a belief that it is not possible to be a human person without ' "owning" a human body, soul, mind and will' (ibid. 278). Body and soul are clearly concrete particulars, parts of a person. Thus, as Leftow puts it, 'abstract-nature incarnation takes place only if concrete-nature incarnation does' (ibid. 279). There seems to me to be reason to doubt this. For we might hold that (whether we think of natures as particulars or universals) abstract-nature incarnation merely amounts to this: that the second person of the Trinity becomes a body, or becomes a soul, or becomes something that is identical with the conjunction of body and soul (this last being, as we shall see, Swinburne's view—a view that seems to defend abstract-nature incarnation without concrete nature incarnation). The case would be analogous to that of any human person, given relevant claims in the philosophy of mind. The divine person begins to exemplify human nature, such that the *only* concrete object is the person.

In an important paper, Trenton Merricks has suggested something very like this. He presents two options. Suppose a dualist account of human nature is true, such that a human person somehow includes both body and soul. Merricks assumes an account of dualism that identifies a human person as a soul related to one body in such-and-such a way, and not related to any other body in just that way. So rather than say that the Son of God, in the Incarnation, gains a (concrete) human soul, we should rather say that the Son of God *becomes* a human soul (Merricks 2007: 293). Or, if we make physicalist assumptions about human nature, denying that a human person includes a soul, then we should claim not that the Son of God gains a body, but that he *becomes* a body:

> Physicalism has a straightforward account of embodiment. You have a body if and only if you are identical with that body. I assume that, in the Incarnation, God the Son is related to the body of Jesus just as you and I are related to our respective bodies. So, given physicalism, God the Son, in the Incarnation, is identical with the body of Jesus.   (ibid. 294)

It would be possible to argue similarly on the assumption that a human person is a composite of body and soul: the divine person becomes a human body–soul composite. (I made a similar suggestion a few years ago in Cross 2003, and, as we shall see, something analogous is defended by Swinburne.) I take it that, depending on the preferred theory of properties, all of these could count as cases of abstract-nature assumption without concrete-nature assumption. On the physicalist view, for example, the sum of physical parts that is Christ constitutes a human *person* (the second person of the Trinity), not a concrete human *nature*. As Merricks (ibid. 294) puts it, 'to say that the Son became a physical object is just to say that he came to have physical properties'. On theological grounds, Merricks prefers the physicalist option, since he believes that, on dualist assumptions, it is impossible to give an account (other than an entirely ad hoc and unsatisfactory one) of the way in which the Son of God could come to have only the body of Jesus (ibid. 282–94). On the physicalist view, abstract-nature assumption without concrete-nature assumption entails that there are no parts had in common by one and the same person pre- and post-incarnation. Putting it bluntly, a person who previously lacked any proper physical parts comes to be constituted of a collection of such parts. Something analogous obtains in the case of the dualist options too. If a human person is a soul, then the divine person becomes a soul; if a person is a body–soul composite, the divine person becomes that composite (on this see Cross 2003, and the account of Swinburne, that I discuss below). Before the incarnation, the person had no proper parts; after it, he comes to be constituted of body and soul as proper parts. It is not clear to me that this is incoherent. It is not obvious that something at first part-free could not come to gain parts over time—be those parts entirely physical, or physical and non-physical.

Clearly, this abstract-nature approach will not in itself better allow for putatively contradictory properties to belong to one and the same thing than any of its rivals; neither is it intended to do so by its originators. I suggested above that this is the fundamental problem for a defence of the coherence of the Incarnation, and thus such views do not address the central problem raised by the doctrine of the Incarnation. (This does not entail that the view could not allow for, say, more than one mind or will in Christ: as suggested by some of the church Fathers, Christ may have a series of distinct human wills, and he may too have a highly unusual and unique will associated with his divine status.) Thus Merricks (2007: 299): 'Physicalism is silent on how to reconcile Christ's divinity with his apparently not knowing the hour of his return (Matt. 24: 36)'. And I doubt that any view that maintains that the natures are akin to properties (rather than concrete parts) will allow for such putatively contradictory properties, be these properties universals or particulars (tropes). For there simply are not different parts—in effect different substances—to which we could ascribe the relevant inconsistent properties.

4. Restriction Solutions

A range of treatments of the problem concedes that the only way forward is to 'trim' the list of attributes necessary for being human and/or divine. More popular are those that trim the list of human attributes. As Swinburne notes:

Our criteria for use of the word 'human' are just not precise enough for there to be a right answer as to whether the possession of powers far beyond those of normal humans [e.g. a power to move mountains on distant continents just by willing, or to know what is going on in distant galaxies without using a telescope or listening to what others tell him] would rule out someone from being a human.   (Swinburne 1994: 28)

The most extensive example of the use of this strategy is by Thomas Morris. Morris makes a significant distinction between being 'merely' human, and being 'fully' human:

The kind-nature exemplified distinctively by all human beings is that of humanity. To be a human being is to exemplify human nature. An individual is fully human just in case he fully exemplifies human nature. To be merely human is not to exemplify a kind-nature, a natural kind, distinct from that of humanity; it is rather to exemplify humanity without also exemplifying any ontologically higher kind, such as divinity.   (Morris 1986: 66)

The point here is that something that is fully but not merely human lacks certain imperfect properties commonly (but not necessarily) associated with human beings: for example, contingency, peccability, fallibility, limitations on power. These properties are had by persons that are merely human, but not by other human persons. It seems to me that this is the correct way forward, and in principle there seems to be no reason why we should assume that a being that fails to exemplify these common limitations fails to be human.

Still, it seems that we need to modify too our classical understanding of the divine nature, and perform some analogous 'trimming' here as well. For example, many theists hold God to be immutable and impassible. Clearly, anything that is human is mutable and (on the face of it) passible. These are modal attributes, and thus had (if at all) throughout the duration of the existence of whatever possesses them. I infer, therefore, that, in the absence of the success of the kinds of solution canvassed in the first three sections of this chapter, no divine person is immutable or impassible (other than in the weak sense of being indestructible and morally reliable, and being such that nothing happens to him that he could not avoid). The same goes for timelessness. Anything that is human is temporal; nothing can be first timeless and then temporal; no divine person is essentially non-human; so no divine person is timeless. And if it be doubted that anything that is human is temporal, it at least cannot be doubted that Christ was, since he changed through time, sometimes eating, sometimes drinking, sometimes laughing, and sometimes weeping. As Morris (ibid. 70) notes, there are still further problems too. For example, there are some scriptural data that seem to suggest that the Son of God was ignorant (Matt. 24: 36) and perhaps even fallible (Matt. 16: 28), and that he was subject to temptation (which latter might require either the mistaken belief that he could sin, or indeed that he could sin, and so that he was either fallible or peccable: see Heb. 4: 15).

Some theologians infer that the Son of God gave up his omniscience, and perhaps infallibility, when he became incarnate. And it is not infrequent for these same theologians to hold (again on the basis of scriptural data) that the incarnate Son of God failed to be omnipotent too. These sorts of Christology are known as 'kenotic', on the basis of the early Christian hymn in Phil. 2: 5–11, according to which Christ, in becoming incarnate, 'emptied' (*ekenōsen*) himself (Phil. 2: 7). Curiously, the clearest and best exponent of this view is a thinker who emphatically rejects it, namely Thomas Morris. Morris (ibid. 94–5) considers three ways of developing the position. First, we could simply assume that the relevant divine attributes are non-essential. God is merely contingently omniscient and omnipotent, such that any divine person could fail to exemplify these properties.[5] (Perhaps they could not all do so at once, or at least do so and continue to sustain the universe in existence, since these properties may be required for sustaining it.) If we do not want to abandon the claim that God has his attributes necessarily, then we would claim instead that each relevant divine attribute has a 'kenotic clause,' such that 'a being would be said to be, for example, omniscient just in case that being naturally (in the sense of "ordinarily" or "typically") knows all true propositions *and* fails to know any true proposition only when freely and temporarily restricting its knowledge... [where] the kenotic clause is the clause following the italicized connective' (ibid. 97–8). This of course allows God to be omniscient even while incarnate, but, as Morris (ibid. 99) points out, this 'seems to amount to no more than a verbal maneuver which departs dramatically from the traditional concept of omniscience'. A third option retains the traditional definition of each divine attribute, but claims that what God has (necessarily) is not the attribute but the attribute qualified by 'kenotic limitation possibilities' (ibid.). For example, God has 'the property of being omniscient-unless-freely-and-temporarily-choosing-to-be-otherwise' (ibid.). This strategy has proved popular amongst kenoticists,[6] though Morris (ibid. 100–1) rejects it on the grounds that it still involves a considerable departure from traditional views of the divine nature.

Morris rejects the first strategy on the grounds that it is inconsistent with even a weak view of divine immutability (one endorsed by Morris) according to which 'any individual who has a constitutive attribute of deity can never begin to have it, and can never cease to have it' (ibid. 97). Of course, it can be objected to this that Morris has, in offering this weak account of immutability, already significantly departed from the God of classical theism, since the account is perfectly consistent with the view that being/becoming incarnate involves change. This is in accordance with the position outlined above, according to which we learn from the doctrine of the Incarnation that no divine person is timeless, immutable, or impassible. This move does not entail the kind of kenoticism that Morris rejects, of course, although it does push away from classical theism in the way suggested above. Swinburne (1994: 230–1) offers a further consideration against the kenotic strategy, namely, that 'the hypothesis of the existence of a being who has the divine properties essentially... is much simpler than the hypothesis of the existence of a kenotic God'. Our evaluation of this will depend on our judgment as to the success of those models of the Incarnation that attempt to make it compatible with God's possession of all traditional divine attributes essentially. It seems to me that omnipotence can be dealt with easily: Christ is necessarily omnipotent, though there is only a limited amount that he can bring about by means of standard human powers. In principle, I can see no objection to Christ's being necessarily omniscient as well, since it is by no means apparent to me that being human requires being limited in knowledge. But on the face of it this is precluded by reasonably secure scriptural data about Christ's life, according to which he was ignorant (and possibly even mistaken), and subject to temptation. Considerations such as these lead Morris, Swinburne, and others to introduce a further element to their theories, and I turn to this in the next section. As we shall see, there are various replies to this worry in both Morris and Swinburne.

5. TWO-MINDS SOLUTIONS

Two-minds solutions build on the kind of material dealt with in the previous section—particularly, the insight that certain divine properties are compatible with failing to be merely human—but make particular modifications to deal with Jesus's apparently limited knowledge. The basic suggestion is that the divine person includes two 'minds', or two 'systems of belief', or two 'consciousnesses'. The position has been defended at length by Thomas Morris. On the position, we can identify in Christ 'something like two distinct ranges of consciousness. There is first what we can call the eternal mind of the Son with its distinctively divine consciousness.... And in addition there is a distinctly earthly consciousness that...drew its visual imagery from what the eyes of Jesus saw, and its concepts from the languages that he learned' (Morris 1986: 103–4). Morris uses the example of those cases of multiple personality, discussed in psychoanalytic research, in which one personality has full cognitive access to the experiences of the others, to argue that there could be an 'asymmetric accessing relationship' between the divine and human minds in Christ (ibid. 106), such that the divine mind has access to all the thoughts and experiences contained in the human mind, though not conversely. Clearly, as Morris acknowledges, the divine mind needs more than mere access to the human mind, since each divine person has such an asymmetric accessing relationship with every created mind. So Morris (ibid. 162) argues that there is in addition a 'unity of cognitive and causal powers productive of the contents of each mind'. Such a view gives unity of person, presumably because it gives unity of mental *subject*: persons are mental subjects; minds on this view are merely collections of mental items such that the mental items have some kind of unity relation to each other alone,[7] such that the relevant unity relationship does not require unity of mental subject, but merely of the mental items within one consciousness.

On this view, having two minds does not entail being two persons: 'Ordinarily, minds and persons are individuated in a one-one correspondence.... So among mere humans, the individuation of two minds at any one time will suffice for the identification of two persons. But this leaves open the possibility that outside that context, there is no such one-one correlation' (ibid. 157). Given some of the insights of psychoanalysis in relation to divided minds, there does not seem to be an overwhelming problem with this distinction between minds and persons (I consider some of these claims in a little more detail below). But these insights do not help deal with the problem of the divine person's including incompatible beliefs, since they do not account for a person's *consciously* holding incompatible beliefs. So Morris (ibid. 159) maintains that not all beliefs included in the human mind are contained in the divine mind: 'Most theologians who take seriously the real humanity of Jesus...will want to allow at least the possibility that the full belief-set of the earthly mind of Jesus...did not even constitute a proper subset of the belief-set ingredients in the omniscient mind.' But there is nevertheless a Christological problem here: the Christological point is supposed to be that the divine *person* has all these beliefs as his own, so maintaining that not all the beliefs contained in the human mind are included in the divine mind does not prevent those beliefs from belonging to the *person*. As Tim Bayne (2001: 137) succinctly puts it, 'Consciousnesses don't believe things, people do.'[8] Conversely, if it is held that the relevant beliefs do not belong to the divine person, it will be hard to resist the conclusion that there are two mental subjects in Christ: the divine person, and a subject for the false human beliefs too.

Suppose that we accept this last conclusion, namely that there are two mental subjects in Christ—something that Bayne's analysis of Morris's position seems to require. In this case, it looks as though we need to make a further distinction in order to avoid Nestorianism: namely, a distinction between mental subjects and persons. How might we make this distinction? The anti-Nestorian desideratum is that human attributes and experiences be ascribed to the divine person: that they are his beliefs and his experiences. But it is not clear that this requires that *all* human attributes and experiences be attributed to the divine person. Perhaps most are; but any that raise otherwise insoluble contradiction-problems could be mental experiences of some other mental subject without being experiences of the divine person, much as Morris implicitly suggests.

The Incarnation would on this view consist of two overlapping mental subjects, such that some of the attributes of one would be attributes of the other—something I attempted to defend a few years ago (in Cross 2002: 318–23).[9] We might in this context think of some of the experiences of one mind—the human—flowing to the other—the divine:[10] i.e. being such that they are the experiences of the divine mental subject himself. And we might think that unity of person requires *maximal* flow: that is to say, the experiences of the human mental subject flow to the divine person unless there are *logical* reasons why they cannot (e.g. because the beliefs of the human mental subject are incompatible with beliefs of the divine mental subject). So maximality of unavoidable flow (within the logical constraint just mentioned), and not mere voluntary overlap of minds, would be required in order to avoid the danger of two distinct persons. On this view, any two mental subjects, united in as strong a sense as is metaphysically possible, count as one person—or, better, only the recipient subject counts as a person; the other is a mental subject that fails to be a person, because most of its experiences automatically maximally flow to some other entity: they are not uniquely its experiences.[11] This distinction between mental subjects and persons need not present insurmountable problems: after all, some such distinction seems to be implicitly at work in the passages in Morris, examined above, where the problem of contradictory beliefs is considered. It fits neatly too with cases of divided minds where it seems plausible to maintain that there is one person but two mental subjects (for example, in cases in which neither mind appears to have any access to the experiences of the other). This account of the Incarnation perhaps presents problems for that explicitly offered by Morris, since he identifies persons as subjects of mental properties. But this would merely constitute a local objection to the accounts offered by Morris (in terms of internal coherence), rather than a global objection to two-minds Christologies as such. All that would be required of Morris would be a distinction between persons and mental subjects.

In any case, there is another well-known defence of a two-minds Christology that avoids making any of these moves, because the account defends the two-minds Christology while avoiding making a distinction, whether implicit or explicit, between persons and mental subjects. The view is defended by Swinburne. Before I consider the way in which his account avoids any sort of distinction between persons and mental subjects, we need (in order to understand his position) to grasp certain metaphysical commitments that he espouses. According to Swinburne (1994: 25–6), a human being is a humanly embodied soul and a humanly animated soul. Soul and body are two substances, and each is an instantiation of distinct bundles of universal properties. The bodily properties are instantiated in matter (ibid. 11 42–3, 46), and the soul's properties are instantiated in something that is individuated by a 'thisness' or 'haecceity' (ibid. 39–42). Personal identity derives from the identity of the soul, in the sense that the soul is the 'thisness' of the human person. In the case of the Incarnation, the Son of God takes on a human body, and in gaining a relationship to a body (of the kind usually had by a soul to its body), the Son of God begins to instantiate human mental properties in addition to his divine mental properties. The Son is the 'thisness' that determines the identity of the embodied person. On this view, the Word becomes a composite of body and soul, such that the soul, which previously constituted the Son alone, becomes a part of the relevant human composite. The idea, in short, is that the Word gains a contingent part—a body—that he previously lacked.[12]

Given this, what does Swinburne have to say about the Son's essential omniscience? Swinburne accepts a version of the two-minds theory, and thus maintains that a solution can be found in the shape of a person having two systems of belief, or somehow including two consciousnesses. The example—taken from Freudian psychotherapy—is of a person who, while clearly acting on the basis of certain (true) beliefs, refuses to allow these beliefs into her consciousness, and indeed consciously (and falsely) believes the opposite of the relevant beliefs. In this case, the subject's two belief-systems are to some extent separate, in the sense that she does not admit some of her beliefs to consciousness (ibid. 201). So the person does not consciously simultaneously believe that p and not-p. I take it that this is uncontroversial: it does not imply that the same person *consciously* has incompatible beliefs. Only one of the beliefs is consciously entertained. For this reason Swinburne prefers to categorize the other 'belief' not properly as a belief but as an *inclination to believe*. The object of such an inclination is a proposition that 'does not form part of a general view of the world, but merely guides the subject's actions in certain circumstances'—as in the case of a person who acts on certain inclinations to believe without consciously having the contents of such inclinations as beliefs of hers (ibid. 202).[13] The key point, however, turns out to be not that the inclinations are not consciously entertained. Rather, they fail to count as beliefs because they are not expressive of the subject's overall world-view. If asked to give an account of her beliefs about the world, the subject would *not* include in that account any of those propositions that count merely as inclinations to belief.

Swinburne spells out what this implies for the case of Christ. In becoming incarnate, the divine person takes on a human belief-system, one that comes to include a set of propositions that would under normal circumstances form the beliefs of a human person. In the case of Christ, this set of propositions forms merely inclinations to belief, for some of the propositions (the false ones) do not constitute the divine person's world-view.[14] Christ's human actions (including 'thoughts consciously entertained connected with the brain') are performed 'in the light of his human belief system' (ibid.). Christ, then, is one person with two consciousnesses. But while remaining essentially omniscient, and consciously so, the divine person consciously keeps this knowledge from forming part of the human belief-system. So Christ's human actions are performed on the basis of a belief-system that, first, does not include the belief that the belief-system is included in the divine belief-system in this way; and, secondly, includes some inclinations to false beliefs. But since inclinations to belief are not beliefs, there is no danger of the divine person's having false beliefs: as Swinburne (ibid.) puts it, 'his divine knowledge-system will inevitably include the knowledge that his human system contains the beliefs [i.e., inclinations to belief] that it does; and it will include those among the latter which are true'. And since the inclinations to belief in the human belief-system are not beliefs, there is no worry about two mental subjects: beliefs that p, on the one hand, and inclinations to believe that not-p, on the other, can belong to one and the same mental subject, namely, in this case, the divine person.

The way in which Swinburne sets out the metaphysics of his theory has nevertheless given commentators some theological unease. For as he himself acknowledges, at first glance his view might seem to be Apollinarian, since it denies to Christ a human soul (see ibid. 196–7)—a view of Apollinarius's that was condemned at the first Council of Constantinople (381 CE). Swinburne claims that if Christ had a human soul in this sense, he would be two individuals or persons—something that he rightly holds cannot have been intended by early church councils when they affirmed that Christ had a 'rational soul'. Rather, according to Swinburne (ibid. 252), what is intended is that Christ has a human 'way of thinking and acting'; and it is certainly the case that this is what Apollinarius wished to deny. And surely Swinburne is right about this. The Son of God is not identical with the rational soul thus understood: the Son is the composite of body and soul, and the identity of the person derives from the Son's 'thisness'. Since human souls generally individuate human persons, there is no soul (in Swinburne's sense of 'soul') other than the Son in the Incarnate Christ. But this does not mean that there is no sense in which the Incarnate Christ has a human soul in the way required by the councils. Swinburne allows that there is a different but legitimate sense of 'soul'—one that is accepted by Aristotle—according to which a soul is 'a way of thinking and acting'—namely, a *human* way of thinking and acting. And Swinburne's view of course requires that the Word acquired such a soul; he holds too that the early church councils require that the Word acquired such a soul, and that the councils would deny that the Word acquired a soul in Swinburne's sense of 'soul'. This too is correct. Swinburne's express claim is that the Son began to instantiate *human* mental states, and this is something that Apollinarius was not prepared to countenance. So on this reading, the charge of Apollinarianism is unjust. In any case, it is important to realize that Swinburne's two-minds solution is in principle independent of the metaphysics he outlines: we could wholly deny his view about human identity and still find his two-minds solution fruitful and appealing.

Overall, Swinburne's distinction between beliefs and inclinations to belief provides, it seems to me, a more elegant way of dealing with the Nestorian worry than the one I proposed above, and that I found implicitly by Morris too, according to which we need to make a distinction between persons and mental subjects. But if Swinburne's distinction between beliefs and inclinations to believe is felt to be unsatisfactory, I believe that distinguishing mental subjects from persons is still probably sufficient to deal with the Nestorian problem.

Modern discussion in philosophical theology on the doctrine of the Incarnation still represents to some extent work in progress. But it has, I believe, shown where best to look for solutions, and what the likely shape of such solutions will be: namely, first, an abandonment of a strong form of classical theism, and secondly the clarification of the relation between persons and minds, and perhaps between both of these and mental subjects. On the first of these issues, we need to abandon divine impassibility, immutability, and timelessness. The two-minds views that I consider above all seem to entail this kind of modification to classical theism (at least with regard to impassibility, immutability, and timelessness). And it is surely right to worry about the kinds of concern that philosophers raise. Coherence is, after all, a necessary condition for truth, and theological 'wisdom', or appeals to the necessarily 'mysterious' nature of the doctrine, should not be an excuse for failing to worry about possible fundamental difficulties with this central locus of Christian theology. I have tried to suggest here that the most hopeful strategy for dealing with possible contradictions lies in a combination of something like Morris's merely human/fully human distinction with a modification of classical theism, such that no divine person is timeless, or immutable, or impassible. Excluding contradictory pairs of attributes does not, of course, entail abandoning Chalcedon by adopting a 'one-nature' Christology. After all, the Christologies I am advocating do not involve denying that Christ has all properties necessary and jointly sufficient for being human (i.e. a human nature), and all properties necessary and jointly sufficient for being divine (i.e. a divine nature). The point is merely that these lists of properties cannot contain contradictory pairs.

On the second point—the clarification of the relation between persons, mental subjects, and minds, the proposals made above are certainly not inconsistent with the claim made at Constantinople III that Christ has two wills and two energies—two modes of acting, or two kinds of causal power—divine and human. Talk of divine will and divine power here is roughly a way of saying that Christ can do things (e.g. miracles) that only God can do; and talk of human will and human power is roughly a way of saying that Christ can do things (e.g. talk, touch things) that human beings can do. And talk of two wills does not entail any serious conflict—even I, for example, can have short-term goals different from and incompatible with my long-term goals. What I cannot do, of course, is simultaneously act in a way that achieves two incompatible goals—and neither can an incarnate divine person. Nestorianism is avoided both by the maximal-flow proposal, and by Swinburne's distinction between beliefs and inclinations to belief. The capacity of the maximal-flow proposal to avoid Nestorianism perhaps remains controversial, since what counts as Nestorianism is not a settled matter, either today or in the light of the objections raised in early-church orthodoxy (e.g. by Cyril of Alexandria). Overall, the achievements thus far of this theological 'research project' (so to speak—governed as it is by shared aims, materials, methods, and assumptions) seem to be orthodox; but it is not yet clear that further work is not required to show this.

Notes

Thanks to the editors of the volume for comments, and especially to Brian Leftow and Joseph Jedwab. Jedwab's insightful feedback greatly improved the whole of this chapter. Leftow's comments greatly helped me deal with issues in sect. 3. We await eagerly Jedwab's important Oxford doctoral dissertation on the whole issue. It should of course be added that neither Leftow nor Jedwab would endorse the conclusions I come to here.

1. This reading of Chalcedon is not universal amongst scholars. Sarah Coakley (2006: 246 n. 1), for example, notes that 'In the Chalcedonian definition itself it is not clear that the *hypostasis* is to be straightforwardly identified with the pre-existent Logos [i.e. the Word], since it (the *hypostasis*) is mentioned only in the context of its being the point of "concurrence" of the humanity and the divinity. . . . The explicit identification of the *hypostasis* with the Logos is made only later, at the second Council of Constantinople [in 553].' But in Chalcedon, Christ is the 'point of "concurrence" ', and in the Council the Son of God (referred to as the Word) is identified with Christ, as just noted. Thus, the Word is the subject of whatever properties Christ is the subject of—and this amounts to the claim that the hypostasis is the Word.

2. The worry about the particularity of the Incarnation receives an extensive treatment in Morris 1986: 163–86; the question of the evidential basis for the Incarnation ibid. 187–204, and especially in Swinburne 1994: 216–38 and Swinburne 2003. I ignore these further debates here, because it seems to me that the most important philosophical work has focused on the coherence issue, and because this question (unlike the others) seems to be a specifically philosophical problem, one that cannot be tackled without certain intellectual specializations of a kind typically had by philosophers and philosophically minded theologians.

3. Brian Hebblethwaite endorses this relative identity approach too, though he rather confusingly chides Richard Swinburne for accepting what is in effect a reduplicative analysis without accepting relative identity (Hebblethwaite 2005: 65–6). I discuss Swinburne's position below, and suggest why Hebblethwaite's criticism is misguided.

4. I thank Joseph Jedwab for this way of spelling out the relevant distinction between parts and properties. For a different attempt that strikes me now as less clear and elegant, see Cross forthcoming.

5. For other endorsements of kenotic views by modern philosophers of religion, see e.g. Davis 1983: 118–31, 2006; Evans 1996: 132–6, 2002, 2006a; Feenstra 1989, 2006; Forrest 2000; and Thompson and Plantinga 2006.

6. See e.g. its endorsement in Feenstra 2006: 152.

7. I thank Joseph Jedwab for this way of putting the matter.

8. A two-minds view related to Morris's can be found in Brown 1985. But Brown's account seems to involve some unresolved issues. For example, he associates minds with natures (ibid. 265), but also talks of e.g. the divine nature experiencing things 'through the medium of the human nature' (ibid. 266)—suggesting that minds for Brown are mental subjects (subjects of mental experiences), and thus, on the face of it, persons. But Brown's contribution nevertheless represents an important first step on the way to the more fully developed two-minds solutions found in Morris and Swinburne.

9. My motivation in this case was to provide some kind of defence of medieval Christologies, which generally concern themselves with metaphysical rather than psychological accounts of what it is to be a person. Thus, for the medievals, there is no sense in which persons should be identified with mental subjects. This medieval view raises questions exactly analogous to the ones I am now considering in relation to Morris's view. And this, at the least, demonstrates that there are opinions close to Morris's view, and generally considered to be orthodox, that require something like the distinction that I am now proposing. The modern debate brings with itself, quite rightly, additional insights that require further discussion.

10. I borrow talk of 'flow' from Brown 1985: 264–5.

11. It may be that this account of the Incarnation, and of maximal mental flow between two subjects, will require some further finessing of the doctrine of the Trinity, since it may be that there is such maximal flow between the divine persons' mental experiences too, and the criterion is not intended to show that there is just one divine person. But that is a topic for a different paper.

12. It is hard to keep together all Swinburne's claims here. On the one hand, as we saw above, he insists that natures are universals. On the other hand, he holds that the Word becomes a human soul that has an (individual) body. The body, as an individual, cannot be a universal, or part of a universal. Furthermore, Christ's human soul is supposed to be, like any human soul, an individual essence, a thisness: the individuator of a human person. Like any human soul, it is also supposed to be a mental subject. But an individual essence is a (non-universal) property: that is to say, an abstract object, whereas a mental subject is supposed to be a concrete object. (Again, I thank Jedwab for this point.) But this constitutes a worry about his general philosophical anthropology rather than a specific objection to his Christological outworking of this anthropology.

13. It is perhaps for this reason that Hebblethwaite believes that Swinburne is committed to a use of qua-qualifiers that requires him to be committed to relative identity. But this is not right: Swinburne claims that we can partition beliefs into different consciousnesses, and that we can do so without endorsing either relative identity or ascribing conflicting conscious beliefs to one and the same person.

14. I am not sure whether Swinburne holds that all Christ's human beliefs are in fact inclinations to belief, or whether only the false ones are. Swinburne introduces the distinction to deal merely with the problem of contradictory beliefs, but ends up arguing without qualification that 'the "beliefs" belonging to the human perspective would be mere inclinations to belief' (Swinburne 1994: 202–3). The true propositions contained in the human belief-system would seem to be expressive of the divine person's world-view, and thus count as fully-fledged beliefs.

REFERENCES

ADAMS, MARILYN MCCORD (2006). *Christ and Horrors: The Coherence of Christology*, Current Issues in Theology. Cambridge: Cambridge University Press.

BAYNE, TIM (2001). 'The Inclusion Model of the Incarnation: Problems and Prospects', *Religious Studies* 37: 125–41.

BLOUNT, DOUGLAS K. (2002). 'On the Incarnation of a Timeless God', in Ganssle and Woodruff (eds.), 236–48.

BROWN, DAVID (1985). *The Divine Trinity*. London: Duckworth.

BURRELL, DAVID (2004). Review of Cross 2002, *Speculum* 79: 467–9.

COAKLEY, SARAH (2006). 'Does Kenosis Rest on a Mistake?', in Evans (ed.), 2006*b*: 246–64.

CROSS, RICHARD (2002). *The Metaphysics of the Incarnation: Thomas Aquinas to Duns Scotus*. Oxford: Oxford University Press.

—— (2003). 'Incarnation, Omnipotence, and Action at a Distance', *Neue Zeitschrift für systematische Theologie und Religionsphilosophie* 45: 293–312.

—— (forthcoming). 'Parts and Properties in Christology', in Martin Stone (ed.), *Reason, Faith and History: Essays for Paul Helm*. Aldershot: Ashgate.

DAVIS, STEPHEN T. (1983). *Logic and the Nature of God*. London: Macmillan.

—— (2006). 'Is Kenosis Orthodox?', in Evans (ed.), 2006*b*: 112–38.

—— KENDALL, DANIEL, and O'COLLINS, GERALD (eds.) (2002). *The Incarnation: An Interdisciplinary Symposium on the Incarnation of the Son of God*. Oxford: Oxford University Press.

EVANS, C. STEPHEN (1996). *The Historical Christ and the Jesus of Faith: The Incarnational Narrative as History*. Oxford, Clarendon Press.

—— (2002). 'The Self-Emptying of Love: Some Thoughts on Kenotic Christology', in Davis, Kendall, and O'Collins (eds.), 246–72.

—— (2006*a*). 'Kenotic Christology and the Nature of God', in Evans (ed.), 2006*b*, 190–217.

—— (ed.) (2006*b*). *Exploring Kenotic Christology: The Self-Emptying of God*. Oxford: Oxford University Press.

FEENSTRA, RONALD J. (1989). 'Reconsidering Kenotic Christology', in Ronald J. Feenstra and Cornelius Plantinga, Jr. (eds.), *Trinity, Incarnation and Atonement: Philosophical and Theological Essays*, Library of Religious Philosophy. Notre Dame: University of Notre Dame Press, 128–52.

—— (2006). 'A Kenotic Christological Model for Understanding the Divine Attributes', in Evans (ed.), 2006*b*: 139–64.

FORREST, PETER (2000). 'The Incarnation: A Philosophical Case for *Kenosis*', *Religious Studies* 36: 127–40.

GANSSLE, GREGORY E., and WOODRUFF, DAVID M. (eds.) (2002). *God and Time: Essays on the Divine Nature*. New York: Oxford University Press.

HEBBLETHWAITE, BRIAN (2005). *Philosophical Theology and Christian Doctrine*, Exploring the Philosophy of Religion. Malden: Blackwell.

HICK, JOHN (ed.) (1977). *The Myth of God Incarnate*. London: SCM.

LEFTOW, BRIAN (2002). 'A Timeless God Incarnate', in Davis, Kendall, and O'Collins (eds.), 273–99.

MCCABE, HERBERT (1987). *God Matters*. London: Geoffrey Chapman.

MERRICKS, TRENTON (2007). 'The Word Made Flesh: Dualism, Physicalism, and the Incarnation', in Peter van Inwagen and Dean Zimmerman (eds.), *Persons Human and Divine*. Oxford: Oxford University Press, 281–300.

MORRIS, THOMAS V. (1986). *The Logic of God Incarnate*. Ithaca: Cornell University Press.

SENOR, THOMAS (2002). 'Incarnation, Timelessness, and Leibniz's Law Problems', in Ganssle and Woodruff (eds.), 220–35.

STUMP, ELEONORE (2003). *Aquinas*, The Arguments of the Philosophers. London: Routledge.

SWINBURNE, RICHARD (1994). *The Christian God*. Oxford: Clarendon Press.

—— (2003). *The Resurrection of God Incarnate*. Oxford: Oxford University Press.

TANNER, KATHRYN (2001). *Jesus, Humanity and the Trinity: A Brief Systematic Theology*, Scottish Journal of Theology Current Issues in Theology. Edinburgh: T. & T. Clark.

TANNER, NORMAN P. (ed.) (1990). *Decrees of the Ecumenical Councils*, 2 vols. London: Sheed & Ward; Georgetown, Washington DC: Georgetown University Press.

THOMPSON, THOMAS R., and PLANTINGA, CORNELIUS, JR. (2006). 'Trinity and Kenosis', in Evans (ed.), 2006b: 165–89.

VAN INWAGEN, PETER (1994). 'Not by Confusion of Substance but by Unity of Person', in Alan G. Padgett (ed.), *Reason and the Christian Religion: Essays in Honour of Richard Swinburne*. Oxford: Clarendon.

WILLIAMS, C. J. F. (1967). 'A Programme for Christology', *Religious Studies* 3: 513–24.

CHAPTER 21

THE RESURRECTION OF THE BODY

TRENTON MERRICKS

Rabbinic Judaism, Christianity, and Islam agree that there is life after death. More-over, all three religions agree that we shall not spend eternity as mere spirits or as disembodied souls. Instead, we shall have hands and feet and size and shape. For we shall have bodies. And not just any bodies. Each of us will have the very same body that he or she had in this life, although that body will be 'glorified'. Each of us can have the same body because, at some point in the future, all those bodies that have died will rise again to new life. That is, dead bodies will be resurrected. Indeed, we ourselves shall be resurrected. This is the doctrine of the resurrection of the body.

This chapter will focus on two questions about the doctrine of the resurrection, questions that will occur to most philosophers and theologians interested in iden-tity in general, and in personal identity in particular. The first question is: *How?* How could a body that at the end of this life was (e.g.) frail and feeble be the very same body as a resurrection body, a body that will not be frail or feeble, but will instead be glorified? Moreover, how could a body that has passed out of existence—perhaps as a result of decay or cremation—come back into existence on the Day of Resurrection?

The second question is: *Why?* Why would anyone want a resurrection of the body? And even if the resurrection delivers something that we want—maybe one's current body has some sentimental value and so having it back would be nice—we might still wonder why any religion would give the doctrine a central place, as Judaism, Christianity, and Islam all do.

CHANGE AND TEMPORAL GAPS

I have a body. And it is the very same body that I had earlier today. It is even the same body I had as a child. That is why, for example, my foot now bears a scar from an injury I suffered as a toddler. Again, the body I have now is numerically identical with—is one and the same object as—the body I had as a child. To deny this would imply, I think quite implausibly, that I literally lost one body and then acquired another at some point or other between my childhood and now.

Of course, my body is now quite different from how it was when I was a child. It has changed in size and in shape and in many other ways. That is why someone who had last seen my body when I was a child would not recognize it today. Again, my body has persisted through enormous amounts of change. And so has every other human body, at least every other body that has been around for any appreciable amount of time. So too have many other objects.

We are familiar with a single object's being one way, even though it was or will be a very different way. So the doctrine of the resurrection's implication that one and the same body is one way at death (e.g. sickly) but will be a very different way at resurrection (e.g. glorified and healthy) should not strike us as strange. So let us assume that there is nothing worrisome about this implication.[1]

Dead bodies often pass out of existence. For example, some dead bodies decay completely; others are cremated; some are even eaten by wild animals. But, given the doctrine of the resurrection, even those bodies that have gone out of existence will one day rise—and so will one day exist—again. Thus the doctrine of the resurrection implies a 'temporal gap' in the career of many bodies.[2]

To understand better what a temporal gap is supposed to be, consider this story: you build a time machine that can send you—and your body—to 'the future'. You push the *start* button. You disappear. You then reappear at some later date. That is, this machine sends you to some future time, allowing you to 'skip' all the times between now and then. Thus this machine causes a temporal gap in your life, and also in the career of your body. Or consider a watch that is disassembled, perhaps for cleaning. Assume that, as a result, it ceases to exist. Assume further that when its parts are reassembled, the watch comes back into existence. If all these assumptions are right, the watch 'jumps' a temporal gap *via* disassembly and reassembly.

The doctrine of the resurrection implies a temporal gap in the career of many bodies. So objections to a temporal gap in a body's career are thereby objections to the doctrine of the resurrection. We shall consider two such objections.

Suppose, first, that, necessarily, whenever identity holds between an object at one time and an object at another time, something must *account for* or *ground* that identity. And suppose, second, that nothing could account for, or ground, identity's holding across a temporal gap between a body that has (e.g.) been cremated and a resurrection body. These two suppositions jointly rule out the coming back into existence on Resurrection Day of a body that has been cremated. So these two suppositions amount to an objection to the doctrine of the resurrection.

A compelling account of what grounds the identity of a resurrection body with that of a cremated body would undermine this objection. And a number of accounts have been offered. Over the centuries, the most common account among Christian philosophers and theologians, an account that was also countenanced by Islamic and Jewish thinkers, has been this: on the Last Day, God will gather up the very small bits that composed a body at death and will 'reassemble' them, which will thereby bring the body that died back into existence (see Bynum 1995; Smith and Haddad 2002).[3]

One potential problem with this account is that even a body's smallest parts might themselves sometimes go out of existence. For example, perhaps some of those parts get converted (as in nuclear explosions) from matter to energy. If this were to happen, then those parts would not be around for reassembly on the Last Day, and so that body—given this account—could not be resurrected.[4] But every body is supposed to be resurrected.

Another objection to resurrection as reassembly trades on the many ways in which the small parts of one body can end up as parts of another body. The most sensational versions of this objection involve cannibalism. A cannibal eats me, incorporates parts of my body into his, and then dies. So some of the small bits that composed my body at my death also composed the cannibal's body at his death. As a result, when Resurrection Day arrives, God cannot (totally) reassemble both the cannibal's body and mine. So—given resurrection as reassembly—God cannot resurrect both my body and the cannibal's body. But, again, every body is supposed to be resurrected.

In the second century, Athenagoras replied to this objection by insisting that human flesh is not digestible. As a result, he would have maintained, the very small bits that compose my body at death never could become parts of a cannibal's body. So on Resurrection Day my body shall be the only one with a claim to those bits, even if a cannibal ate me and then died (Bynum 1995: 33). Unfortunately for Athenagoras's bold reply, human flesh is (so I understand) digestible.

A final, and I think deeper, problem with resurrection as reassembly was pointed out at least as far back as Origen (ibid. 64–6). It is that our bodies are constantly changing with respect to the very small bits that compose them. (This is one way

in which our bodies are quite different from inanimate objects such as watches.)
Therefore, a body's identity from one moment to the next is not a matter of having
exactly the same very small parts. So it seems to be a mistake to claim that its
identity from death to resurrection is a matter of having exactly the same very small
parts.

Look at it this way. Because my body is constantly changing its very small parts,
it might be that none of the atoms that was a part of my body when I was 5 years
old is now a part of my body. Let us suppose that none is. Now suppose that today
God gathers together all those atoms that composed my body when I was 5 years old
and reassembles them. This would produce a body, a body that looks just like mine
did when I was 5 years old. But that body would not—could not—be my body. For
that body is over there, where God did the reassembling, but my body is right here
(cf. van Inwagen 1978: 120).

We know for sure that reassembling the atoms that composed my body when
I was 5 years old, if done today, would not produce my body. This suggests that
reassembling those same atoms, if done on the Day of Resurrection, would not
produce my body. And this suggests, in turn, that reassembling the atoms that
will compose my body when I die, if done on the Day of Resurrection, would not
produce my body. At any rate, I conclude that a Resurrection Day reassembly (of
last parts, or indeed of parts from any time during a body's life) would not ground
or account for the identity of a resurrection body with a body that existed in this
life.

Here is an alternative to resurrection as reassembly, an alternative first endorsed
by early rabbis. Each body has an indestructible bone at the base of its spinal cord,
and even if a body goes out of existence at some point after death, that body will
come back into existence when a resurrection body is constructed around that bone
(Bynum 1995: 54; cf. Smith and Haddad 2002: 131). Unfortunately for this proposal,
there is no indestructible bone at the base of the spinal cord, no bone that survives
cremation, decay, and every other threat to a dead body's existence.[5]

Some might suggest that my current body will be identical with whatever resurrection body has the *same (substantial) soul* as is had by my current body. But a soul
is not part of a body. And I doubt that the identity of one physical object (such as a
body) might be entirely a matter of the identity of a second object (such as a soul)
when that second object is not itself a part of the first object. In this regard, taking
a soul to be the guarantor of bodily identity is less plausible than taking the bone
from the base of the spinal cord to be that guarantor. For at least that bone is a part
of the relevant body.

Moreover, explaining bodily identity across a temporal gap in terms of the same
soul seems to presuppose that having the same soul is sufficient for being the same
body. This straightaway entails that it is impossible for a soul to switch bodies.
But, surely, if there really are souls, it is possible for a soul to switch bodies.
(Some even argue for the existence of the soul by way of the alleged possibility

of a person's—and so, presumably, a soul's—switching bodies (see e.g. Swinburne 1986: 151).) And, finally, as will become clear in the next section, the doctrine of the resurrection itself provides a reason to deny that bodily identity across a temporal gap is secured by having the same soul.

We have briefly considered three accounts of what might ground the identity of the resurrection body with the body had in this life. I do not think that any of these three accounts—or any other extant account—is plausible.[6] Nor do I have a novel account of my own to offer. But, as I shall now point out, none of this implies that the above objection to the doctrine of the resurrection is successful.

Recall that that objection assumes, first, necessarily, something must account for or ground every instance of identity over time; and, second, nothing could account for or ground identity across (at least some) resurrection-induced temporal gaps. As I have argued elsewhere, possibly, some instances of identity over time have no ground. Moreover, it would be no surprise if the identity of a body had in this life with a resurrection body were just such an instance (see Merricks 2001b). If so, then the first assumption of the above objection to the resurrection is false, and so that objection fails.

Moreover, suppose we concede, just for the sake of argument, that something or other must account for, or ground, every instance of identity over time, including every instance that would result from a coming resurrection. Then believers in the resurrection can block the above objection by denying that objection's second assumption. That is, they can simply conclude that there will be something in virtue of which each resurrection body will be identical with a body had in this life, something that will ground or account for that identity. Crucially, they can conclude this even given their inability to discover that ground, an inability evidenced by the failure of proposed accounts such as reassembly. After all, no one should presume to know exactly how God pulls off any miracle, including the resurrection of the body.

A second objection to the temporal gaps implied by the doctrine of the resurrection, and so a second objection to the doctrine itself, claims that a certain condition is necessary for bodily identity over time. Moreover, this objection adds, when it comes to the purported identity of a body that has (e.g.) been cremated with a body that will exist on Resurrection Day, this condition cannot be satisfied.[7]

There are various species of this second objection, each differing from the others with respect to what is alleged to be necessary for bodily identity over time. One familiar allegation is that *spatiotemporal continuity* is thus necessary. This allegation is equivalent to the claim that, first, spatial continuity is thus necessary and, second, temporal continuity is thus necessary.[8] The claim that temporal continuity is thus necessary just is the claim that one and the same body cannot exist at two times without existing at all the times in between. And that claim just is the claim that temporal gaps in a body's career are impossible.

So the thesis that spatiotemporal continuity is necessary for bodily identity over time says exactly that 'spatial continuity' is necessary for bodily identity over time and, moreover, that temporal gaps in a body's career are impossible. Given that this is what it says, the thesis that spatiotemporal continuity is necessary for bodily identity over time presupposes that temporal gaps in a body's career are impossible. So that thesis is a question-begging reason to conclude that such temporal gaps are impossible. So it is not a good reason for that conclusion.

Some have suggested that, necessarily, the way a body is at one time must appropriately *cause* the way a body is at a later time, if the body at the later time is to be identical with the body at the earlier time.[9] This suggestion threatens temporal gaps in a body's career, and so threatens the doctrine of the resurrection, only if the relevant sort of causation cannot occur across a temporal gap.

Suppose, once more, that the time machine sends you to the future. You arrive in the future with a familiar tattoo on your leg. That tattoo's being on your leg was caused not only by a youthful lapse of judgment, but also—and more importantly—by your having that very tattoo on your leg before entering the time machine. This implies that causation can occur across a temporal gap, since the way your leg was before time travel causes it to be a certain way after time travel. In fact, this seems to be just the sort of causation that is allegedly necessary for bodily identity over time.

Now some might object that the time machine story just told is absolutely impossible. But I do not see why we should agree with them.[10] More generally, and more to the point, I see no compelling reason to conclude that there is any condition that is *both* necessary for bodily identity over time *and also* cannot possibly be satisfied across a temporal gap. On the other hand, the considerations raised above do not show that there is no such condition. As far as those considerations go, we should be agnostic about the existence of such a condition.

Similarly, I think that, although we might have hunches one way or the other, philosophical reasons of the sort surveyed above deliver nothing conclusive about the possibility of the temporal gaps implied by resurrection. As far as standard philosophical reflection on these matters goes, resurrection of the cremated or decayed human body might be possible, but then again it might not be possible.

Of course, those who believe in the resurrection in the first place do not believe in it because of standard philosophical reflection. Rather, we believe that God has revealed that there will be a resurrection of the body, a resurrection that—given cremation, decay, etc.—implies bodily identity across a temporal gap. And to the extent that revelation justifies belief in the resurrection, I think it also justifies belief in bodily identity across a temporal gap. So it likewise justifies the conclusion that there are no necessary conditions for bodily identity that cannot possibly be satisfied across a temporal gap.

BODIES AND PERSONS

Even in polite company, one may admit to believing in life after death, at least if one's beliefs are appropriately spiritual, involving leaving one's body behind, heading toward the light, and so on. Such beliefs are controversial, of course, but most people will maintain eye contact with you, and perhaps even murmur sympathetically, while you express your hope that, for example, your spirit will live on past the grave. Alas, the resurrection is another matter altogether. At least, my own experience suggests that averted eyes and an awkward silence are the typical results of expressing one's hope that, at some time after one's death, every dead body, including one's own, will come back to life.

The idea of a coming resurrection of every body seems strange not just to the non-religious, but also to many of the religious, including many who believe that Jesus Christ rose from the dead. Perhaps discomfort with the idea of many bodies rising from the dead is why—I merely speculate—my childhood Sunday school teachers never asked me to memorize this passage from the New Testament, which concerns events around the time of Christ's death and resurrection: 'The tombs also were opened and many bodies of the saints who had fallen asleep were raised. After [Christ's] resurrection they came out of the tombs and entered the holy city and appeared to many' (Matt. 27: 52–3, NRSV). At any rate, it is safe to assume that the signs at sporting events that read 'John 3: 16' will not soon be replaced with signs saying 'Matthew 27: 52–3'. Lots of bodies rising from the dead is just too strange.

Nevertheless, Christianity, Islam, and traditional rabbinic Judaism all teach that lots of bodies—in fact, every human body that has ever died—will rise from the dead on the Last Day. Moreover, this teaching is central to all three religions. For example—and now I narrow my focus to Christianity—the Apostle's Creed closes with an affirmation of 'the resurrection of the body, and the life everlasting'.[11] And here are the final words of the Nicene Creed: 'I look for the resurrection of the dead, and the life of the world to come. Amen.'[12]

These creeds are short documents, meant to summarize the most important points of Christian theology. And resurrection of the body gets explicit mention in both, which I take to be evidence of the centrality of the doctrine of the resurrection to Christianity. This centrality should bring to mind some of the questions that opened this chapter: Why should anyone want there to be a resurrection of the body? And why would any religion have that doctrine at its heart?

I shall defend an answer to these questions. My defense begins with a three-step argument, each step of which is plausible, though controversial. The first step says that each of us—each human person—has *physical properties*. For example, you literally have a certain weight. You likewise have a certain shape. You have a certain location in space. And so on.[13]

The second step says that you are neither heavier than nor lighter than your body; that is, your weight is the same as your body's weight. Moreover, you are not one shape, and your body another; rather you and your body have the same shape. Nor are you off in one corner of the room, while your body is to be found in another; instead, you are located just where your body is located.

The third step says that there is only one human-shaped object exactly and entirely located where you are exactly and entirely located, and, more generally, only one object with all of the physical properties had by you and had by your body. Once we have taken these three steps, we must conclude that you are *identical with* your body.

So if the above argument is sound, you are identical with your body. (And even if it is not sound, it is still illuminating, clarifying what your being identical with your body amounts to.) At any rate, let us suppose, just for the sake of argument, that you really are identical with your body. More generally, let us suppose, for the sake of argument, that each of us is identical with his or her body.

As was noted in the preceding section, most dead bodies (eventually) cease to exist. This implies, given our supposition that each of us is identical with his or her body, that most of us shall cease to exist after death. And this implies that, for most of us, our only hope for existence after death is the hope that our bodies (i.e. we ourselves) will come back into existence. Moreover, this implies that, for all of us, our only hope for life after death is the hope that our bodies (i.e. we ourselves) will live again, that is, that our bodies will be resurrected. The doctrine of the resurrection of the body—despite its appearing quite strange at first glance—is as motivated as belief in life after death itself.

Look at it this way. Suppose you know that you are about to die. And you hope that death is not the end. Add that you know that you are one and the same thing as your body. Then your hope for life after death should have a very clear focus. You should hope that your body (i.e. you yourself) will one day live again. Your body's living again will not happen on its own, of course. It will take a miracle, especially if your body passes out of existence by way of (e.g.) cremation. But that miracle— and, more generally, God's raising every dead body—will not be merely some sort of spooky sideshow. Instead, it will be your only shot at life after death.

Or suppose that a close friend has just died. Suppose that you know for certain that your friend was identical with his or her body. Then you have only one hope for seeing your friend again: the resurrection. Your only hope is the hope that, someday, God will raise the dead. Thus we see once more that our being identical with our bodies makes the motivation for, and importance of, the doctrine of the resurrection perfectly clear.

If we are bodies, then when our bodies are resurrected, *we ourselves* are resurrected. This result fits with the way the creeds couple belief in resurrection with belief in everlasting life, and also with the way various passages of Scripture describe the resurrection. Consider:

At that time Michael, the great prince, the protector of your people, shall arise. There shall be a time of anguish, such as has never occurred since nations first came into existence. But at that time your people shall be delivered, everyone whose name is found written in the book. Many of those who sleep in the dust of the earth shall awake, some to everlasting life, and some to shame and everlasting contempt.   (Dan. 12: 1–2, NRSV)

Do not be astonished at this; for the hour is coming when all who are in their graves will hear [the Son of Man's] voice and will come out—those who have done good, to the resurrection of life, and those who have done evil, to the resurrection of condemnation.

(John 5: 28–9, NRSV)

For the Lord himself, with a cry of command, with the archangel's call and with the sound of God's trumpet, will descend from heaven, and the dead in Christ will rise . . .

(1 Thess. 4: 16, NRSV)

If we take the above passages at face value—or take any of a number of others at face value (e.g. Matt. 14: 12–14; Acts 24; 1 Cor. 15)—it is not just dead bodies that will be raised to life, but dead people. Our being identical with our bodies makes perfect sense of the idea that the resurrection of our bodies will be the resurrection of us.[14]

What if we were not identical with our bodies? Then it would be hard, if not impossible, to make sense of the idea that dead *people* will be resurrected. Moreover, the importance of the doctrine that, on the Day of Resurrection, one gets a body *identical with the body one had in this life* would be difficult to explain. Indeed, I cannot think of any plausible explanation at all, much less one that rivals the very straightforward and absolutely compelling explanation that flows directly from the claim that each of us is identical with his or her body.

I think that all of this gives those of us who believe in the resurrection of the body—and who are committed to its importance—a good reason to conclude that we are identical with our respective bodies. Thus we have a new reason to conclude that each of us is identical with his or her body, a reason in addition to my three-step argument above that began with the claim that we have physical properties.[15]

This is but one reason to conclude that each of us is identical with his or her body. I believe that there are further reasons to endorse this conclusion. And there are, of course, alleged reasons to reject this conclusion, including some specifically theological reasons. Below I shall respond to a few reasons one might offer for rejecting this conclusion. But I do not pretend to respond to every such reason, just as I do not pretend to present every reason one might have for affirming that each of us is identical with his or her body.[16]

Let us begin with what I suspect is the most common reason that many Christians, and others, deny that a human person is one and the same thing as his or her body. They deny this because they want to make sense of life after death, life after the destruction of one's body. And they think that this can be done only if one is not the body that will be destroyed, but instead something else, such as a soul. But as should now be perfectly clear, this 'reason' is no good. On the contrary, I argued above that we are identical with our bodies precisely because this identity makes the best sense of specifically Christian claims surrounding life after death, even life after the destruction of one's body. (Our being identical with our bodies is, I confess, entirely inconsistent with the pictures of life after death found in, for example, pagan Greek philosophy and the movie *Ghost*.)

Let us turn to another objection. On the view I am here suggesting, we cease to exist at (some point after) death and then come back into existence on the Day of Resurrection. Put otherwise, my view implies that we jump ahead in time from our death to the Day of Resurrection, skipping all the times in between. And some might object that Christians are committed not just to life after death, but to life after death *and before resurrection*.

Some might thus object because of certain scriptures. For example, the book of Revelation speaks of souls, under the altar, prior to the Day of Resurrection:

When he opened the fifth seal, I saw under the altar the souls of those who had been slaughtered for the word of God and for the testimony they had given; they cried out with a loud voice, 'Sovereign Lord, holy and true, how long will it be before you judge and avenge our blood on the inhabitants of the earth?' They were each given a white robe and told to rest a little longer . . .   (Rev. 6: 9–11, NRSV)

This passage, taken completely literally, suggests that martyrs exist as souls between death and resurrection (and also that souls can wear robes). But I think we should not take this passage completely literally. And the same goes for other passages that seem to suggest that we shall exist after our death but before our resurrection.[17]

I say this partly because I take different passages literally, such as those that say that dead people are raised to life. And I say this partly because I am convinced by the above explanation of the motivation for, and centrality of, the doctrine of the resurrection. In the background here is my opinion that the emphasis on resurrection as our hope for eternal life is more central to Christian Scripture and creed than is the idea of an 'intermediate existence' between death and resurrection.

Some might respond that intermediate existence is required for a practice central to the devotional lives of many Christians: seeking the intercession of the saints. Most of the saints have died, but have not yet been resurrected. (The exceptions that prove the rule are, assuming her assumption, the Blessed Virgin Mary, along with any Saint that never died in the first place, such as unfallen angles.) So—if human beings do not exist between death and resurrection—most of the saints do not now exist. This seems to threaten the practice of asking the saints for help.

But consider the following. I ask Saint Frideswide to pray for me, to ask God to grant a certain request. God, being omniscient, knows that I have asked her this. So suppose that God, after the resurrection, will communicate my request to her. She will then ask God to have granted my petition. God even now knows that she will do this. And so he now grants my petition, on account of Frideswide's future intercession. And so it goes, in general, with how the saints intercede for us.

This seems to accommodate the practice, and efficacy, of asking the saints for help. More generally, I think that it offers one way of securing the 'communion of saints'. But none of this requires that the saints exist right now. So I conclude that the various practices involving the saints do not require that they exist between death and resurrection.

Of course, the 'mechanism' for saintly intercession I have just outlined is not what petitioners are likely to have in mind. But I am not sure what mechanism, if any, they do have in mind. After all, those who seek the help of the saints do so not only in many languages, but also often completely silently. How are the saints to know what is being asked of them? I think that the best answer is that God, in his omniscience, knows what is requested of each saint, and somehow communicates that to him or her.

So I suspect that, whatever we say about the existence of human beings between death and resurrection, any petitions that reach the saints do so by 'going through God' in some way or other. But once we concede this, I see nothing objectionable about the mechanism I have suggested. And that mechanism is consistent with each saint—like each of us—jumping ahead in time from his or her death to the Day of Resurrection.

Notes

Thanks to Mike Bergmann, Tom Flint, Mark Murphy, Mike Murray, Mike Rea, and Nick Wolterstorff.

1. Merricks 1994 discusses, and defends, identity through change. Some might object that, while identity can be preserved through ordinary change, one's glorified resurrection body will be so different from one's current body that that resurrection body cannot be identical with the body one has now. But I reply that we do not know enough about what a resurrection body will be like to conclude this, especially when we recall that some ordinary change is quite stunning, as when a single body goes from being the body of an infant to that of a full-grown adult.

2. In what follows, I shall say that the doctrine of the resurrection implies a temporal gap in the career of many bodies. This is shorthand for the claim that that doctrine *and the fact that many dead bodies go out of existence* jointly imply such gaps. My own view is that a human body ceases to exist immediately after dying (see Merricks 2001a: 53). But nothing I say below turns on this view. The arguments below require only that at least some human bodies cease to exist at some point or other after dying.

3. We shall consider objections to resurrection as reassembly. But, at least until quite recently, virtually no self-styled believer in the resurrection would have raised the following objection: 'What is the *point* of reassembly? Why even *try* to account for the identity of a resurrection body with a body had in this life? After all, resurrection bodies need not be numerically identical with bodies had in this life.'

Virtually no one would have thus objected because debates among believers in the resurrection have been over *how* (not *whether*) a body that has ceased to exist will secure identity with a resurrection body. Again, over almost all the past two thousand years, those debates have uniformly presupposed that the very body that dies (and perishes) will rise again. This is why I say that, according to the doctrine of the resurrection, the very body that dies will rise again. Christians have another reason to insist that the very body that dies will rise again: they believe that Christ's body at crucifixion, that is, the body that was crucified on the cross, is one and the same as the body that walked out of the tomb; and they believe that our resurrection will be patterned after Christ's.

4. Objection: Those parts could come back into existence on the Day of Resurrection and so be available for reassembly. Reply: To do that, the parts themselves would have to jump a temporal gap. But they could not jump a temporal gap by way of reassembly, since the idea here is that when they convert to energy (or otherwise cease to exist), so too do all their parts (if they have parts at all). So this objection requires that there are ways other than reassembly to jump a temporal gap. Thus this objection in defense of resurrection as reassembly undermines, at least to some extent, the motivation for resurrection as reassembly.

5. Bones perish when a body is cremated. But some smaller parts of a body do not. For example, an electron that is now part of my body would not perish if my body were now cremated. Thus one might suggest that there is some very small part—a certain electron, say, as opposed to a very hard bone—of each body such that that body would come back into existence, if a resurrection body were constructed around that electron.

   This suggestion is afflicted by analogues of the problems that afflict resurrection as reassembly. First, that electron itself might go out of existence, precluding resurrection of the relevant body. Second, that electron might become part of another body, as a result of (e.g.) cannibalism; this demonstrates, among other things, that having that electron as a part is not sufficient for being the body that originally had it. Third, human bodies are constantly changing their very small parts, including the electrons that compose them; so it seems mistaken (if not positively bizarre) to say that bodily identity across a temporal gap could be entirely a matter of having a single special electron as a part.

6. Hud Hudson 2001: 190 offers a memory-based account of a physical person's jumping the temporal gap between that person's death and resurrection (cf. John Locke 1975: 542; *Essay*, 4. 3. 6). But this is not—as Hudson himself agrees—even a purported account of a *body's* jumping a temporal gap. Peter van Inwagen 1978, unlike Hudson, does believe that the very body that has died will be resurrected. And van Inwagen offers an account of how this could be. But his account rejects my assumption that dead bodies typically cease to exist. Rather, according to his account, each dead body is squirreled away somewhere by the Lord to await resurrection, while a replica decays (or is cremated, etc.) in its stead.

7. This second objection turns on (alleged) *necessary* conditions for identity over time. The first objection—the objection in terms of what grounds or accounts for trans-gap bodily identity—turned on (alleged) *sufficient* conditions for identity over time. Unlike the first objection, this second objection cannot be blocked by denying that identity across temporal gaps must be grounded. Nor can it be blocked, again unlike

the first objection, by admitting ignorance about how God will resurrect long-gone bodies.

8. More precise statements of spatiotemporal continuity are offered by, among others, George Mavrodes 1977: 37 and Eli Hirsch 1982: 15–21.

9. Van Inwagen 1978 not only endorses this causal requirement, but also turns it into a new objection to resurrection as reassembly, an objection in addition to those considered above. The key to van Inwagen's objection is that, he argues, the reassembly of a dead body's last parts is not sufficient for the body that has died to cause, in the relevant way, the features of the body that results from reassembly.

10. Dean Zimmerman defends the possibility of the relevant sort of causation occurring across a temporal gap. Zimmerman 1999: 204 summarizes his defense thus: 'Of course the supposition that causal processes can be spatiotemporally gappy in this way is contentious. But it should be much less so than it once was, for the following reasons: there is no a priori reason to think it is impossible, and some a posteriori reason to think it happens; the theories of causation which imply that it is impossible have been exploded; and the most promising theories still in the water can accommodate it.'

11. The doctrine of the resurrection is also central to Islam and Judaism. Smith and Haddad 2002: 63 tell us: 'The promise, the guarantee, of the day at which all bodies will be resurrected and all persons called to account for their deeds and the measure of their faith is the dominant message of the Qur'an . . .' The Basic Principles of Moses Maimonides are widely taken to articulate the central beliefs of rabbinic Judaism. The thirteenth and final principle affirms the resurrection of the dead.

12. The Athanasian Creed tells us that, at Christ's coming, 'all men shall rise again with their bodies.'

13. Our having physical properties does not imply that our only properties are physical. For example, our having physical properties is consistent with our having mental properties, even if those mental properties are themselves in no way physical. Thus our having physical properties is consistent with 'property dualism' about the mental.

14. I am not saying that the human authors of Scripture, or those who formulated the creeds, believed or meant to teach that we are identical with our bodies. I am saying that they believed and meant to teach that our bodies will be resurrected, that this is intimately related to our hope for life after death, and that dead people will rise again. Because I believe what they taught, I conclude—for reasons given in this chapter—that we are identical with our bodies.

Compare my approach here to Scripture and the creeds with the following. A document written in 1350 describes those dying all around the author; the dying experience nausea, fever, and other symptoms of bubonic plague. Because we believe what the author had to say, we might conclude—for reasons that a pathologist might give—that those people had an infection caused by the bacterium *Yersinia prestis*. Of course, the author of that document did not believe or mean to say anything about that bacterium; the author had never even heard of bacteria.

15. I have just argued from the doctrine of the resurrection to the claim that we are identical with our bodies. That claim implies that we lack (substantial) souls. This is why I said, in the preceding section, that the doctrine of the resurrection provides a reason to deny that bodily identity across a temporal gap is secured by having the same soul.

Those who deny that we are identical with our bodies might say that they have no idea why the doctrine of the resurrection is important, even though it is important. Perhaps this is a reasonable thing for them to say. And they might add that saying this is analogous to saying that they have no idea what grounds bodily identity across a temporal gap, even though (some might maintain) something must ground it. But I do not think that the cases are appropriately analogous. As I argued in the previous section, there is nothing remotely like a genuinely live option that, if true, would deliver a full and satisfying account of what grounds the identity of a resurrection body with a body that was (e.g.) cremated. So an appeal to ignorance here is unavoidable for believers in the resurrection, at least for those who think there must be some ground for bodily identity across a temporal gap. On the other hand, there is (what I take to be) a genuinely live option that, if true, would deliver a full and satisfying account of the importance of the doctrine of the resurrection: namely, the identity of a person with his or her body.

16. For example, the Incarnation provides considerations that bear on the identity of a person with his or her body, but I shall not discuss them in this paper. Plantinga 1999 and Leftow 2002 both object that the Incarnation cannot be squared with the claim that human persons are identical with their bodies. But, on the contrary, I argue (Merricks 2007) that it is easier to reconcile the Incarnation with the claim that human persons are identical with their bodies than with any other thesis about the relation of a person to his or her body.

17. My dying results in my literal non-existence. Nevertheless, to die is to jump ahead in time to the Day of Resurrection. Thus I could think to myself, as I am about to die, that so far as things seem to me—and only because of the resurrection of the body—this day I shall be with the Lord in paradise (cf. Luke 23: 43).

REFERENCES

Bynum, Caroline Walker (1995). *The Resurrection of the Body in Western Christianity 200–1336*. New York: Columbia University Press.

Hirsch, Eli (1982). *The Concept of Identity*. Oxford: Oxford University Press.

Hudson, Hud (2001). *A Materialist Metaphysics of the Human Person*. Ithaca: Cornell University Press.

Leftow, Brian (2002). 'A Timeless God Incarnate', in Stephen T. Davis, Daniel Kendall, and Gerald O'Collins (eds.), *The Incarnation*. Oxford: Oxford University Press.

Locke, John (1975). *An Essay Concerning Human Understanding*, ed. Peter H. Nidditch. Oxford: Clarendon.

Mavrodes, George I. (1977). 'The Life Everlasting and the Bodily Criterion of Identity', *Noûs* 11: 27–39.

Merricks, Trenton (1994). 'Endurance and Indiscernibility', *Journal of Philosophy* 91: 165–84.

——— (2001a). *Objects and Persons*. Oxford: Clarendon.

——— (2001b). 'How to Live Forever without Saving Your Soul: Physicalism and Immortality', in Kevin Corcoran (ed.), *Soul, Body, and Survival: Essays on the Metaphysics of Human Persons*. Ithaca: Cornell University Press.

MERRICKS, TRENTON (2007). 'The Word Made Flesh: Dualism, Physicalism, and the Incarnation', in Peter van Inwagen and Dean Zimmerman (eds.), *Persons: Human and Divine*. Oxford: Oxford University Press.

PLANTINGA, ALVIN (1999). 'On Heresy, Mind, and Truth', *Faith and Philosophy* 16: 182–93.

SMITH, JANE IDLEMAN, and HADDAD, YVONNE YAZBECK (2002). *The Islamic Understanding of Death and Resurrection*. Oxford: Oxford University Press.

SWINBURNE, RICHARD (1986). *The Evolution of the Soul*. Oxford: Clarendon.

VAN INWAGEN, PETER (1978). 'The Possibility of Resurrection', *International Journal for Philosophy of Religion* 9: 114–21.

ZIMMERMAN, DEAN (1999). 'The Compatibility of Materialism and Survival: The "Falling Elevator" Model', *Faith and Philosophy* 16: 194–212.

CHAPTER 22

....

HEAVEN AND HELL

....

JERRY L. WALLS

In the introduction to their anthology of readings about heaven, Carol and Philip Zaleski observe that the classical view of philosophy represented by the likes of Plato and his followers was that our highest calling as human beings is the eternal contemplation of truth, beauty, and goodness. So understood, the Zaleskis observe that 'philosophy itself... is nothing less than the quest for heaven'.[1]

While versions of the doctrines of heaven and hell appeared in a number of ancient cultures long before Christ was born,[2] the Christian account of heaven raised the significance of the quest for truth, beauty and goodness to new heights. The ultimate destiny of every person is either eternal joy of unimaginable glory and delight or eternal misery of unspeakable horror. The distinctively Christian account of God with its attendant doctrines of Trinity, incarnation, and atonement, gave particular shape to the hope for heaven and the horror of hell. Heaven is the climax and perfection of an intimate relationship with a personal God whose very nature is love. This love was revealed definitively in the incarnation, atonement, and resurrection of Jesus, and the salvation thereby provided will reach its highest end in the blissful experience of seeing the Trinity.[3] The choice either to receive this salvation or to reject it is a matter of momentous importance. It is precisely the prospect of losing a good so extraordinary that makes hell so terrible. The truth was never so beautiful, and the stakes never so high in the quest to find the truth and follow after the good.

With the prospects for happiness and misery so magnified, the meaning of our lives and the significance of our choices are both elevated to dramatic proportions. Indeed, both heaven and hell have stirred the imagination of western culture for centuries, inspiring great literature as well as visual art. Moreover, heaven and hell have played an undeniable role in the moral foundations of western culture, providing direction as well as hard motivation in the form of ultimate sanctions.

Despite this impressive pedigree, heaven and hell have faded from the consciousness of many people in recent times. Citing what he sees as 'irreversible changes' in our ways of thinking and perceiving the world, Harvard theologian Gordon Kaufman opines that 'I don't think there can be any future for heaven and hell'.[4] For an example of the loss of heavenly belief in recent times that may be of particular interest to philosophers, consider the autobiographical musings of one of the greatest practitioners of the discipline in the twentieth century, namely, W. V. Quine.

I may have been nine when I began to worry about the absurdity of heaven and eternal life, and about the jeopardy I was incurring by those evil doubts. Presently I realized that the jeopardy was illusory if the doubts were right. My somber conclusion was nonetheless disappointing, but I rested with it. . . . Such, then, was the beginning of my philosophical concern. Perhaps the same is true of the majority of philosophers.[5]

Unfortunately Quine does not tell us why he found the idea of heaven and eternal life absurd, but seems to assume it is obvious or at least that he can take it for granted among his fellow philosophers. Nor does he tell us why he thinks the majority of philosophers were awakened from their dogmatic slumber by similarly skeptical doubts about the reality of heaven. Regardless, it is hard to exaggerate the difference between seeing the quest for heaven as the very goal of philosophy, and seeing the absurdity of heaven as the dawning moment of philosophical awakening.

If Quine's speculation is true that the majority of philosophers were initiated into philosophical thinking by the absurdity of heaven, or even if they share his view on the matter, we should hardly expect to find much recent philosophical literature on the subject. And judging by that criterion alone, Quine's speculation has a lot to be said for it, for contemporary philosophers have given scant attention to heaven, to put it mildly. Indeed, more surprisingly, heaven has even lost its imaginative grip on many people who would still profess to believe in it. In their history of heaven, Colleen McDannell and Bernhard Lang observe that 'although fundamentalists would discard the suggestion that heaven no longer is an active part of their belief system, eternal life has become an unknown place or a state of vague identity'.[6]

When we turn our attention to hell, we discover that it has suffered perhaps even more from benign neglect. In the centuries since the Enlightenment, hell has melted down from a hard-cast theological conviction into an emotionally charged caricature of revivalism. For many, hell exists primarily as a parody, surviving in popular culture through numerous 'Far Side' cartoons and an occasional episode of 'The Simpsons'. In 1985, Martin Marty published an article tellingly entitled 'Hell Disappeared. No One Noticed. A Civic Argument'.[7] Marty's article takes aim at those who want to return prayer to schools as a means of restoring moral values, and argue that we can do so without endorsing any particular religion. Marty points out, however, that the belief that God punishes evil behavior, not only now but hereafter, has always been an essential component of any morally relevant view of God. Unfortunately the doctrine of hell is no longer 'culturally available', so there is no substantive sense in which God can be restored to public schools and civic life. As part of his evidence that hell is no longer available to contemporary culture, Marty pointed out that a bibliographical search of recent literature turned up almost nothing on the subject.[8]

In the past several years, however, hell has returned with a vengeance—or without a vengeance, depending on how the doctrine is understood! Indeed, just six years after Marty's article appeared, *U.S. News and World Report* ran an article entitled 'Hell's Sober Comeback', in which it claimed that 'hell is undergoing something of a revival in American religious thought', even among theologians.[9] Were Marty to do a bibliographical search today he would find plenty of material on hell. Indeed, he would discover a lively debate on the nature of hell, not only among theologians and biblical scholars but among philosophers as well. Moreover, there are signs of renewed interest in heaven as well, although philosophical literature on hell is far more prevalent to date, perhaps because hell presents more urgent difficulties.

No doubt there are several factors involved in the revival of interest in heaven and hell, but for our purposes, one factor deserves highlighting. The last two or three decades of the twentieth century witnessed a remarkable resurgence in the field of philosophy of religion and philosophical theology. In addition to first-rate work in traditional areas of concern such as the problem of evil and theistic arguments, Christian philosophers have gone beyond generic theism and engaged distinctively Christian beliefs and doctrines as well. Much of this work has challenged the sort of minimalist and agnostic theology represented by liberal theologians such as Kaufman, and more fundamentally it has examined and criticized the philosophical and intellectual foundations of such theology. Many of the alleged 'irreversible changes' that Kaufman and his fellow liberal theologians hold sacred are no longer viewed as such by many of the best Christian philosophers. These intellectual changes suggest the possibility that serious belief in God as well as the larger framework of Christian belief could become more pervasive in our society to the degree that even hell could again become 'culturally available'. Let us now turn our attention more carefully to the doctrine of hell.

TRADITIONAL VERSUS CONTEMPORARY DEFENSES OF HELL

Hell has always posed a challenge for theologians and Christian philosophers for fairly obvious reasons. If God is all powerful as well as perfectly good and loving, it is hard to see why he would consign anyone to eternal punishment. So put, the problem of hell is best situated as part of the larger problem of evil and the project of theodicy. Indeed, as Alfred Freddoso has observed, the difficulty of reconciling even the possibility of anyone's going to hell with the existence of God is 'ultimately the most troublesome form which the problem of evil can take for the orthodox Christian'.[10]

Traditionally this problem has been met, at least among western theologians, by defending eternal hell primarily as a matter of retributive justice that God imposes on deserving sinners. The essential argument for understanding hell in this fashion can be put simply as follows.

(1) Any sin against God is infinitely serious.
(2) An infinitely serious sin deserves a proportionate punishment, which must also be infinite.
(3) God is perfectly just.
(4) Therefore, God must punish any sin that is not atoned for with infinite punishment.

Among classical theologians who have defended hell on these grounds are Augustine, Aquinas, Anselm, and Jonathan Edwards.

Anselm's version of this account of hell was formulated as part of his famous explanation of the atonement of Christ, an observation that illustrates that the doctrines of heaven and hell are organically connected to the larger body of Christian doctrine, particularly the doctrine of salvation. His explication of why the atonement is necessary hinges on his perception of the gravity of sin, and on this matter Anselm leaves us in no doubt that he sees it as infinitely serious. He makes the point most vividly by contending that it would be better to let the whole world perish, and come to nothing, even an infinite number of such worlds, than do the smallest thing against God's will. Jonathan Edwards gave a distinct twist to the argument by casting it in terms of God's infinite loveliness, honorableness, and authority. These attributes place us under an obligation to return to him a proportionate amount of love, honor, and obedience. If we fail in this obligation, then again, we merit infinite punishment. There are other variations on this argument, less famous than the formulations of Anselm and Edwards, but they share in common the attempt to show that sin is infinitely serious. Among these variations are the claims that sin harms God infinitely, that sin harms oneself infinitely, that sin harms other creatures infinitely, and that sin harms an infinite number of creatures.

The punishment that classical theologians pictured as the fitting retribution for such sin is horrific beyond description. In elaborating the misery of the damned, they typically distinguished between the 'pain of loss' and the 'pains of sense'. The former of these refers to the pain that naturally occurs from being separated from God, while the latter was typically understood to include fire of agonizing intensity. Indeed, all conditions of the damned are such as to contribute to what we might call maximal misery. For instance, in commenting on the composition of light and darkness in hell, Aquinas contends that 'The disposition of hell will be such as to be adapted to the utmost unhappiness of the damned. Therefore both light and darkness are there, insofar as they are most conducive to the unhappiness of the damned.'[11]

The thought of such horror is even more excruciating when we add the traditional claim that hell is eternal and that there is no possibility of escape, either by repentance, or suicide, or annihilation. Naturally speaking, such suffering could not be borne, but God will supernaturally keep body and soul together, and thus force the damned to bear, paradoxically, unbearable agony and torment. Leaving aside vivid imagery, we can sum up the traditional view of hell in three propositions.

(TH1) Some persons will never repent of their sins, and therefore will not be saved.

(TH2) Those who remain impenitent at death will be consigned to hell, a place of consummate misery that is the just punishment for sins they commit in this life.

(TH3) There is no salvation after death so there is no end to hell by repentance nor is there an end to it by suicide or annihilation.

This third claim can be taken in two distinct ways, either as contingently true or as necessarily true. Taking it the former way, it would be possible to repent and escape hell, or to be annihilated, but as a matter of fact, none will ever do so. This could be epistemically certain even though metaphysically contingent, if it were, for instance, revealed by God to be true.[12] On the latter reading, it is impossible to escape hell by repentance, and likewise impossible to commit suicide or be annihilated. Moreover, the impossibility of escaping hell by repentance could be due either to the fact that repentance is psychologically or metaphysically impossible for the damned, or to the fact that God would no longer (could no longer?) accept their repentance.[13]

Although the defenders of this conception of hell number among the most influential of western theologians, it has come under fire among recent and contemporary philosophers and theologians and would find relatively few defenders today. Even most of those who would defend hell as a matter of retributive justice are not inclined to hold that the punishment of hell includes literal fire or must cause consummate misery. They would accordingly amend (TH2) to state that hell is a place of misery, without adding that it must be of the consummate variety.

But more fundamentally, the notion of eternal hell as a matter of just punishment has been largely rejected by contemporary philosophers. The so-called proportionality objection to hell contends that infinite punishment is radically out of proportion to any sins that finite beings could commit. Much of the recent discussion has been devoted, accordingly to attacking premise (1) of the argument above. Now if premise (1) of the above argument is rejected, the argument obviously fails. Moreover, the second and third claims of the traditional view of hell are undermined as well.

Among contemporary philosophers who have subjected the notion that our sins deserve infinite punishment to searching criticism are Marilyn Adams, Jonathan Kvanvig, and Charles Seymour.[14] A broad consensus has emerged from this work that the punishment model of hell is not the best way to defend the doctrine. This is not to deny that there have been attempts to defend a punishment model, but those who have taken this line have not typically tried to make the case for infinite punishment. James Cain, for instance, defends the claim that eternal punishment, even punishment that causes intense suffering, is compatible with God's justice, but he offers models to show that endless experiential suffering could be finite.[15]

In view of the emerging consensus rejecting the traditional punishment model of the doctrine, philosophers have turned to other ways to show how eternal hell can be compatible with God's perfect love and power. The most common strategy has been to appeal to libertarian freedom to explain how human beings may be separated from a loving God, even forever, and may consequently experience eternal unhappiness. This is the view I have defended, along with several other philosophers.[16]

It is worth noting at this point that the traditional view of hell sketched above has often been defended by theologians who were determinists and consequently did not accept libertarian freedom, most notably Augustine and Edwards, and perhaps Aquinas as well. Now the denial of libertarian freedom exacerbates the problem of hell, for the sins that merit eternal punishment on this view are sins that the damned were determined by God to commit. Those who hold this view have the added difficulty of explaining how sinners who were determined to commit the sins they did could be deserving of such a fate. This combination of divine determinism and the traditional punishment model of hell is a mix that generates glaring moral difficulties that have frequently served as a ready target for critics of orthodox Christianity. The appeal to libertarian freedom is accordingly a double benefit, for it not only provides an alternative to the traditional punishment model of hell, but also repudiates the doctrine of divine determinism often associated if not identified with orthodox theology, at least of the Protestant variety.

The heart of the view of hell that invokes libertarian freedom is that we have the capacity to reject God, and may persist in doing so to the point that we are forever separated from him. C. S. Lewis famously summed up this view when he wrote 'that the damned are, in one sense, successful, rebels to the end; that the doors of hell are locked on the *inside*'.[17] More recently, Richard Swinburne has argued that our freedom gives us the ability, over time, to form the sort of character that we no longer desire God and the good. The essence of damnation, as he sees it, 'is a loss of good, not an inflicted evil; and it is not so much a punishment inflicted from without as an inevitable consequence of a man allowing himself to lose his moral awareness'.[18] Put in terms of the traditional distinction noted above, this view emphasizes the pain of loss rather than the pain of sense. Indeed, Swinburne thinks the New Testament is ambiguous on the matter of whether hell must include any pains of sense, and suggests that perhaps annihilation is the appropriate end for those who reject God.

In a similar vein, Kvanvig has defended what he calls 'the issuant conception of hell',[19] so named because he believes the doctrine of hell should 'issue' from the same attribute of God as the doctrine of heaven. The common claim is that hell issues from God's justice whereas heaven issues from God's love. It is Kvanvig's contention that heaven and hell both issue from divine love. However, he holds that all of us face the ultimate free choice of whether we will live in relation to God or live independently of him. The latter choice is actually an illusory one, for none of us can actually do so, and to so choose is actually to opt for annihilation. But not all those who reject God choose annihilation in a clear and settled way, and it is precisely in his love that God allows them to remain in existence.[20] Kvanvig appropriately characterizes his view as a 'composite' one since it allows both eternal separation from God and annihilation as possible final ends for the damned.[21]

Seymour has also defended a conception of hell that emphasizes libertarian choice, as is evident from the fact that he calls his position 'the freedom view'. Unlike some others who stress freedom, Seymour believes it is important for hell to include pains of sense as well as the pain of loss. This is reflected in his basic definition of hell, namely, 'an eternal existence, all of whose moments are on the whole bad'.[22] The importance of freedom for his view comes into focus in his rejection of the traditional arguments that the sins committed in this life could be sufficient to warrant eternal punishment. Rather, according to Seymour, what keeps sinners in the perpetual suffering of hell is that they continue to sin. In principle, sinners could repent and escape hell, so if they remain in hell, it is due to their free choice to persist in sinning.

The notion of continuing sin in hell has been clearly illustrated by Michael Murray, who gives the example of a criminal who is given a twenty-year sentence, but then commits further crime while in prison. Although none of his crimes taken alone deserve a life sentence, the cumulative sentence for his ongoing crimes is never completed. Likewise, the 'unchecked sinful desires' of the damned may 'continue to lead them to sin even in hell and so continue to mount penalties which are never satisfied'.[23] This account of what keeps people in hell, it is worth noting, is compatible with the contingent version of (TH3). There is no end of hell for those who go there, but it is due to their own choice.

The attempt to defend the contingent version of (TH3) by appealing to the continuing sin model has been challenged by Kenneth Himma.[24] Taking Murray as his foil, Himma contends that the proportionality problem is not solved if one holds that hell is eternal for all who enter it and there is no escape for those who die without salvation. Before developing his main argument, he points out that whether the suffering of hell is disproportionate depends on both the duration and the intensity of that suffering. Like most recent philosophers, he agrees that if hell is intensely painful, as it would be if it included literal fire, as well as eternal, it would be a disproportionate punishment for any sins we might commit in this life. He also considers two distinct 'separation' conceptions of hell. In the first, the damned are unaware that God exists and therefore unaware that they are separated from him. Their only punishment is that they are deprived of the infinite good of communion with God, though they do not know this. The other separation model includes awareness of what is lost by those excluded from communion with God. This knowledge increases the suffering of the damned because they would regret their loss as well as the choices that led to their condition.

Now Himma contends that it seems likely on the separation-with-knowledge conception that some persons could escape hell because not all would choose to persist in sin. Sincere advocates of other religions who genuinely seek the truth, as well as ethical unbelievers, for instance, are persons who would be likely to repent if they discovered that their mistaken choices had led to their separation from God. The separation-without-knowledge view does not fare much better but for different reasons. While persons without the relevant knowledge would not be likely to repent, it seems unjust to keep them in hell because they have no realistic chance to reform themselves. Thus, Himma concludes that the continuing sin scenario does not provide an adequate defense of the traditional view that there is no end of hell for those who die without salvation. His argument does not lead to universalism, but it does leave open the possibility, if not probability, that at least some of the inhabitants of hell would eventually find their way to heaven. And if he is right about this, there is good reason to think (TH3) is not even probably true, let alone epistemically certain.

In drawing this section to a conclusion, note that the views of Himma, Kvanvig, Lewis, Seymour, and Walls agree in denying (TH3), the third claim of the traditional view listed above. Kvanvig, and perhaps Lewis, think it is possible to escape hell by making choices that lead to annihilation. Moreover, Himma, Kvanvig, Lewis,[25] Seymour, and Walls think that sinners in hell can in principle repent, and if they do so, they will be accepted by God. Of course, this claim is also compatible with the contingent version of (TH3). However, my own reason for denying (TH3) altogether is that I believe it is likely that some persons who die without receiving salvation will do so after death. My position hinges on my argument that it follows from God's perfect love and goodness that he will give all persons 'optimal grace', the best opportunity they can have to be saved, and only if they decisively reject grace will they finally be damned. It seems apparent to me on empirical grounds that many persons have not received optimal grace or made a decisive choice in this life, so it seems likely that many will do so in the next life.[26]

The point I want to emphasize now, however, is that if sinners are forever lost, either because of annihilation or their persistent refusal of grace, their fate depends on their continuing choices rather than only upon choices they made in this life. There is thus an appropriate match between their ongoing choices and their on-going existence in hell, or annihilation, which resolves the proportionality problem.

CHALLENGES TO FREEDOM ACCOUNTS OF HELL

While the appeal to freedom provides ways to relieve the notion of eternal hell of its most pressing moral difficulties and to allow fresh formulations of the doctrine, these new formulations have not escaped criticism. Indeed, a growing number of Christian philosophers and theologians are challenging the first claim of the traditional doctrine of hell (TH1) and advancing universalism, the view that all persons will eventually be saved.

The topic of universalism has been on the table as part of the contemporary discussion in the field of philosophy of religion at least since the publication of John Hick's landmark work *Evil and the God of Love*. In that work, in which Hick defended an Irenaean view of theodicy over against the Augustinian view that has predominated in western theology, he also argued for universal salvation as a 'practical certainty'. Given his view that human free choices are undetermined, along with his view that 'the thoughts and actions of free beings are in principle unknowable until they occur',[27] Hick could not go so far as to rule out the possibility that some may never be saved. Thus, it is metaphysically and logically possible that all may not be saved, and whether or not this is so must remain epistemically uncertain, even for God. But given the infinite resources of God's love, his perfect understanding of his creatures, and endless time to work on them, Hick says it seems *morally* impossible that God could fail in his quest to save them all, and therefore practically certain that he will succeed.[28]

More recently, philosophical advocates of universalism have mounted stronger assaults against the barrier of human freedom in making their case that all will be saved. One of these is Marilyn Adams, who also has given significant attention to the issues of hell and universalism as part of her larger work on theodicy. Judging this debate to have grown stale, Adams, like Hick over a generation ago, attempts in a recent work to offer new resources for theodicy and to point it in some fresh dir-ections. Among her more radical suggestions is that sin is primarily a metaphysical problem rather than a moral one. One aspect of this problem particularly pertinent to our concerns is what she calls the 'size gap' that separates us from God. Failure to appreciate the reality of this size gap causes us to exaggerate the dignity of human nature as something so sacrosanct that not even God may legitimately interfere with it.

Adams sees this tendency especially manifested in what she calls 'mild' versions of the doctrine of hell that emphasize our freedom to reject God and the corresponding misery that is the natural consequence of that choice. She complains that this view treats God and human adults as moral peers, and objects that giving us the right to damn ourselves is not the appropriate sort of respect for God to pay to the likes of us. Whereas this account pictures the relationship between us and God with the analogy of parents and adult children, Adams suggests that a better model would be the relationship between a mother and an infant or a toddler. On Adams's preferred model, there is no meaningful sense in which the child is free or responsible, nor is there any basis for objecting to interfering with his choices.

It is easy to see how this undermines the freedom view of hell and allows Adams to argue that God can save everyone. Given the size gap between us and God on her picture, human freedom poses no obstacle to universalism. If God needs to override our freedom and causally determine things in order to prevent some of his children from eternal damnation, this is 'no more of an insult to our dignity than a mother's changing a diaper is to the baby'.[29]

While this move does indeed eliminate human freedom as a barrier to universal salvation, the question is whether Adams has paid too high a price to achieve this result in her willingness to minimize, if not sacrifice, moral categories. It is also doubtful if her mother–infant image of the divine human relationship does justice to the biblical picture of that reality. It is not insignificant that the Bible often portrays the divine–human relationship with the image of a husband and wife or a lover and his beloved, and sin is pictured as unfaithfulness to this relationship. This image certainly suggests that God desires and expects far more from us in terms of behavior, including responsible moral behavior, than a mother could ever expect from an infant in diapers or a toddler.[30]

Another philosopher who has mounted a sustained attack on the doctrine of eternal hell is Thomas Talbott. In addition to philosophical arguments, he has also given significant attention to biblical exegesis in making his case for universalism.[31] This is vital to the overall case because for many believers, the matter is decisively settled by clear biblical teaching. Typical of this line of thought is Peter Geach, who took Christ's teaching as 'perfectly clear' that 'many men are irretrievably lost' and insisted on this basis that 'universalism is not a live option for a Christian'.[32]

By sharp contrast, Talbott wants to argue that universalism is the *only* option for a Christian. His philosophical case for this strong claim is largely focused on his argument that the notion that anyone could choose eternal hell is finally incoherent because there simply is no intelligible motive to explain such a choice. Now this is not to deny that we can choose evil in the short run. Obviously we can do so, typically under the illusion that this will bring us the happiness we crave. Talbott insists, however, that God will eventually shatter the illusion that motivates the choice of evil by bringing home to us a hard-edged reality check. The more we choose evil, the more miserable we will become. Under the impact of 'greater and greater misery'[33] we will reach a point that we cannot bear it any longer and turn to God, the true source of the happiness we are seeking.

Talbott's argument for this conclusion hinges crucially on his account of what is involved in the free choice of an eternal destiny. The essence of such a choice is that it must be fully informed in such a way that once the person making the choice gets what he wants, he never regrets his choice. This requires that the choice must be free from ignorance and illusion both initially as well as in the long run. The person making it must fully understand what he has chosen and freely persist in that choice.

With this account of what is involved in choosing an eternal destiny clearly on the table, Talbott thinks there is an obvious and crucial asymmetry between choosing fellowship with God in heaven as an eternal destiny, on the one hand, and choosing eternal misery in hell, on the other. Whereas it is overwhelmingly clear that it is possible to choose the first option because there are readily intelligible motives for it, the latter is not possible because it makes no sense at all to say that a rational creature could knowingly persist in the choice of eternal misery.

Next, in addition to his view of what is involved in freely choosing an eternal destiny, Talbott's argument for universalism also depends on his view that the New Testament picture of hell is 'a forcibly imposed punishment rather than a freely embraced condition', that it is 'unbearable suffering'.[34] Indeed, Talbott chides those who say hell is a freely embraced condition for holding a view that 'in effect takes the hell out of hell, as least as far as the damned are concerned'.[35] The claim that hell is unbearable misery underwrites his claim that it is unintelligible that anyone could persist in freely choosing it forever. Rather, the misery of hell will eventually move even the most hardened sinners freely to choose heaven for their eternal destiny.

It is important to stress that Talbott affirms a libertarian view of freedom at least in the sense that he agrees that 'creaturely freedom could never exist in a fully deterministic universe'.[36] He has deep reservations, however, about standard views of libertarian freedom that assert two essential claims.

(1) a person S performs an action A freely at some time t **only** if it should also be within S's power at t to refrain from A at t; and
(2) it is within S's power at t to refrain from A at t only if refraining from A at t is psychologically possible for S at t.[37]

Talbott challenges the second of these claims by drawing a distinction between the *power* to do something and the *psychological capability* of doing it. This distinction is a third component of his argument for universalism. As he notes, in narratives of dramatic conversions, such as those of St Paul and C. S. Lewis, 'the final act of submission seems to occur in a context where the alternative is no longer psychologically possible at all'.[38] Another relevant illustration of the difference between power and psychological ability is Augustine's account of how the redeemed in heaven will no longer even be tempted to sin or disobedience. Does this mean they will no longer be free or that they lack the power to sin? No, they will not lack the power to sin, even though they will no longer be psychologically capable of sinning. Because they will see with such perfect clarity that God is the true source of happiness and sin the cause of misery, sin will lose all appeal and will no longer remain a live option for them.[39]

To sum up Talbott's view in relation to the traditional view of hell sketched above, it is clear that he rejects both (TH1) and (TH3). However, he affirms a version of (TH2). While he may not agree that the suffering of hell is consummate misery, he does insist that it is unbearable suffering that no one could freely choose to undergo forever. Thus, for Talbott, the notion of eternal hell is deeply incoherent, and universalism is not merely possibly true, nor even practically certain as it is for Hick; it is necessarily true.

The Coherence of Eternal Hell

Talbott's challenge to recent versions of the doctrine of eternal hell is a powerful one that requires an answer, so let us consider it more carefully. Let us begin with his distinction between power and psychological ability, a distinction I am inclined to accept. Even with this distinction clearly in hand, there are serious problems with Talbott's claim that all persons can be brought freely to repent in a non-deterministic sense under the pressure of forcibly imposed punishment. The central difficulty with this claim is that the notion of 'greater and greater misery', misery that does not have a distinct limit, destroys any meaningful notion of a free choice. The reason for this is that finite beings such as ourselves are not built with the capacity to absorb ever-increasing misery. At some point in the process of being dealt greater and greater misery we would inevitably crack and would either be coerced to submit or be psychologically and mentally shattered or perish altogether.[40] Appealing to Talbott's distinction will not help, for we have neither the power nor the psychological capability to stand up under constantly increasing misery, regardless of whether that misery is of the physical or emotional variety. In other words, there is a limit to how much pressure our freedom can bear. Where exactly that limit lies is perhaps something only God could know, but clearly there is such a limit.

Now this point is particularly interesting in light of a distinction Talbott himself has drawn between two kinds of compulsion. The right kind of compulsion, which he defends, is illustrated in dramatic conversions such as that of C. S. Lewis, who had a sense of God closing in on him in such a way that it seemed impossible for him to do otherwise than submit.[41] By contrast, he repudiates the sort of compulsion advocated by Augustine, who was prepared to use the sword to persuade the Donatists to return to the church. He spells out the distinction as follows: 'A stunning revelation such as Paul reportedly received, one that provides clear vision and *compelling evidence*, thereby altering one's beliefs in a perfectly rational way, does not compel behavior in the same way that threatening with a sword might.'[42] As Talbott goes on to note, swords are not evidence, so they provide no rational reason to alter one's beliefs. Conversion at sword's point is neither rational nor morally acceptable, nor is it free in any meaningful sense of the word.

Talbott's distinction is another one I am inclined to accept, but precisely this distinction poses problems for him, given his insistence that hell is a matter of 'forcibly imposed punishment', and 'unbearable suffering'. The traditional accounts of the suffering of hell that Talbott professes to endorse surely include physical pain of a rather intense variety. If he does not believe this, he should not pretend to be espousing the traditional understanding of what makes hell literally unbearable. But if he really does support the traditional view, then he owes us some explanation of how forcibly imposed punishment that produces unbearable suffering is not the wrong kind of compulsion that he repudiates. Without this sort of explanation, his view suffers from obvious inconsistency. This point holds, incidentally, even if Talbott thinks the misery of hell is purely psychological and spiritual. If conversion at sword point is objectionable, then it is surely equally objectionable to compel repentance by any sort of forcibly imposed misery, even if that misery is 'only' spiritual and psychological.

But there is another difficulty with Talbott's account of the proper kind of compulsion, namely, his appeal to 'compelling evidence' that alters beliefs in a perfectly rational way. The difficulty is not in the claim that evidence can so alter our beliefs. Indeed, it is arguably the very heart of rationality to be willing to alter one's beliefs in light of appropriate evidence, especially if that evidence is staring you in the face! The problem is in the claim that such evidence can ever be truly compelling, a problem that is very much compounded by the fact that religious truth claims are highly contested, including the claim that God even exists.

This is not to deny that there is substantial evidence in favor of Christian faith. Indeed, it is arguable that a certain amount of evidence is necessary in order to keep faith from being an irrational or arbitrary commitment. However, it is also arguable that the evidence must fall short of being truly compelling for our response to be free. Pascal represented such a balance when he wrote the following: 'But the evidence is such as to exceed, or at least equal, the evidence to the contrary, so that it cannot be reason that decides us against following it, and can therefore only be concupiscence and wickedness of heart.'[43]

At the end of the day, for Pascal, neither belief nor unbelief is simply a matter of evidence or recognition of certain facts. Belief requires a heart that is rightly disposed, and unbelief exposes a wicked heart. And if this is correct, then evidence alone can never be compelling for genuine faith. The evidence can be compelling in the more modest sense that it makes clear the disposition of our hearts. However, neither evidence that is compelling in this sense nor unbearable suffering can guarantee the sort of free response that God desires from us. Evidence can never be compelling in the sense that Talbott's argument requires and unbearable suffering cannot elicit the sort of repentance that is rationally motivated and morally free.

Now in response to these sort of criticisms, Talbott has clarified his position in some important respects. First, he has made clear that those who repent under the pressure of ever-increasing misery finally have no choice but to turn to God, so this choice is not free in the libertarian sense. The choices we make to reach this point are free in the libertarian sense, but the ironic result of these choices is that they take us to a point where the only thing we can do is repent of those choices.

Second, and more importantly, Talbott has explained just what he means by the 'unbearable suffering' and the 'forcibly imposed punishment' of hell. And it is now clear that what he means by these terms is very different from how they are typically understood in traditional accounts of hell, despite what some of his previous writings suggested. To illustrate the sort of suffering he has in mind, he invites us to consider the example, inspired by a well-known movie plot, of a married man who foolishly has an affair with an unstable woman. When the affair ends, she takes out her revenge by murdering his wife and child (he does not mention the fate of the bunny rabbit).[44] We can imagine that the man's subsequent guilt, sorrow, and profound sense of loss would be an unbearable suffering that God could use to move him to repent, and 'insofar as God uses the man's suffering as a means of correction, or as a means to repentance, we can again say that the man has endured a *forcibly imposed punishment* for his sin'.[45] He goes on to point out that 'the good in the worst of sinners—the indestructible image of God if you will—can itself become a source of unbearable torment'. The 'good' Talbott has in mind is especially our moral nature, our conscience, that causes us to feel guilt and regret and thereby spurs us to repentance.

Now these clarifications are indeed helpful for gaining an accurate picture of Talbott's position but unfortunately, these very clarifications expose further difficulties for his case for necessary universalism. The most glaring problem is that his explanation of what he means by unbearable torment no longer sustains his claim that all sinners must inevitably reach a point where resistance would no longer be possible. This claim was tenable so long as we took him to mean that the forcibly imposed punishment of hell is a matter of ever-increasing suffering of such intensity that no one could bear it indefinitely. Ironically, however, Talbott seems to have tamed the bear of unbearable suffering and made it quite possible to embrace.

Consider his example of the foolish philanderer. Granted that his actions and the consequences that followed would surely cause him great misery, it is still highly doubtful that his repentance would be inevitable. No doubt Talbott is right: God could use his suffering as a way to show him the folly of his actions and to move him in the direction of repentance. But there is nothing in the case as described that makes it inevitable that he will remain on the road to repentance and truly come to see the error of his ways. Indeed, we can easily imagine that rather than sincerely repenting and reforming, he might become angry and embittered if he thought God allowed the murder of his family in order to punish him for his affair. Rather than viewing God as a just judge who rightly created a moral universe where actions have consequences, he might come to see God as a vengeful deity more deserving of scorn than worship and obedience.

Similar points can be made about Talbott's observation that the good in sinners can become the source of unbearable torment. Again, the question is whether there is any way to relieve this torment, or whether it invariably must become greater and more intense. Contrary to Talbott's scenario of ever-increasing misery, it is a well-known psychological reality that we do have the power to dull and desensitize our consciences. One way we can do this is by deliberately choosing to continue performing those very acts that caused our guilt and remorse in the first place. Moreover, we can rationalize our actions or restructure our values in such a way that our conscience no longer bothers us. Such choices require a significant degree of self-deception, and indeed, the ability to deceive ourselves may be an essential component in our freedom to love God or not.

As Talbott himself has observed, we have the freedom, 'expressed in thousands of specific choices, to move incrementally either in the direction of repentance and reconciliation or in the direction of greater separation from God, and that freedom God always respects'.[46] Now if this is true, the question that begs to be answered is why such incremental movement must inevitably arrive at a point where our illusions would be shattered and repentance would be unavoidable. Intuitively, it seems just the opposite would occur. If we can move further and further from God, this would mean we would become more and more hardened in sin, correspondingly less and less aware of his goodness, and therefore less and less likely to repent and be reconciled to him. Objectively, such a person would become ever more miserable as he moved ever further from a loving relationship with God, but subjectively his hardness of heart could make the misery more tolerable.

Of course, God could intervene and circumvent the natural hardness of heart that would develop as we moved ever further from him. Moreover, he could impose other sorts of pain on us, such as ever more intense physical agony with each incremental move away from himself. Were God to impose such suffering on us, then at some point everyone would reach a point where they would crack and have to submit to God. But given Talbott's distinction between two kinds compulsion, he would presumably reject this as the wrong variety.

What this means is that Talbott has a dilemma on his hands, indeed, a hell of a dilemma. He must choose between his clarified account of divinely imposed misery and his claim that all sinners must inevitably arrive at a place where resistance to God is no longer possible. Given his clarified account of forcibly imposed punishment, there is no convincing reason why rebellious sinners could not go on rejecting God forever. But if he reverts to the claim that the suffering of hell induces repentance through the imposition of pain and agony so intense that it is literally impossible for anyone to bear it, then he will be endorsing the 'wrong' kind of compulsion. Moreover, this view of the pains of hell is at odds with his claim that God grants us the freedom to move ever further away from him. In order to maintain his case for necessary universalism, Talbott must choose the horn of the dilemma that involves embracing the sort of compulsion that he would prefer to repudiate. Otherwise, his case for necessary universalism fails.[47]

OBJECTING TO HEAVEN

As noted above, the doctrine of heaven has not received as much attention from philosophers as hell has. Nevertheless, there have been some interesting challenges raised against the Christian hope of eternal joy. Ironically, one of these can be generated from the argument just developed. Suppose it is not merely possibly true that some will be lost forever, but, as many traditional theologians have contended, some, perhaps many, surely will be. If this were true, would it not detract from the joy of the saved? As stated by Eric Reitan, the crux of the argument, which goes back at least to the nineteenth-century theologian Friedrich Schleiermacher, 'is that the eternal damnation of anyone is incompatible with the salvation of any, because knowledge of the sufferings of the damned would undermine the happiness of the saved'.[48]

Obviously, the argument assumes that the saved would not only be aware of the damned but would also empathize with their miserable condition. Since the saved would be fully transformed and perfected in love, they would surely have a deep love for all persons and desire their salvation. So if any remain separated from God, none could experience the perfect happiness that is supposed to characterize heaven. Indeed, the argument can be extended to claim that not even God himself could be fully happy if some are forever lost.[49] Although this argument is usually cast as an argument against eternal hell, it can also be used against the doctrine of heaven since it says in essence that heaven and eternal hell are incompatible.

There have been several attempts to blunt the force of this argument by suggesting various scenarios in which eternal hell can be compatible with perfect happiness.[50] For instance some have proposed that the blessed are not aware of the lost either because they are in a state of such overwhelming bliss that they would never think of them, or because the memory of them has been eliminated. Others have argued that the saved will see the nature of evil with such perfect moral clarity that they will not be disturbed by the reality of damnation. They will clearly understand the damned have freely chosen their fate, and if they will not repent, they cannot be allowed to hold heaven hostage. The damned can refuse to accept God's invitation to joy but they cannot have the right or power to spoil the happiness of those who have accepted the invitation simply because they will not.

A second objection to heaven that is being advanced in contemporary literature focuses on the historical origins of the doctrine. In the spirit of Nietzsche's suspicious reading of the 'genealogy' of morality, some recent historians have written histories of the afterlife that purport to show that doctrines of heaven (and hell) were formulated with the fuel of dubious motivations.[51] J. Edward Wright, for instance, argues that Jewish and Christian visions of heaven were often prompted by a desire to prove God's special favor for their group. And while these visions did indeed inspire hope for members of the chosen group, they also created 'a dangerous sense of superiority over outsiders by dehumanizing or demonizing them'.[52] Similarly, Alan Segal has contended that doctrines of the afterlife not only mirror the values of the societies that hold them, but also 'have benefited a particular social class and served to distinguish the purveyors of the idea from their social opponents'.[53]

While it is no doubt true that many persons who have held and promoted beliefs about heaven have been at least partially motivated by the dubious sort of motivations cited by Wright and Segal, there is more to the story, even as told by them. As Wright notes, the idea of the afterlife in Judaism originally grew out of bedrock convictions about the ultimate reality of God's goodness and justice. The treacherous injustice of this life poses an obvious challenge to these convictions and they could be sustained only if this life is not the last word.[54] Now if the deepest roots of belief in heaven are tied up with convictions about God's moral nature, then the hope of heaven at its best is motivated by our highest and best aspirations for goodness and justice. This part of the story provides resources to critique dubiously motivated belief in heaven where it occurs as well as to challenge histories of the doctrine that unduly emphasize such motivation.

The final objection to heaven I shall mention is a poignant one, with more than a touch of irony. In a famous article entitled 'The Makropulos Case: Reflections on the Tedium of Immortality', Bernard Williams contended 'that an endless life would be a meaningless one, and that we could have no reason for living eternally a human life'.[55] As Williams sees it, the hope of eternal happiness is actually an incoherent one, because no matter what delights heaven might hold, inevitably it would eventually become boring. Whereas previous generations have looked forward to heaven as the profound cure for what ails us in this life, Williams says there is no cure. The boredom and meaninglessness that haunt this life now threaten heaven as well, so perhaps the best we can hope for is to die 'shortly before the horrors of not doing so become evident'.[56]

A number of responses to the boredom challenge have been offered in the recent literature.[57] I am inclined to think, however, that the crux of the issue comes down to whether or not we find the idea of God intelligible, whether or not we believe that a being whose very nature is to be ecstatically happy has existed from all eternity, and will do so forever. If there is such a God, the hope that he might share his infinite happiness with us is a rational one, even if it hard fully to imagine in our current situation. Indeed, perhaps the fact that we fear boredom, even in heaven, is a telling mark of how far we have fallen from our intended relationship with God. The fact that Williams suggests that we should abandon the hope of heaven and find the meaning of our lives in a timely death before boredom completely sets in is, moreover, a stark indicator of how far our hope for happiness and meaning have fallen.

Recall Quine's autobiographical musing in which he recalled that the loss of his juvenile faith in heaven was attended by a sense of disappointment. This is hardly surprising. Anyone who has had even a glimpse of the beauty that heaven might hold or has felt even a murmur of the hope of eternal joy stirring in his heart could hardly fail to be disappointed if he came to believe it was not real. While heaven has received scant overt attention in recent philosophical literature, it does sometimes enter the conversation in some backhanded ways that betray this disappointment. This comes through most tellingly perhaps, in the various secular substitutes for heaven that secular philosophers have offered. Indeed, what is perhaps most striking is how secular philosophers sometimes advance the extraordinary claim that they actually have something better than heaven, a claim more notable for its bravado than its plausibility.[58]

Once the concept of heaven has entered our hearts and minds, there is no alternative to disappointment if it is not real. Heaven holds out the hope of perfect happiness, a depth and intensity of joy beyond what we can fully imagine, that is literally without end. Never to know such joy, to deny it could even exist, to claim that finite joy with a timely death is the best possible outcome, all of these are disappointing to the highest dreams for happiness we have dared to dream. Only heaven makes possible an understanding of life not finally resigned to disappointment.

Notes

1. *The Book of Heaven*, ed. Carol and Philip Zaleski (New York: Oxford University Press, 2000), 5.
2. See J. Edward Wright, *The Early History of Heaven* (New York: Oxford University Press, 2000); Alan F. Segal, *Life After Death: A History of the Afterlife in Western Religion* (New York: Doubleday, 2004).

3. For a recent explication of this idea that draws on classic resources, see John Saward, *Sweet and Blessed Country* (Oxford: Oxford University Press, 2005), 15–55.

4. Cited by Kenneth L. Woodward, 'Heaven', *Newsweek* (27 March 1989), 54.

5. W. W. Quine, *The Time of My Life* (Cambridge: MIT, 1985), 14.

6. Colleen McDannell and Bernhard Lang, *Heaven: A History* (New York: Vintage, 1990), 351–2.

7. *Harvard Theological Review* 78: 3–4 (1985), 381–98.

8. 'Hell Disappeared', 393.

9. 'Hell's Sober Comeback', *U.S. News and World Report* (25 March 1991), 56. Nine years later, hell was the cover story in the same magazine. See Jeffery L. Sheler, 'Hell Hath No Fury', *U.S. News and World Report* (31 January 2000), 44–50.

10. Alfred J. Freddoso (ed.), *The Existence and Nature of God* (Notre Dame: University of Notre Dame Press, 1983), 3. Although hell has not been defined with 'orthodox' precision in anything like the way Christology has been defined in the Councils of Nicea and Chalcedon, the doctrine of eternal hell is nevertheless a matter of broad consensus among orthodox Christians of all the major traditions.

11. *Summa Theologiae*, Suppl. to III q. 97 a. 4.

12. This assumes, of course, that God knows future contingents.

13. Charles Seymour analyzes Aquinas's arguments for the claim that the damned are 'frozen in their wickedness' and unable to repent. He contends that although Aquinas's argument appears at first to be metaphysical, it rests on the moral premise that the damned deserve eternal punishment for past sins. See his *A Theodicy of Hell* (Dordrecht: Kluwer Academic, 2000), 167–70.

14. Marilyn McCord Adams, 'Hell and the God of Justice', *Religious Studies* 11 (1975): 433–47; Jonathan L. Kvanvig, *The Problem of Hell* (Oxford: Oxford University Press, 1993), 25–66; Seymour, *A Theodicy of Hell*, 37–94.

15. James Cain, 'The Problem of Hell', *Religious Studies* 38 (2002), 355–62.

16. Jerry L. Walls, *Hell: The Logic of Damnation* (Notre Dame: University of Notre Dame Press, 1992), 113–38.

17. C. S. Lewis, *The Problem of Pain* (New York: Macmillan, 1962), 127.

18. Richard Swinburne, *Responsibility and Atonement* (Oxford: Clarendon, 1989), 182. See also 'A Theodicy of Heaven and Hell', in *The Existence and Nature of God*, 46–52.

19. Kvanvig, *The Problem of Hell*, 112.

20. Eleonore Stump has also defended a variation of the view that God in his love sustains the damned in existence. See 'Dante's Hell, Aquinas's Moral Theory and the Love of God', *Canadian Journal of Philosophy* 16 (1986), 181–98.

21. Kvanvig, *The Problem of Hell*, 151–9. Kvanvig notes, incidentally, that sometimes C. S. Lewis's comments about hell implied that the damned could be annihilated: see 121–3.

22. Seymour, *A Theodicy of Hell*, 161.

23. Michael J. Murray, 'Heaven and Hell', in Michael J. Murray (ed.), *Reason for the Hope Within* (Grand Rapids: Eerdmans, 1999), 293.

24. Kenneth Himma, 'Eternally Incorrigible: The Continuing-Sin Response to the Proportionality Problem of Hell', *Religious Studies* 39 (2003), 61–78.

25. In *The Great Divorce*, Lewis's fantasy novel of sinners in hell who take a bus ride to heaven, one of the characters explains that if any choose to remain in heaven and leave the grey town (hell) behind, then it is purgatory. See *The Great Divorce* (San Francisco: Harper, 2001), 68.

26. See Walls, *Hell*, 83–105. Seymour also takes this view: see *A Theodicy of Hell*, 167. See also Andrei A. Buckareff and Allen Plug, 'Escaping Hell: Divine Motivation and the Problem of Hell', *Religious Studies* 41 (2005), 39–54.

27. John Hick, *Evil and the God of Love* (San Francisco: Harper & Row, 1966), 343. Gordon Knight has recently argued that 'open theists', those theists who hold that God cannot have infallible knowledge of our future free choices, should embrace 'contingent universalism'. See Gordon Knight, 'Universalism for Open Theists', *Religious Studies* 42 (2006), 213–23.

28. Hick, *Evil and the God of Love*, 343–4. If God is necessarily good, and something is *morally* impossible, then it should be *metaphysically* impossible as well, for God's nature limits what is metaphysically possible. For further criticism of Hick, see Walls, *Hell*, 70–81.

29. Marilyn McCord Adams, *Horrendous Evils and the Goodness of God* (Ithaca: Cornell University Press, 1999), 157.

30. See Katherin A. Rogers, 'The Abolition of Sin: A Response to Adams in the Augustinian Tradition', *Faith and Philosophy* 19 (2002), 69–84.

31. Talbott lays out his biblical argument in Robin A. Parry and Christopher Partridge (eds.), *Universal Salvation? The Current Debate* (Grand Rapids: Eerdmans, 2003), 15–52. This volume also includes critiques of Talbott's universalism by several authors representing different disciplines, including philosophy. Talbott's biblical arguments are critiqued by I. Howard Marshall and Thomas F. Johnson. The book also includes Talbott's replies to his critics.

32. Peter Geach, *Providence and Evil* (Cambridge: Cambridge University Press, 1977), 123–4. Geach thought it less clear that the ultimate fate of the lost is eternal misery rather than destruction.

33. Thomas Talbott, 'Freedom, Damnation and the Power to Sin with Impunity', *Religious Studies* 37 (2001), 420.

34. Ibid. 417.

35. Ibid. 429–30.

36. Ibid. 426.

37. Ibid. 426.

38. Ibid. 426.

39. Thomas Talbott, 'On the Divine Nature and the Nature of Divine Freedom', *Faith and Philosophy* 5 (1988), 13.

40. Some traditional theologians have held that God supernaturally sustains the damned in such a way that he causes them to endure what they could not otherwise endure in order to maximize their misery. Of course, Talbott assumes no such thing and would surely reject such a notion.

41. Talbott quotes passages from Lewis's spiritual autobiography to make this point. See C. S. Lewis, *Surprised by Joy* (New York: Harcourt Brace Jovanovich), 224, 229.

42. Talbott, 'Freedom', 427.

43. Blaise Pascal, *Pensées*, trans. A. J. Krailsheimer (London: Penguin, 1966), no. 835.

44. Presumably he has in mind the movie 'Fatal Attraction', although the wife and child do not share the same fate as the bunny rabbit in this film.

45. Talbott, 'Misery and Freedom: Reply to Walls', *Religious Studies* 40 (2004), 218.

46. Ibid. 221–2.

47. This section reiterates and summarizes some of the key points in two papers in which I criticize Talbott's views. For further argument of these points, see my 'A Hell of a Choice: Reply to Talbott', *Religious Studies* 40 (2004), 203–16; and 'A Hell of a Dilemma: Rejoinder to Talbott', *Religious Studies* 40 (2004), 225–7.

48. Eric Reitan, 'Eternal Damnation and Blessed Ignorance: Is the Damnation of Some Incompatible with the Salvation of Any?', *Religious Studies* 38 (2002), 429.

49. I have responded to this line of the argument in *Hell*, 106–10. I argue, moreover, that if God can be perfectly happy despite eternal hell, then the saved may share his perspective and also be perfectly happy. For Reitan's critique of my argument, see 'Eternal Damnation and Blessed Ignorance', 432–4.

50. In the article just cited, Reitan surveys and criticizes several of these arguments. It is worth noting, incidentally, that this problem is one that would not have bothered many classical theologians. Indeed, the likes of Augustine and Aquinas argued that contemplating the misery of the damned would provide a contrast that would actually enhance the joy of the saved. See D. P. Walker, *The Decline of Hell* (Chicago: University of Chicago Press, 1964), 29.

51. For Nietzsche's own thoughts along this line, see *The Birth of Tragedy & The Genealogy of Morals*, trans. Francis Golfing (New York: Anchor, 1956), 178–85.

52. J. Edward Wright, *The Early History of Heaven* (Oxford: Oxford University Press, 2000), 202; see also 137, 157, 163, 177.

53. Alan Segal, *Life After Death: A History of the Afterlife in Western Religion* (New York: Doubleday, 2004), 699; see also 11, 16, 68, 243, 292, 344.

54. Wright, *The Early History of Heaven*, 158, 191–2. See also Segal, *Life After Death*, 271–2.

55. Bernard Williams, 'The Makropolus Case: Reflections on the Tedium of Immortality', in John Martin Fischer (ed.), *The Metaphysics of Death* (Stanford: Stanford University Press, 1993), 81.

56. Williams, 'Makropolus', 92.

57. Garth Hallett surveys six proposed solutions to this difficulty in ' "The Tedium of Immortality" ', *Faith and Philosophy* 18 (2001), 279–81. See also John Martin Fischer, 'Why Immortality is Not So Bad', *International Journal of Philosophical Studies* 2: 2 (1994), 257–70; Jerry L. Walls, *Heaven: The Logic of Eternal Joy* (New York: Oxford University Press, 2002), 193–200; Arthur O. Roberts, *Exploring Heaven: What Great Thinkers Tell us About Our Afterlife With God* (San Francisco: Harper, 2003), 112–28.

58. I have documented a number of these secular substitutes for heaven. See my *Heaven*, 177–85.

CHAPTER 23

THE EUCHARIST: REAL PRESENCE AND REAL ABSENCE

ALEXANDER R. PRUSS

1. INTRODUCTION

THE Eucharist has traditionally been the center of Christian liturgical life. Typically the liturgy includes Jesus' words from the Last Supper: 'This is my body' and 'This is my blood.' Until the Reformation, most Christians took these words at more or less face value—the Eucharist *is* Christ's body and blood, which is joined with the whole of Christ, and so in the Eucharist Christ nourishes his followers with himself.

The Eucharist lies at the center of a vast array of deep, philosophically charged theological questions. The Eucharistic event appears triggered by certain physical actions by the priest, on the Catholic and Orthodox views, or by the congregation and its presider on some Protestant views. Prior to these actions what is present is just bread and wine, devoid of intrinsic spiritual significance, but afterwards there is 'the body and blood of Christ'. Are the actions of the human agents given a supernatural power of producing such an effect or does God produce the effect entirely by himself on the occasion of these actions? Likewise, is the reception of the

Eucharist a cause of the occurrence of grace, or does God simply happen to choose to provide grace on the occasion of the receiving of the Eucharist? And if it is a means, then in what way does this causality work?

What does it mean to 'eat' and 'drink' in general and what significance is to be found in the idea of Christ giving himself to us to be eaten and drunk? How does the Eucharist cause both physical and spiritual nourishment, and potentially even drunkenness? Do Christ's body and blood become a part of the physical body of the believer, do they revert to ordinary bread and wine just prior to being digested, do they cease to be present, or are Christ's body and blood transubstantiated again, this time into the flesh and blood of the recipient?

When Christ's words are spoken in the Eucharistic liturgy, who counts as their speaker? To whom, if to anyone, does 'my' refer in 'This is *my* body'?[1] Is it an indexical? How does the apparently demonstrative 'this' gain reference to the invisible reality here?

In the Catholic tradition, the Eucharist is seen as a sacrifice, fulfilling the prophecy of Malachi that in messianic times a sacrifice will be offered from the rising to the setting of the sun. Yet according to the Letter to the Hebrews, Christ's sacrifice is the only sacrifice in messianic times. Catholic theology attempts to reconcile these two claims by saying that the sacrifice of the altar and the sacrifice of Calvary are one and the same sacrifice. What, then, are the identity and individuation conditions for sacrifices? Is there on a deep level a single act of self-giving that Christ undertook, and if so, how is it related to the events of the altar and those of Calvary? Are they perhaps manifestations of that act? Are they parts of it? Catholic devotion talks of being present at Mass as a way of being present at Calvary. Can this be literally true, space-time being bridged in a supernatural way? Or does the Eucharistic liturgy simply represent Calvary, and if so, what philosophical account can be given of the nature of this representing—is it conventional or in some way natural, for instance?

Next come the ontological issues surrounding the question: What actually happens that makes it true to say that 'the body and blood of Christ' comes to be present?

The ontologically simplest answers are ones that take this presence to be non-literal. Thus, one might simply stay on a naturalistic level and say that Christ's body and blood are 'present' in the congregation's thoughts, and are represented by the bread and wine. Or one might say that at communion, God gives the recipient of the Eucharist graces that ultimately flow from the sacrifice of Christ's body and blood on the cross, and so the body and blood are 'present' through their effects.

There are, however, serious theological difficulties with these two solutions. The most obvious is that, as far back as we can trace it, Christians have generally taken it that the 'presence' is to be understood in a more substantive way, and have made the Eucharist a central part of their Christian worship, as is already seen in the New Testament (see e.g. Acts 2: 42 and 1 Cor. 10). If one believes that the Christian church is guided by the Holy Spirit, at least in the central aspects of Christian life, this creates at least a strong presumption in favor of a more substantive interpretation.

Furthermore, the New Testament overall has a strong emphasis on the reality of Christ's body and blood, in contrast to gnostics who saw the flesh as something unbecoming, and also contains Christ's promise to abide with Christians. It would be fitting indeed for this abiding also to be bodily in some way.

Thus one should take seriously the idea of Christ's body and blood being present in a non-metaphorical way, 'really present'. The doctrine of 'real presence' presents several questions. First, we may wonder about the sense of 'present' here. While we have taken 'presence' as not metaphorical, there may still be multiple senses of presence. Is Christ's body and blood 'spatially present' in the same sense in which the bricks of the church building are 'spatially present'? Or is there some other non-metaphorical way of being present that is applicable? How can Christ's body and blood be simultaneously present in multiple, disconnected places? Is a part here and a part there, or is the whole present in each place?

A parallel question concerns what happens to the bread and wine. It certainly appears as if bread and wine are present after consecration. Some take this appearance at face value, and insist that not only is Christ's body and blood present, but so are bread and wine. This is 'consubstantiation'. Others insist that the appearance alone is present, and bread and wine are really absent. This conjunction of the real presence of Christ's body and blood and the non-existence of bread and wine is, according to Pope Paul VI's 1968 'Credo of the People of God', at the core of the doctrine of 'transubstantiation'.

If consubstantiation holds, we have two options. First, by analogy with the incarnation, we could have 'impanation'. Just as one and the same person is both a human and God, one and the same entity is both bread and body, and likewise for wine and blood, or maybe one and the same entity is both Christ and bread, as well as both Christ and wine. Or one might have co-presence, in which case bread and body are in the same place, and wine and blood are in the same place. The co-presence version is subject to the objection that 'this' in 'This is my body' would seem to more appropriately apply to the *visible* of the two substances, namely bread, if there were two substances there.

If, on the other hand, transubstantiation holds, we have several further questions. Is there a real connection between the bread and wine and the body and blood, with, say, the bread and wine literally becoming transformed, or do bread and wine simply cease to exist, being followed by the coming-present of the body and blood? What makes it be the case that bread and wine are present? Is an illusion miraculously caused in the minds of the people present? Or is it that the causal powers of the bread and wine are somehow sustained, so that light bounces off just as it did before? If so, what are these causal powers grounded in? Are they now the causal powers of Christ's body and blood? Are they the causal powers of God? Are they self-standing causal powers, present in the same place as the body and blood?

Or had bread and wine received a power of affecting future events at a time at which they no longer exist?

To discuss even half these questions would take a book. For present purposes, then, I shall focus simply on the question of whether the doctrine of the real presence of Christ's body and blood, and likewise the doctrine of the real absence of bread and wine, can be defended philosophically. I shall argue for an affirmative answer, and I shall do so by considering a variety of metaphysical models, including that of Aquinas. It will appear, thus, that transubstantiation is a philosophical possibility. If it is possible for two substances to be in the same place at the same time, consubstantiation will be a philosophical possibility as well. Of course, the question of actuality is a theological one.

For brevity, I will usually speak of the body rather than the blood. There is here yet another question that I shall not address, which is whether the presence of the body brings along with it the presence of the blood and *vice versa*. The Catholic tradition answers this affirmatively, and in the 13th Session of the Council of Trent adds that the soul and divinity are present along with the body. On Aquinas's view, the blood, soul, and divinity are present on account of their union with the body which is eucharistically present where the bread used to be (*Summa Theologiae* III q. 76 a. 1).

2. REAL PRESENCE

2.1. The Problem

According to the doctrine of the real presence, Christ is present wherever the Eucharist is validly[2] celebrated. By any plausible criteria of validity, the Eucharist is validly celebrated at the same time in multiple places. Therefore, the doctrine of the real presence seems to imply that Christ is present in multiple places at once. Moreover, according to orthodox Christianity, Christ currently exists bodily in heaven. If a body can exist only in a place, and no earthly place is also a heavenly place, then we can conclude that Christ is present in multiple places at one time from his being present on earth in the Eucharist and in heaven.

Assuming a body is a material object, it seems that the doctrine of real presence leads to:

(M) A material object can be simultaneously wholly located in more than one place.

This multilocationist thesis will need to be examined. But before we do that, we should examine strategies for holding on to the claim that Christ's body is really present in the Eucharist without being committed to (M).

2.2. First Anti-Multilocation Strategy: Partial Presence

Leibniz, while not himself a Catholic, for ecumenical purposes and/or to gain a wider following for his views, attempted to show that his metaphysics was compatible with the Catholic doctrine of transubstantiation. To that end, in his correspondence with Des Bosses (Leibniz 1989: 197 ff.), Leibniz claimed that his monadic metaphysics was compatible with the idea—to which he was not committed—that a material substance required the existence of a 'substantial chain'. The basic item in Leibniz's ontology is the *monad*, which is a substance that has no parts. The soul of a human being is a monad, and all material reality is in some sense built up out of monads as well.

Leibniz then suggests extending this ontology by introducing substantial chains. These are entities of an ontological type different from a monad, that tie together multiple monads. More precisely, to each substantial chain there corresponds a collection of monads that are its *members*, i.e. which stand in a special *member-of* relation to the chain. Chains can lose and acquire members, and monads can come to be and cease to be the members of chains. Thus chains can survive replacement of their parts, in the way in which we think organic bodies can. A material substance, then, is at any given time constituted by both a substantial chain and its member monads. If *a* and *b* are material substances, at the same or different times, then they are identical if and only if they have the same chain. A good way to think of the chain is as a Leibnizian analogue to a scholastic substantial form, but perhaps without the form's causal efficacy.

Leibniz's proposal, then, was to say that in the Eucharist the monads of the bread and wine become members of the chain that constitutes Christ's body. Thus, Christ's body grows to include the monads that were previously the monads of the bread and wine. This metaphysical event, we may note, has no observable consequences in Leibniz's thought, because the relations between chains and their monads are not observable.

Leibniz's account shows a way to understand real presence that blocks the argument from real presence to (M) by affirming that Christ's body is present in more than one place but denying that it is *wholly* located in more than one place. Instead, a part of Christ's body is in heaven and another part of his body is on earth. Because the monads of the bread that is consecrated in different places are distinct, one part is present at one Eucharistic liturgy and another at another.

We need not accept the full monadic system to see the attractiveness of Leibniz's account. The account requires only a primitive metaphysical relation that constitutes something as a part of a real whole. This might be a relation to other parts, or to a form, or to some central and irreplaceable part. What happens at consecration, then, is that the parts of the bread acquire such relations as make them be parts of the body of Christ.

Does this account do justice to real presence, or does real presence require the presence of all of Christ's body? Plausibly, it is not necessary for *all* of a person to be in a room for the person to count as really present in the room. If a witness to a marriage were required to be in the church in which the marriage happened, and due to the crowd the witness stood in the church near the doorway, and as it happened had stuck his foot outside the doorway during the exchange of the vows, we would not, I think, deny that he was present in church for the vows. In fact, if due to the crowd he was able to have only his *head* in the church, I think we would say that he was present.

On the other hand, if the part of the witness present in the church were the tip of his little finger, we would be rather less confident that he was in the church. It seems that we count someone as present in a place provided that a significant portion of her is there, such as a head. What portion is significant may be contextual—for the presence of a witness in a place it may be the part bearing the eyes and ears, or perhaps the eyes or ears themselves, while for the presence of a runner receiving an award on a podium a foot might be enough.

But if the parts of the bread become parts of Christ's body, they do not seem to become organically important parts. As far as we can tell, they do not engage in any organic interaction with Christ's heavenly body. Thus on the Leibnizian account, what is present in the Eucharist seems to be an insignificant portion of Christ's body. If there is no organic interaction there, the part present seems to be more like a hair than a heart. Moreover, it is a part that Christ could easily do without, since moments earlier he did not have it, and nonetheless had a fully complete, indeed glorified, body.

Thus this kind of partial presence would not only not be doing justice to the idea of a real presence, but would also not match the devotional tradition's focus on Christ's self-giving to us in the Eucharist—here one thinks of the common image in Christian art of the pelican legendarily feeding its young with blood from her breast—since his giving us his hair to eat would not seem to have the kind of depth of self-giving that is ascribed to the Eucharist. Moreover, it would appear that on the Leibnizian view, Christ should have said 'This is a part of my body' rather than 'This is my body.'

A different partial presence approach that avoids multilocation would be that different parts of Christ's heavenly body come to be present instead at different Eucharistic liturgies, still connected to the whole of the body of Christ via the relations that constitute them as parts thereof, and these parts are then not present in heaven. Thus, the more consecrated hosts there are, the less of Christ there is in heaven, unless the parts left behind in heaven grow to compensate.

This would lead to the odd question of which part of Christ comes to be present at which liturgy, different parts being present at different ones. Perhaps more worrisomely, a view on which the parts of the heavenly body of Christ left heaven and came back to earth would not seem to do justice to the *triumph* of the resurrection, through which Christ received a complete glorified body, and reigns in that body in heaven.

A further absurdity that results from any partial presence view is that although St Paul warns about gorging at eucharistic liturgies (1 Cor. 11: 21–2), on these views one really does receive more of Christ the more one eats and drinks at the liturgy, and so Paul's warning would end up being a warning not to receive too much of Christ.

The existence of partial presence views nonetheless shows that the argument from real presence to (M) requires that the doctrine of real presence be taken as saying that Christ's body is *wholly* located where the eucharistic bread used to be.

2.3. Second Anti-Multilocation Strategy: Placeless Presence

A common phrase among Catholic theologians is that Christ is present 'sacramentally' in the Eucharist. For this to block the argument for (M), we need the claim that a sacramental presence is not only not the same as presence in a place, but does not even entail it. Someone who thinks that sacramental presence is just a special case of standard spatial presence when this happens to occur in the context of a sacrament can agree that Christ is present 'sacramentally', but cannot use 'sacramental presence' to escape the inference to (M). Nonetheless, the predominant view among Catholic theologians, including St Thomas Aquinas, has apparently been that sacramental presence does not entail 'local presence', i.e. presence as in a place. This view is not magisterially binding on Catholics, but it is important and must be examined.

Let us, then, consider the family of 'placeless presence' views of the real presence—views on which Christ's body in the Eucharist, while real, is not locally present as in a place and the inference of (M) is blocked. On a placeless presence view, Christ's body is really present in the Eucharist on account of standing in a presence relation R to some anchoring entity y. It is essential to the account that the anchoring entity y either be the place of the Eucharist or be unproblematically present there, and then it is on account of the R-relatedness to y that Christ counts as really present. The anchoring entity y might be the accidents of the bread, or the congregation, or even a place in space, depending on the details of the view.

We require, then, an explanation of the presence relation R and of the anchoring entity y which makes it clear why it is that x's standing in relation R to y is a real presence of x in or at y. I shall say that a relation R such that x's standing in R to y is a real presence of x in or at y is a 'real presence relation'.

Examples of relations that are not real presence relations include 'symbolic presence' where x is symbolically present at y provided that a symbol of x is present at y as well as 'mental presence' where x is mentally present at y provided that x is thinking about being at y. In fact, we can see that these cannot be real presence relations because (*a*) an unreal entity can be symbolically present in a real place, Sherlock Holmes being these days symbolically present, by virtue of a statue, outside the Baker Street underground station, and (*b*) a real person can be mentally present in an unreal place, C. S. Lewis arguably having been mentally present in Narnia.

Say that a relation R is 'weakly locational' provided that x's standing in R to y entails that either y is not anywhere or x is spatially present where y is. Here, a strongly locational relation would be one where the first disjunct can always be dropped. An example of a weakly but not strongly locational relation is the relation of a trope to the entity having the trope: when the entity is spatial, we can say that its tropes are where it is, but when the entity is non-spatial, this would make no sense.

The defender of a placeless presence view must find a real presence relation R that is not even weakly locational. For if the relation in question *is* weakly locational, then it seems we can derive (M) just as well as in the case of standard local presence. For the anchoring entity y had better be where the Eucharist takes place, or else we cannot say that Christ's body is really present in the Eucharist, and so Christ's standing in R to the anchoring entity would entail Christ's being locally present where the Eucharist is being celebrated if R were weakly relational.

It is not immediately clear that there are any real presence relations that are not weakly locational. To see the difficulty in finding such a relation, consider Aquinas's discussion of God's omnipresence. Unlike Hud Hudson in this volume, rather than ascribing local presence to God everywhere, Aquinas says: 'He is in all things by His power insofar as all things are subject to His power. He is in all things by His presence insofar as all things are bare and open to His eyes. He is in all things by His essence insofar as He is the cause of being for all things, as has been explained' (*Summa Theologiae* I q. 8 a. 3, trans. Freddoso). If we take omnipresence in each of Aquinas's three senses to be a real presence everywhere, then we now seem to have three examples of real presence relations that are not weakly local.

However, what counts as a real presence in the case of one entity, say God, might not count as a real presence in the case of another entity. According to a causal interpretation of Newtonian physics, distant astronomical objects are capable of instantaneously moving other objects. The sun would thus be present in the earth by (gravitational) power, if all it means to be present by power in y is that one can or does affect y. But this way of speaking seems metaphorical: we generally could not say that the sun is *really* present in the earth without being quite misleading, even if Newtonian physics happened to be true. Likewise, no matter how much I observe a room from the outside, I am not *really* present in it. Thus it seems that either being present by power and observation are simply not real presence relations, or they are real presence relations in the case of God but not in the case of a material object such as a star, a living human (who may be more than material but is also material), or a body.

The case of presence by 'essence' requires some more discussion. We could simply take Aquinas to be saying that when x causes y to exist, then x is present by essence at y. If so, then this will generally not be a real presence when x is an object in space. There is a sense in which Michelangelo is present in the David, but he is not *really* present. But Aquinas appears to be referring not just to God's causing entities to come-to-be, but God's continual creation of entities—his efficaciously willing them to continue in existence. Creatures are more intimately related to God qua creator than the David is to Michelangelo. The continual dependence seems crucial here. But if so, then this form of presence would simply be a more hallowed case of being present somewhere by continuing immediate action. However, that will in general not be a real presence in the case of a material object. The sun continually acts on the earth gravitationally, and even if this action were immediate as in Newtonian physics, it would not make the sun be *really* present in the earth. Hence this option does not help, either.

The task of finding a relation that is not weakly locational but nonetheless a real presence relation in the case of a material object like a body is prima facie difficult. Moreover, there is some prima facie reason to suspect that no such relation can be found. For while we may be willing to admit with Aquinas that God (or an angel) is present where he is acting, and we may even take this to be a real presence, the reason we might take it to be a real presence is that there is no way for a being that is in no way material to be *locally* present anywhere, and presence by action is a natural analogue for such a being. But in the case of a material object, which *is* capable of being spatially present somewhere, it seems likely that we should say that it is *really* present in any location or in any located thing only if it is there *spatially*. That seems to be the lesson of looking at the three modes of omnipresence above.

However, this argument is based on a defeasible expectation that no relation that is not weakly locational will be a real presence relation. Aquinas appears to provide a counterexample to this expectation (*Summa Theologiae* III q. 76 a. 5). According to Aquinas, ordinary material substances have dimensions that they occupy. The dimensions of an object consist in the inner geometric configuration of the parts of the object, and can be thought of as basically the size and shape, or extension (in the Cartesian sense), of the object. We can intuitively visualize the dimensions of an object as the object's three-dimensional filled-in outline, which changes as the object changes its shape and/or size, but remains unchanged as the object moves rigidly through a flat space. But we need to be careful with this visual image, because we cannot say that the dimensions are a material object—they are, in the ordinary case, just an accident of some substance. For a substance to *have* such-and-such dimensions is for it to be shaped and sized thus and so.

Ordinarily, a substance, say a frog, *has* its dimensions, i.e. the dimensions are an accident (roughly, a non-essential trope) of it. In virtue of the substance's having the dimensions, we can say that the substance is *in* these dimensions. What makes it be the case that a material substance is found in a place P is that the substance is in the dimensions D, and D is in turn located in P. There are ordinarily thus two steps in locating a substance: Find its extension, and then see where that extension lies. If we think of the frog's filled-in outline, which is the shape and size of the frog and moves with the frog, then it makes sense to say that the frog is *in* its filled-in outline, and that filled-in outline is *in* a place.

There are, then, two things that the substance is really present in: it is *directly* present within the dimensions D, and *thereby* mediately present in P. The substance is then said by St Thomas to be 'substantially' present in D and 'locally' present in P.

We can find plausible the claim that the presence of a substance in a place is mediated by its dimensions if we accept that the size and shape of an entity are intrinsic properties of the entity (we shall see in sect. 2.4 that if we deny this claim, we get another account of real presence). An intrinsic property is one such that an entity's having that property is not a matter of anything beyond the entity, but simply of how the entity itself is. If the dimensions are intrinsic, plausibly they are not dependent on location. On the other hand, what counts as the location of an entity depends on the entity's shape and size—if I grew to gigantesque proportions I would no longer be wholly in this room, for instance. This makes it plausible that the location depends on the dimensions. Moreover, to locate something in a place we need only relate its filled-in outline to the place in such a way that the relation makes it true that the object's filled-in outline is there, i.e. we need to locate the object's *dimensions* in the place. Hence, it is plausible that it is the dimensions that are directly locally present.

Aquinas's move in the case of the Eucharist, then, is to insist that while the substance of bread has turned into the body of Christ, the accidents of bread—including most significantly its dimensions—have remained in existence when there is no longer any subject that they are the accidents of, the body of Christ *not* having these accidents. (It is, of course, ontologically quite surprising that an accident could survive the perishing of its object—this is an issue that will be discussed in sect. 3—but for now let us grant this possibility.)

What we then have are the dimensions of bread that are directly present on the altar as in a place, and then the body of Christ is substantially present in these dimensions, in the way in which the substance of bread had been present in them. The body of Christ, however, is not present locally on the altar, whether directly or indirectly. It is not present directly locally, because material substances are only directly present in their dimensions—it is only through the dimensions' presence that they are present anywhere. And the body of Christ is not indirectly present locally, because to be indirectly present locally in P, a substance must *have* dimensions that are directly locally present in P. But the dimensions in question are not ones that Christ's body *has*, though it is contained in them 'substantially'.

To summarize, Aquinas is first analyzing the ordinary notion of the presence of a substance in a place through two presence relations: a substance's being substantially present in dimensions and these dimensions being present in space. He then claims that one way for a substance to be present in its dimensions is just for these dimensions to be *its* dimensions. But, he claims, that this is just a special case of the more general relation of 'substantial presence', and the body of Christ stands in that more general relation to the dimensions that the bread had, without actually *having* these dimensions.

The presence of Christ's body in the dimensions is *real*, since it is supposed to be the same kind of presence that an ordinary material substance has in its dimensions, and that had better count as a 'real presence' if it is to mediate the ordinary substance's real, local presence in a place. The substantial presence of the body in the dimensions, thus, would count as a real presence. The account also has the merit of explaining why it is that when the eucharistic host is moved, Christ's body continues to be present there. If it were simply an invisible presence directly in some location in space, it would take an additional miracle for the minister's hand to relocate it. But the body is not relocated when the host is moved, because it is not present in a place, but present in the dimensions, which continues to be the case when these dimensions are relocated by the minister's hand. Moreover, the account fits with the Catholic and Orthodox tradition that when the accidents of bread cease to exist, e.g. due to rot or digestion, Christ's body ceases to be present.

There are, nonetheless, at least two difficulties with Aquinas's account.

1. The idea of accidents existing without a substance is problematic. This will be discussed in sect. 3.

2. Can something be *substantially* present within dimensions that are not its own dimensions, and in a way that does not give rise to a local presence? Consider a putative case of being present within the dimensions of something else: I am present within the dimensions of the room. But this is not a substantial presence. I am present within the dimensions of the room by virtue of my own dimensions and the spatial connection between them and those of the room. But substantial presence is not mediated in this way. Moreover, my presence in the dimensions of the room entails a local presence.

Consider now this argument: 'substantial presence' either is or is not meant in the same sense when we say that x is substantially present in the dimensions it has as when we say that x is substantially present in the dimensions that are not its dimensions. If the two are *not* meant in the same sense, then it does not seem we have good reason to agree that substantial presence is a real presence relation. For while we agree that being substantially present in one's own dimensions *is* an instance of real presence—it has to be since it mediates local presence for substance—we can no longer conclude from this that the second kind of substantial presence, where something is present within dimensions that are not its own, is a real presence relation. Moreover, we no longer have a grasp on this second kind of substantial presence. We might be able to do something if there is an analogy between the two kinds of substantial presence, but it would be an analogy difficult, I suspect, to set up.

Suppose, on the other hand, that 'substantial presence' is meant in the same sense in the two cases. Then it seems that substantial presence *is* a strongly locational presence relation. For it seems that what makes it be true that an ordinary substance is found in a place is the pair of facts that it is in its dimensions and that these dimensions are in the place. But the same would be true, and in the same sense, even if these were not *its* dimensions, as long as it was substantially present in them, and hence it seems that the same inference about being found in a place could be made.

But perhaps what makes it be true that an ordinary substance is found in a place is not some more general relation of 'substantial presence' in virtue of which it is *in* its dimensions which are in that place, but more simply that it *has* the dimensions which are in that place, whereas Christ's body stands in the more general relation of substantial presence to the dimensions of the bread but does not *have* these dimensions. This is what Aquinas would say. But at this point, I fear, it is quite unclear what it means for a substance to be 'in' its dimensions in the mode of 'substantial presence'. We unproblematically have a concept of ordinary substances *having* dimensions. But if their being *in* the dimensions is anything other than their *having* these dimensions, it seems very difficult to understand what their being in these dimensions consists in.

These difficulties are not knock-down arguments. But what they suggest is that Aquinas might be better off allowing that Christ's body is locally present on the altar, in virtue of being substantially present in the dimensions that are locally present on the altar. This would seem to force an acceptance of (M). However, this acceptance should not be problematic to someone friendly to Aquinas's view, since it does not seem to be any more difficult to be in more than one place than to be in more than one set of dimensions. Such a modified view that denies (M) would be, it seems, fully consonant with the Catholic tradition of transubstantiation.

Furthermore one might think that shape and size are *not* intrinsic properties of an entity, but instead depend on the location of the parts, with location being a relational property (this will be discussed further in sect. 2.5). If one takes this view, then one will not see locatedness as mediated by being within dimensions, and Aquinas's view will not be attractive. However, one can still take one of the views of the next two sections.

2.4. Third Strategy: Curved Space

The argument from real presence to (M) makes another assumption that has not yet been noted. It assumes that if Christ is wholly located on one altar and wholly located on another altar or in heaven, then Christ is wholly located in two places.

For validity, this inference requires the claim that the same place cannot be on two altars or on an earthly altar and in heaven at the same time.

This claim seems quite plausible, but is not clearly true. Observe first that a person might be wholly located in two buildings at once. Thus, the Royal British Columbia Museum contains a wooden house ceremonially belonging to the descendants of Chief Kwakwabalasami, and someone within that house would be in two buildings at once. Moreover, then the *place* where the person would be would itself be in two houses. But if a place could be in two buildings at once, it seems plausible that a place could be on two altars at once. Of course that would require a special spatial relationship between the two altars. Imagine, for instance, a large altar whose surface seen from above was a wooden rectangle surrounded by a larger stone surface. It might turn out that the wooden rectangle had its own independent legs, and was originally consecrated as a separate altar, and then became a part of a larger altar without losing its initial consecration. Then something lying on top of the wooden rectangle would by lying on two altars at once—the larger one of stone and wood, and the smaller one just of wood.

This response may seem flippant—analytic (or, I think equivalently, scholastic) philosophy at its worst. But actually there is a serious point here. To make the argument for (M) go through we need substantial claims about the structure and arrangement of altars and heaven.

For consider one plausible way of making the argument go. We might note that the eucharistic liturgy can be simultaneously celebrated in two non-overlapping buildings, and conclude that therefore Christ's body will be present in two non-overlapping buildings, and hence in two places. However, there is an ambiguity in 'non-overlapping buildings'. In one sense, two buildings are non-overlapping provided the walls do not overlap. This cannot be the sense meant, because a common place might be found in two buildings that are not overlapping in *this* sense, if, say, one building is entirely within the other, and so the argument for (M) would be invalid.

In a second sense, two buildings are non-overlapping provided the spaces within them are non-overlapping. Then we cannot fault the inference that if Christ's body is present wholly in one building as well as wholly in the other, then it is wholly in each of two non-overlapping places. But we now need a second argument to show that the liturgy can be celebrated in two buildings that have no common place. On the face of it this seems obvious empirically: surely if the liturgy is celebrated at St Peter's in Rome and in the National Shrine in Washington, it is celebrated in two buildings that have no common place.

But how would we argue that St Peter's and the National Shrine have no common place? The best way I can see—and one whose failure will be illustrative of the failures of other ways—would be to note that a straight line segment can be drawn between any pair of points one of which is wholly in St Peter's and the other wholly in the National Shrine, and the line segment will have positive length. This argument, however, presupposes the premise that when a line segment of non-zero length can be drawn between point A in space and point B in space, then A and B are distinct. This premise is empirical, and we do not at present actually know if it is in general true. For all we know, the space of the universe has a geometry such that if you go far enough in any one direction you will come back to where you started.

Of course, all I am saying continues to look as though it is in the worst tradition of analytic nit-picking. After all, granted, it may be that if you go billions of light years in a straight line you will come back to where you started, but we know the topology near the earth is roughly euclidean, and going a mere several thousand miles will surely not get you back to where you started.

But remember that we are considering a situation that is, professedly, a miracle. A miracle can involve violations of the laws of physics, though not of the laws of logic. The topology of space, as long as it is logically consistent, is a matter of physics—this is the foundation of relativity theory, at least when generalized to space-time. Thus unless one can show that there is no logically consistent topology that could allow the same place to be found on an altar in Italy and on an altar in the United States, the argument that real presence implies (M) has a serious gap.

And in fact it does seem quite possible to give such a topology by using a mathematical construction known as a quotient space. A quotient space construction 'identifies' together points of the original space to form a new space. For instance, as a topological space, take the surface of a long rectangular strip running from left to right. We might identify together corresponding points on the left end of the strip and on the right end, identifying the top left point with the top right point, and so on. The result of such identification is a new topological space which is no longer a rectangle but a loop. As you keep on going leftward, you come to, as it were, the points on the left edge. But these got identified with points on the right edge. And since *those* points had something to the left of *them* (namely, points near the right edge of the original strip), you can continue going leftward, and come around in a loop.

We can likewise identify together the points in the space occupied by the pre-consecration wafer in Italy and the points in the space occupied by the pre-consecration wafer in the United States, and thus construct from our standard, non-miraculous, semi-euclidean space a quotient space in which there is a place surrounded by *both* Italy *and* the United States. We could more easily visualize this if our space were two-dimensional instead of three. Just bend space until the wafer-shaped place in Italy lines up with the wafer-shaped place in the United States, and glue the two places into one. It appears this can be made mathematical sense of.[3] But then God could miraculously ensure that after consecration our world's space is just like the quotient space, and that matter continues to behave as expected. A bit more work would be needed to account for the four-dimensionality of space-time, but there does not appear to be any serious obstacle there.

The same quotient space move could be done with more than one wafer, as well as with the wafers and Christ's body in heaven. Christ's body would come to be present on the altar, then, in the sense that the points in the space just around the eucharistic host would come to be neighbors of points in heaven. It would become literally true that a little piece of heaven is on earth. The only thing one needs to do to form the quotient space is to have a one-to-one correspondence between each set of points where a wafer is before consecration and the points in Christ's heavenly body.

Of course a number of miracles would be needed to keep particle movements as observed. And one may think this story implausibly difficult. But of course it makes little sense to say that one thing is more difficult to an omnipotent God than another.

One might, however, have a general preference for theological accounts that involve fewer invisible miracles. This preference would have to take the form of the claim that if there are two accounts of how some doctrinal claim could be true, then the account involving fewer miracles should be chosen. If so, then this account has plausibility if one with fewer miracles cannot get off the ground. But whether there is another account or not, the existence of this account shows that an argument against the real presence from the denial of (M) cannot be made to work. For the real presence indeed *is* important enough that God would bend space itself to make heaven be present on earth if that were needed to make it possible. Hence if none of the other solutions work, this one *is* available. The Kingdom of Heaven would then be present among us in a more literal sense than one might have initially thought possible.

2.5. Bilocation

But suppose that Aquinas's 'substantial presence' solution is held indeed to involve a local presence, contrary to Aquinas's words, that no better sense of real but placeless presence can be found, and that we do not want to allow space to have strange topologies. In that case, the defender of real presence must accept (M). Is the acceptance of (M) absurd? I shall argue in the negative.

There are, after all, coherently describable cases of bilocation. As Koons (2005) points out, time travel is one such case—if one were contemporaneous with one's teenage self, one would be bilocated, once as an adult and once as a teenager. Another case given by Koons is Feynman's supposition that all particles of the same type are one, multilocated particle.

The primary difficulty is with making sense of what it could mean for something to be wholly located in more than one place. We need to distinguish a case where x is wholly located in places P and Q from a case where x is located in both P and Q

simply because x is big enough so that some of it is in P and some of it is in Q (cf. the Leibnizian model of the real presence).

Readers familiar with the concept of an object's being wholly present in a region of space-time may want to observe that this concept is to be distinguished from the concept of being *wholly located* in a place P at a time t. The concept of being wholly present has received significant attention in the recent literature (an excellent survey is provided by Crisp and Smith 2005). The main metaphysical use of the concept of being wholly present is to distinguish between two views of how an object persists over time. On the endurantist or three-dimensionalist view, all of an ordinary material object is present at every time at which the object exists, and hence ordinary material objects are three-dimensional. On the perdurantist view, objects are four-dimensional—they extend through space and time. At any given time t at which the object exists, it has a special part known as a *stage*, which exists only at t, and is a complete three-dimensional cross-section through the four-dimensional object. Only that three-dimensional cross-section of the ordinary object exists at t. Thus, the endurantist holds that ordinary material objects are *wholly present* at every time at which they exist, while the perdurantist denies this. The concept of an object x's being *wholly located* in a place P at a time t, however, is meant to be neutral between endurantism and perdurantism, and is compatible with the idea that x might have parts existing at *other* times which are not present at time t. Being wholly located in a place at a time is meant simply to capture the intuitive notion of all of the object at that time being there. If endurantism is true, then to be wholly located and wholly present somewhere at a time is one and the same thing. If perdurantism is true, then it *may* be that being wholly located in a place at a time is the same as for the relevant stage to be wholly present in that place.

It is tempting to define something as wholly located in a place P at a time t provided that some of the parts of the object at t are in P and none of them are outside P. If this were true, (M) could not hold. However, one can reasonably object to such a definition by insisting that the question of whether x is wholly in P should depend only on x and on what happens in P, not on what does or does not happen outside P, e.g. whether any of the parts of x are found there as well.

An obvious definition that does justice to this intrinsicness requirement (cf. Koons 2005) is:

(W1) An entity is wholly located in P if and only if either it is simple—i.e. without any parts—and present in P or each of its parts is present in P.

Since the whole is where all the parts are, we can then say that the whole is in P.

A difficulty with this definition is an ambiguity in 'all the parts'. If we mean all the parts that exist at the given time t, then multilocation is only possible when the object has the same parts in all one's locations. In particular, the kind of multilocation that is involved in time travel will be ruled out, because the adult time traveler who visits her teenage self has cells that the teenager does not and *vice versa*. If, on the other hand, we mean all the parts that are found in P, then it follows that we are trivially wholly located wherever any of our parts is present, so that being wholly located reduces to being present, which seems implausible.

There is a large literature attempting to define the concept of being wholly present in a way that avoids analogues of these difficulties, and if one wanted to come up with a *definition* of being wholly located one could draw on that literature. However, there is no need for that. For even though (W1) is perhaps not a good *definition* of being wholly located in P, it yields a perfectly fine *sufficient* condition:

> (W2) An entity is wholly located in P at t if either it is simple—i.e. without any parts—and present in P at t or each of the parts it has at t is present in P at t.

This is all we need in the case of the Eucharist because there the possibility that an entity may have more parts at one of its multiple locations than at another may not come up. Rather, we can simply say that each of the parts that Christ's body now has is found in each of the multiple locations of the Eucharist.

A more serious difficulty with bilocation is the possibility of differences in intrinsic properties. If I am present in more than one place at a time, I might be red all over as found in one place and green all over as found in another, which would imply that I am simultaneously red all over and green all over. One response, defended by Koons 2005, is that the problem here is no bigger than the problem of intrinsic change for an eternalist, i.e. for someone who believes that the past and future are equally as real as the present. The problem of change, raised by Lewis 1986: 204 is generated by the fact that an entity might have contradictory properties at different times, say, being round at one time and square at another.

There are two familiar positions on the problem of change. A perdurantist believes that I am present at a time in virtue of a temporal slice of me being present there. In the bilocation case, I might suppose that something like an organically complete slice is present in one location and another slice is present in the other. In the case of the Eucharist, though, this would lead to a possibly unsatisfactory variant on the partial presence view of Leibniz: for one slice of Christ's body is present in heaven, then, and another on the altar.

An endurantist, on the other hand, believes I am wholly present at each time at which I exist, and thus he is already accepting that I am wholly present in disjoint regions of space-time. But if so, then why can't two of these locations in which I am wholly present happen to be simultaneous, in which case I would be wholly located in two disjoint regions of space? As Koons points out, anything the endurantist eternalist might say about the problem of change can be said here.

The problem of change for the endurantist is, basically, that an object that is wholly present at each of t_8 and t_9 might be both positively charged all over and negatively charged all over, at t_8 and t_9 respectively, which seems absurd. However, an endurantist might resolve the problem by indexing properties to times: e.g. *being positively charged at t_8*, and *being negatively charged at t_9*. Well, for bilocation one simply indexes them not to times but to times and positions: *being positively charged at t_8 as located in P* and *being negatively charged at t_9 as located in Q*. Or the endurantist might say that what seemed to be intrinsic, non-relational properties such as being electrically charged in fact do include relations to points in time. Thus, the object might stand in a *positive-charge-at* relation to t_8 but in a *negative-charge-at* relation to t_9. Again, the bilocationist can likewise make properties be relational to positions and points in time: an object might stand in a *positive-charge-at-...-and-as-located-in* relation to $<t_8, P>$ but in a *negative-charge-at-...-and-as-located-in* relation to $<t_9, Q>$.

(And when we realize that, given General Relativity, times are just maximal spacelike hypersurfaces, it might well seem not to be any more problematic to index properties to subsets of these hypersurfaces (a subset of a spacelike hypersurface being an encoding of both a place and a time) or to make them relative to such subsets, than it is to index or relate them to whole hypersurfaces.)

But actually it seems plausible that these complications are not needed. These complications were introduced to take care of the problem of intrinsic properties and multilocation. But actually, according to the standard view of transubstantiation, it is not at all clear that we need to allow for the body of Christ to have different intrinsic-like properties as located on the altar and as located in heaven. It is tempting to say that the body of Christ has, say, whiteness and roundness as found on the altar but not as found in heaven. But on the standard view, these are *not* properties of Christ's really present body. It is not Christ's body that looks white and is round—there is just an appearance (the Latin term used by the Council of Trent is *species*) of whiteness and roundness, but this is not an appearance *of* the body of Christ. In general, then, it may well be that Christ's body does not directly acquire new intrinsic properties by virtue of consecration (there may be indirect acquisition, e.g. because Christ's human brain might be affected by his divine knowledge of the fact of consecration). It simply comes to be additionally present in a new place. If this is right, then the problem of different intrinsic properties at different locations of a multilocated entity simply does not arise in the case of the Eucharist.

If shape and size, however, count as intrinsic properties, then this solution would be difficult. For Christ's heavenly body is surely larger than a wafer. Moreover, Christ is wholly located in the Eucharist—he does not, for instance, invisibly stick out outside the host. It seems to follow that if Christ is spatially present, he is present as round and circular. Aquinas, however, would block this inference by saying that Christ is *present in* the dimensions of the bread, but that he does not *have* these dimensions, and in fact, nothing has them, because the one thing that had them— the substance of the bread—is no longer in existence. How successful this would be would depend on whether one can make sense of being present in dimensions that one does not have.

But in fact shape and size are not intrinsic properties. We learn from Einstein that shape and size depend on reference frame, for instance. We might also argue that the shape and size of an object supervenes on the positions of its parts. If so, then we might take the shape and size as *constituted* by facts about the positions of the parts. But the position of an entity may well be relational, consisting in the relation between the entity and a point in space on an absolutist view of space, or the relation between the entity and other entities on a relational view. (For other arguments for the non-intrinsicness of shape, see Skow 2007.)

Consider the following quick argument against the shape and size of an object being intrinsic properties. Consider an object that is a large circular ring, one light day in radius (i.e. it takes light one day to travel from the center to the edge). The diameter of the ring, then, is two light days: this is the distance between two opposite edges. But suppose that God creates *ex nihilo* a massive star right in the middle of the ring, and consider the situation five minutes later. The ring is not intrinsically changed by the creation of the star in its middle, because physical effects, including gravitational ones, propagate at most at the speed of light, and it would take about a day for light to travel from the star to the ring. About a day later, the ring will be intrinsically changed, but it is as yet unchanged. However, the ring's size *has* changed. For the insertion of the star has warped space-time near the star, and so the distance between two opposite edges of the ring is no longer what it used to be. Therefore, the size of the ring is not an intrinsic feature of it. It depends on the structure of space-time beyond the space-time occupied by the matter of the ring itself. Likewise, if the star pops into existence off-center, the ring will no longer be circular in the classical sense of a circle as a set of points equidistant to a center. It appears that size and shape are not intrinsic.[4]

One difficulty here is that there seem to be intrinsic properties of an organic entity that directly depend on its shape and size; but how can an intrinsic property directly depend on an extrinsic one? The heart would not work if it were as thin as a wafer, for instance. There is a connection between the spatial configuration of parts and their causal interconnection. However, this is not a problem given divine omnipotence if the dependence is nomic and not logical. For it may be that the causal interconnections between the multilocated parts of Christ's body depend only on the spatial interconnections that the parts have as found in heaven, and not as found in the Eucharist.

It may also be the case that we can distinguish an internal shape and size of an object, defined by spatial relations between parts of the object where these relations in an appropriate sense 'do not leave' the object (in the way in which the relations between the opposite parts of the ring 'left' the ring by entering into the space in the middle) and the external shape of an object, defined by spatial relations between the parts of the object and things outside the object (either space itself or other objects).

(See also McDaniel 2003.) If so, then it might be that the internal shape and size is something intrinsic but the external one is not. One might be suspicious of even the idea that the internal shape and size is intrinsic (e.g. the arguments of Skow 2007 would still apply), but even if we grant the intrinsicness, it is not clear that a problem for multilocational accounts of real presence results.

For the main difficulty is, presumably, that Christ is, let us suppose, five feet tall while the Eucharistic host is, let us suppose, an inch in diameter, and there is a disparity of shape. However, we *can* imagine a space where the inside of an area is in some sense bigger than the outside, and whose internal geometry is different from what one might expect from the outside. Imagine an infinite, flat two-dimensional space. Think of this as a rubber sheet. Draw a small circle. Now keep the edges of the circle fixed, but stretch the rubber within the circle into a large bubble whose diameter is much larger than that of the circle (for visualizing this, we stretch the sheet into the third dimension; to avoid making use of an extra dimension, we could simply modify the metric). The resulting space is flat, except for a circle that pinches off a large balloon. Then there is a real sense in which the inside of the area is larger than the outside: the outside is a small circle, but the diameter of the bubble within is larger. Moreover, the geometry inside may be quite different from what we expect from the outside.

We can now give two model metaphysical views of location on which we can get real presence by multilocation. On the first model, space (or space-time—the same things can be said in a more relativistic framework, but for simplicity I just deal with space) consists of points. There is also a primitive relation L that can hold between an extended entity x and a non-empty set P of points in space at any given time. We can read LxP as 'x is wholly located at P'. Given this, what happens in the real presence on the present model is that the internal causal relations and intrinsic properties of Christ's body remain as they were, but Christ's body comes to be additionally L-related to the area in space to which the bread was previously related. Location is defined by a primitive relation between an object and a non-empty set of points, and while normally a material object is thusly related to only one set of points, miraculously it can come to be thusly related to more than one set. This seems to be a coherent story about locatedness and of what it would mean for Christ's body to come to be locally present in more than one place without changing in internal relations and intrinsic properties.

On the second model, space is constituted by a network of relations between things in space. The exact nature of these relations will depend on the details of the relational view. One option is the following: We have a relation $Rxyd$ which means that the distance between objects x and y is d. It might, further, make sense to suppose that a pair of points can stand in more than one such relation if space is non-euclidean: thus there might be more than one distance between two points. For consider the two different 'straight line' distances between Washington and the North Pole (assuming for simplicity the earth is a perfect sphere): one is obtained by measuring the length of the trip directly north from Washington to the North Pole, and the other is obtained by measuring the length of the 'straight line' (or more precisely 'great circle') trip south from Washington to the South Pole and then up to the North Pole on the other side of the globe. Thus it might well be that two points have more than one distance between them: for instance, a distance 'the short way' and a distance 'the long way'.[5]

The location and shape of an entity x might well then be constituted by all the $Rzyd$ relations where z ranges over the parts of x and y ranges over entities other than the parts of x. On this model, real presence is again no difficulty to an omnipotent being who can bring it about that if $Rxyd$ held with x a part of the pre-consecration bread and y something outside it, then now Rx^*yd holds where x^* is some part of Christ's body, and that every part of Christ's body enters into one of these new relations. It appears possible to make this coherent.

Observe that Christ's body then comes to be at a positive distance from itself: if the distance between one eucharistic host and another is 100 meters, then it will be the case that R(Christ's body)(Christ's body)(100m). But there is no difficulty in something being a positive distance from itself: an object on a perfect sphere is both at zero distance from itself and at a positive distance (just walk straight in any direction and you'll come back where you started).

Thus it seems possible to produce coherent metaphysical models of how a multi-location of Christ's body might work in a eucharistic context. Until we decide what is the right metaphysics of location, we cannot say which model is correct. But at least we have reason to think that there is nothing in any way obviously contradictory about the hypothesis of a real multilocation.

Two further remarks are in order. The first is that Catholic teaching holds that Christ whole and entire is present in each part. This requires *massive* multilocation, where in fact Christ comes to be wholly located in the place where any part of the eucharistic bread was. But this in turn simply requires more L or R relations on the above models.

The second remark is that we are now in a position to see that there are prima facie two kinds of bilocation. The first we might call *robust* bilocation. This is the kind of bilocation that would obtain if you went back in time and were simultaneous with your past self. The robust bilocation of a person would be a doubling of mental capacity and a doubling of centers of consciousness. In robust bilocation, the entity at each location can have what at least intuitively seems to be different intrinsic properties (though they may turn out to be relational). Robust bilocation is what generates the problem of intrinsic properties, as well as the challenge of coming up with an account of 'wholly located' that allows a different mix of parts to be in each of two places at each of which the entity is wholly present.

But if the eucharistic real presence is a bilocation, it is probably not a robust bilocation. One way to see this is to note that the cessation of the existence of a person as wholly located in one place in a case of robust bilocation is very much like a death. If you go back in time to meet your younger self and then you die while in the past, then you *have* died, though oddly enough you continue to be alive at the location of your younger self. But the consumption of the Eucharist is not seen by the Christian tradition as *this closely* akin to the death of Christ, given that Christ is now glorified, though it might well be seen as *representing* that sacrificial death.

In non-robust bilocation, on the other hand, the same entity comes to be present in multiple places, but has the same intrinsic properties in each of those locations (except perhaps shape and size if we are forced to concede shape and size to be intrinsic). If the entity is a person, centers of consciousness and mental capacity are not multiplied, but all that happens is that the person becomes related locationally to multiple places. If you need to be active at meetings of two different committees at the same time, you need robust bilocation—you need a different set of mental capacities to be available to each committee, for instance. If you just need to fill out the quorum of each of two different committees but do not need to participate in both discussions, non-robust bilocation will do. Un-bilocating after the two meetings in the non-robust case will not be like a death—you will just be once again present in one place instead of two.

Non-robust bilocation seems to have significantly fewer philosophical difficulties than robust bilocation. And if the eucharistic real presence needs bilocation at all, it only needs the non-robust kind.[6]

3. REAL ABSENCE

According to Catholic dogma, not only is Christ's body really present, but bread is really absent. All that remains of it are the 'appearances' ('species') of bread. These have the same effect on measuring instruments as bread does, but the substance is no longer there.

Aquinas's metaphysical view was that what remains are the *accidents* of bread. These accidents are not the accidents of any substance any more. They are not the accidents of bread since there no longer is any bread. But neither are they the accidents of Christ's body or of any third substance such as the air (note that the accidents remain interrelated: in fact all the accidents other than the dimensions inhere in the dimensions according to *Summa Theologiae* III q. 77 a. 2). The idea of accidents not attached to a substance seems to play havoc with Aristotelian categories on which accidents are precisely what exists in a substance. However, Aquinas modifies that traditional definition to say that 'it belongs to the quiddity or essence of accident "to have existence in a subject" ' (*Summa Theologiae*, III q. 77 a. 1 ad. 2). The analogy of the four-leggedness of a sheep might help. It belongs to the essence of a sheep to have four legs. But a particular sheep might have only three. 'Essence' in this context does not refer to what the entity *must* have, but to that which it in some sense *should* have given what it is like, but might in fact lack. Thus an accident is the sort of thing that should have a subject, but God can miraculously bring it about that it does not.

Aquinas's argument for this possibility is that substances cause their accidents, and yet God is closer to each thing than its non-divine cause, so he can directly preserve the being of the accidents even absent the substance (*Summa Theologiae* III q. 77 a. 1). Accidents, thus, cannot be seen as properties—for only *something* can have a property. Rather, Aquinas sees accidents as real beings, albeit ones dependent on a substance in a deep way.

We can perhaps do better. Suppose one believes the past is real, in the sense that Alexander's warhorse Bucephalus exists, though not in the present-tense sense of 'exists' but in a tenseless sense. We can introduce this tenseless sense of 'exists' by two examples. When we say that a solution to the equation $x^2 + x = 9$ 'exists', we are not saying anything about the *time* of its existence—the word 'exists' is really tenseless (even though grammatically in English it looks like the present tense). Likewise, when we say that the root of World War II 'lies' in the discontent of the German people after World War I, we are not implying that this discontent is something *present*—we are using 'lies' in a tenseless sense, that does not imply pastness, presentness, or futurity. If this is right, then likewise the bread and wine *exist*, though pastly, after consecration, and the conclusion that the accidents of bread exist without a subject can be blocked without affirming that the accidents are accidents of Christ's body or the air or suchlike. For why cannot an accident have its subject exist *pastly* if the past is real and past existence is bona fide existence? Certainly an *appearance* can survive that which it is the appearance of. One hears a lightning strike after the strike is already over and it is quite possible to see the light from a distant star that in some reference frames has long ago perished. If the sound of the lightning strike and the sight of the star count as accidents, then it seems accidents *can* exist while their subjects no longer do.

Aristotelians do think of accidents as effects of substances. If we accept that effects need not be simultaneous with their causes, then seeing the accidents as continuing to exist as effects of the bread does not seem all that absurd.

Alternatively, one might identify accidents with certain dispositions. Thus, the accident of being positively electrically charged might be identified with the disposition to attract negative charges and repel positive ones in an appropriate way. Seen this way, the accidents of bread can persist after the cessation of the bread if God arranges some other way for these dispositions to subsist. (It might not be the numerically same causal powers, depending on the criteria of individuation of dispositions. But it is not clear that it is necessary to insist on numerical identity here.)

If it is possible for there to be bare dispositions without a substance, so that there might be a disposition in a region of space to bend light in a particular way, there is no difficulty here at all. Or it might be that God *directly* effects everything these dispositions did, so that all the same counterfactuals remain true as were previously true. If all we mean by saying that there is such-and-such a disposition is that certain counterfactuals (such as that negative charges would be attracted in a particular direction) hold and have a truth-ground of the fact of their holding, then the dispositions can indeed be said to continue existing. It is also philosophically possible, though there might be theological difficulties here,[7] that some third substance comes to be the ground of these causal powers. Finally, perhaps there could be dispositions grounded in the power of a pastly existing substance, like the pastly existing bread.

The possibility of the accidents of bread inhering in Christ or Christ's body, on the other hand, would seem to require something like *robust* bilocation, with its attendant problems of intrinsic properties. And if these problems were solved, the view might nonetheless be theologically problematic, if it be thought unfitting that the *glorified* Christ become small and round (this was apparently a standard medieval objection to certain views).

Interestingly, Aquinas distinguishes between the accidents of bread and the properties that follow from its essence, such as its ability to nourish us. It is only the accidents that remain. The ability to nourish, then, must be miraculously supplied by God. Here, I think, we might make a theological improvement. Why not say that *Christ's body* gains the ability to nourish us? If so, then we can understand why Christ says in the Gospel of John (6: 55) that his flesh is true food.

The main philosophical challenge of the doctrine of the real absence of bread and wine is to explain how it is that the appearances of bread and wine are there, with the same physical interactions happening as happened prior to consecration. As we saw several explanations are available.

At the same time, one might ask a non-metaphysical question: are not the appearances of bread and wine *deceptive* absent the substance of bread and wine? Aquinas notes that our senses are not deceived. They see the accidents, and the accidents are there. A similar thing can be said on dispositional views—it really is true that there is a disposition to deflect light rays in the way bread does, and so on. Of course an inference to the existence of a subject for these accidents would be incorrect. But faith can guard the Christian from such an inference. And we *need* the appearances of bread and wine 'because it is not customary, but horrible, for men to eat human flesh, and to drink blood. And therefore Christ's flesh and blood are set before us to be partaken of under the species of those things which are the more commonly used by men, namely, bread and wine' (*Summa Theologiae* III q. 75 a. 5).

4. Conclusions

There are no metaphysical difficulties with symbolic presence. We have seen that it is possible to make sense of transubstantiation, understood as the conjunction of real presence and real absence. Granted, to make such sense we need to make metaphysical assumptions. But there is more than one set of metaphysical assumptions that will do. And clever thinkers can no doubt find others. It would also be possible to make sense of consubstantiation, provided that we can make sense of impanation—Christ becoming bread—or that it is possible for two distinct material objects to be wholly located throughout the same place at the same time.

Notes

1. These two questions arose in conversation with Terence Cuneo.
2. 'Valid' here is a technical term from Catholic canon law. An apparently sacramental action is *valid* provided that it is done in such a way, by such a person, with such intentions, and under such circumstances as guarantee, given God's plan, the sacramental effect—in this case, Christ's real presence. The exact conditions believed to be necessary for the validity of a eucharistic celebration differ between denominations.
3. Here is one way to do the construction mathematically. It is only going to yield topological and not metric properties, but with some work metric properties can be handled. First take some one-to-one correspondence between points within the wafer in Rome and points within the wafer in Washington, and define the relation $\sim$ on points in space as follows: $x \sim y$ if and only if either $x = y$ or x and y correspond under the aforementioned one-to-one correspondence. A topological space consists of a set S of 'points' and a set O of subsets of S, known as 'open sets', where O is closed under finite intersections, and infinite unions, and contains S. Let S be our space and O its topology. Define a new space S^* containing all the points of S minus those found in the wafer in Washington. Let U be a set in O. Define U^* as the set of all points x in S^* that stand in relation $\sim$ to some point of U. We can now let O^* be the set of all sets of the form U^* where U is in O. It is easy to see that U^* is also closed under finite intersections and infinite unions, and contains S. The desired quotient space, then, consists of S^* and O^*.
4. For mathematically more sophisticated discussions of intrinsicness and relativity, see Bricker 1993 and Butterfield 2005.
5. If we want to be precise, we can say that $Rxyd$ provided that there is a geodesic (a generalization of a straight line) between x and y of length d.
6. This also allows an additional escape from a worry that Hud Hudson 2005: 113–16 raises for the multilocationist. If multilocation is possible, is it not a more parsimonious theory of the world to suppose there is only one particle in existence, multilocated at 10^{80} regions, and doing different things in different regions? However, this would seem to require *robust* multilocation. In any case, I do not think Hudson's worry is very pressing. The theory that the universe consists of a single multilocated particle would surely generate absurd consequences for the moral life, which is surely good enough reason for rejecting it, once we grant, as we should, that we have genuine moral knowledge of our duties (we have the right to be more confident about the wrongness of torturing persons for fun than about just about any scientific theory). For instance, it is unclear how there could be multiple embodied persons in such a world.

7. One worry is that 'this' gets its reference from the visible accidents when these are attached to a substance. If there were some third substance in view, then 'This is my body' might seem to refer to that substance, which would be incorrect.

REFERENCES

AQUINAS, THOMAS (1920). *Summa Theologica*. Transl. the Fathers of the English Dominican Province, <www.newadvent.org/summa>, accessed 28 May 2008.

—— (undated). *Summa Theologiae*, trans. A. J. Freddoso, <http://www.nd.edu/~afreddos/ summa-translation/TOC.htm>, accessed 28 May 2008.

BRICKER, PHILLIP (1993). 'The Fabric of Space: Intrinsic vs. Extrinsic Distance Relations', *Midwest Studies in Philosophy* 43: 271–93.

BUTTERFIELD, J. (2005). 'Against *Pointillisme* about Geometry', <http://philsci-archive. pitt.edu/archive/00002552/01/APG1.pdf>, accessed 28 May 2008.

CRISP, THOMAS M., and SMITH, DONALD P. (2005). ' "Wholly Present" Defined', *Philosophy and Phenomenological Research* 71: 318–44.

HUDSON, HUD (2005). *The Metaphysics of Hyperspace*. Oxford: Clarendon.

KOONS, ROBERT C. (2005). 'On Being in Two Places at the Same Time', unpublished.

LEIBNIZ, G. W. (1989). *Philosophical Essays*, ed. and trans. R. Ariew and D. Garber. Indianapolis: Hackett.

LEWIS, DAVID (1986). *On the Plurality of Worlds*. Oxford: Blackwell.

McDANIEL, KRIS (2003). 'No Paradox of Multi-Location', *Analysis* 63: 309–11.

PAUL VI (1968). 'Credo of the People of God', <http://www.vatican.net/holy_father/paul_vi/ motu_proprio/documents/hf_p-vi_motu-proprio_19680630_credo_en.html>, accessed 28 May 2008.

SKOW, BRADFORD (2007). 'Are Shapes Intrinsic?' *Philosophical Studies* 133: 111–30.

PART V

NON-CHRISTIAN PHILOSOPHICAL THEOLOGY

CHAPTER 24

....

JEWISH
PHILOSOPHICAL
THEOLOGY

....

DANIEL H. FRANK

In 1783, at the height of the Enlightenment, the Jewish savant Moses Mendelssohn
wrote *Jerusalem, or On Religious Power and Judaism*. It is an apologetic work,
attempting to make the case for inclusion of Jews and Judaism in modern European
social and political life. Jews had long been debarred on account of their strange
ways and practices, antithetical to Christianity. Seemingly irrational and anachron-
istic, Judaism needed to undergo reform, if ever Jews were to be full participants
in the modern age. What form should Judaism take to shed itself of its past? What
precisely is 'traditional' Judaism that stands in the way of reform? Minimally we
can say that traditional Judaism is at least a certain set of practices supportive of
anti-idolatrous worship, of a strict monotheism that requires obedience to the one
God, creator of heaven and earth. Such practices are quotidian, from daily prayers
to digestion of food to washing of hands to sexual practices. All these activities have
the effect of sanctifying the mundane, and support the notion that Jews are a 'holy'
people in the service of the one God.

Given this, one might well suppose that the requisite reform of Judaism would
entail an abrogation of its 'outdated' practices. Jews should commence to eat
both with and like their non-Jewish brethren, to work on the seventh day, etc.
As one peruses the history of Jewish life in the post-Enlightenment period, it is
certainly the case that many western European Jews, and somewhat later, Jews in

the Americas, reformed their religion in just these ways. Full inclusion in civic life, and civil society, seemed to require a level of assimilation to contemporary ways that necessitated the abandonment of traditional practices. And so Jews and Judaism reformed themselves. At this point one may begin to wonder what *beliefs* are underwritten by such revised practices. As noted, a very strict monotheism is underwritten by traditional practices. A strong dichotomy between secular and divine, creation and creator is mandated. What happens to such binary oppositions when traditional practices, whose sole purpose is to support these oppositions, are undercut? What one sees in much of Jewish reform, especially in its initial stages in the mid-nineteenth century, is a diminishing of the strict monotheism of earlier times. The *via negativa* of Maimonides, which more than anything underscores the unfathomable otherness of God and our epistemological fallibility, gives way in some influential modern quarters to an understanding of God as an *ethical* ideal.[1] Whatever one may make of this gloss, it indexes God to our moral imagination, and worse, from a traditional vantage point, it makes God a partner in collective action. It tends to understand God as caring about what we care about, and even suffering along with us.

In addition, of course, there have also been deeply anti-religious reforms of Judaism, of which political Zionism, secular Jewish nationalism, is the best example. Political Zionism (there are also religious versions of Zionism) has as its goal the establishment and continuing existence of the Eretz Israel, the land of Israel. The nation-state replaces God as the goal of human action, and with it the binary opposition between secular and divine completely collapses.

So, there are many ways of Jewish reform, but interestingly Mendelssohn's brief on behalf of Judaism does not call for a reform of Jewish *practice*. Famously he writes,

Among all the prescriptions and ordinances of the Mosaic law, there is not a single one which says: *You shall believe or not believe.* They all say: *You shall do or not do.* Faith is not commanded, for it accepts no other command than those that come to it by way of conviction. All the commandments of the divine law are addressed to man's will, to his power to act. In fact, the word in the original language that is usually translated as *faith* [*emunah*] actually means, in most cases, *trust, confidence,* and firm reliance on pledge and promise…Commandments and prohibitions, reward and punishment are only for actions, acts of commission and omission which are subject to a man's will…Hence, ancient Judaism has no symbolic books, no *articles of faith.* No one has to swear to symbols or subscribe, by oath, to certain articles of faith. Indeed, we have no conception at all of what are called *religious oaths*; and according to the spirit of true Judaism, we must hold them to be inadmissible.[2]

This is a remarkable passage. In it Mendelssohn defends Judaism at the bar of the Enlightenment, but not as we might expect. He does not call for a reform of religious practice and ritual. Rather, in understanding that the olive branch offered to Jews is grounded in a commitment to religious toleration, Mendelssohn responds in kind, that Judaism (as a tolerant faith) does not command belief, and that the (eternal) commandments are injunctions to *act* in certain specifiable ways. For Mendelssohn, that Judaism knows of no articles of *faith* entails that Jews can be (practicing) Jews *and* loyal citizens of modern states. Jews are not bound by 'religious oaths', which would render them servants to an authority other than the state. Their 'obedience' to God takes the form of living a certain way of life, with supra-political goals. But these goals in no way compromise or lessen loyalty to the state. For Mendelssohn, Jewish religious practice and ritual is eternal, the goals of the commandments and prohibitions. By contrast, beliefs are not, and cannot be, commanded, and this point of empirical psychology entails for Jews considerable latitude in belief, even as they practice the religion of their forebears. The demand upon Jews to express their loyalty to the secular state is feasible for Mendelssohn since there is no conflict of interest. One is reminded here of a similar discussion when John Kennedy, a devout Catholic, was a candidate for the Presidency. A worry arose about divided loyalties; from whom would he take his orders—from Rome or from the Constitution of the United States? Analogous with Mendelssohn, JFK's response was that his ability to uphold the Constitution and be a solid citizen was compatible with being a Catholic. In both cases, a bifurcated existence, living a life whose trajectories are at once political and supra-political, is not only a possibility, but a necessity, if ever certain prejudices were to be overcome.

If Mendelssohn is right that his ancestral religion is incompatible with 'orthodoxy', then prima facie Judaism would appear to be unpromising territory for (normative) *theological* speculation. Indeed, 'Jewish philosophical theology', the very topic at hand, would seem to be a non-starter. Often Judaism is characterized as 'orthopraxic', this in distinction to Christianity, whose commitment to articles of faith and creeds are clear. The emphasis in Judaism is on practice, actions that are commanded and prohibited, not on rectification of belief. The perennial (anti-Semitic) charge of the 'unspirituality' of Judaism seems to point in the same direction, supposing that Jews go about their daily lives in an utterly 'bloodless', emotionally lifeless way. Detractors of Judaism might try to capture this point by reference back to Mendelssohn's remarks about the Hebrew term *emunah*. In wishing to establish the case for 'freethinking' in Judaism, and in so doing to indicate the compatibility of Judaism with the Enlightenment ideal of unencumbered thought, Mendelssohn is at pains to gloss *emunah* (faith) as trust and confidence. In the place of faith and articles of faith, Mendelssohn substitutes firm trust grounded in promises. Jews made a promise at Sinai to keep commandments, and this promise and pledge provides the eternal foundation for their living in a certain way. The psychological point being made here about the direct object of imperatives is not new with Mendelssohn. It can be found in Locke's *Letter on Toleration* (1689) and in medieval Jewish circles in the late fourteenth century anti-Maimonidean, Hasdai Crescas. The point is simply that belief cannot be commanded, and it is quite pointless to found a society on a set of beliefs, and to demand of the citizenry articles of faith. Rather, the goal should be goodness and rectitude of actions, and prima facie this latter is compatible with a certain doxastic freedom.

As noted, such an act-centeredness might be construed as an emotionally dead, somnambulistic going through the motions. Certainly Mendelssohn never entertained this thought, wishing instead to present Judaism and Jews as open-minded and modern. But the issue is now joined, about the undogmatic nature of Judaism, and its presumed inhospitality to dogmatics and even theological speculation. What are we to make of Jewish (philosophical) theology?

A Medieval Prolegomenon

If we turn back to the medieval period, when Jews and Judaism were not vying for a spot at a (modern) secular table, we might imagine we would see Judaism in an unapologetic mode, not intent on (*ex hypothesi*) effacing dogmatic, credal commitments. With a view to maintaining group loyalty, we might expect a certain presumption of orthodoxy and credal commitment. The first great work of medieval Jewish philosophy, *The Book of Doctrines and Beliefs*, written in the first half of the tenth century in Baghdad by Saadya Gaon, is a work of Jewish kalam (dialectical theology).[3] It presents in considerable detail discussions of a standard set of issues such as creation of the world, the nature and unity of God, divine justice, freedom and determinism, and divine reward and punishment. In its own way this work is an apology, a defense of traditional Judaism, but the defense is of a certain way of *understanding* Judaism, namely as committed to a distinct set of philosophical theses, noted above. Saadya's project is manifestly not a defense of (what Mendelssohn would call) 'articles of faith'.

Saadya has well been called 'the revolutionary champion of tradition'.[4] The 'revolutionary' nature of his book lies in its underlying assumption that Judaism—traditional (rabbinic) Judaism—is in fact (reducible to) a set of doctrines and thus amenable to systematic theological speculation. It was due to Saadya that a defense of Judaism took the form of a Mu'tazilite (Greek-inspired) theological discussion of such issues as creation *ex nihilo*, the absolute oneness of God, free will, and divine reward and punishment. What might have been, for the religious fundamentalist, a reactionary call to cease philosophizing becomes in Saadya's hands a rich philosophical fare of argument and counterargument. Saadya's book is a full participant in contemporary intellectual life, while it defends traditional Judaism. Jewish philosophical theology is born.

The very title of Saadya's philosophical magnum opus clarifies his innovation. *The Book of Doctrines and Beliefs* was written in Arabic under the title *Kitab al-Amanat wa'l-I'tiqadat*. It was first translated into Hebrew in 1186 by Judah ibn Tibbon as *Sefer ha-Emunot ve-ha-De'ot*. Focusing on the title, both in Arabic as well as Hebrew, reveals much about the purpose of the book as a whole. *Amanat* (Hebrew *emunot*) are beliefs held on the basis of scriptural authority. Contrarily, *i'tiqadat* (Hebrew *de'ot*) are the very *amanat* subjected to rational reflection and critical scrutiny. The purpose of Saadya's book is thus 'to enable the reader to reach a stage where the *Amanat* ("doctrines," i.e. of Judaism) become the object of *I'tiqadat* ("conviction," i.e. faith based on speculation)'.[5] In the introduction to the ten chapters, or treatises, that make up the text, Saadya indicates the dynamic of the book when he says that 'the believer who blindly relies on tradition will turn into one basing his belief on speculation and understanding'.[6]

Viewed this way, the trajectory of Saadya's project reminds one of Aristotle's general (dialectical) way of proceeding philosophically.[7] Both Aristotle and Saadya commence with the status quo, generally the untutored beliefs and customary actions of the neophyte, and proceed to transport the 'student' to the point where he begins to understand the grounds for those very beliefs and actions. In his own way, Saadya wishes to turn (mere) belief, or even confusion, into rationally grounded conviction. As we shall soon see, we should likewise understand Maimonides' own philosophical project in *The Guide of the Perplexed*. It is Aristotelian in the way just noted, since it is addressed to a traditional Jew, described as 'perfect in his religion and character' (introduction to the *Guide*), who, on account of naively having accepted traditional beliefs, has finally become perplexed by the 'externals of the law' (its literal meaning), by 'having studied the sciences of the philosophers'.[8] Traditional, unreflected-upon beliefs square off against natural science and philosophy, with apparently disastrous effect. And so it becomes Maimonides' grand project in the *Guide*, as it was Saadya's some centuries earlier in his book, to clarify the tradition in such a way that its 'philosophicality' is revealed, and the addressee's perplexity is removed. In fact, it is just this unearthing of the 'philosophicality' of Scripture that so annoyed Spinoza in the *Tractatus Theologico-Politicus* (1670).[9]

What is to be noted right at the outset of Jewish theology in the medieval period is its penchant for philosophical argumentation, for advancing an understanding of Judaism on philosophical grounds. This is not to suggest that philosophical theology did not have its detractors, those who viewed such speculation as suspect, as leading to possible antinomianism. Rather the suggestion is that credal formulation, the development of a kind of catechism, is not the desideratum of theologians. At this point we might recall Mendelssohn's comment that 'ancient Judaism has ... no articles of faith'.

I have spoken above of the medieval philosophical project as one of 'unearthing' the 'philosophicality' of Scripture. The metaphor should be pressed. The medieval philosophers are, in their own way, archaeologists. They wish to root out the deepest layer of truth, beneath the surface. Beneath the literal meaning of biblical text, likewise underlying spatio-temporal phenomena, are deep truths and regulative ideals.

And these truths are to be teased out by philosophical acumen. They are manifestly not *emunot*, dogmatically held beliefs; rather they are the grounds for belief, and this is why Aristotle is so dear to them and why natural theology, grounding belief in science, is pronounced.

It is important now to turn at some length to the very greatest of the medieval Jewish philosophers, Maimonides (1138–1204). The reason for so doing is simple. He is taken to have commenced Jewish dogmatics, the enunciation of principles ('foundations of faith'), acceptance of which defines a Jew as such, and brings about salvation.[10] In his commentary on *Pereq Heleq*, the tenth chapter of the Mishnaic tractate *Sanhedrin*, Maimonides outlines thirteen foundations of the law. The thirteen foundational principles are belief in God's existence, unity, incorporeality, ontic priority (creation *ex nihilo*), that only God may be worshipped, that prophecy exists, that Mosaic prophecy is unique, that the Torah is revealed, that the Torah is eternal, that God has knowledge of human acts, that God rewards and punishes, that the Messiah will come, and finally that there will be resurrection of the dead. The actual list and number of principles is less important than the rather simple terminological point that Maimonides' refers to them as *qawa'id al-i'tiqad* (foundations of belief). It is important to recall that this precise terminology is that used by his predecessor Saadya, when the latter laid out his own philosophical defense of Judaism. The point I am now stressing is that Jewish dogmatics is not what we might think it is, an unmediated belief in a set of doctrines, acceptance of which defines a Jew as such. On the contrary, as we can infer from Saadya himself, belief is the conclusion of rational speculation, hard mental work. And the reward is salvation. Indeed, Maimonides understands love of God as a function of knowing him,[11] and such knowledge is (scientific) knowledge of his (beneficent) creation. In this regard, Maimonides and his great detractor, Spinoza, join hands. Both understand the *summum bonum* as an *amor Dei intellectualis*.

At the end of the medieval period, Isaac Abrabanel agreed with Maimonides on this, and his thought on the matter clarifies the issue at hand. Abrabanel asserts, 'Maimonides did not count as a positive commandment the form of the belief and its truth, but, rather, knowledge of those things which bring one to acquire beliefs' (*Principles of Faith* [*Rosh Amanah*], trans. Kellner, p. 155). On this passage Menachem Kellner comments, 'According to Abrabanel, when Maimonides codifies as commandments the obligation to accept that God exists, is one, and is incorporeal, he means that we are commanded to apply ourselves to the study of physics and metaphysics so as to become convinced of the truth of the claims that God exists, is one, and is incorporeal.'[12] Kellner's gloss here on Abrabanel is a good one and provides a way for precisely understanding Maimonides' own position. When Maimonides commands belief in divine existence, unity, etc., he commands the undertaking of a process of study by which one will be led by the light of reason to see that God is a necessary existent, is one, etc. Maimonides does not command belief in the sense of enjoining one to stop what she is doing at the moment and to commence believing something. Recall the point made earlier by Mendelssohn that belief cannot be commanded. So Maimonides too does not command belief *ex nihilo*, but rather an activity (of scientific inquiry) that will result in firmly established convictions.

This very process has *practical* implications. Maimonides' project can be understood as suggesting that something more than mere behavior counts as normative. Like Aristotle, he sets the bar for virtue high, requiring an understanding of reasons or principles of action. For Maimonides, the law itself has reasons, and to achieve human excellence, one must ascertain those reasons to the extent that a human can. Short of this, one is not a Jew *in a normative sense*. Maimonides knows better than anyone that being a Jew de facto does not require the arduous intellectual program just outlined. In this latter sense, one needs only to be born of a Jewish mother or to have converted according to traditional practice, but ever the intellectual elitist, Maimonides demands more. He requires that Jews go beyond the given, beyond easy acceptance of the law and behavior commensurate with it. He demands that we come to see why we do what we do, and to see what the scientific and cosmological foundations for our actions are. The project here is not different from Maimonides' grand project of discovering *ta'amei ha-mitzvot*, the reasons for the commandments. And this latter project is itself commanded.

Ta'amei ha-Mitzvot (the Reasons for the Commandments): A Case Study in Jewish Philosophical Theology

In what follows I present a case study of Jewish philosophical theology, in which I show how Maimonides explicates the reasons for the revealed commandments. Prima facie some of the commandments appear to be quite arbitrary and irrational, and we shall see how Maimonides deals with this. Further, and this is a very important point, this 'theoretical' discussion in legal philosophy about the reasons for the commandments has manifestly practical implications, specifically aretaic implications about the inculcation and establishment of certain dispositions.

We moderns tend to share with Kant the notion of morality as a struggle, a struggle against those impulses that would overwhelm us. To the victor belongs the praise. In this regard, the rabbinic sages are no different from us. According to them, *l'fum tza'arah agrah* [the reward is according to the pain] (*Avot* 5. 23). In reflecting upon this rabbinic dictum, however, Maimonides is struck by its apparent inconsistency with the philosophical, Aristotelian view, which explicitly accords the self-controlled person (the *enkrates*), the one who successfully battles against the pull of contrary impulses, merely second place to the virtuous (temperate) person, this latter being one who has no bad appetites to overcome and who takes pleasure in the doing of virtuous acts.[13]

In facing this apparent inconsistency between the respective philosophic and rabbinic evaluations of virtue and self-control, Maimonides, in *Shemonah Peraqim* (*Eight Chapters*, the introduction to his (early) commentary on Mishnah Avot) 6, brings about, in his own words, 'a wonderful reconciliation' between the two positions. Maimonides harmonizes the philosophic and rabbinic positions by distinguishing between two types of law, generally accepted laws and the ceremonial and ritual laws labeled *huqqim*. The rabbinic praise of self-control, he notes, has reference solely to the ritual laws such as *sha'atnez* (prohibiting the wearing of certain mixed fabrics) and the eating of meat with milk. But as for the universal and customary prohibitions, such as those against murder and theft, both the philosophers and the rabbis agree that the virtuous person, without wayward desires, is to be ranked higher than the one who succeeds in controlling his desires.

Yet a problem lurks beneath this apparent 'reconciliation'. The argument depends upon a radical dualism between laws universally accepted for their intrinsic rationality and those accepted for no reason other than their origin in a divine command. This radical distinction, however, cannot be squared with the view that Maimonides presents in *Guide* 3. 26, that *all* the laws, including the *huqqim*, derive from God's *wisdom*, not from his will alone.[14]

What is to be done about this inconsistency? In overcoming one inconsistency, Maimonides appears to be ensnared in another. To get our bearings on the nuanced discussion in the *Guide*, we need to take a look back at *Shemonah Peraqim* 6. In focusing on the reconciliation that Maimonides there effects between the philosophers and the rabbis, we tend to overlook what motivates the inconsistency in the first place. The whole problem between the philosophers and the rabbis arises because the latter have rank-ordered self-control above Aristotelian virtue in some cases. Why? An obvious answer might be that praise of self-control, of successful struggle against contrary impulses, underscores in a stark and vivid way the heteronomous character of the law (specifically, the *huqqim*), and obedience to it celebrates the duty to obey the divine will in spite of human disinclination.

In support of this gloss of the rabbinic ranking, one might point to Maimonides' explicit rabbinic references in chapter 6. As Rabbi Gamaliel said, 'Let a man not say, "I do not want to eat meat with milk, I do not want to wear mixed fabric ... but [let him rather say] I want to, but what shall I do—my Father in heaven has forbidden me." '[15] This rabbinic statement might be understood as magnifying God, his law, and obedience to it, all at the expense of humans, and their nature. This gloss, however, is one-sided.

Second to no one in pointing out the unbridgeable gulf that separates the human from the divine (the very thrust of his celebrated 'negative' theology), Maimonides is not making *this* point here. Far from glorifying God, the rabbis praise humankind. In presumably agreeing with the rabbinic praise of self-control and the rank-ordering of it over virtue in some instances, Maimonides is *eo ipso* countenancing the struggle in which the self-controlled person engages and emerges victorious. Again, in context, the rabbis *forbade* a person to say in respect of, for example, eating meat with milk: 'I would not naturally yearn to commit this transgression, even if it were not prohibited by the law.' The point stressed is anthropocentric in its intent, a point about human beings and the 'naturalness', the 'givenness', of certain human inclinations. Better to have recalcitrant desires (in certain situations) than no desires at all, given that, according to the rabbis and Maimonides, 'if it were not for the law, they [the *huqqim*] would not be bad at all'. Since there is no intrinsic rationality to the *huqqim*, it is quite natural for human beings to jib at obedience to them. So, the *Shemonah Peraqim*.

As one turns from the *Shemonah Peraqim* to the *Guide*, Maimonides' philosophical magnum opus, I would emphasize that even when in 3. 26 Maimonides re-evaluates his earlier (dualist) position concerning the nature of the law, he maintains a view of it that is attentive to the nature of humankind. Even as Maimonides points out the general intelligibility of the law, contrary to the *Shemonah Peraqim*, he is aware of the limits to which human nature can be brought under the rule of reason.[16] Maimonides' entire discussion concerning the reasons for the commandments strives not only to elicit the general intelligibility of all the laws, but to maintain some sort of distinction between the *mishpatim* (the intelligible ones) and the *huqqim* (the ritual, ceremonial laws).

As much as countering the Ash'arite (voluntarist) claim that all the laws are the product solely of God's will, as well as the Mu'tazilite view that only *some* of the laws are the product of divine will, Maimonides is also concerned to forestall (what we might call) 'hyperrationalism', the rationalist philosopher's attempt to discover reasons for absolutely everything. In the present case, it is quite pointless, according to Maimonides, to search for the reason why a lamb rather than a ram was used for a certain sacrifice, or why a certain number of lambs was sacrificed.[17]

Searching for the reason for every particular proves to be vain, for there was never a reason for God's choice in the first place. The quest for reasons here is a nonstarter. While Maimonides is clear that historical knowledge (of time and place) is certainly helpful in gaining an understanding of the reasons for the law,[18] he is equally insistent that 'no cause will ever be found for the fact that one particular sacrifice consists in a lamb and another in a ram and that the number of the victims should be one particular number'.[19] Although one might explain our ignorance by appealing to the historical distance from Temple days, or to our incapacity as (mere) mortals to fathom God's plan, I myself think such explanations are forced. They artificially place the burden of responsibility for our lack of understanding upon *us*.

Yet Maimonides holds explicitly that it is not any kind of human limitation, biological or historical, that precludes our finding the reasons for the particulars in the laws of sacrifice. Rather, the reason is wholly non-empirical; indeed, it is one of logical necessity. The reason why some number of lambs (seven) rather than another number (eight) was chosen for sacrifice is simply that for the law (of sacrifice) to be instantiated, that is, for there to *be* a law, some choice had to be made. But no other 'reason' is to be found. We may wish to say that the choice was 'reasonless', without (rational) preference, but we need to be clear that this lapse of rationality does not limit the wisdom of God, nor does it covertly signal a return to the kalamic (specifically, the Mu'tazilite) position regarding the law.

In sum, the fact that some laws are the product of reasonless choice, enforced by logical necessity, does not compromise divine wisdom. God is wise, and so is his law, even in those situations in which he chooses, perforce, without preference. Given this, Solomon's traditional wisdom concerning grounds for the commandments (*ta'amei ha-mitzvot*) is confirmed: it rightly extends to 'the utility of a given commandment in a general way, not an examination of the particulars'.[20]

The question remains: in a section devoted to a discussion of the (general) intelligibility of the laws, why should Maimonides wish *also* to emphasize their residual want of reason? As noted, one reason is to forestall hyperrationalism, the desire to find reasons for every particular. Another reason, a possible consequence of the foregoing, is Maimonides' desire to forestall (possible) antinomianism, that is, non-performance of the commandments.[21] Although there is a deep need and even duty for those able to inquire into the reasons for the commandments to do so, there is an equal need, Maimonides seems to suggest, to recognize *limits* to the inquiry. Not to recognize limits is to court antinomianism. In the case of the non-philosophical masses, an unbounded inquiry into reasons might well lead to confusion and hence to a failure of belief and a consequent disregard of the commandments. For the philosophical elite too, the inquiry might well culminate in antinomianism, for in not discovering a reason for some particular, the intellectual might query God's wisdom and, as a result, withhold his assent to the commandment. For these reasons, then, there is a need for Maimonides to state explicitly that the law is in part inscrutable.

When all is said and done, however, I think that there remains another reason for Maimonides' desire to emphasize that some of the laws are in their particularity without reason, although still the consequence of divine wisdom. Recall our earlier discussion concerning the grounds for the distinction between generally accepted laws and the *huqqim* (the ceremonial and ritual laws). We noted the problematic mapping of this distinction onto Maimonides' approving of the rabbinic praise of self-control, his desire in effect to allow for human nature and inclination. With the rabbis of old, Maimonides urges an awareness that certain human inclinations are natural and, although to be overcome by obedience to the law, not to be scorned. This doctrine found in the (early) *Shemonah Peraqim* is not entirely absent in the (late) *Guide*, even though the *Guide* presents itself as a considerably more ascetic, immoderate, work than the earlier one.[22]

A relatively modest point buttresses Maimonides' critique of hyperrationalism and his correlative struggle against all forms of antinomianism. Human beings need the law to achieve certain political as well as spiritual and intellectual ends.[23] The law provides a teleological framework for the good life, but a good *human* life, one in accord with human nature. I suggest that the non-teleological aspects of details of particular commandments, their 'matter', are highlighted by Maimonides as paradigmatic of our corporeality, that part of us that is 'natural' and cannot be brought under the rule of reason. As matter provides limiting conditions on the attainment of the ideal, so the *huqqim*, specifically the particulars of these commandments, in their indeterminateness and recalcitrance to the otherwise teleological nature of the law, are emblematic of our finite nature, even as they are no limitation upon God's.

Thus, there is in Maimonides' discussion of the reasons for the commandments a deep realization that we are, after all, merely human. With the limits of human nature in mind, we must also understand his remarks about the limits of the inquiry concerning the grounds for the commandments. While Maimonides is second to none in urging those capable to ground their actions in wisdom, he is equally concerned to point out that some things just are: they have no reason. And we should act accordingly.

SOME GENERAL (AND TENTATIVE) CONCLUSIONS ABOUT JEWISH PHILOSOPHICAL THEOLOGY

Are there any substantive conclusions we can draw from this brief excursus through the thoughts of some major Jewish philosophers? One conclusion might be a healthy revision of the very notion of philosophical theology. I think that the subject is generally conceived to be a highly theoretical one, having little to do with actions and living one's life. The (philosophical) theologian is the person who wonders about the nature of God, divine power and knowledge, the creation (or eternity) of the world, and the implications of this on divine freedom, etc. The list goes on and on, and there can be no doubt that the medieval Jewish philosophers from Saadya onwards address these issues. But perhaps what is overlooked is how these 'theoretical' discussions appear to support some rather practical, moral, and even political considerations. At the very beginning of this chapter, we noted Mendelssohn's claim that the only commandments that Judaism knows are commands to act and to refrain. He stresses as strongly as he can, and for the apologetic reasons we noted, that Judaism has no 'articles of faith', no commands to believe.

From this 'orthopraxic' perspective we can at least draw the conclusion that unmediated belief, 'orthodoxy' in a very literal sense, will have little purchase. And in turning to two giants of Jewish philosophical theology, Saadya and Maimonides, we noted that for them, the most important intellectual task, for those able to engage in it, is to ground the requisite beliefs in reason. This is nicely captured by Saadya, who indicates that the goal of his philosophical magnum opus is to lead one from unreflective to grounded belief. Saadya, and Maimonides as well, do not wish to impose 'correct' belief, for just the very reason that Mendelssohn suggests. It cannot be done. Thus, the command laid upon one wishing to achieve the *summum bonum* is to engage in natural philosophy (science), the study of the divine creation, and to gain from this endeavor such knowledge of God that it is possible to obtain. And, as we have seen explicitly in the case of Maimonides' philosophy of law, there is an injunction to ascertain the reasons for the commandments, at least in their general form. The telos is not to follow the law blindly, any more than one is commanded to believe that the world is created, but rather to ponder the very grounds for the proposition in question.

The attainment of this wisdom has itself practical ramifications. In both Saadya's and Maimonides' philosophical works, the focus on particular 'theoretical' points in semantic theory, epistemology, cosmology, prophetology, legal theory, and so forth tends to obscure the overall non-theoretical telos of their respective works. Consider the *Guide*. However conventional the literary form of the work is, an epistle to a beloved student, troubled by a deep existential crisis, one must take the topos seriously. Maimonides is not writing for himself, nor is the *Guide* to be understood as a patchwork of theoretical minitreatises on the aforementioned topics. This is not in the least to deflate or to overlook the brilliance of Maimonides' contributions to a variety of deep and difficult philosophical and scientific topics, but rather to contextualize those discussions in the appropriate way. Everything in the *Guide* subserves the end of showing the addressee that, properly understood, his religion—his traditional way of life, one circumscribed by halakhic (legal) norms—is philosophically defensible. And this latter point is not a theoretical one, offered for its own sake, but manifestly a moral and even political one. In responding to the addressee's worries, his perplexity, the *Guide* repositions him squarely within the community, from which as a deeply troubled 'intellectual' he is temporarily estranged.

The very order of presentation of philosophical topics in the *Guide* is another way one may see the overall (practical) trajectory of the project. The *Guide* is a tripartite work, commencing with philosophy of (divine) language and a finitist epistemology consistent with that semantics, followed by cosmology, philosophical psychology, and metaphysics, and finally concluding in the third part with legal theory and moral and political philosophy. This very procession maps on precisely to the ordering of the edited Aristotelian corpus, and as importantly to the practical thrust of (post-Aristotelian) Hellenistic philosophy generally. From Epicurus to Sextus Empiricus, the point of doing science and philosophy is to achieve a state of repose. In its own way Spinoza's *Ethics* is a part of this grand tradition of engaging in deeply difficult study for the sake of happiness.

The suggestion here is not that the Jewish philosophical theologians we have been interrogating are aiming at *ataraxia* (unperturbedness), but rather that their 'theoretical' discussions subserve practice. The project of understanding the reasons for the commandments is undertaken so as to better ground a communal life, much as Aristotle's *Ethics* is offered in the service of one well on her way to effective citizenship. Further, I think that if we read sensitively between the lines of Maimonides' celebrated discussion of divine attributes in the first part of the *Guide*, we shall discover that his semantic theory is offered inter alia to deflate a certain impetuosity, a naive epistemological optimism about the (unlimited) scope and powers of human knowledge. Such 'pride', intellectual presumption, ends in perplexity. For a full picture of what Maimonides is up to, the delineation of the bounds and limits of human wisdom (and laying out the semantic correlate to this epistemological finitism) must be harnessed to the aretaic point about character reformation. In sum, for Maimonides, the doctrine of divine attributes entails a certain humility as its desideratum.

So, it can be seen, at least on the basis of the few authors we have discussed, that Jewish philosophical theology muddies the grand dichotomy of theory and practice. Study is commanded for the sake of moral and social reform. And the law itself becomes most effective in a human life when obedience follows on consideration of its grounds.

Notes

Primary source material for Jewish philosophical theology, including philosophical exegesis of Scripture, may be found in: D. Frank, O. Leaman, and C. Manekin (eds.), *The Jewish Philosophy Reader* (London: Routledge, 2000); M. Walzer, M. Lorberbaum, N. Zohar (eds.), *The Jewish Political Tradition* (New Haven: Yale University Press, 2003–); C. Manekin (ed.), *Medieval Jewish Philosophical Writings* (Cambridge: Cambridge University Press, 2007). Further secondary reading in Jewish philosophical theology, and its history, include: C. Sirat, *A History of Jewish Philosophy in the Middle Ages* (2nd edn.) (Cambridge: Cambridge University Press, 1990); D. Frank and O. Leaman (eds.), *History of Jewish Philosophy* (London: Routledge, 1997); S. Nadler and T. Rudavsky (eds.), *The Cambridge History of Jewish Philosophy: From Antiquity through the Seventeenth Century* (Cambridge: Cambridge

University Press, forthcoming); D. Frank and O. Leaman (eds.), *The Cambridge Companion to Medieval Jewish Philosophy* (Cambridge: Cambridge University Press, 2003); K. Seeskin (ed.), *The Cambridge Companion to Maimonides* (Cambridge: Cambridge University Press, 2005); M. Morgan and P. Gordon (eds.), *The Cambridge Companion to Modern Jewish Philosophy* (Cambridge: Cambridge University Press, 2007).

1. This view is most prominently associated with the neo-Kantian, Hermann Cohen, whose major Jewish philosophical treatise is *Religion of Reason out of the Sources of Judaism* (1919).
2. *Jerusalem, or On Religious Power and Judaism*, trans. A. Arkush (in D. Frank. O. Leaman, and C. Manekin (eds.), *The Jewish Philosophy Reader* (London: Routledge, 2000), 349).
3. Saadya Gaon, *The Book of Doctrines and Beliefs*, abridged edn. A. Altmann, with new introduction by D. Frank (Indianapolis: Hackett, 2002).
4. R. Brody, *The Geonim of Babylonia and the Shaping of Medieval Jewish Culture* (New Haven: Yale University Press, 1998), 235 ff.
5. Saadya Gaon, *Book of Doctrines*, 20.
6. Ibid. 30.
7. As Tom Flint reminds me, the trajectory of Saadya's project stands comparison with Anselm's a century later.
8. Maimonides, *The Guide of the Perplexed*, abridged edn. J. Guttmann, trans. C. Rabin, with new introduction by D. Frank (Indianapolis: Hackett, 1995), 41.
9. See *Final note*.
10. A comprehensive treatment is found in M. Kellner, *Dogma in Medieval Jewish Thought: From Maimonides to Abravanel* (Oxford: Littman Library of Jewish Civilization, 1986).
11. *Guide* 3. 51.
12. M. Kellner (trans.), Isaac Abrabanel, *Rosh Amanah* [*Principles of Faith*] (Oxford: Littman Library of Jewish Civilization, 1982), 79.
13. *Nicomachean Ethics* [*NE*] 1. 8 (1099a7–12); 1. 13 (1102b27); 2. 3 (1104b3–8); 7. 9 (1151b32–1152a6).
14. *Guide* 3. 26.
15. *Sifra* to Leviticus 20: 26.
16. *Guide* 3. 8; 3. 33.
17. Ibid. 3. 26.
18. Ibid. 3. 49: 'The fact that there are particulars the reason for which is hidden from me and the utility of which I do not understand, is due to the circumstance that things known by hearsay are not like things one has seen . . .'
19. Ibid. 3. 26. For a possible source for this latter point, see *NE* 5. 7 (1134b20–3).
20. Ibid.
21. For a full discussion of this point, see J. Stern, 'The Idea of a *Hoq* in Maimonides' Explanation of the Law', in S. Pines and Y. Yovel (eds.), *Maimonides and Philosophy* (Dordrecht: Nijhoff, 1986), 92–130.
22. For remarks on the reasons for this 'developmental' scheme in Maimonides' ethical theorizing, see H. Davidson, 'The Middle Way in Maimonides' Ethics', *Proceedings of the American Academy for Jewish Research* 54 (1987), 31–72; D. Frank, 'Anger as a Vice: A

Maimonidean Critique of Aristotle's Ethics', *History of Philosophy Quarterly* 7 (1990), 269–81.

23. *Guide* 2. 40

Final note: In large measure Jewish philosophical theology presumes the 'philosophicality' of Scripture, the view that Scripture is amenable to philosophical reconstruction. A good way to enter this debate is to read Spinoza's stinging critique of the philosophical-theological project (Spinoza, *Tractatus Theologico-Politicus*, chs. 1–7), followed by Maimonides' defense of it in *The Guide of the Perplexed*.

CHAPTER 25

....

ISLAMIC PHILOSOPHICAL THEOLOGY

....

OLIVER LEAMAN

ISLAM as a distinct religion started in the seventh century CE when the Prophet Muhammad received a series of messages from God, according to Islam. He in turn communicated those messages to the local Arabs in his part of the Arabian peninsula and after some difficult periods managed to establish a community of believers, the Muslims. They rapidly went on to conquer the neighboring areas, and converted the local inhabitants to the new religion. Islam, however, does not really see itself as a new religion, but as a culmination of earlier religions, based as they are on earlier revelations.

As Islam spread, there was growing contact with centers of civilization in the Arab world and Persia that were in one way or another imbued with Greek culture. This led to a fierce reaction by many Muslims, rejecting that foreign and unbelieving culture for the more familiar and authentically Islamic sciences of grammar, law, the traditional sayings of the Prophet and his Companions, and theology. Yet the very real material advances of Greek culture, in particular in medicine and science, impressed many Muslims, and there was evidently much enthusiasm for what could be learned from the developed cultures that were rapidly incorporated into the Islamic empire. The caliph al-Ma'mun, who reigned from 813 to 833 CE, was a significant advocate of Greek thought, and founded an institution in Baghdad whose main purpose was translating Greek texts into Arabic. Often these translations came about through translation of a Greek text first into Syriac, and then into Arabic. Early translations included works of Aristotle, commentaries on him, summaries of many of Plato's dialogues, and later Greek elaborations of their work, and many works in the standard Neoplatonic curriculum.

This translation project was itself controversial, with some arguing that logic is only a tool employed by philosophy, and has no other implications. Other thinkers hostile to philosophy argued that logic is inevitably contaminated with it and so should not be used. Al-Ghazali (AH 450–505/1058–1111 CE), a steadfast critic of philosophy, displayed his independence by both accepting logic as a useful technique and rejecting the philosophy then current which based itself very much on that logic. He firmly took the view that logic is independent of philosophy and could, in fact, be derived from scripture itself rather than a Greek source. There was also a controversy about whether logic is independent of language, obviously a not unrelated issue. Right at the start of Islamic philosophy there was a celebrated debate in Baghdad between al-Sirafi and Ibn Bishr Matta on whether knowing the grammar of a particular language is more useful than knowing logic that takes itself to form the foundation of all language itself. By the nineteenth century Peripatetic philosophy had become part of the Arabic *Nahda* or Renaissance, often seen as a symbol of modernity and the growing identification with the non-Islamic world. After all, the philosophical thought of Islam found a significant role in Europe in the medieval period, and is often argued to have played an important part in the European explosion of science and intellectual thought in general. The works of Ibn Rushd (Averroes) and Ibn Sina (Avicenna) were in the curriculum of the Christian and Jewish worlds for many centuries, there were many translations of even the same text and they seem to have played a significant role in the development of philosophy and theology in Europe as a whole.

There are three main schools of thought in Islamic philosophy, and they all have theological consequences.

PERIPATETICISM (*FALSAFA*)

Peripateticism or *mashsha'i* philosophy in the Islamic world is very much based on Greek thought, and in particular Neoplatonism. This was really established at the time of al-Kindi (d. 252/866) and is often said to have come to an end with Ibn Rushd, who represented the height of Peripatetic thought in al-Andalus, the Iberian peninsula under Muslim rule.

Al-Farabi (257–380/870–950), commonly referred to as the second teacher (after the first in significance, Aristotle, or sometimes Ibn Sina), played a defining role in establishing Peripatetic philosophy in the Islamic intellectual curriculum. He identified philosophy with the deep grammar of language, and as decisive in dealing with intellectual issues as compared with the other Islamic sciences. This led to two significant problems. It downplayed the role of the religious scholars in the competition for who had the most powerful conceptual equipment, always a potent issue in religious thought. The other was that philosophy threw up conclusions that are apparently in opposition to accepted understandings of Islam within the community of believers. We shall see how al-Ghazali came to list precisely these conclusions and challenge the role of philosophy accordingly.

Ibn Rushd (520–95/1126–98) was unusual for his rejection of mysticism, which by contrast was something that was adopted by most of the other Peripatetic thinkers. He also rejected much Neoplatonism, which he clearly saw as incompatible with Aristotelian thought, and attempted to represent in his philosophy a more genuine form of Aristotelianism. He had few followers in the west of the Islamic world. The attack his style of philosophy had received at the hands of al-Ghazali had swung the intellectual debate away from philosophy in the style of the Peripatetics towards a more theologically centered form of work. It is difficult to know whether al-Ghazali's work was really so influential, because it did not have much effect on the survival of Peripateticism in the Persian world, where that style of Peripatetic thought continued to play an important part in the philosophical curriculum. This was despite the fact that al-Ghazali, like so many Islamic philosophers, was Persian and was held in high regard in general in philosophical circles in the Persian world.

Ibn Rushd responded to al-Ghazali's *Incoherence of the Philosophers* with his *Incoherence of the Incoherence*, but there can be no doubting that al-Ghazali managed to identify some very difficult issues for the Peripatetic tradition. There are three propositions on which the Peripatetics tend to agree, and they all constitute novel and inappropriate views from an Islamic point of view, according to al-Ghazali. They are all also invalid, he argues, even if one accepts their premises and their philosophical principles. We shall return to this point, but first let us look briefly at what he called the heretical and logically invalid views, and to which he took such exception.

The first is the eternity of the world, a thesis apparently found in Aristotle and generally shared by the philosophers. The world is eternal because time is a function of motion, in that if there were no motion, the concept of time would not make sense. Before the world existed there was no motion and so no time, and so the world could not have been created at a particular time. For a similar reason it could not be destroyed, since then motion would cease and so would time, and there cannot be a last time. The picture of creation was very much one of emanation, where a constant overflowing of grace from the divine produces lower forms of existence, the earth being the lowest.

The second thesis al-Ghazali highlights is that of the immortality of the soul, and only the soul, rather than the soul and body. The sort of immortality that the philosophers tended to defend was spiritual and far from the religious account in the Qur'an and the *hadith*. Philosophers had difficulty in seeing how the matter of bodies could be reconstituted after death, whereas the mind, with its links to abstract issues and higher realms of being, could be understood to have some form of immortality. This is because of the principle that when one knows something, the knower, the known object and the act of knowing are all the same, a view the Islamic philosophers attributed to Aristotle. So if one comes to know something that is permanent and unchanging, that part of one that does the knowing might also lay a claim to share in its immortality.

The third thesis that al-Ghazali found so threatening to Islam is the idea that God cannot know the ordinary events that take place in the world. This means, as he says, that God would not know that Muhammad prophesied, or whether one deserved to be rewarded or otherwise in the next world. The thesis also goes right against a constant theme of the Qur'an, that God knows everything that happens. For the philosophers God's knowledge of ordinary events is a problem because if he knew of changing things, then this means he changes, or at least his thoughts do, and this goes against the idea that he is unchanging. It also makes him too much like us, in having something like a sensory system. After all, how could he see what happens in the world if he has no eyes? Now, of course they suggest that a more sophisticated understanding of what it is for God to know needs to be adopted to understand the nature of divine knowledge, something that al-Ghazali seems to be denying. When the Qur'an talks of God knowing what happens in the world, the philosophers argued, the meaning is not that he knows in much the same way that we know, but rather that he knows in a special and unique sort of way. But al-Ghazali is surely quite correct in thinking that there has to be in any system of thought that calls itself Islamic some access of God to the world of generation and corruption. The attack on the Peripatetics' account of divine knowledge is perhaps his weakest criticism, though, since they of course accept that God knows what happens in the world, albeit via a more sophisticated route. Al-Ghazali also advocates a more sophisticated route to interpreting these three basic aspects of religion, and so can hardly complain that the philosophers suggest something similar. He also accepts that one should not always understand literally what one reads in the Qur'an, and the anthropomorphic language to be found there should not be taken to suggest that God is really like us. What is really at issue is two distinct approaches to understanding how to make sense of the Qur'an, and what implications those different approaches possess.

One of al-Ghazali's main targets is Ibn Sina (370–428/980–1037), who formulated the main features of philosophy in the Islamic world during the early centuries of the discipline. He presented the Neoplatonic line, albeit with many variations, and there are features of Neoplatonism that fit in very easily with Islam. The emphasis on the One, for example, links up nicely with the monotheism of Islam. Islam emphasizes throughout the significance of belief in one deity, someone who must not be linked with partners, a being who is the One from which everything else comes. For the Neoplatonists the chief problem is explaining how there came to be many things in the world, given that only One thing exists originally entirely by itself. They provide a theory in accordance with which it thinks about itself, since there is nothing else worth thinking about as far as it is concerned (anything else being less perfect), and it is this that gets us to the existence, eventually, of many other things. What keeps the universe in existence is the constant thought that emanates from the One and has the various effects lower down the ontological scale that eventuate in our world and in us. It is not difficult to see how the One could be linked with the God of Islam, nor how this sort of theory can be taken to express our links with what is higher than us in a perfectly acceptable way from a religious point of view. God is connected with everything that exists through producing thought that subsequently produces everything else. So he is connected to the world, but in a way that does not interfere with his perfect unity and independence of that world. Variations of this Neoplatonic model were employed by Islamic thinkers for a long time by those working within all traditions of philosophy, and retained their role, as we shall see, in *ishraqi* and Sufi thought right up to now, at least to a degree. *Ishraqi* thought is based on the concept of light and uses this as the leading idea on which to base its metaphysics, while Sufism is Islamic mysticism. They both see themselves as transcending Peripatetic thought. The notion of divine grace emanating through the levels of being is rich in its implications for explaining the relationship between a transcendent deity who nonetheless is seen as involved in our level of existence in some way, while also beyond that existence and entirely independent of our world.

MYSTICISM

Mysticism or Sufism in Islamic philosophy is employed as a philosophical technique very generally. Some thinkers such as Ibn Sab'in (614–69/1217–70) even went to the lengths of arguing that philosophy that was analytical could not be of value since reality is basically one, and dividing it up to examine it bit by bit is to misunderstand it profoundly. (Of course, this itself is an analytical argument.) The mystical thinker Ibn al-'Arabi (560–638/1165–1240) pursued this line and represented himself as burying the old Peripatetic form of thought when he carried the bones of Ibn Rushd back to al-Andalus for burial on the back of a donkey. But most philosophers combined mysticism with Peripatetic philosophy, arguing that these are just two different philosophical methodologies, and mysticism goes deeper into the nature of reality.

The application of Sufism to philosophical issues can be seen today in the work of Seyyed Hossein Nasr. He argues that mysticism represents a constant thread in philosophy and religion and a way of thinking we need to recapture if we are going to be able to appreciate the world as a spiritual as well as material realm. The trouble with analytical thought, he argues, is that it denies the role of God in the world, and sees it primarily as a material realm to be understood by science. Nasr uses traditional ideas based on Sufism to discuss such issues as ecology, ethics, and the nature of philosophy itself.

Illuminationism

Illuminationist (ishraqi) thought comes from the term *ishraq*, which is linked with the idea of the East, and represents something of a combination of Peripatetic thought and mysticism. One of the limitations they thought existed in Aristotelian ways of doing philosophy is its tendency to break down concepts into simpler components as a way of understanding them better. The *ishraqi*s argued against the principle that reasoning starts with definition in terms of genus and differentia, a process of explaining something by reducing it to its smaller parts and so defining the concept at issue. Illuminationist thinkers such as al-Suhrawardi (549–87/1154–91) argue that this is to explain the unknown in terms of something even less known. That is, if one does not understand the concept itself, then there is no reason to think that one will understand its constituent parts any better, at least until they are in turn broken down into yet smaller parts and so on ad infinitum. They also seek to demote deductive knowledge, the sort of knowledge one gets from using the principles of syllogistic reasoning, with knowledge by presence, which is knowledge so immediate that it cannot be doubted. That is, the radiance in one's mind from the item of knowledge is so strong that one cannot doubt it. An example often given is of one's awareness of the self that underlies all one's other experience. One cannot doubt that it is there since it makes such a strong claim on one's attention. Light comes into the picture since the idea is that such knowledge is lit up in a way that makes it impossible to doubt or ignore, and this is because light flows through the universe and brings to existence and awareness a range of levels of being. The differences between things can be described in degrees of luminosity or light, not in terms of their essences. God is often aligned with the Light of Lights, the light that is the source of all other light and that does not itself receive light, rather like Aristotle's unmoved mover, that other things move around but does not itself move. This form of philosophy was particularly popular in the Persian world, where it was combined in varying degrees with aspects of mysticism and even Peripateticism. Mulla Sadra (979–1050/1572–1640), whose thought has dominated the Persian philosophical curriculum since his time, used all three forms of philosophy in his writings, as became very much the style of much Persian philosophy.

What were the leading issues of Islamic philosophical theology? Here we will concentrate on the Peripatetic tradition, since it is clearest what its implications are for issues in religion, and it often established the basic presuppositions of Sufism and Illuminationist thought also.

ETHICS

There was an involved debate about the objectivity or subjectivity of ethical rules, in particular over the issue of whether an action is just if and only if God says that it is just, or whether it is just in itself, both issues that arise in similar forms in Islamic theology. The Mu'tazilites argued that God's actions are based on an objective notion of justice, and so God has to act to reward the innocent and punish the evil. Their opponents, the Ash'arites, argued that it is a mistake to insist that God has to act in any way whatsoever, and that whatever he does is right. It is right because he does it, not because he follows some objective rules of morality. This point comes out in a very nice story by al-Juwayni (419–78/1028–85) which is often used to show the shallowness of the Mu'tazilite theory. This involves three people who die. One is evil and goes to hell, one would have become evil, so God kills him as a child and he goes to the *barzakh*, the realm in between heaven and hell, so avoiding hell, while another who has lived well goes to heaven. The child complains that he missed the opportunity of going to heaven by dying early, although God informs him that had he lived he would have been evil and gone to hell. The sinner in hell complains that God should have killed him while a child so that at least he would have avoided hell and earned the *barzakh*. This example is often taken to show that the idea that there is only one possible idea of justice, that expounded by the Mu'tazilites, and that it represents the general principle on which God has to operate, is vacuous. God could decide to intervene directly in our lives to prevent us from developing in the ways in which we otherwise would do, but he also might not. That is true of us also; we can often intervene to help or hinder others, and we sometimes do and sometimes do not. There are reasons for what we do, but those reasons do not have to be seen as determining the action.

Politics

How to reconcile the social virtues that arise through living in a community and the intellectual virtues that tend to involve a more solitary lifestyle was a deeply felt issue, since so many philosophers had difficulties in being accepted by their local communities, especially by the political authorities. Their means of expressing themselves often set them against the ordinary believer. Why should the philosophical thinker who can grasp the truth primarily through the use of reason be part of the social and religious activities of the community? They often argued that philosophy represents the truth in a pure form, whereas religion is a working of that truth in a way that makes it digestible and comprehensible to the community in general. The implication might be that the philosophers really regarded religion as significant only for the masses and not for the intellectual elite, and so were not sincere in their apparent adherence to religion. During a period when religious and social identity were so closely connected, this gave rise to questions about the real religious beliefs of the philosophers, and their sincerity was often questioned. Although the philosophers were undoubtedly keen for prudential reasons to link up with the practices of the community, this is clearly a different form of attachment than was normal, and gave rise sometimes to suspicion concerning their real beliefs.

Political philosophy looked to Greek thinkers for ways of discussing the nature of the state, and often combined Aristotelian and Platonic political ideas with notions from the Qur'an and other Islamic texts. This was not difficult since it enabled them to argue that the state ought to be concerned with both the material and the spiritual welfare of its inhabitants. The philosopher would be the best ruler because he could understand dispassionately what is in the general interest, and ensure that religion is used to teach the community in general how to behave so that its welfare is enhanced. This sort of elitism was widely shared by a range of philosophies. Even Sufi and Illuminationist thinkers were largely of the opinion that only a limited group of people could understand precisely how the state ought to operate, and that traditional religion was an important source of information for the people as a whole.

The Soul

The nature of the soul, the thinking part of human beings, was a particularly important issue from a religious point of view. Many Peripatetic thinkers followed Aristotle in regarding the soul as the form of a person, as the way in which we are organized and not something distinct that is part of us. This implies that once the body or matter dies, the soul or form of the matter no longer exists since it then has nothing to inform. Yet Islam has a strong notion of an afterlife, graphically described in the Qur'an and the traditional sayings as a physical afterlife, and the soul and body would in some sense be regarded as eternal in that afterlife. It might be suggested that the Qur'anic view is largely allegorical, so that our actions in this life have consequences that extend further than this life, and a good way of communicating this to people who think that matter is important is through talking about having an afterlife in the sense of eternal souls. Other thinkers tended to use a Platonic account of the soul as something eternal and immaterial, and this also seems to contradict the Qur'anic account of the afterlife as a physical sort of place, as heaven or hell or what lies in between. Many of the Peripatetics (*falasifa*) argue that the religious language is physical because for most people that is what is important in their lives. It is a way of explaining to everyone why it is important for us to behave well, whereas a more spiritual grasp of the links between this world and the next one is achievable only by a few intellectuals or spiritually advanced individuals, and should not be widely broadcast.

LOGIC

Logic became a particularly lively topic of debate between those who saw it as just a tool to be used, and others who regarded it as bringing an ideology with it. For the former, even poetry was taken to have some sort of a logical structure, since poetry is writing that is expected to have a conclusion, perhaps the eliciting of an emotion, and it sets out to achieve this conclusion by a careful and logical organization of language. In fact, each type of writing has a logical structure that describes how it is supposed to operate, and what the appropriate rules are. These rules will differ for each area. The logic of theology is dialectical, for example, and takes a particular proposition as true, because it occurs in a text that is accepted as true, and works out what the logical implications of that text are. But since the text could be wrong, it is only accepted within a particular context; the status of the conclusion that one derives is always a bit dubious. Law and many of the other Islamic sciences are dialectical in this sense, and philosophers often have an account of knowledge that does not include those sciences as representing the very highest type of knowledge. The main difference between philosophers and ordinary people is that philosophers are capable of understanding the structure of these arguments better than everyone else. Ordinary believers tend to be very influenced by imagination and their senses; they are emotional and reliant on tradition, so they are not really able to understand arguments that come from those who are able to see behind ordinary experience to what exists at a deeper level, analytically or spiritually, or indeed both. The philosophers are unique in having access to what might be called the gold standard of argument, the demonstrative syllogism, where one proceeds logically from definitions to entirely certain conclusions. The rest of the community, including the religious scholars, only have a vague grasp of how reasoning really operates.

THE DOUBLE TRUTH ISSUE

One of the shocking implications that was derived from Ibn Rushd in Christian Europe was the idea that religion and reason are entirely separate areas of thought. A proposition may be true in one and false in another, a view often attributed to Ibn Rushd. Although he certainly did not argue in this way, he did suggest that there are different routes to the truth, to the same truth, and these routes may be quite distinct from each other. This is an important topic for the *falasifa* as a whole, since for them many issues and ideas can be seen from a variety of perspectives, each of which represents where the individual is coming from, each of which links up with the truth, and all of which are different. For example, al-Farabi points out that the religious understanding of the prophet is that he is someone of excellent moral character chosen by God to transmit a message. From the philosophical point of view he is someone of equally sound moral character whose intellect is in line with the active intellect and so knows how to persuade an audience of a particular point of view. By the active intellect is meant the highest level of conceptual thought that is accessible by human beings. The philosopher and the believer both listen to the same message, that provided by the prophet, and analyze what they hear differently, but both are right. The philosopher understands the rational basis of the prophetic message, while the ordinary believer is impressed with its emotional power. Does this mean that the former has a better grasp of the meaning of the message than the latter?

It would be wrong to see the philosopher's view as primarily intellectual and abstract and the other as merely 'user-friendly', since the sort of language that surrounds religious ideas such as prophecy is hardly simple and perspicuous. Often theology is more complex than philosophy, and the views of the ordinary believer more complicated than those of the thinker who can organize his thought into clear and distinct categories, or thinks he can. This was very much the point of the *falasifa*, the Islamic philosophers in the Peripatetic tradition, that each way of talking was valid, although they surely also thought that the philosophical account was more accurate than many of the alternatives. What is worth noting here is that the idea of there being different routes to the truth takes seriously the principle that the way we frame our beliefs fits in with who we are and what we think we know, and so for different people different ways of framing those beliefs are appropriate.

Some thinkers who could not express their thought in the politically correct way paid the ultimate price, and the example of Socrates and his fate at the hands of the Athenians had more than a historical resonance for many in the Islamic world. Al-Farabi comments that Socrates did not have significantly different views from those of Aristotle, but Socrates was executed while Aristotle remained in political favor throughout his life. The mistake that Socrates made was to express himself clearly, in ways that anyone could understand, and that led to people thinking that he was being subversive. Aristotle prudently expressed his ideas in difficult and complex language, so only those capable of really understanding his presentation could come near to grasping his views.

QUR'ANIC LOGIC

It is difficult to say when philosophical and theological speculation started in Islam. From a very early stage there are reports of the Prophet, and those close to him, being questioned on issues of interpretation, and these reports have been codified as the *hadith* or traditions. The theoretical level of these remarks is not high, although they are of great interest, and very helpful in fixing how to carry out actions in a way that fits in with Islam. They often relate to the practice or *sunna* of the Prophet, and his actions are often taken to be exemplars for Muslims, since although he was undoubtedly a human being, as the final prophet he is as close to perfection as a human being can be and well worth copying.

But it is the Qur'an itself that is generally taken to be the main guide for both behavior and speculation and the Qur'an frequently describes itself as clear (16. 103) and also as wonderfully or miraculously constructed. Indeed, the miraculous nature of the text is often cited as a proof of Islam itself, in that a human being could not have produced anything like it, and so it must have originated with God. This claim is made quite often in the Book itself, and has been frequently reproduced afterwards, and it is an interesting and unusual claim for a religion to make about its central text. Islam challenges those of other faiths and of none to show how the Book could have come about except directly from God.

The other claims made in the Book describe our relationship with God, what God has done for us, what he expects in return, how the world started and how it will end, and the nature of various beings such as angels, jinn, human beings, and other natural creatures. These claims raise theoretical difficulties once we wonder how to reconcile them with aspects of theory coming from elsewhere, such as Greek philosophy, and we have looked already at some of these debates. It is worth pointing out that in the Qur'an itself there is a heavy emphasis on the significance of knowledge and a constant demand that the hearer and reader consider and ponder over what he or she finds in the Book. Islam makes a range of theoretical claims backed up by comments made in the Book and elsewhere, although whether the comments are supposed to prove demonstratively that those claims are true is another matter. Like all major religious books, the Qur'an is not primarily a theoretical work, although it does contain ideas and arguments that are capable of and have undergone theoretical elaboration.

Some of these Qur'anic ideas very quickly became contentious. The first concerns the nature of the succession to the Prophet as head of the community. The debate over succession led to the split that has persisted ever since between the Shi'a (*shi'at 'Ali*, party of 'Ali), who thought that the leadership should be restricted to the family of the Prophet, and the Sunnis, who argue that a much wider category of candidacy for leadership could be considered. Like a lot of theoretical arguments, this has considerable practical ramifications, and determines who the political authority should be and how this sort of issue should be determined. The Shi'ites have continued to look to leadership from those closely linked with the descendants of the Prophet, and the succession of imams or spiritual leaders who are linked with 'Ali. The majority Sunnis on the contrary regard as the appropriate authorities those selected in some other way, by a consensus of those qualified to judge, perhaps, or through some political process, depending very much on the particular school of Sunni thought that is accepted.

Another theoretical debate that swiftly arose was over the nature of determinism and freedom. Are human beings free to act, or are their actions determined by God? Both sorts of language are found in the Qur'an and the remarks of the Prophet and his Companions, but the final position is a matter of debate. This is a good example of a theological debate that quickly became philosophical, in that it started by looking at scriptural passages and trying to understand their implications, and ended up by exploring the rational foundations of each position. The determinist can find plenty of Qur'anic passages that suggest that God makes everything happen, even the fact whether we believe in him or otherwise. This implies, though, that one cannot be held responsible for one's actions, yet the Qur'an goes into long and highly descriptive detail of the day of judgment and the afterlife of reward and punishment. How can this life be a realm of testing if God determines everything that happens? Yet the idea that people have free will has difficult implications also, in that it could be taken to suggest that they are in charge of things rather than God.

The nature of belief itself became a significant topic. What makes a person a Muslim? What does he or she have to believe? Do they have to do anything to provide evidence of that belief? Can a sinner be a Muslim, or is such a person ruled out by virtue of behavior? The early centuries of Islam saw the introduction of creeds, statements that listed the basic beliefs that a Muslim has to accept if he or she can really claim to be a Muslim. As one might expect, these differ from each other and represent the conflict of ideas that took place within the Islamic community over which theological and political group best represented genuine Islam.

The role of theory in Islam has always been controversial, as in other religions. There are on the one hand theoretical techniques for resolving issues that come from within the Islamic tradition itself and make up the Islamic sciences. These include Arabic grammar, particularly important since the revelation was provided in Arabic. If people are to understand the revelation, they have to know the language and its grammar. Difficulties of interpretation can be resolved, sometimes through an investigation of language itself. Then there is the analysis of the order in which revelations appeared, since some later ones might abrogate the earlier, or be linked with the occasion in which they were given for a more comprehensive understanding of them. Some are Meccan, some Medinan, some have passages from both places, and many are related to particular historical events, and it is held to be important to know the history to fix the precise meaning of many of the verses. The *hadith* or Traditions are helpful in providing even more history on what important people at the time had to say on difficult issues.

TRADITION (*TAQLID*) AND ARGUMENT

There has been a long discussion in Islam about the significance of following tradition or *taqlid*. Clearly any religion requires interpretation, and there are some authorities that are likely to be more reliable. They are the people to follow when it comes to seeking an understanding of what the religion means and expects one to do. In any area, it was argued, one should seek to follow the expert, since if one knew what to do one would not need to ask an expert in the first place. But who is an expert? The Qur'an is full of injunctions to its hearers and readers to consider, think, reason, and that is presumably because Muslims are supposed to use their rational faculties to work out what the text means and indeed what everything means, insofar as they can. There are limits to what one can work out oneself, however, and it is here that there is a need for guidance.

Taqlid has an important role in that there are people who can help one understand a text and its contemporary relevance if one is unable to grasp this owing to a lack of knowledge of the whole book and its context and other appropriate sources of information. It is rational to follow authorities under such circumstances, and to do so is not blind obedience; it is submitting oneself to the authority of another when one has good grounds for doing so. Those good grounds are established rationally.

The Qur'an is full of arguments, and many of them have as their basis the idea that God, the ultimate creator, knows the nature of everything in the world, and especially his human creatures, and that he has brought about a type of creation that is specifically designed to be in the interests of his creatures. As one might expect, the creator then establishes rules that he expects people to obey if they are to get the best out of this world and the next. The text constantly provides reasons for believing what it asserts. God wishes to communicate with his creation, he does this through messengers, and yet his creatures often reject what he has to say. This rejection is not because of any doctrine of original sin, but because God has made everyone differently and so is not surprised at the differences in their responses to him. He could have made everyone the same, and thus avoided this sort of diversity of opinion (2. 118; 10. 19; 16. 93) but chose not to do so. The differences between people are important learning opportunities, since in comparing ideas we learn a great deal about our own beliefs.

Does the text really argue for the existence of God? Not very seriously. God's existence is taken to be an obvious and natural fact, based on what we observe around us all the time, and nature, like the verses of the Qur'an, is full of 'signs (*ayat*) for people who understand' (2. 164). There is quite a bit of argument about why we should believe in the existence of one God as opposed to many gods, and why associating partners with God (*shirk*) is to be rejected totally. There are also many arguments in the Book for resurrection, a basic doctrine given the importance of rejecting materialism and the belief that our deaths are followed by nothing more than the collapse and decay of our bodies. These are based on the idea that God can do anything, and on our experience of nature in which life often follows death. The materialist who believes that all there is is this life has no reason to believe in God and his message. There are also many arguments for the prophethood of the Prophet himself, and much of this clearly replicates the sort of to and fro of debate that took place in Mecca and Medinah when Islam was becoming established in the early years. The issue of who should succeed the Prophet, the source of the Sunni/Shi'i split, is of course discussed widely.

The range of arguments to be found in theology vary in form. The Peripatetic philosophers, the *falasifa* such as Ibn Rushd and his predecessors such as al-Farabi, used the organon or system of Aristotle as an example of how such arguments may vary in form and in particular in the general nature of their conclusions. It was widely accepted that there is a hierarchy of argumentative strength, with demonstration at the top of the scale, where one operates with true premises and uses them to arrive at validly derived and entirely general conclusions. Then comes dialectic, where the premises one uses are those supplied by the side with which one is debating, and so one has no independent reason to think they are true. After this a number of other argument types follow, rhetoric and poetry, for example, where the point is to change people's minds by the use of imagination and appeals to the emotions, and where the validity of the conclusion may be quite limited, restricted to a particular audience within a specific context. That does not mean that there is anything wrong with the argument. It is a perfectly acceptable argument of its type, but not up to the rigor of demonstration or even dialectic. Philosophy was identified with demonstration, while theology was more closely linked with dialectic, since it is based on a book that is accepted by a particular community but not necessarily universally. Religion for ordinary people follows weaker rules of reasoning such as rhetoric and poetry, since it is designed to move people emotionally, and does not rely on advanced reasoning skills to be understood. The point of religion is to communicate with everyone and so although the message should be based on sound reasoning, the particular form that the general language takes will be able to stimulate the imagination.

REASONS AND CAUSES

The fact that reasons may explain but not determine subsequent actions was not accepted by al-Ghazali, advocate though he was of the use of logic in theology and of its incorporation as a natural part of Islamic thought. Al-Ghazali criticized thinkers such as Miskawayh (320–421/932–1030) for believing that God had reasons to establish certain rituals and rules that fit in with human nature. Miskawayh suggests that many of the rites of Islam have the purpose of strengthening the links between believers, so that religion uses social norms to encourage and strengthen religious observance. Al-Ghazali argues on the contrary that God institutes rules just because that is what he wants to do; there is no necessity for him to align himself with our social instincts, nor even to employ them. Where al-Ghazali goes awry here is thinking that because God may have had reasons for what he did, those reasons would make his actions governed by them. He would be forced by the reasons to act in a particular way. The Mu'tazilites did in fact argue in this way that God has to follow certain principles of morality in his behavior; he has to have justice in mind when he acts. Al-Ghazali rejected that theory, arguing plausibly that it is an error to think that God must have a particular purpose in mind that we can understand when he does something. But he went too far in suggesting that God could have nothing in mind when he does something. For al-Ghazali, all God wants to do in telling us how to act is demonstrate his power and the necessity on our part to obey him. However, having reasons for action only constrains us if they inevitably result in particular actions, but God cannot be forced to act in this way, and nor can we.

One might think that the case for God would be different here than it is for us. We are finite and changing creatures with a partial view of the world and ourselves. None of this is true of God; he is perfect, infinite and understands everything. Yet for him also reasons do not determine. There are many things he can do and might wish to do given the same set of facts. Rationality and beneficence do not inevitably lead to particular actions. When the angels are told by God to bow down to Adam (2. 30–4) and they complain saying that Adam and his descendants will wreck the earth if they get power over it, the angels have a point. But God replies that he understands this and will send human beings a guide. The notion of a guide is important here. A guide guides, he indicates the right direction and the appropriate ways to determine the right direction. The guide does not force people to obey him nor even to accept him. The guide brings a message, but messages get distorted and twisted, or are just quite honestly misunderstood. God provides general advice and instructions to his creation, but there is a great deal of freedom for people to make their own decisions and take their own risks. This explains the significant role of theology and philosophy. The reasons they accept as significant in controlling their actions do not point to a set of clear and distinct propositions, since if they did there would be no variety of understandings of religion, or even of Islam. Since the Qur'an tells us sometimes to respect diversity in humanity and forbids us from compelling religious allegiance, the idea that reasons are not followed inevitably by particular actions and beliefs is presumably well taken.

Muslims, like those in other religious traditions, are interested in finding rational explanations for what they find in their faith. We often overemphasize the role of faith in religion, but although it is significant, many other issues remain. Faith cannot tell us how to resolve apparent difficulties in reconciling religion with what we know or suspect to be true in other parts of our life. Sometimes we believe something to be true on religious grounds but have good scientific or even personal reasons nonetheless to doubt its truth. This sort of issue needs to be resolved, and the only means at our disposal is the use of rationality and the principles of theology and philosophy as applied to religion and what is related to it.

That does not mean that how one resolves these issues is obvious, since it will depend on the particular theory that is accepted. Some theologians think that one should base any difficulties in interpreting religious texts on other religious texts, in particular by interpreting the Qur'an in terms of the Qur'an. Others argue that one ought to give a great deal of respect to the traditional sayings of the Prophet and his Companions, as they have come down to us. Among these sayings, the *hadith*, one has to distinguish between those that are more reliable and those that are less so, itself very much a rational investigation. Regarding the Qur'an, one also has to consider which verses might be thought to abrogate which others, and for that one has to have some theory of which verses are later than others. One requires, in fact, a historical grasp of the events associated with the revealing of the various Qur'anic passages, so that one can understand better the context in which they were given. One also needs an opinion on the role that independent judgment might be called upon to play, together with who in the Islamic community one recognizes as an authority, and how far that authority extends. This merely skims the surface of some of the hermeneutic issues that arise in trying to understand Scripture, and as we have seen there is also a wide range of more general philosophical techniques available to us.

A way in which the different theorists in Islam are often characterized is in terms of their being either rationalists or traditionalists or something else, but in fact it goes with the commitment to theory that one uses reason to try to make clear how one is resolving problems and why that way of doing it is the right way. Islamic philosophical theology has always in the past been a lively arena for rational discussion and controversy, and there is every sign that it will continue to have the same sort of character in the future.

BIBLIOGRAPHY

(A source of general bibliographical information can be found in 'A Guide to Bibliographical Resources' in S. Nasr and O. Leaman (eds.), *History of Islamic Philosophy* (London: Routledge, 1996), 1173–9), which is followed by a list of general introductions to Islamic philosophy.)

ABDUL-RAOF, H., 'The Linguistic Architecture of the Qur'an', *Journal of Qur'anic Studies*, 2/2 (2000), 37–51.

AL-BAQILLANI, ABU BAKR MUHAMMAD, *I'jaz al-Qur'an*. Beirut: Dar Ihya' al-'Ulum, 1994.

CRAGG, K., *The Event of the Qur'an*, 2nd edn. Oxford: Oneworld, 1994.

FAKHRY, M., *A Short Introduction to Islamic Philosophy, Theology, and Mysticism*. Oxford: OneWorld, 1997.

GWYNNE, R., *Logic, Rhetoric, and Legal Reasoning in the Qur'an: God's Arguments*. New York: RoutledgeCurzon, 2004.

HAHN, L., et al. (eds.), *The Philosophy of Seyyed Hossein Nasr*. Chicago: Open Court, 2001.

HA'IRI YAZDI, M., *The Principles of Epistemology in Islamic Philosophy: Knowledge by Presence*. Albany: State University of New York Press, 1992.

HOURANI, G., *Reason and Tradition in Islamic Ethics*. Cambridge: Cambridge University Press, 1985.

IZUTSU, T., *God and Man in the Koran: Semantics of the Koranic Weltanschauung*. Tokyo: Keio Institute of Cultural and Linguistic Studies, 1964.

—— *Ethico-Religious Concepts in the Qur'an*. Montreal: McGill University Press, 1966.

JOMIER, J., *The Great Themes of the Qur'an*. London: SCM, 1997.

AL-JUWAYNI, *Kitab al-irshad ila qawati al-adilla fi usul al-i'tiqad*, ed. M. Musa and A. 'Abd al-Hamid. Cairo, 1950.

LEAMAN, O., *Averroes and his Philosophy*. Oxford: Oxford University Press, 1990.

—— *Brief Introduction to Islamic Philosophy*. Oxford: Polity, 1999.

—— *Introduction to Classical Islamic Philosophy*. Cambridge: Cambridge University Press, 2001.

—— *Islamic Aesthetics: An Introduction*. Edinburgh: Edinburgh University Press, 2004.

—— (ed.), *Biographical Dictionary of Islamic Philosophers*. London: Continuum, 2006.

—— (ed.), *The Qur'an: An Encyclopedia*. London: Routledge, 2006.

MUTAHHARI, M., *Fundamentals of Islamic Thought*, trans. R. Campbell. Berkeley, Calif.: Mizan, 1985.

NASR, S., and LEAMAN, O. (eds.), *History of Islamic Philosophy*. London: Routledge, 1996.

PETERS, F. E. (ed.), *The Arabs and Arabia on the Eve of Islam*. Brookfield: Ashgate, 1999.

AL-QURTUBI, ABU 'ABD ALLAH MUHAMMAD, *al-Jami' li ahkam al-Qur'an*. 20 vols. Beirut: Dar al-Kitab al-'Arabi, 1997.

RAHMAN, F., *Major Themes of the Qur'an*. Chicago: Bibliotheca Islamica, 1980.

—— *Islam and Modernity: Transformation of an Intellectual Tradition*. Chicago: University of Chicago Press, 1982.

ROBINSON, N., *Discovering the Qur'an: A Contemporary Approach to a Veiled Text*. London: SCM, 1996.

AL-SUHRAWARDI, *The Philosophy of Illumination*, trans. John Walbridge and Hossein Ziai. Provo: Brigham Young University Press, 1999.

AL-ZAMAKHSHARI, ABU AL-QASIM, *al-Kashshaf*. 4 vols. Beirut: Dar al-Kutub al-'Ilmiyyah, 1995.

ZEBIRI, K., 'Towards a Rhetorical Criticism of the Qur'an', *Journal of Qur'anic Studies* 5 (2003), 95–120.

CHAPTER 26

CHINESE (CONFUCIAN) PHILOSOPHICAL THEOLOGY

JOHN H. BERTHRONG

PREAMBLE

The Voice of the Turtle

The sun's rays glint first on the mountains to the west, then, moments later, touch the thatched roofs of the temples and pit dwellings that follow the curve of the Huan. The river, still in shadow at the foot of the earthen cliff, winds to the southeast between clearings of sprouting millet, on its way to merge with the powerful He. The year is the eleventh of Wu Ding's reign, the season spring, the day xinwei, eighth of the week.

Filtering through the portal of the ancestral temple, the sunlight wakens the eyes of the monster mask, bulging with life on the garish bronze tripod. At the center of the temple stands the king, at the center of the four quarters, the center of the Shang world. Ripening millet glimpsed through the doorway shows his harvest rituals have found favor. Bronze cauldrons with their cooked meat offerings invite the presence of his ancestors, their bodies buried deep and safely across the river, but their spirits, some benevolent, some not, still reigning over the royal house and the king's person. One is angry, for the king's jaw ached all the night, is aching now, on the eve of his departure to follow Zhi Guo on campaign against the Pa-fang.

Five turtle shells lie on the rammed-earth altar. The plastrons have been polished like jade, but are scarred on their inner sides with rows of oval hollows, some already blacked by fire. Into one of the unburned hollows, on the right side of the shell, the diviner Que is thrusting a brand of flaming thorn. As he does so, he cries, 'The sick tooth is not due to Father Jia!' Fanned by an assistant to keep the glowing tip intensely hot, the stick flames against the surface of the shell. Smoke rises. The seconds slowly pass. The stench of scorched bone mingles with the aroma of millet wine scattered in libation. And then, with a sharp, clear *puk*like sound, the turtle, the most silent of creatures, speaks.   (Keightly 1983: 1)

Centuries later, Master Kong (Kongzi 孔子 551–479 BCE, or as he is known in the west, Confucius) is recorded to have observed in the *Lunyu* 論語, or the *Analects* as they are known in English, that

3. 13: Wang-sun Jia inquired of Confucius, quoting the saying
       'It is better to pay homage to the spirit of the stove
       Than to the spirits of the household shrine.'

'What does this mean?'
   The Master replied: 'It is not so. A person who offends against *tian* 天 has nowhere else to pray.'

7. 23: The Master said, '*Tian* 天 has given life and nourished excellence (*de* 德) in me—what can Huan Tui do to me!'

11. 12: Zilu asked how to serve the spirits [*gui* 鬼] and the gods [*shen* 神]. The Master replied, 'Not yet being able to serve other people, how would you be able to serve the spirits?' Zilu said, 'May I ask about death?' The Master replied, 'Not yet understanding life, how could you understand death?'   (Translations from Ames & Rosemont 1998: 85, 116, 144)

2. 4: The Master said, 'At fifteen I set my mind on learning; at thirty, I took my place in society; at forty, I became free of doubts; at fifty, I understood Heaven's Mandate; at sixty, my ear was attuned; at seventy, I could follow my heart's desires without overstepping the bounds of propriety'.   (Slingerland 2003: 9)

EISEGETICAL EXEGESIS

Do we really know what the fictional diviner Que thought when he was divining or who he was consulting when he made his charge to the spirits upon the command of King Wu Ding? If we follow Keightly's wonderful recreation of the ritual, the turtle, that most silent of creatures, finally does indeed speak. While we can never know if Keightly's imaginative reconstruction is anywhere near accurate, heated turtle plastrons do make this kind of *puk*-like sound. Who does the turtle speak for? Is it the high spirit of the ancestors, *shangdi* 上帝? Is it *tian* 天 supernal heaven? Or some other powerful spirit? What is the nature of Chinese religion in its formative phase?

Wilfred Cantwell Smith wrote with oracular insight when considering the specific case of Confucianism, 'For the moment, we may simply observe once again that the question, "Is Confucianism a religion" is one that the west has never been able to answer, and China never able to ask' (Smith 1991: 69). The question of the nature of Chinese religion in general and Confucianism in particular lingers whenever there is an ecumenical discussion of divine, supernal matters. All religious traditions are unique yet the Chinese case seems to occupy a different niche. It is obvious that the Shang kings (*c.*1750–1040 BCE) believed they could contact the spirits, divine beings who were the cause of good or woe in the Shang world.

Moving forward a millennium, the first two quotes from Master Kong (Confucius) are often cited in order to demonstrate that he shared a set of beliefs about and even veneration for a set of early Zhou dynasty (*c.*1040–249 BCE) religious ideals such as *tian* 天 supernal heaven and various minor and major spirits *gui* 鬼 and gods *shen* 神. With a typical Confucian flair Master Kong observes that if *tian* has given him a mission in life and helped to nourish his ethical virtue, what could such a mere odious ruffian as Huan Tui do to him? Master Kong was convinced that only a person who has offended *tian* had no one to pray to and no protection from the vicissitudes of an imperfect and dangerous world. Scholars see in such passages in the *Lunyu* connections to the archaic Shang and Zhou religious worldview reconstructed by Keightly.

The account we have of Master Kong's religious sensibility is tantalizingly vague and ambiguous about the precise nature of his religious beliefs and practices. He cherished and promoted the inherited rituals of the Zhou and yet prefers not to speak about prodigies or strange events. He is most famous as the 'first teacher' and reveres *tian* as intimately connected to the virtue of his own life and conduct. As his students lamented, we simply have not heard about the religious vision of the master in any fulsome fashion save for a clear piety towards *tian* and a commitment to the moral life. We also know that he makes only one claim to fame when pressed by his students to tell them in what he excels: others are wiser, braver, faster, stronger, more intelligent, but no one loves learning *xue* 學 more than Master Kong. This love of learning is one key element of Confucian 'theology' or reflection on the supernal path *tiandao* 天道. Any great Jewish rabbi would understand the religious aura of pious and persevering learning. To revere *tian* is to set one's mind-heart *xin* 心 on learning.

Contrariwise, the third quote, *Lunyu* 11. 12, is cited to prove that Master Kong did not believe in the spirits and gods. However, such an inference is not clear in the text. The most that can be drawn suggestively from the quote is an agnostic view of how the spirits and gods interact with human beings. Remembering that *tian* not only gives us life but also nourishes *de* 德 virtue, I interpret the passage to mean that Kongzi is reminding his audience that whatever role the spirits and gods play in the world, the proper charge or supernal mandate *tianming* 天命 for a person was to cultivate humane virtue *ren* 仁. If a person persistently cultivates virtue, then what is there to worry about in relationship to the spirits, gods and even *tian*? As Herbert Fingarette (1972) so elegantly observed, for Master Kong the secular is the sacred and the axiology of ethical self-cultivation trumps any kind of *bhakti* devotion to the spirits, gods, and *tian*. This does not mean that we lack a natural or cultivated piety towards the spirits and gods, but that our primary task is to learn how to serve our fellow human beings in the way we would ourselves like to be treated in order to create a flourishing, harmonious, and shining human society.

The famous outline of a cultivated life given in *Lunyu* 2. 4 is paradigmatic for what a person must do in order to create and live within a flourishing human society. The path of self-cultivation begins with *xue* 學 and at the end of life embodies the ability to follow the desires of the mind-heart and never to overstep the bounds of propriety. The attuned mind-heart also hears something else, what in the western tradition we would call the music of the spheres. The cultivated person has found how to walk the supernal path of being fully human by means of personal self-cultivation of virtue and through the ordering of society and an appreciation of the supernal heaven's mandate *tianming* 天命, a developed attention to the mind-heart's desires and a mature sense of propriety. We will argue that this pithy statement encapsulates the salient features of being religious following the Confucian Way—from learning, cultivating a moral path, conforming to supernal heaven's mandate, and the consummate balance of desire, propriety, and the goal of humane harmony in society.

What is truly fascinating about the Confucian tradition is that, unlike so many other Eurasian religions, later Confucians did not make the obvious—at least obvious to the Children of Abraham—extension from the veneration of *tian* to veneration of an omnipotent and omniscient God. Although known and remembered in the classics, the gambit of worshiping or consulting a monotheistic high god embraced so strongly by the western Asian religions is declined by the Confucians, even though being religious has been and remains integral to the Confucian Way. The Confucians may not have a 'theology' if by this we demanded an affirmation of a monotheistic creator, sustainer, and redeemer of the cosmos. Confucians do have what modern Chinese scholars have called a 'Daology', a way to follow the Dao with reverence, creativity, and propriety by means of elaborating the notion of *tiandao* 天道 the supernal path or way of heaven.

The early classical canon has been called the Confucian classics but at the time these early texts were composed they were simply the cultural records in many genres for the emerging intellectual elite of the Shang, Zhou, and Han dynasties (*c.*1750 BCE to 220 CE). Other considerations beyond a focused reverence for *tian* as a high god won out in the development of the Confucian Way *rudao* 儒道 when compared to west and south Asian religions and even extensive segments of the Daoist world as well. While there is a wonderful exfoliation of religious themes and traits over the next three millennia of Confucian history, what is striking is just how different Confucianism is from Daoism, Buddhism, and the other religious theologies and cumulative traditions of Eurasia. In his epic history of Chinese science Joseph Needham (1954–) once observed that in Confucianism we have a creation without a creator and we could add to this, a religion without supernatural theism. As we shall see, the later Neo-Confucians (Song and post-Song developments, i.e. 960 to the twentieth century) and the modern New Confucians Mou Zongsan (1909–95) and Tu Wei-ming (1940–) are explicit in defending the religious dimension of the Confucian Way.

CONFUCIAN RELIGIOSITY

The literature about the complexity of discerning what 'religion' means in the Chinese setting is vast and growing daily as more and more students of Chinese thought both in China and the Chinese Diaspora ponder this question they are often asked by western scholars of religion.[1]

What could 'theology' mean for Confucians? Theology is certainly a Christian enterprise, though many other cultural traditions have clear analogs to such Christian endeavors; for instance Indian sages such as Shankara and Ramanuja wrote treatises that any western theologian who learned something of the Hindu world-view would instantly recognize as theological reflection. We cannot remain confined by the comfortable western religious lexicography when we review the Confucian canon[2] and how it was interpreted and practiced for thousands of years as a form of being 'religious'. While it is true that we can discover pervasive and persuasive analogs to western norms and forms of theological discourse in Daoism and Buddhism, the truly hard nut to crack remains the Confucian tradition. That is why it is so important to ponder the nature of Confucian religious discourse.

Whitehead (1996: 67–8) wrote, 'To-day there is but one religious dogma in debate: What do you mean by God? And in this respect to-day is like all its yesterdays.' Whitehead informs us that when we talk about religion, we are talking about our notion of God or what Tillich labeled our object of ultimate concern or what people hold to be the most supernal, divine reality. By subtly changing the focus from God to an exploration of the Chinese supernal matrix we can then readily include, as worthy markers of supernal reality, such concepts as *tian*, the Dao, or the *taiji* 太極 the Supreme Polarity [Ultimate] beloved of Song (960–1279) Confucian masters.

We will now focus our attention on the Confucian tradition as the test case for explicating theology as the science or study of supernal things or events in the Chinese cultural context. Confucianism is a western term invented by the early Jesuit scholar-missionaries in order to catalog the various forms of religious theory and practice they found in late Ming China (1560–1644). Of course, earlier Chinese intellectual historians asked the same sorts of questions about how to classify the various teachings of the golden age of Chinese thought in the Zhou dynasty. Scholars such as Sima Tan and Ban Gu created bibliographical categories of intellectual teachings and lineages, for instance, such as the designations of *ru* 儒 and *dao* 道 designating what we now call Confucian and Daoist discourse. However, *ru* originally probably meant a scholar and *dao* simply someone who followed the *dao* exemplified in texts such as the *Daodejing* or the *Zhuangzi*. In contemporary Chinese we find terms such as *rudao* 儒道, *rujao* 儒教, *rujia* 儒家, and *ruxue* 儒學, all of which can be roughly translated as the Confucian Way, Confucian teaching, the Confucian school, and Confucian learning. When modern Chinese scholars discuss the cumulative Confucian tradition they use *rujia* Confucian school for the totality of the tradition and *rujiao* if they want to specify or recognize the religious dimensions of the tradition. The most common sophisticated response about the religious traits of the tradition now is to recognize that while Confucianism is not a religion per se if the model of religion is the template of the monotheisms of Judaism, Christianity, or Islam, nonetheless there are certainly religious elements or dimensions of the cumulative Confucian tradition that are religious. As Tu Wei-ming (1989) has argued, rather than trying to define Confucianism as a religion it is better to ask, what does being religious mean for a Confucian? 'Being religious, in the Confucian perspective, informed by sacred texts such as the *Zhongyong*, means being engaged in the process of learning to be fully human. We can define the Confucian way of being religious as *ultimate self-transformation as a communal act and as a faithful dialogical response to the transcendent*' (ibid. 94). Tu's statement is considered a classic modern definition of Confucian spirituality. The task is to travel from the 'puk' voice of the sacred turtle in the Shang to the affirmation of the Confucian way of being religious affirmed by a modern New Confucian scholar such as Tu Wei-ming.

THE CONFUCIAN WAY OF BEING RELIGIOUS

A fascinating historical question to ponder is, how did the classical Chinese *ru* become transformed from the Shang court diviners into the social system of modern New Confucians in China and the East Asian Diaspora? We must remember that Confucianism also played a vital role in the cultural, social, political, and religious life of Korea, Japan, and Vietnam as well as China. As a religious question, the

Confucian Way is a long and complicated journey of the human *xin* 心 (mind-heart) seeking to embody the supernal reality of the cosmos.

In order to simplify the task of discerning the *ru* way of being religious I am pausing at three critical locations in the history of the development of the Confucian Way. The first epoch, *Classical Confucianism*, is the foundation or classical period represented by Master Kong, Master Meng (Mencius), Master Xun 荀子, and the *Zhongyong* 中庸. These Confucian masters and texts are considered essential elements of the golden age of classical Chinese philosophy (*c.*551–221 BCE). The second era, *Neo-Confucianism*, is the great revival of Confucianism thought and praxis during and after the Song dynasty (960–). Song and post-Song thought is celebrated as the second golden age of Confucian religious speculation and is indebted to the interaction of generations of Confucian scholars with their learned Daoist and Buddhist cousins. It is impossible to think of Neo-Confucianism (Song and post-Song Confucian discourse) without the impact and influence of Daoism and Buddhism. Neo-Confucianism is a bridge between the classical and modern periods. The third temporal portal we will enter is the modern period (1911 to the present) dominated by the encounter with the west. In the world of contemporary Confucian thought the third epoch is distinguished from its classical and Neo-Confucian ancestors by being labeled *New Confucianism*—that is, a Confucianism revived, transformed, and renewed by its encounter with western culture, politics, religion, and philosophy. We will select the work of Mou Zongsan and Tu Wei-ming as paradigms for the contemporary Confucian art of being religious.

CLASSICAL CONFUCIANISM: MENGZI, XUNZI, AND THE *ZHONGYONG*

The second great classical Confucian master after Kongzi was Mengzi 孟子 (*c.*371–289 BCE). Although Master Meng protested that he disliked the philosophically contentious nature of his age, it was his duty to refute all the false schools and to place the true *ru* learning of self-cultivation, propriety, and ritual back in their proper place by following the insights found in Kongzi. Ideas that were merely hinted at by Master Kong are elaborated and expanded by Mengzi to give the first relatively comprehensive philosophical exposition of the Confucian Way.

Against adversaries as diverse as Mozi and his utilitarian rejection of Confucian ritual conduct, Yang Zhu and his sophistic defense of egoism, together with wandering Daoists who rejected any value whatsoever in the moral deportment of a Confucian worthy, Mengzi's defense of the Confucian Way highlighted a number of concepts that were to remain at the core of Confucian religious and philosophical discourse. Two critical concepts Mengzi defined and defended from a Confucian perspective were *xing* 性 as human nature, dispositions, or tendencies, and *xin* 心 as the human mind-heart. Mengzi argued against all-comers that the supernal *xing* was the matrix of the four seeds of the virtues of humanity, righteousness or justice, ritual propriety, and wisdom or discernment. Using botanical metaphors, Mengzi argued that if a person successfully cultivated these four cardinal virtues then there would be progress along the path of true virtue and a person could realize the authentic Confucian way.

However, the task of such cultivation had to take place somewhere, and the locus of the cultivation of the four seeds of virtue was in the mind-heart. One of the most fascinating things about Mengzi's vision is his various strategies for helping us to nurture the mind-heart, to reform or temper less than perfect desires and inclinations in order to embrace the cultivation of the four virtues as the proper path of becoming human. If Master Kong professed the necessity to follow the path of the Dao, his disciple Mengzi showed what innate seeds of morality human beings needed to embody in order to allow them to become virtuous and provided guidance by means of the careful praxis of self-cultivation contained in our *xing* human nature.

In a tantalizing passage, Master Meng, in responding to a question from a student about his own forms of excellence, is recorded to have made the following response. By naming the truly protean concept of *qi* 氣[3] as an object of ethical cultivation, he evokes an almost mystical sense of the power of Confucian self-cultivation of the mind-heart, itself constituted by the *qi* of the cosmos.

May I ask what your strong points are?

I have an insight into words. I am good at cultivating my 'flood-like *qi*' [*haoran chi qi* 浩 然 之 氣].

May I ask what this 'flood-like *qi*' is?

It is difficult to explain. This is a *qi* which is, in the highest degree, vast and unyielding. Nourish it with integrity and place no obstacle in its path and it will fill the space between Heaven and Earth. It is a *qi* which united rightness and the Way.   (Lau (trans.), *Mencius*, 1984: i. 57–8)

Master Meng makes two points. The first is that he has insight into words, and this means that he understood the role of philosophical disputation about the true nature of the Dao. But secondly, more than merely having insight into words, he had the ability to cultivate his flood-like *qi*. His disciple is as perplexed by what Mengzi means by this *qi* as we and countless Confucian scholars have been over the centuries. Although to proffer some 'obvious' exegesis is the height of folly, it does appear that if one can achieve this feat of the cultivation of the flood-like *qi* then the person will be in tune with heaven and earth in manifest *yi* 義 rightness or righteous justice within the matrix of the Dao. In short, such a person can achieve oneness with the very flow of the cosmos in the highest degree. This truly is a teaching about self-cultivation that becomes part of the Confucian religious quest. In fact, based on Mengzi's teachings, many of the great mystics of the Confucian tradition have counted themselves as followers of Master Meng in seeking to cultivate the flood-like *qi*.

The third of the great classical Confucians was Xunzi (*c*.310–238 BCE). Because Master Xun had the audacity to contradict Master Meng concerning *xing* 性 by declaring that human nature or dispositions were odious and perverse, he was banished from the inner circle of the 'orthodox' founders of the Confucian way. However, it is wise to remember that this banishment was only formalized in the Song dynasty; prior to the rise of Neo-Confucianism Master Xun was considered one of the greatest of the classical Confucians. Given the range of his works, from poetry, ritual theory, ethics, military theory, and epistemology, he was by far and away the most systematic and coherent of any of the early Confucian masters.

It was also Xunzi who resolutely rejected the supernatural theological path. What was at least ambiguous in the religious speculation of Kongzi and Mengzi takes a decidedly naturalist turn in Xunzi. We are no longer in the realm of spirits and gods; we are in the world of human contrivance. Even the human good comes, according to Master Xun, not from innate seeds of virtue implanted in our mind-hearts by heaven but rather is the outcome of conscious human effort or *wei* 偽, contrived action as conformed and shaped by ritual action *li* 禮 and *yi* 義 justice/righteousness.

John Knoblock, the meticulous translator and commentator on Xunzi, translates the chapter *tianlun* 天論 as 'Discourse on Nature'. While Xunzi can use *tian* in the older sense of heaven, for the most part, he means nature as the orderly structure of the natural world.

17. 1 The course of Nature is constant; it does not survive because of the actions of a Yao: it does not perish because of the actions of a Jie. (Yao is a paragon of virtue whereas Jie is an exemplar of perversity—my explanation of these two important figures and not in Knoblock's translation.)

17. 2b The constellations follow their revolutions; the sun and moon alternately shine; the four seasons present themselves in succession; the Yin and Yang enlarge and transform; and the wind and rain spread out everywhere. . . . We do not perceive the process, but we perceive the result—this indeed is why we call it 'divine'.

17. 5 Heaven does not suspend the winter because men dislike cold weather. Earth does not reduce its broad expanse because men dislike long distances. The gentleman does not interrupt his pattern of conduct because petty men rant and rail. Heaven possessed a constant Way; Earth has an invariable size; the gentleman has constancy of deportment.

(Knoblock 1994: iii. 14–17)

Notwithstanding his commitment to a naturalist cosmos, Xunzi was more than a narrow rationalist or strict materialist—there is still an element of the supernal in his cosmos. Moreover, his form of naturalism is expansive and holistic in that it continues to commingle the grand triad of heaven, earth, and humanity as essential for the flourishing of the cosmos. What he explains is a creation without a super-natural creator: creation is the coordinated work of heaven, earth, and humanity, each playing its own primordial role in the cosmic drama. As with so many later Confucians, Master Xun can be religious without invoking the transcendent powers of a creator God.

Xunzi had a vision of the world as grand ritual inspired by powerful poetry and music. He was also moved by the virtue or process of *cheng* 誠, true integrity, a term crucial to his theory of self-cultivation. In his chapter on 'Nothing Unseemly' he included this hymn to self-realization that demonstrates how true a Confucian he really is, and wherein his religious sensibility really lies.

As for the gentleman's cultivation of the mind-heart, there is nothing better than *cheng* 誠 (true sincerity or self-realization), for he who perfects true integrity/sincerity need do nothing else than allow humanity to be maintained and justice acted upon. With the realization of the mind-heart and the maintenance of humanity, they become manifest, and being manifest they are spirit-like, and being spirit-like they are capable of transforming; with the realization of the mind-heart and the practice of justice, there is order, and when there is order, clarity, and with clarity there is change. The transformations and changes act together and this is what is called the Virtue of Heaven ... Heaven and Earth are great, but without true integrity they cannot transform the ten thousand things; although the sage has knowledge, yet lacking true integrity, he is out of touch. The exalted ruler is indeed eminent, and yet, without true integrity, he is lowly. Therefore true integrity is what the gentleman seeks to approach, and is the root of the cultivation of affairs. Only when he rests in the perfection of true integrity will he assemble the like minded to himself ... After having succeeded [in perfecting true integrity] the character of the person is completed and has progressed such a long way that does not revert to its origins, and this is transforming.

(*A Concordance to the Xunzi* 1996: 1; for an alternative translation,
see Knoblock 1988: i. 177–8)

It would not be an exaggeration to call this Master Xun's hymn to *cheng*. If Kongzi and Mengzi show us an emerging form of Confucian spirituality, Xunzi provides us a way to cultivate our mind-heart so that we can put ourselves in tune with the constancies and transformation of the Dao.

THE *ZHONGYONG*

In the *Zhongyong*[4] we clearly perceived the creative holistic and expansive religiosity of the classical Confucian period. If Xunzi provides us with a hymn to *cheng*, the

Zhongyong is an extended religious meditation on the role of *cheng* in acknowledging and discerning the secular as the sacred. 'What *tian* 天 commands (*ming* 命) is called natural tendencies (*xing* 性); drawing out these natural tendencies is called the proper way (*dao* 道); improving on this way is called education (*jiao* 教)' (Ames and Hall 2001: 89). The *how* of this method of instruction for improving the way in order to follow the Dao and obey the natural tendencies of *tian* delineates the function of *cheng* 誠. No other classical text better exemplifies the religious dimension of the notion of sincerity or self-actualization that is the process of *cheng*.

Ames and Hall translate *cheng* by calling it 'creativity'[5] in order to stress the processive and generative nature of the religious vision of the text. 'Creativity (*cheng* 誠) is the way of *tian* (天 之 道); creating is the proper way of becoming human (人 之 道). Creativity is achieving equilibrium and focus (*zhong* 中) without coercion; it is succeeding without reflecting'; 'and only if one can assist in the transforming and nourishing activities of heaven and earth can human beings take their place as members of the triad' (ibid. 104 and 105). As a form of classical Confucian spirituality, this is pretty exalted company indeed and bespeaks of the holistic, relational, and creative supernal discernment of a holistic and expansive Confucian humanism in its most robust religious sensibility.

'Thus, the utmost creativity (*zhicheng* 至 誠) is ceaseless.... This process of utmost creativity is in full display without manifesting itself, changes without moving, and realizes without doing anything.... The way of heaven and earth can be captured in one phrase: Since events are never duplicated, their production is unfathomable' (ibid. 107).

It is this unfathomable nature of the Dao that provides what the New Confucian scholar Mou Zongsan calls the supernal dimension of the Confucian Way. Mou (1994) sees this as a form of immanent transcendent, yet it is so productive, unceasing, and unfathomable that it is surely as 'divine' as Xunzi asserted in his description of *cheng* in the cosmos.

The journey from Kongzi to the *Zhongyong* illustrates the outline of classical Confucian spirituality; a theology of the secular as the sacred; of a holistic and expansive humanism that seeks to find a creative place for humanity in the ceaseless transformations of the Dao. It is a Trinitarian theology to be sure, yet it is a natural, non-theistic spirituality that locates the supernal Dao through the interaction of *tian*, earth, and humanity. Furthermore, along with locating the supernal in this primordial triad, it suggests that the truly supernal or divine is the proper coordination of the cosmos founded and funded by this triad of heaven, earth, and humanity.

We now must move forward more than a millennium to take up the thread of the story again in the Song dynasty, the second golden epoch of the Confucian Way.

THE SONG REVIVAL

The second great epoch of the Confucian Way began in the late Tang and gained momentum to influence in the Northern Song (960–1126 CE). It is important to remember that the contemporary New Confucians of the third epoch are the direct descendants of the great masters of the Tang, Song, Ming, and Qing dynasties. Many western students of Confucianism have a marked preference for the classical period even though the Song–Ming masters argued that they were faithfully reviving and restoring the grand classical Confucian tradition that had been partially eclipsed by the arrival of the Buddhist dharma in China in all its resplendent Mahāyāna glory and the flourishing of various indigenous Daoist sects.

Later in the Qing dynasty (1644–1911) many great Confucian scholars revolted against what they considered the metaphysical excesses of the Neo-Confucian masters. Great thinkers such as Wang Fuzhi (1619–92), Dai Zhen (1724–77), and the equally impressive Japanese scholar Ogyū Sorai (1666–1728), protested that the Song–Ming masters had won a pyrrhic victory over their Buddhist and Daoist cousins by incorporating too much of the metaphysics of the Buddhists and Daoists in Song and Ming Confucian philosophy. For instance, the whole of Zhu Xi's complicated theory of the abstract nature of *li*, coherent principle, was taken to be a perfect example of borrowing a Buddhist idea and applying it inappropriately to Confucian philosophy. This is the same charge that many western scholars also level against the Neo-Confucians: the Song philosophers muddied the waters of the perfectly good classical Confucianism with a hodgepodge of Buddhist and Daoist metaphysics that ought to be left behind by modern Confucians. The problem is that even the great Qing and Japanese scholars had to unlearn Song–Ming Neo-Confucianism before they could begin to try to purify the Buddhist-tainted works of scholars such as Zhang Zai (1020–77), Zhu Xi (1130–1200), and Wang Yangming (1472–1529). The irony is that many contemporary New Confucians see absolutely no reason to abandon any of the religious, historical, aesthetic, and philosophical achievements of the Song–Ming masters *or* the critical Qing and Japanese scholars.

We will briefly review two examples of how the Northern Song and Southern Song masters appropriated, expanded, and renewed the teachings of their respected Zhou dynasty teachers concerning the supernal way. The two writings reviewed are the justly famous 'Western Inscription' of Zhang Zai and 'The Treatise on the Completion of the Mind-heart' by Zhu Xi.

Zhang Zai was one of the greatest of the Northern Song masters, and with his strong affirmation of the role of *qi* vital energy as the key concept of his philosophy, he was deeply appreciated by the later Qing scholars because of this commitment to the dynamic, concrete nature of the cosmos. Zhang is lauded for writing the famous short essay the 'Western Inscription'.[6] Not only does the 'Western Inscription' capture the cosmic scope of Song cosmology, axiology, and ethics, it also has an unmistakable religious sensibility that has inspired the entire Confucian tradition.

Although the 'Western Inscription' is not a long document, I will select the passages that are the most important for the future 'theological' development of the Song tradition.

The Western Inscription

Heaven is my father and Earth is my mother, and even such a small creature as I finds an intimate place in their midst.

Therefore that which fills the universe I regard as my body and that which directs the universe I consider as my nature.

All people are my brothers and sisters, and all things are my companions.

The great ruler (the emperor) is the eldest son of my parents (Heaven and Earth), and the great ministers are his stewards. Respect the aged—this is the way to treat them as elders should be treated. Show deep love to the orphaned and the weak—this is the way to treat them as the young should be treated. The sage identifies his character with that of Heaven and Earth, and worthy is the most outstanding man. Even those who are tired, infirm, crippled, or sick; those who have no brothers or children, wives or husbands, are all my brothers who are in distress and have no one to turn to.

When the time comes, to keep himself from harm—this is the care of a son. To rejoice in Heaven and to have no anxiety—this is filial piety at its purest.

He who disobeys [the Principle of Nature] violates nature. He who destroys humanity is a robber...

One who knows the principles of transformation will skillfully carry forward the undertakings [of Heaven and Earth], and one who penetrates spirit to the highest degree will skillfully carry out their will...

Wealth, honor, blessing, and benefits are meant for the enrichment of my life, while poverty, humble station, and sorrow are meant to help me to fulfillment.

In life I follow and serve [Heaven and Earth]. In death I will be at peace.

(Chan 1963: 497–8)

The classical Confucian virtues are all reconfirmed, but within a spiritual vision of the cosmos that expands its sense of concern consciousness from the immediate family and clan to the whole of humanity and beyond to all the things or events of the world. Both blessings and difficulties are the methods by which the Dao strengthens the sage and the worthy. If one is successful in this spiritual, moral, and intellectual quest, then as Zhang says with such eloquence, even 'In death I will be at peace.' If this is not an evocation of a supernal religious sensibility, a meditation on how a person ought to deport him or herself in the presence of the Dao, the reader is deaf to the spiritual yearnings of the Northern Song mind-heart.

Later in the Southern Song, the greatest of the Neo-Confucian masters was Zhu Xi. It was his interpretation of the Song legacy that became the foundation of the Chinese civil service from 1313 to 1905. Moreover, through his extensive writings on ritual praxis, he influenced not only the philosophical development of Song–Ming thought but also had a profound impact on the ritual and spiritual life of the Chinese, Korean, Japanese, and Vietnamese people. Although he was known as a champion of *li* 理, coherent principle, pattern and order, he was also profoundly implicated in the study and cultivation of *xin* 心, the mind-heart of humanity. The spiritual aspect of Master Zhu's teachings emerges in works such as:

Treatise on the Completion of the Mind-heart
[*Jinxin shuo* 盡心 說]

'The completion of the mind-heart [*xin* 心] is knowing nature. Knowing nature is knowing heaven' [from Mengzi] and hence we affirm that a person can know the mind-heart when the person knows nature and this capacity to know the nature is to know heaven. Now, heaven is the spontaneity of coherent principle and the source from which human beings are born. Nature is the essence of coherent principle which the person receives to become a person. The mind-heart is the way a human being controls the person and fully sets forth this coherent principle. 'Heaven is great and boundless' [quoting Zhang Zai] and nature receives [this boundless nature] completely. Therefore the essence of a person's fundamental mind-heart is itself expansive and without limitation. Only when it is fettered by the selfishness of concrete things, hemmed in by seeing and hearing pettiness, does it become concealed and incomplete. A person can in each event and in every thing exhaustively examine their coherent principles until one day the person will penetratingly comprehend them all without anything being left out: then a person can complete the broad essence of the fundamental mind-heart. The reason for a person's nature being what it is and the reason for heaven being supernal heaven is not beyond this and is connected in its unity.

(Zhu Xi 2002: xxiii. 3273)

The *Treatise*[7] encapsulates not only the outlines of Zhu's mature philosophical interpretation of the role of *xin*, but it shows the structure of Confucian spirituality, the knowledge, comprehension, and unity of supernal things, as it were. The three major elements are learning, action, and discernment through the cultivation of the mind-heart. *Tian* is the source of coherent principle and its manifestation is human nature *xing*. When we understand our nature, we understand our coherent principle *li*, and when we understand our coherent principle we will penetratingly comprehend the holistic interconnections of heaven, earth, and humanity. The method for the encompassing envisagement of the coherent principle of supernal heaven depends upon the proper ethical cultivation of the mind-heart. The mind-heart is potentially expansive and limitless in its powers of knowledge and holistic discernment if it can overcome selfishness and the pettiness of unexamined things and events. Even Xunzi would have found little trouble with this formulation: he would simply add that the proper way to overcome selfishness and pettiness of spirit is always and everywhere by ritual civility and righteousness. The unity of learning, action, and discernment of the proper axiological values of self-cultivation remain as the core of the Confucian search for *tian*, the marker of supernal things or events in a holistic world-view.

THE NEW CONFUCIAN MOU ZONGSAN'S 牟宗三 RELIGIOUS THOUGHT

The traditional Confucian world, a culture that stretches back to the primordial sages of antiquity, Kongzi, the baroque philosophical edifices of the Song–Ming masters, the harsh critiques of the Qing Evidential Research scholars, all came crashing down under the hammer blows of the colonial west. By 1905 the civil service examinations, based on Zhu Xi's interpretation of the Confucian Way, were abolished and in 1911 the empire itself was extinguished.

In 1949 when Chairman Mao, standing in Tiananmen Square, proclaimed that the Chinese people had stood up in order to liberate themselves from their semi-colonial status to the western powers and Japan, he did not make his announcement in the name of a revived Confucianism. Mao proclaimed that modern China would follow the Marxist path and that Confucianism was fit only, and barely that, for the museum of intellectual history as a disgraced example of the worst of feudal ideology. Many non-Marxist scholars would have agreed with Mao's assessment of the negative future for Confucianism even if they did not embrace his passionate messianic version of Marxism.

Nonetheless, the reports of the demise of Confucianism were premature to say the least. By the early 1920s a small group of scholars, while recognizing that a great deal of Confucian culture was in need of drastic reform, began the process of reviving and reforming the Confucian Way as had Kongzi, Mengzi, Xunzi, and the Song–Ming masters before them. This group of scholars, now into its fourth generation, has become a vigorous force in China and the Chinese Diaspora. In order to distinguish it from its classical and Neo-Confucian ancestors, it is now called the New Confucian movement.

While there are many distinguished reformers within New Confucianism, most agree that Mou Zongsan (1909–95) was the most comprehensive and creative philosopher of the second generation. Mou was more than a philosopher per se; he also defended the religious nature of the Confucian Way and tried to show that it was both a spiritual and philosophical tradition worthy of respect as it underwent a drastic reformation in the twentieth century. Mou was a passionate defender of Confucianism; he was also a harsh critic and pointed out that a renewed Confucianism must and should include a place for democratic theory and political practice; the development of ecumenical and modern scientific learning; and a complete rejection of its patriarchal mistreatment of women. Only a thoroughly modern and reformed Confucianism could stand a chance of finding a place again in the mind-hearts of the Chinese people. One crucial element of Mou's reform project was to examine the religious and spiritual dimension of the Confucian Way *rudao* 儒道.

In the twelfth lecture of *The Special Features of Chinese Philosophy*, Mou (1994: 125) provides a concise discussion of his understanding of the religious dimensions of the Confucian Way:

According to our way of seeing things, a culture cannot but have a foundational inner spirituality. This is the power of the creative spirit of culture, and it is where the special nature of the culture resides ... this motive power is religion and it does not matter in what form. Following this we can say that the motive power of the foundation of the life-values of a culture are necessarily found in religion.

Mou hypothesized that if Confucianism is a religion or way of being religious, it must satisfy the broad functional features of any religion. There are two such traits: (1) Any religion 'should perfect the duties of the proper way of everyday life' (ibid. 126). Mou strongly affirms that this is the case for the Confucian Way with its great emphasis on the moral cultivation of the five cardinal virtues, social rituals, and pedagogies for 'the proper conduct of daily life' (ibid. 127) it has devised over the centuries to sustain human flourishing. (2) A religious way of being human must be a path of living spirituality, something more than a secular path of conduct, though such a practical, even mundane path is critical to the holistic vision of the spiritual quest. 'But the reason why a religion is a religion is not merely on this level, for it also has yet another necessary function to fulfill ... A religion must stimulate the incipient seeds of a person's spirituality towards transcendence, to point out a path of spiritual life' (ibid. 128). In short, a religion has both daily praxis and a coherent and supernal principle that govern its teachings and structures.

According to Mou the two foundational traits of Kongzi's spirituality are the traits of *ren* 仁, supported by nature *xing* 性 and the supernal way *tiandao* 天道. *Ren* has both the meaning of the moral code of the five cardinal virtues, namely *ren* 仁 humaneness, *yi* 義 righteous justice, *li* 禮 ritual action or civility, *zhi* 知 discernment or wisdom, and *xin* 信 faithfulness, and an even deeper, spiritual meaning as well. *Ren* is 'the fundamental root of creativity' (ibid. 130) or, as he earlier in the text glosses his own formulation in English, 'creativity itself' 創造性得本身(ibid. 32). Therefore, '*Ren* is the essence of the myriad things of the cosmos and in the primary sense it is not a substance but rather spiritual' (ibid. 131).

Mou adds that for something to be spiritual, it must have two traits: intuition and perseverance. 'It [intuition] has the meaning of morality. From the perception of yielding, intuition is the sense that life does not head into a deadlock, is not constricted, and is the opposite of the meaning that something is dead and without feeling' (ibid. 131). In his earlier discussion of creativity itself, Mou defines it as unceasing generativity, *shengsheng buxi* 生生 不 息 (ibid. 31). The mind-heart yields to the dictates of the true intuition of generativity and moral connection and this is what Mou calls perseverance without ceasing in the cultivation of the way of creativity itself. Moreover, this is the unceasing movement of *tian*, or *tianming* 天命, as the 'profound and unceasing' urgency of the decree, *ming* 命, of the creativity of *tian* (ibid. 131). If we follow *tianming* Mou believed that we will cultivate the essence of creativity itself as *ren*.

Human beings are given *xing* 性 as a set of basic dispositions and if these are cultivated correctly, Mou affirmed that a person can conform the mind-heart to *tiandao* itself (ibid. 131 ff.). Mou goes on to point out that this form of Confucian spirituality does not focus on a creator god, though such an idea was clearly present in the early classical literature. Confucian religious thought simply took a different direction. Because of their emotional nature, human beings often take their feelings of despair or joyous piety and turn them into a prayer to God. Again, while Mou understands and approves of this kind of religious insight, it simply and historically is not what the Confucians did with their spiritual sense of supernal or divine things (ibid. 133 ff.).

If Confucians decline the life of prayer to a supreme Creator God, then wherein does the main thrust of Confucian spirituality direct itself? 'I answer that it lies in the question of how the person goes about embodying the Way of Heaven' (ibid. 135). Mou links the primordial 'how' of embodying *tiandao* to his notion of inter-subjectivity *zhuguanxing* 主 觀 性 (ibid.). 'If we open up the idea of inter-subjectivity, then what is above and what is below become unified. The inter-subjective nature and the objective nature are correlated and the virtue of the *Dao* becomes the praxis of the mind-heart' (ibid.). The ultimate goal of the cultivation of inter-subjectivity is to become a sage, the person who assists in the unceasing creative activity of the cosmos and becomes one with heaven and earth. In one sense Confucianism is humanistic in its focus on the embodying of the *Dao*. But this is a holistic humanism that is open to *tiandao* and *tianming*. It has both an immanent and transcendent focus and is hence a profound form of spirituality. Confucianism definitely has incredibly strong religious dimensions in that the truly cultivated person seeks to become a sage, to be conjoined as one with the Way of Heaven analogous to a Buddhist *bodhisattva* or a Daoist Immortal. While it is often asserted that Confucianism is an overly optimistic faith, Mou counters that the task of self-cultivation is extremely difficult, so much so that only a sage or worthy can achieve such a feat. Most human beings have limits to their ability to perfect the mind-heart; the path is long and the burden is heavy. But the true Confucian never desists from asking, in any situation, how he or she can advance towards the Way of Heaven (ibid. 135 ff.). Mou (and other New Confucians of his generation) provide the context for the current discussions underway in China and the Chinese Diaspora about Confucian spirituality.

Tu Wei-ming has an oft-quoted definition of being religious that is inspired by Mou's defense of the religious dimension and spirituality of the Confucian Way.

Being religious, in the Confucian perspective, informed by sacred texts such as *Chung-yung* [*Zhongyong*], means being engaged in the process of learning to be fully human. We can define the Confucian way of being religious as *ultimate self-transformation as a communal act and as a faithful dialogical response to the transcendent* [italics in the original]. This is also the Confucian prescription for learning to be fully human . . . we can say that Confucian religiosity is expressed through the infinite potential and the inexhaustible strength of each human being for self-transcendence.   (Tu [Du] 1989: 94)

Tu's formulation of 'being religious' as a Confucian adds the trait 'communal act' as constitutive of the tradition, namely the need to act within what Tu calls a fiduciary community. Tu's notion of 'being religious' meshes perfectly with Mou's argument that the religious dimension of the Confucian way is in the method of *how* a person embodies *tiandao*. Of course Mou recognized this need for communal religious solidarity, and for him the prime exemplar of this trait is his notion of inter-subjectivity, the fusions of subject and object relations between the myriad things. For Mou and Tu the task of being religious is unthinkable without a person's interaction with other people, society, and the natural world. The classic formulation is that a Confucian must be a sage within, a king without *neisheng waiwang* 內聖外王.

THE FUTURE OF THE CONFUCIAN TASK FOR BEING RELIGIOUS

For a modern Confucian religious thinker, the issue is, as Mou clearly understood, 'the question of "how" the person goes about embodying the Way of Heaven' (Mou 1994: 135). Tu Wei-ming glosses this task of embodying the *tiandao* as the quest for learning how to be fully human. Any contemporary Confucian spiritual reflection must cohere with this primordial Confucian insight into *how* the human person is conjoined through self-cultivation with the most spiritual, transcendent, and supernal traits of the Dao.

Lunyu 15. 29 says, 'The Master said, "Human beings can broaden the Way—it is not the Way that broadens human beings"' (Slingerland 2003: 185). It is this kind of insight that has always separated the Confucian religious tradition from the great theistic teachings of west and south Asia. Nonetheless, a sampling of modern New Confucians such as Mou Zongsan and Tu Wei-ming illustrates why *Lunyu* 15. 29 remains relevant to the current New Confucian revival project. One can imagine many changes or transformations of the Confucian Way in the future, but one cannot imagine that Confucians will turn the saying around to affirm that it is the Way that broadens human beings, even if Confucians are concerned to discern how they should respond to the Way of Heaven. It is precisely this note of immanent transcendence that many western thinkers find appealing as they struggle to overcome the feeling that the western religious path has overemphasized the nature of God as the wholly other, the completely transcendent One of worship. If the Jesuits and early Protestants found the *Zhongyong*'s thesis that heaven, earth, and humanity form a living trinity to be heretical, then modern men and women find this an increasingly plausible notion about how to be spiritual in the world that modern science reveals to us.

We now wander into speculation about the future of a tradition. This is a hard business and I profess no abilities at prophecy. Moreover, the Confucian Way has been dramatically challenged over the last 150 years, perhaps more so than in any other period of its long journey. Confucians have experienced other great transformations before with marked success. The first triumph was in its classical period with the teachings of the late Zhou masters Kongzi, Mengzi, and Xunzi. The second grand transformation occurred when the late Tang and Northern Song Neo-Confucians responded to the religious and philosophical challenges of Daoists and Buddhists, creating a form of religious, intellectual, and social life that lasted for more than eight hundred years as the dominant ideology of the Chinese empire. The official examination system ensured the continuity and homogeneity of the legal state and social mores throughout the empire. The radical impact of the west since 1842 has provoked a third great transformation, one that is really only its first phases now as the New Confucian movement and reformation. It is truly a reformation because all the New Confucians realize and affirm that they must find a method for a positive engagement with modern democratic theory and practice, ecumenical science, the changing roles of women in the modern world and an appropriate response to globalization and the ecological crisis globalization announced via its rapid industrialization and pollution of the earth.

Notwithstanding all the pressures for change, some things will remain constants in New Confucianism: (1) learning as an act of religious piety; (2) the praxis of civility through ritual actions and patterns of social behavior; (3) discernment of the ultimate moral good, the transcendent and supernal elemental moral seeds that are as immanent in the human mind-heart as they are transcendently supernal; (4) self-cultivation of the mind-heart in order to cultivate the Dao for oneself in service to others; and (5) the ongoing search for the harmony *he* 和 of human flourishing. The path is long and New Confucians, as much as their ancestors, will be called upon to discern what constitutes the merely mundane from the morally necessary and to seek a way to move from what is to what ought to be.

Confucianism has returned with a vengeance to the cultural agenda of China and the Chinese Diaspora. But then, so many things are flourishing in China, including monumental architectural and building projects such as the Three Gorges Dam; the fastest train the world in Shanghai; a newly discovered love of the automobile; amazing industrialization linked to an equally amazing pollution of the environment; successful though closely supervised revivals of Daoism, Buddhism, and Christianity; and a renewed pondering of the meaning of the Confucian Way. In fact, the Chinese government, on the model of France's Alliance française and Germany's Goethe Institutes, is now in the process of establishing hundreds of Confucius Institutes in the western world. One wonders what Chairman Mao would make of all of this. Bookstores are crammed with large sections on Confucian thought and the practical applications of this ancient wisdom. Everyone is asking, what can Confucianism contribute to the flourishing of modern China? No one has a complete or coherent answer.

One common criticism of New Confucianism when it is compared to the revivals of Daoism, Buddhism, and Christianity is that there has been precious little renewal or reformation of the public side of the Confucian Way. At one level this is not hard to understand. The Chinese government, though now relatively friendly to the revival of certain aspects of the Confucian Way, is vigilant about any large religious or cultural movement gaining too much public support and influence beyond the careful monitoring and control of the government. The Chinese civil service has definitely *not* revived the study of the Four Books as the basis of government service,[8] though even the highest governmental officials are pleased to quote from the Confucian classics when it suits their purposes. The cynical among Confucian scholars note that the government loves to cite those aspects of the Confucian Way that encourage a hard-working, educated population dedicated to social harmony and the continued material development of a unified country. Criticism of state policy is not high on the government's list of things needed in the Confucian revival.

When the government decided that it was timely to allow the teaching of literary Chinese again in the private schools,[9] public schools, and universities, the Four Books and the other classics again resumed their centuries-long role as common textbooks to instruct modern Chinese students in the crafts of reading classical and early modern literature, poetry, history, and philosophy. The criticism is often made that there has been a commendable renewal of *neisheng*, the sage within, in terms of the modern critical study of the Confucian tradition but previous little of the *waiwang*, or king without, in the sense of public ritual or policy. One of the tasks of a Confucian scholar has always been to speak truth to the powerful, even at the risk of great personal harm.

Even amidst all these problems of social orientation, policy formation, and reformed ritual praxis, most Chinese intellectuals acknowledge that Confucianism is definitely a major part of the Chinese cultural DNA. For instance, there is legislation in China that mandates that children must care for their aged parents: *xiao* 孝, filial piety, it appears, is even a good Chinese Communist virtue. A specter is haunting the Chinese intellectuals: what about the spiritual resources of the Confucian tradition? Some choices are obvious. Zhang Zai's 'Western Inscription' has become the favorite manifesto for the ecological movement and is seen as precisely the sort of indigenous spiritual resource the Chinese people will need to remember while they grapple with the incredible ecological crisis provoked by the amazingly rapid industrialization of China.

The other side of the coin is the recognition of the revival of Confucian scholarship. As we have seen, one of the critical traits of spirituality is learning. While merely arcane research is never commended (even though it is admired by other scholars), learning as a way to embody the *tiandao* is still foundational to the survival and revival of Confucianism in all its aspects, including the religious; nor is such a form of spirituality unknown in the west. For thousands of years the rabbis have taught that the study of Torah is a sacred act, a way of discerning God's will in the midst of the daily life of the people. As the Chinese people, and Koreans, Japanese, Vietnamese, and even assorted westerners, ponder the spiritual dimensions of the Confucian Way in the midst of its third epoch, just as with Kongzi and Zhu Xi, new forms of Confucian 'theology' or reflection on supernal, divine matters will flourish—though what this renewed appropriation of *tiandao* 天道 will become is something left to present and future generations to determine.

With its emphasis on immanent transcendence, New Confucianism also speaks to the nervous culture of the west. Many people search for a spirituality that allows for the full development of humanity and a sense of connection to the environment nurtured by a commitment that makes a religious place for them within the holistic and ontologically unified cosmos illumined by modern ecumenical science. People want a unity of heaven, earth, and humanity in order to find a balance and harmony for their lives. With this kind of yearning, there will always be a place for being religious in a Confucian mode.

NOTES

Save for the names of authors and book titles, I have modified all texts and translations to use the contemporary pinyin Romanization system for consistency.

1. Actually this is always more of a problem with the elite segments of the Chinese world; Chinese popular and local religions look very religious with all kinds of rites, revealed texts, gods and goddesses, spirits, ghosts, demons, tightly organized religious hierarchies and societies, priests, art, temples—in short, all the functional elements we would expect from a 'religious' tradition. In particular it is the emerging Confucian elite and literati culture that diverges from the commonplaces of Eurasian religious history.

   For two excellent large collections of material on the question of the religious nature of Confucianism, see Yao 2003 and Tu (Du) and Tucker 2003–4. For general accounts of the historical and religious issues involved see Berthrong 1994, 1998, 2000.

2. The Confucian Canon began with the recognition of five great classical texts, but by the Song dynasty (960–1279) eight more early texts had been added for a total of thirteen texts. From the Song on, when people refer to the canon, it would be these thirteen early texts and would be known in the west as the Thirteen Confucian Classics. All the texts were composed, according to critical scholarship, at least by the Han period (221 BCE–220 CE).

3. *Qi* defies any easy translation: it can accurately be translated as vapor, force, action, material force, vital force, vital energy, matter-energy—and many other reasonable suggestions have been made over the centuries. If there is a truly metaphysical or cosmological term in the Chinese philosophical lexicography, *qi* is it. It is simply assumed by most indigenous Chinese philosophical and religious traditions to be one of the foundational traits of the cosmos, the very vital stuff or vital force or vital material energy out of which all the ten thousand things, the favorite term used to designate everything that is, arises, and perishes. It becomes a particular element of analysis, as we shall see, with the Song Neo-Confucians.

4. It is impossible to say just when the current text of the *Zhongyong* was composed. Tradition holds that it is after Kongzi and before Mengzi and Xunzi. However, it could be as late as the early Han dynasty for all that. I have chosen to place it after Xunzi not because I have a better insight into its textual history but because I want to follow up on the theological/spiritual point about *cheng* raised by Master Xun.

5. If translating *cheng* as creativity seems a stretch, Andrew Plaks (*Ta Hsüeh and Chung Yung* trans., 2003) suggests 'integral wholeness' in his 2003 translation of the *Zhongyong* (*Chung Yung*), which neatly captures the expansive humaneness of the process of *cheng*. Wing-tsit Chan 1963 stays much closer to the common meaning of *cheng* and translates *cheng* as being sincere, with the recognition that only through sincere commitment to the highest ethical values can we learn to become fully human.

6. It was called the 'Western Inscription' because it was inscribed on the western wall of Zhang's study.

7. Mou 1968–9: iii. 439–47 has an extended commentary on the essay. He contends that it clearly shows how far Zhu Xi has departed from the correct teachings of Cheng Hao and Hu Hong. Levey 1991, in his superb dissertation, is much less sure that Zhu got it wrong.

8. It is important to remember that the Four Books were the bedrock, the core of the texts used by all students seeking to join the imperial civil service from 1313 to 1905.

9. For instance see a BBC Internet article at <http://news.bbc.co.uk/1/hi/world/asia-pacific/7169814.stm>, accessed 10 June 2008, about the teaching of Confucianism in private schools.

REFERENCES

AMES, ROGER T., and ROSEMONT, HENRY, JR. (1998). *The Analects of Confucius: A Philosophic Translation*. New York: Ballantine.

——and HALL, DAVID L. (2001). *Focusing on the Familiar: A Translation and Philosophical Interpretation of the Zhongyong*. Honolulu: University of Hawaii Press.

Berthrong, John H. (1994). *All Under Heaven: Transforming Paradigms in Confucian–Christian Dialogue*. Albany: State University of New York Press.

—— (1998). *Transformations of the Confucian Way*. Boulder: Westview.

—— and Berthrong, Evelyn Nagai (2000). *Confucianism: A Short Introduction*. Oxford: Oneworld.

Chan, Wing-tsit (1963). *A Source Book in Chinese Philosophy*. Princeton: Princeton University Press.

A Concordance to the Xunzi (1996). *A Concordance to the Xunzi*. The Chinese University of Hong Kong Institute of Chinese Studies. Hong Kong: Commercial.

Fingarette, Herbert (1972). *Confucius—the Secular as Sacred*. New York: Harper & Row.

Keightley, David N. (ed.) (1983). *The Origins of Chinese Civilization*. Berkeley: University of California Press.

Knoblock, John (1988–94). *Xunzi: A Translation and Study of the Complete Works*. 3 vols. Stanford: Stanford University Press.

Lau, D. C. (trans.) (1984). *Mencius*, trans. D. C. Lau. 2 Vols. Hong Kong: The Chinese University Press.

Levey, Matthew A. (1991). 'Chu Hsi as a "Neo-Confucian": Chu Hsi's Critique of Heterodoxy, Heresy, and the "Confucian" Tradition', Ph.D. Dissertation. Chicago: University of Chicago.

Mou, Zongsan (1968–9). *Xinti yu Xingdi* 心體 與 性 體 [Mind and Nature]. 3 vols. Taipei: Zhengjing Shuju.

—— (1994). *Zhongguo Zhexue de tezhi* 中 國 哲 學 得 特 質 [Special Traits/Features of Chinese Philosophy]. Taipei: The Student Book Company.

—— (2003). *Spécificités de la philosophie chinoise*, trans. d'Ivan P. Kamenarovic and Jean-Claude Pastor. Paris: Éditions du Cerf. [French trans. of Mou 1994.]

Needham, Joseph (1954–). *Science and Civilisation in China*. 8 vols. Cambridge: Cambridge University Press.

Plaks, Andrew (trans.) (2003). *Ta Hsüeh and Chung Yung (The Highest Order of Cultivation and On the Practice of the Mean)*, trans. with an introduction, Andrew Plaks. London: Penguin.

Slingerland, Edward (trans.) (2003). *Confucius Analects with Selections from Traditional Commentaries*. Indianapolis: Hackett.

Smith, Wilfred Cantwell (1991). *The Meaning and End of Religion*. Fortress edn. Minneapolis: Fortress.

Tu Wei-ming [Du Weiming] (1989). *Centrality and Commonality: An Essay on Confucian Religiousness*. Albany: State University of New York Press.

—— and Tucker, Mary Evelyn (eds.) (2003–4). *Confucian Spirituality*. 2 vols. New York: Crossroad.

Whitehead, Alfred North (1996). *Religion in the Making*. New York: Fordham University Press.

Yao, Xinzhong (ed.) (2003). *Encyclopedia of Confucianism*. 2 vols. London: Routledge-Curzon.

Zhu Xi 朱 熹 (2002). *Zhuzi quan shu* 朱子 全 書 [The Collected Works of Master Zhu], ed. Zhu Jieren, Yan Zuozhi, Liu Yongxiang. 27 vols. Shanghai: Shanghai gu ji chu ban she & Anhui jiao yu chu ban she.

Index